Global Politics in a Changing World

Global Politics in a Changing World

A Reader

Fourth Edition

Richard W. Mansbach

Iowa State University

Edward Rhodes

Rutgers University

Houghton Mifflin Harcourt Publishing Company   Boston   New York

Publisher: Suzanne Jeans
Executive Editor: Traci Mueller
Marketing Manager: Edwin Hill
Discipline Product Manager: Lynn Baldridge
Development Manager: Jeffrey Greene
Associate Project Editor: Carrie Parker
Senior Media Producer: Lisa Ciccolo
Art and Design Manager: Jill Haber
Cover Design Manager: Anne S. Katzeff
Senior Photo Editor: Jennifer Meyer Dare
Senior Composition Buyer: Chuck Dutton
New Title Project Manager: Susan Peltier
Editorial Assistant: Sareeka Rai
Marketing Assistant: Samantha Abrams
Editorial Assistant: Jill Clark

Cover image: © David Muir/Master file

Printed in the U.S.A.

Library of Congress Control Number: 2008926613

ISBN-10: 0-618-97451-2
ISBN-13: 978-0-618-97451-1

1 2 3 4 5 6 7 8 9-CRS-12 11 10 09 08

 # CONTENTS

**Part Three A NEW SECURITY AGENDA IN
                  A GLOBALIZED WORLD**

Part Four THE SUBJECTIVE DIMENSION: IDENTITIES AND LOYALTIES

 # PREFACE

These are exciting times to study global politics. We remain in a period of turbulent transition. We are witnessing the simultaneous evolution of war and the global security agenda, rapid change in our world's political institutions, and the emergence of increasingly divergent, competing, and sometimes dangerous conceptions of identity. In today's world issues like terrorism and crime, nuclear proliferation, human rights, economic security and development, migration and refugees, and environmental protection compete for attention in global negotiations alongside more traditional issues of war and peace; concerns are mounting about the ability of nation-states and international institutions to manage or solve the problems facing ordinary people, or even to survive; and ethnic, gender, and cultural identities vie with those based on citizenship, leading to new patterns of political organization and action.

Just as rapid and unpredictable changes necessitated earlier editions of this book, their continuation and acceleration demands a fourth edition. Even more than was the case when earlier editions of this book were published, there is a disconnect between many international relations textbooks and the reality of what is happening "out there" as reported in newspapers and other news media. To understand the nature of global politics, we believe it is crucial to avoid a narrow perspective that looks only at sovereign territorial states interacting in a state system dominated by anarchy, mistrust, and military rivalry—a view that reveals only part of the story, and a shrinking part at that. A broader focus helps make sense of events such as continued insurrection in Iraq and the destruction of New York's World Trade Center by suicidal fanatics. The latter vividly drove home to most Americans how tightly knit into the mesh of world politics their lives had become and prompted the realization that national security could no longer be thought of simply in terms of wars between nation-states. The dangers confronting us, and our efforts to deal with them, are increasingly complex. As today's headlines suggest, we are witnessing new examples and even new forms of cooperation, as states develop regional and global institutions and practices that help them address a widening agenda of transnational threats to survival and well-being, and as they work together to derive benefits from the tightening interconnectedness of globalization. Even while some states, like the United States, find ways to survive and thrive in today's turbulent transition, other states have imploded, leaving armed militias, nongovernmental organizations, transnational corporations, and international agencies to play an increasing and ever more complicated role in providing security and shaping everyday life.

Thus, our aim in selecting readings for this volume, as in previous editions, was to connect the concepts that help us understand global political life with real world events. We have sought to introduce students to some of the exciting new ways that social scientists are viewing the world—for example, through the insights of feminist scholars and through analysis of how identities are constructed. At the same time, by presenting illustrative and contemporary news stories within the context of conceptual discussions of global politics, this text provides a stimulus for discussion, debate, and discovery, and enables students to see the events of the day as part of a larger, more understandable process of change.

We find that news accounts, read in the light of the conceptual writings that frame each chapter, offer a variety of exciting teaching possibilities, including their use as mini-case studies. In this role, they provide material for individual or group classroom activities, such as debates or role-playing exercises, and invite a wide range of writing assignments, such as critical reviews, pro-and-con analyses, policy memos, and longer reports. We have deliberately sought news stories that will not only expose students to the enormous diversity of global politics but that will, by the problems they pose, challenge students to develop a range of skills including critical reading, analytical thinking, and moral reasoning.

Structure of the Book

To facilitate these objectives, each chapter begins with an introductory narrative by the editors, providing background and placing the issue in its global context. These introductions are followed by one or two in-depth essays per chapter, generally from journals such as *Foreign Affairs, Foreign Policy,* and *International Security,* each introduced and summarized by the editors. These essays offer a conceptual foundation for students as they consider the transformation under way in global politics. In two chapters, in-depth essays dealing with international finance and gender were commissioned especially for this text.

Shorter descriptions and reports of contemporary events from newspapers and newsmagazines such as the *Financial Times* of London, the *New York Times,* the *Washington Post,* the *Wall Street Journal,* or *The Economist* follow these essays. These brief excerpts provide material that enables students to explore and investigate the conceptual points of the longer essays.

Each chapter ends with a series of suggested topics that encourage students to challenge their assumptions and use logic as they think about the issues. These topics can be used in class discussion and as preparation for exams and papers.

Organization and Changes in the Fourth Edition

In light of the continued velocity of change, over half of the readings from the third edition have been replaced. We have made use of many insightful suggestions from those who have assigned past editions in their courses, including the recommendation that we focus on the problems created by growing migration and immigration. As a result, a new chapter, "Immigrants, Refugees, and Diasporas: Movements Across Borders," introduces readers to the problems associated with population movements. In addition, this edition places greater emphasis on the questions of clashing civilizations and economic development.

The new edition retains the four-part division that has been so successful in previous editions. Thus, following an introductory chapter on the ways in which global politics has and has not changed, Part One focuses on war, especially the increasing importance of civil strife and terrorism and the fast-growing danger of major war resulting from the proliferation of nuclear and biological weapons. The themes of disintegration and integration of political authority remain the focus of Part Two, which examines how global politics is pulling nations and peoples apart at the same time that new forces and institutions are emerging to stitch them together again. These chapters address the spread of democracy as a global institution, "failed states," intergovernmental organizations, transnational institutions such as transnational corporations and nongovernmental groups that link people around the world, and the growing importance of individual human rights in international law.

The challenges to the institutions described in Part Two take the form of new or changing issues that are largely beyond the coping capacity of individual states. Part Three consists of five chapters that examine the issues involved in the "New Security Agenda in a Globalized World"—for example, transnational crime, disease, global warming, globalized economic and financial markets, poverty, and migration and refugees—and how they have redefined and enlarged the core meaning of security in global politics.

These new or altered challenges to human well-being and to traditional sources of authority have been accompanied by new definitions of who "we" are and new boundaries between "us" and "them." Thus, Part Four, "The Subjective Dimension: Identities and Loyalties," contains three chapters consisting mainly of new selections that focus on the growing importance of culture and "identity politics" in today's turbulent world. Conceptual and case materials examine the variety of ways people identify and divide themselves in global politics, the ideologies that legitimate those identities, and the implications of these identities for order and stability around the world. Increasingly, people think of themselves not only as citizens or subjects of sovereign states but also as members of other identity groups based on religion, tribe, ethnicity, and (as Samuel Huntington argues) civilization. Gender, too, is important in how we construct our identity and has a major impact on the way we regard and behave toward others. Finally, pressures toward global homogenization are not only shaping how people understand and define themselves but are prompting a backlash as well, as individuals and cultures strive to protect their differences or values they believe to be imperiled.

Acknowledgments

Our thanks go to those at Houghton Mifflin who have been so generous with their time and effort, including Traci Mueller, Jeff Greene, Carrie Parker, and Mary Dalton-Hoffman. Thanks also go to those who, in reviewing this manuscript, have improved it by their suggestions and emendations, including David Edelstein, Georgetown University; Kenneth J. Mijeski, East Tennessee State University; Lori Solomon, Ohio State University; Boyka Stevanova, University of Texas, San Antonio; and Elizabeth Wishnick, Montclair State University. This book is dedicated to our siblings: Peter, Laurence, Harker, and James.

R. W. M.
E. R.

Global Politics in a Changing World

Chapter 1

CONTINUITY AND CHANGE IN GLOBAL POLITICS

Students today face a world that must seem alien to their parents. There is no longer a Soviet Union and no superpower rivalry keeping the world balanced on the brink of World War III. Fear of nuclear holocaust, so prominent during the Cold War, has receded, even as fear of terrorism has grown, particularly since September 11, 2001. The power of communism as a competitive international ideology has vanished, and new concerns about Islamic fundamentalism have emerged. Japan and Germany have become economic superpowers and China will soon join them. Europe is poised to move beyond economic integration toward political unity. The North American Free Trade Agreement (NAFTA) and other regional treaties and organizations are integrating markets and reshaping the economies of the Americas and Asia. "Globalization" is the new buzzword, and "outsourcing" the economic concern of the day.

Although many of the changes of the last few decades have been positive, pointing toward the spread of peace, prosperity, democracy, and human rights around the world, other developments have been worrisome. While Americans have largely focused on the problem of terrorism, around the globe ethnic conflict and civil war have emerged as serious challenges to world peace. A variety of new, very different issues increasingly dominate the global agenda—for example, the proliferation of weapons of mass destruction and the danger of nuclear accidents, human rights violations and genocide, the AIDS epidemic, international refugees and uncontrolled migration, transnational drug trafficking and crime, "hot money" and monetary stability, poverty and economic underdevelopment, and aging populations, global warming, and environmental degradation. The political institutions we have relied on to provide order and facilitate cooperation are meeting mixed success in dealing with these new challenges.

In years to come, we will look back on this era as one in which the world was fundamentally altered: simultaneous integration and fragmentation of political authority are taking place at a dramatic pace, as the old breaks down and new arrangements are made. A period of turbulent transformation, like the ones that followed the fall of Rome, the Thirty Years' War of the seventeenth century, and the two world wars of the twentieth century, is now under way. Events since the end of the Cold War have made clear that the modern system of global politics based on independent sovereign states is eroding and evolving, and new political processes and institutions are acquiring importance.

The Origins and Consequences of the State System

In this reader we describe our subject as global, not international, politics. We do so because "international" restricts our vision to the interactions of national governments.

Until recently, limiting one's view in this way was accepted practice. Most observers viewed the world through the lens of an intellectual tradition that focused attention on the activities of nation-states and on the international "state system" created by their interactions. This tradition reflected events in Europe between the fifteenth and seventeenth centuries that resulted in the development of highly capable, centralized, territorially defined units we call "states." Emerging at a time when technological, economic, and military developments were making war increasingly destructive, the early European states were successful in controlling political activities and imposing order within their own borders, in building up wealth and military power, and in intimidating their neighbors. Observing this success and fearing for their own survival, others quickly mimicked the political and economic measures that had resulted in this centralization of authority, and the state system of organized political life spread. Other types of political actors and organizations became less significant. Over the course of several centuries, European states not only came to dominate political life on that continent but gradually, through a combination of conquest and colonization, expanded their influence to the remainder of the world.

From a Feudal System to a State System   Understanding how this state system and the idea of sovereignty embedded in it emerged helps us to recognize that the state system represented a particular historical solution to problems of providing order and security rather than an inevitable, universal, or unchangeable reality. It also helps us to understand the transformation under way today.

Europe's state system had its roots in the turmoil that followed the collapse of the Roman Empire, and European states had their origins in the territorial holdings of powerful nobles during the Middle Ages. Under feudalism, those who owned land also enjoyed political power over those who lived on their lands. The property or fiefs of feudal lords ranged from holdings as small as a village to huge estates scattered across vast distances. This feudal system was hierarchically organized: in theory at least, every lord owed political loyalty and service to those above him in the feudal hierarchy and was, in turn, owed allegiance and service by lesser lords. In return for the loyalty and service given to them, nobles owed their vassals protection from attack or violence. At the top of the feudal hierarchy stood the pope in Rome and the Holy Roman Emperor in Germany, both claiming to be rightful successor to the emperors of the Roman Empire and to exercise dominion over a united Christian world.

Despite the apparent clarity of hierarchical relationships, the feudal system invited constant struggle, and it offered at best imperfect security. Feudal lords routinely waged private wars against each other and against lords nominally above or below them in the feudal hierarchy. These wars were fought to settle disputes or to acquire greater wealth. Ordinary people regularly found themselves victims of this fighting and subject to conflicting claims of loyalty.

By the end of the fifteenth century, both the fiction of a unified Europe ruled by an emperor or pope and the notion that lesser lords could defend either themselves or their subjects against the predation of more powerful royal families were increasingly challenged. The Protestant Reformation that began in 1519 marked a rebellion against the Roman Church's authority and attracted the support of lords who sought to free themselves from papal interference in their affairs. Religious conflict swept Germany in 1546, and a number of German princes used the opportunity to gain independence from the Holy Roman Empire. The war was settled by the Peace of Augsburg (1555), which, by declaring that Lutheran princes might impose their religion on subjects regardless of the preferences of the emperor, was a giant step toward legitimating the idea of state sovereignty. Equally important, with the failure of the Catholic Church to stamp out Protestantism, the medieval unity of Christendom and the belief that all of the Christian world was, or ought to be, a single political unit was shattered.

The Peace of Westphalia, which ended the bloody strife of the Thirty Years' War (1618–1648), is frequently described as marking the emergence of the modern system of sovereign states. The Thirty Years' War inflicted unprecedented levels of destruction on Central Europe and undermined both the bottom and the top of the old feudal order. The inability of lesser lords and princes to protect subjects or to wage war effectively was clearly demonstrated. At the same time, the inability of the Holy Roman Emperor to impose his will, even in league with major Catholic allies both in Germany and across Europe, confirmed the hollowness of the old hierarchical system. The Peace of Westphalia helped ratify the sovereign state by giving major princes in the Holy Roman Empire the right to conduct their own foreign affairs and to conclude treaties with other rulers. Although the emergence of a system of independent sovereign states, each exercising effective independent centralized political control over a clearly defined territory, was a long and gradual process, scholars often date the birth of the modern state system from the year of the Peace of Westphalia and call it the "Westphalian" system.

In the following centuries, the sovereign state, originally a European invention, was globalized. Advances in technology enabled Europeans to extend their territorial reach outward, first to the Americas and later to Asia, the Middle East, and Africa. And where European colonies were established, European political institutions followed, replacing traditional patterns of authority and security. At one time or another during the eighteenth, nineteenth, and early twentieth centuries, most of the world was part of one of the vast empires ruled by competing European states. Great Britain, France, Spain, and the Netherlands struggled with one another to seize the resources of North America; Spain and Portugal imposed their rule over nearly all of South and Central America; Africa was carved up by Britain, France, Germany, Italy, Portugal, and the king of the Belgians; Britain exerted dominion over the Indian subcontinent and colonized Australia; the Netherlands conquered the Indonesian archipelago; and France seized much of Indochina. In Northeast Asia, Japan modeled itself on the European states and began to build an empire of its own, while after its war with Spain in 1898 the United States acquired the Philippines and Puerto Rico.

As the European empires retreated in the twentieth century, they left rudimentary European-type states in their wake. The boundaries of these new postcolonial states, however, followed the colonial frontiers drawn by the Europeans and frequently separated members of the same tribal groups and enclosed members of disparate groups. The consequences of the artificial boundaries that had been drawn would become clear in the ethnic strife within and across state borders that has plagued global politics since the end of the Cold War.

State Sovereignty   The idea of state sovereignty was at the heart of the state system and provided the justification for monarchs' behavior toward lesser nobles and toward one another. During the centuries when Europe's states were solidifying, sovereignty was embodied in the monarch himself and meant that, within the boundaries of his state, the monarch was the supreme authority (with the exception of God, who granted the king a "divine right" to rule). Sovereignty had both external and internal implications. Externally, since each king was the supreme authority within his kingdom, sovereignty necessarily meant that all kings were legally equal and that none had the right to interfere in another's internal affairs. Internally, direct control of the tools of military power and the development of bureaucracies able to administer the law and to collect taxes meant that monarchs could exercise significant control over what went on within the boundaries of their kingdoms.

The idea of sovereignty made it possible to distinguish between "domestic" (intrastate) and "international" (interstate) politics. This had not been the case in the Middle Ages, when numerous secular and religious authorities might have responsibility for or rule over the same or overlapping territory. Instead of the feudal world's confused map of tangled allegiances and authorities, in which a single individual might owe loyalty to a number of different warring institutions or leaders, the concept of sovereignty permitted the drawing of neat, clean maps, in which each bit of territory and each person living on it belonged to one, and only one, state.

Since early modern states were regarded as the exclusive property of their rulers, Europe's eighteenth-century kings regularly traded provinces and populations with little concern for inhabitants' well-being or preferences. However, following the French Revolution in 1789, the ideas of "nation" (a community of people with a shared culture and history, that is, a group of people who regard themselves as sharing a common identity and purpose) and "state" were united, and sovereignty shifted from dynasties to the body of citizens more generally. The notion of a "nation-state," which gained popularity during the nineteenth and twentieth centuries, implied that a state served the interests of a particular national group.

The doctrine of state sovereignty had several important consequences for the study of international relations. First, it ratified the state itself as the principal unit of international relations and regarded relations among states as creating an international system. Under international law, only states enjoyed legal status. Nowhere is sovereignty enshrined more clearly than in the United Nations Charter. According to Article 2, paragraph 1: "The Organization is based on the principle of the sovereign equality of all its Members." The implication is spelled out in paragraph 7: "Nothing contained in the present Charter shall authorize the United Nations to intervene in matters which are essentially within the domestic jurisdiction of any state. . . ."

A second logical corollary of the claim that each state was sovereign was the assertion that the international system was "anarchic." In this context, anarchy merely means the absence of an accepted higher authority: that no state recognized the right of any other state, or any other actor, to tell it what it must do. This anarchy, the absence of an accepted higher authority, means that states must depend on themselves ("self-help") for security and that the failure of other states to carry out their promises and agreements must always be regarded as a real possibility. Anarchy means that the order that exists in global politics reflects the power of sovereign states to protect and advance their interests, and it means that states always see war as a possibility if disputes cannot be settled by other means.

A third implication of sovereignty was an emphasis on "national interest" as the driving force behind state policies. Rather than pursue the well-being of the world as a whole, each state is expected to act in what it perceives as its own best interests. Indeed, each state's need to ensure its own security under conditions of anarchy is seen as creating an overriding national interest in increasing the state's power relative to its neighbors.

A fourth corollary was that the only way to prevent powerful states from threatening one another's survival was through countervailing power. To prevent any single state from becoming strong enough to conquer all of its neighbors, a "balance of power" had to be maintained. States had to be constantly vigilant and to band together, and even go to war if necessary, to limit the ambitions of powerful neighbors. In other words, each state's sovereignty could be preserved only by using war or the threat of it to ensure a balance of power in the system.

A fifth implication of state sovereignty was that all states would be driven by the same logic in their behavior and would behave similarly. Because all states, regardless of their particular ideology or culture, needed to protect themselves against possible attack by neighbors, it was assumed that foreign policy was determined almost entirely by external factors, particularly the distribution of power. This meant that domestic features such as whether or not a country was democratic, followed free-market economic principles, or was predominantly Christian or Islamic would make little difference in its definition of national interest and therefore the policies it followed.

A sixth consequence of state sovereignty was the claim that domestic and interstate politics could be neatly separated. The domestic arena was usually idealized as a well-ordered and peaceful environment, controlled by a single government that enjoyed a monopoly of legitimate authority and the means of coercion and violence. The conflictual, anarchic international arena, by contrast, was the realm of foreign policy. Unlike domestic policy, foreign policy was seen as dictated principally by necessity, fear, and self-aggrandizement rather than by justice, morality, or altruism. In contrast to the feudal system, in which all violence was between nobles within the same empire or Christian world and was in this sense intracommunal, the state system distinguished between violence *within* states (rebellion or civil war), which was not supposed to occur, and violence *between* states (war), which was a normal, if unfortunate, feature of politics.

The Changing Nature of Global Politics

For some three hundred years, international politics was equated with the European-originated state system. During this time, relations among Europe's states and the extension of European empires and rivalries to other continents meant that sovereign states continued to be the focus of the study of global politics and that the threat of war among them remained the overriding concern of scholars and practitioners. Most states were preoccupied with their military power relative to others, and many leaders followed balance-of-power policies, employing shifting alliances to counter threats posed by other states. The most important events in global politics in this period were the great wars, centered in Europe but waged on a global scale: the Revolutionary and Napoleonic Wars (1792–1815), World War I (1914–1918), World War II (1939–1945), and the Cold War (1947–1991).

The nineteenth century, however, saw an erosion of the classical balance-of-power European state system. The industrial revolution and the growing power of nationalism made war a riskier and more devastating enterprise than in the past, greatly complicated the measurement of power and skewed its distribution, and increased the impact of domestic factors on foreign policy. At the same time, the development of transnational economic ties and the emergence of ideologies, like Marxism, that crossed national boundaries reduced the impermeability of state frontiers and created new links among societies. Many of the changes in global politics that began in the nineteenth century accelerated in the twentieth and became visible at the end of the Cold War, which had pitted communism against capitalism and the Soviet Union and its allies against the United States and its allies.

Redefining "Security"   For reasons we will explore, recent decades have witnessed a redefinition of the concept of security in global politics. Historically, security was equated with the capability of a state to protect its territory and subjects from military aggression by other states. This meant that security could only be attained by increasing military power, joining alliances, and/or appeasing foes.

For most of the history of the state system, land was a key source of wealth and power, and states had a great incentive to extend their territorial boundaries. More territory meant more men for the army and more land to exploit for raw materials and on which to grow food. More territory also meant greater protection from possible invasion or additional opportunities to initiate aggression oneself. Not surprisingly, the major European powers found themselves repeatedly at war for territories like Silesia, Alsace and Lorraine, and the Rhineland, which offered economic and military benefits to whoever possessed them.

Territorial disputes, however, create special barriers to cooperation. Fights over territory are essentially "zero-sum games": the more of a territory that one country seizes, the less of it that is available to other countries. When the United States seized California from Mexico in 1848, the amount of territory the United States acquired was exactly equal to the amount that Mexico lost. Zero-sum situations like these, where the size of the pie is fixed and states are simply trying to decide how it is to be divided, are inherently conflictual, since interests are incompatible.

Although any definition of security must still take account of military threats from other countries and potentially zero-sum conflicts of interest like those over territory, in today's tightly connected world it must take account of much else as well. Nonmilitary dangers and situations in which one side's gain does not necessarily mean an equal loss to the other side are increasingly common.

Today, many of the dangers threatening us are not posed or created directly by other states, and events occurring entirely within the borders of other states, even states far away, may endanger our well-being. Ethnic and tribal strife, for example, have forced millions of people to become refugees, swamping the economic and political capacity of neighboring states. Diseases such as AIDS, SARS, Ebola, and drug-resistant tuberculosis threaten to spread around the world. Our species' well-being and even survival are jeopardized by intensifying ecological crises such as global warming, which threatens to raise sea levels enough to submerge island nations like Fiji and the Maldives and to inundate heavily populated coastal regions of countries like China, Bangladesh, and the United States. Rapid population growth in the developing world is straining the planet's capacity to feed itself and dispose of its wastes, and profligate use of resources by wealthier nations adds to a global environmental problem that is beyond the ability of any single state to solve. Economic concerns, too, have assumed a higher place on the global agenda. Prosperity is increasingly determined by decisions of faraway individuals and corporations, largely outside the control of individual states. In today's world, international trade and finance issues are receiving the attention formerly reserved for questions of war and peace because they directly affect whether ordinary people in nations around the globe will be able to live happy, meaningful lives, or even to avoid destitution or starvation.

This new, broader sense of what is necessary to ensure human safety and well-being challenges notions of security based on mutual respect for sovereignty. It means that states more and more often perceive that the safety and well-being of their citizens is being threatened by events within the borders of other states. As a consequence, the principle that states should not interfere in each other's domestic affairs is increasingly ignored. For example, the United States regularly violates this stricture when it demands that the government of Afghanistan stop the activities of groups such as al-Qaeda within its borders, ban the cultivation of opium poppies within its territory, and halt its repressive treatment of women; when it insists that China improve its human-rights record in return for trade privileges; or when it takes action against European-based companies that operate in Cuba. So do the United Nations (UN) and its affiliated agencies like the International Monetary Fund (IMF) when dealing with human rights, economic development, and environmental issues. The UN was not reluctant to intervene in South Africa's domestic sphere in opposing that country's apartheid policy, and the IMF routinely forces states to alter their economic policies as a condition for receiving loans. Such intrusions significantly limit the sovereign independence of target states and in some cases, as when the IMF forces loan recipients to adopt austerity policies, may even threaten to bring about the government's overthrow.

Dilemmas of Collective Action Many of the issues on the new, broader security agenda cannot be dealt with effectively by individual states. Instead, they require collective action by many, sometimes even all, states. Ecological threats such as global warming and disappearing rain forests offer a good illustration of the problem. Carbon dioxide emissions, which are the main source of global warming, are produced in a variety of ways, the most important of which is by automobiles. Reducing such emissions would benefit everyone; individually, however, each of us would prefer that others make the sacrifice necessary to reduce carbon dioxide while we continue our own carbon dioxide–producing activities. Many Americans, for example, would be happiest if global warming could be prevented by reduced automobile use in Europe and the developing world, without limits on automobile use or stricter emissions controls in the United States. At the same time, Americans naturally worry that if they make the sacrifices required to reduce carbon dioxide production, other nations will simply increase their carbon dioxide–producing activities and global warming will occur anyway. Even though they fear global warming, many Americans therefore are reluctant to make the sacrifices necessary to counter this threat. The decision by President George W. Bush to back out of an international agreement, the Kyoto Protocol, that the United States had earlier signed reflects this logic. The Kyoto Protocol called for states around the world, including the United States, to reduce the emission of the "greenhouse gases" responsible for global warming. In part, President Bush's decision was based on the argument that, compared to poorer, less developed countries, the United States was being asked to pay a disproportionate share of the cost of slowing global warming.

Or consider the problem of global deforestation. The world's tropical rain forests absorb a great deal of carbon dioxide and are important sources of oxygen. In addition, they are home to a wide variety of plant and animal life. Their destruction exacerbates a number of environmental problems that cross national boundaries, including soil erosion, desertification, and global warming. However, much of the rain forest that has not already been destroyed is located in a relatively few economically less developed countries, such as Brazil and Indonesia. Why, these countries reason, should they sacrifice their own nations' economic development for the good of other nations, many of which have already achieved a standard of living far higher than theirs? Why should they not have the right to cut down their jungles to provide new land for farmers and timber for export? In general, there is tension between developing and developed countries regarding environmental issues. Developing countries argue that wealthy countries produce far more waste per capita than they do and already enjoy prosperity. Developed countries respond by contending that rapidly expanding population and economic growth in the developing world create the greatest burdens on the world's environmental health.

Threats to security like these pose "dilemmas of collective action." In a dilemma of collective action, if each actor pursues its own selfish best interests, the result is something that is worse for *everyone,* including the actors acting selfishly. On the one hand, individual actors share a common interest in enhancing the general welfare by cooperating with one another to overcome collective problems and will suffer if these problems go unsolved. On the other hand, each state wishes to avoid paying its share to solve the problem and wants absolute guarantees that others will do at least their fair share. In the absence of a higher authority able to assure that each actor contributes its share, actors may evade their responsibilities, both because they fear being taken advantage of by others and because, if possible, they would like to take advantage of others. Finding ways to overcome these dilemmas of collective action and work together to solve common problems is one of the major tasks of global politics.

As dilemmas of collective action suggest, the anarchic nature of the international system, in which sovereign power is divided among individual states, impedes cooperative settlements, even when common interests exist. Since anarchy means that there is no higher authority to make sure that states carry out their promises, trust is low. In this situation, every actor fears that, regardless of the commitments or treaties its neighbors may have made, they may break their word if it is in their short-term interest to do so. The absence of higher authority is a structural obstacle to cooperation. New political arrangements and institutions are necessary if these dilemmas and the new security agenda are to be dealt with effectively.

Conflict, Cooperation, and the New Security Agenda In contrast to a world in which most problems are seen as zero-sum, a world in which actors are individually unable to ensure their citizens' security and in which there are numerous dilemmas of collective action places a premium on cooperation. In "variable-sum games" the *size* of the pie, as well as how it is divided, depends on the policies pursued by actors. This is a good description of the world that is now emerging.

Territory, for example, has become less important as a source of wealth and military power. Increasingly, these depend on advanced technology and global trade. Trade and technology, however, are not fixed the way territory is. The creation of technology and growth in trade can be fostered by cooperation among actors. The liberal global economic policies that have been pursued by Western democracies since World War II underscore the value of working together cooperatively to increase the total size of the pie. The collapse of the Soviet Union has been explained in part by its isolation from the global trading system the United States and its allies created after World War II and by the Soviet Union's failure to keep abreast of technological change. By contrast, the willingness of China's communist regime, beginning in the 1970s, to open up the country to global trade and investment triggered rapid economic growth that has made it a major player in the global economic system.

It is important to recognize that trade and investment are *collectively* beneficial. Unlike territory, trade and investment offer great opportunities for cooperation. Indeed, in the absence of cooperation everyone loses. If actors squabble over how to divide the pie and refuse to work together, the pie shrinks in size. For example, during the Great Depression of the 1930s, countries sought to protect domestic industries from foreign competition by erecting tariff barriers and to increase their share of world trade by reducing the value of their currency compared to the currencies of others (thereby making their goods cheaper overseas while making it more expensive to buy imported goods at home). As countries emulated one another in using these "beggar-thy-neighbor" policies, the net result was a contraction of global trade. Exchanges of goods and services that would have profited *all* countries, and contributed to world employment, were prevented. This not only increased the severity of the Depression but ultimately contributed to political instability in countries like Germany and Italy, which made them easy prey for demagogues like Adolf Hitler and Benito Mussolini.

In a world in which variable-sum games offer incentives for cooperation, political institutions and organizations provide the tools that make this cooperation possible. The proliferation of global and regional economic institutions after World War II facilitated interstate economic cooperation and helps to explain the rapid recovery and growing prosperity of Europe and Japan, which in turn led to greater prosperity for Europe's and Japan's trading partners, including the United States. Under American leadership, the General Agreement on Tariffs and Trade (GATT), the World Bank, and the IMF reduced trade barriers, provided loans for reconstruction, and stabilized currency rates. This facilitated rapid growth in global trade and the emergence of new public and private institutions that stimulated greater economic activity worldwide.

The emergence of cooperative institutions to solve common problems has not been limited to the economic sphere. A combination of new transnational threats to security and the growing capacity of people in different countries to communicate and work together has produced a proliferation of transnational organizations dealing with a wide range of issues. In the environmental arena, for example, groups such as Greenpeace and World Wildlife Fund mobilize people directly for political ends. These organizations constitute a genuine global civil society that exists independently from the traditional pattern of state-to-state relations.

This suggests a final reason why pressure for global cooperation is growing. Individuals have an increasing capacity to make their opinions known to others and to work together globally, both through their states and directly. In recent years, democracy has spread from North America, Western Europe, and Japan to Latin America, where a number of military regimes have returned political power to civilians, and to the former Soviet-bloc states of Eastern Europe. The seeds of democracy have also been planted in Russia and in a number of African societies. But even where democracy is absent, growing literacy rates and mass media expose peoples to the wider world in which they live, mobilize them to place pressure on governments to look out for their welfare, and enable them to communicate directly with citizens of other societies. To be sure, improved literacy and knowledge do not necessarily result in a preference for peaceful, rather than violent, solutions to conflicts of interest. They do, however, mean greater awareness of the complex ways in which people around the world depend on each other and greater pressure to develop governmental and nongovernmental institutions to solve problems that transcend borders.

Integration and Fragmentation   One of the major trends in the world today is toward greater transnational integration. The well-being of human beings everywhere is affected by actions of other individuals around the globe. People are increasingly aware of this interdependence and have recourse to a growing variety of institutions and organizations other than states.

Some of these new or increasingly important institutions are "intergovernmental organizations" (IGOs), that is, organizations that have states as members. These IGOs not only serve as forums for negotiation but also attempt to hold their member states to commitments they may have made and to enforce the decisions made by the group as a whole. The growing authority of economic institutions like the World Trade Organization (WTO), the successor to the GATT, and the European Union (EU) reflects a major process in global politics, that is, the surrender by states to global and regional actors of selected responsibilities and the centralization of specific tasks. Thus, when NAFTA came into force in 1992, the United States, Mexico, and Canada agreed to surrender a measure of independence in making economic policy in order to enjoy the collective economic growth promised by free trade. Although integration of this sort is taking place mainly in the developed world and is further advanced in economic issues than in political or military ones, the trend marks growing recognition that states are poorly equipped to respond effectively to the challenges created by growing interconnectedness of peoples everywhere.

Also drawing the world together in a complicated network of relationships that cut across national borders are a variety of other nonstate actors. We have already referred to some nongovernmental organizations (NGOs), like Greenpeace and the World Wildlife Fund, that have ordinary people from nations around the world as members and that address the concerns of "global citizens." Other border-spanning nongovernmental organizations are motivated by profit rather than by public policy concerns. In the modern world, in which the global economy is linked by immense transnational corporations (TNCs) like Sony, Shell, and IBM that can take advantage of wage and cost differentials around the world, the prosperity of workers in a country may be largely determined by investment and market decisions that are beyond the control of that state's government, or indeed the government of any single state. Increasingly, global trade involves the movement of goods and services among corporations and among corporate subsidiaries rather than among states. Particularly when these transnational corporations collude with each other, their power may dwarf that of states, and states may be forced to adapt their policies to meet the demands or accommodate the interests of transnational corporations rather than pursuing other preferred policies.

Thanks to technology, the world of finance has become global, too. Just as corporations can move raw materials and finished products around the globe to take advantage of lower wages, higher skills, and better markets, so also can investors move vast sums of money around the world to obtain higher or safer yields and to benefit from minute changes in currency rates. In fact, using cyberspace, they can do this virtually instantaneously. What this means is that, despite the importance of such matters in determining national prosperity and coping with inflation or unemployment, governments lack the resources to control macroeconomic (monetary) policies in their own countries if foreign investors seek to undermine them. The funds that investors can shift dwarf the resources available to governments.

The integration taking place in today's world involves more than economics, though. More than ever before, ordinary people are introduced to a global, rather than purely national, culture. People all over the world are exposed to foreign mass media—television, radio, films—and many people in wealthy countries are connected by the Internet, the facsimile machine, global advertising, and jet aircraft.

Such exposure erodes cultural differences and homogenizes the tastes and habits especially of young people in urban areas. Today, it is possible to travel around the world eating at McDonald's, sleeping at Hilton hotels, and never being exposed to local customs and tastes. The fear that cultural homogenization will bring with it liberal Western attitudes that erode morals and local values and unravel the fabric of local communities has produced a backlash in countries like Afghanistan, Iran, and China, where even satellite dishes have been outlawed. Islamic fundamentalism—that is, belief that a community should be governed according to the dictates of the Muslim holy book, the Koran—represents another response to the inroads of secular modernity. And nowhere is the struggle between new and old more vividly reflected than in the efforts of some Islamic governments to limit the autonomy of women, especially middle-class urban women who have been educated and have professional aspirations.

One reaction to economic centralization and cultural homogenization in recent years has been the rediscovery of cultural "roots" and the reassertion of ethnic, religious, tribal, and other identities to resist the rootlessness of modernity. Identity politics plays a growing role in providing psychological security to people who fear and loathe the remote forces that reduce their economic status and erode the ethics and tastes that have held sway in their communities, sometimes for centuries.

And identity politics is central to a second major global process, fragmentation of states. Although civil strife plagued states such as Vietnam, South Africa, Indonesia, and Nigeria prior to the end of the Cold War, it has become a virtual epidemic in recent years, especially in the developing world where Europeans imposed artificial frontiers in previous centuries. Ethnic, tribal, religious, and racial cleavages have exploded in such countries as Bosnia, Somalia, Rwanda, Congo, Liberia, Sierra Leone, and Sudan, accompanied by the virtual collapse of state institutions.

The combination of these integrative and disintegrative pressures is transforming global politics before our eyes. Old institutions—old organizations and patterns of behavior—are increasingly overwhelmed as their legitimacy is called into question and as new problems arise that they are ill equipped to handle. At the same time, new institutions are emerging. Understanding where this process is leading—how human needs will be met around the world and how we will come to view ourselves and our relations to one another—is the challenge facing us as inhabitants of this world and members of this global community.

From a State-Centric to a Turbulent World

In this chapter and those that follow, we provide two types of readings. Each chapter begins with one or more general pieces drawn from the academic literature to lay out the contours of the issue that the chapter addresses. Following this, shorter, current pieces are presented that vividly describe or reflect particular aspects of the issue; in many cases, these are drawn from news sources, and they show how the issue impacts our lives today.

1.1 Turbulence in World Politics: A Theory of Change and Continuity

James N. Rosenau

In our first reading, political scientist James Rosenau describes a rapidly changing world of diminishing state authority and capacity in which sovereignty means less and less. He argues that change in recent years has been so dramatic as to make the term *international politics* obsolete. Instead, he speaks of "postinternational politics" to express the idea that today's world is far more complex than a system of sovereign states.

Rosenau argues that for the first time in three hundred years turbulent change has altered the three major dimensions, or "parameters," of global politics. The first of these parameters reflects people's capabilities: people today are better educated than their ancestors and are constantly exposed to the world around them because of modern technologies such as televisions, satellite dishes, and computers. As a result, they can understand their own interests and can participate directly in global politics, rather than relying on their states.

The second parametric change, Rosenau argues, is the rise of new actors that operate alongside of and interact with the older state system. To serve their interests, people organize into a variety of nonstate groups like Amnesty International. The third change that Rosenau points to is that people today no longer automatically accept authority. Governments and authority figures can no longer assume that people will blindly follow their commands; instead, they have to earn citizens' loyalty or else suffer the fate of the Soviet Union, which collapsed in 1991.

Rosenau emphasizes two sources of these changes: the revolution in microelectronics that has made possible instantaneous and inexpensive communication and the emergence of issues like environmental pollution that affect everyone. New technologies enable people to communicate and travel quickly. New issues foster the creation of nonstate groups to tackle them; the authority of these groups is reinforced by states' inability to solve problems. The authority of new groups and institutions grows as the authority of states declines. Ironically, Rosenau concludes, these changes are at the same time promoting greater fragmentation and greater integration in global politics.

Previewing Postinternational Politics

The very notion of "international relations" seems obsolete in the face of an apparent trend in which more and more of the interactions that sustain world politics unfold without the direct involvement of nations or states.

So a new term is needed, one that denotes the presence of new structures and processes while at the same time allowing for still further structural development. A suitable label would be *postinternational politics*. . . . Postinternational politics is an appropriate designation because it clearly suggests the decline of long-standing patterns without at the same time indicating where the changes may be leading. It suggests flux and transition even as it implies the presence and functioning of stable structures. . . . It reminds us that "international" matters may no longer be the dominant dimension of global life, or at least that other dimensions have emerged to challenge or offset the interactions of nation-states. And, not least, it permits us to avoid premature judgment as to whether present-day turbulence consists of enduring systemic arrangements or is merely a transitional condition.

Accordingly, the term will henceforth be used to designate the historical era that began after World War II and continues to unfold today. It is a shorthand for the changes wrought by global turbulence; for an ever more dynamic interdependence . . . for the centralizing and decentralizing tendencies that are altering the identity and number of actors on the world stage; for the shifting orientations that are transforming authority relations among the actors; and for the dynamics . . . that are fostering new arrangements through which the diverse actors pursue their goals. . . .

Turbulent Change   Doubtless every era seems chaotic to the people who live through it, and the last decades of the twentieth century are no exception. It is as if Spaceship Earth daily encounters squalls, downdrafts, and wind shears as it careens into changing and unchartered realms of experience. Sometimes the turbulence is furiously evident as thunderclouds of war gather or the lightning of a crisis streaks across the global sky; but often the turbulence is of a clear-air kind, the havoc it wreaks unrecognized until after its challenges have been met or its damage done.

In seeking here to account for this turbulence in world politics and the changes that it both reflects and promotes, the analysis will focus on the underlying and enduring dynamics out of which daily events and current issues flow. Some of the dynamics are located at micro levels, where individuals learn and groups cohere; others originate at macro levels, where new technologies are operative and collectivities conflict; and still others derive from clashes between opposing forces at the two levels—between continuity and change, between the pulls of the past and the lures of the future, between the requirements of interdependence and the demands for independence, between centralizing and decentralizing tendencies within and among nations. . . .

. . . Turbulence is . . . more than the commotion that accompanies shifts in major variables. Such fluctuations make up the day-to-day life of any system, be it social or meteorological. Just as shifts from cloudiness to showers to sunshine constitute normal weather patterns, so do electoral shifts from right to center to left or industrial shifts from high to moderate to low productivity form standard political and economic patterns. . . . When the system's boundaries no longer contain the fluctuations of the variables, however, anomalies arise and irregularities set in. . . . These are the hallmarks of turbulence. Meteorologically, it appears in the form of hurricanes, tornadoes, tidal waves, droughts, and other "abnormalities" of nature that transform the terrain across which they sweep. Socially, it is manifested in technological breakthroughs, authority crises, consensus breakdowns, revolutionary upheavals, generational conflicts, and other forces that restructure the human landscape in which they erupt.

It follows that uncertainty is a prime characteristic of turbulent politics. While the fluctuations of variables usually adhere to recognizable patterns, regularities disappear when turbulence sets in. At such times, the structures and processes of world politics enter a realm without prior rules or boundaries. Anything may happen, or so it seems, as demands are intensified, tensions exacerbated, relationships transformed, policymaking paralyzed, or outcomes otherwise rendered less certain and the future more obscure.

Closely related to the uncertainties associated with political turbulence is the pace at which it moves. Unlike conventional diplomatic or organizational situations, which evolve in the context of formal procedures, cautious bargaining, and bureaucratic inertia, those beset by turbulent conditions develop rapidly as the repercussions of the various participants' actions cascade through their networks of interdependence. Sustained by the complexity and dynamism of diverse actors whose goals and activities are inextricably linked to each other, and facilitated by technologies that transmit information almost instantaneously, turbulent situations tend to be marked by quick responses, insistent demands, temporary coalitions, and policy reversals. . . .

Viewed in this context, it is not surprising that, in 1988, protests and uprisings followed quickly upon each other in Soviet Armenia, the West Bank, Poland, Burma, and Yugoslavia, or that the same time span was marked by regimes being shaken up in the Soviet Union, Chile, Haiti, and Lebanon. Likewise, and no less conspicuous, 1988 witnessed cascades of cooperation: within weeks of each other, negotiations to end wars were initiated in Afghanistan, Angola, Central America, Cambodia, the Western Sahara, and the Persian Gulf. The winds of turbulence, in short, can propel postinternational politics in many directions, through the world's diplomatic and legislative chambers, where compromises are reached, no less than through its streets and battlefields, where conflicts are joined. . . .

It could be argued that high complexity and high dynamism are not new to world politics, that global wars, revolutions, and depressions reflect such conditions, and accordingly, that change has always been at work in world politics. In order to differentiate the familiar and commonplace changes from the profound kind of transformations that seem to be occurring today, one other attribute of political turbulence needs to be noted—namely, it involves parametric change. . . . [W]hen the orientations, skills, relationships, and structures that have sustained the parameters of world politics begin to crumble . . . the course of events is bound to turn turbulent.

Three dimensions of world politics are conceptualized as its main parameters. One of these operates at the micro level of individuals, one functions at the macro level of collectivities, and the third involves a mix of the two levels. The micro parameter consists of the orientations and skills by which citizens . . . link themselves to the macro world of global politics. I refer to this set of boundary constraints as the *orientational* or *skill* parameter. . . . [T]he *structural* parameter . . . refers to the constraints embedded in the distribution of power among and within the collectivities of the global system. The . . . *relational* one . . . focuses on the nature of the authority relations that prevail between individuals at the micro level and their macro collectivities.

All three of these parameters are judged to be undergoing such a thoroughgoing transformation today as to bring about the first turbulence in world politics since comparable shifts culminated in the Treaty of Westphalia in 1648. . . . In the case of the structural parameter, the transformation is marked by a bifurcation in which the state-centric system now coexists with an equally powerful, though more decentralized, multi-centric system. . . . In the case of the relational parameter, the long-standing pattern whereby compliance with authority tends to be unquestioning and automatic is conceived to have been replaced by a more elaborate set of norms that make the successful exercise of authority much more problematic, thus fostering leadership and followership conflicts within and among state and nonstate collectivities that can fairly be judged as amounting to a series of authority crises which, in both their pervasiveness and their scale, are new and global in scope. Lastly . . . the analytic skills of individuals have increased to a point where they now play a different and significant role in world politics. . . .

. . . Earlier eras have witnessed wars that shifted global structures from multipolar to bipolar foundations and revolutions that undermined the prevailing authority relationships; but not since the seventeenth century have circumstances arisen in which the values of all three of these fundamental parameters underwent reinforcing realignments. . . .

The Sources of Change   What are the forces at work . . . that drive these parametric transformations? Five seem particularly relevant. One involves the shift from an industrial to a postindustrial order and focuses on the dynamics of technology, particularly on those technologies associated with the microelectronic revolution that have made social, economic, and political distances so much shorter, the movement of ideas, pictures, currencies, and information so much faster, and thus the interdependence of people and events so much greater. A second engine of global change is the emergence of issues—such as atmospheric pollution, terrorism, the drug trade, currency crises, and AIDS—that are the direct products of new technologies or of the world's greater interdependence and are distinguished from traditional political issues by virtue of being transnational rather than national or local in scope. A third dynamic is the reduced capability of states and governments to provide satisfactory solutions to the major issues on their political agendas, partly because the new issues are not wholly within their jurisdiction, partly because the old issues are also increasingly intertwined with significant international components . . . and partly because the compliance of their citizenries can no longer be taken for granted. Fourth, with the weakening of whole systems, subsystems have acquired a correspondingly greater coherence and effectiveness, thereby fostering tendencies toward decentralization (what I call *subgroupism*) at all organizational levels that are in stark contrast to the centralizing tendencies (here regarded as *nation-statism* or *transnationalism*) that marked the early decades of [the twentieth] century and those that preceded it. Finally, there is the feedback of the consequences of all the foregoing for the skills and orientations of the world's adults who comprise the groups, states, and other collectivities that have had to cope with the new issues of interdependence and adjust to the new technologies of the postindustrial order; with their analytic skills enlarged and their orientations toward authority more self-conscious, today's persons-in-the-street are no longer as uninvolved, ignorant, and manipulable with respect to world affairs as were their forebears. . . .

. . . One of the five dynamics, the shift in micro capabilities and orientations, is deemed to be more powerful than the other four. . . . That is, although world politics would not be on a new course today if the microelectronic and other technological revolutions had not occurred, if the new interdependence issues had not arisen, if states and governments had not become weaker, and if subgroupism had not mush-roomed, none of these dynamics would have produced parametric change if adults in every country and in all walks of life had remained essentially unskilled and detached with respect to global affairs. . . . Without the micro transformations . . . none of the others could have emerged on a worldwide scale, and in this sense the enlargements of the capacities of citizens is the primary prerequisite for global turbulence. . . .

. . . Once the micro level shifts began . . . alterations in the status of states, governments, and subgroups were bound to follow, as people became receptive to the decentralizing consequences inherent in their growing capacity to locate their own interests more clearly in the flow of events. The subtlety of these interactive processes is perhaps most clearly evident in the links between the expansion of cit-izen skills and the technologies made available by the microelectronic revolution. If one asks what the advent of instantaneous communications and information retrieval—of satellites bringing pictures of ongoing events into homes everywhere and of computers storing, processing, and disseminating information heretofore unknown and ungatherable—may be doing to individuals as actors on the global stage, the answer seems inescapable that the new technologies have had a pro-found, if not always desirable, impact upon how individuals perceive, comprehend, judge, enter, avoid, or otherwise interact with the world beyond their workplace and home. . . . No longer does the translation of commitment into action await word brought by stagecoach that like-minded citizens are banding together or that leaders discern an opportunity for effective participation. Today, events and the words about them are, in effect, simultaneous occurrences. Unlike any prior time in history, therefore, citizens are now able to intrude themselves readily into a situa-tion anywhere in the world, because information about its latest twists and turns is immediately at hand. . . .

Indeed . . . the ability to mobilize those skills and orientations is so much greater and speedier than in the past that the practical effect is an expanded capacity for identify-ing and articulating self-interests and participating effectively in collective action. . . .

The Technological Dynamic   . . . [P]olitical systems are also subject to a broad array of changes originating in the economy and society, all of which are also sufficiently dynamic to spur still further changes once they have been absorbed by the polity.

. . . [T]hree dynamics are conceived to be especially relevant as exogenous sources of global turbulence. . . . [O]ne is the pressures created by extensive changes in the struc-ture and size of populations in recent decades. A second involves the shifting availabil-ity and distribution of natural resources, especially those related to the generation of energy. The third derives from the . . . consequences of technologies in all fields of human endeavor, from information processing to medicine, biogenetics and agriculture.

Since it has also contributed to the shifts in population and natural resources, technology is perhaps the most powerful of the exogenous dynamics. . . . Tech-nology has expanded the capacity to generate and manipulate information and knowledge even more than the ability to produce material goods, leading to a situation in which the service industries have come to replace the manufacturing industries as the cutting edge of societal life. It is technology, too, that has so greatly diminished geographic and social distances through the jet-powered airliner, the computer, the orbiting satellite, and the many other innovations that now move people, ideas, and goods more rapidly and surely across space and time than ever before. It is technology that has profoundly altered the scale on which human affairs take place, allowing more people to do more things in less time and with wider repercussions than could have been imagined in earlier eras. It is technology, in short, that has fostered an interdependence of local, national, and international communities that is far greater than any previously experienced.

1.2 Bloggers May Be the Real Opposition

The Economist

The microelectronics revolution, as Rosenau observes, is one of the factors at the heart of the shift from international to postinternational politics. This revolution is profoundly changing the meaning of borders and boundaries in today's world by allowing individuals around the globe not simply to gather and analyze information in ways that previously only states and other large, bureaucratic institutions were able to do, but also to communicate with others around the world, ignoring political divisions and unchecked by political authorities. In addition to being a force driving globalization, however, this microelectronic revolution also fundamentally shifts the balance of power between ordinary individuals and the states and elites that govern them. As the following story from the British news journal *The Economist* observes, the ability of state leaders to control what ordinary people know and think is now challenged—not only by advocates of greater democracy, but by advocates of fundamentalist religion and by various ethnic, ideological, and class-based groups—thanks to the new technology. For better and for worse, the power to question authority is much more real today than in the past few centuries.

T hey call themselves *pyjamahideen*. Instead of galloping off to fight holy wars, they stay at home, meaning, often as not, in their parents' houses, and clatter about computer keyboards. Their activity is not as explosive as the self-styled jihadists who trouble regimes in the region, and they come in all stripes, secular liberal as well as radical Islamist. But like Gulliver's Lilliputians, youthful denizens of the internet are chipping away at the overweening dominance of Arab governments.

In Egypt, for instance, blogging has evolved within the past year from a narcissistic parlour sport to a shaper of the political agenda. By simply posting embarrassing video footage, small-time bloggers have blown open scandals over such issues as torture and women's harassment on the streets of Cairo. No comment was needed to air widespread disillusionment with last month's referendum to approve constitutional changes, after numerous Egyptian websites broadcast scanned images of a letter from one provincial governor to junior bureaucrats, ordering them to vote yes. (The government claimed a 27 percent turnout, with three-quarters approving; critics claim fewer than 5 percent voted.)

The Muslim Brotherhood, Egypt's main Islamist group and most powerful opposition force, has countered a recent government crackdown not with street protests, but far more effectively with a web-based campaign to help its arrested members. More playfully subversive, an anonymous blogger has drawn a rave following for his spoof version of Egyptian politics, which pictures the country as a village ruled by an ageing headman. Through overblown praise of this exalted leader, and of his plans for his son to inherit the post, the blogger runs mocking circles around the suspected ambitions of Egypt's 78-year-old president, Hosni Mubarak.

Such pinpricks have yet to puncture the dominance of any Arab state. But with internet access spreading even to remote and impoverished villages, and with much of its "user-generated content" pitched in pithy everyday speech rather than the high classical Arabic of official commentary, the authorities are beginning to take notice. In February, an obliging Egyptian court fired a shot across the bows of would-be web dissidents by sentencing 22-year-old Abdelkarim Suleiman to four years in jail. A law student in Alexandria, he had strayed by penning bitter critiques of Egypt's main centre of Islamic learning, al-Azhar University, and of Mr. Mubarak, and posting them on his personal blog.

Bahrain, another country that hides authoritarian rule behind a veneer of democratic practice, has taken to summoning bloggers for questioning, and tries to make them register with the police. Saudi Arabia, which blocks thousands of websites, has silenced many web critics with quiet warnings. Syria's most prominent web activist, who runs a news service reporting opposition, as well as government views, recently quit the country for similar reasons. But like the controversial opinions of Mr. Suleiman, the Alexandria blogger, the real story of what goes on in Syria is still on the web, for anyone inclined to find it.

Sovereignty, Borders, and Real Life

1.3 Why The World Isn't Flat

Pankaj Ghemawat

While the spread of literacy and the development of information and communication technology may indeed be leveling the world, giving increased power to ordinary people (at the expense of sovereign states and their leaders) and allowing individuals around the world to work together for profit or to solve shared problems, Harvard Business School professor Pankaj Ghemawat warns against assuming that national boundaries and global geography no longer matter. The reality is more complex than that. As Rosenau would put it, the possibilities and pressures for global integration coexist with possibilities and pressures for fragmentation. Indeed, national and local loyalties, and national and local political and economic institutions, not only continue to matter but are strengthened by the sense of alienation and fears of powerlessness that a truly global world creates.

"Ideas will spread faster, leaping borders. Poor countries will have immediate access to information that was once restricted to the industrial world and traveled only slowly, if at all, beyond it. Entire electorates will learn things that once only a few bureaucrats knew. Small companies will offer services that previously only giants could provide. In all these ways, the communications revolution is profoundly democratic and liberating, leveling the imbalance between large and small, rich and poor." The global vision that Frances Cairncross predicted in her *Death of Distance* appears to be upon us. We seem to live in a world that is no longer a collection of isolated, "local" nations, effectively separated by high tariff walls, poor communications networks and mutual suspicion. It's a world that, if you believe the most prominent proponents of globalization, is increasingly wired, informed, and, well, "flat."

It's an attractive idea. And if publishing trends are any indication, globalization is more than just a powerful economic and political transformation; it's a booming cottage industry. According to the U.S. Library of Congress's catalog, in the 1990s, about 500 books were published on globalization. Between 2000 and 2004, there were more than 4,000. In fact, between the mid-1990s and 2003, the rate of increase in globalization-related titles more than doubled every 18 months.

Amid all this clutter, several books on the subject have managed to attract significant attention. During a recent TV interview, the first question I was asked—quite earnestly—was why I still thought the world was round. The interviewer was referring of course to the thesis of *New York Times* columnist Thomas L. Friedman's bestselling book *The World Is Flat*. Friedman asserts that 10 forces—most of which enable connectivity and collaboration at a distance—are "flattening" the Earth and leveling a playing field of global competitiveness, the likes of which the world has never before seen.

It sounds compelling enough. But Friedman's assertions are simply the latest in a series of exaggerated visions that also include the "end of history" and the "convergence of tastes." Some writers in this vein view globalization as a good thing—an escape from the ancient tribal rifts that have divided humans, or an opportunity to sell the same thing to everyone on Earth. Others lament its cancerous spread, a process at the end of which everyone will be eating the same fast food. Their arguments are mostly characterized by emotional rather than cerebral appeals, a reliance on prophecy, semiotic arousal (that is, treating everything as as sign), a focus on technology as the driver of change, an emphasis on education that creates "new" people, and perhaps above all, a clamor for attention. But they all have one thing in common: they're wrong.

In truth, the world is not nearly as connected as these writers would have us believe. Despite talk of a new, wired world where information, ideas, money, and people can move around the planet faster than ever before, just a fraction of what we consider globalization actually exists. The portrait that emerges from a hard look at the way companies, people, and states interact is a world that's only beginning to realize the potential of true global integration. And what these trend's backers won't tell you is that globalization's future is more fragile than you know.

The 10 Percent Presumption

The few cities that dominate international financial activity—Frankfurt, Hong Kong, London, New York—are at the height of modern global integration; which is to say, they are all relatively well connected with one another. But when you examine the numbers, the picture is one of extreme connectivity at the local level, not a flat world. What do such statistics reveal? Most types of economic activity that could be conducted either within or across borders turn out to still be quite domestically concentrated.

One favorite mantra from globalization champions is how "investment knows no boundaries." But how much of all the capital being invested around the world is conducted by companies outside of their home countries? The fact is, the total amount of the world's capital formation that is generated from foreign direct investment (FDI) has been less than 10 percent for the last three years for which data are available (2003–05). In other words, more than 90 percent of the fixed investment around the world is still domestic. And though merger waves can push the ratio higher, it has never reached 20 percent. In a thoroughly globalized environment, one would expect this number to be much higher—about 90 percent, by my calculation. And FDI isn't an odd or unrepresentative example. . . .

A Strong National Defense

If you buy into the more extreme views of the globalization triumphalists, you would expect to see a world where national borders are irrelevant, and where citizens increasingly view themselves as members of ever broader political entities. True, communications technologies have improved dramatically during the past 100 years. The cost of a three-minute telephone call from New York to London fell from $350 in 1930 to about 40 cents in 1999, and it is now approaching zero for voice-over-Internet telephony. And the Internet itself is just one of many newer forms of connectivity that have progressed several times faster than plain old telephone service. This pace of improvement has inspired excited proclamations about the pace of global integration. But it's a huge leap to go from predicting such changes to asserting that declining communication costs will obliterate the effects of distance. Although the barriers at borders have declined significantly, they haven't disappeared.

To see why, consider the Indian software industry—a favorite of Friedman and others. Friedman cites Nandan Nilekani, the CEO of the second-largest such firm, Infosys, as his muse for the notion of a flat world. But what Nilekani has pointed out privately is that while Indian software programmers can now serve the United States from India, access is assured, in part, by U.S. capital being invested—quite literally—in that outcome. In other words, the success of the Indian IT industry is not exempt from political and geographic constraints. The country of origin matters—even for capital, which is often considered stateless.

Or consider the largest Indian software firm, Tata Consultancy Services (TCS). Friedman has written at least two columns in the *New York Times* on TCS's Latin American operations: "[I]n today's world, having an Indian company led by a Hungarian-Uruguayan servicing American banks with Montevidean engineers managed by Indian technologists who have learned to eat Uruguayan veggie is just the new normal," Friedman writes. Perhaps. But the real question is why the company established those operations in the first place. Having worked as a strategy advisor to TCS since 2000, I can testify that reasons related to the tyranny of time zones, languages, and the need for proximity to clients' local operations loomed large in that decision. This is a far cry from globalization proponents' oft-cited world in which geography, language, and distance don't matter.

Trade flows certainly bear that theory out. Consider Canadian-U.S. trade, the largest bilateral relationship of its kind in the world. In 1988, before the North American Free Trade Agreement (NAFTA) took effect, merchandise trade levels between Canadian provinces—that is, within the country—were estimated to be 20 times as large as their trade with similarly sized and similarly distant U.S. states. In other words, there was a built-in "home bias." Although NAFTA helped reduce this ratio of domestic to international trade—the home bias—to 10 to 1 by the mid-1990s, it still exceeds 5 to 1 today. And these ratios are just for merchandise;

for services, the ratio is still several times larger. Clearly, the borders in our seemingly "borderless world" still matter to most people.

Geographical boundaries are so pervasive, they even extend to cyberspace. If there were one realm in which borders should be rendered meaningless and the globalization proponents should be correct in their overly optimistic models, it should be the Internet. Yet Web traffic within countries and regions has increased far faster than traffic between them. Just as in the real world, Internet links decay with distance. People across the world may be getting more connected, but they aren't connecting with each other. The average South Korean Web user may be spending several hours a day online—connected to the rest of the world in theory—but he is probably chatting with friends across town and e-mailing family across the country rather than meeting a fellow surfer in Los Angeles. We're more wired, but no more "global."

Just look at Google, which boasts of supporting more than 100 languages and, partly as a result, has recently been rated the most globalized Web site. But Google's operation in Russia (cofounder Sergey Brin's native country) reaches only 28 percent of the market there, versus 64 percent for the Russian market leader in search services, Yandex, and 53 percent for Rambler.

Indeed, these two local competitors account for 91 percent of the Russian market for online ads linked to Web searches. What has stymied Google's expansion into the Russian market? The biggest reason is the difficulty of designing a search engine to handle the linguistic complexities of the Russian language. In addition, these local competitors are more in tune with the Russian market, for example, developing payment methods through traditional banks to compensate for the dearth of credit cards. And, though Google has doubled its reach since 2003, it's had to set up a Moscow office in Russia and hire Russian software engineers, underlining the continued importance of physical location. Even now, borders between countries define—and constrain—our movements more than globalization breaks them down. . . .

The champions of globalization are describing a world that doesn't exist. It's a fine strategy to sell books and even describe a potential environment that may someday exist. Because such episodes of mass delusion tend to be relatively short-lived even when they do achieve broad currency, one might simply be tempted to wait this one out as well. But the stakes are far too high for that. Governments that buy into the flat world are likely to pay too much attention to the "golden straitjacket" that Friedman emphasized in his earlier book, *The Lexus and the Olive Tree*, which is supposed to ensure that economics matters more and more and politics less and less. Buying into this version of an integrated world—or worse, using it as a basis for policymaking—is not only unproductive. It is dangerous.

1.4 Our Borderless World

Moisés Naím

By contrast to Pankaj Ghemawat in the preceding selection, Moisés Naím, the editor of the journal *Foreign Policy,* stresses the reduced—or at least changed—significance of political borders in today's world. It may be comforting to imagine a world divided clearly and unambiguously by the the dark and impermeable maplines representing the boundaries of sovereign states. But which borders matter, in what ways, for which purposes, and for what people is in flux. True, states continue to exist and continue to divide the world along their borders. And true, individuals continue to exhibit loyalty to their national group and continue to expect a state to protect "their" nation's interests and customs. At the same time, however, the forces of integration and fragmentation that Rosenau discusses are making borders porous. Ideas, goods, and sometimes (although not always) people are able to move more and more freely across them. The result is a world in which state borders and national loyalties have not disappeared but in which interactions across borders serve to unite as well as divide.

A country's borders should not be confused with those familiar dotted lines drawn on some musty old map of nation-states. In an era of mass migration, globalization and instant communication, a map reflecting the world's true boundaries would be a crosscutting, high-tech and multidimensional affair.

Where is the real U.S. border, for example, when U.S. customs agents check containers in the port of Amsterdam? Where should national borders be marked when drug traffickers launder money through illegal financial transactions that crisscross the globe electronically, violating multiple jurisdictions? How would border checkpoints help record companies that discover pirated copies of their latest offering for sale in cyberspace—long before the legitimate product even reaches stores? And when U.S. health officials fan out across Asia seeking to contain a disease outbreak, where do national lines truly lie?

Governments and citizens are used to thinking of a border as a real, physical place: a fence, a shoreline, a desert or a mountain pass. But while geography still matters, today's borders are being redefined and redrawn in unexpected ways. They are fluid, constantly remade by technology, new laws and institutions, and the realities of international commerce—illicit as well as legitimate. They are also increasingly intangible, living in a virtual and electronic space.

In this world, the United States is adjacent not just to Mexico and Canada but also to China and Bolivia. Italy now borders on Nigeria, and France on Mali.

These borders cannot be protected with motion sensors or National Guard troops.

Naím, Moisés, "Our Borderless World," *Washington Post National Weekly Edition,* June 5–11, 2006, p. 22. Reprinted by permission of the author.

Political unions, economic reforms and breakthroughs in technology and business came together to revolutionize the world's borders during the 1990s.

It was a decade during which a global passion for free markets erupted. From Latin America to Eastern Europe, politicians and their electorates felt that prosperity was possible by enticing foreigners to invest, tourists to visit, traders to import and export, banks to move funds freely in and out of countries, and businesses to operate free of heavy regulations.

It was also a decade when nations with long histories of conflict or animosity surprised the world by dismantling or rearranging their borders through political unions and trade agreements. The European Union kicked into high gear; Argentina, Brazil and rival South American nations formed a regional customs union; and Mexico joined Canada and the United States in their own trade agreement. These efforts sought to maximize economic growth and political harmony (or so the leaders hoped).

Meanwhile, new technologies were vastly reducing the economic and business importance of distance and geography. The only prices that dropped faster than shipping a cargo container from Shanghai to Los Angeles were those for sending e-mail, making phone calls, or rapid-firing text and images across borders.

With borders much more fluid, opportunities for profit multiplied and cross-border activity boomed. Suddenly it seemed normal to invest in Thailand, visit China, trade in exotic currencies, take seasonal jobs in different countries or download stolen software from Bulgarian Web sites.

Even something as simple as buying a counterfeit Prada handbag on the streets of Manhattan or Washington represented the final step in a long journey of border crossings. The bag's original design—probably acquired or stolen in Europe—was transported electronically or physically to China. There, the leather, zippers, belts and buckles were procured and assembled into tens of thousands of counterfeit handbags. The finished products were then smuggled onto containers officially carrying, say, industrial valves, to ports such as Naples or New York.

Once the handbags reached these final markets, street merchants took over—often African immigrants who themselves were smuggled across borders by human-trafficking networks. Yes, the poorly paid street vendors are usually as illegal as the goods they're peddling. Meanwhile, the overall counterfeit enterprise reaped enormous cash profits that were converted into bank deposits and laundered across the globe electronically, again trespassing across multiple borders.

These changes reflected a severe and acute new asymmetry: borders became harder for governments to control, and easier and more lucrative for violators to bypass. Anyone seeking to cross them found it easier to do so, while government agencies floundered in their efforts to regulate the new world they had helped create.

Today's borders are violated, enforced and remade not only on the ground but also in cyberspace, multilateral agencies and the virtual world of international finance.

Consider the most mundane of examples: the ATM. When an immigrant living in the United States sends her ATM card to her children in the Philippines and they draw money from her U.S. checking account, where has the transaction taken place? Did the kids cross a border to tap the funds from an American bank? In a sense, they did—the ubiquitous ATM has become a powerful, easy-to-use, border-crossing tool. Often, such crossings are perfectly legal. But not always.

National boundaries are also being transformed by new—or newly empowered—international institutions. For example, when the World Trade Organization's 149 member states agree on the reduction of tariff rates around the globe, our time-honored beliefs about controlling sovereign borders are upended. On trade, the borders that matter may be drawn at the WTO headquarters in Geneva as much as anywhere else.

The fluid, unpredictable nature of modern borders is evident even among the most geographically isolated and remote nations on Earth. Try landlocked Bolivia and Afghanistan. Their rugged geography and poor roads make internal travel exceedingly difficult and time-consuming. Yet narco-traffickers regularly and swiftly connect Bolivia's remote Chapare region, where coca is cultivated, with Miami or New York, where cocaine is consumed (with a processing stopover in the jungles of Colombia and a transshipment detour to a deserted beach in Haiti). And in Afghanistan, opium traffickers seamlessly link the Deshu district in the lawless Helmand province with elegant consumers in London or Milan.

Even for experienced travelers, reaching Chapare or Deshu is a tough pro-position. But location and geography now matter less and less for traffickers or for anyone seeking to violate national borders. In major cities across the globe, the availability of banned merchandise stands as a monument of sorts to nations' eroding sovereignty—no matter the billions of dollars that governments spend seeking to keep such goods from reaching their shores and penetrating their borders.

In 2004, the *Guardian* published a dispatch from the banks of the Yalu River, on the border between China and North Korea. "Here and there shadowy figures can be seen on both sides of the misty river quietly carrying out an illegal—but thriving—trade in women, endangered species, food and consumer appliances," wrote Jonathan Watts.

If a paranoid police state such a North Korea is incapable of controlling its borders and deterring illicit trade, there seems to be little hope for open, democratic, and technologically advanced nations seeking to uphold their sovereign borders. This issue gained urgency in the United States in particular after the terrorist attacks of Sept. 11, 2001, when security concerns became paramount.

Yet the paradox of policing borders in a high-tech, globally integrated era is that today, less sovereignty may equal more protection. In order to reinforce national boundaries and combat terrorism, one of the most effective tools a government can deploy is collaboration with other nations—in effect, ceding or "pooling" certain aspects of their sovereignty.

That is no easy task. It requires partnering with less efficient, less democratic and less trustworthy nations and sharing information, technology, intelligence and decision-making power. In many quarters—Washington and beyond—the notion of diluting national sovereignty verges on treason.

But if sovereignty is indeed a hallowed concept, it has become a somewhat hollow one, too. Traditional borders are violated daily by countless means, and virtual borders seem even more permeable and misunderstood. "Closing the border" may appeal to nationalist sentiments and to the human instinct of building moats and walls for protection. But when threats travel via fiber optics or inside migrating birds, and when finding ways to move illegal goods across borders promises unimaginable wealth or the only chance of a decent life, unilateral security measures have the unfortunate whiff of a Maginot line.

1.5 Cities Mesh Across Blurry Border, Despite Physical Barrier

Marc Lacey

As *New York Times* reporter Marc Lacey points out in the following news story, the U.S.-Mexican border offers a good illustration of the ties that exist across political boundaries in today's world. Real life, its problems, and its achievements—jobs, family ties, education, housing prices, pollution, crime, art, culture—have found ways to ignore boundaries and barriers. In dealing with any of these, the distinction between domestic and international quickly becomes problematic.

Mexican authorities complained recently that American construction workers putting up a barrier on the border between Mexico and the United States had trespassed into Mexico a full 33 feet.

Promising an investigation of the diplomatic brouhaha, the American ambassador, Antonio O. Garza, Jr., reassured the Mexicans, who are livid that the barrier is going up in the first place, that any improper step across the line was unintentional. "The U.S. is sensitive to Mexican concerns," Mr. Garza said.

The accusation involved an episode in February east of here, near the Mexican border city of Agua Prieta and the Arizona town of Douglas. But it drove home a point that might be more evident in Tijuana than anywhere else: the border is a blurry one, no matter what barriers may be going up to keep people from illegally crossing it.

A case in point is Kurt Honold Morales, a citizen and resident of both countries, who drives his Mercedes sports utility vehicle with California plates around Tijuana, where he works.

Mr. Honold, a 46-year-old telecommunications executive, recently became the mayor of Tijuana, when the elected mayor resigned to run for governor and Mr. Honold, a business associate and the mayor's No. 2, stepped in to fill the unexpired term.

"We're connected, border or no border," Mr. Honold said, noting that his children go to San Diego schools and that his family has held season tickets for the San Diego Chargers for more than 30 years.

On a host of issues, there is no separating San Diego, the largest city along the border, from Tijuana, the biggest municipality on the Mexican side.

They are linked economically, with Tijuana's assembly plants, or maquiladoras, helping to fuel growth on both sides of the border. High home prices in San Diego have pulled up Tijuana's real estate as well.

When it comes to the environment, it is difficult to say where Mexico ends and United States begins. Air pollution knows no borders, and heavy rains in Tijuana send sewage and industrial waste down the Tijuana River into the United States.

A former congressman once used a bulldozer to try to push sewage back to Mexico, but that was no permanent fix. For years, an American-financed sewage treatment plant on the Tijuana side has been considered the best solution, although now support is increasing for a plant to process waste on the American side.

There are other cross-border irritants. When San Diego announced that it was replacing a leaky section of the canal that carries water into the city from the Colorado River, Mexicans complained loudly because their farmers had been irrigating their crops with the leakage for decades.

Mr. Honold, whose German-Mexican father was born in San Diego, is hardly the only person whose life straddles the border.

There is Elisa R. Peñaloza-Aguirre, also a dual citizen, who teaches in a San Diego elementary school but moved to Tijuana a year ago for the lower home prices and so that her children would become fluent in Spanish as well as English.

"There are tons of people who commute back and forth," said Ms. Peñaloza-Aguirre, one of 88,252 regular crossers who have a special American pass that allows them to use a fast lane at the California-Mexico border.

There is metal border fencing running the length of Tijuana, but that does not stop people from trying to poke holes in the barriers, both literally and figuratively.

For years, the San Diego-Tijuana Border Initiative, a binational anti-drug organization, held its meetings right at the fence, with American members sitting on chairs on their side and their Mexican colleagues on the other. "The drug problem does not stop at the border," said Veronica Baeza, the group's executive director.

But American authorities soured on the meetings after Sept. 11, 2001, Ms. Baeza said. Now the sessions are rotated between the cities, though Mexicans without visas cannot attend the ones in San Diego.

It is hard to find a Mexican who supports the barriers going up along the border. Many are offended by such an approach, even those like Tijuana's mayor, who will be able to cross back and forth no matter how high the walls are built.

On the other hand, Representative Duncan Hunter, a Republican who represents part of the San Diego area and is a candidate for president, has said building a wall between Mexico and the United States will be among his highest priorities if he wins. One of his campaign advisers, Lois Eargle, a county official in South

Carolina, recently boasted about the advice she gave an illegal immigrant seeking legal aid for an abused child.

"I told her the best thing for her to do was to get back to Mexico," Ms. Eargle said.

Luis Ituarte, a third-generation Tijuanan who lives in Tijuana half the week and Los Angeles the other half, has a much more relaxed view of the border.

Just recently, his Border Council of Arts and Culture rented a house in Tijuana just a few steps from the border to use as a cultural center. Recently, it was the site of a cross-border poetry reading. Using bull-horns, poets from Mexico and the United States recited their work from their respective countries.

"Air doesn't need a passport," Mr. Ituarte said. "Light doesn't need a passport. Art should not need a passport either."

Mr. Ituarte, who is a citizen of Mexico and permanent resident of the United States, chose the site of the cultural center not just for its proximity to the border. The house was seized by Mexican authorities several years ago when it was discovered that drug traffickers had dug a hole in the concrete floor and a tunnel that crossed under the border to a parking lot in San Ysidro, Calif.

"What better place to try to connect two cultures," he said. "We want to break this wall in a subliminal way, if we can't break it physically."

The Twenty-First-Century State?

1.6 We Need Rules for Sovereign Funds

Jeffrey Garten

While most observers of today's world stress the weakened capacity of states relative to their own people and to other actors on the world stage such as transnational corporations, it should be clear that states, too, can take advantage of the opportunities that globalization offers and can adapt in interesting and provocative ways. States may survive and flourish in the twenty-first century, but they may end up looking quite different, and behaving very differently, from today's states. In the final selection, Yale University trade and finance professor Jeffrey Garten talks about a new business that states are increasingly getting into—the international investment business. Traditionally, political scientists have thought of states as being in the business of providing security to their people, selling their citizens protection against each other (crime) and outsiders (an invasion or military attack) and charging these citizens tax dollars and obedience to the state's laws in return. But the distinction between states and other business enterprises may be becoming increasingly blurred. As Garten points out, many states are increasingly getting into the overseas investment game, taking the money they may have accumulated and buying and selling stakes in businesses around the world. The possibility that states may acquire large stakes, or even controlling interests, in companies operating outside their borders and may use these investments for political purposes is troubling. Sovereign wealth funds (SWFs)—investment funds that are owned by states—blur not only the boundaries between states, but the boundaries between public and private that Americans usually take for granted.

The growth of government-owned investment companies, often called sovereign wealth funds, has caused a lot of hand-wringing in the U.S. and Europe—and rightly so.

Washington has asked the International Monetary Fund and World Bank to establish a code of good practice for SWFs. Berlin is eyeing new legislation to deal with these funds, modelled on U.S. procedures for screening incoming foreign direct investment. Brussels is considering a European-wide set of guidelines. But so far no western government has had the courage to admit that dealing with SWFs may require departures from the conventional liberal orthodoxy concerning global trade and investment flows. Yet this is precisely what is needed.

When relatively few SWFs existed, such as Singapore's Temasek Holdings or the Kuwait Investment Authority, the challenge they posed to the global financial system and to market-based cross-border investment was small. But now sovereign funds in countries such as Saudi Arabia and Russia are becoming active, Beijing is establishing the government-owned China Investment Corporation, and Japan and South Korea are contemplating similar SWFs. Moreover, the amounts under sovereign management could soar from about $2,500bn today to $12,000bn in 2015, according to Morgan Stanley.

These funds are going to have the ability to buy any global company, to create panic in markets if they move too precipitously, even to dwarf the political clout of international financial institutions. They can no longer be ignored.

The agenda for dealing with SWFs must take account of disturbing trends in the global marketplace. For all the backslapping among finance officials and private bankers about the benefits of increasing globalisation and the diversification of risk via securitisation and high-technology derivatives, the fact is that the capital markets have become increasingly opaque.

Between the growth of impossible-to-value derivatives, the phenomenal increase in secretive hedge funds and the multiplying layers of connections among different markets, a critical assumption underlying a liberal economic order—that market participants have the information they need to make rational decisions—is being jeopardised.

This is where sovereign wealth funds come into the picture. Yes, they are only part of the global financial black box, but because they are driven by governments, they nevertheless compel immediate attention. As they expand their presence, they could undercut another key premise of a global market—that it is dominated

Garten, Jeffrey, "We Need Rules for Sovereign Funds," *Financial Times,* August 8, 2007, p. 9. Reprinted by permission of the author.

by private participants seeking to maximise their welfare and that of their shareholders.

Of course, in 2007, sovereign funds may seek to invest excess foreign exchange reserves or extraordinary profits from oil for nothing more than higher returns than would be earned from U.S. Treasuries. But who knows what the governments of countries such as China, Russia and Saudi Arabia may look like a decade from now, and what their political motivations might be?

In the first instance, the U.S. and European Union should harmonise their policies rather than pursue their usual go-it-alone response to important global issues. Among the principles that Washington and Brussels ought to consider are these:

Transparency is the key. In order to be treated as normal investors, SWFs should be obliged to publish internationally audited reports on their entire portfolios at least twice a year. They should disclose the precise mechanisms by which they themselves are regulated in their home countries—including the specific individuals charged with that oversight. From the SWF disclosures we should know the fund's investment philosophy, its corporate governance process and its risk management techniques.

Reciprocity should be required. If western host countries are going to treat SWFs like any other market participant, the economy of the SWF's home country must be as open as the country in which the SWF aspires to invest. In addition, if a sovereign fund was established because of currency manipulation in the host country that led to excess reserve creation (China), or if it is the result of strident resource nationalism (Russia), or if it is due to monopolistic pricing practices (Saudi Arabia), then consultations should be initiated between the two governments to reduce these policy distortions.

Ownership guidelines are essential. SWFs should not own more than 20 percent of any company in the U.S. or Europe, without a decision of the host government to go higher. The underlying premise must be that SWFs are political entities and should be treated as such.

Many in global financial markets will see these proposals as having a protectionist thrust. However, it would be equally dangerous to pretend that governments will always invest like normal market participants, or that without effective rules, the growing activity of SWFs will not set off an even larger protectionist backlash than the rules themselves would create.

Others will worry that the U.S. will jeopardise much-needed funding for its large current account deficits. It is equally possible, though, that predictable rules could facilitate capital flows. One thing is for sure: it will become more difficult to deal with SWFs once they become an entrenched feature of the world economy. Now is the time to act.

Suggested Discussion Topics

1. Explain the key steps in the evolution of Europe's state system and its expansion to incorporate the rest of the world. What forces led to or shaped the emergence of a state system and its globalization? Do you think the emergence

of separate, individually sovereign states and a global system composed of sovereign states was inevitable? Do you think it will continue? Why might it continue and why might it change? Do you think the three parameter shifts that Rosenau discusses will affect the state system? If so, is this good or bad?

2. Define state sovereignty. What are the key features of a sovereign state? Why does the sovereignty of states imply the anarchy of the state system? What does anarchy imply about the potential for conflict and cooperation between states? Are today's nation-states sovereign in a meaningful sense? Explain your thinking. Some observers see international organizations such as the UN, or developments such as the emergence of a "global market" and the increasing importance of market forces, as undermining state sovereignty. Do you agree?

3. What role does the sovereign state play in your life? What do you rely on the state for, and what do you turn to other organizations or institutions for? Do you think this state of affairs will change?

4. How has the meaning of national security been altered in recent years? What does it mean to you to be "secure"? What threats or dangers do you need to be protected from? As an ordinary person, how do you protect yourself from these dangers? What political institutions or organizations do you rely on for protection?

5. What is meant by "dilemmas of collective action," and why is it difficult to get states to cooperate in solving collective problems? Can you think of examples of collective action problems in the world today, or in your daily life? How are these dilemmas solved?

6. Compare the forces in global politics that are pushing in the direction of integration of peoples with those causing fragmentation of many states. What examples of integration and fragmentation do you see in the world today? How do you expect these forces to work during your lifetime? In what ways do you think the world will be more integrated and in what ways more fragmented fifty years from now?

7. Do you think borders are declining in importance? Explain your thinking and cite evidence that supports it. If we are moving toward an increasingly borderless world, will we need a "world government" to solve the problems and resolve the disputes that arise? Why or why not? In the wake of the September 11, 2001 terrorist attacks, do you think national borders ought to be strengthened? What are the costs and benefits of living in a world with strengthened international borders? What would strengthened borders involve and mean in the case of San Diego and Tijuana? Be prepared to debate the pros and cons of making—or trying to make—this border more impermeable.

8. Should states be able to buy investments in other countries? For example, should the Chinese state be allowed to buy a stake in McDonald's? Or in General Motors? Or in Microsoft? Or in Lockheed Martin (the largest arms manufacturer in the world)? Should the Chinese state be allowed to buy a controlling stake in such companies? How does it transform the nature of the state if the state is in the business not only of trying to protect its people but of playing global investment or financial markets for profit and power?

Chapter 2

OUT OF CONTROL?
THE RISE OF POSTMODERN
WAR AND TERRORISM

For centuries, the prospect of war among sovereign states has been regarded by scholars and practitioners as the most critical issue in global politics. In the absence of higher authority, war was seen as a legal right and as the final arbiter of disputes among sovereign states. War or the threat of war was the ultimate remedy available to states to defend themselves from aggression, enforce their rights, or secure their interests. As a result, even in times of peace, states had to prepare for war.

Given the prevalence of war in global politics, some scholars have assumed that war is rooted in unalterable conditions, perhaps man's fallen nature or the absence of central authority. At best, these scholars, frequently termed "realists," believe that the scope and duration of war can be limited by creating a balance of power. By contrast, other scholars, often called liberals (or derided as "idealists" and "utopians" by members of the first school), view war as preventable, perhaps through education, international law, economic development, economic integration, or democracy.

One thing is clear, however: war (defined as organized violence) and the threat of war have been present in most historical periods and in most places. As far back as we have recorded history, roughly five thousand years, we have a record of war. With only a very few exceptions, such as contemporary Costa Rica and Iceland, all countries have had armed forces, and many of the most important technological developments over the past several hundred years were achieved with military objectives in mind. Indeed, the beginning of the Western tradition in global politics is often ascribed to the Greek general and historian Thucydides, who described in detail the symptoms, causes, and consequences of the Peloponnesian War between the Greek city-states of Athens and Sparta and their respective allies in the fifth century B.C.

Much of our understanding of war, however, grows out of the roughly 350 years of "modern" history since the Treaty of Westphalia ended the Thirty Years' War (1618–1648). By the end of that epochal struggle, Europe was in shambles, its economy devastated and its population decimated by disease. In the shadow of that war, in which civilians had been victims as much as soldiers and the distinction between military campaigning and organized banditry was often hard to make, the leaders of Europe's newly emerging territorial states set out to limit war, especially its consequences for civil society. They sought to differentiate clearly between "legitimate" warfare by professional warriors undertaken in the interests of states and "illegitimate" crime against civilians and the domestic order. Professional armies were created, dressed in special uniforms, limited by international law in how they fought, and clearly distinguished from civilian populations. The soldiers' task was to protect the state and further its national interests in an anarchic global system. War, in other words, was to be waged by a clearly defined group of professional soldiers, answering to a clearly identified sovereign authority, according to a clearly specified set of rules that limited the violence done. Ordinary citizens, unless they were impressed into military service and except for the requirement that they pay taxes to support the army, would be largely free from the consequences of their rulers' decisions to wage war and would be protected from whatever fighting might go on around them. In this way, war was to be a rational instrument in the hands of state leaders, available when other instruments proved inadequate to achieve the state's political ends.

This view of war as a rational instrument of national policy was articulated eloquently by the Prussian military theorist Karl Maria von Clausewitz (1780–1831). Clausewitz is famous for his argument that war must be regarded as an extension of politics—that it is one of the instruments at the disposal of states in their efforts to get what they want from other states—and for his "trinitarian" view of war, which distinguishes among the soldiers who fight the war and are the legitimate target of violence during war, the leaders of the state who direct the war, and the populace whose taxes and industry support the war. His view of war as something that can be monopolized by states and limited to avoid harm to civilians grew out of the fact that war in Europe in his era was the business of professional soldiers formed into regiments. These regiments were employed and carefully controlled by states and were isolated from civilians. In this way, kings could keep peace at home without running the risk that soldiers would loot the countryside as they often had during the Thirty Years' War.

The Clausewitzian conception of war remained largely unquestioned until the experiences of World War I (1914–1918) and World War II (1939–1945) demonstrated the difficulty of keeping wars limited and controlled. As these wars showed, changes in technology and in how people interacted with political authority—an explosive combination of improved military weaponry, an increased ability of economies to raise and support mass armies, and growing popular nationalism—made it difficult to employ war as a rational means for achieving limited political objectives. Ensuring that the violence of war would remain under control was proving increasingly difficult for states.

During the Cold War, direct military confrontation between the United States and the Soviet Union was avoided largely because both sides recognized that it was virtually impossible to use nuclear weapons as rational instruments of national policy and that in a direct conflict between the superpowers it would be difficult to refrain from using these weapons. In other words, leaders realized that a war between the superpowers would probably escalate out of their rational control and that the destruction to both societies would probably greatly exceed any rational political benefit. Despite the Strategic Defense Initiative (SDI or, as it was popularly known, "Star Wars") begun by President Ronald Reagan in an effort to develop an antiballistic missile (ABM) defense against a possible Soviet attack, a high-confidence national missile defense (NMD) shield to protect civilians from a nuclear attack has not been possible. As a consequence, the potentially catastrophic nature of war, even for the strongest military powers, continues to have a chilling effect on the use of war as an instrument of politics. Nonetheless, as the Iraqi invasion of Kuwait in 1990 (and the subsequent "Desert Storm" war in the Persian Gulf that pitted an American-led international alliance against Iraq) illustrated, war is still sometimes used by states as a method to advance their national interest, and states remain concerned about the danger that other states will resort to war.

Although the experience of the 1990–91 "Desert Storm" war suggests that the kind of politically purposeful violence, controlled and limited by states, that Clausewitz wrote about still exists in today's world, more and more of the "wars" taking place around the world do not fit this model. One element of the turbulent political transformation under way is the increasing fragmentation of political authority and the breakdown of political control over the use of violence.

Even during the Cold War, some conflicts demonstrated that Clausewitz's distinction among governments, soldiers, and ordinary people was difficult to preserve in the modern world. The American defeat in Vietnam and the Soviet defeat in Afghanistan, for example, confronted states with the problem of irregular warfare waged by guerrillas in which the distinction between civilians and soldiers was muddied. Recent experiences in Iraq have underscored these earlier lessons, reminding Americans that "war" may pit American military forces against adversaries other than the army of another sovereign state. Far from ending the violence, the defeat and destruction of the Iraqi army at the hands of the American coalition forces, and the effective dissolution of the Ba'athist Iraqi state, merely marked a prelude to the more protracted and bloody violence in which various militias, political factions, ethnic groups, and religious sects fought among themselves and against American and coalition troops. The goals of the combatants have been varied, shifting, and sometimes unclear; their targets have frequently been unarmed innocents, and even in cases in which the targets were other combatants, significant "collateral" casualties have been viewed as acceptable; and the weapons of choice have often been bombs or explosive devices that have been indiscriminate in their killing effect. In dealing with this kind of civil violence, the United States has resorted to a variety of tactics, including interrogation procedures like those employed at Abu Ghraib, that violate traditional norms.

In recent years, doubts about war being the preserve and rational tool of sovereign states have been intensified by the virtual collapse of states like Somalia, Congo, and Yugoslavia, and the upsurge in violence within or across states in which civilians are the principal targets and in which youthful fighters (often children armed with modern weapons and high on drugs) kill, loot, and rape in the name of some vague ethnic or national slogan, or often for no higher motive at all.

The "postmodern wars"—or what Herfried Münkler refers to as the "new wars"—that are increasingly commonplace today thus challenge the notion that wars are waged *by* sovereign states *against* sovereign states to enhance the power and well-being *of* sovereign states. While some wars may fit this Clausewitzian image, many do not. If we mistakenly assume that all wars will be "like" Desert Storm, we are in danger of overlooking or misinterpreting many of the forces that are tearing apart today's turbulent world.

"War," the prominent military historian John Keegan recently argued, "is not the continuation of policy by other means." In his view, war is an extension of culture rather than politics, and Clausewitz's belief that war is a matter of "state interests" and "rational calculation" reflects European culture of the eighteenth century and particular political conditions at the time Clausewitz lived. What Clausewitzian war attempted to do was to limit and carefully control human violence: not to eliminate it altogether or outlaw it, but to make it the special responsibility of the state, to prohibit nonstate actors ("rebels," "freebooters," and "brigands") from engaging in it, and to limit the suffering it brought to ordinary people. It may be argued that this is what war *should* look like, and it may be the case that war sometimes *does* look like this, but it is not true that war is always this sort of rational, political activity. War is a social act, and the role it plays in a society and the meaning ascribed to it vary from culture to culture.

Nowhere is the changing nature of war and its cultural roots more visible than in the proliferation of global terrorism. The events of September 11, 2001, brought home to Americans one of the most shocking features of today's global turbulence: terrorism. Like postmodern war, the upsurge in terrorism around the world reflects the darker side of the three parametric changes in today's world noted by James Rosenau in Chapter 1: first, the greater empowerment of individuals and small groups of people, enabling them to carry out actions (for good or evil) that before could be accomplished only by large hierarchic, bureaucratic organizations like states; second, the rising capability and importance of nonstate actors, and the declining ability of states to exert meaningful sovereignty, or rule, over these other actors; and, third, the declining tendency of individuals to give unquestioning, automatic loyalty to states and their increasing tendency to challenge—by violent means if necessary—authorities and relationships they regard as unfair or illegitimate. In today's world, terrorism can be understood as one of the manifestations of the political disintegration triggered by rapid technological, economic, and social change.

Terrorism, of course, is not a new phenomenon, nor is it a tactic limited to extremist groups like Osama bin Laden's al-Qaeda network. Terrorism—the use of indiscriminate violence against innocent individuals in an effort to create a climate of fear that encourages other individuals or political actors to yield to the terrorists' demands—is a tactic employed by the strong as well as by the weak, and by states as well as by nonstate groups. Nazi Germany and the Soviet Union under Stalin, for example, used terror against occupied nations and their own people as a means of silencing dissent and deterring opposition to their political agendas. What is different in today's world is the increasing ability of nonstate actors to carry out major acts or even campaigns of terror, their increasing willingness to use these tools and tactics as a means of changing the status quo, and the increasing globalization of terrorism. Ironically, this last development reflects the increased *integration* of world politics and the recognition that the relevant or important audience for terrorists to influence may be in other countries or even on other continents. Whereas rebels in Sierra Leone chop off the hands of innocent civilians as a means of terrorizing the rest of the population of Sierra Leone into submission, the Irish

Republican Army bombs targets in Britain as a means of undermining British support for Unionists in Northern Ireland, and Palestinian Hezbollah terrorists bomb embassies and cultural centers in Argentina as a means of drawing world attention to (and bringing world pressure to bear on) Israel and its actions in the Middle East. What varies is the size of the stage on which these terrorists operate, and today, increasingly, the whole world is a relevant stage for political action.

What makes terrorism different from other forms of political violence is that it is explicitly and directly aimed at innocent individuals. By demonstrating the vulnerability of innocent individuals—and the willingness of the terrorists, whether they represent the state itself or some nonstate terrorist group, to hurt innocent people—terrorist activities seek to *coerce:* that is, they aim to *deter* or *compel* others. The goals of terrorism can vary enormously. Indeed, depending on one's political stance, one person's "terrorist" may be another person's "freedom fighter." Some groups that use terrorism (for example, the Irish Republican Army, the Palestine Liberation Organization, or the Tamil Tigers of Sri Lanka) seek independence or autonomy for their national, religious, or ethnic group. Others, like the Shining Path in Peru, are ideologically motivated. But, like states when they use terrorist measures, all of these organizations link violence to clear political objectives. Although we may be shocked by their willingness to use violence and regard as immoral their willingness to hurt random, innocent individuals, these terrorists are not "crazy": their actions are not irrational, however much we may disapprove of them. Terrorists simply refuse to acknowledge the boundaries and limits that are commonly placed on political violence. In particular, they refuse to acknowledge Clausewitz's trinitarian distinction, which differentiates between soldiers, political leaders, and civilians: terrorists regard civilians as legitimate, indeed perhaps necessary, targets of violence.

The transformation of war in today's world also involves increasing reliance on private military contractors to assist or replace the state's own armed forces. Critics describe some of these private military contractors as mercenaries, as guns for hire who provide their services (that is, their ability to kill, conquer, and coerce) to the highest bidder. Other private military contractors provide less lethal, but nonetheless vital, assistance to states or their armies, delivering food and supplies, providing infrastructure support, or maintaining and repairing equipment. In some cases, as in Sierra Leone, governments faced with civil war have relied on private military contractors to restore order. The United States has not been immune to this trend toward outsourcing military activities. Its operations in Iraq have involved extensive reliance on private military contractors, most controversially including reliance on private security firms like Blackwater to protect American officials and visitors and the operations of American firms in Iraq.

This privatization of military activities marks an extraordinary reversal in modern history. Perhaps the central feature in the emergence of the modern state in the seventeenth century was the move away from "renting" or hiring military forces and toward creating permanent forces under the direct control of the state, as part of the effort by sovereigns to monopolize control of the tools of violence. Arguably, the return of armies for hire is at least in part a consequence of the weakening, and even failure, of many states in today's world, and is a symptom of and contributing factor to the decline of a sovereign state system. The rise of private military contractors also reflects technological changes that make it possible for relatively nonbureaucratic, relatively nonhierarchical corporations to compete with states in building the tools for violence.

A final element in today's postmodern violence is the possibility of using virtual weapons to inflict damage. Nations are increasingly reliant on the Internet, and it does not take guns to attack the Internet. Cyberwarriors sitting at keyboards can attack a nation's critical infrastructure electronically without ever setting foot on that nation's territory or ever engaging in physical violence. Similarly, the Internet can be an enormously useful tool to groups seeking to mobilize resources necessary to wage war. Unlike physical territory, no state is sovereign over the Internet, and the Internet's increasing importance creates a new dimension of warfare and new challenges for the world's political institutions.

2.1 The New Wars

Herfried Münkler

In the first selection, German political scientist Herfried Münkler examines the reasons for and consequences of the rise of postmodern or "new" wars. As he explains, these wars are fundamentally different from the trinitarian model of war conceived of by Clausewitz.

In a process that long went unnoticed by the public, war has gradually changed its appearance over the past few decades. The classical model of war between states, which still largely marked the Cold War scenarios, appears to have been discontinued: states have given up their de facto monopoly of war, and what appears ever more frequently in their stead are para-state or even partly private actors (from local warlords and guerrilla groups through firms of mercenaries operating on a world scale to international terror networks) for whom war is a permanent field of activity. Not all but many of these are military entrepreneurs, who wage war on their own account and find various ways of obtaining the necessary funds. They sometimes receive financial backing from wealthy private individuals, states or émigré communities; they may sell drilling and prospecting rights on territory under their control, engage in drugs or human trafficking, or extort protection and ransom money; and, without exception, they profit from aid supplied by international agencies, since they control—or at least have access to—the refugee camps. But, wherever their resources come from, the financing of war is always an important element in the actual fighting—unlike in the classical conflicts between states. The change in modes of funding is a crucial reason why the new wars may

Excerpts from Herfried Münkler, from *The New Wars*, translated by Patrick Camiller (Cambridge, UK: Polity Press, 2005), pp. 1–31. Reprinted by permission of Polity Press Ltd.

stretch over decades, with no end in sight. Thus, if we are to understand the distinctive features of these new wars, we must always take into account their economic foundations. . . .

Ethnic-cultural tensions, and increasingly also religious convictions, play an important role in the new wars. Without ethnic and religious conflicts, the wars of the last decade in the Balkans, as well as those in the Caucasus and Afghanistan, would have developed differently or never have broken out in the first place. Such ideologies are a resource for the mobilization of support, and in recent times warring parties have fallen back on them to an increased extent. Clearly this is bound up with the fact that other sources of motivation and legitimation for the use of military force, which were prominent in earlier conflicts, have meanwhile been pushed to one side. This is especially true of social-revolutionary ideologies, which would have much greater significance if—as we still repeatedly hear it said—poverty and destitution really were the main cause of these wars. No doubt the uneven distribution of wealth is also relevant in the new wars, but it is by no means the case that military conflicts are most common where the poverty is more abject. Indeed, it may be argued that desperate want becomes more likely the longer military entrepreneurs have settled in a region and exploited its resources; and that the ending of a war brings with it no hope of political stability and economic recovery. The specific economy of the new wars, together with their long duration, ensures that the exhausted and devastated regions in question will never get back on their feet without extensive outside aid.

In view of the obscurity of the reasons for conflict and the motives for violence, I prefer to use the poorly defined but open-ended concept of "new wars"—although I am well aware that they are not so new and in many respects even involve a return of something thoroughly old. A comparison with earlier forms of warfare may help us to work out the *differentia specifica* of these wars. First of all, they need to be distinguished from the classical war between states that still often shapes contemporary images of war. But there is also the question of whether they can in a sense be described as a return to a stage prior to Europe's early modern statization of war; a look at that earlier period is a suitable way of bringing out similarities with the conditions in which the state is *no longer* what it was then *not yet*: the monopolist of war.

The constellations of the Thirty Years' War, in particular, exhibit many parallels with the new wars. It involved a characteristic mixture of private enrichment and hunger for personal power, political drives for expansion into neighbouring states, intervention to save and protect certain values, as well as internal struggles for power, influence and domination in which religious-denominational connections played by no means the smallest role.

In most of the major wars of our time—leaving aside the few instances of classical inter-state conflict between China and Vietnam, Iraq and Iran, or Ethiopia and Eritrea—we find similar combinations of values and interests, and of state, parastate and private actors. The main feature is a multiplicity of interest groups which expect to derive more disadvantages than advantages from a lasting renunciation of violence, and which therefore find nothing to suit them in peace. The wars in sub-Saharan Africa (from southern Sudan through the Great Lakes region and the Congo over to Angola), the wars associated with the collapse of Yugoslavia, the armed conflicts throughout the Caucasus (most notably in Chechnya), the wars in Afghanistan since the early 1980s: all these bear much greater resemblances to the Thirty Years' War than to the inter-state wars of the eighteenth to twentieth centuries.

This kind of historical comparison may help to bring out the specificities of the new wars. We should examine three developments here. First, there is the already mentioned *de-statization* or privatization of military force, which has become possible because the direct pursuit of war is less expensive than in the past; light weapons can be obtained everywhere on favourable terms and no lengthy training is required in their use. This cheapening has to do with the second characteristic of new wars, the greater *asymmetry* of military force, so that the adversaries are as a rule not evenly matched. There are no longer war fronts, and, therefore, few actual engagements and no major battles; military forces do not lock horns and wear each other down, but spare each other and direct their violence mostly against civilians. One aspect of this asymmetry is that certain forms of violence that used to be tactically subordinate to a military strategy have acquired a strategic dimension of their own. This is true of guerrilla warfare, as it has developed since the end of the Second World War, and especially of terrorism. This brings us to the third characteristic tendency of the new wars: namely, a successive *autonomization* of forms of violence that used to be part of a single military system. As a result, regular armies have lost control over the course of war; to a considerable extent it is now in the hands of players for whom war as a contest between like and like is an alien concept. . . .

The Old Empires and The New Wars

Nearly all wars that have claimed our attention for a shorter or longer time over the past ten to twenty years have developed in the margins and breaches of the former empires that ruled and divided the world until the early part of the last century. Thus, the Balkan wars linked to the break-up of Yugoslavia were most intense and lasted longest where the Austro-Hungarian and Ottoman empires collided with each other up to the early twentieth century, constantly shifting their spheres of influence in a succession of minor and major wars. Much the same is true of the armed conflicts and wars that have flared up in the Caucasus and elsewhere on the southern flank of the former Soviet Union, essentially in regions where the expanding Tsarist Empire and the shrinking Ottoman Empire contended with each other for supremacy from the eighteenth century onwards, and where it was only with great difficulty, and never on a permanent basis, that the Russians succeeded in bringing the mountain peoples under their sway. The eventual collapse of the Ottoman Empire at the end of the First World War led not only to the emergence of the Balkans and Caucasus as zones of war and conflict, but also to numerous confrontations in the Middle East, of which the Palestinian conflict has long been the most significant and dangerous.

As to Afghanistan, it retained into the twentieth century the role it had developed in the nineteenth as a buffer zone between the advancing Tsarist Empire and the British-ruled Indian subcontinent. . . .

Finally, almost all the wars in South East Asia and Black Africa—from Indonesia through Somalia to Guinea or Sierra Leone—take place in regions which, until after the Second World War, were ruled by European colonial powers. Here, clashes between different states have been due not so much to frontiers inherited from the colonial period as to internal disputes over political influence and social-economic policy. Along with ethnic conflicts, which can be partly traced back to pre-colonial times and were used by the colonial powers to ensure their domination, religious and cultural differences not infrequently play quite a considerable role. Of course, in conflicts that often stretch over decades, these differences are so powerfully overlaid by power politics and economic rivalries that it is only rarely possible to decide what is a cause and what is a mere occasion. Moreover, warring parties are only too happy to exploit these differences as an ideological resource for the recruitment of followers and the mobilization of support. Even where people have lived smoothly side by side for decades in multicultural, multi-ethnic communities—as in Bosnia, for example—the outbreak of open violence turns ethnic and religious divisions into faultlines of a friend-enemy definition. In short, ethnic and religious oppositions are not usually the cause of a conflict, but merely reinforce it. It is hard to define the precise mixture of personal cravings for power, ideological convictions and ethnic-cultural oppositions that keep the new wars smouldering away, often for no recognizable goal or purpose. This skein of motives and causes makes it especially difficult to end these wars and to create a lasting peace.

Our first look at the geographical distribution and density of wars in the late twentieth and early twenty-first centuries shows that where a stable state came into being, as in Western Europe or North America, zones of lasting peace have developed, but that war has become endemic mainly in regions where a major empire held sway and then fell apart. It is true that, there too, new states immediately took their place in the world organization of the United Nations, but the great majority have proved to be weak and incapable of withstanding much pressure. These parts of the world have not seen the emergence of robust state forms similar to those of Europe. There can no longer be any doubt that the many processes of state formation in the Third World, or in the periphery of the First and the Second World, have been a failure.

One of the main reasons for this failure is certainly the lack of incorruptible political elites who view the state apparatus as a source of tasks and duties rather than as a vehicle for personal enrichment. In many regions, the "capture" of the state has served to increase the power or wealth of individuals, the two usually fitting together without difficulty. Contrary to a view widely heard in discussion of the causes of the new wars and the scope for ending them, poverty as such by no means points to a danger of escalating violence and war; the most that can be said is that the juxtaposition of desperate poverty and immeasurable riches is a significant indicator that conflicts within a society are likely to develop into open civil war. And the likelihood that such civil wars will not end after a short sharp outbreak of violence, but will grow into protracted transnational wars, increases with the suspicion that the disputed territory contains mineral resources whose sale on the world market would enrich those who are trying, if necessary through violence, to bring it under their control. Potential wealth is much more significant than chronic poverty as a cause of wars. A further factor may be revenue from affluent émigré communities, whose interests and loyalties may lead them to fund one or more of the warring parties and therefore increase their staying power.

In the emergence of new wars, none of the several causes may be singled out as the really decisive one, and so the various monocasusal approaches (updated theories of imperialism or neocolonialism, explanations in terms of ethnic or religious contradictions) fall short of the mark. Yet the impenetrable web of motives and causes, which often leaves no prospect of lasting peace, is a direct consequence of the fact that it is not states but para-state players that confront one another in the new wars. . . .

In the agrarian subsistence economy that marked large parts of early modern Europe, wars would die down after a certain (considerable) time—once the country was ruined, the fields devastated and supplies consumed. But the picture is not the same in the new wars. They are linked in many ways to the world economy, through the phenomenon known as "shadow globalization," and are able to draw from it the resources necessary for their continuation. This is not the least reason why the American political and strategic theorist Edward Luttwak's idea of simply allowing the new wars to burn themselves out (in the hope that, after the exhaustion of the resources deployed in them, there would be a greater prospect of establishing a stable and lasting peace) so quickly turned out to be illusory. The embargo policy pursued for a time by the West as well as the United Nations failed in almost every case to confirm the prognosis that increased consumption of resources in wars would put an end to them more swiftly; for the warring parties usually managed to acquire the wherewithal, either by relying upon an ideological ally or a strategically interested regime, or by gaining access to the new forms of shadow globalization. This also explains why almost one in four of these wars has lasted longer than ten years. In Angola the fighting has gone on for thirty years, in Sudan for at least twenty and in Somalia for more than fifteen. The war in Afghanistan, if it is now really over, will have lasted twenty-four years, while those in eastern Anatolia and Sri Lanka are approaching their twentieth year. Without support from outside powers, and especially without shadow globalization, this would scarcely have been possible. Shadow globalization, as the term is used here, includes the émigré communities that support either or both warring parties by means of money transfers, all manner of businesses, the recruitment of volunteers and the reception of wounded or exhausted fighters. The creation of refugee camps in neighbouring countries or under UN protection has played an important role in almost every one of the new wars. Refugee camps are by no means simply war's "refuse dumps"; they are also its supply centres and reserve forces, where humanitarian aid from international organizations is at least partly converted into resources for the continuation of war.

Short Wars Between States, Long Wars Within Societies

The long duration of the new wars scarcely differentiates them from the state-building wars of early modern Europe, which could also draw upon resources from external forces motivated by religious or ideological factors. In sharp contrast, the inter-state wars in Europe from the mid-seventeenth to the early twentieth century were, with a few exceptions, rather short; both sides sought to resolve their dispute through a battle that would pave the way for subsequent peace negotiations. Napoleon and the elder Moltke, in particular, brought to perfection this form of warfare based upon the concentration of forces in space and time. War was both declared and concluded in accordance with certain rules. It therefore had a precise definition in time, beginning with the declaration of war and ending with the peace settlement. Although the First and especially the Second World War often broke these conventions, it is this model of inter-state conflict which still essentially shapes our idea of war: that is, a contest between soldiers fought in accordance with the codified laws of war. Only if some acts are not permitted in war can there be talk of war crimes that must be punished.

This has all changed in the new wars, whose course is determined by the dispersion, not the concentration, of forces in space and time, usually in accordance with the principles of guerrilla warfare. The distinction between front, rear and homeland breaks down, so that fighting is not restricted to a small sector but may flare up anywhere. A potentially decisive confrontation with the enemy is avoided at all costs, either because of a perceived unevenness of forces or because one's own troops are not suited to such warfare. The kind of combatant who dominates nearly all the new wars would have had no place in those that shaped the course of European history in the eighteenth to twentieth centuries. Typically, then, the new wars lack what characterized the inter-state wars: the decisive battle which, for Clausewitz, was the "real centre of gravity of the war":

> The great battle takes place for the sake of itself, for the sake of the victory which it is to give, and which is sought for with the utmost effort. Here on this spot, in this very hour, to conquer the enemy is the purpose in which the plan of the War with all its threads converges, in which all distant hopes, all dim glimmerings of the future meet; fate steps in before us to give an answer to the bold question.

Such questions are not posed in the new wars; there is no time or place where all the threads converge and a decisive result is sought.

Nearly every party in the new wars follows the principles of what Mao Zedong called "protracted warfare." For Mao, however, the tactic of withdrawal and dispersion after lightning attacks was only a means to wear down a numerically and technologically superior enemy, to sap its strength in order eventually to achieve equilibrium, so that the initially weaker side might then gradually move on to the strategic offensive and seek a military resolution of the war. Most players in the new wars, on the other hand, content themselves with what Mao called "strategic defensive"; that is, they use military force essentially for self-preservation, without seriously looking for a military resolution to the war. If both sides conduct the war with this aim in mind, then clearly, with sufficient internal or external funding, it can theoretically last for ever. Often it is no longer even identifiable as war, since there is scarcely any fighting and the violence, as it were, seems to be dormant. But then it suddenly breaks out anew, and the war may acquire fresh intensity before dying down again and appearing to come to an end. The concept of "low-intensity wars" is supposed to express just this concatenation. . . .

Whereas classical inter-state wars were separated from peace by legal acts such as a declaration of war and a peace agreement, and whereas they knew no intermediate status between war and peace (as Hugo Grotius pointed out in his great work *De iure belli ac pacis*), the new wars have neither an identifiable beginning nor a clearly definable end. Only very rarely is it possible to set a date on the cessation of violence, or on its flaring up again. Classical wars ended with a legal act which assured people that they could adjust their social and economic behaviour to conditions of peace; most of the new wars, by contrast, come to an end when the overwhelming majority of people behave as if there were peace, and have the capacity over time to compel the minority to behave in that way too. The problem is, of course, that in such cases the defining power rests not with the majority but with a minority. Where there is no state executive powerful enough to impose the will of the majority, the ones who decide on war or peace are those most prepared to resort to violence. They hold the initiative and impose their will on everyone else. Thus, another reason for the protracted nature of internal and transnational wars is that, if even small groups are unhappy with the emerging peacetime conditions, it is an easy matter for them to rekindle the flames of war. Since, in intra-state wars, every group capable of violence must be won over to the renunciation of violence, peace *agreements* ending the war are replaced by peace *processes* in which the warring parties have to be sworn to mutual consumption of the peace dividend. As a rule, however, these peace processes are successful only if an outside arbiter is capable of suppressing the violent options (if necessary through superior force), and if sizeable funds are introduced to make the dividend sufficiently attractive. This being so, it is scarcely surprising that peace processes end more often in failure than in success.

Victim Totals, Refugee Camps, Epidemics

In the wars that were fought up to the early part of the twentieth century, roughly 90 percent of those killed or wounded would have been defined as combatants under international law. In the new wars at the end of the twentieth century, the profile of victims has been almost the exact opposite: some 80 percent of the killed and wounded were civilians and only 20 percent were soldiers on active service. One explanation for this turnaround should be sought in the decline in the number of inter-state wars and the dramatic rise in the number of intra-state and transnational wars. But that is not all there is to it. More critical is the fact that, in the new wars, force is mainly directed not against the enemy's armed force but against the civilian population, the aim being either to drive it from a certain area (through "ethnic cleansing" and perhaps even the physical annihilation of whole sections of the population) or to force it to supply and support certain armed groups on a permanent basis. In the latter case, which is typical of the new wars, the boundaries between working life and the use of force become blurred. War becomes a way of life: its players make a living out of it, and not infrequently amass considerable fortunes. In any event, in the short term, wars come to involve robbery and plunder, in the medium term, forms of slave labour, and in the long term, the development of shadow economies in which exchange and violence are inseparably bound up with each other. Hence, the belligerents and groups associated with them have an increasing interest in the continuation of war, and the means of forcibly asserting this interest are no longer the decisive battle but the massacre. Unlike on the battlefield, where an armed opponent capable of putting up a fight is forced to submit to the political will of the other side, extreme violence is used here to intimidate an unarmed civilian population into doing whatever the armed group commands. The economy of robbery and plunder nearly always rests upon an extensive organization of fear. The new wars exhibit a distinctive management of fear, which the armed side constructs and organizes against the unarmed. This leads to a widespread breakdown of discipline among the armed group: soldiers become looters for whom the laws of war or any kind of military code of punishment no longer enter the picture; and a strong sexualization of violence produces phenomena ranging from almost daily orgies or veritable strategies of rape through to the ever more common mutilation of victims and the displaying of body parts as war trophies. "The war," Hans Christoph Buch reported from Liberia:

> is turning things inside out. This metaphor becomes literally true when you look at the severed head that replaces traffic lights at a road junction in Monrovia, telling drivers not to proceed any further. Only on closer inspection do I realize that the rope strung across the street, which blocks access to the bridge, is in fact the intestines of the dead man, whose headless body sits as a macabre still life on an office chair.

Especially characteristic of the new wars, however, is the association of military violence with starvation and epidemics. From the late seventeenth century onwards the statization of war, and the strategic orientation to its earliest possible resolution, broke up the premodern troika of famine, pestilence and war (also represented, for example, in the Horsemen of the Apocalypse) and entailed that times of war were no longer necessarily accompanied by disastrous famines and epidemics. By contrast, in most wars of the last twenty years, those who are unable to get food by force of arms are condemned to starve or to face death from disease amid the wretched hygiene conditions of the refugee camps—a tendency sometimes reinforced by the use of economic sanctions to bring belligerent regimes into line without actually applying force against them. Regularly it is young children, women and old people who pay the highest price, even if they are not direct victims of military violence. And since only part of this price—or none of it—is included in the final tally of the costs of war, the percentage of civilians among the casualties should probably be set higher than it is.

It is no accident, then, if the new wars are visible to us mainly through the refugee flows, slum camps and famished populations, but not in fighting between armies and decisive battles. The trickling of military violence to the outer reaches of the social capillary system has turned war into a phenomenon that is not only without beginning or end but also without any clear contours. The new wars know no distinction between combatants and non-combatants, nor are they fought for any definite goals or purposes; they involve no temporal or spatial limits on the use of violence. Intra-state wars have a strong tendency to jump across the boundaries of the region in which they originated and to turn into transnational wars in the briefest space of time. And, finally, the players in these wars enter into myriad links with international organized crime—whether to sell war booty, to dispose of illegal goods or to provide themselves with weapons and ammunition—so that the question of whether certain forms of violence are acts of war or merely criminal acts can be posed in different ways. But what does "crime" mean, when there is no longer a state structure? The war in Colombia is probably the most conspicuous example of this kind of diffuseness, but the Chechen war is also conducted by both sides in such a way that it is no longer clear where the boundary lies between acts of war and ordinary violent crime. . . .

To have separated the use of force from commercial activity, and to have imposed that distinction as a trend in society, is one of the often overlooked achievements of the state, brought about only because it had a de facto monopoly on war. This suggests that the new wars should be defined first of all in contrast to classical inter-state wars, and that what is new and distinctive about them should be analysed within that framework.

Privatization and Commercialization: Warlords, Child Soldiers, Firms of Mercenaries

The de-statization of war, which finds its plainest expression in the growth of para-state and private players, is driven not least by the spreading commercialization of military force. One of the elements in the new wars is the state's loss of its monopoly of military force. When it features in them at all, it does so only together with private firms which, partly for ideological reasons but mainly for robbery and plunder, have joined the ranks of the belligerents. The much-feared "Chetniks," those paramilitary groups and gangs who fought as volunteers on the Serbian side in the wars accompanying the disintegration of Yugoslavia, acted in many cases out of primarily economic motives: the booty from the houses of those they drove out and murdered enabled them for a while to live a life about which they could only dream as ordinary civilians. The new wars give contemporary relevance to the motto variously attributed to the Spanish general Spinola, the mercenary leader Ernst zu Mansfeld and the Swedish king Gustavus Adolphus: that war must continually feed war. Paramilitary units, warlord troops, local militias and mercenary bands are not equipped and paid by functioning states that tax part of the social surplus, but usually have to find ways of supplying themselves. Increased use of violence against civilians is a direct result of this, but it is the only means that armed groups have of supporting themselves. Moreover, in civil wars it is the most effective means, since anyone under arms not only has better chances of survival, but can also live better and more securely when life's necessities are primarily distributed *manu militari*.

Local warlords and transregional entrepreneurs come forward as the main protagonists and profiteers in the de-statization of war. Those, in particular, who control and are able to plunder large areas of a collapsed state claim for themselves the chief attributes of state power—not, of course, to push forward the arduous process of state building, but to garner the additional advantages that come from international recognition (economic support, access to international markets and the possibility of transferring their ill-gotten gains abroad to protect them from rival warlords). In the case of warlords, then, the claim to the attributes of state power does not involve tying themselves down or taking on new obligations out of which a state-building process might develop over time. It is merely a continuation of booty-hunting by other means. . . .

"International relief for the poor, starving population is an inexhaustible source of profit to the warlords," writes Ryszard Kapuściński. "From each transport they takes as many sacks of wheat and as many litres of oil as they need. For the law in force here is this: whoever has weapons eats first. The hungry may take only that which remains." International aid has thus frequently become part of the local war economy: what was supposed to relieve hunger and poverty becomes a resource of war.

Along with the warlords, child soldiers have made their entry into the new wars. The UN estimates their total number around the world at approximately 300,000. The fact that children, many of them under fourteen years, can be used at all in military hostilities is due not least to the technical development of firearms, whose average weight has continually fallen at the same time that firing frequency has increased. They have also been shrinking in size, so that many look as if they were specially designed for children rather than adults. Children do not need a long period of training before they can be deployed as fighters, and their comparatively undemanding nature and low awareness of risks make them a cheap and effective instrument in the application of force. The Khmers Rouges in Cambodia used such soldiers no less than various groups in Afghanistan and the warlords in Black Africa. These adolescents, for their part, often consider a gun as the only means of getting food and clothing, or as the simplest way of acquiring desirable consumption goods and status symbols.

One major impetus behind the new wars is the combination of structural unemployment and the disproportionately high representation of young people in the total population who are largely excluded from the peace economy. They are not subject to the disciplining mechanisms of regular work, nor do they have access to the world of consumption. Peter Scholl-Latour, repeating the explanations given him by an African interlocutor, asks: "So how can a child soldier of twelve or fourteen, who would otherwise vegetate as a street urchin or a casual labourer, do better than terrorize adults with his kalashnikov and demonstrate his omnipotence by shedding blood?" Such power fantasies, which these armed adolescents can act out without hindrance, play an important role along with the overcoming of hunger and destitution. . . .

A final element in the fantasies of omnipotence is the free rein given to sexual needs. These gun-toting adolescents have been responsible for many particularly gruesome rapes and mutilations of sexual organs. Michael Ignatieff, who knows better than almost anyone else how to combine reportage with analysis, has pointed out that the increased cruelty and brutality of the new wars is essentially due to the increased involvement of these armed youngsters. "In most traditional societies," he writes:

> honour is associated with restraint, and virility with discipline. . . . The particular savagery of war in the 1990s taps into another view of male identity—the wild sexuality of the adolescent male. Adolescents are supplying armies with a different kind of soldier—one for whom a weapon is not a thing to be respected or treated with ritual correctness but instead has an explicit phallic dimension. To traverse a checkpoint in Bosnia where adolescent boys in dark glasses and tight-fitting combat khakis wield AK-47s is to enter a zone of

toxic testosterone. War has always had its sexual dimension—a soldier's uniform is no guarantee of good conduct—but when a war is conducted by adolescent irregulars, sexual savagery becomes one of its regular weapons.

Ignatieff's account may also be expressed in figures. While international organizations estimate that 20,000 to 50,000 women were raped in the Balkan wars of the last ten years, Human Rights Watch set the corresponding figure during and after the genocide in Rwanda at more than a quarter of a million. The violence used against civilians in the new wars is mainly violence against women. Practices range from "ethnic cleansing" strategies (which are associated with systematic rape) through destruction of the cohesion and moral norms of a society (rape especially stigmatizes young women and makes them alien bodies within the community) to extension of the demand for war booty to include forced sexual intercourse with women and girls in newly occupied territory. The descent into sexual barbarism of which Ignatieff speaks can be seen mainly where new wars shatter and ravage societies with a traditionally rigid sexual morality. Here the opportunities for sex at the point of a gun are especially tempting, and the social consequences especially devastating, since the social groups in question can no longer reproduce once a large part of their young women have undergone the stigma of rape.

In addition to the emergence and growth of warlordism and the deployment of cut-price child soldiers, the tendency to privatize and commercialize war is apparent not least in the wider involvement of mercenaries in nearly all these wars— from the West European adventures and fortune hunters who on their own initiative joined one of the parties in the Balkan wars, usually for rather low remuneration, through to the highly professional London-based security businesses with branches around the world, such as the Control Risks Group, Defence Systems Ltd, Sandline International, Saladin Security, Gurkha Security Guards and, above all, Executive Outcomes, which can supply well-trained military personnel as well as aircraft and helicopters and elaborate security systems. Among their clients are heads of state who can no longer rely on their own army and presidential guard to crush uprisings, as well as internationally active corporations that turn to mercenaries to protect their production sites in hotbeds of war and insurrection. In Africa there is a widely held view that a single Executive Outcomes mercenary is worth as much as a whole company of native soldiers. The new war mercenaries also include the Mujahedin of Chechnya and Bosnia, Afghanistan and Algeria, who are paid out of the petrodollars of Arab states or private individuals to fight for the maintenance of religious bonds and cultural values. . . .

From Mujahedin networks to contingents of hastily recruited fighters, from distinguished-looking security firms linked to the top addresses in the arms trade through to rowdy adventurers noted for their overindulgence in alcohol and for going weeks without washing to preserve the traces of battle: none of these consists of state subjects fighting out of a mixture of political duty and patriotic attachment to a cause, but rather of individuals driven mainly by financial gain, a lust for adventure and a range of ideological motives. There can be no doubt at all that this motley group—whose pay may only cover immediate necessities but may also reach the heights of $15,000 a month—is removing more and more of the limits to the violence and brutality of war. The Hague Land Warfare Convention, together with the Geneva Convention and the prohibitions and restrictions contained in its additional protocols, are scarcely ever respected in the new wars. The main reason for this is that the countries that form the traditional target group for war-related and international law are of little significance for the course of the new wars. The so-called regular armies, which officially defend the state, are mostly nothing other than marauding bands, and the half-state, half-private players are not really subject to the sanctions threatened under international law, especially as few powers are willing to enforce the law, to arrest war criminals and, eventually, to organize costly court proceedings that may last for years. The passing notion that world politics was generally changing for the better, after the end of the East–West conflict and the decline in the number of inter-state wars, has thus turned out to be a great illusion. The number of wars has increased over the longer term, and the chances are diminishing that violence can be contained by legislation and the courts. While many intellectuals in Western Europe and North America reflected on global internal policy, global civil law and democratic peace, war has torn down the protective fencing and established itself as an independent presence on the periphery of the zones of prosperity, a—quantitatively if not formally—new mode of income generation. War enables many people to make a living: it provides them with a means of generating considerable income in the short term and of living out blocked fantasies without restraint; it also endows a few with huge fortunes and indescribable wealth. It might be objected that things have always been so, that they were much the same in traditional inter-state wars. But the crucial difference is that what used to be a concomitant of war, more or less pronounced in each particular instance, has become the central focus and true goal of many new wars.

2.2 The Global Menace of Local Strife

The Economist

Much of today's violence pits tribal and ethnic groups against one another, but is such violence merely the result of old hatreds? The following selection from the British news magazine *The Economist* argues that the reasons for such violence are far more complex. Poverty, the essay suggests, is a root cause and, when combined with poor governance, creates the conditions in which corrupt leaders can manipulate ethnic and tribal differences for their own profit.

In a confetti of medicines, pens and second-hand shirts, armed looters rage through Bunia's main market-place. Startled, the local dogs stop feeding on the rotting human corpses scattered among the empty fruit and vegetable stalls. The mob, which is also looking for food, finds none, and moves on. The pack resumes feeding in quick, delicate bites.

Once a prosperous gold town, ringed by fertile green hills, Bunia, in eastern Congo, was ransacked and deserted last week. Where one gold-trader had his shop, only a gold-paint picture of a pair of scales remains. Every other stall has been gutted, too; boy warriors with AK-47s clamber in and out of jagged holes in once smoothly plastered walls.

The cyclone struck after the Ugandan army, a plunderous occupying force, withdrew. The two largest local tribes, the Hema and the Lendus, then began to fight for control. First, Lendu militiamen poured into town, killing Hemas and burning their houses. Days later, Hema warriors counter-attacked and chased the Lendus away. No one can say how many died, but the fighting seems to have put at least 250,000 people to flight.

The death toll since Congo's war began in 1998 is higher, at between 3.1m and 4.7m, than in any other ongoing war. But otherwise the conflict is typical of today's wars. The combatants are mostly irregular militias, their victims mostly unarmed, and the fighting has gone on for nearly five years. A century ago most conflicts were between nations, and 90 percent of casualties were soldiers; today almost all wars are civil, and 90 percent of the victims are civilians.

Civil wars are much more common than they were forty years ago. This is mainly because, back then, most of the countries currently fighting were colonies, so powerful outside forces imposed stability. Counting only wars with more than 1,000 violent deaths, about one country in eight is embroiled in one. This proportion peaked around 1990, after the superpowers stopped bankrolling rebels who attacked each other's allies. But post-cold-war peacemaking seems to have fizzled, and civil wars are getting longer. An average conflict lasts eight years, more than twice the norm before 1980.

Why is this happening? Some blame tribalism: a pleasingly simple thesis that both seems to fit the facts, and gives outsiders an excuse for indifference and inaction. But the reality is more complex. Tribes often quarrel, but ethnic passions on their own are rarely enough to stoke a full-blown war. The Hema and the Lendus, for example, have been trying to wipe each other out only since Uganda started arming rival tribal militias in 1999, in the hope of controlling the mineral-rich region around Bunia. If tribalism is the problem, ethnically homogenous countries should be peaceful—but look at Somalia.

Or at Sudan, whose civil war is often seen as a simple conflict between Arab Muslims and black non-Muslims. The view from the battlefield is cloudier, however. Last year, your correspondent met David Matwok, a young militiaman in the pay of Sudan's Arab government, who was lying on his back on the savannah with both legs broken by bullets. Mr. Matwok was a member of the Nuer tribe; so were the rebels who had shot him, during a pitched battle. The battlefield had seen Nuer fight Nuer before: among the still-bleeding corpses were scattered human vertebrae and clean-picked skulls, like golf balls on a vast green fairway. Every bone had once belonged to a Nuer.

And why were they fighting? According to the rebel commander, "Even where you are sitting, there is oil." Money trumps kinship. Mr. Matwok begged for water, but his fellow tribesmen told him they hoped wild animals would eat him.

All wars are different, of course. Each arises from a unique combination of causes, and each requires a different sort of solution. Nonetheless, by looking at what the most conflict-prone places have in common, it is possible to identify likely risk factors. This, in turn, might help to prevent wars in the future.

What Causes Wars?

A new study by Paul Collier of the World Bank and others, which examines the world's civil wars since 1960, concludes that although tribalism is often a factor, it is rarely the main one. Surprisingly, the authors found that societies composed of several different ethnic and religious groups were actually less likely to experience civil war than homogenous societies.

However, in multi-ethnic societies where one group forms an absolute majority, the risk of war is 50 percent higher than in societies where this is not the case. This is perhaps because minorities fear that even if the country is democratic, they will be permanently excluded from power.

The most striking common factor among war-prone countries is their poverty. Rich countries almost never suffer civil war, and middle-income countries rarely. But the poorest one-sixth of humanity endures four-fifths of the world's civil wars.

The best predictors of conflict are low average incomes, low growth, and a high dependence on exports of primary products such as oil or diamonds. The World Bank found that when income per person doubles, the risk of civil war halves, and that for each percentage point by which the growth rate rises, the risk of conflict falls by a point. An otherwise typical country whose exports of primary commodities account for 10 percent of GDP has an 11 percent chance of being at war. At 30 percent of GDP, the risk peaks at about one in three.

Why are poor, stagnant countries so vulnerable? Partly because it is easy to give a poor man a cause. But also, almost certainly, because poverty and low or negative growth are often symptoms of corrupt, incompetent government, which can provoke rebellion. They are also common in immature societies, whose people have not yet figured out how to live together.

Natural resources tend to aggravate these problems. When a state has oil, its leaders can grow rich without bothering to nurture other kinds of economic activity. Corrupt leaders often cement their support base by sharing the loot with their own ethnic group, which tends to anger all the other groups.

Most countries have what Mr. Collier calls "ethnic romantics who dream of creating an ethnically 'pure' political entity." If oil is found beneath their home region, their calls for secession suddenly start to sound attractive to those who live there, and abhorrent to everyone else. Oil was one reason why Biafra tried to secede from Nigeria, and why the Nigerian government fought so hard to prevent it.

Secessionist leaders in Aceh, an oil-endowed part of Indonesia, told potential supporters that secession would make them as rich as the people of Brunei. This ten-fold exaggeration raised expectations that were impossible to meet, which may explain why the rebels went back to war despite a peace deal in December promising Aceh autonomy and 70 percent of the cash from its oil and gas.

Guns Cost Money

Laurent Kabila, the rebel who overthrew the dictator Mobutu Sese Seko, once boasted that all he needed to mount a revolution was $10,000 and a satellite telephone. He was exaggerating. Recruiting soldiers in Congo (which was then called Zaire) is cheap, because the country is so poor, but it is not that cheap. Guns have grown less costly since old Soviet armouries emptied on to the black market, but they are not free. In fact, Kabila had a budget in the millions, partly because he enjoyed the backing of a foreign power, Rwanda, and partly because he used his sat-phone to sell mineral rights he did not yet control to unscrupulous foreign firms.

Rebellions almost always start for political reasons. But since sustaining even the crudest guerrilla war requires cash, rebel leaders have to find ways of raising the stuff. Many, including most in Africa, receive money from neighbouring governments hostile to the one they are fighting. Some rebel groups are supported by an ethnic diaspora whose members, since they live abroad, do not have to endure the consequences of the wars they help fund.

In countries with abundant natural resources, however, rebels have less need to beg. Alluvial diamonds, the sort that can be plucked from riverbeds without sophisticated mining equipment, have financed rebel groups in Angola and Sierra Leone. Illegal logging, another low-tech business, fuels fighting in Liberia and Cambodia. In Congo, half a dozen national armies and countless rebel groups have fought over some of the world's richest deposits of gold, cobalt, diamonds and coltan.

In countries with high tariffs, rebels can make money by seizing a stretch of border and charging smugglers less than the government would. Afghan fighters, for example, have prospered from the protectionism of Afghanistan's neighbours. Rebel areas are also ideal for growing drugs. An estimated 95 percent of the world's opium comes from war-torn nations, and Colombia's rebels thrive on coca.

Rebels rarely pump oil. It requires capital, skills and technology, and the firms that have these things prefer to deal with legitimate governments. But rebels can still profit from oil, by extorting money from oil firms. One technique, popular in Colombia and Nigeria, is to kidnap their employees and demand ransoms. Another is to threaten to blow up pipelines. Firms usually pay up. During the 1990s, European companies handed over an estimated $1.2 billion to rebel extortionists, a sum far greater than official European aid to the governments of the countries in question. Ransom insurance, now available, has the effect of raising ransom demands, and so increases the profits to be made from violence.

From Comrades-in-Arms to Cosa Nostra

Rebellions rarely begin as criminal business ventures, but they often mutate into them. Their leaders can grow fabulously rich. By one estimate, Jonas Savimbi, the late Angolan guerrilla chief, amassed $4 billion from selling diamonds, ivory and anything else his men could steal. Besides paying for bullets, such profits give rebel commanders a powerful incentive to keep fighting. Says Mr. Collier: "Asking a rebel leader to accept peace may be a little like asking a champion swimmer to empty the pool." Savimbi only laid down his weapons for good when he was shot dead.

War creates a vicious circle. When rebel groups start to make money, they attract greedy leaders. At the same time, war makes it harder for peaceful people to earn a living. No one wants to build factories in war zones. People with portable skills flee, and those with money stash it offshore. Peasants find it hard to farm when rebels keep plundering their villages.

Poverty fosters war, and war impoverishes. In Congo, a combination of violence and official neglect has all but destroyed the country's roads, telephones and organs of government. Whole regions are cut off from the centre. Rubaruba Zabuloni, for example, has been fighting for nearly 40 years. A dwarfish 69-year-old with a crew-cut and a black fur hat, he leads a 7,000-man militia in the hills above Lake Tanganyika. In the 1960s, he fought with Che Guevara; in later years, the Soviet Union continued to send arms. He is unaware of the demise of either.

The big foreign armies involved in Congo's war have more or less made peace, and a new central government is gradually forming. But dozens of smaller, local conflicts continue to blaze. They are fought with low-tech weapons: machetes, bows and a few guns. An endless cycle of atrocities creates an endless cycle of grudges, which fuel more micro-wars. "When we kill a Rwandan," said Mr. Zabuloni's personal witchdoctor, "we fry up his penis and eat it. It makes you fearless. Would you like to try it?"

Being a rebel footsoldier is no way to make a fortune, but it may be better than the alternative, particularly if the alternative is to be a rebel footsoldier's victim. One of the gun-waving boys in Bunia put it pithily. Asked why he chose to take up arms, Singoma Mapisa fiddled shyly with his new Seiko watch—a happy acquisition on a Congolese soldier's pay of nothing—and replied: "The Lendus murdered my parents. How else could I survive?" He was later seen pilfering two Mickey Mouse satchels, which could prove useful if he ever goes to school.

A typical civil war leaves a country 15 percent poorer than it would otherwise have been, and with perhaps 30 percent more people living in absolute poverty. The damage persists long afterwards. Skills and capital continue to flee, because people do not trust the peace: half of newly peaceful countries revert to war within a decade.

Infant mortality also remains high, not least because war nurtures disease. Refugees carry malaria from areas where the population is immune to a particular strain to areas where it is not. One study found that for each 1,000 refugees who flee from one tropical country to another, the host country suffers an extra 1,406 cases of malaria.

Rampaging armies are also efficient vectors for AIDS. Soldiers are more likely than civilians to be infected, and too often inclined to spread the virus forcibly. One study found that halving military manpower correlates with a one-quarter reduction in HIV among low-risk adults. Some researchers even blame war for the first spread of the AIDS pandemic, conjecturing that a small localised infection was carried far and wide through mass rape during the Ugandan civil war of the 1970s.

Besides scattering refugees and spreading disease, civil wars often disrupt trade across whole regions. Congo's war blocked the river along which the Central

African Republic's trade used to flow, aggravating the CAR's economic malaise and perhaps contributing to a recent succession of coup attempts by unpaid soldiers. In all, having a neighbour at war reduces economic growth by about 0.5 percent each year.

Give Peace a Chance

Since countries prone to civil war are poor, stagnant places, anything that promotes growth ought to help. Governments in poor countries should strive to keep corruption, inflation and trade barriers low, while attempting to build better health, education and legal systems.

To guard against future insurgency, governments of newly peaceful countries often keep lavishing cash on the army. Military spending averages 4.5 percent of GDP in the first decade of peace, down from 5 percent during the war, but up from 2.8 percent before it. Such spending actually increases the risk of another war, because it wastes resources that could improve people's lives, and signals to rebels and people alike that the government is preparing for another war.

Spending on health and education, by contrast, seems to provide an immediate boost to the economy of a newly peaceful nation. This is surprising. The benefits of social spending usually take years to show up in the growth figures. But in countries emerging from war, a new school or clinic shows that the government is serious about peace, which buoys confidence and may encourage private investment.

Once war gathers pace, the vicious circle is hard to break. Intervention by proper armies with orders to shoot to kill can work: British troops helped save Sierra Leone, and the French legionnaires in Côte d'Ivoire have reduced the carnage there. The UN, whose peacekeepers are often ill-prepared for actual fighting, has a less impressive record. In Bunia last week, 700 Uruguayan peacekeepers were unable to prevent a massacre outside their barracks because their mandate was too feeble. The UN managed to broker a ceasefire on May 16th, but the only reason the fighting has stopped in Bunia is that one side has won. Out in the hills, the killing continues.

Targeting the Innocent: Terrorism

2.3 Strategies of Terrorism

Andrew H. Kydd and Barbara F. Walter

Since September 11, 2001, perhaps the most visible face of our world's global violence, at least for most Americans, has been the rise of terrorism. The bloody consequences of terrorism are often so horrific that it would be a relief to be able to chalk these acts up as those of madmen or fanatics, or to be able to conclude that they were irrational or self-defeating. As political scientists Andrew Kydd and Barbara Walter argue, however, terrorism often represents a quite intelligent and well-reasoned—if bloody—approach to achieving political objectives. While some of the foot soldiers in terrorist campaigns may indeed be fanatical or motivated by a rage so strong as to prevent a careful calculation of costs and consequences, the political leaders organizing the terrorist campaign are likely to be coolly calculating. Kydd and Walter bluntly note that "terrorism often works." The use of indiscriminate violence against innocent individuals can persuade third parties to make the concessions or take the steps that the terrorists seek. By analyzing the sorts of goals terrorists may be seeking and the ways that terrorist violence may be useful in achieving these goals, we can gain a better understanding both of our vulnerability to this sort of political strategy and of the best ways to counteract it.

Terrorism often works. Extremist organizations such as al-Qaeda, Hamas, and the Tamil Tigers engage in terrorism because it frequently delivers the desired response. The October 1983 suicide attack against the U.S. Marine barracks in Beirut, for example, convinced the United States to withdraw its soldiers from Lebanon. The United States pulled its soldiers out of Saudi Arabia two years after the terrorist attacks of September 11, 2001, even though the U.S. military had been building up its forces in that country for more than a decade. The Philippines recalled it troops from Iraq nearly a month early after a Filipino truck driver was kidnapped by Iraqi extremists. In fact, terrorism has been so successful that between 1980 and 2003, half of all suicide terrorist campaigns were closely followed by substantial concessions by the target governments. Hijacking planes, blowing up buses, and kidnapping individuals may seem irrational and incoherent to outside observers, but these tactics can be surprisingly effective in achieving a terrorist group's political aims. . . .

Terrorism works not simply because it instills fear in target populations, but because it causes governments and individuals to respond in ways that aid the terrorists' cause. The Irish Republican Army (IRA) bombed pubs, parks, and shopping districts in London because its leadership believed that such acts would convince Britain to relinquish Northern Ireland. In targeting the World Trade Center and the Pentagon on September 11, al-Qaeda hoped to raise the costs for the United States of supporting Israel, Saudi Arabia, and other Arab regimes, and to provoke the United States into a military response designed to mobilize Muslims around the world. . . .

The core of our argument is that terrorist violence is a form of costly signaling. Terrorists are too weak to impose their will directly by force of arms. They are sometimes strong enough, however, to persuade audiences to do as they wish by altering the audience's beliefs about such matters as the terrorist's ability to impose costs and their degree of commitment to their cause. Given the conflict of interest

Excerpts from Andrew H. Kydd and Barbara F. Walter, "The Strategies of Terrorism," *International Security* 31:1 (Summer 2006), pp. 49–80. © 2006 by the President and Fellows of Harvard College and the Massachusetts Institute of Technology.

between terrorists and their targets, ordinary communication or "cheap talk" is insufficient to change minds or influence behavior. If al-Qaeda had informed the United States on September 10, 2001, that it would kill 3,000 Americans unless the United States withdrew from Saudi Arabia, the threat might have sparked concern, but it would not have had the same impact as the attacks that followed. Because it is hard for weak actors to make credible threats, terrorists are forced to display publicly just how far they are willing to go to obtain their desired results.

There are five principal strategic logics of costly signaling at work in terrorist campaigns: (1) attrition, (2) intimidation, (3) provocation, (4) spoiling, and (5) outbidding. In an attrition strategy, terrorists seek to persuade the enemy that the terrorists are strong enough to impose considerable costs if the enemy continues a particular policy. Terrorists using intimidation try to convince the population that the terrorists are strong enough to punish disobedience and that the government is too weak to stop them, so that people behave as the terrorists wish. A provocation strategy is an attempt to induce the enemy to respond to terrorism with indiscriminate violence, which radicalizes the population and moves them to support the terrorists. Spoilers attack in an effort to persuade the enemy that moderates on the terrorists' side are weak and untrustworthy, thus undermining attempts to reach a peace settlement. Groups engaged in outbidding use violence to convince the public that the terrorists have greater resolve to fight the enemy than rival groups, and therefore are worthy of support. . . .

The Goals of Terrorism

For years the press has portrayed terrorists as crazy extremists who commit indiscriminate acts of violence, without any larger goal beyond revenge or a desire to produce fear in an enemy population. This characterization derives some support from statements made by terrorists themselves. For example, a young Hamas suicide bomber whose bomb failed to detonate said. "I know that there are other ways to do jihad. But this one is sweet—the sweetest. All martyrdom operations, if done for Allah's sake, hurt less than a gnat's bite!" Volunteers for a suicide mission may have a variety of motives—obtaining rewards in the afterlife, avenging a family member killed by the enemy, or simply collecting financial rewards for their descendants. By contrast, the goals driving terrorist organizations are usually political objectives, and it is these goals that determine whether and how terrorist campaigns will be launched.

We define "terrorism" as the use of violence against civilians by nonstate actors to attain political goals. . . .

Although the ultimate goals of terrorists have varied over time, five have had enduring importance: regime change, territorial change, policy change, social control, and status quo maintenance. Regime change is the overthrow of a government and its replacement with one led by the terrorists or at least one more to their liking. Most Marxist groups, including the Shining Path (Sendero Luminoso) in Peru, have sought this goal. Territorial change is taking territory away from a state either to establish a new state (as the Tamil Tigers seek to do in Tamil areas of Sri Lanka) or to join another state (as Lashkar-e Tayyiba would like to do by incorporating Indian Kashmir into Pakistan). Policy change is a broader category of lesser demands, such as al-Qaeda's demand that the United States drop its support for Israel and corrupt Arab regimes such as Saudi Arabia. Social control constrains the behavior of individuals, rather than the state. In the United States, the Ku Klux Klan sought the continued oppression of African Americans after the Civil War. More recently, antiabortion groups have sought to kill doctors who perform abortions to deter other doctors from providing this service. Finally, status quo maintenance is the support of an existing regime or a territorial arrangement against political groups that seek to change it. Many right-wing paramilitary organizations in Latin America, such as the United Self-Defense Force of Colombia, have sought this goal. Protestant paramilitary groups in Northern Ireland supported maintenance of the territorial status quo (Northern Ireland as British territory) against IRA demands that the territory be transferred to Ireland.

Some organizations hold multiple goals and may view one as facilitating another. For instance, by seeking to weaken U.S. support for Arab regimes (which would represent a policy change by the United States), al-Qaeda is working toward the overthrow of those regimes (or regime change). As another example, Hamas aims to drive Israel out of the occupied territories (territorial change) and then to overthrow it (regime change). . . .

Attrition: A Battle of Wills   The most important task for any terrorist group is to persuade the enemy that the group is strong and resolute enough to inflict serious costs, so that the enemy yields to the terrorists' demands. The attrition strategy is designed to accomplish this task. In an attrition campaign, the greater the costs a terrorist organization is able to inflict, the more credible its threat to inflict future costs, and the more likely the target is to grant concessions. During the last years of the British Empire, the Greeks in Cyprus, Jews in Palestine, and Arabs in Aden used a war of attrition strategy against their colonizer. By targeting Britain with terrorist attacks, they eventually convinced the political leadership that maintaining control over these territories would not be worth the cost in British lives. Attacks by Hezbollah and Hamas against Israel, particularly during the second intifada, also appear to be guided by this strategy. In a letter written in the early 1990s to the leadership of Hamas, the organization's master bomb maker, Yahya Ayyash, said, "We paid a high price when we used only sling-shots and stones. We need to exert more pressure, make the cost of the occupation that much more expensive in human lives, that much more unbearable."

Robert Pape presents the most thorough exposition of terrorism as a war of attrition in his analysis of suicide bombing. Based on a data set of all suicide attacks from 1980 to 2003 (315 in total), Pape argues that suicide terrorism is employed by weak actors for whom peaceful tactics have failed and conventional military tactics are infeasible because of the imbalance of power. The strategy is to inflict costs on the enemy until it withdraws its occupying forces: the greater the costs inflicted, the more likely the enemy is to withdraw. Pape asserts that terrorists began to recognize the effectiveness of suicide terrorism with the 1983 Hezbollah attack against

U.S. Marines in Beirut that killed 241 people. Since then, suicide terrorism has been employed in nationalist struggles around the world. . . .

A war of attrition strategy is more effective against some targets than others. Three variables are likely to figure in the outcome: the state's level of interest in the issue under dispute, the constraints on its ability to retaliate, and its sensitivity to the costs of violence.

The first variable, the state's degree of interest in the disputed issue, is fundamental. States with only peripheral interests at stake often capitulate to terrorist demands; states with more important interests at stake rarely do. The United States withdrew from Lebanon following the bombing of the marine barracks because it had only a marginal interest in maintaining stability and preventing Syrian domination of the country. In that case, the costs of the attack clearly outweighed the U.S. interest at stake. . . .

The second variable, constraints on retaliation, affects the costs paid by the terrorists for pursuing a war of attrition. Terrorist organizations almost always are weaker than the governments they target and, as a result, are vulnerable to government retaliation. The more constrained the government is in its use of force, the less costly an attrition strategy is, and the longer the terrorists can hold out in the hopes of achieving their goal. . . .

The third variable is a target's cost tolerance. Governments that are able to absorb heavier costs and hold out longer are less inviting targets for an attrition strategy. Terrorist organizations are likely to gauge a target's cost tolerance based on at least two factors: the target's regime type and the target's past behavior toward other terrorists. Regime type is important because democracies may be less able to tolerate the painful effects of terrorism than non-democracies. Citizens of democracies, their fears stoked by media reports and warnings of continued vulnerability, are more likely to demand an end to the attacks. In more authoritarian states, the government exerts more control over the media and can disregard public opinion to a greater extent. . . .

Perhaps the most important example of a terrorist group pursuing an attrition strategy is al-Qaeda's war with the United States. In a November 2004 broadcast, bin Laden boasted, "We gained experience in guerilla and attritional warfare in our struggle against the great oppressive superpower, Russia, in which we and the mujahidin ground it down for ten years until it went bankrupt, and decided to withdraw in defeat. . . . We are continuing to make America bleed to the point of bankruptcy." . . .

Intimidation: The Reign of Terror   Intimidation . . . is most frequently used when terrorist organizations wish to overthrow a government in power or gain social control over a given population. It works by demonstrating that the terrorists have the power to punish whoever disobeys them, and that the government is powerless to stop them.

Terrorists are often in competition with the government for the support of the population. Terrorists who wish to bring down a government must somehow convince the government's defenders that continued backing of the government will be costly. One way to do this is to provide clear evidence that the terrorist organization can kill those individuals who continue to sustain the regime. By targeting the government's more visible agents and supporters, such as mayors, police, prosecutors, and pro-regime citizens, terrorist organizations demonstrate that they have the ability to hurt their opponents and that the government is too weak to punish the terrorists or protect future victims.

Terrorists can also use an intimidation strategy to gain greater social control over a population. Terrorists may turn to this strategy in situations where a government has consistently refused to implement a policy a terrorist group favors and where efforts to change the state's policy appear futile. In this case, terrorists use intimidation to impose the desired policy directly on the population, gaining compliance through selective violence and the threat of future reprisals. In the United States, antiabortion activists have bombed clinics to prevent individuals from performing or seeking abortions, and in the 1960s racist groups burned churches to deter African Americans from claiming their civil rights. In Afghanistan, the Taliban beheaded the principal of a girls school to deter others from providing education for girls. . . .

Provocation: Lighting the Fuse   . . . Provocation helps shift citizen support away from the incumbent regime. In a provocation strategy, terrorists seek to goad the target government into a military response that harms civilians within the terrorist organization's home territory. The aim is to convince them that the government is so evil that the radical goals of the terrorists are justified and support for their organization is warranted. This is what the Basque Fatherland and Liberty group (ETA) sought to do in Spain. For years, Madrid responded to ETA attacks with repressive measures against the Basque community, mobilizing many of its members against the government even if they did not condone those attacks. As one expert on this conflict writes, "Nothing radicalizes a people faster than the unleashing of undisciplined security forces on its towns and villages." . . .

The United States in September 2001 was ripe for provocation, and al-Qaeda appears to have understood this. The new administration of George W. Bush was known to be hawkish in its foreign policy and in its attitude toward the use of military power. In a November 2004 videotape, bin Laden bragged that al-Qaeda found it "easy for us to provoke this administration." The strategy appears to be working. A 2004 Pew survey found that international trust in the United States had declined significantly in response to the invasion of Iraq. Similarly, a 2004 report by the International Institute for Strategic Studies found that al-Qaeda's recruitment and fundraising efforts had been given a major boost by the U.S. invasion of Iraq. In the words of Shibley Telhami, "What we're seeing now is a disturbing sympathy with al-Qaeda coupled with resentment toward the United States." The Bush administration's eagerness to overthrow Saddam Hussein, a desire that predated the September 11 attacks, has, in the words of bin Laden, "contributed to these remarkable results for al-Qaeda." . . .

Spoiling: Sabotaging the Peace   . . . Terrorists resort to a spoiling strategy when relations between two enemies are improving and a peace agreement threatens the terrorists' more far-reaching goals. Peace agreements alarm terrorists because they understand that moderate citizens are less likely to support ongoing violence once a compromise agreement between more moderate groups has been reached. Thus, Iranian radicals kidnapped fifty-two Americans in Tehran in 1979 not because relations between the United States and Iran were becoming more belligerent, but because three days earlier Iran's relatively moderate prime minister, Mehdi Bazargan, met with the U.S. national security adviser, Zbigniew Brzezinski, and the two were photographed shaking hands. From the perspective of the radicals, a real danger of reconciliation existed between the two countries, and violence was used to prevent this. A similar problem has hampered Arab-Israeli peace negotiations, as well as talks between Protestants and Catholics in Northern Ireland. . . .

Outbidding: Zealots Versus Sellouts   Outbidding arises when two key conditions hold: two or more domestic parties are competing for leadership of their side, and the general population is uncertain about which of the groups best represent their interests. The competition between Hamas and Fatah is a classic case where two groups vie for the support of the Palestinian citizens and where the average Palestinian is uncertain about which side he or she ought to back. . . . Groups competing for power have an incentive to signal that they are zealots rather than sellouts. Terrorist attacks can serve this function by signaling that a group has the will to continue the armed struggle despite its costs.

Conclusion

Terrorist violence is a form of costly signaling by which terrorists attempt to influence the beliefs of their enemy and the population they represent or wish to control. They use violence to signal their strength and resolve in an effort to produce concessions from their enemy and obedience and support from their followers. They also attack both to sow mistrust between moderates who might want to make peace and to provoke a reaction that makes the enemy appear barbarous and untrustworthy. . . .

Our analysis suggests that democracies are more likely to be sensitive to the costs of terrorist attacks, to grant concessions to terrorists so as to limit future attacks, to be constrained in their ability to pursue a lengthy attritional campaign against an organization, but also to be under greater pressure to "do something." This does not mean that all democracies will behave incorrectly in the face of terrorist attacks all the time. Democratic regimes may possess certain structural features, however, that make them attractive targets for terrorism.

Hiring an Army: Mercenaries and Private Military Contractors

2.4 The Private Surge

Steve Fainaru

States are increasingly outsourcing—hiring private corporations to perform military functions or to perform nonmilitary functions essential to the continued effectiveness of their armies—rather than having their armies do these duties themselves. This return to the practice of hiring private armies worries many observers, particularly in the wake of revelations in fall 2007 that troops provided by Blackwater, one of the largest private security firms operating in support of American activities in Iraq, may have indiscriminately shot innocent Iraqi civilians while conducting security operations. Recalling the history of mercenary forces in the period before the rise of the modern state, and the more recent history of mercenary forces in emerging and weak states in Africa, observers are also concerned about the larger implications for the state system.

In the next reading, *Washington Post* reporter Steve Fainaru examines the role of private contractors assisting the United States in Iraq, the increasing militarization of these contractors, and the expanding roles they have assumed.

Private security companies, funded by billions of dollars in U.S. military and State Department contracts, are fighting insurgents on a widening scale in Iraq, enduring daily attacks, returning fire and taking hundreds of casualties that have been underreported and sometimes concealed, according to U.S. and Iraqi officials and company representatives.

While the military has built up troops in an ongoing campaign to secure Baghdad, the security companies, out of public view, have been engaged in a parallel surge, boosting manpower, adding expensive armor and stepping up evasive action as attacks increase, the officials and company representatives say. One in seven supply convoys protected by private forces has come under attack this year, according to previously unreleased statistics; one security company reported nearly 300 "hostile actions" in the first four months.

The majority of the more than 100 security companies operate outside of Iraqi law, in part because of bureaucratic delays and corruption in the Iraqi government licensing process, according to U.S. officials. Blackwater USA, a prominent North Carolina firm that protects U.S. Ambassador Ryan C. Crocker, and several other companies have not applied, U.S. and Iraqi officials say. Blackwater says that it obtained a one-year license in 2005 but that shifting Iraqi government policy has impeded its attempts to renew.

The security industry's enormous growth has been facilitated by the U.S. military, which uses the 20,000 to 30,000 contractors to offset chronic troop shortages. Armed contractors protect all convoys transporting reconstruction materiel, including vehicles, weapons and ammunition for the Iraqi army and police. They guard key U.S. military installations and provide personal security for at least three commanding generals, including Air Force Major General Darryl A. Scott, who oversees U.S. military contracting in Iraq and Afghanistan.

"I'm kind of practicing what I preach here," Scott said in an interview on the use of private security forces for such tasks. "I'm a two-star general, but I'm not the most important guy in the multinational force. If it's a lower-priority mission and it's within the capabilities of private security, this is an appropriate risk trade-off."

The military plans to outsource at least $1.5 billion in security operations this year, including the three largest security contracts in Iraq: a "theaterwide" contract to protect U.S. bases that is worth up to $480 million, according to Scott; a contract for up to $475 million to provide intelligence for the Army and personal security for the U.S. Army Corps of Engineers; and a contract for up to $450 million to protect reconstruction convoys. The Army has also tested a plan to use private security on military convoys for the first time, a shift that would significantly increase the presence of armed contractors on Iraq's dangerous roads.

"The whole face of private security changed with Iraq, and it will never go back to how it was," says Leon Sharon, a retired Special Operations officer who commands 500 private Kurdish guards at an immense warehouse transit point for weapons, ammunition and other materiel on the outskirts of Baghdad.

U.S. officials and security company representatives emphasize that contractors are strictly limited to defensive operations. But company representatives in the field say insurgents rarely distinguish between the military and private forces, drawing the contractors into a bloody and escalating campaign.

The U.S. Military has never released complete statistics on contractor casualties or the number of attacks on privately guarded convoys. The military deleted casualty figures from reports issued by the Reconstruction Logistics Directorate of the Corps of Engineers, according to Victoria Wayne, who served as deputy director for logistics until 2006 and spent 2½ years in Iraq.

Wayne describes security contractors as "the unsung heroes of the war." She says she believes the military wants to hide information showing that private guards have been fighting and dying in large numbers because it would be perceived as bad news.

"It was like there was a major war being fought out there, but we were the only ones who knew about it," Wayne says.

After a year of protests by Wayne and logistics director Jack Holly, a retired Marine colonel, the casualty figures were included. In an operational overview updated last month, the logistics directorate reported that 132 security contractors and truck drivers had been killed and 416 wounded since fall 2004. Four security contractors and a truck driver remained missing, and 208 vehicles were destroyed.

Only convoys registered with the logistics directorate are counted in the statistics, and the total number of casualties is believed to be higher.

"When you see the number of my people who have been killed, the American public should recognize that every one of them represents an American soldier or Marine or sailor who didn't have to go in harm's way," Holly said in an interview.

According to the logistics directorate, attacks against registered supply convoys rose from 5.4 percent in 2005, to 9.1 percent in 2006, to 14.7 percent through May 10 [2007]. The directorate has tracked 12,860 convoys, a fraction of the total number of private supply convoys on Iraqi roads.

"The military are very conscious that we're in their battle space," says Cameron Simpson, country operations manager for ArmorGroup International, a British firm that protects 32 percent of all nonmilitary supply convoys in Iraq. "We would never launch into an offensive operation, but when you're co-located, you're all one team, really."

ArmorGroup, which started in Iraq with 20 employees and a handful of SUVs, has grown to a force of 1,200—the equivalent of nearly two battalions—with 240 armored trucks; nearly half of the publicly traded company's $273.5 million in revenue last year came from Iraq. Globally, ArmorGroup employs 9,000 people in 38 countries.

The company, with headquarters at a complex of sandstone villas near Baghdad's Green Zone, is acquiring a fleet of $200,000 tactical armored vehicles equipped with two gun hatches and able to withstand armor-piercing bullets and some of the largest roadside bombs.

The U.S. Labor Department reported that ArmorGroup has lost 26 employees in Iraq, based on insurance claims. Sources close to the company say the figure is nearly 30. Only three countries in the 25-nation coalition—the United States, Britain and Italy—have sustained more combat-related deaths.

In spring 2004, Holly built the logistics network for Iraq's reconstruction from scratch. The network delivered 31,100 vehicles, 451,000 weapons and 410 million rounds of ammunition to the new Iraqi security forces, and items as varied as computers, baby incubators, school desks and mattresses for every Iraqi government ministry. The network came to rival the military's own logistics operation.

Holly also discovered he was at the center of an undeclared war.

He assembled a small private army to protect material as it flowed from border crossings and a southern port at Umm Qasr to the 650,000-square-foot warehouse complex at Abu Ghraib and on to its final destination.

"The only way anything gets to you here is if somebody bets their life on its delivery," says Holly, a burly civilian with a trimmed gray beard who strikes a commanding presence even in khakis, multicolored checked shirts and tennis shoes. "That's the fundamental issue: nothing moves anywhere in Iraq without betting your life."

The most dangerous link in Holly's supply chain is shipping. It requires the slow-moving convoys to navigate Iraq's dangerous roads. Holly erected a ground-traffic control center in a low-slung trailer near his office in Baghdad's Green Zone. The security companies monitor their convoys in air-conditioned silence, which is shattered by a jarring klaxon each time a contractor pushes a dashboard "panic button," signaling a possible attack.

On May 8, 2005, after dropping off a load that included T-shirts, plastic whistles and 250,000 rounds of ammunition for Iraqi police, one of Holly's convoys was attacked. Of 20 security contractors and truck drivers, 13 were killed or listed as missing; five of the seven survivors were wounded. Insurgents booby-trapped four of the bodies. To eliminate the threat, a military recovery team fired a tank round into a pile of corpses, according to an after-action report.

The convoy had been protected by Heart Security, a British firm that used unarmored vehicles. Within a month, another Hart-led convoy was hit. The team leader informed the ground-control center by cellphone that he was running out of ammunition. He left the cellphone on as his convoy was overrun.

"We listened to the bad guys for almost an hour after they finished everybody off," Holly said.

The attacks represented a turning point in the private war.

Holly vowed he would never again use unarmored vehicles for convoy protection. He went to his primary shipper, Public Warehousing Co. of Kuwait, and ordered a change. PWC hired ArmorGroup, which had armed Ford F-350 pickups with steel-reinforced gun turrets and belt-fed machine guns.

Other companies followed suit, ramping up production of an array of armored and semi-armored trucks of various styles and colors, until Iraq's supply routes resembled the post-apocalyptic world of the "Mad Max" movies.

ArmorGroup started in Iraq in 2003 with four security teams and 20 employees. It now has 30 mechanics to support its ground operation. "It's a monster," said Simpson, the country operations manager, strolling past a truck blown apart by a roadside bomb.

ArmorGroup operates 10 convoy security teams in support of Holly's logistics operation. The company runs another 10 to 15 under a half-dozen contracts, as well as for clients who request security on a case-by-case basis, Simpson says.

The company charges $8,000 to $12,000 a day, according to sources familiar with the pricing, although the cost can vary depending on convoy size and the risk. For security reasons, the convoys are limited to 10 tractor-trailers protected by at least four armored trucks filled with 20 guards: 4 Western vehicle commanders with M-21 assault rifles and 9mm Glock pistols, and 16 Iraqis with AK-47s.

The Western contractors, most with at least 10 years' experience, are paid about $135,000, the same as a U.S. Army two-star general. The Iraqis receive about a tenth of that.

"Every time I think about how it was at the beginning, arriving here with a suitcase and $1,000, and there was no one else around, it's just incredible," Simpson says. "Nobody envisioned that private security companies would be openly targeted by insurgents."

ArmorGroup prides itself on a low-key approach to security. Its well-groomed guards travel in khakis and dark blue shirts. The company's armored trucks are adorned with stickers issued by the Interior Ministry, where the company is fully licensed. Holly's former deputy, Victoria Wayne, says ArmorGroup turned down an opportunity to use more powerful weaponry as the insurgent threat increased.

"As a publicly traded company, they didn't want to be perceived as a mercenary force," she says.

But the company is under constant attack. ArmorGroup ran 1,184 convoys in Iraq in 2006; it reported 450 hostile actions, mostly roadside bombs, small-arms fire and mortar attacks. The company was attacked 293 times in the first four months of 2007, according to ArmorGroup statistics. On the dangerous roads north of Baghdad, "you generally attract at least one incident every mission," Simpson says.

Allan Campion, 36, who joined ArmorGroup after 18 years in the British infantry, says one of his convoys was recently attacked three times on a two-mile stretch outside Baghdad. One bomb exploded near the team leader's vehicle, but the convoy managed to continue, he says. Within minutes, another bomb exploded, followed by small-arms fire.

A firefight ensued as the convoy continued through the "kill zone," Campion says.

"We were still moving, so whether you've hit anybody or not, it's very hard to say," he says.

With the insurgents employing more lethal roadside bombs, ArmorGroup has responded by changing tactics and spending $6.8 million to bolster its armor. Its new armored "Rock" vehicles are built on Ford F-550 chassis and are favored by ArmorGroup because of a V-shaped hull that provides better protection against roadside bombs.

Chris Berman, a former Navy SEAL who helped design the Rock for North Carolina–based Granite Tactical Vehicles, says its main deterrent is its twin gun hatches. "That gives you twice as much firepower," Berman says. "With two belt-fed machine guns in there, that's enough to chew up most people."

 War by Electron: Cyberwar

2.5 Cyber Attack Vexes Estonia, Poses Debate

Christopher Rhoads

The information and communication revolution has also changed the nature of war in today's world. In the following *Wall Street Journal* article, reporter Christopher Rhoads talks about a 2007 cyber attack on Estonia, a small northern European state bordering on Russia. After the Estonian government authorized the removal of a Soviet war memorial honoring the Red Army's defeat of the Nazis—an act that angered many Russians and strained Estonia's already difficult relations with

Russia—the Estonian government and Estonian businesses found their computers under massive cyber attack. While the Estonian government suspected the Russian government of organizing or facilitating these attacks, this was impossible to prove. Nonetheless Estonia, a NATO member, brought this situation to the alliance's attention, and the attack prompted states around the world to think about their vulnerability to cyber attack.

A cyber attack on the Baltic country of Estonia will likely shape a debate inside many governments over how such attacks should be considered in the context of international law and what sort of response is appropriate.

The Estonian government compares the episode, which it has blamed on Russia, to an act of war. The Kremlin has denied any Russian government involvement.

Since the end of April, the unprecedented cyber attack has crippled Web sites operated by Estonian government ministries, banks, media outlets and other companies. The "denial of service" attacks swamp Web sites with so many hits they are forced to shut down.

The attack comes as the U.S. and other governments are mulling how to respond to cyber attacks. "There is a discussion over how cyber aggression should fit into current law and whether a conventional attack would be suitable retaliation," said Johannes Ullrich, chief technology officer at the SANS Institute, a Bethesda, Md., Internet-security company that tracks threats to the Internet.

In meetings this week, Estonia brought the attack before the North Atlantic Treaty Organization [NATO] and the European Union. NATO has dispatched a cyber-crime expert to Estonia.

The Estonian government said it traced much of the traffic that inundated its Web sites to Russian computers. The government also said it found on the Internet instructions in Russian on how to carry out the action. The Estonian foreign minister initially accused the Kremlin of orchestrating the attack. Lately, the government has softened that position, alleging the attacks came from Russia but that it has no evidence implicating the Kremlin.

"If a bank or an airport is hit by a missile, it is easy to say that is an act of war," said Madis Mikko, a spokesman for the Estonian defense ministry. "But if the same result is caused by a cyber attack, what do you call that?"

The attack began on April 27, shortly after Estonia removed a Soviet statue from downtown Tallinn that commemorated Red Army soldiers killed by the Nazis in World War II. The incident inflamed relations between the two countries. In Moscow, pro-Kremlin youth groups blockaded the Estonian embassy and harassed the Estonian ambassador. Estonia, with a population of 1.3 million, was formerly a part of the old Soviet Union.

In the early days of the attack, government Web sites that normally receive around 1,000 visits a day were receiving 2,000 visits every second, according to Mr. Mikko. The onslaught shut down some Web sites for half an hour, others for several hours or more, according to government officials. "They tried to cut us off from the rest of the world," Mr. Mikko said.

Estonia is particularly vulnerable to such an attack because of its heavy use of the Internet. Over two-thirds of the population has access to broadband. More than 80 percent of the country's tax returns are filed online and most Estonians pay their bills via the Internet.

"This is a threat to the security of our country," said Sten Hansson, the information-technology adviser to the Estonian prime minister. He added that while servers within the country have been able to restore usage for most of the sites, there are still delays, particularly for users outside the country trying to access Estonian sites.

Russian entities have gained a reputation in recent years for similar attacks, using what are called "botnets." They consist of a group of computer simultaneously controlled—sometimes thousands at once—by an unauthorized user, who illicitly takes them over without the knowledge of the computer owner. The infected computers are then directed to deluge the target with traffic.

"Russia has a fairly long track record for this kind of activity," said Joe Stewart, a security researcher with SecureWorks Inc., an Atlanta Internet-security company.

2.6 A World Wide Web of Terror

The Economist

As the following news story from the British journal *The Economist* reports, the Internet has been an important tool for transnational terrorist groups.

By his own admission, he never fired a single bullet or "stood for a second in a trench" in the great *jihad* against America. Yet the man who called himself "Irhabi007"—a play on the Arabic word for terrorist and the code-name for James Bond—was far more important than any foot soldier or suicide-bomber in Iraq. He led the charge of *jihad* on the Internet.

In doing so, Irhabi007 was a central figure in enabling al-Qaeda to reconstitute itself after the fall of the Taliban and its eviction from Afghanistan. Al-Qaeda ("the base") and its followers moved to cyberspace, the ultimate ungoverned territory, where jihadists have set up virtual schools for ideological and military training and active propaganda arms.

Irhabi007 pioneered many of the techniques required to make all this happen. He was a tireless "webmaster" for several extremist websites, especially those issuing the statements of the late Abu Musab al-Zarqawi, the leader of al-Qaeda in Iraq. Intelligence agencies watched powerlessly as Irhabi007 hacked into computers, for instance appropriating that of the Arkansas Highway and Transportation

Department to distribute large video files, and taught his fellow cyber-jihadists how to protect their anonymity online.

Despite his celebrity, this was not good enough for Irhabi007. "Dude," he complained to a fellow cyber-jihadist (who called himself "Abuthaabit") during one encrypted web chat, "my heart is in Iraq."

Abuthaabit: How are you going to have enough to go there?

Irhabi007: I suppose someone gotta be here!

Abuthaabit: This media work, I am telling you, is very important. Very, very, very, very.

Irhabi007: I know, I know.

Abuthaabit: Because a lot of the funds brothers are getting is because they are seeing stuff like this coming out. Imagine how many people have gone [to Iraq] after seeing the situation because of the videos. Imagine how many of them could have been shaheed [martyrs] as well.

Irhabi007's desire for real action may have led to his downfall. He was not only involved in a dispersed network of *jihadi* propaganda, but also, it seems, in a decentralised web of terrorist plots. In October 2005 police in Bosnia arrested a cyber-jihadist who called himself "Maximus," a Swedish teenager of Bosnian extraction called Mirsad Bektasevic. He and three others were later sentenced to jail terms of up to 15 years for plotting attacks that were to take place either in Bosnia or in other European countries.

Among the material recovered from Mr. Bektasevic's flat, police found 19 kg of explosives, weapons, a video with instructions for making a suicide vest and a video recording of masked men proclaiming their membership of "al-Qaeda in northern Europe". On his computer they found evidence of contacts with other jihadists across Europe. Among them was Irhabi007.

Two days later, British police raided a flat in a terraced house in west London next to one of the rougher pubs in Shepherd's Bush. After an altercation, they arrested Younis Tsouli. The elusive Irhabi007 turned out to be the 22-year-old son of a Moroccan tourism board official and a student of information technology. Two other men, also students, were arrested at the same time, although Mr. Tsouli had never met them except on the Internet.

The trial of Mr. Tsouli and his co-defendants—Waseem Mughal, a British-born graduate in biochemistry (aka Abuthaabit), and Tariq al-Daour, a law student born in the United Arab Emirates—came to an end this month when they belatedly pleaded guilty to charges of incitement to murder and conspiracy to murder. The court also heard that Mr. al-Daour ran a £1.8 m credit-card fraud and used the funds to buy equipment for *jihadi* groups. Mr. Tsouli and Mr. Mughal used stolen credit-card numbers to set up *jihadi* websites. Mr. Tsouli was sent to jail for ten years; the others received shorter sentences.

There have been several arrests in Denmark, where a 17-year-old man of Palestinian origin was convicted last February for his involvement in Mr. Bektasevic's plot. Three others were found guilty, but the jury's verdict was overturned. Irhabi007 has also been reported to be linked to plots in America, where two men living in Atlanta, Georgia, have been charged with planning attacks against civilian and military targets in and around Washington, DC, including the Capitol, the World Bank, the George Washington Masonic Memorial and a fuel depot. According to the indictment, the two men—Syed Ahmed, 21, and Ehsanul Sadequee, 19—sent Irhabi007 photographs of the proposed targets, and also travelled to Canada to meet fellow plotters and discuss attacks.

Many of the details are still subject to court restrictions. But these interlinked investigations underline the words of Peter Clarke, the head of the counter-terrorism branch of London's Metropolitan Police, who said in April that his officers were contending with "networks within networks, connections within connections and links between individuals that cross local, national and international boundaries."

In light of this month's failed attempts to set off car bombs in London and at Glasgow airport, allegedly by a group of foreign doctors and other medical staff, one exchange of messages found on Irhabi007's computer, in a folder marked "*jihad*," makes intriguing reading. "We are 45 doctors and we are determined to undertake jihad for Allah's sake and to take the battle inside damaged America, Allah willing," ran part of it.

The message purported to set out a plot to attack a naval base, apparently Mayport in Jacksonville, Florida, with the aim of achieving the "complete destruction" of the *U.S.S. John F. Kennedy,* an aircraft carrier, and 12 escort vessels, as well as blowing up "clubs for naked women" around the base. "The anticipated number of pig casualties is 200–300," said the author, unidentified except for the boast that he had been discharged from the Jordanian army. He claimed to have the support of a pilot who would provide air cover for the operation, but he lacked one essential piece of information that he asked Irhabi007 to provide: a guide for making car bombs. The FBI said it had investigated the plot at the time and found it to be "not credible."

Nevertheless, the capability of the Internet to promote terrorism is worrying intelligence agencies. According to America's National Intelligence Estimate in April 2006, "The radicalisation process is occurring more quickly, more widely and more anonymously in the Internet age, raising the likelihood of surprise attacks by unknown groups whose members and supporters may be difficult to pinpoint."

Bomb.com

Past technological innovations, such as telephones or fax machines, have quickly been exploited by terrorists. But the information revolution is particularly useful to them. To begin with, encrypted communications, whether in the form of e-mail messages or, better still, voice-over-internet audio, make it much harder for investigators to monitor their activity. Messages can be hidden, for instance, within innocuous-looking pictures.

More important, the Internet gives jihadists an ideal vehicle for propaganda, providing access to large audiences free of government censorship or media filters, while carefully preserving their anonymity. Its ability to connect disparate *jihadi* groups creates a sense of a global Islamic movement fighting to defend the global *ummah*, or community, from a common enemy. It provides a low-risk means of taking part in *jihad* for sympathisers across the world.

The ease and cheapness of processing words, pictures, sound and video has brought the era not only of the citizen-journalist but also the terrorist-journalist. Al-Qaeda now sends out regular "news bulletins" with a masked man in a studio recounting events from the many fronts of *jihad,* whether in Iraq, Afghanistan, Chechnya or Palestine. *Jihadi* ticker-tape feeds provide running updates on the number of Americans killed (about ten times more than the Pentagon's death toll).

Battlefield footage of American Humvees being blown up to shouts of "Allahu Akbar!" (God is Great) appear on the Internet within minutes of the attacks taking place. The most popular scenes are often compiled into films with musical soundtracks of male choirs performing songs such as "Caravans of Martyrs." Jihadists have even released a computer video game, "Night of Bush Capturing," in which participants play at shooting American soldiers and President George Bush. Inevitably, experts say, jihadists have also started to create "residents" in the virtual world of Second Life.

As well as war fantasies, there is sometimes also a dose of sexual wish-fulfilment. A video recording by a Kuwaiti ideologue, Hamid al-Ali, declares that a martyr in the cause of *jihad* goes to paradise to enjoy delicious food, drink and a wife who will "astonish your mind" and much else besides; her vagina, apparently, "never complains about how much sex she had," and she reverts back to being a virgin.

The Internet is awash with communiqués from insurgent groups extolling their own success or denouncing rivals. Even the most hunted figures, such as Ayman al-Zawahiri, the second-most-senior figure in al-Qaeda, regularly put out video statements commenting on political developments within just a few days.

In short, the hand-held video camera has become as important a tool of insurgency as the AK-47 or the RPG rocket-launcher. As Mr. Zawahiri himself once put it in an intercepted letter to Zarqawi, "More than half of this battle is taking place in the battlefield of the media." Or as one *jihadi* magazine found on Irhabi007's computer explained: "Film everything; this is good advice for all mujahideen [holy warriors]. Brothers, don't disdain photography. You should be aware that every frame you take is as good as a missile fired at the Crusader enemy and his puppets." Just before his arrest, Irhabi007 had set up a website that, he hoped, would rival YouTube, to share *jihadi* videos. He called it Youbombit.com.

Of Jihad and Camels

The Internet's decentralised structure, with its origins in military networks designed to survive nuclear strikes, now gives *jihadi* networks tremendous resilience. *Jihadi* websites constantly come and go, sometimes taken down by service providers only to reappear elsewhere, sometimes shifted deliberately to stay ahead of investigators. As one expert put it: "It's like the old game of Space Invaders. When you clear one screen of potential attackers, another simply appears to take its place."

The number of extremist websites is increasing exponentially, from a handful in 2000 to several thousand today. Some are overtly militant, while others give *jihad* second place to promoting a puritanical brand of piety known as "salafism," that is modelled on the earliest followers of the Prophet Muhammad and regards later developments as degenerate. Most are in Arabic, but some have started to translate their material into English, French and other languages to reach a wider audience.

The most headline-grabbing material on the Internet is the military manuals—whether as books, films or PowerPoint slides—giving instruction on a myriad of subjects, not least weapons, assassination techniques, the manufacture of poisons and how to make explosives. But intelligence agencies say there is nothing like having hands-on experience in a place like Iraq, or at least a training camp. In the latest attempted attacks in London and Glasgow, for example, the attackers clearly botched the manufacture of their car bombs even though many of the alleged plotters were well educated.

Still, internet-based compilations such as the vast and constantly updated "Encyclopedia of Preparation," as well as militant e-magazines such as the *Tip of the Camel's Hump* (used to mean "the pinnacle") found on Irhabi007's computer, make it easier for self-starting groups around the world to try their hand at terrorism. The Dutch counter-terrorism office, which publishes many of its studies on extremism, concludes that the existence of virtual training camps "has the effect of lowering the threshold against the commission of attacks."

Many *jihadi* websites put their most inflammatory information and discussions in password-protected areas. Here participants can be gradually groomed, invited to take part in more confidential discussions, drawn into one-on-one chats, indoctrinated and at last recruited to the cause.

But the very anonymity that the Internet affords jihadists can also work against them; it lets police and intelligence agencies enter the jihadists' world without being identified. Many postings to web forums are filled with (rightly) paranoid postings about who is watching. A lengthy posting on a Syrian *jihadi* site in 2005, entitled "Advice to Brothers Seeking *Jihad* in Iraq," said raw recruits offering only "enthusiasm or impetuousness or love of martyrdom" were no longer wanted. Instead, the mujahideen needed money and experienced fighters, but they should not assume that the smuggling routes through Syria were safe. It advocated communicating in secret through trusted sources in mosques rather than on the Internet, noting that "this forum, like the others, is under . . . surveillance; any information is obviously not secret, so any individuals you meet and correspond with on the forums cannot be trusted at all."

Contributors to *jihadi* websites are regularly told not to divulge secrets. When news of Irhabi007's arrest emerged last year, some for the postings stressed the need for greater caution online. One of these, signed by "Badr17," gave the warning "Trust in Allah, but tie your camel."

Open University of Jihad

One of the most prolific al-Qaeda strategists is Abu Musab al-Suri. He is now in American custody, but his 1,600-page opus, "The Global Islamic Call to

Resistance," survives. It advocates the creation in the West of self-starting, independent terrorist cells, not directly affiliated to existing groups, to stage spectacular attacks.

For many who study the *jihadi* websites, however, the bigger danger is indoctrination. The Dutch domestic intelligence service, the AIVD, regards the Internet as the "turbocharger" of *jihadi* radicalisation. Stephen Ulph, a senior fellow at the Jamestown Foundation, an American research institute that monitors terrorism, says the Internet provides an open university for jihadists. At least 60 percent of the material on *jihadi* websites deals not with current events or with war videos, but instead concerns ideological and cultural questions. Jihadists, Mr. Ulph says, are fighting less a war against the West than "a civil war for the minds of Muslim youth." In this process of radicalisation, "the mujahideen attract the uncommitted armchair sympathiser, detach him from his social and intellectual environment, undermine his self-image as an observant Muslim, introduce what they claim is 'real Islam,' re-script history in terms of a perennial conflict, centralise *jihad* as his Islamic identity, train him not only militarily but also socially and psychologically."

A key text is the ever-expanding e-book, "Questions and Uncertainties Concerning the Mujahideen and Their Operations," which seeks to arm jihadists with responses to questions and doubts about their actions, ranging from the admissibility of killing Muslims, the use of weapons of mass destruction and the acceptability of shaving one's beard for the sake of *jihad*. "It is important we do not get distracted by focusing on organisations rather than against ideology," argues Mr. Ulph.

The point is underlined in a study by the Combating Terrorism Centre at America's military academy at West Point, which has tried to "map" the most important ideological influences by searching citations in *jihadi* online documents. Top of the list is Ibn Taymiyya, a scholar who lived at the time of the medieval Mongol invasions. He strove to return Islam to the pure faith of Muhammad's followers, advocated *jihad* to repel foreign invaders and taught that Mongol leaders who converted to Islam were not really Muslims because they did not implement *sharia*. These ideas strike a chord with today's jihadists, who see Americans as the new Mongols.

Osama bin Laden does not make the top ten most-cited figures, even among modern authors. Abu Muhammad al-Maqdisi, the theorist jailed in Jordan (and who directly inspired Zarqawi), is regarded as a higher authority. And Mr. Zawahiri, the ubiquitous Internet propagandist who is often described as the real brains behind al-Qaeda, does not even figure in the jihadists' intellectual universe.

Western intelligence agencies trawl the Internet to look for evidence of terrorist plots, but lack the resources or desire to challenge the wider ideology. In a global network, outside the control of any single government, attempts to close down extremist sites are little more than short-lived harassment. What is needed is a systematic campaign of counter-propaganda, not least in support of friendly Muslim governments and moderate Muslims, to try to reclaim the ground ceded to the jihadists.

"Intelligence agencies are dealing with the problem once people have manifested themselves as existing terrorists," says Professor Bruce Hoffman, an expert on terrorism at Georgetown University. "We have to find a way to stanch the flow.

The Internet creates a constant reservoir of radicalised people which terrorist groups and networks can draw upon."

So Irhabi007 may be off the Internet, but others like him remain. Among the most prolific is a figure who roams the web by the name of, yes, Irhabi11.

Suggested Discussion Topics

1. Clausewitz argued that war was "a continuation of policy by other means." Do you think this is a useful way to think about war in today's world? Why or why not? In what ways might Clausewitz's ideas about war have been shaped by the time and culture in which he lived? Have different societies and different ages had different views about the role of violence, who has the right to use it, against whom, and for what purposes?

2. Since the Treaties of Westphalia in 1648, states have attempted to monopolize the use of violence, disarming or destroying other types of political actors that have attempted to use force to press their demands. States have also tried to limit the impact of violence by organizing armed forces into disciplined, professional regiments and creating "laws of war" that sought to ensure that interstate violence would involve only these professional military forces and leave civilians largely unharmed. Do you think that states will be successful in continuing to maintain this monopoly on violence and in limiting warfare? Explain what factors or arguments lead you to your conclusion.

3. What are the principal features of the "new wars" described by Münkler? What are the key economic factors in these wars—in determining who fights them, where they are fought, and how they are fought?

4. What, besides national interest, may motivate war in the postmodern world? What does this imply about how wars will be fought and how they will (or won't) end? What kinds of wars, over what kinds of objectives, might involve your country?

5. What kinds of wars do you think the United States should be preparing for—another Desert Storm or the kinds of violence described in this chapter? Why?

6. What is terrorism, and what makes it different from other forms of war or political violence? What, if anything, makes the destruction of the World Trade Center different from, say, the Japanese attack on Pearl Harbor in 1941? From the American bombing of Hiroshima and Nagasaki during World War II, which together killed more than 100,000 civilians? From General William T. Sherman's famous "march to the sea" during the American Civil War, in which a swath of Georgia was laid to waste? From the assassination of the Austrian Archduke Franz Ferdinand by a Serbian anarchist in 1914 (an assassination that triggered World War I)? From the destruction of a U.S. Marine Corps barracks in Lebanon by a suicide bomber during the U.S. intervention in that country in the early 1980s?

7. Is the practice of terrorism changing in today's world? If so, in what ways and for what reasons? Do you think terrorism will become more common during

your lifetime? If so, why? And if not, why not? What can be done to reduce the likelihood and the impact of terrorism? How should the United States deal with the problem of terrorism?

8. Why have we seen an increase in the number of private military contractors and an expansion of the roles they serve? What are the advantages and disadvantages to states of outsourcing military activities? Should private companies that sell private armies be regulated? If so, by whom? What restrictions would you consider placing on the activities of private military contractors? If a private company with a private army like Blackwater does something wrong (for example, is responsible for killing innocent civilians) who should be held responsible, and by whom? If the alternative to relying on corporations like Blackwater were a return to the draft (in order to replace Blackwater's personnel), what would your recommendation be? Are there other alternatives that you can imagine?

9. Does the return of mercenary armies represent a threat to the state system?

10. Is a cyber attack an act of war? How can states protect themselves against cyber attacks of the sort that Estonia experienced in 2007? If states can identify the parties responsible for these attacks, and if they are outside the state's jurisdiction, what should states do?

11. Given the use of the Internet by terrorist groups, should the Internet be more closely regulated? If so, by whom? What sorts of regulations might you envision? What would be the costs and benefits of these regulations? How feasible would they be?

Chapter 3

Weapons of Mass Destruction: Thinking About the Unthinkable, Again

The prospect of war casts a shadow over our lives. Today, individuals around the world live in fear not only of the increasingly endemic violence of postmodern war and the possibility of terrorism, but of the enormous danger posed by weapons of mass destruction (WMD). Nuclear weapons, biological weapons, and chemical weapons are described as weapons of mass destruction because they have the potential to kill large numbers of people indiscriminately. Although these weapons could be used like traditional weapons, targeted against opposing armies or military bases, they are better suited for attacking civilians, destroying the political or economic basis of a society by inflicting large numbers of casualties and terrorizing or demoralizing the remaining population. Perhaps ironically, the existence of these weapons has transformed, and continues to transform, global politics, increasing the pressure on states and nations around the world to cooperate even while they continue to compete with each other. Any war involving unlimited use of these weapons would be a disaster in which there would be no meaningful victors: both sides would emerge with their societies shattered. Rather than a win-lose proposition, such a war would be a lose-lose situation. As a consequence, avoiding such a war becomes a *shared* problem. Indeed, recent studies suggest that because of the potential environmental effects of a nuclear war—caused by the smoke, soot, and particles thrown into the atmosphere by nuclear explosions and burning cities— even a war between two *other* states might be disastrous. Thus, avoiding nuclear wars becomes a shared problem for the entire world. Similarly, a biological attack involving viruses like smallpox would threaten not simply the society at which it was aimed but societies around the world.

The atomic age began in 1945 when, at the end of World War II, the United States dropped atom bombs on the Japanese cities of Hiroshima and Nagasaki. These bombs were based on the principle of atomic fission; that is, their explosive power derived from the energy released when large uranium or plutonium atoms broke apart. The destructive power of such bombs was roughly equivalent to that of tens of thousands of tons of a conventional explosive like TNT. Four years later, in the midst of the Cold War, the Soviet Union demonstrated its capacity to make atomic weapons too by exploding an atomic device. Over the next few years, both the United States and the Soviet Union proceeded to develop hydrogen or thermonuclear (or nuclear, for short) weapons based on the principle of nuclear fusion. These bombs, which relied on the energy released when hydrogen atoms fused together into helium atoms, were hundreds or thousands of times more powerful than early atomic weapons and could be made relatively cheaply and in large numbers. During the next four decades, the world lived under an atomic/nuclear sword of Damocles, fearful that the Cold War would explode into a nuclear World War III.

During the Cold War, the superpowers acquired enormous arsenals of nuclear weapons, as well as substantial stockpiles of chemical and biological weapons. Between them, they accumulated as many as 50,000 nuclear warheads, along with sophisticated aircraft and missiles to deliver them. Over time, it became clear that weapons of mass destruction were of little use except in deterring a general or all-out war between the superpowers or dissuading others from using such weapons first, against either oneself or one's allies. As both superpowers developed ways to protect their nuclear weapons from an enemy attack, a situation of *mutual deterrence* emerged, based on the threat of mutual assured destruction (MAD). MAD meant that the superpowers could not destroy one another's nuclear weapons in a surprise attack, and that any nuclear blow invited devastating retaliation in a "second strike": in other words, an all-out nuclear war was guaranteed to be a no-win proposition, regardless of whether one attacked first or second.

In 1962, the United States and the Soviet Union found themselves in a dangerous crisis over the secret Soviet deployment of missiles to Cuba. More than any other single event, the Cuban missile crisis persuaded leaders on both sides of the Iron Curtain of the dangers posed by nuclear weapons in a world in which events might spiral out of control. Immediately after the crisis, the superpowers established the Moscow-Washington hot line, a teletype link that let leaders communicate with each other in case of a similar crisis.

The superpowers also recognized that it was always possible that a technological breakthrough would endanger the stability of MAD, that the arms race consumed scarce resources, and that, as long as the superpowers had large numbers of nuclear weapons aimed at each other, mutual fear and suspicion would remain. For these reasons, the second half of the Cold War was marked by a variety of arms-control and disarmament agreements designed to ensure the stability of MAD, reduce pressures to engage in arms racing, and ameliorate antagonisms and worries. The first of these agreements, the Limited Nuclear Test Ban Treaty, was reached less than a year after the Cuban missile crisis. It prohibited testing nuclear weapons in the atmosphere, under water, or in outer space. An even more important breakthrough followed in 1972, when the first Strategic Arms Limitation Treaty (SALT) accords were signed. SALT I limited the number of offensive missiles and antiballistic missiles (ABMs, missiles that would shoot down attacking missiles in flight) the superpowers could have. The limitation on ABMs was particularly significant, effectively guaranteeing that each side would leave its own people defenseless, in a sense making them hostages to ensure its own good behavior. Seven years later SALT II created additional limitations and restricted the technological improvements that the superpowers could make in their weapons systems.

Although SALT II remained unratified because of the Soviet invasion of Afghanistan, both sides adhered to the treaty.

The 1987 Intermediate-range Nuclear Forces (INF) Treaty, which eliminated U.S. missiles in Europe able to reach targets in the Soviet Union and Soviet missiles able to reach the territory of American allies in Europe and Asia, was a first small step in the direction of genuine nuclear disarmament. A second, much larger step was the 1991 Strategic Arms Reduction Treaty (START I), which required the superpowers to cut their nuclear warheads by almost one-third. The reductions agreed to in 1992 under the START II pact were still more dramatic, calling for a further 50 percent reduction in U.S. and Russian nuclear arsenals. Since then, both the United States and Russia have continued to reduce the size of their nuclear arsenals.

While the realization that a large-scale nuclear war would be disastrous for both sides served as the foundation for the nuclear relationship between the superpowers from the mid-1960s onward, at least some American decision-makers have been profoundly uncomfortable with the notion that protection of the American people and survival of the American nation depended on the forbearance of an opponent, particularly one sometimes described as an "evil empire." Without any defenses, the United States could not defend itself against a nuclear missile attack. It could only hope to dissuade an adversary from launching a nuclear attack by making clear that if American society were destroyed, Soviet or Chinese society would be destroyed in retaliation. To alter this MAD relationship and to give the United States some sort of meaningful defense against attack, in 1983 President Ronald Reagan initiated the Strategic Defense Initiative to develop the technological capability to destroy attacking missiles. Although "astrodome" defenses (defenses that would be able to defend America successfully against a significant missile attack) have been viewed by most knowledgeable observers as technologically infeasible, post-Reagan administrations have continued, with greater or lesser enthusiasm, to invest in missile defense programs, despite the political problems this has caused for U.S. relations with Russia and with its own allies.

The end of the Cold War changed the nature of the problem posed by weapons of mass destruction. Increasingly, the most pressing issues have become the fear of some sort of accident or the proliferation of such weapons to rogue states and nonstate terrorists. Rather than seeing each other principally as enemies, Americans and Russians have come to focus on their common concern in stopping the spread of nuclear weapons, technology, and material and retaining tight control over what exists: although Americans and Russians may (and do) disagree about who should pay the economic and diplomatic costs of improving security and preventing or slowing proliferation, accidents and nuclear proliferation are recognized by both sides as a non-zero-sum game—in this case, one in which costs will exceed gains. By providing states or terrorists with weapons of mass destruction, proliferation results in a further fragmentation and disintegration of global authority and order that endangers everyone. The effort to stem proliferation involves strengthening old institutions and creating new ones to combat this fragmentation and disintegration.

Even during the Cold War the United States and the Soviet Union cooperated to try to limit the spread of nuclear weapons. In 1968, the Nuclear Nonproliferation Treaty

(NPT) bound those signatories that possessed nuclear weapons to refrain from exporting them and those signatories that did not possess them to refrain from acquiring them. Despite the NPT and a 1995 agreement to extend the NPT in perpetuity, the problem of nuclear proliferation has grown, especially as it becomes more and more difficult to prevent the diversion and enrichment of nuclear fuels from power plants for weapons use. By the end of the Cold War, the United States, Russia, France, Great Britain, and China were declared nuclear powers. In 1998, India and Pakistan crossed the nuclear threshold by conducting nuclear weapons tests. With the breakup of the Soviet Union, Belarus, Kazakhstan, and Ukraine also temporarily had nuclear weapons, until agreeing to surrender them to Russia for destruction. South Africa developed nuclear weapons and then chose to dismantle them. Israel almost certainly has nuclear weapons, and Iraq came close to developing them before its defeat in the Persian Gulf War when it was forced to give up its capacity to do so. North Korea also has a capacity to make nuclear weapons, and Iran is widely seen as trying to join the nuclear club.

The spread of chemical and biological weapons may be even more dangerous than nuclear proliferation, because they are relatively easy and inexpensive to make and can be hidden without difficulty. This fact was brought home with urgency in the autumn of 2001 when letters contaminated with anthrax spores killed several Americans. The Biological Weapons Convention (1972) and the Chemical Weapons Convention (1993) call for the destruction of these weapons and prohibit their production. After a delay, the U.S. Senate finally ratified the latter treaty in 1997. Still, at least seventeen nations are suspected to be conducting research into biological weapons, and many more have the ability to make and use chemical weapons.

Thus, though in some ways an old issue, in today's world WMD represent a novel set of challenges. The proliferation of nuclear, chemical, and biological weapons poses a collective problem for people around the globe. A variety of new actors, many of them domestic or transnational players rather than states, and a range of new institutions are involved, both positively and negatively. Because of its power, the United States will have to play an important role in developing and implementing responses to the proliferation of WMD, but its ability to solve this problem unilaterally is limited.

3.1 The New Threat of Mass Destruction

Richard K. Betts

In the first selection, Columbia University political science professor Richard Betts examines the way the threat of mass destruction has changed in today's world, noting that although the danger of a U.S.–Russian war is much lower than was the danger of a U.S.–Soviet conflict during the Cold War, the overall risk that WMD will be used may actually be higher. Further, he reasons, the old strategies for dealing with the danger posed by WMD—mutual deterrence and arms control—may not work well today, given the changed nature of the threat. WMD (and biological weapons in particular) may be becoming the preferred weapon of the weak, rather than a tool available only to the strong. New domestic and foreign policies may be needed to cope with this development.

During the Cold War, weapons of mass destruction were the centerpiece of foreign policy. Nuclear arms hovered in the background of every major issue in East-West competition and alliance relations. The highest priorities of U.S. policy could almost all be linked in some way to the danger of World War III and the fear of millions of casualties in the American homeland.

Since the Cold War, other matters have displaced strategic concerns on the foreign policy agenda, and that agenda itself is now barely on the public's radar screen. Apart from defense policy professionals, few Americans still lose sleep over weapons of mass destruction (WMD). After all, what do normal people feel is the main relief provided by the end of the Cold War? It is that the danger of nuclear war is off their backs.

Yet today, WMD present more and different things to worry about than during the Cold War. For one, nuclear arms are no longer the only concern, as chemical and biological weapons have come to the fore. For another, there is less danger of complete annihilation, but more danger of mass destruction. Since the Cold War is over and American and Russian nuclear inventories are much smaller, there is less chance of an apocalyptic exchange of many thousands of weapons. But the probability that some smaller number of WMD will be used is growing. Many of the standard strategies and ideas for coping with WMD threats are no longer as relevant as they were when Moscow was the main adversary. But new thinking has not yet congealed in as clear a form as the Cold War concepts of nuclear deterrence theory. . . .

The points to keep in mind about the new world of mass destruction are the following. First, the roles such weapons play in international conflict are changing. They no longer represent the technological frontier of warfare. Increasingly, they will be weapons of the weak—states or groups that militarily are at best second-class. The importance of the different types among them has also shifted. Biological weapons should now be the most serious concern, with nuclear weapons second and chemicals a distant third.

Second, the mainstays of Cold War security policy—deterrence and arms control—are not what they used to be. Some new threats may not be deterrable, and the role of arms control in dealing with WMD has been marginalized. In a few instances, continuing devotion to deterrence and arms control may have side effects that offset the benefits.

Third, some of the responses most likely to cope with the threats in novel ways will not find a warm welcome. The response that should now be the highest priority is one long ignored, opposed, or ridiculed: a serious civil defense program to blunt the effects of WMD if they are unleashed within the United States. Some of

Betts, Richard K., "The New Threat of Mass Destruction," *Foreign Affairs,* January/February 1998, pp. 26–41. Reprinted by permission of Foreign Affairs. © 1998 by the Council on Foreign Relations, Inc. <www.Foreign Affairs.org>.

the most effective measures to prevent attacks within the United States may also challenge traditional civil liberties if pursued to the maximum. And the most troubling conclusion for foreign policy as a whole is that reducing the odds of attacks in the United States might require pulling back from involvement in some foreign conflicts. American activism to guarantee international stability is, paradoxically, the prime source of American vulnerability.

This was partly true in the Cold War, when the main danger that nuclear weapons might detonate on U.S. soil sprang from strategic engagement in Europe, Asia, and the Middle East to deter attacks on U.S. allies. But engagement then assumed a direct link between regional stability and U.S. survival. The connection is less evident today, when there is no globally threatening superpower or transnational ideology to be contained—only an array of serious but entirely local disruptions. Today, as the only nation acting to police areas outside its own region, the United States makes itself a target for states or groups whose aspirations are frustrated by U.S. power.

From Modern to Primitive

When nuclear weapons were born, they represented the most advanced military applications of science, technology, and engineering. None but the great powers could hope to obtain them. By now, however, nuclear arms have been around for more than half a century, and chemical and biological weapons even longer. They are not just getting old. In the strategic terms most relevant to American security, they have become primitive. Once the military cutting edge of the strong, they have become the only hope for so-called rogue states or terrorists who want to contest American power. Why? Because the United States has developed overwhelming superiority in conventional military force—something it never thought it had against the Soviet Union.

The Persian Gulf War of 1991 demonstrated the American advantage in a manner that stunned many abroad. Although the U.S. defense budget has plunged, other countries are not closing the gap. U.S. military spending remains more than triple that of any potentially hostile power and higher than the combined defense budgets of Russia, China, Iran, Iraq, North Korea, and Cuba.

More to the point, there is no evidence that those countries' level of military professionalism is rising at a rate that would make them competitive even if they were to spend far more on their forces. Rolling along in what some see as a revolution in military affairs, American forces continue to make unmatched use of state-of-the-art weapons, surveillance and information systems, and the organizational and doctrinal flexibility for managing the integration of these complex innovations into "systems of systems" that is the key to modern military effectiveness. More than ever in military history, brains are brawn. Even if hostile countries somehow catch up in an arms race, their military organizations and cultures are unlikely to catch up in the competence race for management, technology assimilation, and combat command skills. . . .

Finally, unchallenged military superiority has shifted the attention of the U.S. military establishment away from WMD. During the Cold War, nuclear weapons were the bedrock of American war capabilities. They were the linchpin of defense debate, procurement programs, and arms control because the United States faced another superpower—one that conventional wisdom feared could best it in conventional warfare. Today, no one cares about the MX missile or B-1 bomber, and hardly anyone really cares about the Strategic Arms Reduction Treaty. In a manner that could only have seemed ludicrous during the Cold War, proponents now rationalize the $2 billion B-2 as a weapon for conventional war. Hardly anyone in the Pentagon is still interested in how the United States could use WMD for its own strategic purposes. . . .

Choose Your Weapons Well

Until the past decade, the issue was nuclear arms, period. Chemical weapons received some attention from specialists, but never made the priority list of presidents and cabinets. Biological weapons were almost forgotten after they were banned by the 1972 Biological Weapons Convention. Chemical and biological arms have received more attention in the 1990s. The issues posed by the trio lumped under the umbrella of mass destruction differ, however. Most significantly, biological weapons have received less attention than the others but probably represent the greatest danger.

Chemical weapons have been noticed more in the past decade, especially since they were used by Iraq against Iranian troops in the 1980–88 Iran-Iraq War and against Kurdish civilians in 1988. Chemicals are far more widely available than nuclear weapons because the technology required to produce them is far simpler, and large numbers of countries have undertaken chemical weapons programs. But chemical weapons are not really in the same class as other weapons of mass destruction, in the sense of ability to inflict a huge number of civilian casualties in a single strike. For the tens of thousands of fatalities as in, say, the biggest strategic bombing raids of World War II, it would be very difficult logistically and operationally to deliver chemical weapons in necessary quantities over wide areas.

Nevertheless, much attention and effort have been lavished on a campaign to eradicate chemical weapons. This may be a good thing, but the side effects are not entirely benign. For one, banning chemicals means that for deterrence, nuclear weapons become even more important than they used to be. That is because a treaty cannot assuredly prevent hostile nations from deploying chemical weapons, while the United States has forsworn the option to retaliate in kind.

In the past, the United States had a no-first-use policy for chemical weapons but reserved the right to strike back with them if an enemy used them first. The 1993 Chemical Weapons Convention (CWC), which entered into force last April [1997], requires the United States to destroy its stockpile, thus ending this option. The United States did the same with biological arms long ago, during the Nixon administration. Eliminating its own chemical and biological weapons practically precludes a no-first-use policy for nuclear weapons, since they become the only WMD available for retaliation. . . .

One simple fact should worry Americans more about biological than about nuclear or chemical arms: unlike either of the other two, biological weapons combine maximum destructiveness and easy availability. Nuclear arms have great killing capacity but are hard to get; chemical weapons are easy to get but lack such killing capacity; biological agents have both qualities. . . .

Like chemical weapons but unlike nuclear weapons, biologicals are relatively easy to make. Innovations in biotechnology have obviated many of the old problems in handling and preserving biological agents, and many have been freely available for scientific research. Nuclear weapons are not likely to be the WMD of choice for non-state terrorist groups. They require huge investments and targetable infrastructure, and are subject to credible threats by the United States. An aggrieved group that decides it wants to kill huge numbers of Americans will find the mission easier to accomplish with anthrax than with a nuclear explosion. . . .

Deterrence and Arms Control in Decline

An old vocabulary still dominates policy discussion of WMD. Rhetoric in the defense establishment falls back on the all-purpose strategic buzzword of the Cold War: deterrence. But deterrence now covers fewer of the threats the United States faces than it did during the Cold War.

The logic of deterrence is clearest when the issue is preventing unprovoked and unambiguous aggression, when the aggressor recognizes that it is the aggressor rather than the defender. Deterrence is less reliable when both sides in a conflict see each other as the aggressor. When the United States intervenes in messy Third World conflicts, the latter is often true. In such cases, the side that the United States wants to deter may see itself as trying to deter the United States. Such situations are ripe for miscalculation.

For the country that used to be the object of U.S. deterrence—Russia—the strategic burden has been reversed. Based on assumptions of Soviet conventional military superiority, U.S. strategy used to rely on the threat to escalate—to be the first to use nuclear weapons during a war—to deter attack by Soviet armored divisions. Today the tables have turned. There is no Warsaw Pact, Russia has half or less of the military potential of the Soviet Union, and its current conventional forces are in disarray, while NATO is expanding eastward. It is now Moscow that has the incentive to compensate for conventional weakness by placing heavier reliance on nuclear capabilities. The Russians adopted a nuclear no-first-use policy in the early 1980s, but renounced it after their precipitous post–Cold War decline.

Today Russia needs to be reassured, not deterred. The main danger from Russian WMD is leakage from vast stockpiles to anti-American groups elsewhere—the "loose nukes" problem. So long as the United States has no intention of attacking the Russians, their greater reliance on nuclear forces is not a problem. If the United States has an interest in reducing nuclear stockpiles, however, it is. The traditional American approach—thinking in terms of its own deterrence strategies—provides no guidance. Indeed, noises some Americans still make about deterring the Russians compound the problem by reinforcing Moscow's alarm.

Similarly, U.S. conventional military superiority gives China an incentive to consider more reliance on an escalation strategy. The Chinese have a long-standing no-first-use policy but adopted it when their strategic doctrine was that of "people's war," which relied on mass mobilization and low-tech weaponry. Faith in that doctrine was severely shaken by the American performance in the Persian Gulf War. Again, the United States might assume that there is no problem as long as Beijing only wants to deter and the United States does not want to attack. But how do these assumptions relate to the prospect of a war over Taiwan? That is a conflict that no one wants but that can hardly be ruled out in light of evolving tensions. If the United States decides openly to deter Beijing from attacking Taiwan, the old lore from the Cold War may be relevant. But if Washington continues to leave policy ambiguous, who will know who is deterring whom? Ambiguity is a recipe for confusion and miscalculation in a time of crisis. For all the upsurge of attention in the national security establishment to the prospect of conflict with China, there has been remarkably little discussion of the role of nuclear weapons in a Sino-American collision.

The main problem for deterrence, however, is that it still relies on the corpus of theory that undergirded Cold War policy, dominated by reliance on the threat of second-strike retaliation. But retaliation requires knowledge of who has launched an attack and the address at which they reside. These requirements are not a problem when the threat comes from a government, but they are if the enemy is anonymous. Today some groups may wish to punish the United States without taking credit for the action—a mass killing equivalent to the 1988 bombing of Pan Am Flight 103 over Lockerbie, Scotland. Moreover, the options the defense establishment favors have shifted over entirely from deterrence to preemption. The majority of those who dealt with nuclear weapons policy during the Cold War adamantly opposed developing first-strike options. Today, scarcely anyone looks to that old logic when thinking about rogues or terrorists, and most hope to be able to mount a disarming action against any group with WMD. . . .

From the Limited Test Ban negotiations in the 1960s through the Strategic Arms Limitation Talks, Strategic Arms Reduction Talks, and Intermediate-range Nuclear Forces negotiations in the 1970s and 1980s, arms control treaties were central to managing WMD threats. Debates about whether particular agreements with Moscow were in the United States' interest were bitter because everyone believed that the results mattered. Today there is no consensus that treaties regulating armaments matter much. Among national security experts, the corps that pays close attention to START and Conventional Forces in Europe negotiations has shrunk. With the exception of the Chemical Weapons Convention, efforts to control WMD by treaty have become small potatoes. The biggest recent news in arms control has not been any negotiation to regulate WMD, but a campaign to ban land mines. . . .

The 1968 Nuclear Nonproliferation Treaty remains a hallowed institution, but it has nowhere new to go. It will not convert the problem countries that want to obtain WMD—unless, like Iraq and North Korea in the 1980s, they sign and accept the legal obligation and then simply cheat. The NPT regime will continue to impede access to fissile materials on the open market, but it will not do so in novel or more effective ways. And it does not address the problem of Russian "loose nukes" any better than the Russian and American governments do on their own.

Civil Defense

Despite all the new limitations, deterrence remains an important aspect of strategy. There is not much the United States needs to do to keep up its deterrence capability, however, given the thousands of nuclear weapons and the conventional military superiority it has. Where capabilities are grossly underdeveloped, however, is the area of responses for coping should deterrence fail.

Enthusiasts for defensive capability, mostly proponents of the Strategic Defense Initiative from the Reagan years, remain fixated on the least relevant form of it: high-tech active defenses to intercept ballistic missiles. There is still scant interest in what should now be the first priority: civil defense preparations to cope with uses of WMD within the United States. Active defenses against missiles would be expensive investments that might or might not work against a threat the United States probably will not face for years, but would do nothing against the threat it already faces. Civil defense measures are extremely cheap and could prove far more effective than they would have against a large-scale Soviet attack.

During the Cold War, debate about antimissile defense concerned whether it was technologically feasible or cost-effective and whether it would threaten the Soviets and ignite a spiraling arms race between offensive and defensive weapons. One need not refight the battles over SDI to see that the relevance to current WMD threats is tenuous. Iraq, Iran, or North Korea will not be able to deploy intercontinental missiles for years. Nor, if they are strategically cunning, should they want to. For the limited number of nuclear warheads these countries are likely to have, and especially for biological weapons, other means of delivery are more easily available. Alternatives to ballistic missiles include aircraft, ship-launched cruise missiles, and unconventional means, such as smuggling, at which the intelligence agencies of these countries have excelled. . . .

A ballistic missile defense system, whether it costs more or less than the $60 billion the Congressional Budget Office recently estimated would be required for one limited option, will not counter these modes of attack. Indeed, if a larger part of the worry about WMD these days is about their use by terrorist states or groups, the odds are higher that sometime, somewhere in the country, some of these weapons will go off, despite the best efforts to stop them. If that happens, the United States should have in place whatever measures can mitigate the consequences.

By the later phases of the Cold War it was hard to get people interested in civil defense against an all-out Soviet attack that could detonate thousands of high-yield nuclear weapons in U.S. population centers. To many, the lives that would have been saved seemed less salient than the many millions that would still have been lost. It should be easier to see the value of civil defense, however, in the context of more limited attacks, perhaps with only a few low-yield weapons. A host of minor measures can increase protection or recovery from biological, nuclear, or chemical effects. Examples are stockpiling or distribution of protective masks; equipment and training for decontamination; standby programs for mass vaccinations and emergency treatment with antibiotics; wider and deeper planning of emergency response procedures; and public education about hasty sheltering and emergency actions to reduce individual vulnerability.

Such programs would not make absorbing a WMD attack tolerable. But inadequacy is no excuse for neglecting actions that could reduce death and suffering, even if the difference in casualties is small. Civil defenses are especially worthwhile considering that they are extraordinarily cheap compared with regular military programs or active defense systems. Yet until recently, only half a billion dollars—less than two-tenths of one percent of the defense budget and less than $2 a head for every American—went to chemical and biological defense, while nearly $4 billion was spent annually on ballistic missile defense. Why haven't policymakers attended to first things first—cheap programs that can cushion the effects of a disaster—before undertaking expensive programs that provide no assurance they will be able to prevent it?

One problem is conceptual intertia. The Cold War accustomed strategists to worrying about an enemy with thousands of WMD, rather than foes with a handful. For decades the question of strategic defense was also posed as a debate between those who saw no alternative to relying on deterrence and those who hoped that an astrodome over the United States could replace deterrence with invulnerability. None of those hoary fixations address the most probable WMD threats in the post–Cold War world.

Opposition to Cold War civil defense programs underlies psychological aversion to them now. Opponents used to argue that civil defense was a dangerous illusion because it could do nothing significant to reduce the horror of an attack that would obliterate hundreds of cities, because it would promote a false sense of security, and because it could even be destabilizing and provoke attack in a crisis. Whether or not such arguments were valid then, they are not now. But both then and now, there has been a powerful reason that civil defense efforts have been unpopular: they alarm people. They remind them that their vulnerability to mass destruction is not a bad dream, not something that strategic schemes for deterrence, preemption, or interception are sure to solve. . . .

. . . It is not in the long-term interest of political leaders to indulge popular aversion. If public resistance under current circumstances prevents widespread distribution, stockpiling, and instruction in the use of defense equipment or medical services, the least that should be done is to optimize plans and preparations to rapidly implement such activities when the first crisis ignites demand. . . .

Is Retreat the Best Defense?

No programs aimed at controlling adversaries' capabilities can eliminate the dangers. One risk is that in the more fluid politics of the post–Cold War world, the United States could stumble into an unanticipated crisis with Russia or China.

There are no well-established rules of the game to brake a spiraling conflict over the Baltic states or Taiwan, as there were in the superpower competition after the Cuban missile crisis. The second danger is that some angry group that blames the United States for its problems may decide to coerce Americans, or simply exact vengeance, by inflicting devastation on them where they live.

If steps to deal with the problem in terms of capabilities are limited, can anything be done to address intentions—the incentives of any foreign power or group to lash out at the United States? There are few answers to this question that do not compromise the fundamental strategic activism and internationalist thrust of U.S. foreign policy over the past half-century. That is because the best way to keep people from believing that the United States is responsible for their problems is to avoid involvement in their conflicts.

Ever since the Munich agreement and Pearl Harbor, with only a brief interruption during the decade after the Tet offensive, there has been a consensus that if Americans did not draw their defense perimeter far forward and confront foreign troubles in their early stages, those troubles would come to them at home. But because the United States is now the only superpower and weapons of mass destruction have become more accessible, American intervention in troubled areas is not so much a way to fend off such threats as it is what stirs them up.

Will U.S. involvement in unstable situations around the former U.S.S.R. head off conflict with Moscow or generate it? Will making NATO bigger and moving it to Russia's doorstep deter Russian pressure on Ukraine and the Baltics or provoke it? With Russia and China, there is less chance that either will set out to conquer Europe or Asia than that they will try to restore old sovereignties and security zones by reincorporating new states of the former Soviet Union or the province of Taiwan. None of this means that NATO expansion or support for Taiwan's autonomy will cause nuclear war. It does mean that to whatever extent American activism increases those countries' incentives to rely on WMD while intensifying political friction between them and Washington, it is counterproductive.

The other main danger is the ire of smaller states or religious and cultural groups that see the United States as an evil force blocking their legitimate aspirations. . . . Cold War triumph magnified the problem. U.S. military and cultural hegemony—the basic threats to radicals seeking to challenge the status quo—are directly linked to the imputation of American responsibility for maintaining world order. Playing Globocop feeds the urge of aggrieved groups to strike back.

Is this a brief for isolationism? No. It is too late to turn off foreign resentments by retreating, even if that were an acceptable course. Alienated groups and governments would not stop blaming Washington for their problems. In addition, there is more to foreign policy than dampening incentives to hurt the United States. It is not automatically sensible to stop pursuing other interests for the sake of uncertain reductions in a threat of uncertain probability. Security is not all of a piece, and survival is only part of security.

But it is no longer prudent to assume that important security interests complement each other as they did during the Cold War. The interest at the very core—protecting the American homeland from attack—may now often be in conflict with security more broadly conceived and with the interests that mandate promoting American political values, economic interdependence, social Westernization, and stability in regions beyond Western Europe and the Americas. The United States should not give up all its broader political interests, but it should tread cautiously in areas—especially the Middle East—where broader interests grate against the core imperative of preventing mass destruction within America's borders.

 # Nuclear Proliferation

3.2 Bombs Away

The Economist

While nuclear proliferation has, in recent years, proceeded most rapidly in Asia—where India, Pakistan, and North Korea have pushed ahead with nuclear weapons programs—it is the Middle East that most troubles many observers. Concerns (which proved unfounded) that Iraqi dictator Saddam Hussein was pressing ahead with the development of nuclear weapons provided the justification for the American-led invasion of Iraq. Now, as the following article from *The Economist* discusses, it is the prospect of a nuclear-armed Iran that most worries many American and other Western leaders.

America and many other countries are convinced that Iran is trying to build nuclear weapons. But Iran denies this, and after the intelligence bungles in Iraq such claims need to be examined with care. The Iranians remind the world that their soldiers were victims of Saddam's poison-gas attacks during the Iran-Iraq war, and that they never retaliated in kind. Ayatollah Khamenei, the supreme leader, has gone so far as to issue a *fatwa* (religious decree) declaring the possession or use of WMD in general, and nuclear weapons in particular, to be illegal under Islamic law.

Furthermore, Iran's leaders point out that unlike existing nuclear-weapons states in their neighbourhood, such as Pakistan, India and Israel, Iran has signed the Nuclear Non-Proliferation Treaty (NPT). It has therefore submitted itself to inspections by the International Atomic Energy Agency (IAEA), the treaty's watchdog. When asked why a country overflowing with oil and gas should want nuclear energy, Iran answers that its oil revenues will one day diminish and that in the meantime nuclear energy at home would free more petrol for export. Besides, say the Iranians, America and other Western countries were happy to help the shah establish a nuclear industry before the revolution. Why should what America deemed to make economic sense at that time be thought absurd now?

It should also be noted in Iran's defence that the nuclear agency has as yet found no conclusive evidence that Iran is running a nuclear-weapons programme. In a report to the IAEA's governors last March, Mohammed ElBaradei, its director-general, said only that until Iran gave the agency more information about its nuclear activities—some of which it kept secret for many years—his agency would "not be able to provide assurance regarding the exclusively peaceful nature of all of Iran's nuclear activities." In short, the IAEA has no firm evidence that Iran is trying to make a bomb, but it has plenty of suspicions and cannot give it a clean bill of health.

The IAEA, however, is a cautious organisation with a mixed record. In the 1980s it failed to detect Iraq's nuclear-weapons programme at a time when it was in fact making rapid progress. In Iran, the agency's attempts to monitor nuclear activities have been hampered by years of deception. And Iran's credibility suffered a massive blow in 2002 when a dissident group, perhaps tipped off by Western spies, revealed that the country had built two nuclear facilities in secret without informing the IAEA. One of these, in Arak, was a heavy-water reactor, just the thing for making plutonium, which is one way to fuel an atomic bomb. The other, at Natanz, was a facility for enriching uranium, which is the other way of doing it.

It is true, as Iran says, that the centrifuges at Natanz can also make the less enriched fuel that a nuclear reactor would need for producing electricity. But since Iran does not yet have any such reactors (other than the one the Russians have built for it at Bushehr, which comes with Russian-supplied fuel), why the rush to enrich? Why try to keep both Arak and Natanz secret? And why has Iran apparently co-operated with both North Korea and A. Q. Khan, Pakistan's notorious nuclear-weapons smuggler?

Iran's answer to these questions is that it was forced to keep these nuclear activities secret because America was intent on blocking its civil nuclear programme, even though having such a programme was its "inalienable right" under the NPT. Iran also argues that under the letter of the law it was not required to disclose the existence of these facilities until uranium enrichment actually began—which, it says, it intended to do.

In 2003, embarrassed by the discovery of its secret facilities, Iran agreed to implement the "additional protocol" of the IAEA, making its facilities available for fuller inspection. After negotiations with Britain, France and Germany it agreed to suspend uranium enrichment. But it continued to insist on its right to resume it, and in August 2005, the month of Mr. Ahmadinejad's inauguration, it did so—even though the three European governments had offered it economic and civilian-nuclear help in exchange for stopping permanently. In June 2006 the incentives on offer for nuclear compliance were both broadened (all five permanent members of the Security Council, and Germany, endorsed them) and sweetened. Condoleezza Rice said that if Iran accepted, America would drop its long-standing refusal to negotiate directly with Iran and open talks on a wide range of subjects.

From America's perspective this was a big concession. And yet, for one reason or another, Iran did not bite. And in the past years its readiness to pay a growing price for its determination to press on with enrichment and so master the entire nuclear-fuel cycle has inevitably added to suspicion of its intentions. Part of that price has been losing the diplomatic protection that Russia and China had previously given it in the Security Council. In July 2006 the council ordered Iran to suspend enrichment. Its refusal resulted in two further resolutions—in December 2006 and March

2007—imposing modest sanctions, with a third now in preparation. And yet the centrifuges spin defiantly on. Little wonder that the working assumption in many capitals is that Iran wants the bomb.

If that assumption is correct, how soon might it get one? Mr. Ahmadinejad keeps claiming that Iran has already passed the stage of no return in its attempts to master enrichment, but continues to deny that Iran wants the bomb. "We have broken through to a new stage and it is too late to push us back," he said in June. Most outside experts, however, are sceptical about how much progress Iran has made.

A common estimate is that in order to produce enough fissile material for a basic device, Iran would have to run an array of some 3,000 centrifuges at high speed for more than a year. Mr. ElBaradei told a meeting of the IAEA last month that Iran already had between 1,700 and 2,000 centrifuges running, and predicted that this number could rise to 3,000 by the end of July. But the amount of uranium hexafluoride—the gas put into the machines for enrichment—has been relatively small, suggesting to some analysts, including the IAEA, that Iran is not yet confident of its ability to spin them at full speed.

One respected expert, David Albright, president of America's Institute for Science and International Security, reckons Iran would be lucky to be able to enrich enough uranium for a bomb by 2009 and that to complete all the other steps necessary to make a usable weapon could take another year or more. Israel says that if Iran's programme went very smoothly, it could have a bomb by 2009. Mr. ElBaradei, who makes no secret of his belief that it would be "crazy" to launch a pre-emptive attack on Iran, says an Iranian bomb, if that is what Iran wants, is between three and eight years away.

Reasons for Wanting the Bomb

So what if Iran got the bomb? Wouldn't its only purpose be to deter? Iran does after all have a history of being bullied and invaded. In the 19th century Britain and Russia played their "great game" on its territory. Britain and America engineered the coup that unseated an elected prime minister, Muhammad Mossadegh, in 1953. After Iraq's invasion in 1980 the United Nations did precious little to help Iran. And in 2002 Iran found itself listed as part of George Bush's "axis of evil," at a time when America had just sent one army into neighbouring Afghanistan and prepared to send another into neighbouring Iraq.

All this—plus loose talk in Washington, DC, about "regime change" in Iran— may have convinced the country's leaders that Iran needs a bomb simply to make potential attackers think twice. But if Iran has reason to want a bomb, others have bigger reasons to fear it. Israel is foremost of these. Whereas Israel had good relations with the shah, Ayatollah Khomeini regarded the creation of the Jewish state as an unforgiveable sin and said that all Muslims had a duty to reverse it.

On Israel, Iran has indeed shown less flexibility than the Palestinians themselves. It denounced Yasser Arafat's espousal of a two-state solution as a betrayal and it continues to arm and train groups such as Hamas, Islamic Jihad and Hizbullah that say they want to destroy Israel. During the reformist period, President Khatami softened Iran's stand, implying that it might respect whatever solution the

Palestinians accepted, but Mr. Ahmadinejad, in numerous Holocaust-denying speeches calling for or predicting Israel's eradication, has returned Iran noisily to the true faith.

These pronouncements have led commentators in the West to ask whether Iran's president is a new Hitler with genocidal designs. But a close look shows them to be ambiguous. It is not clear, for example, whether he really doubts that the Holocaust occurred or merely why such an event should have been allowed to justify Israel's creation. In the blogosphere, translators hold lively debates about whether he really did call for Israel to be "wiped off the map" or just "removed from the pages of time," a phrase which some people seem to think sounds less fierce. In the mind of Mr. Ahmadinejad, are Israel and its people to disappear in some violent event? Or is it merely the "Zionist regime" that is to come to an end—perhaps peacefully, after the Palestinian refugees have returned and decided by referendum?

If Israel is to disappear, will Iran be the agent of its destruction? It is hard to say: from time to time, Mr. Ahmadinejad and other officials have said explicitly that Iran poses no threat to Israel. Last month the president said that it was the Lebanese and the Palestinians who had "pressed the countdown button for the destruction of the Zionist regime." A week later the Speaker of the *majlis*, Gholam-Ali Haddad-Adel, said during a visit to Kuwait that Mr. Ahmadinejad's comments did not mean that Iran intended to attack Israel, only that "the Zionist entity" was on a "natural course of disintegration."

For all the ambiguity, such talk helps to sow fear in Israel and corresponding delight in Arab countries, where Mr. Ahmadinejad may now be more popular than he is at home. To that extent it has been a rational instrument of foreign policy. Such talk may also stem from a rational domestic calculation: hurling dire threats against Israel in the Khomeini manner helps rekindle the revolutionary fire that was allowed to cool under the reformists.

As to whether Mr. Ahmadinejad is a new Hitler, one point to note is that he is neither Iran's dictator nor the master of its nuclear programme, which comes under the supervision of the supreme leader. That may not be so very reassuring. It implies that even if Mr. Ahmadinejad were to shut up, or lose his job, the nuclear danger will remain.

Since Israel does not admit to having nuclear weapons, its detailed thinking on nuclear matters is rarely ventilated in public. But most of those Israeli experts willing to talk rate the chances of an Iranian nuclear attack as low. Despite Mr. Ahmadinejad, most consider Iran to be a rational state actor susceptible to deterrence.

Knowing that Israel already possesses a very large nuclear arsenal, Iran would have to be ready to sacrifice millions of its own people to destroy the Jewish state, unless it was sure that in a first strike it could destroy Israel's ability to strike back. That would be hard, given that Israel is reported to have put nuclear weapons at sea on submarines, and has built sophisticated anti-missile defences expressly to protect its second-strike power. Furthermore, if Iran did obtain nuclear weapons, America might be willing to offer Israel (and other allies in the region) additional reassurance by saying—for whatever such a promise can be worth—that it would regard a nuclear attack on its ally as an attack on itself.

The Calculus of Destruction

Nonetheless, Ehud Olmert, its prime minister, has said that Israel cannot live with a nuclear-armed Iran. Whatever its policymakers think, its people have been spooked by Mr. Ahmadinejad. And the sheer disparity in size between the countries (Iran's population is more than ten times Israel's, and its land area 75 times as big) leads some Israelis to question whether stable deterrence is possible between them. Israelis are haunted by a remark of Ayatollah Rafsanjani's in 2001, musing that a single nuclear weapon could obliterate Israel, whereas Israel could "only damage" the world of Islam.

Could ordinary life in Israel continue under such a threat? Even if Iran did not use its bomb, might not possession of it embolden it to attack Israel by conventional means, either directly or by using its allies in Syria, Lebanon and the Palestinian territories? A further danger is that once Iran went nuclear, others in the region, such as Egypt, Syria, Saudi Arabia and Turkey, might feel compelled to follow. Hard as it would be for Israel to establish a deterrent balance with Iran, a cat's cradle of Middle Eastern nuclear face-offs would be an even darker nightmare.

Added together, these considerations might still tempt an Israeli government to try to knock out Iran's nuclear facilities before it can finish building a bomb. The Israelis have worked for years to obtain the weapons for such a strike, spending billions to procure long-range variants of the F15 and F16 fighter-bomber, for example. On the other hand, senior Israelis know that this would be fraught with danger.

Iran's nuclear targets are much further from Israel than was Iraq's Osiraq reactor, which Israeli aircraft destroyed in 1981. Most are more than 1,200 km (750 miles) away, and Israel's aircraft would have to fly even farther to avoid Jordanian or Iraqi airspace. That, according to a study by Ephraim Kam of Israel's Institute for National Security Studies, would require refuelling on both the outward and return flights, adding to the danger of interception. Osiraq, moreover, was a single target. Since there would be many this time, the attacking force would have to be large. And to cause serious damage, the aircraft might have to attack more than once.

Even a successful strike would not be the end of the story. For as the IAEA's Mr. ElBaradei keeps saying, "you can't bomb knowledge." Iran would be likely not only to retaliate with its long-range rockets but also to begin at once to rebuild its nuclear capability, just as Iraq did with extra urgency after Israel's destruction of Osiraq. That might not take long, says Mr. Kam: Iran has its own nuclear raw material and already possesses much of the relevant knowledge and technology. Having spent only three years building Natanz from scratch, it could probably rebuild it much faster with the experience it has gleaned.

More worrying still is the possibility that Iran has secret nuclear sites outsiders do not know about: the existence of Arak and Natanz, remember, was not discovered until fairly recently. That could render an attack on the known ones pointless. And Mr. Kam is surely right that an Israeli strike might unite Iran's people behind the regime and its nuclear aspirations.

Another alternative for Israel might be to attack Iran in order to start a sequence of events in which America eventually joins the fray. The Americans, naturally, would find the military job much easier than Israel. The Americans have a motive, too: not fear of annihilation, but fear that nuclear-armed Iran would knock a hole in what is left of the non-proliferation regime and challenge American interests in the energy-rich Middle East. After Iraq, however, no American president could doubt that such an attack would deepen Muslim hatred of America. And Iran is not without means of retaliation, even against the superpower. It could strike America's already hard-pressed forces in Iraq, direct terrorism at America's friends or disrupt tanker traffic through the Persian Gulf, so causing mayhem in the energy markets.

That is why American and Israeli politicians alike, while refusing to take the threat of military action "off the table," are probably being completely honest when they insist that force is a last resort and that they would prefer to stop Iran by means of diplomacy sharpened by economic sanctions. But can sanctions do the job, and can they do it in time?

 ## Ballistic Missile Defense

3.3 U.S. Missile Defense

International Institute for Strategic Studies

One possible response to nuclear proliferation—indeed, to any continued existence of nuclear weapons—is to build defenses against them. In his "Star Wars" speech of 1983, President Ronald Reagan made the case for developing the technology to protect the United States against a nuclear missile attack: "I call upon the scientific community in our country, those who gave us nuclear weapons, to turn their great talents now to the cause of mankind and world peace: to give us the means of rendering nuclear weapons impotent and obsolete." Today, concerns about the possible acquisition by North Korea and Iran of nuclear weapons have spurred renewed American interest in ballistic missile defenses. As the following analysis by the London-based International Institute for Strategic Studies notes, however, American efforts to build defenses have complicated U.S. relations with Russia and with America's NATO allies.

In January 2007, the United States opened formal discussions with Poland and the Czech Republic about stationing components of the U.S. missile defence programme on their territory. Radar equipment would be stationed on a former military base in the Czech Republic, while Poland would host interceptor missiles. Their purpose would be to defend the U.S. mainland against missiles launched

Strategic Comments by IISS Strategic Comments, April 2007, pp. 1–2. © 2007 by Taylor & Francis Informa UK Ltd—Journals. Reproduced with permission of Taylor & Francis Informa UK Ltd—Journals in the format Text-book via Copyright Clearance Center.

from Iran. The two sites would enlarge the architecture of the Ballistic Missile Defence System (BMDS) protecting the United States, which currently consists of a network of sensors and missiles stretching from Japan to Alaska. Two other European governments are hosting BMDS components: early-warning radars are to be upgraded at Thule in Greenland, a territory of Denmark, and at Fylingdales in the United Kingdom. The Czech Republic and Poland have yet to give their consent, and meanwhile Britain has expressed interest in hosting the interceptors.

Missile Shield Development

While the U.S. government has pursued missile defences since the 1950s, the immediate predecessor to BMDS—in its purpose if not in its precise architecture—was the National Missile Defense (NMD) programme. Created by the U.S. Department of Defense during Bill Clinton's presidency, the original NMD design consisted of a network of missiles, as well as land- and space-based sensors. It was intended to intercept enemy missiles directed at civilian areas in the so-called "midcourse" stage of their ballistic curve, that is at or near their highest altitude, after they had separated from the boosters and before they began the descent toward the target. NMD co-existed with a number of separate missile defence programmes such as Terminal High-Altitude Area Defense (THAAD) and shorter-range theatre systems intended to protect troops in the field. However, early in his presidency George W. Bush reorganised these efforts, eliminating the barriers between the various programmes and creating one unified Pentagon agency, the Missile Defence Agency (MDA). Today's BMDS is thus a system of systems, incorporating components of the original NMD but amalgamating them with other plans aimed at intercepting missiles in other stages of flight (either the initial "boost" phase or the "terminal" stage).

In practical terms, the backbone of today's BMDS relies heavily on former NMD components. The U.S. has 11 (soon to be 15) midcourse interceptors deployed, nine based at Fort Greely, Alaska, and two at Vandenberg air force base in California. Several sea-based radars of various ranges and two types of land-based radars are either already connected to the grid, or will be soon. Work on other parts of the programme such as THAAD and the *Patriot* missile continues. Some are far more technologically mature than the midcourse interceptors, however, not all are yet integrated into the seamless system envisaged under the BMDS concept.

The proposed sites in Poland and the Czech Republic have their roots in the NMD system. The X-band radar considered for the Brdy military base in the Czech Republic is designed to track and illuminate incoming missiles, and then to assess whether they have been successfully destroyed. It would use a long and narrow beam to stay with its distant, small and fast-moving targets. The interceptors in Poland would be a new two-stage missile similar to those in Alaska, capable of defending against "long and intermediate range ballistic missile attack." Midcourse interceptors are designed to destroy incoming missiles in the middle portion of their ballistic curve, at high altitudes outside the earth's atmosphere. The interceptor missile's booster launches a small "kill" vehicle into space, which smashes into the incoming missile and destroys it. It is not clear how different the flight characteristics of the new missile would be from the existing interceptor—unlike the Fort Greely missiles, which have three stages, these will have two, which may suggest a shorter range.

Russia's Concerns

Even though the Polish and Czech sites would represent a relatively modest expansion of the BMDS, and are not the first missile defence sites in Europe, the U.S. request caused a stir. Russia responded angrily, apparently concerned that the sites would pose a danger to its strategic forces. Chief of the General Staff General Yuri Baluyevsky called the U.S. plans "inexplicable" and hinted that Moscow might withdraw from the Intermediate Range Nuclear Forces Treaty. Russia's Commander of Strategic Missile Forces Colonel General Nikolay Solovtsov went a step further, stating that his forces were capable of targeting the Czech and Polish facilities.

Washington asserts that not only is the BMDS not aimed against Russia, but that it in no way affects Russia's ability to launch a mass nuclear strike. Besides the disproportion in numbers—only ten interceptors are likely to be placed in Poland compared with several thousand missiles on the Russian side—the U.S. says that the system's design means it is ill-suited as protection against a strike from Russia. Placing midcourse interceptors in Central Europe may actually lessen their utility against Russia's nuclear arsenal. This is because midcourse interceptors are designed to hit targets outside the atmosphere, and it is not clear that nuclear missiles launched from western parts of Russia would reach that altitude before crossing over Poland. The MDA chief, Lieutenant General Henry A. Obering, said that the Polish site was too close to Russia to allow sufficient time to intercept a Russian launch.

Washington responded to the criticism by intensifying efforts to soften Russia's stance. U.S. Secretary of Defense Robert Gates visited Moscow on 23 April and briefed President Vladimir Putin and the new Russian defence minister, Anatoly Serdyukov, on the proposed new bases. In spite of these talks, tensions have continued to rise. In his 26 April state of the nation speech to parliament, Putin declared a "moratorium" on Russia's observance of the Conventional Forces in Europe Treaty—a move he directly linked to U.S. missile defence plans. In a subsequent meeting with Czech president Václav Klaus, Putin dismissed U.S. claims that Iran posed a missile threat, and threatened further countermeasures. Russian concern is partly based on the possibility that the BMDS could pose a risk to Russia in the long run if, at some point in the future, its capability were to grow. However, this seems a long way off. Tests of the underlying technology against only single-warhead missiles have yielded such mixed results that the programme's critics in the U.S. argue that it should not have been deployed. Only six out of 11 flight tests of the midcourse interceptor have succeeded, and these have tested more mature technology than that planned for the Polish site. Phil Coyle, former Pentagon chief tester, now affiliated to the Washington-based Center for Defense Information has commented that "these missile defences have no demonstrated capability to defend Europe, Russia, or the U.S. from Iranian attack under realistic operational conditions. As such, the claims being made by the MDA for a European missile defence site are unrealistic."

NATO Involvement?

Several European governments expressed worries about the rising tensions, though there were few signs of a U.S.-European divide developing on the subject. Outgoing French President Jacques Chirac said that Europe must be careful to prevent new dividing lines on the continent, but there was little public debate in pre-election France on missile defence. Germany's position was divided along party lines—the debate between the "grand coalition" parties was driven by differing views on Russia and the United States rather than the particulars of the U.S. proposal. Defense Minister Franz Josef Jung, a Christian Democrat, spoke out in favour of building a NATO-wide missile defence system, while the foreign minister, Frank-Walter Steinmeier, a Social Democrat, warned that U.S. facilities must not start a new arms race in Europe. Chancellor Angela Merkel said in early April that the issue needed to be dealt with through NATO. Accordingly, American, Czech and Polish officials briefed allies at a 19 April meeting of the North Atlantic Council.

The proposal, while designed specifically to protect the U.S., sparked discussion in Europe about the position of NATO, which has taken steps towards having alliance-wide missile defence capabilities. It raised new questions about how a system designed to protect the U.S., but with additional elements in Europe, would fit into future NATO systems. NATO Secretary-General Jaap de Hoop Scheffer told the *Financial Times* that the alliance must not offer "A-league and B-league" levels of protection; a NATO missile defence system would have to cover all allies with equal reliability. It is assumed at NATO's Brussels headquarters that the U.S. BMDS would feature heavily in any NATO missile defence programme, which would in turn tie European nations more closely into U.S. plans. Because of the proximity of southern Europe to expected sources of threat such as Iran, the U.S. system would need to be complemented with shorter-range missile defences, possibly on the basis of NATO's theatre missile defence (TMD) system. The November 2006 Riga summit tasked de Hoop Scheffer with producing a study assessing missile threats to NATO; an earlier study commissioned by NATO had concluded that it was technically feasible to construct a missile shield covering all allied territory against a limited strike from a rogue nation. A contract for a short-range TMD system was awarded by NATO in 2006 and is due to reach operational capability by 2010.

Progress at NATO on an allied missile defence system suggests that a significant number of European countries are worried about the threat from ballistic missiles. However, the American proposals may meet obstacles within Poland and the Czech Republic. While official responses to the U.S. proposal were generally positive, public support for hosting U.S. bases was low. The governments will want to avoid referendums on the subject. Complicating its cause, the U.S. Department of Defense appeared to have handled its approach clumsily, presuming agreement before fully exploring the governments' positions. Radek Sikorski, Polish defence minister until February 2007 and a staunch advocate of close transatlantic links, wrote in the *Washington Post* that the U.S. should not take Poland for granted, that Europe was a far greater contributor to the Polish economy than was the U.S., that Poland needed to be sure that its security interests would be protected and that Washington "should tell NATO how it intends to include the Central Europe base in the alliance's missile defence architecture." The U.S., Sikorski wrote, needed to "see the world through the eyes of its allies and offer them a partnership that enhanced the security of both."

The Consequences of a "Limited" Nuclear War

3.4 Climate Effects of Nuclear War

Alan Robock

While Americans have typically focused on the consequences of a nuclear, biological, or chemical attack *on the United States,* and on the measures that the United States might take to deter or defeat such an attack, in today's world a nuclear war between other nations that did not target America might well have huge consequences for America. In the following article written for this volume, Nobel Prizewinning meterologist Alan Robock analyzes some of the likely consequences for the global environment of a nuclear war between India and Pakistan.

The first nuclear war, in which the United States dropped two atomic bombs on innocent people in Hiroshima and Nagasaki, Japan, in 1945, so shocked the world that in spite of the massive buildup of these weapons since then, they have never been used in war again. These direct effects were startling enough, but in the mid-1980s research conducted jointly by Western and Soviet scientists discovered that if a third of the then-existing nuclear arsenal were used, a nuclear winter would result.

The direct effects of nuclear weapons, blast, radioactivity, fires, and extensive pollution, would kill hundreds of millions of people, but only those near the targets. However, the fires would have another effect. Cities and industrial targets would produce massive amounts of dark smoke. The fires themselves would loft the smoke into the upper troposphere, 5–15 km (3–9 miles) above the earth's surface, and then absorption of sunlight would further heat the smoke, lifting it into the stratosphere, a layer where the smoke would persist for years, with no rain to wash it out. Calculations with climate models showed that there would be so much smoke that

Robock, Alan, "Climate Effects of Nuclear War." Reprinted by permission of the author.

it would block out sunlight, plunging the world into cold and dark, killing crops and producing worldwide famine. This effect was named "nuclear winter" in the first paper on the subject in 1983 by Richard Turco and colleagues.

Recognition of these potentially catastrophic consequences, not only for the superpowers but also for distant uninvolved countries, was important in ending the arms race between the United States and the Soviet Union. The realization that more people could die in China or India from climatic effects of a superpower war than in the superpowers combined was a startling wake-up call. That the nuclear winter research was conducted jointly by Soviet and American scientists, with the same results, was a powerful message to the world that the science was valid, and not influenced by narrow political goals.

The overall size of the world's nuclear arsenals peaked in 1986, five years before the breakup of the Soviet Union. There still remain, however, tens of thousands of nuclear weapons in the world. And while the size of the American and Russian arsenals has declined, many additional countries have acquired nuclear weapons. Their ability to build nuclear weapons has stemmed in part from the availability of highly enriched uranium and plutonium, a consequence of the spread of nuclear reactors for power generation, which has been a result of a misguided international atomic energy policy. In addition to the original nuclear powers (the United States and the Soviet Union, now Russia), and the three earlier declared nuclear powers (Britain, France, and China), four other countries now have nuclear weapons: Israel, India, Pakistan, and North Korea. Furthermore, Iran is widely assumed to be seeking nuclear weapons, and other countries are considering acquiring them. It is not difficult to obtain the knowledge of how to construct nuclear weapons; all that is needed is the will and the nuclear material. Right now forty more countries possess enough enriched uranium and/or plutonium to quickly assemble nuclear weapons, and there is enough to make 100,000 nuclear weapons.

Given this proliferation and possible future proliferation of nuclear-armed states, colleagues and I have examined the probable effects of a regional nuclear war between new nuclear weapons states. Because the nuclear winter calculations conducted twenty years ago used much smaller computers and simpler climate models than available today, we also were curious to find out if using modern models would change our older results, by addressing some of the unknowns from then, and to find out if the current nuclear arsenal could still produce nuclear winter.[1]

---

[1] For a fuller account of this research, see: Alan Robock, Luke Oman, Georgiy L. Stenchikov, Owen B. Toon, Charles Bardeen, and Richard P. Turco, "Climatic Consequences of Regional Nuclear Conflicts," *Atm. Chem. Phys.*, **7** (2007), 2003–2012; Alan Robock, Luke Oman, and Georgiy L. Stenchikov, "Nuclear Winter Revisited with a Modern Climate Model and Current Nuclear Arsenals: Still Catastrophic Consequences," *J. Geophys. Res.*, **112** (2007), D13107, doi:10.1029/2006JD008235; Alan Robock, Owen B. Toon, Richard P. Turco, Luke Oman, Georgiy L. Stenchikov, and Charles Bardeen, "The Continuing Environmental Threat of Nuclear Weapons: Integrated Policy Responses Needed," *EOS*, **88** (2007), 228, 231, doi:10.1029/2007ES001816; Alan Robock, "Climate Effects of a Regional Nuclear Conflict," *IPRC Climate*, **7** (2007), no. 1, 16–18; Owen B. Toon, Richard P. Turco, Alan Robock, Charles Bardeen, Luke Oman, and Georgiy L. Stenchikov, "Atmospheric Effects and Societal Consequences of Regional Scale Nuclear Conflicts and Acts of Individual Nuclear Terrorism," *Atm. Chem. Phys.*, **7** (2007),1973–2002; and Owen B. Toon, Alan Robock, Richard P. Turco, Charles Bardeen, Luke Oman, and Georgiy L. Stenchikov, "Consequences of Regional-Scale Nuclear Conflicts," *Science*, **315** (2007), 1224–1225.

We conducted simulations with a state-of-the-art general circulation model of the climate. For the first time we were able to include a complete calculation of not only atmospheric but also oceanic circulation, and the entire atmosphere from the surface up through the troposphere, stratosphere, and mesosphere, to an elevation of 80 km (50 miles). We cannot know how many nuclear weapons would be used in a conflict (hopefully none), so we considered three artificial, but possible, scenarios. One was a nuclear conflict between India and Pakistan, each using fifty Hiroshima-sized weapons (15 megatons explosive power), dropped on the targets in each country that would produce the largest amount of smoke. This would be only 0.3 percent of the current global nuclear arsenal, or 0.03 percent of the explosive power of the current nuclear arsenal. The second scenario was the entire current nuclear arsenal used in a conflict between the United States and Russia, and the third involved use of one third of the current nuclear arsenal, also targeted at the United States and Russia. The second scenario is the same as the baseline scenario we used twenty years ago.

Our results were startling. We found that the first scenario would produce climate change unprecedented in recorded human history, with global temperatures plummeting instantly to values colder than the Little Ice Age of the sixteenth to nineteenth centuries, with precipitation reductions and growing seasons shortened by several weeks in the midlatitudes of the northern hemisphere. One reason the climatic effects are so large is that the growth of megacities in the developing world has produced much more fuel for nuclear fires than realized previously. Whereas nuclear winter theory shows that the superpowers threaten the existence of the rest of the world, now newly emergent nuclear powers threaten the former superpowers, perhaps not with extinction, but with serious consequences, including drought and famine.

The second and third scenarios, of a nuclear war between the United States and Russia, would still produce a nuclear winter. But in contrast to earlier results, we found that the effects would last for longer than a decade for all three scenarios. For the first time we have computer power sufficient to conduct many ten-year simulations. Our climate model allows the response in the ocean to account correctly for heat storage and changes of ocean currents to give the proper time response. But most important, the vertical extent simulated in the model allows us to show that the smoke would be lofted into the stratosphere and stay there for years, much longer than realized before.

The United States and Russia are signatories to the Strategic Offensive Reductions Treaty, which commits both to a reduction to 1700–2200 deployed nuclear weapons by the end of 2012. This continuing reduction of nuclear weapons is to be commended, but our results show that even much more modest nuclear arsenals leave the possibility of a nuclear environmental catastrophe. In addition, serious additional attention is needed to the problem of nuclear proliferation. The story summarized here shows that the world has reached a crossroads. Having survived the threat of global nuclear war between the superpowers so far, the world is increasingly threatened by the prospects of regional nuclear war. The consequences of regional-scale nuclear conflicts are unexpectedly large, with the potential to become global catastrophes. The combination of nuclear proliferation, political instability, and urban demographics may constitute one of the greatest dangers to the stability of society since the dawn of humans.

Biological Weapons

3.5 With Custom-Built Pathogens Come New Fears

Joby Warrick

The world's attention has largely focused on the dangers of nuclear weapons. Biological weapons, however, may prove easier to manufacture, harder to defend against, and more deadly than nuclear weapons. Even more frightening, the danger is evolving and growing. In the next selection, *Washington Post* reporter Joby Warrick examines the threats that new biotechnology may make possible.

Eckard Wimmer knows of a shortcut terrorists could someday use to get their hands on the lethal viruses that cause Ebola and smallpox. He knows it exceptionally well, because he discovered it himself.

In 2002, the German-born molecular geneticist startled the scientific world by creating the first live, fully artificial virus in the lab. It was a variation of the bug that causes polio, yet different from any virus known to nature. And Wimmer built it from scratch.

The virus was made wholly from nonliving parts, using equipment and chemicals on hand in Wimmer's small laboratory at the State University of New York here on Long Island. The most crucial part, the genetic code, was picked up for free on the Internet. Hundreds of tiny bits of viral DNA were purchased online, with final assembly in the lab.

Wimmer intended to sound a warning, to show that science had crossed a threshold into an era in which genetically altered and made-from-scratch germ weapons were feasible. But in the four years since, other scientists have made advances faster than Wimmer imagined possible. Government officials, and scientists such as Wimmer, are only beginning to grasp the implications.

"The future," he says, "has already come."

Five years ago, deadly anthrax attacks forced Americans to confront the suddenly real prospect of bioterrorism. Since then the Bush administration has poured billions of dollars into building a defensive wall of drugs, vaccines and special sensors that can detect dangerous pathogens. But already, technology is hurtling

Warrick, Joby, "With Custom-Built Pathogens Come New Fears," *Washington Post National Weekly Edition,* August 7–13, 2006, pp. 8–9. © 2008, *The Washington Post.* Reprinted with permission.

past it. While government scientists press their search for new drugs for old foes such as classic anthrax, a revolution in biology has ushered in an age of engineered microbes and novel ways to make them.

The new technology opens the door to new tools for defeating disease and saving lives. But today, in hundreds of labs worldwide, it is also possible to transform common intestinal microbes into killers. Or to make deadly strains even more lethal. Or to resurrect bygone killers, such the 1918 influenza. Or to manipulate a person's hormones by switching genes on or off. Or to craft cheap, efficient delivery systems that can infect large numbers of people.

"The biological weapons threat is multiplying and will do so regardless of the countermeasures we try to take," says Steven M. Block, a Stanford University biophysicist and former president of the Biophysical Society. "You can't stop it, any more than you can stop the progress of mankind. You just have to hope that your collective brainpower can muster more resources than your adversaries."

The Bush administration has acknowledged the evolving threat, and last year it appointed a panel of scientists to begin a years-long study of the problem. It also is building a large and controversial lab in Frederick, where new bioterrorism threats can be studied and tested. But overall, specific responses have been few and slow.

The U.S. Centers for Disease Control and Prevention has declined so far to police the booming gene-synthesis industry, which churns out made-to-order DNA to sell to scientists. Oversight of controversial experiments remains voluntary and sporadic in many universities and private labs in the United States, and occurs even more rarely overseas.

Bioterrorism experts say traditional biodefense approaches, such as stockpiling antibiotics or locking up well-known strains such as the smallpox virus, remain important. But they are not enough.

"There's a name for fixed defenses that can easily be outflanked: they are called Maginot lines," says Roger Brent, a California molecular biologist and former biodefense adviser to the Defense Department, referring to the elaborate but short-sighted network of border fortifications built by France after World War I to prevent future invasions by Germany.

"By themselves," Brent says, "stockpiled defenses against specific threats will be no more effective to the defense of the United States than the Maginot line was to the defense of France in 1940."

Wimmer's artificial virus looks and behaves like its natural cousin—but with a far reduced ability to maim or kill—and could be used to make a safer polio vaccine. But it was Wimmer's techniques, not his aims, that sparked controversy when news of his achievement hit the scientific journals.

As the creator of the world's first "de novo" virus—a human virus, at that—Wimmer came under attack from other scientists who said his experiment was a dangerous stunt. He was accused of giving ideas to terrorists, or, even worse, of inviting a backlash that could result in new laws restricting scientific freedom.

Wimmer counters that he didn't invent the technology that made his experiment possible. He only drew attention to it.

"To most scientists and lay people, the reality that viruses could be synthesized was surprising, if not shocking," he says. "We consider it imperative to inform society of this new reality, which bears far-reaching consequences."

One of the world's foremost experts on poliovirus, Wimmer has made de novo poliovirus six times since his groundbreaking experiment four years ago. Each time, the work is a little easier and faster.

New techniques developed by other scientists allow the creation of synthetic viruses in mere days, not weeks or months. Hardware unveiled last year by a Harvard genetics professor can churn out synthetic genes by the thousands, for a few pennies each.

But Wimmer continues to use methods available to any modestly funded university biology lab. He reckons that tens of thousands of scientists worldwide already are capable of doing what he does.

"Our paper was the starting point of the revolution," Wimmer says. "But eventually the process will become so automated even technicians can do it."

Wimmer's method starts with the virus's genetic blueprint, a code of instructions 7,441 characters long. Obtaining it is the easiest part: the entire code for poliovirus, and those for scores of other pathogens, is available for free on the Internet.

Armed with a printout of the code, Wimmer places an order with a U.S. company that manufactures custom-made snippets of DNA, called oglionucleotides. The DNA fragments arrive by mail in hundreds of tiny vials, enough to cover a lab table in one of Wimmer's three small research suites.

Using a kind of chemical epoxy, the scientist and his crew of graduate assistants begin the tedious task of fusing small snippets of DNA into larger fragments. Then they splice together the larger strands until the entire sequence is complete.

The final step is almost magical. The finished but lifeless DNA, placed in a broth of organic "juice" from mushed-up cells, begins making proteins. Spontaneously, it assembles the trappings of a working virus around itself.

While simple on paper, it is not a feat for amateurs, Wimmer says. There are additional steps to making effective bioweapons besides acquiring microbes. Like many scientists and a sizable number of biodefense experts, Wimmer believes traditional terrorist groups such as al-Qaeda will stick with easier methods, at least for now.

Yet al-Qaeda is known to have sought bioweapons and has recruited experts, including microbiologists. And for any skilled microbiologist trained in modern techniques, Wimmer acknowledges, synthetic viruses are well within reach and getting easier.

"This," he says, "is a wake-up call."

The global biotech revolution underway is more than mere genetic engineering. It is genetic engineering on hyperdrive. New scientific disciplines such as synthetic biology, practiced not only in the United States but also in new white-coat enclaves in China and Cuba, seek not to tweak biological systems but to reinvent them.

The Holy Grail of synthetic biologists is the reduction of all life processes into building blocks—interchangeable bio-bricks that can be reassembled into new forms. The technology envisions new species of microbes built from the bottom up: "Living machines from off-the-shelf chemicals" to suit the needs of science, says Jonathan Tucker, a bioweapons expert with the Washington-based Center for Non-Proliferation Studies.

"It is possible to engineer living organisms the way people now engineer electronic circuits," Tucker says. In the future, he says, these microbes could produce cheap drugs, detect toxic chemicals, break down pollutants, repair defective genes, destroy cancer cells and generate hydrogen for fuel.

In less than five years, synthetic biology has gone from a kind of scientific parlor trick, useful for such things as creating glow-in-the-dark fish, to a cutting-edge bioscience with enormous commercial potential, says Eileen Choffnes, an expert on microbial threats with the National Academies' Institute of Medicine. "Now the technology can be even done at the lab bench in high school," she says.

Along with synthetic biologists, a separate but equally ardent group is pursuing DNA shuffling, a kind of directed evolution that imbues microbes with new traits. Another faction seeks novel ways to deliver chemicals and medicines, using ultra-fine aerosols that penetrate deeply into the lungs or new forms of microencapsulated packaging that control how drugs are released in the body.

Still another group is discovering ways to manipulate the essential biological circuitry of humans, using chemicals or engineered microbes to shut down defective genes or regulate the production of hormones controlling such functions as metabolism and mood.

Some analysts have compared the flowering of biotechnology to the start of the nuclear age in the past century, but there are important differences. This time, the United States holds no monopoly over the emerging science, as it did in the early years of nuclear power. Racing to exploit each new discovery are dozens of countries, many of them in the developing world.

There's no binding treaty or international watchdog to safeguard against abuse. And the secrets of biology are available on the Internet for free, said Robert L. Erwin at a recent Washington symposium pondering the new technology. He is a geneticist and founder of the California biotech firm Large Scale Biology Corp.

"It's too cheap, it's too fast, there are too many people who know too much," Erwin said, "and it's too late to stop it."

In May, when 300 synthetic biologists gathered in California for the second national conference in the history of their new field, they found protesters waiting.

"Scientists creating new life forms cannot be allowed to act as judge and jury," Sue Mayer, a veterinary cell biologist and director of GeneWatch UK, said in a statement signed by 38 organizations.

Activists are not the only ones concerned about where new technology could lead. Numerous studies by normally staid panels of scientists and security experts have also warned about the consequences of abuse. An unclassified CIA study in 2003 titled "The Darker Bioweapons Future" warned of a potential for a "class of new, more virulent biological agents engineered to attack" specific targets. "The effects of some of these engineered biological agents could be worse than any disease known to man," the study said.

It is not just the potential for exotic diseases that is causing concern. Harmless bacteria can be modified to carry genetic instructions that, once inside the body, can alter basic functions, such as immunity or hormone production, three biode-fense experts with the Defense Intelligence Agency said in an influential report titled "Biotechnology: Impact on Biological Warfare and Biodefense."

As far as is publicly known, no such weapons have ever been used, although Soviet bioweapons scientists experimented with genetically altered strains in the final years of the Cold War. Some experts doubt terrorists would go to such trouble when ordinary germs can achieve the same goals.

"The capability of terrorists to embark on this path in the near- to mid-term is judged to be low," Charles E. Allen, chief intelligence officer for the Department of Homeland Security, said in testimony May 4 before a panel of the House Commit-tee on Homeland Security. "Just because the technology is available doesn't mean terrorists can or will use it."

A far more likely source, Allen said, is a "lone wolf": a scientist or biological hacker working alone or in a small group, driven by ideology or perhaps personal demons. Many experts believe the anthrax attacks of 2001 were the work of just such a loner.

"All it would take for advanced bioweapons development," Allen said, "is one skilled scientist and modest equipment—an activity we are unlikely to detect in advance."

Throughout the Western world and even in developing countries such as India and Iran, dozens of companies have entered the booming business of commercial gene synthesis. Last fall, a British scientific journal, *New Scientist,* decided to con-tact some of these DNA-by-mail companies to show how easy it would be to obtain a potentially dangerous genetic sequence—for example, DNA for a bacterial gene that produces deadly toxins.

Only 5 of the 12 firms that responded said they screened customers' orders for DNA sequences that might pose a terrorism threat. Four companies acknowledged doing no screening at all. Under current laws, the companies are not required to screen.

In the United States, the federal "Select Agent" rule restricts access to a few types of deadly bacteria, viruses and toxins. But, under the CDC's interpretation of the rule, there are few such controls on transfers of synthetic genes that can be turned into killers. Changes are being contemplated, but for now the gap is one example of technology's rapid advance leaving law and policy behind.

"It would be possible—fully legal—for a person to produce full-length 1918 influenza virus or Ebola virus genomes, along with kits containing detailed proce-dures and all other materials for reconstitution," says Richard H. Ebright, a bio-chemist and professor at Rutgers University. "It is also possible to advertise and to sell the product, in the United States or overseas."

While scientists tend to be deeply skeptical of government intrusion into their laboratories, many favor closer scrutiny over which kinds of genetic coding are being sold and to whom. Even DNA companies themselves are lobbying for better oversight.

Blue Heron Biotechnology, a major U.S. gene-synthesis company based in subur-ban Seattle, formally petitioned the federal government three years ago to expand the Select Agent rule to require companies to screen DNA purchases. The com-pany began voluntarily screening after receiving suspicious requests from overseas, including one from a Saudi customer asking for genes belonging to a virus that causes a disease akin to smallpox.

"The request turned out to be legitimate, from a real scientist, but it made us ask ourselves: how can we make sure that some crazy person doesn't order something from us?" says John Mulligan, Blue Heron's founder and chief executive. "I used to think that such a thing was improbable, but then September 11 happened."

Some scientists also favor great scrutiny—or at least peer review—of research that could lead to the accidental or deliberate release of genetically modified organisms.

In theory, such oversight is provided by volunteer boards known as institutional biosafety committees. Guidelines set by the National Institutes of Health call on federally funded schools and private labs to each appoint such a board. A 2004 National Academy of Sciences report recommended that the committees take on a larger role in policing research that could lead to more powerful biological weapons.

In reality, many of these boards appear to exist only on paper. In 2004, the non-profit Sunshine Project surveyed 390 such committees, asking for copies of minutes or notes from any meetings convened to evaluate research projects. Only 15 institutions earned high marks for showing full compliance with NIH guidelines, says Edward Hammond, who directed the survey. Nearly 200 others who responded had poor or missing records or none at all, he says. Some committees had never met.

New techniques that unlock the secrets of microbial life may someday lead to the defeat of bioterrorism threats and cures for natural diseases, too. But today, the search for new drugs of all kinds remains agonizingly slow.

Five years after the Sept. 11 attacks, the federal government budgets nearly $8 billion annually—an 18-fold increase since 2001—for the defense of civilians against biological attack. Billions have been spent to develop and stockpile new drugs, most of them each tied to a single, well-known bioterrorism threat, such as anthrax.

Despite efforts to streamline the system, developing one new drug could still take up to a decade and cost hundreds of millions of dollars. If successful, the drug is a solution for just one disease threat out of a list that is rapidly expanding to include man-made varieties.

In a biological attack, waiting even a few weeks for new drugs may be disastrous, says Tara O'Toole, a physician and director of the Center for Biosecurity at the University of Pittsburgh Medical Center.

"We haven't yet absorbed the magnitude of this threat to national security," says O'Toole, who worries that the national commitment to biodefense is waning over time and the rise of natural threats such as pandemic flu. "It is true that pandemic flu is important, and we're not doing nearly enough, but I don't think pandemic flu could take down the United States of America. A campaign of moderate biological attacks could."

Suggested Discussion Topics

1. What was the role of nuclear weapons during the Cold War? In what ways has the end of the Cold War altered the role of nuclear weapons in global politics? Why does the United States still choose to have nuclear weapons? Do you think the world would be better if nuclear weapons had never been invented? Now that the Cold War is over, do you think the United States should get rid of its nuclear weapons? Why or why not? What agreements or institutions or arrangements would you insist upon before the United States gave up its weapons?

2. In what ways do nuclear weapons represent a non-zero-sum problem for the world and for the United States? What kinds of institutions and international regimes have developed to try to solve these non-zero-sum problems? What kinds of treaties have been signed to reduce the danger of nuclear war? How much difference do you think these agreements have made? What additional agreements would you want to see? Now that the Cold War is over, what should the United States do to reduce the likelihood or danger of a nuclear war, or of one that involved chemical or biological weapons? Richard Betts suggests that the United States rethink some of its involvement in world affairs. Do you think this is a good idea? Why or why not?

3. Should we be concerned about the proliferation of nuclear weapons and, if so, why? What can be done to reduce the likelihood of proliferation? Which steps do you think are most likely to be useful?

4. If negotiations aimed at preventing an Iranian nuclear capability fail, should the United States use military force to prevent Iran from becoming a nuclear-armed power? Be prepared to debate whichever side of this question your instructor assigns you to take.

5. Should the United States press ahead with missile defenses? What are the costs and what are the benefits of continuing to try to develop and deploy missile defenses? What would be the costs and benefits of adopting a more multilateral approach to building missile defenses?

6. Would a nuclear war between India and Pakistan, or between India and China, or between China and Pakistan, endanger the United States? Why or why not? If you believe such a war would threaten the United States, what can or should the United States do to prevent it?

7. If a nuclear or biological war anywhere in the world has the potential to threaten the rest of the world, does this affect the role in world governance that ought to be assigned to the United Nations? Does it imply that the United States can or should play the role of the world's policeman?

8. What can be done to prevent or limit the dangers of biological warfare? Should biotechnology be limited or controlled? As a practical matter, how could this be done, and who would do it?

Chapter 4

DEMOCRACY: A GLOBAL INSTITUTION?

One of the most important elements in the turbulent transformation of global politics now underway has been the spread of democracy. The end of the Cold War and the political developments of the decade that followed have been heralded as a great victory for liberal democracy. These developments include the disintegration of the Soviet Union, the collapse of communist rule in Russia and nearly everywhere in Eastern Europe, the opening of the Chinese economy, and a return to free elections across Latin America and in an increasing number of states in Africa and Asia. Indeed, the notion that the subjects of a state ought to be able to control that state—that whatever its claims to sovereignty, no state ought to be able to wield arbitrary, unchecked power over the people it rules—has in the years since the end of the Cold War become something of a global norm, receiving at least lip service nearly everywhere in the world. While precise definitions of democracy may be hotly debated, three of the basic requirements for democracy are widely recognized: that the authority of the state must rest on some sort of explicit or implicit contract between the state and the people it governs, setting limits on what the state can demand in return for the benefits it provides (i.e., that there be a constitution); that within the state the power to pass laws, to judge these laws, and to enforce these laws ought not be concentrated in the same hands lest this lead to abuse of citizens' rights (i.e., that there be a division of powers); and that procedures need to be established to allow the people to determine who among them will govern, and to remove individuals from office if their decisions are not made with the consent of the people (i.e., that there be free elections).

Exactly what difference the diffusion of democratic values and the spread of democratic institutions makes has been widely debated. One prominent observer, political scientist Francis Fukuyama, argued even before the collapse of the Soviet Union that the imminent spread of democracy would mark an "end of history." In his view, the victory of liberal democracy in the Cold War and humanity's rejection of liberal democracy's last serious ideological challenger, communism, meant that the world's political evolution was reaching an end. While memorable events would still continue to occur, history was at an end in the sense that liberal democracy's triumph represented the final stage in humanity's efforts to create political order. In Fukuyama's view, the remaining opposition to liberal democracy was anachronistic and backward-looking and would, in the end, die away. Not all observers are so optimistic about the permanence and finality of liberal democracy, of course, and Fukuyama's proposition remains contentious.

The implications of democracy for world peace and for how states deal with each other have also been hotly debated. Political scientists have studied what has been called "the democratic peace"—the fact that, historically, democracies have been unlikely to fight other democracies (even though democracies seem about as likely as nondemocracies to engage in some sort of war). What it is about liberal democratic states that might make them better able to resolve disputes among themselves without a resort to war continues to be studied. Also being studied is the impact that the process of *democratization* has on political life and on the way global politics is conducted. Even among scholars who agree that liberal democracy and the empowerment of individuals that liberal democracy makes possible are morally desirable, there is concern that the process of transforming nondemocratic societies and polities into democratic ones may be unpleasant and dangerous. Democratization is destabilizing. It undermines traditional patterns of authority and traditional institutions that, however abusive or undesirable, did provide a certain amount of predictability and order in daily life. The decay or overthrow of these institutions creates uncertainty and danger, the potential for both political violence and the spread of crime, and a risk of economic turmoil as individuals worry about the safety of their investment in both human and physical capital. The efforts by competing political leaders to mobilize newly enfranchised populations or to create or maintain mass political support during the turbulent transition from old nondemocratic political institutions toward democratic ones may result in these leaders pursuing more intransigent or aggressive foreign policies and a greater danger of war. Thus even optimists, who believe that liberal democracy will be triumphant and stable in the long run and will bring with it a significant propensity toward peace, may well be concerned that in the short run the spread of democratic values and institutions may mean the world is in for a bumpy ride.

For the world's great liberal democratic states (such as the United States, the states of the European Union, and Japan), the notion that democratic institutions can be spread globally creates a real dilemma. On one hand, these states accept the idea of sovereignty—the idea that each state has the right to determine and order its internal affairs as it sees fit. On the other hand, if human beings have an inalienable natural right to freedom, and to democratic institutions that are necessary if they are to enjoy this freedom, don't people everywhere owe it to their fellows, wherever these fellow human beings may live, to ensure that they, too, have access to democratic institutions and are ruled over by democratic governments? That is, isn't there a moral obligation to intervene, to ensure that others experience the blessings of democratic liberty?

For many around the world, these issues were brought to a head by the U.S. invasion of Iraq in 2003. Although a number of justifications for this invasion were given, one of the most prominent was that it was necessary to eliminate tyranny in Iraq and that it would result in the establishment of democracy there—and, indeed, that it would start a democratic domino effect across the region, and perhaps elsewhere, forcing nondemocratic governments to transform themselves into democracies or risk overthrow. Even among those observers who accepted the value of democracy, however, the American decision to invade Iraq and install a new government there raised troubling questions. Did one nation have the right to impose its values on others? Could one nation impose its values on another at an acceptable cost? And could liberal democracy—the notion that individuals and societies have the right to make choices for themselves—be imposed from outside, or was this a contradiction in terms?

The spread of democracy is thus one of the major developments in global politics and one of today's major political issues. Ironically, democracy seems to be bringing both order (in the form of stable governments, working to serve the will of their people) and disorder (as traditional systems of governing societies are undermined), and to be bringing people around the world together in a common institution even while it is splitting them apart over the question of whether states should impose democracy on other states.

4.1 History Is Still Going Our Way

Francis Fukuyama

In the first selection, political scientist Francis Fukuyama argues that liberal democracy is the wave of the future. Writing days after the September 11, 2001, Islamic fundamentalist attack on the World Trade Center and Pentagon, Fukuyama admits that his prediction of "the end of history" may have been premature, but he argues that in the end it will still prove right. He contends that modernization, with the liberal democratic values and norms that are its companions, will overcome the parochial passions of religion, ethnicity, and the like. In his view, today's struggle pits lingering remnants of the past against the inevitable future—not civilization against civilization.

A stream of commentators has been asserting that the tragedy of September 11 proves that I was utterly wrong to have said more than a decade ago that we had reached the end of history. The chorus began almost immediately, with George Will asserting that history had returned from vacation, and Fareed Zakaria declaring the end of the end of history.

It is on the face of it nonsensical and insulting to the memory of those who died on September 11 to declare that this unprecedented attack did not rise to the level of a historical event. But the way in which I used the word *history*, or rather, History, was different: it referred to the progress of mankind over the centuries toward modernity, characterized by institutions like liberal democracy and capitalism.

March of History

My observation, made back in 1989 on the eve of the collapse of communism, was that this evolutionary process did seem to be bringing ever larger parts of the world toward modernity. And if we looked beyond liberal democracy and markets, there was nothing else towards which we could expect to evolve; hence the end of history. While there were retrograde areas that resisted that process, it was hard to find a viable alternative type of civilization that people actually wanted to live in after the discrediting of socialism, monarchy, fascism, and other types of authoritarian rule.

This view has been challenged by many people, and perhaps most articulately by Samuel Huntington. He argued that rather than progressing toward a single global system, the world remained mired in a "clash of civilizations" where six or seven major cultural groups would coexist without converging and constitute the new fracture lines of global conflict. Since the successful attack on the center of global capitalism was evidently perpetrated by Islamic extremists unhappy with the very existence of Western civilization, observers have been handicapping the Huntington "clash" view over my own "end of history" hypothesis rather heavily.

I believe that in the end I remain right: modernity is a very powerful freight train that will not be derailed by recent events, however painful and unprecedented. Democracy and free markets will continue to expand over time as the dominant organizing principles for much of the world. But it is worthwhile thinking about what the true scope of the present challenge is.

It has always been my belief that modernity has a cultural basis. Liberal democracy and free markets do not work at all times and everywhere. They work best in societies with certain values whose origins may not be entirely rational. It is not an accident that modern liberal democracy emerged first in the Christian West, since the universalism of democratic rights can be seen in many ways as a secular form of Christian universalism.

The central question raised by Samuel Huntington is whether institutions of modernity such as liberal democracy and free markets will work only in the West, or whether there is something broader in their appeal that will allow them to make headway in non-Western societies. I believe there is. The proof lies in the progress that democracy and free markets have made in regions like East Asia, Latin America, Orthodox Europe, South Asia, and even Africa. Proof lies also in the millions of Third World immigrants who vote with their feet every year to live in Western societies and eventually assimilate to Western values. The flow of people moving in the opposite direction, and the number who want to blow up what they can of the West, is by contrast negligible.

But there does seem to be something about Islam, or at least the fundamentalist versions of Islam that have been dominant in recent years, that makes Muslim societies particularly resistant to modernity. Of all contemporary cultural systems, the Islamic world has the fewest democracies (Turkey alone qualifies), and contains no countries that have made the transition from Third to First World status in the manner of South Korea or Singapore.

There are plenty of non-Western people who prefer the economic and technological part of modernity and hope to have it without having to accept democratic politics or Western cultural values as well (e.g., China or Singapore). There are others who like both the economic and political versions of modernity, but just can't figure out how to make it happen (Russia is an example). For them, transition to Western-style modernity may be long and painful. But there are no insuperable cultural barriers likely to prevent them from eventually getting there, and they constitute about four-fifths of the world's people.

Islam, by contrast, is the only cultural system that seems to regularly produce people, like Osama bin Laden or the Taliban, who reject modernity lock, stock and barrel. This raises the question of how representative such people are of the larger Muslim community, and whether this rejection is somehow inherent in Islam. For if the rejectionists are more than a lunatic fringe, then Mr. Huntington is right that we are in for a protracted conflict made dangerous by virtue of their technological empowerment.

The answer that politicians East and West have been putting out since Sept. 11 is that those sympathetic with the terrorists are a "tiny minority" of Muslims, and that the vast majority are appalled by what happened. It is important for them to say this to prevent Muslims as a group from becoming targets of hatred. The problem is that dislike and hatred of America and what it stands for are clearly much more widespread than that.

Certainly the group of people willing to go on suicide missions and actively conspire against the U.S. is tiny. But sympathy may be manifest in nothing more than initial feelings of *Schadenfreude* at the sight of the collapsing towers, an immediate sense of satisfaction that the U.S. was getting what it deserved, to be followed only later by pro forma expressions of disapproval. By this standard, sympathy for the terrorists is characteristic of much more than a "tiny minority" of Muslims, extending from the middle classes in countries like Egypt to immigrants in the West.

This broader dislike and hatred would seem to represent something much deeper than mere opposition to American policies like support for Israel or the Iraq embargo, encompassing a hatred of the underlying society. After all, many people around the world, including many Americans, disagree with U.S. policies, but this does not send them into paroxysms of anger and violence. Nor is it necessarily a matter of ignorance about the quality of life in the West. The suicide hijacker Mohamed Atta was a well-educated man from a well-to-do Egyptian family who lived and studied in Germany and the U.S. for several years. Perhaps, as many commentators have speculated, the hatred is born out of a resentment of Western success and Muslim failure.

But rather than psychologize the Muslim world, it makes more sense to ask whether radical Islam constitutes a serious alternative to Western liberal democracy for Muslims themselves. (It goes without saying that, unlike communism, radical Islam has virtually no appeal in the contemporary world apart from those who are culturally Islamic to begin with.)

For Muslims themselves, political Islam has proven much more appealing in the abstract than in reality. After 23 years of rule by fundamentalist clerics, most Iranians, and in particular nearly everyone under 30, would like to live in a far more liberal society. Afghans who have experienced Taliban rule have much the same feelings. All of the anti-American hatred that has been drummed up does not translate into a viable political program for Muslim societies to follow in the years ahead.

The West Dominates

We remain at the end of history because there is only one system that will continue to dominate world politics, that of the liberal-democratic West. This does not imply a world free from conflict, nor the disappearance of culture as a distinguishing characteristic of societies. (In my original article, I noted that the posthistorical world would continue to see terrorism and wars of national liberation.)

But the struggle we face is not the clash of several distinct and equal cultures struggling amongst one another like the great powers of 19th century Europe. The clash consists of a series of rearguard actions from societies whose traditional existence is indeed threatened by modernization. The strength of the backlash reflects the severity of this threat. But time and resources are on the side of modernity, and I see no lack of a will to prevail in the United States today.

4.2 The Return of Authoritarian Great Powers

Azar Gat

Does the collapse of communism mean the triumph of democracy? Most critics of Francis Fukuyama's "end of history" argument have focused on the challenge posed by fundamentalist religions, such as Islam, or by non-Western cultures that are resistant to democracy. But it is also the case that capitalism is not necessarily synonymous with democracy. A number of great powers in the past have been nondemocratic capitalist states. Azar Gat, a professor at Tel Aviv University, argues that states such as China and Russia may retain or return to authoritarian political institutions even while embracing capitalism and that the global triumph of democracy is hardly assured.

The End of the End of History

Today's global liberal democratic order faces two challenges. The first is radical Islam—and it is the lesser of the two challenges. Although the proponents of radical Islam find liberal democracy repugnant, and the movement is often described as the new fascist threat, the societies from which it arises are generally poor and stagnant. They represent no viable alternative to modernity and

Gat, Azar, "The Return of Authoritarian Great Powers," *Foreign Affairs,* July/August 2007, pp. 59–69. Reprinted by permission of *Foreign Affairs.* © 2007 by the Council on Foreign Relations, Inc. <www.ForeignAffairs.org>.

pose no significant military threat to the developed world. It is mainly the potential use of weapons of mass destruction—particularly by nonstate actors—that makes militant Islam a menace.

The second, and more significant, challenge emanates from the rise of nondemocratic great powers: the West's old Cold War rivals China and Russia, now operating under authoritarian capitalist, rather than communist, regimes. Authoritarian capitalist great powers played a leading role in the international system up until 1945. They have been absent since then. But today, they seem poised for a comeback.

Capitalism's ascendancy appears to be deeply entrenched, but the current predominance of democracy could be far less secure. Capitalism has expanded relentlessly since early modernity, its lower-priced goods and superior economic power eroding and transforming all other socioeconomic regimes, a process most memorably described by Karl Marx in *The Communist Manifesto*. Contrary to Marx's expectations, capitalism had the same effect on communism, eventually "burying" it without the proverbial shot being fired. The triumph of the market, precipitating and reinforced by the industrial-technological revolution, led to the rise of the middle class, intensive urbanization, the spread of education, the emergence of mass society, and ever greater affluence. In the post–Cold War era (just as in the nineteenth century and the 1950s and 1960s), it is widely believed that liberal democracy naturally emerged from these developments, a view famously espoused by Francis Fukuyama. Today, more than half of the world's states have elected governments, and close to half have sufficiently entrenched liberal rights to be considered fully free.

But the reasons for the triumph of democracy, especially over its nondemocratic capitalist rivals of the two world wars, Germany and Japan, were more contingent than is usually assumed. Authoritarian capitalist states, today exemplified by China and Russia, may represent a viable alternative path to modernity, which in turn suggests that there is nothing inevitable about liberal democracy's ultimate victory—or future dominance.

Chronicle of a Defeat Not Foretold

The liberal democratic camp defeated its authoritarian, fascist, and communist rivals alike in all of the three major great-power struggles of the twentieth century—the two world wars and the Cold War. In trying to determine exactly what accounted for this decisive outcome, it is tempting to trace it to the special traits and intrinsic advantages of liberal democracy.

One possible advantage is democracies' international conduct. Perhaps they more than compensate for carrying a lighter stick abroad with a greater ability to elicit international cooperation through the bonds and discipline of the global market system. This explanation is probably correct for the Cold War, when a greatly expanded global economy was dominated by the democratic powers, but it does not apply to the two world wars. Nor is it true that liberal democracies succeed because they always cling together. Again, this was true, at least as a contributing factor, during the Cold War, when the democratic capitalist camp kept its unity, whereas growing antagonism between the Soviet Union and China pulled the communist bloc apart. During World War I, however, the ideological divide between the two sides was much less clear. The Anglo-French alliance was far from preordained; it was above all a function of balance-of-power calculations rather than liberal cooperation. . . . Studies of democracies' alliance behavior suggest that democratic regimes show no greater tendency to stick together than other types of regimes.

Nor did the totalitarian capitalist regimes lose World War II because their democratic opponents held a moral high ground that inspired greater exertion from their people, as the historian Richard Overy and others have claimed. During the 1930s and early 1940s, fascism and Nazism were exciting new ideologies that generated massive popular enthusiasm, whereas democracy stood on the ideological defensive, appearing old and dispirited. If anything, the fascist regimes proved more inspiring in wartime than their democratic adversaries, and the battlefield performance of their militaries is widely judged to have been superior.

Liberal democracy's supposedly inherent economic advantage is also far less clear than is often assumed. All of the belligerents in the twentieth century's great struggles proved highly effective in producing for war. During World War I, semiautocratic Germany committed its resources as effectively as its democratic rivals did. After early victories in World War II, Nazi Germany's economic mobilization and military production proved lax during the critical years 1940–42. . . . All the same, from 1942 onward (by which time is was too late), Germany greatly intensified its economic mobilization and caught up with and even surpassed the liberal democracies in terms of the share of GDP devoted to the war (although its production volume remained much lower than that of the massive U.S. economy). Likewise, levels of economic mobilization in imperial Japan and the Soviet Union exceeded those of the United States and the United Kingdom thanks to ruthless efforts.

Only during the Cold War did the Soviet command economy exhibit deepening structural weaknesses—weaknesses that were directly responsible for the Soviet Union's downfall. The Soviet system had successfully generated the early and intermediate stages of industrialization (albeit at a frightful human cost) and excelled at the regimentalized techniques of mass production during World War II. It also kept abreast militarily during the Cold War. But because of the system's rigidity and lack of incentives, it proved ill equipped to cope with the advanced stages of development and the demands of the information age and globalization.

There is no reason, however, to suppose that the totalitarian capitalist regimes of Nazi Germany and imperial Japan would have proved inferior economically to the democracies had they survived. The inefficiencies that favoritism and unaccountability typically create in such regimes might have been offset by higher levels of social discipline. Because of their more efficient capitalist economies, the rightwing totalitarian powers could have constituted a more viable challenge to the liberal democracies than the Soviet Union did; Nazi Germany was judged to be such a challenge by the Allied powers before and during World War II. The liberal democracies did not possess an inherent advantage over Germany in terms of economic and technological development, as they did in relation to their other great-power rivals.

So why did the democracies win the great struggles of the twentieth century? The reasons are different for each type of adversary. They defeated their nondemocratic capitalist adversaries, Germany and Japan, in war because Germany and Japan were medium-sized countries with limited resource bases and they came up against the far superior—but hardly preordained—economic and military coalition of the democratic powers and Russia or the Soviet Union. The defeat of communism, however, had much more to do with structural factors. The capitalist camp—which after 1945 expanded to include most of the developed world—possessed much greater economic power than the communist bloc, and the inherent inefficiency of the communist economies prevented them from fully exploiting their vast resources and catching up to the West. Together, the Soviet Union and China were larger and thus had the potential to be more powerful than the democratic capitalist camp. Ultimately, they failed because their economic systems limited them, whereas the nondemocratic capitalist powers, Germany and Japan, were defeated because they were too small. Contingency played a decisive role in tipping the balance against the nondemocratic capitalist powers and in favor of the democracies. . . .

The most decisive element of contingency was the United States. . . . Throughout the twentieth century, the United States' power consistently surpassed that of the next two strongest states combined, and this decisively tilted the global balance of power in favor of whichever side Washington was on. If any factor gave the liberal democracies their edge, it was above all the existence of the United States rather than any inherent advantage. In fact, had it not been for the United States, liberal democracy may well have lost the great struggles of the twentieth century. This is a sobering thought that is often overlooked in studies of the spread of democracy in the twentieth century, and it makes the world today appear much more contingent and tenuous than linear theories of development suggest. If it were not for the U.S. factor, the judgment of later generations on liberal democracy would probably have echoed the negative verdict on democracy's performance, issued by the fourth-century-B.C. Greeks, in the wake of Athens' defeat in the Peloponnesian War.

The New Second World

But the audit of war is, of course, not the only one that societies—democratic and nondemocratic—undergo. One must ask how the totalitarian capitalist powers would have developed had they not been defeated by war. Would they, with time and further development, have shed their former identity and embraced liberal democracy, as the former communist regimes of eastern Europe eventually did? . . .

The question is made relevant by the recent emergence of nondemocratic giants, above all formerly communist and booming authoritarian capitalist China. Russia, too, is retreating from its postcommunist liberalism and assuming an increasingly authoritarian character as its economic cloud grows. Some believe that these countries could ultimately become liberal democracies through a combination of internal development, increasing affluence, and outside influence. Alternatively, they may have enough weight to create a new non-democratic but economically advanced Second World. They could establish a powerful authoritarian capitalist order that allies political elites, industrialists, and the military; that is nationalist in orientation; and that participates in the global economy on its own terms, as imperial Germany and imperial Japan did.

It is widely contended that economic and social development creates pressures for democratization that an authoritarian state structure cannot contain. There is also the view that "closed societies" may be able to excel in mass manufacturing but not in the advanced stages of the information economy. The jury on these issues is still out, because the data set is incomplete. Imperial and Nazi Germany stood at the forefront of the advanced scientific and manufacturing economies of their times, but some would argue that their success no longer applies because the information economy is much more diversified. Nondemocratic Singapore has a highly successful information economy, but Singapore is a city-state, not a big country. It will take a long time before China reaches the stage when the possibility of an authoritarian state with an advanced capitalist economy can be tested. All that can be said at the moment is that there is nothing in the historical record to suggest that a transition to democracy by today's authoritarian capitalist powers is inevitable, whereas there is a great deal to suggest that such powers have far greater economic and military potential than their communist predecessors did.

China and Russia represent a return of economically successful authoritarian capitalist powers, which have been absent since the defeat of Germany and Japan in 1945, but they are much larger than the latter two countries ever were. Although Germany was only a medium-sized country uncomfortably squeezed at the center of Europe, it twice nearly broke out of its confines to become a true world power on account of its economic and military might. In 1941, Japan was still behind the leading great powers in terms of economic development, but its growth rate since 1913 had been the highest in the world. Ultimately, however, both Germany and Japan were too small—in terms of population, resources, and potential—to take on the United States. Present-day China, on the other hand, is the largest player in the international system in terms of population and is experiencing spectacular economic growth. By shifting from communism to capitalism, China has switched to a far more efficient brand of authoritarianism. As China rapidly narrows the economic gap with the developed world, the possibility looms that it will become a true authoritarian superpower.

Even in its current bastions in the West, the liberal political and economic consensus is vulnerable to unforeseen developments, such as a crushing economic crisis that could disrupt the global trading system or a resurgence of ethnic strife in a Europe increasingly troubled by immigration and ethnic minorities. Were the West to be hit by such upheavals, support for liberal democracy in Asia, Latin America, and Africa—where adherence to that model is more recent, incomplete and insecure—could be shaken. A successful nondemocratic Second World could then be regarded by many as an attractive alternative to liberal democracy.

Making the World Safe for Democracy

Although the rise of authoritarian capitalist great powers would not necessarily lead to a nondemocratic hegemony or a war, it might imply that the near-total dominance of liberal democracy since the Soviet Union's collapse will be short-lived and that a universal "democratic peace" is still far off. The new authoritarian capitalist powers could become as deeply integrated into the world economy as imperial Germany and imperial Japan were and not choose to pursue autarky, as Nazi Germany and the communist bloc did. A great-power China may also be less revisionist than the territorially confined Germany and Japan were (although Russia, which is still reeling from having lost an empire, is more likely to tend toward revisionism). Still, Beijing, Moscow, and their future followers might well be on antagonistic terms with the democratic countries, with all the potential for suspicion, insecurity, and conflict that this entails—while holding considerably more power than any of the democracies' past rivals ever did. . . .

But the most important factor remains the United States. For all the criticism leveled against it, the United States—and its alliance with Europe—stands as the single most important hope for the future of liberal democracy. Despite its problems and weaknesses, the United States still commands a global position of strength and is likely to retain it even as the authoritarian capitalist powers grow. Not only are its GDP and productivity growth rate the highest in the developed world, but as an immigrant country with about one-fourth the population density of both the European Union and China and one-tenth of that of Japan and India, the United States still has considerable potential to grow—both economically and in terms of population—whereas those others are all experiencing aging and, ultimately, shrinking populations. . . . As it was during the twentieth century, the U.S. factor remains the greatest guarantee that liberal democracy will not be thrown on the defensive and relegated to a vulnerable position on the periphery of the international system.

 **Dictating Democracy**

4.3 America's Crusade

Edward Rhodes

If, as Fukuyama argues, "history is still going our way"—if, in the end, democracy will win out over nondemocracy—what should our role in that process be? Is there a moral or practical imperative to hurry history along? And if we aren't sure that Fukuyama is right, and if we are concerned that not every society is inevitably

This reading is based on a longer essay by the author, "The Imperial Logic of Bush's Liberal Agenda," which appeared in the Spring 2003 edition of the journal *Survival*.

heading toward democracy, should we intervene to free these nondemocratic societies from the tyrannies that rule them? In the next selection Edward Rhodes, one of the editors of this textbook, raises these questions, explains the Bush administration's answers to them, and examines these answers critically.

Looking around the globe and seeing societies that are living in fear or denied personal freedom, how should the United States react? Given its extraordinary power, do the United States and its democratic friends and allies have a moral obligation to spread the blessings of liberal democracy—using force if necessary? Do they have a national interest in doing so?

Especially in the wake of the American invasion of Iraq and the insurgencies and guerilla violence that have followed, these questions have been hotly debated in America and around the world. To its credit, the Bush administration has made its answers to these questions quite clear. In his June 1, 2002, address at West Point, President George W. Bush laid out his administration's conceptual framework for dealing with the post-September 11 world. This conceptual framework was fleshed out in greater detail in the administration's "National Security Strategy" issued three months later.[1] The speech and strategy evoke American values, argue the universality of human liberty, and attack what they describe as the twin dangers of tyrants and terrorism. They reject the murkiness of moral relativism, distinguish boldly between good and evil, and unabashedly and unhesitatingly align America on the side of good.

America, the president makes clear, has a global duty. Both to protect itself and to be true to its higher calling, America must shoulder the responsibility of constructing a global peace, which can be built only on the foundation of individual human liberty and free societies. The objective of American foreign policy, President Bush makes clear, is nothing less than a transformation of world politics, domestic as well as international, using American power—military as well as economic and political—to build liberal societies and polities. We are, President Bush suggests, at a great watershed in human history. We find ourselves at a turning point like the one at the end of the Thirty Years' War. Then, from the nightmare of uncontrolled warring, pillage, rapine, and plague emerged a new political order, based on sovereign states able to control and limit violence. Today, in the wake of a twentieth century of violence among these sovereign states—a First World War that pitted liberal democratic states against authoritarian ones, a Second World War that pitted them against fascist and militarist ones, and a Cold War that pitted them against communist ones—new political institutions and a new political order can and must be created. "We have," the president notes, "our best chance since the rise of the nation state in the 17th century to build a world where the great powers compete in peace instead of prepare for war."

---

[1] Both of these documents are available on the Web. George W. Bush, "Remarks by the President at 2002 Graduation Exercise of the United States Military Academy, West Point, New York." Available at: <www.whitehouse.gov/news/releases/2002/06/20020601-3.html>. "The National Security Strategy of the United States of America, September 2002." Available at: <www.whitehouse.gov/nsc/nss.html>. All quotations in this reading are taken from these two documents.

With American leadership, the president argues, it is possible to enter into this new world in which humanity achieves, or reachieves, its natural state. "The United States will," he declares, "use this moment of opportunity to extend the benefits of freedom across the globe." "Freedom," the president goes on to explain,

> is the non-negotiable demand of human dignity; the birthright of every person—in every civilization. Throughout history, freedom has been threatened by war and terror; it has been challenged by the clashing of wills of powerful states and the evil designs of tyrants; and it has been tested by widespread poverty and disease. Today, humanity holds in its hands the opportunity to further freedom's triumph over all these foes. The United States welcomes our responsibility to lead in this great mission.

At West Point and in his "National Security Strategy" the president thus made clear his faith that a new world order based on liberalism's cherished values is both necessary and possible. This new liberal order will not construct itself, however. American power will be key in building it. Indeed, more specifically, American *military* power will be key. Order—even a liberal order based on human liberty and on consent—ultimately requires the exercise of power, and in this case the power will need to be America's military might. "It is," he announced in the "National Security Strategy," "time to reaffirm the essential role of American military strength."

Indeed, the president makes clear, the achievement of a peaceful, liberal world order requires not simply American power, and not simply American military power, but a global American military hegemony—a global military predominance that allows it to shape political developments everywhere in the world. "America has, and intends to keep, military strengths beyond challenge—thereby making the destabilizing arms races of other eras pointless, and limiting rivalries to trade and other pursuits of peace."

Three extraordinary features in the Bush administration's conception of American military hegemony and of how this military hegemony can be translated into the achievement of political goals deserve to be underscored. The first is that American military power will have to be used aggressively, not passively. The "best defense is a good offense," the "National Security Strategy" notes. Though the ultimate political goal, of course, is the *defense* of humanity's natural right to freedom, the United States will not hesitate to take the offensive militarily, striking enemies before they can endanger the United States, the free world, or, indeed, the American interest in a liberal world order. In fact, the United States will not hesitate to strike even before enemies are *able* to endanger us or our ability to shape a world in which humanity's birthright of freedom is restored: "in an age where the enemies of civilization openly and actively seek the world's most destructive technologies, the United States cannot remain idle while dangers gather."

Thus, reversing the positions he took in his 2000 election campaign,[2] the president makes both a moral case and a prudential one for aggressive, preventive

---

[2] Condoleezza Rice's January 2000 *Foreign Affairs* article was, and continues to be, widely viewed as the Bush campaign's foreign policy platform. Dr. Rice became National Security Advisor in the first Bush administration and was appointed Secretary of State in 2005. See Rice, "Promoting the National Interest," *Foreign Affairs*, Volume 79, no. 1 (January/February 2000), pp. 45–62.

American military action to destroy tyrants and terrorism around the world, arguing not only against any inward turn toward isolationism but against a continuation of Cold War–era policies of containment and deterrence that would compromise with, rather than rid the world of, these evils. "For much of the last century," the president mused in his West Point speech,

> America's defense relied on the Cold War doctrines of deterrence and containment. In some cases, those strategies still apply. But new threats also require new thinking. Deterrence—the promise of massive retaliation against nations—means nothing against shadowy terrorist networks with no nation or citizens to defend. Containment is not possible when unbalanced dictators with weapons of mass destruction can deliver those weapons on missiles or secretly provide them to terrorist allies.

Second, the "National Security Strategy" makes plain that the liberal order the United States aims to create will, ultimately, rest on *American* military hegemony, not on the combined will and might of the liberal world. American military power, not that of a global liberal coalition, is what will guarantee peace, security, and human freedom around the world. Consensus is desirable, but it is not necessary. Because the global liberal order is essential not only to the world's safety but to America's safety, America's sovereign responsibilities supercede its commitment to international institutions. "While the United States will constantly strive to enlist the support of the international community, we will not hesitate to act alone, if necessary, to exercise our right of self-defense. . . ."

Third, the "National Security Strategy" makes clear that the Bush administration proposes to use American military hegemony not simply aggressively and unilaterally, but globally. In the Bush administration's thinking, a global house divided against itself cannot stand. A world order cannot endure, permanently half illiberal and half free. The imperative to spread liberalism's freedom throughout humanity's global home rests not simply on the fact that freedom is every human's right. It rests also on the fact that the absence of freedom, even in places as remote as Afghanistan, poses a danger to the rest of humanity.

Just as America, with its global military hegemony, possesses the means to help humanity regain its birthright of liberty and thereby move the world toward peace, so too America possesses in its heritage and experience the necessary road map. The "National Security Strategy" makes clear that the new world order will be constructed not only under the beneficial umbrella of America's global military dominance but on the basis of America's blueprint and on the basis of its conceptions of universal values and of order. There is a single truth, and it is America's. Alternative models of social order and political governance are not only morally wrong but are also an impractical basis for moving forward. "The 20th century," President Bush argued at West Point,

> ended with a single surviving model of human progress, based on nonnegotiable demands of human dignity, the rule of law, limits on the power of the state, respect for women and private property and free speech and equal justice and religious tolerance. . . . When it comes to the common rights and needs of men and women, there is no clash of civilizations. The requirements of freedom apply fully to Africa and Latin America and the entire Islamic world. The peoples of the Islamic nations want and deserve the same freedoms and opportunities as people in every nation. And their governments should listen to them.

The Great Crusade

What is perhaps most striking about the president's rhetoric is that it frames the administration's proposed grand strategy in terms of moral imperatives. "Responsibility" and "obligation" figure prominently alongside of "opportunity" in justifying the choices the president urges America make. America's power imposes on it a moral duty. "The United States possesses unprecedented—and unequaled—strength and influence in the world. Sustained by faith in the principles of liberty, and the value of a free society, this position comes with unparalleled responsibilities, obligations, and opportunity. The great strength of this nation must be used to promote a balance of power that favors freedom."

Indeed, in the president's vision, spreading liberty to all nations is a sacred calling that America cannot evade without denying its very essence. This obligation, the Bush administration suggests, must be regarded as the essential element in America's national security strategy from which all else follows.

> In pursuit of our goals, our first imperative is to clarify what we stand for: the United States must defend liberty and justice because these principles are right and true for all people everywhere. . . . Embodying lessons from our past and using the opportunity we have today, the national security strategy must start from these core beliefs and look outward for possibilities to expand liberty.

Note that the obligation the president sees is not simply to defend liberty and justice in America and in other nations where they are currently enjoyed, but to *extend* freedom's blessings to those who have been denied this birthright. Liberty is not to be defended through passive, defensive measures: rather, it is to be secured by actively spreading the liberal faith. There is no suggestion, of course, that this is exclusively or even predominantly a task for American *military* power. In Bush's thinking, however, this mission of expanding the zone of liberty—this crusade to expand the region of the world in which human beings have regained the freedom that is their natural right—and the use of America's military power are inextricably entwined. In the first place, the preservation of America's unchallenged military hegemony is an essential prerequisite for the global political transformation envisioned; in the second place, in those circumstances where the seriousness or immediacy of the threat posed by freedom's potential foes makes it appropriate, military force is one of the available tools.

While America's power imposes a special responsibility, Bush makes clear that the moral duty to defend and extend liberalism knows no borders. Societies and states are not free to eschew liberalism. Indeed all societies and states have a moral duty not only to embrace liberalism themselves but to ensure that individuals in other societies and states are also free to enjoy its blessings. Sovereignty offers no shield or excuse: "No nation owns these aspirations, and no nation is exempt from them." Since the "values of freedom are right and true for every person, in every society," it follows (the president argues) that "the duty of protecting these values against their enemies is the common calling of freedom-loving people across the globe and across the ages."

There is no neutrality or halfway position in this global crusade against liberalism's foes. While American-led, this is a crusade in which all must join.

> In building a balance of power that favors freedom, the United States is guided by the conviction that all nations have important responsibilities. Nations that enjoy freedom must actively fight terror. Nations that depend on international stability must help prevent the spread of weapons of mass destruction.

A Dissent

This call to the American people is emotionally powerful. Let me suggest, however, that it rests on a deeply troubling vision of America and America's role in the world. Worse, the strategy that flows from this vision is profoundly flawed. The road it charts leads only to tragedy, both for the world and for America.

As a practical matter, the vision woefully misunderstands the power that would be required to do what it proclaims it is America's mission to do. Ridding the world of tyrants and terrorists, as the president seeks to do, is not simply a matter of surgical air strikes and guided munitions, of eliminating particular leaders and destroying particular facilities, of employing superior technology and military science. Ridding the world of tyrants and terrorists is a matter of transforming lives and societies around the world. It is a process inseparable from great, long-term, historical developments in culture and economics. Strike down one tyrant or one terrorist and another will grow in his place, unless the environmental niche that allows them to flourish is altered.

But this is only part—and the least fundamental part—of the misunderstanding. Building a peaceful, liberal world order is not simply a matter of ridding the world of all tyrants and terrorists. Liberalism is not simply the absence of illiberal or antiliberal institutions, like tyranny and terrorism. Nor even is liberalism simply the existence of particular democratic and free-market institutions. Liberalism is an entire way of thinking—an entire way of conceiving of the world and human relationships. Liberalism is a philosophy, a set of beliefs. These beliefs—about how individuals should structure their relationships with each other and organize themselves to deal with collective problems, about the "right" way to live in society—do imply particular behaviors and the development of particular institutions. But ultimately liberalism is a value system and mode of thinking that individuals and societies embrace. For a liberal order to function, for liberal institutions to take root, to grow, and to bear fruit, individuals and societies must believe in the "rightness" of liberalism. Acceptance of the gospel of liberalism, and maintaining the vigor of this gospel in communities that have already accepted it, is in the final analysis an internal matter within each individual and each society. It happens—or fails to happen—not because a hegemon wills it, but because of organic developments within human consciousness and societal operations, developments that render liberalism's assumptions plausible and give evidence that its norms will yield the benefits claimed.

Building a new world order is thus truly a millennial task, one that exceeds even America's enormous power. A liberal world free from tyranny and terror may—and hopefully will—come, but it will not come soon, nor will it come as an act of American will. Governance based on consent rather than on force, amity between peoples, and the rule of reason and law cannot be meaningfully imposed or long sustained at gunpoint.

This is not an idealistic or naive call for pacifism. In the violent, imperfect world that exists today, America may need to act—indeed, even to use violence—to protect from harm its own people and others who depend on it. This regrettable need to employ power for self-defense should not, though, be confused with a divine calling to do with power what cannot be done with power. Power's ability to change behavior is well documented. No tyrant, terrorist, or torturer doubts it. Power's ability to change beliefs, though, is far more limited, more indirect, and operates more slowly.

Certainly America's own record ought to give its leaders reason to doubt the efficacy of American power in creating liberal societies. America's experience has not been one to give cause for much optimism. Admittedly, the seriousness of the effort has waxed and waned, and American interest in building liberal institutions has always been uncomfortably entangled with a pursuit of profits, but the history of American intervention in the Caribbean basin over the last century is instructive. The magnitude of American power—economic, military, and political—defies adjectives. And yet, despite the overwhelming American presence and despite repeated interventions, with how much certainty and confidence is the term *liberal* even today applied to states and societies such as Guatemala, Honduras, and Haiti? What should give pause is not simply that American power has been greater in the Caribbean basin than it is likely ever to be in the Middle East, central Asia, or Africa and that America has had a century to inculcate liberalism. America has also better understood the Caribbean basin than it understands the faraway nations it now proposes to bring into the liberal fold, has had the capacity to co-opt effectively the national elites, and has been dealing with societies already profoundly exposed to the liberal tradition. What reason is there to suspect that America will do better in Afghanistan than it has in Haiti?

The two often-touted examples of American success—Germany and Japan—are of course the exceptions that prove the rule. Unfortunately for the Bush administration, the rule is that liberalism develops organically within a society, not that it can be imposed from outside or above. Both Germany and Japan had developed functioning liberal political systems in the 1920s. These succumbed to fascism and militarism in the 1930s, but the American task in the 1940s and 1950s was to restore, not to create, liberalism.

Ultimately, however, the problem with the Bush administration's grand strategy is not simply that we are further from the millennium than we would like to believe, and that our power to bring it about is less than we would hope. The problem is that the strategy that the administration has embraced for achieving the millennium is fundamentally wrong.

Crusading efforts, like the Bush administration's, aimed at imposing liberalism are likely to lead to failure and tragedy for four reasons. In the first place, they misunderstand the nature of liberalism and therefore misdiagnose what most threatens it. Second, efforts to impose liberalism from above or outside in and of themselves undermine or even destroy the international community that is the fruit of liberalism. A liberal hegemon that imposes its will on others through force of arms sacrifices its own legitimacy and undercuts the legitimacy of the liberal order it has sought to advance. Third, however noble the objective for which it is undertaken, an imperial mission threatens the liberal democracy of a republic that chooses to pursue this path. Fourth, the imperial pursuit of a liberal world order presumes a moral clarity that is in fact lacking.

Liberalism's Real War

Ultimately, the Bush administration's understanding of liberalism and of humanity's troubled love affair with it is profoundly flawed. This leads to an underestimation of the difficulties of living the liberal life and to a misunderstanding of what most threatens liberal societies.

The Bush administration refuses to acknowledge the possibility that individuals who are free to choose may not choose what we believe is best for them—or indeed what, by some sort of objective measure (if such a thing is conceivable), is in fact best for them. The phrasing used by the president in the "National Security Strategy" is revealing: we will use our strength, he says, to create "conditions in which all nations and all societies *can choose for themselves the rewards and challenges of political and economic liberty.*" They are free to choose, but only to choose liberalism. There is, in fact, no choice here whatsoever. By denying the possibility that tastes (or even nutritional needs) in political order may vary across societies—or seasons, or ages of life—American policy-makers blind themselves to the possibility that a menu that offers global diners a single choice dictates, not liberates. Though the implicit comparison is not entirely fair (for liberalism surely will not yield the enormity of human suffering and degradation produced by so many totalitarian systems), this is a ballot from which all the inferior candidates have already been removed. For the Bush administration, however, there is no logical inconsistency between freedom and the requirement that the liberal alternative be selected, since it is inconceivable that anyone, given an opportunity to choose freely, would choose any other option.

In this view, the only obstacles to a liberal world—a world of maximal human liberty, of rule by law, of mutually beneficial cooperation between individuals and societies, and of peace—are those imposed by anachronistic political institutions, by exploitative, self-serving tyrants, and by a handful of deluded, violent individuals. Remove these—that is, remove the tyranny of kings (President Woodrow Wilson's achievement in his war to make the world safe for democracy), remove the tyranny of totalitarian states (the great accomplishment of World War II and the Cold War), remove the tyranny of kleptocratic or brutal dictators (the first of America's challenges in today's world), and remove criminal and terroristic elements in political life (the second of today's challenges)—and liberal values and institutions will inevitably triumph. Freed from the chains of tyrants and from the fear of terrorists, the triumph of the human (that is, liberal) will is assured.

This view does not entertain the possibility that the human heart is divided, that the human eye suffers from myopia, or that the human mind is capable of passion and irrationality. This view does not allow the possibility that, even while loving freedom, humans may be motivated by other desires as well—some as healthy as the desire for food and comfort and to guarantee as absolutely as possible the well-being of loved ones or kin, some as dark as a desire to dominate or to savor the pain of others. It does not acknowledge that humans sometimes sacrifice the long-run good for short-term gratification, that they sometimes fail to see that observing the Golden Rule in the short run is (usually) beneficial in the end. It does not admit the possibility that humans can be moved by anger, vengeance, or pique, and that they are susceptible to demagoguery.

In other words, it fails to recognize that the obstacle to the spread of liberalism and (perhaps more immediately worrisome to Americans and our friends who share a commitment to liberal democracy) the threat to liberal values and liberal institutions where they already exist lie within us as well as outside of us. It is not simply illiberal institutions and illiberal individuals that threaten freedom, peace, and cooperation. What endangers liberalism is also the weakness or incompleteness of our own liberal faith and, consequently, our own capacity to adopt illiberal institutions and behavioral patterns.

Liberalism may indeed be the best way to organize our lives, societies, and polities. There are, however, a lot of deluded individuals, societies, and political actors today—as there have always been in the past. One does not have to look to the Muslim world, to the failed states and kleptocracies spotting the map of sub-Saharan Africa, to Confucian societies, to the world's largest democracy, India, or to certain post-Communist states like Serbia to find doubts about liberalism. Even in societies where liberal values and institutions are deeply entrenched one finds challenges. In Western Europe there exist right-wing populist political parties that, while arguably still within the liberal tradition, embrace platforms whose strident nationalism (and in some cases, racism, anti-Semitism, anti-Islamism, and xenophobia) balances their commitment to liberalism. The power of fascism and communism may have been broken, but for the alienated their allure remains.

Indeed, even in America there have always been voices arguing against liberal institutions and liberal values, voices suggesting either that these values are undesirable or that in some times and under some circumstances they need to be sacrificed or limited in order to achieve other equally important values. These voices have sometimes been influential. The United States lived with slavery for its first three generations. It denied women the right to vote until well into the twentieth century. It was home to the Ku Klux Klan. It restricted civil rights for a century after the Civil War. It long accepted racially or ethnically based immigration restrictions. It tolerated McCarthyism. Such a list is not meant as an indictment of America. It is meant only to remind us that even a polity based on Jefferson's stirring Declaration of Independence and incorporating the Bill of Rights in its fundamental constitution is capable of illiberal thought and action.

This warning of the danger that lies within our own selves and within our own society in no way denies that there is a threat to peace and freedom from foreign tyrants and terrorists. It does, however, underscore that tyrants and terrorists are not the *only* threat to liberalism. While quantifying such things is impossible, one might even be tempted to argue that tyrants and terrorists represent by far the smaller threat. For a superpower like the United States, surely there are reasons to suspect that external threats generated by the world's weak and dispossessed will pose less of a challenge than the internal ones posed by an unchecked growth of governmental power, by the breakdown of the family and other vital societal institutions, by alienation from the land and from production, or by racism, sexism, and xenophobia. These *internal* dangers to our liberal democracy are the ones that are most likely to prove fatal to our freedom and to our way of life. Yes, some sort of protection against external threats is necessary—whether this is accomplished through preventive war, reactive war, passive defenses, deterrence, negotiation, or appeasement. But to focus solely on external dangers (and opportunities) is to run the risk of losing the real war. Given human nature, the struggle to build and maintain liberalism at home is a never-ending one.

The Costs, Abroad and at Home

The problem with the grand strategy embraced by the Bush administration, however, is not simply that it focuses exclusively on only one (and probably the lesser) of the threats to liberalism. The problem is that, even in terms of the threat it has identified, the strategy is self-defeating. The strategy is aimed at creating international peace and individual freedom. In fact, it jeopardizes both.

The effort to create a global, liberal empire is already bringing us into conflict with our friends around the world—with those who share the very values that we seek to advance and spread. This is hardly surprising. The growing fissure between the United States and its allies is, in fact, what most realists would predict. As realists observe, there is a tendency for power to balance power. Efforts to create an empire—any sort of empire—are expected to encourage counterveiling power. The harder a sovereign fights to expand its dominion and influence, the larger and stronger will be the coalition that forms against it. The pursuit of empire thus tends to be self-defeating.

Ironically, however, America's crusade to build a global *liberal* empire may be particularly self-defeating. Every appeal to power, every military success, every tyrant overthrown by outside overt or covert force, every terrorist killed and every terrorist lair destroyed, is simultaneously a blow against the enemies of liberalism and a blow against the liberal norms that are being advanced or defended. It may have been necessary to bomb Afghanistan, funnel decisive aid to the rebels fighting the central government, intervene on a massive scale in the nation's political, economic, and social life, and rearrange the nation's domestic politics to ensure the Taliban is kept from power. It may, in the end, have been the course of wisdom to invade Iraq and, at American gunpoint, install a new and hopefully different government. In each case, analysts can balance and policy-makers debate the costs and benefits. Perhaps the benefits outweigh the costs. But it should be clear that the costs are real.

In the end, for the liberal order to be secure and stable, freedom and peace must rest on widespread acknowledgment of the rule of law, rather than the rule of power. A liberal order depends on general acceptance that governance needs to rest on consent, not imposition. Every act of violence, every government or law imposed from outside or without consent from above, is a violation of the norms of liberalism, and each violation weakens the liberal edifice that is being constructed.

The harm is twofold. In the first place, it undercuts efforts to transform illiberal regimes and societies into liberal ones. To preach the right of nations to determine their own destinies and to rule themselves free from arbitrary authority and, at the same time, to dictate these nations' choice of political constitution, government, and domestic policies is, at a minimum, to risk the charge of hypocrisy. There may be reasons why the possession of weapons of mass destruction by Iraq or North Korea is, in the end, unacceptable and why the United States and its liberal allies need to destroy these arsenals and, perhaps, to overthrow the regimes that threatened to build them. But no one should be surprised if one of the lessons drawn from this is that, in the end, the strong do what they will and the weak submit as they must—hardly a lesson that provides a good foundation for the spread of liberal values and institutions. In the second place, a political-military crusade to construct a liberal empire is likely to undermine existing liberal international institutions. Liberal institutions are being asked to act in ways that are fundamentally at odds with their own character and values. Again, it may on balance have been the course of wisdom to undertake a preventive war against Iraq. But surely it is unreasonable to expect NATO (or the larger community of liberal states) to embrace without dissent or extensive soul-searching what was an explicitly aggressive war with the goal of imposing a new government, against an opponent that, however morally repugnant, had not attacked us. These are the sorts of activities that liberalism opposes, not embraces, and that liberal institutions are designed to prevent, not facilitate.

It is thus hardly surprising that the Bush administration's crusade was widely criticized across the liberal world; that states like Germany, which for their own historical reasons are particularly sensitive to concerns about behaving in an illiberal fashion, were especially firm in opposition; and that liberal international institutions have bent only with reluctance to serve this crusade. Indeed, this reluctance to go a-crusading should be taken as a sign of the general health of liberal values and liberal institutions.

Unfortunately, this tension within the liberal world risks splitting it and weakening or destroying the institutions that have been so painstakingly developed over the last half century and longer. One cannot live or travel in Europe without being impressed not only by the breadth and depth of the disillusionment over American policy but by the rate at which the decay in Atlantic relations is accelerating. The American government's explicit willingness, expressed in both word and deed, to part company with liberal institutions, to ignore the international liberal consensus, and to act unilaterally serves to exacerbate this more fundamental problem. How long, given these trends, international liberal institutions will continue to function is unclear. One should not be overly pessimistic. Surely they will last for years, and perhaps for decades. Unlike the open-ended crusade against tyrants and terrorism, however, they do not have the potential to last forever. In the end, either the crusade or the institutions will probably have to be sacrificed.

The fraying and unraveling of the laboriously woven fabric of international institutions is only one of the prices the United States will have to pay for this crusade, though. The cost at home will be dearer still. Indeed, the real tragedy for America is likely to be that the pursuit of liberal imperium conflicts with its own *republican* values. A liberal democratic republic may pursue imperial dominance, but in gaining the whole world it loses its own soul.

The United States has found its previous forays into imperialism deeply divisive. In the past it has, wisely, drawn back, leaving scars that with time healed. Past forays, however, were generally limited in scope—for example, in the Philippines after the Spanish American War. After World War I, America rejected President Wilson's crusade. After World War II, the United States worked to rebuild liberal democracy where depression and war had overthrown it or cast it into doubt, but compromised and engaged with nonliberal forces across the wide reaches of the globe. But it is worth recalling that even the limited wars it did fight—in Korea and Vietnam—and the limited covert efforts it undertook were difficult for the republic to accommodate.

Grey Is a Color, Too

Finally, as a moral matter, the neat distinctions between good and evil that the Bush administration draws so facilely are, in the real world, impossible to make. In enunciating American foreign policy, the president speaks in terms of moral clarities and moral universalities, not of ambiguities, tensions, and tradeoffs. "Some worry," the president mused at West Point,

> that it is somehow undiplomatic or impolite to speak the language of right and wrong. I disagree. Moral truth is the same in every culture, in every time, and in every place. . . . There can be no neutrality between justice and cruelty, between the innocent and the guilty. We are in a conflict between good and evil, and America will call evil by its name. By confronting evil and lawless regimes, we do not create a problem, we reveal a problem.

We cannot, however, evade the need for careful moral judgment by declaring that tyrants and terrorism are, *per se,* bad: however true, this does not mean that all policies to rid the world of tyrants and terrorism are morally acceptable. Nor does it mean that an absence of democratic institutions or the threat of indiscriminate violence is in every case morally intolerable.

We can, for example, condemn, as the president did at West Point, the evil of killing or threatening to kill innocent civilians and still, as the United States did for forty or more years, base our security policy on a threat to kill hundreds of millions of innocent Russians, Chinese, and Eastern Europeans in retaliation for acts of aggression committed by their unaccountable, totalitarian governments. We can condemn Stalin as a brutal and ruthless dictator and still make common cause with him against Nazi Germany and decline to start World War III to free the Soviet Union from his grip.

Life (like foreign policy) is all about living with moral tensions and making troubling moral tradeoffs. It compels us, at times, to compromise with evil. In the first place, it compels us to compromise with evil because the violent act of destroying that evil in itself involves a covenant with evil. In our opposition to terrorists and tyrants we must bear in mind not only the harm our actions might do to the innocent but the danger that in this struggle against evil we become, in some small measure, precisely what we abhor. In the second place, diagnosing an evil does not necessarily mean we can or should then proceed to cut it away. As in surgery on the human body to remove a diseased tissue or organ, the treatment itself involves a violation of the body and trauma to healthy organs. However excellent the doctor's motives, the surgeon's blade, like a criminal's knife, cuts living tissue. At best it creates a wound that invites infection, and leaves scar tissue that may interfere with normal functioning. At worst the surgery may kill. Living with the diseased tissue, or pursuing medical—that is, nonsurgical—treatment that seeks to cure rather than excise the disease, may thus be preferable to surgery. Recognition of the existence of evil does not necessarily suggest the advisability or moral permissibility of action to destroy it.

Where does this leave a nation, like America, that is committed to liberal values and regards freedom as the natural birthright of all peoples? Sadly, there is no millennium at hand. There is no quick fix or single, easy answer. Freedom and peace are possible, but they are not achieved once and for all time, and they are not achieved through a crusade. They are achieved through the daily, often frustrating, and sometimes unrewarding process of compromise, negotiation, and self-restraint. War and violations of freedom are not tumors that can be surgically removed. They are recurring inflammations, the consequence of weaknesses inherent in human nature, that can at times be prevented through forethought and that can at other times be treated. A wise policy aims to strengthen the global body politic to reduce its susceptibility—and our own susceptibility—to these inflammations. But the process of human and societal development is neither rapid nor linear, and it resists efforts to rush it or force it in particular directions. Such an understanding does not condone evil or engage in some sort of confused moral relativism that equates repression with freedom or violence with peace; nor does it deny that violence at times must be countered with violence. It does, however, recognize that amity and peaceful relations between peoples cannot in the end be imposed at gunpoint, and that freedom imposed by imperial diktat is not freedom at all.

4.4 America's Crisis of Legitimacy

Robert Kagan

Within the "West"—that is, within the community of modern, liberal, democratic nations—there has been widening disagreement about how best to build a stable, peaceful world. This disagreement came to a head over the U.S. invasion of Iraq.

As Robert Kagan, a well-known commentator on Euro-American relations at the Carnegie Endowment for International Peace, notes, in Europe the dominant view has tended to be that the key to world peace lies in international institutions, international law, and a respect for national sovereignty. In America, the presumption has tended to be that the foundation for world peace is the existence of human rights and democracy. What is to be done when these two prescriptions conflict? Given America's enormous military power, many Europeans fear that the United States will attempt to act unilaterally, without seeking the legitimacy that might come from consultation with other nations or the approval of international institutions.

Clashing Views

"What kind of world order do we want?" asked Joschka Fischer, Germany's foreign minister, on the eve of the U.S. invasion of Iraq in March 2003. That this question remains on the minds of many Europeans today is a telling sign of the differences that separate the two sides of the Atlantic—because most Americans have not pondered the question of world order since the war.

They will have to. The great transatlantic debate over Iraq was rooted in deep disagreement over world order. . . .

Opinion polls taken before, during, and after the war show two peoples living on separate strategic and ideological planets. Whereas more than 80 percent of Americans believe that war can sometimes achieve justice, less than half of Europeans agree. Americans and Europeans disagree about the role of international law and international institutions and about the nebulous but critical question of what confers legitimacy on international action. These diverging world views predate the Iraq war and the presidency of George W. Bush, although both may have deepened and hardened the transatlantic rift into an enduring feature of the international landscape. . . .

. . . A great philosophical schism has opened within the West, and mutual antagonism threatens to debilitate both sides of the transatlantic community. At a time when new dangers and crises are proliferating rapidly, this schism could have serious consequences. For Europe and the United States to come apart strategically is bad enough. But what if their differences over world order infect the rest of what we have known as the liberal West? Will the West still be the West?

A few years ago, such questions were unthinkable. After the Cold War, the political theorist Francis Fukuyama assumed along with the rest of us that at the end of history the world's liberal democracies would live in relative harmony. Because they share liberal principles, these democracies would "have no grounds on which to contest each other's legitimacy." Conflicts might divide the West from the rest, but not the West itself. That reasonable assumption has now been thrown into doubt, for it is precisely the question of legitimacy that divides Americans and

Robert Kagan, "America's Crisis of Legitimacy," *Foreign Affairs*, March/April 2004, vol. 83, no. 1, pp. 65–67, 78–81. Reprinted with permission of the author.

Europeans today—not the legitimacy of each other's political institutions, perhaps, but the legitimacy of their respective visions of world order. More to the point, for the first time since World War II, a majority of Europeans has come to doubt the legitimacy of U.S. power and of U.S. global leadership. . . .

The problem is that the modern liberal vision of progress in international affairs has always been bifocal. On the one hand, liberalism has entertained since the Enlightenment a vision of world peace based on an ever-strengthening international legal system. The success of such a system rests on the recognition that all nations, big or small, democratic or tyrannical, humane or barbarous, are equal sovereign entities. As Hugo Grotius, Hans Morgenthau, and many others have asked over the centuries, how would international law survive if states could violate one another's sovereignty in the name of propagating democracy, human rights, or any other moral good?

On the other hand, modern liberalism cherishes the rights and liberties of the individual and defines progress as the greater protection of these rights and liberties across the globe. In the absence of a sudden global democratic and liberal transformation, that goal can be achieved only by compelling tyrannical or barbarous regimes to behave more humanely, sometimes through force. Looking back on Kosovo, the genocide in Rwanda, and other crises, UN Secretary-General Kofi Annan aptly framed the modern liberal's quandary. "On the one hand," he asked, "is it legitimate for a regional organization to use force without a UN mandate? On the other, is it permissible to let gross and systematic violations of human rights, with grave humanitarian consequences, continue unchecked?"

Given the tension between these two aspirations, what constitutes international legitimacy will inevitably be a matter of dispute within the liberal world. Immanuel Kant's vision of "perpetual peace" solved the problem in theory, by presuming that all the nations of his imagined international system would be free, liberal republics. But the UN Charter enshrined the "sovereign equality of all its members," even though, in practice, the nature of their governments varies wildly. The present international legal structure, in other words, does not—and arguably cannot—conform to liberalism's goal of ameliorating the human condition by securing individual rights for all.

This is a problem for all modern liberals. But it is a particularly difficult one for Europeans. Having moved beyond the Westphalian order into a postmodern, supranational order, Europe is the Kantian miracle. Ironically, however, although many Europeans now claim to define international legitimacy as strict obedience to the UN Charter and the Security Council, the union they have created transcends the UN's exclusive focus on national sovereignty. As a confederation of free states that subject themselves to interference with their sovereignty, the EU better fulfills the vision of Kant than that of Grotius. The postmodern European order rests on an entirely different political and moral foundation than the one on which the UN was erected.

At the time of the Kosovo war, Blair argued that Europe must fight "for a new internationalism where the brutal repression of ethnic groups will not be tolerated [and] for a world where those responsible for crimes will have nowhere to hide." If this is the "new internationalism," then the "old internationalism" of the UN

Charter is dead. Europeans may have to choose which version of liberal internationalism they really intend to pursue. Whether they do so or not, however, they must at least recognize that the two paths diverge.

For Americans, the choice is likely to be less difficult: the United States is, and always has been, less divided on this question than Europeans are today. By nature, tradition, and ideology, the United States has generally favored the promotion of liberal principles over the niceties of Westphalian diplomacy. Despite its role in helping to create the UN and draft the UN Charter, the United States has never fully accepted the organization's legitimacy or the charter's doctrine of sovereign equality. Although fiercely protective of its own autonomy, the United States has been less concerned about the inviolability of the sovereignty of others. It has reserved for itself the right to intervene anywhere and everywhere. And although it is as capable of self-serving hypocrisy as other nations, the United States has generally justified its interventions in the name of defending the cause of liberalism.

In this sense, the United States is and always has been a revolutionary power, a sometimes unwitting—but nevertheless persistent—disturber of the status quo, wherever its influence grows. From its founding generation onward, the United States has looked at foreign tyrannies as transient and destined to be toppled by the forces of republicanism that its own revolution unleashed. Americans consider hostile tyrannies as fair targets and even allied dictatorships as inherently illegitimate. If most Americans have been oblivious to their own nation's revolutionary impact on the world, the rest of the world has not. In the early nineteenth century, European conservatives such as Klemens von Metternich feared that the American Revolution and the French upheaval it helped spark would ripple outward and fatally engulf their societies. Today, it is the conservative forces of extremism in the Muslim world—the militant fundamentalists—who fear U.S. influence and seek to repel it. And for Europeans, who are consumed with radical changes on their own continent and seek a predictable future in the world beyond, the United States has once again become a dangerous member of the society of nations.

Farewell, Westphalia

In Europe's view, this danger is best encapsulated in the so-called Bush doctrine and in its commitment to confronting the global "axis of evil." Many Europeans and some Americans profess to be shocked that the United States would announce its intention to seek "regime change" in despotic governments, even at the expense of international law and the UN Charter. In light of U.S. history, especially of the previous half-century, however, nothing could be less shocking. The Bush doctrine, such as it is, has naturally sprung out of the United States' liberal revolutionary tradition. If the vision of securing the rights of all peoples risks running afoul of international legal traditions, it should come as no surprise that a liberal nation such as the United States would be even more inclined to set aside those constraints to defend its own soil and citizens against dictators with deadly arsenals.

The problem of legitimacy is a good deal more complex today because the emergence of a unipolar era coincided with two other historical developments: the proliferation of WMD and the rise of international terrorism, both of which seem more threatening to Americans than to Europeans. It is the Bush administration's response to these developments, including the doctrine of "preemption" ("prevention" would be a more accurate term), that has caused the greatest uproar. It has prompted many Europeans, and many others around the world, to call the United States' willingness to take preventive action a prime example of the superpower's disregard for international law and the international order—stark evidence of its new illegitimacy.

But a more compelling way to assess the Bush doctrine is to ask whether new international circumstances might not be forcing Americans, as well as Europeans and even the UN secretary-general, to reexamine traditional international legal principles and definitions of legitimacy. Even before the Bush administration publicly enunciated its policy of preventive war in 2002, a growing body of opinion in both the United States and Europe was arguing that preventive action might at times be necessary to meet new international threats, even if it violated state sovereignty, prohibitions against intervention, and other traditional legal norms. Thinkers as diverse as Michael Walzer and Henry Kissinger concluded that principles left over from Westphalia were inadequate to deal with today's challenges. Even Kofi Annan has suggested that UN members consider developing "criteria for an early authorization of coercive measures to address certain types of threats—for instance, terrorist groups armed with weapons of mass destruction."

Given this growing, if unrecognized, convergence of opinion, the real issue may not be whether prevention is ever justified but rather who may do the preventing and who decides when, where, and how it is handled. In this matter as in many others, Europe objects less to U.S. actions than to what it perceives to be their unilateral character. The dispute over preventive war is, in other words, little more than a restatement of America's unipolar predicament: how can the world's sole superpower be controlled?

 ## Religion and Democracy

4.5 Why God Is Winning

Timothy Samuel Shah and Monica Duffy Toft

While some scholars and politicians debate whether or not liberal democracy can or should be imposed on the world's sovereign states, others wonder whether democracy might not be self-limiting. In an article published in *Foreign Policy*, Timothy Samuel Shah and Monica Duffy Toft point out that democracy tends to empower religion—and while some religious groups might support democracy, others clearly do not. Whether the spread of democracy results in a world in which liberal values are more widely embraced is thus unclear. What seems clearer is that it will result in a world in which religion becomes politically more important.

After Hamas won a decisive victory in January's [2006] Palestinian elections, one of its supporters replaced the national flag that flew over parliament with its emerald-green banner heralding, "There is no God but God, and Muhammad is His Prophet." In Washington, few expected the religious party to take power. "I don't know anyone who wasn't caught off guard," said U.S. Secretary of State Condoleezza Rice. More surprises followed. Days after the Prophet's banner was unfurled in Ramallah, thousands of Muslims mounted a vigorous, sometimes violent, defense of the Prophet's honor in cities as far flung as Beirut, Jakarta, London, and New Delhi. Outraged by cartoons of Muhammad originally published in Denmark, Islamic groups, governments, and individuals staged demonstrations, boycotts, and embassy attacks.

On their own, these events appeared to be sudden eruptions of "Muslim rage." In fact, they were only the most recent outbreaks of a deep undercurrent that has been gathering force for decades and extends far beyond the Muslim world. Global politics is increasingly marked by what could be called "prophetic politics." Voices claiming transcendent authority are filling public spaces and winning key political contests. These movements come in very different forms and employ widely varying tools. But whether the field of battle is democratic elections or the more inchoate struggle for global public opinion, religious groups are increasingly competitive. In contest after contest, when people are given a choice between the sacred and the secular, faith prevails.

God is on a winning streak. It was reflected in the 1979 Iranian Revolution, the rise of the Taliban in Afghanistan, the Shia revival and religious strife in postwar Iraq, and Hamas's recent victory in Palestine. But not all the thunderbolts have been hurled by Allah. The struggle against apartheid in South Africa in the 1980s and early 1990s was strengthened by prominent Christian leaders such as Archbishop Desmond Tutu. Hindu nationalists in India stunned the international community when they unseated India's ruling party in 1998 and then tested nuclear weapons. American evangelicals continue to surprise the U.S. foreign-policy establishment with their activism and influence on issues such as religious freedom, sex trafficking, Sudan, and AIDS in Africa. Indeed, evangelicals have emerged as such a powerful force that religion was a stronger predictor of vote choice in the 2004 U.S. presidential election than was gender, age, or class.

The spread of democracy, far from checking the power of militant religious activists, will probably only enhance the reach of prophetic political movements, many of which will emerge from democratic processes more organized, more popular, and more legitimate than before—but quite possibly no less violent. Democracy is giving the world's peoples their voice, and they want to talk about God.

Divine Intervention

It did not always seem this way. In April 1966, *Time* ran a cover story that asked, "Is God Dead?" It was a fair question. Secularism dominated world politics in the mid-1960s. The conventional wisdom shared by many intellectual and political elites was that modernization would inevitably extinguish religion's vitality. But if 1966 was the zenith of secularism's self-confidence, the next year marked the beginning of the end of its global hegemony. In 1967, the leader of secular Arab nationalism, Gamal Abdel Nasser, suffered a humiliating defeat at the hands of the Israeli Army. By the end of the 1970s, Iran's Ayatollah Khomeini, avowedly "born-again" U.S. President Jimmy Carter, television evangelist Jerry Falwell, and Pope John Paul II were all walking the world stage. A decade later, rosary-wielding Solidarity members in Poland and Kalashnikov-toting mujahedin in Afghanistan helped defeat atheistic Soviet Communism. A dozen years later, 19 hijackers screaming "God is great" transformed world polities. Today, the secular pan-Arabism of Nasser has given way to the millenarian pan-Islamism of Iranian President Mahmoud Ahmadinejad, whose religious harangues against America and Israel resonate with millions of Muslims, Sunni and Shia alike. "We increasingly see that people around the world are flocking towards a main focal point—that is the Almighty God," Ahmadinejad declared in his recent letter to President Bush. . . .

God's comeback is in no small part due to the global expansion of freedom. Thanks to the "third wave" of democratization between the mid-1970s and early 1990s, as well as smaller waves of freedom since, people in dozens of countries have been empowered to shape their public lives in ways that were inconceivable in the 1950s and 1960s. A pattern emerged as they exercised their new political freedoms. In country after country, politically empowered groups began to challenge the secular constraints imposed by the first generation of modernizing, postindependence leaders. Often, as in communist countries, secular straitjackets had been imposed by sheer coercion; in other cases, as in Atatürk's Turkey, Nehru's India, and Nasser's Egypt, secularism retained legitimacy because elites considered it essential to national integration and modernization—and because of the sheer charisma of these countries' founding fathers. In Latin America, right-wing dictatorships, sometimes in cahoots with the Catholic Church, imposed restrictions that severely limited grassroots religious influences, particularly from "liberation theology" and Protestant "sects."

As politics liberalized in countries like India, Mexico, Nigeria, Turkey, and Indonesia in the late 1990s, religion's influence on political life increased dramatically. Even in the United States, evangelicals exercised a growing influence on the Republican Party in the 1980s and 1990s, partly because the presidential nomination process depended more on popular primaries and less on the decisions of traditional party leaders. Where political systems reflect people's values, they usually reflect people's strong religious beliefs.

Many observers are quick to dismiss religion's advance into the political sphere as the product of elites manipulating sacred symbols to mobilize the masses. In fact, the marriage of religion with politics is often welcomed, if not demanded, by people around the world. In a 2002 Pew Global Attitudes survey, 91 percent of

Nigerians and 76 percent of Bangladeshis surveyed agreed that religious leaders should be more involved in politics. A June 2004 six-nation survey reported that "most Arabs polled said that they wanted the clergy to play a bigger role in politics." In the same survey, majorities or pluralities in Morocco, Saudi Arabia, Jordan, and the United Arab Emirates cited Islam as their primary identity, trumping nationality. The collapse of the quasi-secular Baathist dictatorship in Iraq released religious and ethnic allegiances and has helped Islam play a dominant role in the country's political life, including in its recently adopted constitution. As right- and left-wing dictatorships have declined in Latin America and democratization has deepened, evangelicals have become an influential voting bloc in numerous countries, including Brazil, Guatemala, and Nicaragua.

The New Orthodoxies

Far from stamping out religion, modernization has spawned a new generation of savvy and technologically adept religious movements, including Evangelical Protestantism in America, "Hindutva" in India, Salafist and Wahhabi Islam in the Middle East, Pentecostalism in Africa and Latin America, and Opus Dei and the charismatic movement in the Catholic Church. The most dynamic religiosity today is not so much "old-time religion" as it is radical, modern, and conservative. Today's religious upsurge is less a return of religious orthodoxy than an explosion of "neo-orthodoxies."

A common denominator of these neo-orthodoxies is the deployment of sophisticated and politically capable organizations. These modern organizations effectively marshal specialized institutions as well as the latest technologies to recruit new members, strengthen connections with old ones, deliver social services, and press their agenda in the public sphere. The Vishwa Hindu Parishad, founded in 1964, "saffronized" large swaths of India through its religious and social activism and laid the groundwork for the Bharatiya Janata Party's electoral successes in the 1990s. Similar groups in the Islamic world include the Muslim Brotherhood in Egypt and Jordan, Hamas in the Palestinian territories, Hezbollah in Lebanon, and the Nahdlatul Ulama in Indonesia. In Brazil, Pentecostals have organized their own legislative caucus, representing 10 percent of congresspeople. Religious communities are also developing remarkable transnational capabilities, appealing to foreign governments and international bodies deemed sympathetic to their cause.

Today's neo-orthodoxies may effectively use the tools of the modern world, but how compatible are they with modern democracy? Religious radicals, after all, can quickly short-circuit democracy by winning power and then excluding nonbelievers. Just as dangerous, politicized religion can spark civil conflict. Since 2000, 43 percent of civil wars have been religious (only a quarter were religiously inspired in the 1940s and 50s). Extreme religious ideology is, of course, a leading motivation for most transnational terrorist attacks.

The scorecard isn't all negative, however. Religion has mobilized millions of people to oppose authoritarian regimes, inaugurate democratic transitions, support human rights, and relieve human suffering. In the 20th century, religious movements helped end colonial rule and usher in democracy in Latin America, Eastern Europe, sub-Saharan Africa, and Asia. The post-Vatican II Catholic Church played a crucial role by opposing authoritarian regimes and legitimating the democratic aspirations of the masses.

Today's religious movements, however, may not have as much success in promoting sustainable freedom. Catholicism's highly centralized and organized character made it an effective competitor with the state, and its institutional tradition helped it adapt to democratic politics. Islam and Pentecostalism, by contrast, are not centralized under a single leadership or doctrine that can respond coherently to fast-moving social or political events. Local religious authorities are often tempted to radicalize in order to compensate for their weakness vis-à-vis the state or to challenge more established figures. The trajectory of the young cleric Moqtada al-Sadr in postwar Iraq is not unusual. The lack of a higher authority for religious elites might explain why most religious civil wars since 1940—34 of 42—have involved Islam, with 9 of these being Muslim versus Muslim. We need to look no further than Iraq today to see religious authorities successfully challenging the forces of secularism—but also violently competing with each other. Even in a longstanding democracy like India, the political trajectory of Hindu nationalism has demonstrated that democratic institutions do not necessarily moderate these instincts: where radical Hindu nationalists have had the right mix of opportunities and incentives, they have used religious violence to win elections, most dramatically in the state of Gujarat.

The belief that outbreaks of politicized religion are temporary detours on the road to secularization was plausible in 1976, 1986, or even 1996. Today, the argument is untenable. As a framework for explaining and predicting the course of global politics, secularism is increasingly unsound. God is winning in global politics. And modernization, democratization, and globalization have only made him stronger.

4.6 Islamists Suffer as Freedom
Slips Down the Mideast Agenda

Heba Saleh

Nowhere is the complex relationship between democracy and religion more evident than in the Middle East. Even while the United States has used military force to try to bring democracy to Iraq, continued American support of authoritarian regimes—support extended at least in part because of the assistance provided by these regimes to America's "war against terror"—has aligned the United States against democratic movements and religious ones. *Financial Times* reporter Heba Saleh discusses the cross-cutting tensions among democracy, religion, and authoritarian governance.

I n a chilling account of his torture in a Cairo detention facility, Abu Omar, an Egyptian cleric, describes how he was interrogated while naked, blindfolded and hanging upside down by his feet.

"I am recording my testimony from inside my grave," he writes in prison at the beginning of an account that goes on to detail beatings, electric shocks and sexual assault.

Abu Omar was released a few months ago after almost four years in detention. He is currently at the centre of a court case in Italy where prosecutors allege he was snatched from a street in Milan by CIA and Italian security agents, then flown to Egypt to be tortured under the U.S. extraordinary renditions programme.

Four years after U.S. President George W. Bush launched an initiative promising a "forward strategy of freedom" to bring democracy to the Middle East, human rights activists say the war against terror and practices such as extraordinary rendition have underlined the shallowness of America's commitment to democracy and human rights in the Arab world.

Egypt is the most visible manifestation of his dilemma. Despite repeated promises of a democratic transformation, Egyptian authorities have launched yet another crackdown on the Muslim Brotherhood, the largest opposition force in the country. The government has also pushed through constitutional amendments that human rights defenders say mark an alarming regression in civil liberties. The U.S. still voices concern about human rights in Egypt but more privately than in recent years. This message, moreover, is confused and undermined by its own record, including on renditions.

"The U.S. and weak European allies have chosen at this moment in time [to support] repressive, stable, pro-western governments instead of the threat of the unknown—that is, the Islamists having political power," says Sarah Leah Whitson, Middle East director of the U.S.-based Human Rights Watch.

The failure of democratic reforms in Iraq to quell the mounting sectarian violence there, as well as the election of a Hamas-dominated parliament by the Palestinians, appear further to have eroded what remained of Washington's willingness to press for political reforms in countries where Islamists are certain to be main beneficiaries.

Hopes for improvement in democratic rights have been dashed across the region: there is no talk of new elections in Saudi Arabia, which held its first limited nationwide poll in 2005, for example, and some reformers who have demanded constitutional changes have faced renewed pressure.

In Syria, the regime has been cracking down hard, with the courts delivering long jail terms to some dissidents and human rights activists. In Jordan, meanwhile, the government has been accused by Human Rights Watch of breaking its promise to revise restrictive new press laws.

But it is the experience of Egypt, the Arab world's most populous country and once a trendsetter in the region, that activists both inside and outside the country find the most disappointing. "The impact in Egypt has been shocking. With the

U.S. backing down, Cairo thinks it has a license to clamp down on the Muslim Brotherhood," says Ms. Whitson.

Since late last year the government has arrested hundreds of supporters of the Muslim Brotherhood, which has widespread grassroots support despite being illegal. Some 40 members, including senior leaders, have been referred for military trial, in a move criticized by both local and international human rights groups.

Officials charge that the Brotherhood is a danger to democracy and to the cohesion of a society with a sizeable Christian minority. But in elections in 2005 the group outperformed all legal opposition parties: affiliated candidates running as independents won one-fifth of the seats in parliament.

Despite the Brotherhood's electoral success, and its leaders' insistence that they are committed to peaceful politics, the government has maintained its longstanding policy of containing them through periodic arrests.

During elections, such as those for the upper chamber of parliament in June, polling stations are often barred to Brotherhood supporters or even surrounded by riot police and closed.

"I think the government's policy towards the Brotherhood will continue especially after the [Palestinian Islamist group] Hamas takeover of Gaza," says Hafez Abu Saada, head of the Egyptian Organisation for Human Rights. "Gaza has convinced the authorities here that they are doing the right thing and it has also helped convince the west of the Egyptian government's view. There will be more repression, but it will be easier because they won't have to justify it."

Already Egypt has adopted controversial constitutional amendments aimed at blocking further electoral advances by the Islamists. Human rights groups have loudly opposed one particular change intended to pave the way for a new anti-terrorism law that would allow the suspension of key constitutional guarantees of basic rights. The U.S. has criticized the law, but in notably muted fashion.

The authorities contend the changes are necessary in the face of deadly attacks by Islamic militants. They say the new law will be used only in terrorism cases and under judicial supervision. But human rights activists are sceptical.

"This law will be a disaster," says Mr. Abu Saada. "All they would have to say is that they suspect someone of being a terrorist or of planning violence and that will allow all sorts of exceptional measures, giving the security services unlimited powers of arrest and detention." For him and other activists, the fear is that the law will be used to intimidate opposition supporters.

Suggested Discussion Topics

1. Is the triumph of liberal democracy inevitable? Do you think eventually the whole world will embrace democracy? Is fundamentalist Islamic opposition to "the West," manifested in events like the terrorist attack on the World Trade Center and Pentagon, simply the last gasp of another failed ideology, or is it a long-term clash of competing civilizations? Given the opportunity to make an informed choice, would all human beings everywhere choose liberal democracy?

2. Can liberal democracy be imposed from outside, or does it have to develop organically within each individual society? Where liberal democracy does not currently exist, why is this the case? Would removing the existing government and replacing it with one that is popularly elected solve the problem in these countries? What does your answer imply about the future of Iraq?

3. Which is more important in building a peaceful world: respecting sovereignty or ensuring democracy for people everywhere? Be prepared to take whichever side your teacher assigns you in a classroom debate.

4. Does the United States have a moral duty to spread democracy?

5. Azar Gat argues that the triumph of capitalism does not necessarily imply the triumph of liberal democracy and that we may see the emergence of authoritarian capitalist great powers. Do you think that it is possible for an authoritarian government—one that denies ordinary people a meaningful ability to vote, or that does not limit the power of the state to regulate the lives of its people, or that does not include checks and balances on executive power—can survive if the national economy is capitalist? Why or why not? Would authoritarian capitalist great powers be a threat to world peace or to a stable international order? More specifically, do you think the spread of capitalism in Russia and China will yield stable democracies there, and, if not, are you concerned about this?

6. If the triumph of democracy in the Middle East would bring fundamentalist Islamic governments to power, should the United States support democracy?

7. If America's allies in the Middle East oppose Islamic fundamentalists but use torture and terror and are authoritarian rather than democratic, should the United States continue to support these allies?

Chapter 5

FAILED STATES

Given the challenges posed by postmodern war, terrorism, and weapons of mass destruction, and the tensions and opportunities created by the global spread of the idea of democracy, one of the most disturbing trends in global politics today is the decay of political institutions responsible for providing order and safety. The most important of these institutions is the sovereign state itself, which since the seventeenth century has been regarded as the essential provider of security. Around the world today, the virtual collapse of a number of states and the threatened collapse of many others is happening before our eyes, captured by news cameras and reported nightly on television. These "failed states" are unable to provide basic services, like police protection, to their people or to prevent warring groups from fighting among themselves and terrorizing ordinary citizens. People in the territory of these failed states find themselves turning to other individuals or organizations for security and help: to tribal or clan leaders, to local warlords, or even to criminals. This trend, more than any other, reflects the increasing fragmentation of authority in global politics and the piecemeal weakening of traditional political institutions that characterizes today's world.

The collapse of states in today's turbulent global system has many causes. Some African and Asian states are relatively new entities, lacking deep historical roots or ties to the societies they rule and hindered by boundaries imposed by European powers during the colonial period. Those boundaries often left tribal and ethnic groups divided among several states and, in other cases, enclosed rival groups within a single state. With the retreat of European colonialism in the 1950s and 1960s, indigenous leaders tried to build their new states by encouraging nationalism and the development of national economies. With the advantage of hindsight, it is apparent that many of these leaders failed to eliminate older loyalties to clans, tribes, and ethnic groups or to pursue policies that would encourage economic growth. Indeed, throughout Africa, Asia, and the Middle East, governments often became the fiefs of particular tribal and ethnic groups whose control of the state apparatus enabled them to reward members of their group while discriminating against other tribal and ethnic groups. In other cases, state "kleptocracies" emerged, as control of the government was seen as an easy route to personal enrichment, and state bureaucracies were seen primarily as an instrument for shaking down both foreign and domestic businesspeople and making a tidy profit for ministers and bureaucrats. In yet other cases, commitment to "decolonization" or to a socialist ideology prevented the introduction of effective economic development policies that might have assisted national leaders in efforts to mold unified nations and build stable state institutions.

This failure to construct effective states or to create loyalties to the state that transcended or replaced tribal and ethnic loyalties was at least partially hidden during the Cold War, since leaders of these states could rely on outside help and support. During the Cold War, the superpowers sought to gain influence in the developing world by providing military and economic assistance to their "friends." Thus, the United States and the Soviet Union routinely aided leaders and governments they thought favored them in the East-West conflict, underwriting budgets and providing assistance that leaders could use to buy off or repress political opponents or to pursue policies that enriched their particular ethnic or tribal group at the expense of others. With the end of the Cold War, however, the United States and Russia largely lost interest in most poor countries and the flow of foreign aid dried up. Without this outside support, many states have suddenly found themselves vulnerable, lacking strong state institutions or loyalty from the people they governed.

This drying up of superpower support has come at a time when the consequences of decades of poor national governance have been increasingly felt. A potent combination of ethnic hatred manipulated by unscrupulous leaders, intense poverty, population growth, and environmental catastrophe has made a number of African and Asian states effectively ungovernable. Governments have found themselves unable to satisfy even their citizens' most fundamental needs. Indeed, during the 1980s and 1990s, many African states actually suffered a decline in living standards as measured by per capita gross national product, in some cases to below pre-independence levels. Those countries whose institutions of statehood have melted away and whose inhabitants now depend on outsiders for security and the essentials of survival are *failed states*.

One of these, Somalia, located on the Horn of East Africa, became the object of world attention in 1992 as its government vanished and as civil war and famine (the results of which were televised on CNN) engulfed the country. In November 1992 the United Nations authorized humanitarian intervention to restore order, protect relief agencies from the militias of rival clans, and provide humanitarian relief. The following month an international force led by U.S. Marines landed in Somalia to carry out that mission. Although the worst effects of starvation were brought to an end, the mission failed to reunite the country's one hundred clan groups. Following a firefight in the Somali capital of Mogadishu in which a number of American soldiers were killed and their bodies then dragged through the streets, the decision was taken to end the U.S. operation. The last American units pulled out of Somalia in March 1994, and the UN operation ended a year later.

Despite this lack of success in rebuilding a functioning national state, the collapse of state institutions in Somalia and elsewhere has made the world community less reluctant to intervene in domestic politics. There is growing recognition that the boundaries of these countries mean little and that civil strife threatens to spill across international borders and endanger the peace and security of other countries. Violence between ethnic Hutus and Tutsis in Rwanda, for example, spread into neighboring Zaire (now Congo) and helped destabilize the already fragile political order there, triggering a civil war in Congo (and military intervention by various neighbors) that still continues. At this point, putting Congo back together again seems to many outside observers a hopeless task. Recognizing the potential for disorder to spread, international organizations are gradually becoming more willing to inject themselves into such situations. In Cambodia, for instance, a large multinational effort under UN auspices was launched in 1991 to establish a functioning government for the country and prepare for national elections.

Although the breakdown of state institutions is most widespread in Africa—where these institutions were always weakest—even in Europe, the birthplace of the state system, some states have failed or are on the verge of doing so, especially in the Balkans. Bosnia, born in the breakdown of one state (Yugoslavia), was the scene of savage violence among Croatians, Serbs, and Muslims between 1992 and 1995. In neighboring Kosovo, where Serbs ruled a province that was 90 percent ethnic Albanian, violence exploded in 1998 and Serbian government military forces attempted to drive ethnic Albanians out, until Western forces under NATO forced the Serbian forces to withdraw. In Bosnia, "peace," based on de facto partition of the country between ethnic groups, has been maintained only by the presence of a substantial NATO force. Although a recognized state with a seat in the UN General Assembly, Bosnia remains hopelessly divided, and the fact of its sovereignty means little. Kosovo, too, is largely administered by international personnel.

The root problems leading to state failure are largely internal—for example, the absence of effective governmental institutions generally perceived by ordinary people to be legitimate, leaders more interested in looting the state or empowering or enriching their supporters than in the well-being of the general public, and deep divisions within the population along ethnic or religious lines. In some cases, however, external interventions have been the immediate catalyst for state failure. Iraq offers a useful example. The Iraqi state under Saddam Hussein was a bloody, tyrannical one, terrorizing its own people and behaving aggressively towards its neighbors. The removal of Saddam Hussein and the Ba'athist Party that supported him, however, caused the Iraqi state to crumble, leaving warring parties attempting to seize control or to gain autonomy or independence.

The survival of weaker states cannot be taken for granted in the face of enormous social, economic, and political pressures. Increasingly, ordinary individuals in many regions of the world may have to look elsewhere for security as states collapse or are taken over by criminal elements. Lest the picture being painted appear too bleak, however, it is important to recognize that the disintegration of state institutions is only part of the story: as we will note in the chapters that follow, at the same time that postmodern war, terrorism, weapons of mass destruction, and failed states are combining to make life dangerous and human security tenuous, new and newly revitalized political institutions are creating exciting possibilities for global cooperation and political integration.

5.1 Failed States in a World of Terror

Robert I. Rotberg

The first selection, by political scientist Robert I. Rotberg, defines and describes what is meant by "failed states." States, he argues, fail for different reasons, although poor governance and rapacious leaders seem common to them all. Such states are no longer able to provide citizens with essential military, social, or economic services. They can no longer maintain public order. Rotberg, however, does not see state failure as either inevitable or permanent, and he suggests a variety of ways both to prevent state failure and to overcome it after it takes place. All of these suggestions are costly and require ever greater international action.

The Road to Hell

In the wake of September 11, the threat of terrorism has given the problem of failed nation-states an immediacy and importance that transcends its previous humanitarian dimension. Since the early 1990s, wars in and among failed states have killed about eight million people, most of them civilians, and displaced another four million. The number of those impoverished, malnourished, and deprived of fundamental needs such as security, health care, and education has totaled in the hundreds of millions.

Although the phenomenon of state failure is not new, it has become much more relevant and worrying than ever before. In less interconnected eras, state weakness could be isolated and kept distant. Failure had fewer implications for peace and security. Now, these states pose dangers not only to themselves and their neighbors but also to peoples around the globe. Preventing states from failing, and resuscitating those that do fail, are thus strategic and moral imperatives.

But failed states are not homogeneous. The nature of state failure varies from place to place, sometimes dramatically. Failure and weakness can flow from a nation's geographical, physical, historical, and political circumstances, such as colonial errors and Cold War policy mistakes. More than structural or institutional weaknesses, human agency is also culpable, usually in a fatal way. Destructive decisions by individual leaders have almost always paved the way to state failure. President Mobutu Sese Seko's three-plus decades of kleptocratic rule sucked Zaire (now the Democratic Republic of Congo, or DRC) dry until he was deposed in 1997. In Sierra Leone, President Siaka Stevens (1967–85) systematically plundered his tiny country and instrumentalized disorder. President Mohamed Siad Barre (1969–91) did the same in Somalia. These rulers were personally greedy, but as predatory patrimonialists they also licensed and sponsored the avarice of others, thus preordaining the destruction of their states.

Rotberg, Robert, "Failed States in a World of Terror," *Foreign Affairs,* vol. 81, no. 4, July/August 2002, pp. 127–40. Reprinted by permission of Foreign Affairs. © 2002 by the Council on Foreign Relations, Inc. <www.Foreign Affairs.org>.

Today's failed states, such as Afghanistan, Sierra Leone, and Somalia, are incapable of projecting power and asserting authority within their own borders, leaving their territories governmentally empty. This outcome is troubling to world order, especially to an international system that demands—indeed, counts on—a state's capacity to govern its space. Failed states have come to be feared as "breeding grounds of instability, mass migration, and murder" (in the words of political scientist Stephen Walt), as well as reservoirs and exporters of terror. The existence of these kinds of countries, and the instability that they harbor, not only threatens the lives and livelihoods of their own peoples but endangers world peace.

Into the Abyss

The road to state failure is marked by several revealing signposts. On the economic side, living standards deteriorate rapidly as elites deliver financial rewards only to favored families, clans, or small groups. Foreign-exchange shortages provoke food and fuel scarcities and curtail government spending on essential services and political goods; accordingly, citizens see their medical, educational, and logistical entitlements melt away. Corruption flourishes as ruling cadres systematically skim the few resources available and stash their ill-gotten gains in hard-to-trace foreign bank accounts.

On the political side, leaders and their associates subvert prevailing democratic norms, coerce legislatures and bureaucracies into subservience, strangle judicial independence, block civil society, and gain control over security and defense forces. They usually patronize an ethnic group, clan, class, or kin. Other groups feel excluded or discriminated against, as was the case in Somalia and Sierra Leone in the 1970s and 1980s. Governments that once appeared to operate for the benefit of all the nation's citizens are perceived to have become partisan.

As these two paths converge, the state provides fewer and fewer services. Overall, ordinary citizens become poorer as their rulers become visibly wealthier. People feel preyed upon by the regime and its agents—often underpaid civil servants, police officers, and soldiers fending for themselves. Security, the most important political good, vanishes. Citizens, especially those who have known more prosperous and democratic times, increasingly feel that they exist solely to satisfy the power lust and financial greed of those in power. Meanwhile, corrupt despots drive grandly down city boulevards in motorcades, commandeer commercial aircraft for foreign excursions, and put their faces prominently on the local currency and on oversize photographs in public places. . . .

In the last phase of failure, the state's legitimacy crumbles. Lacking meaningful or realistic democratic means of redress, protesters take to the streets or mobilize along ethnic, religious, or linguistic lines. Because small arms and even more formidable weapons are cheap and easy to find, because historical grievances are readily remembered or manufactured, and because the spoils of separation, autonomy, or a total takeover are attractive, the potential for violent conflict grows exponentially as the state's power and legitimacy recede.

If preventive diplomacy, conflict resolution, or external intervention cannot arrest this process of disaffection and mutual antagonism, the state at risk can collapse completely (Somalia), break down and be sundered (Angola, the DRC, and Sudan), or plunge into civil war (Afghanistan and Liberia). The state may also lapse and then be restored to various degrees of health by the UN (Bosnia and Cambodia), a regional or subregional organization (Sierra Leone and Liberia), or a well-intentioned or hegemonic outside power (Syria in Lebanon, Russia in Tajikistan). A former colonial territory such as East Timor can be brought back to life by the efforts and cash infusions of a UN-run transitional administration.

Law and Order

State failute threatens global stability because national governments have become the primary building blocks of order. International security relies on states to protect against chaos at home and limit the cancerous spread of anarchy beyond their borders and throughout the world. States exist to deliver political (i.e., public) goods to their inhabitants. When they function as they ideally should, they mediate between the constraints and challenges of the international arena and the dynamic forces of their own internal economic, political, and social realities. . . .

States are not created equal. Their sizes and shapes, their human endowments, their capacity for delivering services, and their leadership capabilities vary enormously. More is required of the modern state, too, than ever before. Each is expected to provide good governance; to make its people secure, prosperous, healthy, and literate; and to instill a sense of national pride. States also exist to deliver political goods—i.e., services and benefits that the private sector is usually less able to provide. Foremost is the provision of national and individual security and public order. That promise includes security of property and inviolable contracts (both of which are grounded in an enforceable code of laws), an independent judiciary, and other methods of accountability. A second but vital political good is the provision, organization, and regulation of logistical and communications infrastructures. A nation without well-maintained arteries of commerce and information serves its citizens poorly. Finally, a state helps provide basic medical care and education, social services, a social safety net, regulation and supply of water and energy, and environmental protection. When governments refuse to or cannot provide such services to all of their citizens, failure looms.

But not all of the states that fit this general profile fail. Some rush to the brink of failure, totter at the abyss, remain fragile, but survive. Weakness is endemic in many developing nations—the halfway house between strength and failure. Some weak states, such as Chad and Kyrgyzstan (and even once-mighty Russia), exhibit several of the defining characteristics of failed states and yet do not fail. Others, such as Zimbabwe, may slide rapidly from comparative strength to the very edge of failure. A few, such as Sri Lanka and Colombia, may suffer from vicious, enduring civil wars without ever failing, while remaining weak and susceptible to failure. Some, such as Tajikistan, have retrieved themselves from possible collapse (sometimes with outside help) and remain shaky and vulnerable, but they no longer can be termed "failed." Thus it is important to ask what separates strong from weak states, and weak states from failed states. What defines the phenomenon of failure?

The Essence of Failure

Strong states control their territories and deliver a high order of political goods to their citizens. . . .

In contrast, failed states are tense, conflicted, and dangerous. They generally share the following characteristics: a rise in criminal and political violence; a loss of control over their borders; rising ethnic, religious, linguistic, and cultural hostilities; civil war; the use of terror against their own citizens; weak institutions; a deteriorated or insufficient infrastructure; an inability to collect taxes without undue coercion; high levels of corruption; a collapsed health system; rising levels of infant mortality and declining life expectancy; the end of regular schooling opportunities; declining levels of GDP per capita; escalating inflation; a widespread preference for non-national currencies; and basic food shortages, leading to starvation.

Failed states also face rising attacks on their fundamental legitimacy. As a state's capacity weakens and its rulers work exclusively for themselves, key interest groups show less and less loyalty to the state. The people's sense of political community vanishes and citizens feel disenfranchised and marginalized. The social contract that binds citizens and central structures is forfeit. Perhaps already divided by sectional differences and animosity, citizens transfer their allegiances to communal warlords. Domestic anarchy sets in. The rise of terrorist groups becomes more likely. . . .

Total Collapse

Truly collapsed states, a rare and extreme version of a failed state, are typified by an absence of authority. Indeed, a collapsed state is a shell of a polity. Somalia is the model of a collapsed state: a geographical expression only, with borders but with no effective way to exert authority within those borders. Substate actors have taken over. The central government has been divided up, replaced by a functioning, unrecognized state called Somaliland in the north and a less well defined, putative state called Punt in the northeast. In the rump of the old Somalia, a transitional national government has emerged thanks to outside support. But it has so far been unable to project its power even locally against the several warlords who control sections of Mogadishu and large swaths of the countryside. Private entrepreneurialism has displaced the central provision of political goods. Yet life somehow continues, even under conditions of unhealthy, dangerous chaos.

An example of a once-collapsed state is Lebanon, which had disintegrated before Syria's intervention in 1990 provided security and gave a sense of governmental legitimacy to the shell of the state. Lebanon today qualifies as a weak, rather than failed, polity because its government is credible, civil war is absent, and political goods are being provided in significant quantities and quality. Syria provides the security blanket, denies fractious warlords the freedom to aggrandize themselves, and mandates that the usually antagonistic Muslim and Christian communities cooperate. The fear of being attacked preemptively by rivals, or of losing control of critical resources, is alleviated by Syria's imposed hegemony. Within that framework of security, the Lebanese people's traditional entrepreneurial spirit has transformed a failed state into a much stronger one.

The Art of Prevention

Experience suggests that the prevention of state failure depends almost entirely on a scarce commodity: international political will. In part, prevention relies on outsiders' recognizing early that a state's internal turmoil has the potential to be fatally destructive. That recognition should be accompanied by subregional, regional, and UN overtures, followed, if required, by private remonstrations—that is, quiet diplomacy. If such entreaties have little effect, there will be a need for public criticism by donor countries, international agencies, the UN, and regional groupings such as the European Union (EU) or the Association of Southeast Asian Nations. These entities should also cease economic assistance, impose "smart sanctions," ban international travel by miscreant leaders, and freeze their overseas accounts. . . . Furthermore, misbehaving nations should be suspended from international organizations. In retrospect, if the international community had more effectively shunned Siad Barre, Mobutu, Idi Amin of Uganda, or Sani Abacha of Nigeria, it might have helped to minimize the destruction of their states. Ostracizing such strongmen and publicly criticizing their rogue states would also reduce the necessity for any subsequent UN peacekeeping and relief missions. . . .

Getting Nation Building Right

If . . . preventive diplomacy, targeted financial assistance, and other methods of stanching failure prove unsuccessful and a weak state actually fails, earnest efforts at reconstruction are required. . . .

The examples of Tajikistan and Lebanon suggest that failed states can be helped to recover. Even the seemingly hopeless cases, such as Somalia, are not irredeemable. Likewise, the accomplishments of the UN transitional administrations in Cambodia and East Timor, as well as the NATO-UN interim administration in Kosovo, indicate that nation building is possible if there is sufficient political will and targeted external assistance.

In each of the last three cases mentioned above, an international interim administration provided security and developed a rudimentary local police force, patiently trained local administrators across departments, reintroduced legal codes and methods, and helped to rejuvenate and regularize existing economies. The transitional government eventually registered voters and sponsored internationally guaranteed expressions of political choice through the ballot box, thus leading all three countries out of a state of tutelage toward home rule and independence. But in each instance the interim government has been anxious to do its job and leave. Short-term fixes and quick reconstruction efforts were imperative for those who funded the interim administrations. Yet sustainable nation building demands more than a quick fix. It requires a long-term commitment by outsiders to building capacities, strengthening security, and developing human resources. The uncomfortable but necessary lesson of these partially effective attempts is that the revival of failed states will prove more successful if a regional or international organization takes charge and only very gradually relinquishes authority to an indigenous transitional administration. . . .

When a state fails or collapses, it destroys trust and mutilates its institutions. That is why sustained state rebuilding requires time and enduring economic and technical commitments. Rich nations must promise not to abandon state rebuilding before the tough work is finished—before a failed state has functioned well for several years and has had its political, economic, and social health restored. The worst enemy of reconstruction is a premature exit by donors, international agencies, and countries backing reconstruction initiatives. Today's Haiti and Somalia reflect such untimely exit strategies.

5.2 Africa's Revolutionary Deficit

Jeremy M. Weinstein

In many cases, the connection between civil war and state failure is clear. The problem, Stanford professor Jeremy Weinstein observes, is that the cost of starting a war and trying to seize control of the state is so low and the potential gains from looting the national economy are so high. To prevent failed states, the international community needs to make rebellion more costly or difficult to finance.

Somalia is once again on the front page—and the news isn't pretty. Since 2003, the country's seaside capital of Mogadishu has served as an arena for a battle of gladiators, pitting U.S.-backed warlords against gun-toting Islamic revolutionaries. With no capable or legitimate state to counter it, the Union of Islamic Courts emerged victorious last June, only to be felled in December by an enfeebled transitional government, formed in exile and backed by the Ethiopian military. A recent spate of assassination-style killings and suicide bombings herald the arrival of a new resistance movement intent on ejecting these foreign forces and the African Union troops now being dispatched to the country. Caught in the midst of this violent morass is Somalia's long-suffering population of 8.5 million, seeking order from whomever can provide it, simply hoping that the bully who comes out on top will care enough to reverse the country's economic collapse.

Somalia may be garnering headlines today, but the country's strife parallels the bloodshed in far too many of Africa's struggling nations. Violence has engulfed 27 of the 46 counties in sub-Saharan Africa since independence, and the revolutionary movements that emerged to wage these wars of "liberation" and "transformation" have rarely behaved better than the regimes they sought to uproot. In Sierra Leone, the Revolutionary United Front publicly challenged decades of corrupt leadership as it hacked its way through the countryside, killing and maiming thousands of civilians in its quest for control of the nation's diamond mines. After the fall of Mobutu Sese Seko in the Democratic Republic of the Congo in 1997, a patchwork of competing militias and warlords ruled the vast eastern provinces, promising clean government and a return to democracy, while looting homes and raping women at will. In the past 10 years, the story has been no different in Angola, the Central African Republic, Chad, Congo, and Liberia: rebels trampling on civilian populations in their quest to capture the capital.

Why have Africa's civil wars so rarely produced revolutionary movements that fight for the political and economic changes that the population deserves? The answer is as simple as the violence is troubling. In much of Africa, the barriers to entry for rebel movements are simply too low. With states often incapable of projecting power outside of cities and insurgents easily able to finance their own private armies, just about anyone can hoist a flag, arm recruits, and launch a revolution. Building a rebel army should be difficult, in principle, because young people must risk their lives for highly uncertain returns. But in many parts of Africa, initiating a rebellion may be easier than starting a business.

Unlike early nation-states in Europe, where rulers depended on citizens for taxes and built strong states to protect them in return, Africa's state-building process has often gone awry. Seldom do rebel leaders turn to civilians for the resources needed to field private armies. War is becoming cheaper, and the means to wage it flow from illicit trafficking in natural resources, contributions from foreign capitals, or networks of expats—not from the voluntary contributions of those who most need political change. Legitimacy, too, depends not on popular support but simply on achieving control of the capital city, from where access to a seat at the United Nations provides all the protections of sovereignty. With such a system in place, is it really any surprise that civilian populations have been largely ignored by Africa's revolutionaries?

The great irony is that in a part of the world where civil war is endemic, Africa faces a dispiriting shortage of true revolutionaries—members of movements committed to replacing decades of misrule with effective, transparent governance. Only in places where armies have been mobilized with the most meager resources have we witnessed the birth of insurgencies that protect and advocate for the poor. But in countries rich in natural resources, where elites loot the treasury rather than provide public goods for ordinary people, civilians have been cursed with abusive insurgencies. These are environments in which an opportunistic form of rebellion is most attractive—where the barriers to organizing an army are low, the pickings are good, and constructive revolutionary movements tend to be crowded out by criminals.

War must be made more expensive in Africa. That means redoubling efforts to choke the sources of financial support that prop up rebel armies. Stemming the trade in illicit resources is an important first step, but insurgent movements draw heavily on financing provided by neighboring governments. Just as governments were pressured by international nongovernmental organizations to clamp down on the trade in blood diamonds and other illegally traded resources, cross-border support for rebel groups must be unearthed, publicized, and penalized. Civil-society organizations have a role to play, but ultimately governments, acting through the U.N. Security Council, must make external alliances with rebels more costly. Diaspora financing, too, given its origins in rich countries, can be stopped at its source. And the proliferation of small arms and light weapons—technologies that diminish the costs of raising an army—requires urgent international attention. Rich countries continue to be among the most substantial producers and distributors of small arms; they should also demonstrate a clear commitment to stronger export and border controls and more aggressive efforts to dismantle trafficking networks, perhaps in the form of an international arms trade treaty.

Part of the challenge is that sovereignty accrues to whomever mobilizes the guns and men required to take a capital. But sovereignty, with all of its benefits, should be conditional. Putting it into practice, however, means abandoning decades of U.N. impartiality and recognizing that rebel movements, like governments, wear different stripes. A seat at the table should be a privilege, and it should be reserved for those who earn it.

5.3 The Coming Anarchy

Robert D. Kaplan

Robert Kaplan, in the next selection, provides a vivid description of the causes and consequences of state failure today. The author describes how government has become nonexistent in much of West Africa and why he thinks that what is happening in that region may be a harbinger of what may occur elsewhere. Kaplan explains how a number of trends, including rapid urbanization, overpopulation, disease, misrule, poverty, and ethnic hate, have converged to produce a breakdown of civil order and why, as a result, conventional political maps that divide the world into exclusive territorial states are deceptive. The boundaries these maps show are at best irrelevant to the real problems and real lives of people who live there; increasingly, these boundaries are simply fictions. Kaplan believes that the trends he discusses illustrate the decline of the nation-state and augur a future of ungovernable and virtually independent megacities. Not even the United States, Kaplan claims, will be immune from these trends, as the ties that hold the American "nation" together decay and as new loyalties to smaller or larger communities increase in importance.

The Minister's eyes were like egg yolks, an aftereffect of some of the many illnesses, malaria especially, endemic in his country. There was also an irrefutable sadness in his eyes. He spoke in a slow and creaking voice, the voice of hope about to expire. Flame trees, coconut palms, and a ballpoint-blue Atlantic composed the background. None of it seemed beautiful, though. "In forty-five years I have never seen things so bad. We did not manage ourselves well after the British departed. But what we have now is something worse—the revenge of the poor, of the social failures, of the people least able to bring up children in a modern society." Then he referred to the recent coup in the West African country Sierra Leone. "The boys who took power in Sierra Leone come from houses like this." The Minister jabbed his finger at a corrugated metal shack teeming with children. "In three months these boys confiscated all the official Mercedes, Volvos, and BMWs and willfully wrecked them on the road." The Minister mentioned one of the coup's leaders, Solomon Anthony Joseph Musa, who shot the people who had paid for his schooling, "in order to erase the humiliation and mitigate the power his middle-class sponsors held over him."

Tyranny is nothing new in Sierra Leone or in the rest of West Africa. But it is now part and parcel of an increasing lawlessness that is far more significant than any coup, rebel incursion, or episodic experiment in democracy. Crime was what my friend—a top-ranking African official whose life would be threatened were I to identify him more precisely—really wanted to talk about. Crime is what makes West Africa a natural point of departure for my report on what the political character of our planet is likely to be in the twenty-first century.

The cities of West Africa at night are some of the unsafest places in the world. Streets are unlit; the police often lack gasoline for their vehicles; armed burglars, carjackers, and muggers proliferate. "The government in Sierra Leone has no writ after dark," says a foreign resident, shrugging. When I was in the capital, Freetown, last September, eight men armed with AK-47s broke into the house of an American man. They tied him up and stole everything of value. Forget Miami: direct flights between the United States and the Murtala Muhammed Airport, in neighboring Nigeria's largest city, Lagos, have been suspended by order of the U.S. Secretary of Transportation because of the ineffective security at the terminal and its environs. A State Department report cited the airport for "extortion by law-enforcement and immigration officials." This is one of the few times that the U.S. government has embargoed a foreign airport for reasons that are linked purely to crime. In Abidjan, effectively the capital of the Côte d'Ivoire, or Ivory Coast, restaurants have stick- and gun-wielding guards who walk you the fifteen feet or so between your car and the entrance, giving you an eerie taste of what American cities might be like in the future. An Italian ambassador was killed by gunfire when robbers invaded an Abidjan restaurant. The family of the Nigerian ambassador was tied up and robbed at gunpoint in the ambassador's residence. After university students in the Ivory Coast caught bandits who had been plaguing their dorms, they executed them by hanging tires around their necks and setting the tires on fire. In one instance Ivorian policemen stood by and watched the "necklacings," afraid to intervene. Each time I went to the Abidjan bus terminal, groups of young men with restless, scanning eyes surrounded my taxi, putting their hands all over the windows, demanding "tips" for carrying my luggage even though I had only a rucksack. In cities in six West African countries I saw similar young men everywhere—hordes of them. They were like loose molecules in a very unstable social fluid, a fluid that was clearly on the verge of igniting.

"You see," my friend the Minister told me, "in the villages of Africa it is perfectly natural to feed at any table and lodge in any hut. But in the cities this communal existence no longer holds. You must pay for lodging and be invited for food. When young men find out that their relations cannot put them up, they become lost. They join other migrants and slip gradually into the criminal process.". . .

Finally my friend the Minister mentioned polygamy. Designed for a pastoral way of life, polygamy continues to thrive in sub-Saharan Africa even though it is increasingly uncommon in Arab North Africa. Most youths I met on the road in West Africa told me that they were from "extended" families, with a mother in one place and a father in another. Translated to an urban environment, loose family structures are largely responsible for the world's highest birth rates and the explosion of the HIV virus on the continent. Like the communalism and animism, they provide a weak shield against the corrosive social effects of life in cities. In those cities African culture is being redefined while desertification and deforestation—also tied to overpopulation—drive more and more African peasants out of the countryside.

A Premonition of the Future

West Africa is becoming *the* symbol of worldwide demographic, environmental, and societal stress, in which criminal anarchy emerges as the real "strategic" danger. Disease, overpopulation, unprovoked crime, scarcity of resources, refugee migrations, the increasing erosion of nation-states and international borders, and the empowerment of private armies, security firms, and international drug cartels are now most tellingly demonstrated through a West African prism. West Africa provides an appropriate introduction to the issues, often extremely unpleasant to discuss, that will soon confront our civilization. To remap the political earth the way it will be a few decades hence—as I intend to do in this article—I find I must begin with West Africa.

There is no other place on the planet where political maps are so deceptive—where, in fact, they tell such lies—as in West Africa. Start with Sierra Leone. According to the map, it is a nation-state of defined borders, with a government in control of its territory. In truth the Sierra Leonian government, run by a twenty-seven-year-old army captain, Valentine Strasser, controls Freetown by day and by day also controls part of the rural interior. In the government's territory the national army is an unruly rabble threatening drivers and passengers at most checkpoints. In the other part of the country units of two separate armies from the war in Liberia have taken up residence, as has an army of Sierra Leonian rebels. The government force fighting the rebels is full of renegade commanders who have aligned themselves with disaffected village chiefs. A pre-modern formlessness governs the battlefield, evoking the wars in medieval Europe prior to the 1648 Peace of Westphalia, which ushered in the era of organized nation-states.

As a consequence, roughly 400,000 Sierra Leonians are internally displaced, 280,000 more have fled to neighboring Guinea, and another 100,000 have fled to Liberia, even as 400,000 Liberians have fled to Sierra Leone. The third largest city in Sierra Leone, Gondama, is a displaced-persons camp. With an additional 600,000 Liberians in Guinea and 250,000 in the Ivory Coast, the borders dividing these four countries have become largely meaningless. Even in quiet zones none of the governments except the Ivory Coast's maintains the schools, bridges, roads, and police forces in a manner necessary for functional sovereignty. The Koranko ethnic group in northeastern Sierra Leone does all its trading in Guinea, Sierra Leonian diamonds are more likely to be sold in Liberia than in Freetown. In the eastern provinces of Sierra Leone you can buy Liberian beer but not the local brand.

In Sierra Leone, as in Guinea, as in the Ivory Coast, as in Ghana, most of the primary rain forest and the secondary bush is being destroyed at an alarming rate. I saw convoys of trucks bearing majestic hardwood trunks to coastal ports. When Sierra Leone achieved its independence, in 1961, as much as 60 percent of the country was primary rain forest. Now 6 percent is. In the Ivory Coast the proportion has fallen from 38 percent to 8 percent. The deforestation has led to soil erosion, which has led to more flooding and more mosquitoes. Virtually everyone in the West African interior has some form of malaria.

Sierra Leone is a microcosm of what is occurring, albeit in a more tempered and gradual manner, throughout West Africa and much of the underdeveloped world: the withering away of central governments, the rise of tribal and regional domains, the unchecked spread of disease, and the growing pervasiveness of war. West Africa is reverting to the Africa of the Victorian atlas. It consists now of a series of coastal trading posts, such as Freetown and Conakry, and an interior that, owing to violence, volatility, and disease, is again becoming, as Graham Greene once observed, "blank" and "unexplored." However, whereas Greene's vision implies a certain romance, as in the somnolent and charmingly seedy Freetown of his celebrated novel *The Heart of the Matter*, it is Thomas Malthus, the philosopher of demographic doomsday, who is now the prophet of West Africa's future. And West Africa's future, eventually, will also be that of most of the rest of the world.

Consider "Chicago." I refer not to Chicago, Illinois, but to a slum district of Abidjan, which the young toughs in the area have named after the American city. ("Washington" is another poor section of Abidjan.) Although Sierra Leone is widely regarded as beyond salvage, the Ivory Coast has been considered an African success story, and Abidjan has been called "the Paris of West Africa." Success, however, was built on two artificial factors: the high price of cocoa, of which the Ivory Coast is the world's leading producer, and the talents of a French expatriate community, whose members have helped run the government and the private sector. The expanding cocoa economy made the Ivory Coast a magnet for migrant workers from all over West Africa: between a third and a half of the country's population is now non-Ivorian, and the figure could be as high as 75 percent in Abidjan. During the 1980s cocoa prices fell and the French began to leave. The skyscrapers of the Paris of West Africa are a façade. Perhaps 15 percent of Abidjan's population of three million people live in shantytowns like Chicago and Washington, and the vast majority live in places that are not much better. Not all of these places appear on any of the readily available maps. This is another indication of how political maps are the products of tired conventional wisdom and, in the Ivory Coast's case, of an elite that will ultimately be forced to relinquish power.

Chicago, like more and more of Abidjan, is a slum in the bush: a checkerwork of corrugated zinc roofs and walls made of cardboard and black plastic wrap. It is located in a gully teeming with coconut palms and oil palms, and is ravaged by flooding. Few residents have easy access to electricity, a sewage system, or a clean water supply. The crumbly red laterite earth crawls with foot-long lizards both inside and outside the shacks. Children defecate in a stream filled with garbage and pigs, droning with malarial mosquitoes. In this stream women do the washing. Young unemployed men spend their time drinking beer, palm wine, and gin while gambling on pinball games constructed out of rotting wood and rusty nails. These are the same youths who rob houses in more prosperous Ivorian neighborhoods at night. One man I met, Damba Tesele, came to Chicago from Burkina Faso in 1963. A cook by profession, he has four wives and thirty-two children, not one of whom has made it to high school. He has seen his shanty community destroyed by municipal authorities seven times since coming to the area. Each time he and his neighbors rebuild. Chicago is the latest incarnation.

Fifty-five percent of the Ivory Coast's population is urban, and the proportion is expected to reach 62 percent by 2000. The yearly net population growth is 3.6 percent. This means that the Ivory Coast's 13.5 million people will become 39 million by 2025, when much of the population will consist of urbanized peasants like those of Chicago. But don't count on the Ivory Coast's still existing then. Chicago, which is more indicative of Africa's and the Third World's demographic present—and even more of the future—than any idyllic junglescape of women balancing earthen jugs on their heads, illustrates why the Ivory Coast, once a model of Third World success, is becoming a case study in Third World catastrophe.

President Félix Houphouët-Boigny, who died last December at the age of about ninety, left behind a weak cluster of political parties and a leaden bureaucracy that discourages foreign investment. Because the military is small and the non-Ivorian population large, there is neither an obvious force to maintain order nor a sense of nationhood that would lessen the need for such enforcement. The economy has been shrinking since the mid-1980s. Though the French are working assiduously to preserve stability, the Ivory Coast faces a possibility worse than a coup: an anarchic implosion of criminal violence—an urbanized version of what has already happened in Somalia. Or it may become an African Yugoslavia, but one without mini-states to replace the whole.

Because the demographic reality of West Africa is a countryside draining into dense slums by the coast, ultimately the region's rulers will come to reflect the values of these shanty-towns. There are signs of this already in Sierra Leone—and in Togo, where the dictator Etienne Eyadema, in power since 1967, was nearly toppled in 1991, not by democrats but by thousands of youths whom the London-based magazine *West Africa* described as "Soweto-like stone-throwing adolescents." Their behavior may herald a regime more brutal than Eyadema's repressive one.

The fragility of these West African "countries" impressed itself on me when I took a series of bush taxis along the Gulf of Guinea, from the Togolese capital of Lomé, across Ghana, to Abidjan. The 400-mile journey required two full days of driving, because of stops at two border crossings and an additional eleven customs stations, at each of which my fellow passengers had their bags searched. I had to change money twice and repeatedly fill in currency-declarations forms. I had to bribe a Togolese immigration official with the equivalent of eighteen dollars before he would agree to put an exit stamp on my passport. Nevertheless, smuggling across these borders is rampant. *The London Observer* has reported that in 1992 the equivalent of $856 million left West Africa for Europe in the form of "hot cash" assumed to be laundered drug money. International cartels have discovered the utility of weak, financially strapped West African regimes.

The more fictitious the actual sovereignty, the more severe border authorities seem to be in trying to prove otherwise. Getting visas for these states can be as hard as crossing their borders. The Washington embassies of Sierra Leone and Guinea—the two poorest nations on earth, according to a 1993 United Nations report on "human development"—asked for letters from my bank (in lieu of pre-paid round-trip tickets) and also personal references, in order to prove that I had sufficient means to sustain myself during my visits. I was reminded of my visa and currency hassles while traveling to the communist states of Eastern Europe, particularly East Germany and Czechoslovakia, before those states collapsed.

Ali A. Mazrui, the director of the Institute of Global Cultural Studies at the State University of New York at Binghamton, predicts that West Africa—indeed, the whole continent—is on the verge of large-scale border upheaval. Mazrui writes,

> In the 21st century France will be withdrawing from West Africa as she gets increasingly involved in the affairs [of Europe]. France's West Africa sphere of influence will be filled by Nigeria—a more natural hegemonic power. . . . It will be under those circumstances that Nigeria's own boundaries are likely to expand to incorporate the Republic of Niger (the Hausa link), the Republic of Benin (the Yoruba link) and conceivably Cameroon.

The future could be more tumultuous, and bloodier, than Mazrui dares to say. France *will* withdraw from former colonies like Benin, Togo, Niger, and the Ivory Coast, where it has been propping up local currencies. It will do so not only because its attention will be diverted to new challenges in Europe and Russia but also because younger French officials lack the older generation's emotional ties to the ex-colonies. However, even as Nigeria attempts to expand, it, too, is likely to split into several pieces. The State Department's Bureau of Intelligence and Research recently made the following points in an analysis of Nigeria:

> Prospects for a transition to civilian rule and democratization are slim. . . . The repressive apparatus of the state security service . . . will be difficult for any future civilian government to control. . . . The country is becoming increasingly ungovernable. . . . Ethnic and regional splits are deepening, a situation made worse by an increase in the number

of states from 19 to 30 and a doubling in the number of local governing authorities; religious cleavages are more serious; Muslim fundamentalism and evangelical Christian militancy are on the rise; and northern Muslim anxiety over southern [Christian] control of the economy is intense . . . the will to keep Nigeria together is now very weak.

Given that oil-rich Nigeria is a bellwether for the region—its population of roughly 90 million equals the populations of all the other West African states combined—it is apparent that Africa faces cataclysms that could make the Ethiopian and Somalian famines pale in comparison. This is especially so because Nigeria's population, including that of its largest city, Lagos, whose crime, pollution, and overcrowding make it the cliché par excellence of Third World urban dysfunction, is set to double during the next twenty-five years, while the country continues to deplete its natural resources.

Part of West Africa's quandary is that although its population belts are horizontal, with habitation densities increasing as one travels south away from the Sahara and toward the tropical abundance of the Atlantic littoral, the borders erected by European colonists are vertical, and therefore at cross-purposes with demography and topography. Satellite photos depict the same reality I experienced in the bush taxi: the Lomé-Abidjan coastal corridor—indeed, the entire stretch of coast from Abidjan eastward to Lagos—is one burgeoning megalopolis that by any rational economic and geographical standard should constitute a single sovereignty, rather than the five (the Ivory Coast, Ghana, Togo, Benin, and Nigeria) into which it is currently divided.

As many internal African borders begin to crumble, a more impenetrable boundary is being erected that threatens to isolate the continent as a whole: the wall of disease. Merely to visit West Africa in some degree of safety, I spent about $500 for a hepatitis B vaccination series and other disease prophylaxis. Africa may today be more dangerous in this regard than it was in 1862, before antibiotics, when the explorer Sir Richard Francis Burton described the health situation on the continent as "deadly, a Golgotha, a Jehannum." Of the approximately 12 million people worldwide whose blood is HIV-positive, 8 million are in Africa. In the capital of the Ivory Coast, whose modern road system only helps to spread the disease, 10 percent of the population is HIV-positive. And war and refugee movements help the virus break through to more-remote areas of Africa. Alan Greenberg, M.D., a representative of the Centers for Disease Control in Abidjan, explains that in Africa the HIV virus and tuberculosis are now "fast-forwarding each other." Of the approximately 4,000 newly diagnosed tuberculosis patients in Abidjan, 45 percent were also found to be HIV-positive. As African birth rates soar and slums proliferate, some experts worry that viral mutations and hybridizations might, just conceivably, result in a form of the AIDS virus that is easier to catch than the present strain.

It is malaria that is most responsible for the disease wall that threatens to separate Africa and other parts of the Third World from more-developed regions of the planet in the twenty-first century. Carried by mosquitoes, malaria, unlike AIDS, is easy to catch. Most people in sub-Saharan Africa have recurring bouts of the disease throughout their entire lives, and it is mutating into increasingly deadly forms. "The great gift of Malaria is utter apathy," wrote Sir Richard Burton, accurately portraying the situation in much of the Third World today. Visitors to malaria-afflicted parts of the planet are protected by a new drug, mefloquine, a side effect of which is vivid, even violent, dreams. But a strain of cerebral malaria resistant to mefloquine is now on the offensive. Consequently, defending oneself against malaria in Africa is becoming more and more like defending oneself against violent crime. You engage in "behavior modification": not going out at dusk, wearing mosquito repellent all the time.

And the cities keep growing. I got a general sense of the future while driving from the airport to downtown Conakry, the capital of Guinea. The forty-five-minute journey in heavy traffic was through one never-ending shanty-town: a nightmarish Dickensian spectacle to which Dickens himself would never have given credence. The corrugated metal shacks and scabrous walls were coated with black slime. Stores were built out of rusted shipping containers, junked cars, and jumbles of wire mesh. The streets were one long puddle of floating garbage. Mosquitoes and flies were everywhere. Children, many of whom had protruding bellies, seemed as numerous as ants. When the tide went out, dead rats and the skeletons of cars were exposed on the mucky beach. In twenty-eight years Guinea's populations will double if growth goes on at current rates. Hardwood logging continues at a madcap speed, and people flee the Guinean countryside for Conakry. It seemed to me that here, as elsewhere in Africa and the Third World, man is challenging nature far beyond its limits, and nature is now beginning to take its revenge.

Africa may be relevant to the future character of world politics as the Balkans were a hundred years ago, prior to the two Balkan wars and the First World War. Then the threat was the collapse of empires and the birth of nations based solely on tribe. Now the threat is more elemental: *nature unchecked.* Africa's immediate future could be very bad. The coming upheaval, in which foreign embassies are shut down, states collapse, and contact with the outside world takes place through dangerous, disease-ridden coastal trading posts, will loom large in the century we are entering. (Nine of twenty-one U.S. foreign-aid missions to be closed over the next three years are in Africa—a prologue to a consolidation of U.S. embassies themselves.) Precisely because much of Africa is set to go over the edge at a time when the Cold War has ended, when environmental and demographic stress in other parts of the globe is becoming critical, and when the post–First World War system of nation-states—not just in the Balkans but perhaps also in the Middle East—is about to be toppled, Africa suggests what war, borders, and ethnic politics will be like a few decades hence. . . .

The Lies of Mapmakers

. . . It is not only African shanty-towns that don't appear on urban maps. . . . Traveling with Eritrean guerrillas in what, according to the map, was northern Ethiopia, traveling in "northern Iraq" with Kurdish guerrillas, and staying in a hotel in the Caucasus controlled by a local mafia—to say nothing of my experiences in West Africa—led me to develop a healthy skepticism toward maps, which, I began to realize, created a conceptual barrier that prevents us from comprehending the political crack-up just beginning to occur worldwide.

Consider the map of the world, with its 190 or so countries, each signified by a bold and uniform color: this map, with which all of us have grown up, is generally an invention of modernism, specifically of European colonialism. Modernism, in the sense of which I speak, began with the rise of nation-states in Europe and was confirmed by the death of feudalism at the end of the Thirty Years' War—an event that was interposed between the Renaissance and the Enlightenment, which together gave birth to modern science. People were suddenly flush with an enthusiasm to categorize, to define. The map, based on scientific techniques of measurement, offered a way to classify new national organisms, making a jigsaw puzzle of neat pieces without transition zones between them. "Frontier" is itself a modern concept that didn't exist in the feudal mind. And as European nations carved out far-flung domains at the same time that print technology was making the reproduction of maps cheaper, cartography came into its own as a way of creating facts by ordering the way we look at the world.

In his book *Imagined Communities: Reflections on the Origin and Spread of Nationalism*, Benedict Anderson, of Cornell University, demonstrates that the map enabled colonialists to think about their holdings in terms of a "totalizing classificatory grid. . . . It was bounded, determinate, and therefore—in principle—countable." To the colonialist, country maps were the equivalent of an accountant's ledger books. Maps, Anderson explains, "shaped the grammar" that would make possible such questionable concepts as Iraq, Indonesia, Sierra Leone, and Nigeria. The state, recall, is a purely Western notion, one that until the twentieth century applied to countries covering only 3 percent of the earth's land area. Nor is the evidence compelling that the state, as a governing ideal, can be successfully transported to areas outside the industrialized world. . . .

Yet this inflexible, artificial reality staggers on, not only in the United Nations but in various geographic and travel publications (themselves by-products of an age of elite touring which colonialism made possible) that still report on and photograph the world according to "country.". . .

The Last Map

. . . The Indian subcontinent offers examples of what is happening. For different reasons, both India and Pakistan are increasingly dysfunctional. The argument over democracy in these places is less and less relevant to the larger issue of governability. In India's case the question arises, Is one unwieldy bureaucracy in New Delhi the best available mechanism for promoting the lives of 866 million people of diverse languages, religions, and ethnic groups? In 1950, when the Indian population was much less than half as large and nation-building idealism was still strong, the argument for democracy was more impressive than it is now. Given that in 2025 India's population could be close to 1.5 billion, that much of its economy rests on a shrinking natural-resource base, including dramatically declining water levels, and that communal violence and urbanization are spiraling upward, it is difficult to imagine that the Indian state will survive the next century. India's oft-trumpeted Green Revolution has been achieved by overworking its croplands and depleting its watershed.

Norman Myers, a British development consultant, worries that Indians have "been feeding themselves today by borrowing against their children's food sources."

Pakistan's problem is more basic still: like much of Africa, the country makes no geographic or demographic sense. It was founded as a homeland for the Muslims of the subcontinent, yet there are more subcontinental Muslims outside Pakistan than within it. Like Yugoslavia, Pakistan is a patchwork of ethnic groups, increasingly in violent conflict with one another. . . . Karachi is becoming a subcontinental version of Lagos. In eight visits to Pakistan, I have never gotten a sense of a cohesive national identity. With as much as 65 percent of its land dependent on intensive irrigation, with wide-scale deforestation, and with a yearly population growth of 2.7 percent (which ensures that the amount of cultivated land per rural inhabitant will plummet), Pakistan is becoming a more and more desperate place. As irrigation in the Indus River basin intensifies to serve two growing populations, Muslim-Hindu strife over falling water tables may be unavoidable. . . .

Rather than one bold line dividing the subcontinent into two parts, the future will likely see a lot of thinner lines and smaller parts, with the ethnic entities of Pakhtunistan and Punjab gradually replacing Pakistan in the space between the Central Asian plateau and the heart of the subcontinent. . . .

Indeed, it is not clear that the United States will survive the next century in exactly its present form. Because America is a multi-ethnic society, the nation-state has always been more fragile here than it is in more homogenous societies like Germany and Japan. James Kurth, in an article published in *The National Interest* in 1992, explains that whereas nation-state societies tend to be built around a mass-conscription army and a standardized public school system, "multicultural regimes" feature a high-tech, all-volunteer army (and, I would add, private schools that teach competing values), operating in a culture in which the international media and entertainment industry has more influence than the "national political class." In other words, a nation-state is a place where everyone has been educated along similar lines, where people take their cue from national leaders, and where everyone (every male, at least) has gone through the crucible of military service, making patriotism a simpler issue. Writing about his immigrant family in turn-of-the-century Chicago, Saul Bellow states, "The country took us over. It *was* a country then, not a collection of 'cultures.'"

During the Second World War and the decade following it, the United States reached its apogee as a classic nation-state. During the 1960s, as is now clear, America began a slow but unmistakable process of transformation. The signs hardly need belaboring: racial polarity, educational dysfunction, social fragmentation of many and various kinds. William Irwin Thompson, in *Passages About Earth: An Exploration of the New Planetary Culture*, writes, "The educational system that had worked on the Jews or the Irish could no longer work on the blacks; and when Jewish teachers in New York tried to take black children away from their parents exactly in the way they had been taken away from theirs, they were shocked to encounter a violent affirmation of negritude.". . .

. . . "Patriotism" will become increasingly regional as people in Alberta and Montana discover that they have far more in common with each other than they do with Ottawa or Washington, and Spanish-speakers in the Southwest discover a greater commonality with Mexico City. (*The Nine Nations of North America*, by Joel Garreau, a book about the continent's regionalization, is more relevant now than when it was published in 1981.) As Washington's influence wanes, and with it the traditional symbols of American patriotism, North Americans will take psychological refuge in their insulated communities and cultures.

Returning from West Africa last fall was an illuminating ordeal. After leaving Abidjan, my Air Afrique flight landed in Dakar, Senegal, where all passengers had to disembark in order to go through another security check, this one demanded by U.S. authorities before they would permit the flight to set out for New York. Once we were in New York, despite the midnight hour, immigration officials at Kennedy Airport held up disembarkation by conducting quick interrogations of the aircraft's passengers—this was in addition to all the normal immigration and customs procedures. It was apparent that drug smuggling, disease, and other factors had contributed to the toughest security procedures I have ever encountered when returning from overseas.

Then, for the first time in over a month, I spotted business people with attaché cases and laptop computers. When I had left New York for Abidjan, all the businesspeople were boarding planes for Seoul and Tokyo, which departed from gates near Air Afrique's. The only non-Africans off to West Africa had been relief workers in T-shirts and khakis. Although the borders within West Africa are increasingly unreal, those separating West Africa from the outside world are in various ways becoming more impenetrable.

But Afrocentrists are right in one respect: we ignore this dying region at our own risk. When the Berlin Wall was falling, in November of 1989, I happened to be in Kosovo, covering a riot between Serbs and Albanians. The future was in Kosovo, I told myself that night, not in Berlin. The same day that Yitzhak Rabin and Yasser Arafat clasped hands on the White House lawn, my Air Afrique plane was approaching Bamako, Mali, revealing corrugated-zinc shacks at the edge of an expanding desert. The real news wasn't at the White House, I realized. It was right below.

 # Haiti

5.4 UN Troops Fight Haiti's Gangs
One Battered Street at a Time

Marc Lacey

Haiti has represented a clear case of a failing state. While members of the elite and ineffective reformers have struggled to seize and hold political power (with the ultimate power to determine political outcomes effectively residing in Washington), ordinary people have become even more wretchedly poor, vast numbers have fled the country, and gangs (whether "government"-controlled, like the infamous Tontons Macoute, or controlled by local thugs) have ruled the streets. In this situation, efforts to rebuild the state and to impose its authority may require external help. Marc Lacey of the *New York Times* discusses efforts by the United Nations to try to bring order to Haiti.

For years, street gangs have run Haiti right alongside the politicians. With a disbanded army and a corrupted wreck of a police force, successive presidents have either used the gangs against political rivals or just bought them off.

Recently, something extraordinary has occurred. President René Préval decided to take on the gangs and set the 8,000 United Nations peacekeepers loose on them, a risky move that will determine the security of the country and the success of his young government.

"We're taking back Port-au-Prince centimeter by centimeter," said Lt. Col. Abdesslam Elamarti, a peacekeeper from Morocco. "We're pressing these gangs so the population can live in peace."

The offensive by the United Nations forces, who arrived here in 2004 after the ouster of President Jean-Bertrand Aristide, began in earnest in late December. One of the fiercest battles took place on the morning of Jan. 25 with a raid by hundreds of United Nations forces on a gang hide-out on the periphery of Cité Soleil, this sprawling seaside capital's largest and most notorious slum.

After a fierce firefight in which gang members fired thousands of shots, United Nations officials succeeded in taking over the hide-out, a former schoolhouse that gang members had once used to fire upon peacekeepers and to demand money from passing motorists. The United Nations said four gang members had been killed in the battle.

Other raids have followed, and though it is still too early to judge the operation, gang leaders seem to be on the run, and armored United Nations vehicles now rumble through the crowded streets of Cité Soleil.

[Some 700 United Nations peacekeepers raided strongholds in Cité Soleil before dawn on Friday trying to take control of abandoned buildings used by gang members. One person was killed and several others wounded, including two peacekeepers, United Nations officials said.

["There will be no tolerance for the kidnappings, harassment and terror carried out by criminal gangs," Major General Carlos Alberto dos Santos Cruz, the commander of the United Nations forces, said in a statement on Friday. "I will continue to cleanse these areas of the gangs who are robbing the Haitian people of their security."]

The biggest of the United Nations operations have been aimed at one of the most wanted and feared of all the gang leaders, an unlikely and unpredictable power broker in his 20s who goes simply by the name Evans. Evans and his groups have been linked to a rash of kidnappings in the capital, and lately his men have been locked in fierce battles with United Nations peacekeepers.

Within the confines of Cité Soleil, Evans's every whim is enforced with absolute authority. Deeply superstitious, he recently said he suspected cats of bringing him bad luck after one appeared during a raid by United Nations troops on one of his hide-outs, local residents and United Nations officials said.

So he issued an order that all cats were to be killed in his patch of the slum. His gunmen would be rounding them up and roasting them, he told the people. When one woman resisted, he or one of his men shot her, United Nations officials say.

Evans and the other leaders now hide in the maze of tin-roofed shanties that are home to some 300,000 of Haiti's urban poor. Meanwhile, the local population debates which is a more effective strategy for dealing with these young toughs, confronting or conversing with them.

Haiti, the poorest country in the Western Hemisphere, has a long tradition of politics mixed with thuggery. In the 1970s and '80s, François Duvalier and his son Jean-Claude employed the Tontons Macoute, dreaded paramilitary hoodlums.

Mr. Aristide was elected president in 1990 and again in 2000 with the support of the poor. Gang leaders, who act as de facto spokesmen for long-neglected slums, gained entry to the presidential palace and helped dole out jobs and other spoils to their men.

In his initial months in office, Mr. Préval, who had been Mr. Aristide's prime minister as well as president from 1996 to 2001, followed a similarly conciliatory tack. He negotiated with gang leaders, including Evans, inviting them at times to face-to-face meetings in the presidential palace, officials say.

But he has grown increasingly impatient with the gangs as they resisted surrendering their guns and continued wreaking havoc on Port-au-Prince.

The kidnapping spree at the end of last year was the last straw. As the country prepared for Christmas, street thugs began grabbing people off the street, taking them into the slums and demanding ransoms.

Then the kidnappers began singling out children. In one horrible episode, a teenage girl was killed and her eyes were gouged out. Then, a school bus of children was seized by gunmen, prompting many terrified parents to keep their children hidden at home.

Mr. Préval, who has support among Haiti's poor as well as its elite, found his coalition government under attack as well, with opposition politicians in the Senate and Chamber of Deputies denouncing him for allowing the violence. The president changed course, calling off negotiations with the gangsters and giving the United Nations the go ahead to go after them.

Some local resident say that the raids are stirring up the gangs and that innocent people are getting caught up in the cross-fire.

David Wimhurst, the spokesman for the United Nations mission, said that the peacekeepers were careful to single out only combatants and that gang members had themselves killed civilians and then blamed the United Nations.

Not everybody agrees that confrontation is the best way of calming the slums. "The gang men can change," insisted Meleus Jean, 45, a pastor who runs a tiny church in Cité Soleil and who was once almost hit by a stray bullet while delivering a Sunday morning sermon. "I talk to them and I think they are gang men because they have nothing else. Fighting them will not change them."

One of those who has been criticized in the past for dealings with gang members has been Wyclef Jean, the Haitian-American rapper formerly of the Fugees. "The problem is much bigger than the gang leaders," he said in a telephone interview from New York. "I'm not saying they are not part of the problem. When people are killing people, that's a problem. But we don't have enough conversation."

But United Nations officials say the time for talk is over.

"If one of them goes to Préval and says, 'I want to give up,' and waves a white handkerchief, that is fine," said Edmond Mulet, a Guatemalan diplomat in charge of the United Nations mission here. "That's the kind of conversation we want."

At the same time, nobody believes that arresting or killing the gang leaders will be enough to calm Port-au-Prince. The violence is linked, most say, to the dire poverty.

"The people didn't ask to be born here," said Christy Jackson, 42, headmaster of a school in Cité Soleil. "We didn't ask to live like this."

The United States government recently set aside $20 million to create jobs for young people in Cité Soleil once the violence is quelled. In Solino, a neighborhood where the gangsters were chased away, people are being paid to clean garbage from a clogged drainage ditch.

Mr. Jean, the singer, has numerous social projects under way, including a program to bring giant mobile movie screens to poor neighborhoods, which have no cinemas.

Mr. Mulet, of the United Nations, said he believed that the gang leaders were beyond rehabilitation. "They've been killing people, kidnapping people, torturing people, raping girls," he told reporters recently in Washington. "It is very difficult to re-insert into society someone like that. A psychiatric institution would be the best place to place them in the future—after we arrest them."

Even if the gangsters are all rounded up, the country's justice system is ill-equipped to handle them.

Justice is bought and sold in Haiti, with both police officers and judges routinely allowing bribes to determine guilt or innocence. Jails are packed with people awaiting trial, most languishing for years.

On top of that, more and more narcotics have begun flowing through Haiti to the United States, law enforcement officials say. It is Haiti's weakened state that is the big attraction to narcotics traffickers, officials say.

In a recent report on Haiti's woeful law enforcement apparatus, the International Crisis Group, a nonprofit group committed to preventing and resolving deadly conflicts, said that without urgent reform "the current escalation of organized violence and criminality may come to threaten the state itself."

As bullets fly, everyone is under threat. On stray shot pierced the outer wall of a hospital in Cité Soleil recently. "We don't know who shot it," said Marie Yves Noël, the chief nurse. The bullet continued on through the maternity unit and then broke the glass of a pediatrics ward. Nobody was hit.

Iraq

5.5 The 10th Circle

Terry McCarthy

In the following news story from the *Washington Post,* ABC News correspondent
Terry McCarthy discusses the hellish qualities of life in Baghdad after the collapse
of the Iraqi state. In this anarchy, everyday activities now involve rolling the dice of
life and death.

Abu Taha, a portly, smiling man with two young children, lives a couple
of blocks from our house in Baghdad. I arrived here to cover the war for
ABC News last July, and one of the few pleasures I have found is sitting
with him on his flat roof, where he keeps pigeons in a series of coops. In the
evening, as the sun glows orange on the buildings, he releases them, and they fly
wide spirals over the neighborhood, circling the dome of a mosque, ducking below
a brace of Black Hawk helicopters headed for the Green Zone, soaring up over the
Tigris River before returning for the handful of seeds that he throws down for them.
Nowhere else but here, Abu Taha says, does he feel at peace, putting out of his
mind the explosions, gunfire and rocket attacks that shake Baghdad. His birds fly
free over the deadly streets of this city, unhindered by checkpoints, traffic jams,
angry young men with guns and explosives. Only birds can go where they like in
Baghdad these days.

Two and a half weeks ago, two of my friends, Alaa Uldeen Aziz, a cameraman,
and Saif Laith Yousuf, his soundman, were heading home from our bureau. They
were stopped by two cars full of gunmen just 100 yards from Alaa's house, dragged
into the street and taken away. We later discovered they were shot dead. We do not
know whether they were killed because they worked for an American network,
because of their religion or because they happened to be in the wrong place at the
wrong time. Either way, they were innocent victims of the violence that is eating
away at this city's humanity: a father of two young girls who still don't understand
why Daddy isn't coming home, and a man whose fiancee used to call him every
hour on his cellphone to make sure he was okay.

We sat with both their families on a Friday afternoon in a safe area outside their
neighborhood, offering what condolences we could. I had to apologize; neither I
nor any of my colleagues would be able to attend the funerals, because their neighborhood isn't safe for us to enter. Both families understood and said they would

have told us not to come anyway. Left unspoken was the fact that in many parts of Baghdad, to have a foreigner visit your house could endanger everyone there.

Alaa's mother had wanted her son's final resting place next to his father's in a cemetery in central Baghdad. His cousins had to dissuade her: the area is ringed with snipers, and it is too dangerous to set foot in the graveyard now. She wailed at the cruelty of a city that will not even allow her to bury her son.

Danger is everywhere in Baghdad; life here is a continuous series of risk assessments. From the moment people wake up, they have to check whether it is safe to leave the house. Is there an unusual amount of gunfire? Have strangers been seen driving through the neighborhood? Is there something new to be afraid of?

Anything out of the ordinary is cause for fear. A friend who lives in southwest Baghdad says a man recently parked a car on the main street across from his apartment block, then ran away. He was spotted by a butcher, who summoned a U.S. patrol. The troops cordoned off the area and defused what turned out to be a massive bomb inside the suspicious car. The brave butcher was taking a risk either way. He could have had his store blown up, but now he risks a bullet from insurgents for informing the Americans about the car.

The next decision of the morning: is it safe to send the children to school? Have there been bombs on the school route recently? Do the streets feel secure? Any new fliers that insurgents or militias stuck to the walls of the neighborhood overnight? Most parents I talk to keep their children home at least two or three days a week as a precaution.

Then you have to think about yourself. is it safe to drive across the city to go to work? Would it be better to take one's own car or trust a taxi driver? This entails a surprisingly complex calculus. Taxis are more expensive, but the gas lines for private cars are long, and gas stations are frequent targets for bombers. Police at checkpoints tend to search private cars more than they do taxis. But Sunni taxi drivers will not go into Shiite areas, and Shiite taxi drivers will not enter Sunni areas. Sometimes crossing the city requires taking two taxis to get through the sectarian frontiers that have sprung up—unmarked, but known as a matter of life and death to everyone who uses the roads.

The third possibility is to travel by public bus, either the smaller Kias (Korean minibuses) or the larger Tatas (Indian buses). Both have been targeted by suicide bombers; these days, an attendant will normally frisk every male before he gets on board to make sure he is not hiding an explosive vest under his jacket.

Having evaluated all that, the average Baghdad resident is now ready to step outside his or her front door and start the day—in a city that has become hell on Earth. In Baghdad, as in Dante's "Inferno," you step from one circle of hell into another, each worse than the last. A friend who lives in the eastern Shiite slum of Sadr City was talking to a man who had lost a son in a recent bombing. "I am ashamed to talk about it," said the grieving father. "Why?" asked my friend, trying to console the man, assuming he felt his son's death was somehow his fault. The reply silenced him. "Because my neighbor just lost all five of his children in one car bombing."

Car bombs punctuate life here with percussive malevolence. They have become more frequent since the U.S. troop "surge" began three months ago. Loud enough to be heard across much of the city, they quickly throw up a characteristic plume of black smoke, which comes from the instant vaporization of the tires by the heat of the blast.

The bombers bring dread into such humdrum tasks as shopping. Markets were a favorite target for car bombers until Americans began stopping any vehicles driving into markets during shopping hours. Now the insurgents send suicide bombers on foot instead. Few men I know will allow their wives to go to the main markets anymore.

Baghdad also cannot take comfort in prayer. Sunni insurgents have been blowing up Shiite shrines, and Shiite militiamen have responded by attacking Sunnis leaving mosques. As religion has been hijacked by extremists, public prayer by the moderate has become an impossible indulgence; mosques and churches are now mostly empty.

The constant threat of violence has changed the city's face. Driving around Baghdad now is like navigating a video-game maze; to deter the bombers, 12-foot T-walls better suited to a high-security prison line the streets and the exteriors of many buildings. From the window of a moving car, all you see is a continuous band of gray concrete. The occasional breaks in the walls have crash barriers, tire spikes and men with guns crouching behind sandbags, often wearing black ski masks and sunglasses so they cannot be identified. These guards use mirrors on long handles to look under cars for bombs; they have dogs trained to sniff for explosives, even truck-sized X-ray machines that can examine the inside of a vehicle as it passes by. But still the bombers get through. The inverted T-shape of the walls is designed to funnel the blast of a bomb upward, reducing damage to the surrounding area.

Suggested Discussion Topics

1. What are failed states, and what are the main causes behind their failure? Why have the states created in the wake of European colonialism, like those in much of Africa, had difficulty consolidating their power and establishing effective authority over their territory? What can be done to help states that are failing and to prevent other states from experiencing this fate?
2. How do we know when a state has failed? What should we expect states to be able to do—what duties should we, as citizens of a state, expect the state to be able to perform? How would your life be different if the United States failed?
3. What alternatives are there to relying on states? Can other organizations or institutions carry out the duties that states are usually expected to fulfill?
4. To what extent are the superpowers responsible for the failure of states in the developing world, and how did the end of the Cold War affect these countries? What obligation does the global community have to save failed states or to help the people who live in a failed state? Do you think the Western powers have a duty to the people of Africa and Asia, where states have failed or may fail? Why or why not?

5. Robert Kaplan worries that Africa is the future: that the breakdown of states and the increasing irrelevance of borders will become a global phenomenon. Why does he think this is what our future holds? Do you find his argument convincing? Why or why not? To what extent has his prediction of a "coming anarchy" come true?

6. How have regimes sought to hide behind sovereignty, and to what extent should it protect states from external intervention? Does the global community have a right or a duty to intervene in a sovereign state when that state seems to be losing control over what happens within its boundaries or when the state becomes nothing more than a collection of thugs and gangsters? Why or why not? What criteria would you apply in making a decision to intervene?

7. In Haiti, United Nations troops are waging war against local gang leaders. What are the costs and benefits of this sort of international intervention? If the United Nations were to request it, should the United States send its army to help? Explain your thinking.

8. Terry McCarthy describes life in Baghdad. What would it take to end the violence in Baghdad and restore order? Is Iraq currently a failed state? If it is, what would it take to rebuild an Iraqi state? Who should be responsible for this rebuilding?

Chapter 6

SOLVING SHARED PROBLEMS: INTERGOVERNMENTAL ORGANIZATIONS

The litany of postmodern war, terrorism, fears of mass destruction, and failed states provides a bleak picture of global conflict and disintegration. However, this is only a partial picture. Today's turbulence does not simply involve violence, disintegration, and collapse: it also involves the creation of new patterns of cooperation and vibrant growth in political institutions. Although old ways of providing global order are failing, nations and individuals around the globe are discovering new ways to work together. New institutions, and the strengthening of old institutions, counter the effects of fragmentation and help individuals and states cope with issues that are beyond the competence of any one of them alone.

To a large degree, this movement toward enhanced cooperation reflects the changed global political agenda we discussed in Chapter 1. Old zero-sum issues, while still present, must increasingly compete for political attention with variable-sum issues—that is, with issues on which collaboration, while contentious, may be mutually beneficial. These new issues do not mean that conflict no longer exists; they only mean that as problems spill across borders, societies increasingly find themselves interdependent and discover that solutions to the problems they face require joint efforts. Although nations and groups may differ on how the costs of solving the problems they face should be divided, they are likely to recognize that solving these problems requires joint effort.

In this chapter and the next, we will look at some of the institutions and organizations that play an important role in bringing people and groups around the world together and helping them reach agreements to solve some of the non-zero-sum problems they face. In Chapter 7 we will focus on *transnational nongovernmental organizations*: organizations that allow ordinary people in different locations around the world to work together for some common aim, whether it is making profits or saving lives. In this chapter, we will concentrate on *intergovernmental organizations:* organizations consisting of the representatives of member *states*.

Intergovernmental institutions have been around for many years. However, their number increased dramatically in the twentieth century, from fewer than forty in 1909 to almost three hundred today. Most consist of member states from within the same geographic region, but the number of universal international organizations is also growing. Some intergovernmental organizations, such as the Organization of African Unity (OAU) and the Organization of American States (OAS), perform mainly political tasks, whereas others, such as the International Monetary Fund (IMF) and the North American Free Trade Agreement (NAFTA), are mainly economic in nature or, like the North Atlantic Treaty Organization (NATO), are principally military in their focus. A few, like the European Union (EU), have gradually expanded their scope to include a variety of problems, tasks, and activities.

 # The United Nations

6.1 International Organizations: Perspectives on Governance in the Twenty-First Century

Kelly-Kate S. Pease

The most important global international organization is the United Nations, which was founded in 1945 as the successor to the pre–World War II League of Nations. The major organs of the United Nations carry out both political and economic functions and address a variety of social and cultural tasks as well. The most important of these organs, especially in maintaining international peace and security, are the Security Council, which includes the world's major powers (the United States, Russia, China, Great Britain, and France) as permanent members, with the power to veto resolutions they oppose, and the General Assembly, which includes all UN members, each with a single vote. There are also a number of specialized agencies that are associated with the UN but act independently of it. Some have important economic roles, for example, the World Trade Organization (WTO), the International Monetary Fund (IMF), and the World Bank (sometimes more formally referred to as the International Bank for Reconstruction and Development, or IBRD). Others, like the World Health Organization (WHO) or the International Labor Organization (ILO), perform specialized tasks that keep the fabric of international society from unraveling.

During the Cold War, many possible UN activities were frustrated by the rivalry between the United States and the Soviet Union. The end of the Cold War witnessed a revival of UN peacekeeping activity. Cooperation between the United States and Russia allowed a UN–authorized U.S.–led coalition to reverse Iraq's annexation of Kuwait in 1991. In the euphoria that followed the war in the Persian Gulf, UN peacekeepers became involved in a variety of operations, the most important of which were in Angola, Cambodia, Central America, Haiti, Somalia, and Bosnia. By late 1995, the UN was supervising nearly 60,000 troops in sixteen operations. Not only was the UN embroiled in more operations than ever before, but some were far more complex than previous UN operations, involving humanitarian relief (Bosnia, Somalia, and Kurdish areas of Iraq), separating combatants and protecting civilians in civil wars (Croatia, Bosnia, and Somalia), and in a few instances actually running the country for a time (Cambodia and Haiti).

In this chapter's first selection, political scientist Kelly-Kate Pease discusses the organization of the United Nations and the very different perspectives about international organizations and their functions that Realists, Liberals, and Marxists bring to bear. As she explains, these competing theoretical traditions make very different assumptions about what international organizations like the United Nations are likely to be able to achieve, and what it is they are trying to achieve.

The idea of international organization has probably been around since the advent of the first governments. From the writings of ancient Greek philosophers, for example, we learn of military alliances and international trading agreements. And we know that the early Greek city-states Athens, Sparta, and Macedonia once employed a common currency, which required a high degree of international cooperation. Most contemporary scholars, however, point to the Congress of Vienna (1815-1822) as the earliest modern precedent to today's IGO. The Congress of Vienna, a multipurpose IGO, was created by the European great powers to reestablish order and stability on the continent after the Napoleonic Wars. The Congress of Vienna was a forum for international collaboration on European security and commerce. It also strengthened the Rhine River Commission (1804), a bilateral IGO between France and the German confederation. This Commission established navigation rules for the Rhine River and an adjudication board to prosecute individuals accused of violating those rules. Similar river commissions were subsequently created for the Danube and Elbe rivers in central and eastern Europe.

The next important IGO to emerge was the League of Nations (1919–1939), which was established after World War I. The League of Nations was the first twentieth-century multipurpose IGO to have universal membership. The League was organized around three bodies: the Council, the Assembly, and the Secretariat. The Council was the chief executive organ of the League. It consisted of the victors of World War I, together with any four lesser powers that they chose to invite. The Council was mainly responsible for addressing issues relating to international war and threats to international peace. In addition, according to the League's Charter, the Council could "deal at its meetings with any matter within the sphere of action of the League" (Article 4, Section 4). The Assembly functioned as a quasi-legislative body; it, too, was entitled to address any matter within the purview of the League. All members of the League of Nations belonged to the Assembly, and each member could have up to three representatives. The Secretariat served as the League bureaucracy, which was responsible for carrying out League policies and mandates.

In addition to the League's three principal organs, several autonomous and semi-autonomous organizations were established under the League Charter. The Permanent Court of International Justice and the International Labor Organization were created to help member states meet their obligations under the League Charter. Article 13 committed members to submit any matter unsolved by diplomacy to international arbitration or judicial settlement. The Permanent Court of International Justice was established to consider disputes that might arise regarding treaty interpretation or breaches of international obligations assumed under international law. The International Labor Organization (ILO) was created, in part, to help member states meet their social responsibilities. Article 23(a) stated that members of the League "will endeavor to secure and maintain fair and humane conditions of labor for men, women and children, both in their own countries and in all countries to which their commercial and industrial relations extend, and for that purpose will establish and maintain the necessary international organizations." The ILO, one of the few surviving League institutions, remains the central IGO responsible for setting and preserving international labor standards.

The League of Nations, although widely considered a failed experiment, was based on three important principles, which have since been incorporated by its successor, the United Nations. First, the League of Nations embraced the idea of collective security where international security is directly tied to the security of member states. Second, the League established as a norm the peaceful settlement of disputes through such nonviolent measures as mediation, negotiation, arbitration, and adjudication. Third, the League was founded to foster international cooperation in the economic and social realms. The ideals of the League were both novel and innovative. They were also heavily influenced by American values, as one of its principal architects was President Woodrow Wilson. Ultimately, however, the U.S. government chose not to join the organization—a decision that is widely considered to have compromised the League's effectiveness during the interwar period. The League was politically challenged by the Japan–China conflict in Manchuria (1931) and the Italy-Ethiopia conflict (1935). The outbreak of World War II spelled the demise of the League as a viable international organization. However, its legacy lives on.

The post–World War II era has witnessed a massive proliferation of IGOs, as well as other types of international organizations. . . .

The UN System

The UN system was created in 1945 following World War II. The founders of the United Nations sought to strengthen the idea of the multipurpose, universal IGO first envisioned by the League of Nations. The UN was designed to be the center of multilateral diplomacy in postwar world politics. Its central purpose is manifold: to maintain international peace and security; to develop friendly relations among nations; to address economic, social, cultural, and humanitarian problems; and to promote respect for universal human rights. The UN retains the age-old principle of the sovereign equality of all states; however, it also commits members to the non-use of force and the peaceful settlement of disputes.

The UN is a comprehensive IGO to which, effectively, any state can belong. The UN system is structured around six principal organs—the General Assembly, the Security Council, the International Court of Justice (ICJ), the Economic and Social Council (ECOSOC), the Secretariat, and the Trusteeship Council. These organs serve as an umbrella to other UN agencies and autonomous bodies. The six principal organs of the UN, together with its several agencies and autonomous organizations, comprise the UN family of IGOs; collectively, they address just about every conceivable global issue, including war, civil disorder, arms control, trade, development, the environment, and human rights. . . .

The UN is based on several complementary principles. First, the UN is founded on the principle of the sovereign equality of all members. This simply means that each state, at least in legal theory, retains the right to determine its own internal and external affairs. Second, UN members voluntarily accept responsibility to carry out certain international obligations upon joining the UN, one of which is the obligation to settle disputes peacefully. Thus, the third founding principle of the UN is the peaceful settlement of disputes. Fourth, member states agree not to threaten or use force in their international relations. Fifth, the UN is enjoined from intervening in the domestic jurisdiction of member states. . . .

The UN was conceived in the fires of World War II and born in its ashes. In 1944, from August through October, representatives of the "big three" (U.S., UK, and USSR) fleshed out the framework for the UN at the Dumbarton Oaks Conference. The UN's reason for being, its *raison d'être*, is identified in Article 1(1) of the Charter:

> To maintain international peace and security and to that end: to take effective collective measures for the prevention and removal of threats to the peace, and for the suppression of acts of aggression or breaches of the peace, and to bring about by peaceful means, and in conformity with the principles of justice and international law, adjustment or settlement of international disputes or situations which might lead to a breach of the peace.

The devastation of World War II, coupled with the advent of atomic weapons, brought about a renewed sense of urgency in preventing future wars. To bolster this mission, Article 2(4) of the Charter explicitly forbids member states from threatening or using force in their international relations. The exception to this prohibition is found in Article 51. Member states are permitted to use force only in cases of self-defense or for collective self-defense. The international peace and security interests of all member states could be served by effectively outlawing war as a legitimate option of international diplomacy.

Article 2(1) of the UN Charter recognizes the principle of state sovereignty and the territorially based state. Only states may be full members of the UN, and all states are equally sovereign in that their representatives (the government) have the final say within their own territories. Article 2(7) reinforces the principle of state sovereignty by limiting the jurisdiction of the UN: "Nothing contained in the present Charter shall authorize the United Nations to intervene in matters which are essentially within the domestic jurisdiction of any state or shall require the Members to submit such matters to settlement under the present Charter; but this principle shall not prejudice the application of enforcement measures under Chapter VII."

The architects of the UN sought to strike a balance between the status quo of territorially based, sovereign nation-states and the need for international governance and stability. Governments retained sovereignty domestically and agreed to the peaceful settlement of their disputes internationally. This balance is a precarious one. International peace is not necessarily an interest of all states at all times. From ancient Sumer to modern-day Sarajevo, violence has proven to be an effective form of leverage, and the threat of violence a useful tool for obtaining foreign policy goals. Historically, violence has been, in fact, the decisive mechanism of change and the final arbiter of international disputes. Thus, the UN Charter is revolutionary: it challenges long-established international practice by outlawing both the threat and the use of force and by creating a higher authority to maintain international peace as security. The UN Security Council is that higher authority.

The Security Council

Chapter V, Article 24, of the UN Charter gives the Security Council the responsibility for preventing and responding to war: "In order to ensure prompt and effective action by the United Nations, its Members confer on the Security Council primary responsibility for the maintenance of international peace and security, and agree that in carrying out its duties under this responsibility the Security Council acts on their behalf." As identified in Chapter V, the five permanent members of the Security Council are the United States, the United Kingdom, the Union of Soviet Socialist Republics (USSR), France, and the Republic of China. These states were the allied victors of World War II, and their great-power status enabled them to take on a special responsibility for providing international stability in the postwar period. As permanent members, the states retain a continuous seat from session to session; moreover, each possesses an absolute veto, meaning that each can nullify a decision without further discussion. The veto provision was a controversial feature of the UN Charter as it violates the principle of the sovereign equality of states. That is, the permanent members are more sovereign than others: their veto renders UN action against any permanent member impossible and keeps the UN from taking any other action without their consent. But many observers argue that the veto provision was simply necessary. It was there to prevent the UN from starting an enforcement action it could not finish or invoking the name of the UN to use force over a great power's objection, thereby quickly raising a local conflict into a global one. In essence, the structure and the decision-making procedure of the Security Council are fully informed by a strong dose of political pragmatism.

Chapter V also mandates that the ten nonpermanent members of the Security Council be elected by the General Assembly, which is a plenary body. These ten nonpermanent members are elected for two-year terms and retiring members are not eligible for immediate reelection. The architects of the UN wanted the Security Council to represent the entire international community, not just the victors of World War II. By granting the General Assembly the power to elect the remaining members, they provided for a diverse membership in the Security Council, thereby ensuring that alternative viewpoints would be represented. The presidency of the Security Council rotates monthly among members alphabetically (English).

The task of the UN architects was to construct the Security Council as an organizational mechanism that would permit member states to act collectively to deter international aggression and provide a framework for a collective military response should deterrence happen to fail. However, they were faced with the stark reality that the first formalized experiment with collective security had failed dramatically under the League of Nations. Moreover, the principal lesson of World War II was fresh in their minds: do not appease aggressors. The efforts of European leaders to pacify Adolf Hitler at the Munich Conference served only to embolden him. In his quest for an Aryan empire, Hitler went unchecked. Nor did any leader see fit to check Japanese aggression in China and Southeast Asia. Limited war was thus rewarded. In consequence, the international community had faced another world war close on the heels of the first one.

This time around, however, one important new factor was working in favor of collective security—the full cooperation of the United States. In fact, the United States, first under Franklin D. Roosevelt and then under Harry S. Truman, was taking a leadership role in the construction of the UN. Having emerged from the war predominant in military strength and economic power, the United States was willing to commit those resources to the UN, a commitment it never made to the League. Without U.S. participation, the League of Nations remained a fledgling organization, politically weak and hence ineffectual at problem-solving during the inter-war years. Arguably, that weakness was inherent in the League's Charter. Under the League of Nations Charter, for example, the Council could only make recommendations regarding the use of military and economic sanctions. In legal theory, these sanctions were mandatory; in practice, they were voluntary and discretionary. The League, as such, had no power to enforce its recommendations.

The UN Charter, on the other hand, contains much stronger provisions for peace enforcement. First, Chapter VII requires member states to abide by Security Council decisions and to contribute to UN enforcement in general. Second, and more specifically, Article 43 of Chapter VII requires member states to make armed forces available to the Security Council. Article 47 establishes a Military Staff Committee to advise and assist the Security Council in matters relating to military enforcement of Security Council decisions. Through these provisions collective security was institutionalized, at least on paper. Security Council decisions were legally binding. A UN security force and the Military Staff Committee were to be available for Security Council initiatives and to forcibly carry out decisions if necessary.

While the architects of the UN Charter were able to correct for the organizational shortcomings evident in the League's collective security arrangements, they could not change world politics. The Cold War, which pitted two of the most influential of the permanent members against each other, rendered UN collective security arrangements ineffective. The Military Staff Committee, consisting of the Chiefs of Staff of the permanent members, argued about the size and cost of the security force and how much each should contribute. The Military Staff Committee and the security force envisioned in Chapter VII died shortly after their inception. Other security initiatives designed to stabilize the immediate postwar environment also met an early demise. Early efforts to control the spread of atomic weapons were quickly gutted by suspicious enemies. The UN Atomic Energy Commission, the U.S.-sponsored Baruch Plan, and the USSR-sponsored Peace Offensive became little more than propaganda tools in the emerging Cold War. The veto provision led to near-complete paralysis of the Security Council in matters of international security. Thus collective security and arms control gave way to alliances, balance of power, and arms races.

Why did UN collective security falter so dramatically after its inception? . . . The UN Charter provided member states with the organization, but consensus and commitment among the Security Council's permanent members were clearly absent. The lack of consensus was based not merely on practical questions—who contributes what and how much—but on fundamental differences as to how the world ought to be ordered. Perceptions of right and wrong are rarely negotiable. The United States and the USSR and their respective allies had essentially different world views, making any consensus fleeting at best.

Without a consensus, commitment is hard to establish. Member states must be willing to contribute to enforcement actions, even when those actions run contrary to their national interests. They must also be willing to refrain from using force unilaterally. . . .

The lack of consensus and commitment extends beyond the permanent Security Council members. Developing states are less than satisfied with a status quo not of their making. Many such states have been victims of great-power colonialism and, as such, have been forced to fight for self-determination. . . .

The lack of consensus and commitment to collective security is less a problem in principle than a question as to what constitutes aggression. . . .

According to the UN Charter, the only permissible use of force is self-defense. Does this mean force cannot be used against colonial or racist regimes or governments committing genocide against their own people? Does this mean a state must wait to be attacked before it can act to prevent imminent hostilities? Does this mean a state must sit idly by while its citizens are *in extremis* abroad? These questions are troubling, in large part because aggression now appears to have many meanings, none of which is wholly clear. Consequently, international efforts to define aggression have met with little success. And if defining aggression is difficult, then so is determining an appropriate collective response. In effect, the UN is largely silent on these thorny problems. After all, Article 2(7) prohibits the UN from intervening in matters that are essentially within the domestic jurisdiction of states. Sometimes, supraviolence is not the answer to violence.

The complexity of the political landscape in the postwar environment doomed the UN experiment with collective security. The UN Security Council did authorize a military response to the North Korean invasion of South Korea in 1950; however, that response was possible only because the USSR was boycotting the Council to protest the denial of a seat to the newly formed communist Chinese government. When the USSR returned, it used its veto to block any more Security Council decisions.

The Cold War record of the UN Security Council in providing for collective security is, by most accounts, quite poor. However, the UN's *raison d'être* was not completely abandoned. The prevention of violent conflict involves more than just a credible threat of a collective violent response. Breaches of the peace can be prevented through airing of grievances, diplomatic negotiations, mediation, arbitration, confidence building, and other forms of nonviolent conflict resolution. The Security Council, the General Assembly, and the Secretary-General have improvised to approximate the UN's central mission in spite of political exigencies that prevented successful collective security.

The General Assembly

The General Assembly's influence in the realm of international security stems from two Charter provisions—the authority to make recommendations regarding international security issues (Articles 10 and 11) and control of the UN budget (Article 17). During the Cold War, the General Assembly stood as a voice against aggression by condemning illegal uses of force through resolutions. Such resolutions fell far short of the expectations generated by the ideals of collective security and peace enforcement because the General Assembly had neither the authority nor the resources to do any thing about breaches of the peace. Nevertheless, they expressed the conscience of the community and served as a reminder of the main purpose of the UN. The Gerenal Assembly also supported "peacekeeping" by establishing it as a budget priority. . . .

Peacekeeping

Peacekeeping was not envisioned by the architects of the UN Charter. Former Secretary-General Dag Hammarskjöld once joked that peacekeeping was permitted under "Chapter Six and a half." He was referring to the tacit compromise between the UN's role in diplomatic efforts at conflict resolution as outlined in Chapter VI and its role in collective security as it evolved. As collective security arrangements proved increasingly unworkable, the UN's role in nonviolent conflict resolution gained in prominence. . . .

The UN conducted nineteen peacekeeping missions between 1947 and 1989. This figure includes observer missions that monitor cease-fire agreements or election procedures. Peacekeeping can be costly, and such missions have met with varying degrees of success. Most agree, however, that they have saved countless lives, which can have no price tag. Since 1989, UN peacekeeping operations have expanded considerably. The UN has authorized dozens of missions in more than twenty countries including Tajikistan, India, Haiti, Bosnia, Kosovo, and Mozambique. The end of the Cold War marks the beginning of a second generation of peacekeeping that extends beyond observer missions and lightly armed multinational contingents. . . . The end of the Cold War provided the international community with an opportunity for greater cooperation in peacekeeping, and as events began to unfold in the Middle East in 1990, the international community was also able to revisit the idea of collective security. . . .

Mainstream Approaches

Realism and liberalism represent the mainstream approaches to international relations and international organizations. Often thought of as the "conventional wisdom" in international governance, realism and liberalism approximate widely held world views about how the world operates and what the role of international organizations should be within the broader context of world politics. Both approaches are rooted in rich intellectual traditions, and each describes different actors and dynamics in international politics. Not surprisingly, a fierce academic debate has been raging between realists and liberals about their relative importance to international organizations in global governance. . . .

Realism and the Nature of International Organizations

Realists argue that no hierarchy of authority exists in international relations. The international system is characterized by anarchy, where authority resides with each individual state. No international entity exercises jurisdiction over states or reviews their domestic or foreign policy decisions. Anarchy, however, does not mean chaos. The international system is, in fact, quite orderly because a power hierarchy does exist among states. Some states are endowed with a plentitude of resources and, through design or chance, have attained great-power status. . . .

The explanations generated by realism regarding the creation of international organizations suggest that international organizations play one of two roles in the realist world. One role is a marginal one. International organizations matter only at the fringes of world politics. They may foster cooperation in noncontroversial issue areas where states have common interests. However, they rarely constrain state behavior in issue areas where interests are diverse and opposed. In other words, international organizations play little or no role in maintaining international peace and security. Rather, balance-of-power realities dictate whether or not war will break out.

International organizations can also play an intervening role in great-power calculations. International organizations are used by the hegemon and great powers to further their interests in the international system. Other, non-great-power states may also use international organizations to attain goals and to have a voice within the existing system. But, in terms of constraining state behavior, international organizations have little influence. States will bypass or ignore international organizations if their immediate security or important national interests are at stake.

In spite of this rather pessimistic view, international organizations do matter in the realist world. Schweller and Priess point out that international organizations perform several important functions. First, international organizations provide a mechanism for great-power collusion. Great powers usually benefit from the existing order and have an interest in maintaining it. After all, the fact that they are great powers suggests that they are doing well under existing rules and institutions. International organizations may not be useful if great-power interests collide, but do permit great powers to control other states in international systems. Second, international organizations are useful for making minor adjustments within the existing order while the basic underlying principles and norms remain uncompromised. An enduring international order must be flexible to account for changes in national interest and for rising and declining states. Third, international organizations can be agents of international socialization. International organizations legitimize the existing order, thereby gaining the acceptance of the status quo by those who are dominated. Finally, "international institutions are the 'brass ring' so to speak: the right to create and control them is precisely what the most powerful states have fought for in history's most destructive wars" (Schweller and Priess). . . .

Liberalism and the Role of International Organizations

Liberalism is more optimistic than realism about the contributions and independence of international organizations in international relations. Five interrelated roles can be discerned from the liberal approach. First, international organizations help states overcome collective action problems. . . .

Liberals argue that, in spite of the obstacles to collective security, the post–Cold War era has witnessed dramatic steps toward a viable international collective security arrangement. They also point out that a great deal of cooperation fostered by international organizations has existed within the security realm, an area in which realists predict little or no cooperation outside of balance-of-power considerations.

Collective action problems exist in other issue areas ranging from the economy to the environment. The most difficult is the "free rider" problem. A free rider is an actor that benefits from the provision of a public good without contributing anything to providing that good. . . . For example, liberals consider free trade a public good that is provided by the hegemon. The hegemon bears the costs of creating and maintaining the free trading system. In this case, a free rider is a state that benefits from the open markets of other states while at the same time keeping its markets closed to foreign competition. The hegemon usually carries a free rider because the gains associated with the free trading system outweigh the costs of the free rider. However, the balance of that equation shifts as the hegemon's capabilities decline. International organizations can help counter the free rider problem absent the hegemon by identifying unacceptable barriers to trade and providing a neutral forum for settling trade disputes. International organizations can, in a neutral manner, decide when it is permissible to discriminate against foreign goods. Under hegemony, a free rider gets away with free riding because a hegemon is willing to bear the costs. After hegemony, the free rider's position is increasingly untenable and international organizations provide a mechanism for discouraging such behavior.

A second role of international organizations is to promote economic prosperity and global welfare. Ideologically speaking, liberals argue that the world's goods, services, and resources should be distributed by the market. Liberals argue that the market yields the most efficient use of natural resources and the most efficient production of goods and services. Private ownership and private property rights are also important because private citizens and firms are more directly influenced by and can more easily adjust to market changes. Private citizens and firms are also more innovative and dynamic. Through the development of a global market based on comparative advantage, the welfare of the world can be maximized by improving the lot of individuals regardless of their nationality. International economic institutions, like the IMF and the WTO, exist to promote these goals.

International economic institutions have pursued several strategies in order to promote economic prosperity and global welfare. They have sought to reduce barriers to trade through multilateral negotiations. They have sought to eliminate protectionist measures by states, thereby forcing industries either to become efficient or lose out as casualties of the market. They have encouraged states to privatize industries and reduce their regulation of the market. They have development programs that encourage direct foreign investment by multinational corporations. They have provided funding for the creation of export industries that promote economic growth and development. They even help states adjust their economies to the new, global market realities. When international organizations promote global markets, trade, and investment, they are also promoting complex interdependence. Complex interdependence reduces the likelihood of war because the utility of military force in achieving national goals or settling disputes is greatly reduced.

A third role of international organizations is to help societies develop shared values and norms. Interdependence may reduce the chances of violent conflict; however, the problems associated with interdependence cannot be managed or solved unless societies have some common ground. International organizations foster certain values and help to establish certain norms that are conducive to the peaceful settlement of disputes, such as compromise, reciprocity, multilateralism, and the rule of law. International organizations promote democracy and democratic institutions. They promote and protect individual human rights. They promote values associated with a liberal international economic order based on neoclassical economic principles, such as private property rights and limited state involvement. But these values and norms are not universal, nor are they self-evident within or between societies, contrary to the writings of liberal writers. Some societies put the needs of the community over the needs of the individual. Some see the separation of church and state as a bad idea. For others, the state should eliminate private property or at least be responsible for caring for citizens "from cradle to grave," even if it means public ownership of industries or expensive welfare budgets.

For liberals, values and norms must compete in the "free marketplace of ideas" and evolve over time. Liberal values and norms have withstood the test of time, generating unprecedented levels of prosperity and individual freedom. Contemporary international organizations are agents of socialization for a political and economic order through which everyone can benefit. This liberal view contrasts slightly with the realist notion of international organizations of agents of socialization for an international order whereby one state or a group of states dominates lesser states in the international system.

A fourth role of international organizations is integrative and is performed principally by MNCs. MNCs are seen as a figurative needle and thread that binds societies together through the formation of a common global market. The activities of MNCs benefit societies because they bring jobs, industries, managerial skills, and technologies to societies. They are private economic organizations that transcend national boundaries and are responsible only to international stockholders. MNCs are a strong force for economic liberalism in the global economy. They command significant resources and have the ability to influence governments and IGOs. MNCs are interested in limited government involvement and the right to freely move capital to areas where it can be utilized more efficiently. MNCs are committed to capital mobility, and wherever they go they bring liberal ideology and a commitment to human rights with them.

A fifth role performed by international organizations in the liberal world is to provide assistance to the "victims of international politics." These victims include the abject poor, refugees, and those who have experienced environmental disaster, medical epidemics, and war. Liberals see these kinds of crises as being man-made. Choices are made by governments that have important consequences for its citizens. While environmental and medical emergencies may be influenced by nature, the policies and the reactions of governments play a decisive and often aggravating role. International organizations (IGOs and NGOs) seek to provide immediate relief to the victims of such "politics" and to find durable solutions.

In sum, international organizations are prominent features in the liberal land-scape. International organizations help states overcome collective action problems and help promote economic prosperity and global welfare. In addition, interna-tional organizations foster shared norms and values among societies and further economic interdependence. Lastly, international organizations aid the victims of international politics. Rather than being marginal actors, international organiza-tions are at the fore-front of international governance. . . .

Marxism and the Nature of International Organizations

Like many liberals and realists, Marxists argue that international organizations are created through hegemony. . . .

International organizations are mechanisms of capitalist domination and exploitation. The international order established by the United States after World War II was a capitalist system in which the United States had a competitive advan-tage in industrial production. An international system based on liberal (capitalist) economic principles would allow American businesses to penetrate markets world-wide. For traditional Marxists, the root of U.S. hegemony was its ability to impose its capitalist vision. Political, economic, and social organizations reflect the under-lying economic system. Contemporary international relations and organizations are shaped, informed, and reflective of contemporary world capitalism. . . .

The Marxist theoretical approach suggests three interrelated roles for inter-national organizations. For IGOs like the UN, they are political complements to capitalism. Financed and controlled by the capitalist states, they promote a capitalist agenda. The political institutions of the UN, such as the Security Coun-cil and the General Assembly, are hobbled by procedural rules that make them ineffective as organs of international governance. This enables capitalism to expand unchallenged. In an environment of interstate competition and rivalry, capitalists are unfettered by significant international restriction—they are free to seek new outlets for goods and new sources of raw materials and cheap labor. The principles of sovereignty and nonintervention allow the capitalist states to pick and choose when, where, and how the "international community" will act against a state. International intervention usually happens only when there is a compelling economic interest. . . .

The independent economic agencies of the UN, such as the IMF and the World Bank, impose capitalist features such as private property and wage labor on developing societies. These societies are forced to accept the market, rather than the state, as the mechanism for distributing wealth, resources, and values. As long as the market distributes wealth, resources, and values, the owners of the means of production will always benefit at the expense of wage earners. In the context of modern world system theory, the core will always benefit at the expense of the periphery. As long as the IMF and the World Bank continue to demand market reforms in exchange for development and stabilization loans, periphery states will see, at best, maldevelopment and, at worst, chronic underdevelopment. . . .

A second, related role of international organizations is that of mechanism of domination. International organizations are tools that core states use to exploit and control the weak. Periphery societies are controlled politically because they are given a voice in organizations like the UN in which that voice carries very little weight. The decolonization process provided periphery states with the trappings of sovereignty. The newly formed states thus have the right to govern themselves but not the means. Their ruling classes are collaborators with the core states and their interests are tied to the core. The ruling class controls the government and that government is what is represented at the UN. Hence, many UN officials are the elites of periphery states. Their constituencies often include the ruling classes and are committed to capitalist values.

Self-determination is a principle that is recognized only when societies determine for themselves that they will embrace capitalism. Developing states that do not embrace capitalism or who threaten core economic interests are subject to intervention. The UN paid only lip service to the principle of nonintervention when the United States invaded the Dominician Republic, Grenada, and Panama while intervening covertly in Iran, Guatemala, Cuba, Chile, and Nicaragua. All of these states had one of two things in common. Their governments were guided by nationalist or populist sentiments and/or they sought to embrace a different mode of production—socialism or communism. Most of these governments were democratically elected, and those that were not had overthrown extremely brutal dictators or military regimes. Hobbled by its own rules and procedures, the UN did nothing. . . .

A third and closely related role of both private and public international organizations is as developers of hegemony. Traditional Marxists have tended to view hegemony as sheer domination. Hence, international organizations reflect, reinforce, and impose capitalism. However, coercive domination is not an effective means of control, at least in the long run. Effective control comes from the consent of the dominated. Gramscian Marxists see international organizations as important instruments for selling capitalism, an economic mode of production under which the vast majority of the world's people are impoverished, malnourished, and exploited. A tough sell? Not really—not when capitalism is coupled with the ideas of self-determination, human rights, and democracy and is, besides, the only game in town. The implementation of these ideas in the real world suggests that they take a back seat to market capitalism and are sacrificed if they interfere in any significant way with capitalist accumulation. Nevertheless, the ideas are important selling points.

6.2 The United Nations

The Economist

As the United Nations attempts to fulfill its mandate to provide collective security in today's changed world, it faces a number of challenges. As the British news journal *The Economist* notes, the new secretary-general of the United Nations, Ban Ki-moon, needs to deal not only with the pressing, and ever-widening, global security agenda but with the need for institutional reform of the UN itself (including enhancing the UN's ability to carry out peacekeeping operations) and with the problem of managing relations between the UN and its most important members, especially the United States.

Mission Impossible?

Any new job brings challenges: but none quite like those facing Ban Ki-moon, the quiet Korean who has just become the UN's new secretary-general. Rising nuclear demons in Iran and North Korea, a haemorrhaging wound in Darfur, unending violence in the Middle East, looming environmental disaster, escalating international terrorism, the proliferation of weapons of mass destruction, the spread of HIV/AIDS. And then there are more parochial concerns, such as the largely unfinished business of the most sweeping attempt at reform in the UN's history. That effort was started by Kofi Annan, who stepped down this week [January 2007] after ten turbulent years at the helm.

Mr. Ban now picks up the baton. As a member of a "group without a church"— a Christian organisation that emerged in Japan in the early 20th century, whose adherents make the Gospel a source of inspiration for their private and public life—the UN's first Asian secretary-general in 35 years has described himself as "a man on a mission," keen to restore trust between member states and the secretariat, between rich and poor countries, and in the discredited organisation itself. He hoped, he joked to journalists last month, that this would not prove a "Mission Impossible." The world will hope so, too.

Mr. Ban says he wants to concentrate on the goals already set for the UN, rather than find "new frontiers to conquer." That is wise, but frustrating, because the UN's biggest problem is also its most intractable. It lies in the all-powerful Security Council or, more precisely, with its five permanent members. The UN's failure to stop the atrocities in Darfur or the nuclear posturing of Iran and North Korea has stemmed largely from the inability of the so-called P5 to agree on what should be done. If Mr. Ban could simply conjure away the P5's extraordinary powers and privileges, which allow any one of them to paralyse the will of the rest of the world, everything, it seems, could be much easier.

When the UN was created in 1945, its founder-nations—the four main victors of the second world war, America, Britain, China and Russia, plus France—allocated to themselves the only five permanent seats, with veto powers, on what was then an 11-seat Security Council. The other members, all elected by the General Assembly, held two-year non-renewable seats without a veto. Since then, the number of the UN's member states has almost quadrupled from 51 to 192, two-thirds of them in the developing world.

Yet apart from the addition of four more non-permanent seats in 1965, membership of the Security Council, the only UN body whose decisions are binding, has remained unchanged. The system is not only undemocratic, anachronistic and unfair, but also—as Paul Kennedy, professor of history at Yale, suggests in his new book, *The Parliament of Man*—outrageous . Yet it cannot be changed without inviting a veto from one of the very nations whose powers might be diminished.

Change might well be unwise, too. As Mr. Kennedy notes, powerful nations will always be tempted to go their own way. The League of Nations, set up between the two world wars, failed precisely because it was too democratic, too liberal, and toothless. The United States was never a member. Germany and Japan pulled out in 1933, Italy four years later. A different system had to be devised if the potentially isolationist great powers of the post–1945 world were to be kept inside a new world body.

The veto, which America and Russia insisted on as the quid pro quo for their membership of the UN, allows any one of the P5 to block any action brought before the Security Council that it deems contrary to its—or its friends'—interests, without needing to resort to force. If, on the other hand, a country finds itself blocked by a veto (or threatened veto), it can still decide to go it alone, as America did over the invasion of Iraq. Far from being a failure of the UN system, Mr. Kennedy argues, this should be seen as the successful operation of a safety valve. Much better to have an obstructionist America on board than a furious one walking out.

Without American involvement the UN would not amount to much, as successive secretary-generals have recognised. Before taking up his new post, Mr. Ban made it clear that one of his first tasks would be to forge closer relations with the United States. That pledge is an indication of how poisonous they had become under his predecessor.

Restraining the Mighty   The low point came when Washington, ever suspicious of the UN's desire to restrain it, reacted furiously to Mr. Annan's purported failure to deliver UN backing for the Iraq war—not in fact his own doing, but the result of divisions on the Security Council. There followed the $64 billion oil-for-food scandal, and reports of UN peacekeepers sexually abusing the people they had been sent to protect. Congress and the American press had a field day, vying with one another to see how much blame they could dump at Mr. Annan's door. The arrival of John Bolton as America's ambassador to the UN in August 2005 did not help matters; the two men never got on.

Mr. Annan was never in any doubt about the importance of strong American leadership, without which, he said, he saw "no hope of a peaceful and stable future for humanity in this century." At the same time, he insisted, no nation, however powerful, could hope to tackle today's increasingly global threats and challenges alone. Nor—as he declared pointedly in one of many valedictory speeches last month—could a nation "make itself secure by seeking supremacy over all others." Historically, America had been in the vanguard of the global human-rights movement, Mr. Annan noted; but that lead could be maintained only if America remained "true to its principles in the struggle against terror."

Mr. Ban was asked what he thought of such undiplomatic sideswipes at the Bush administration. He replied firmly that they represented Mr. Annan's "personal assessment and insight." South Koreans are used to that sort of thing from Mr. Ban; back home, the former diplomat's tendency to duck awkward questions won him the nickname "the slippery eel."

But he is in an awkward spot. He owes his election as much to the backing of America and China as to his own superbly organised campaign, and dare not offend either of them. At the same time, Mr. Ban knows that he cannot be seen to be too cosy with the American superpower. Mr. Annan, who also started out with American backing, soon showed his independence. Mr. Ban could do the same—especially if, as he claims, he wants to win the trust of the increasingly assertive and obstreperous group of developing countries known as the G77.

For many years after it was set up, in 1964, to represent the interests on trade and development of 77 poor countries, this group was regarded as a fairly negligible force, unable to agree on anything other than more aid and plumper trade concessions. It is now much bigger—131 countries plus China—and bolder, heartened by the growing oil wealth of some of its members and by deepening divisions, on matters ranging from Kyoto to Iraq, between America and its European partners. The abrasive Mr. Bolton, in his 16-month stint at the UN, probably did more than any other single factor to encourage the G77 to get its act together and resist the United States.

Some see the gulf between rich and poor countries as the single most important issue confronting the UN. It is paralysing vital proliferation talks and blocking badly needed reforms. The G77 now sees everything through the distorting lens of the North-South divide. UN management reform? An attempt by rich white countries to gain even more influence over a secretariat already dominated by the North. Greater powers for the secretary-general? A bid to reduce his accountability to the General Assembly, one of the few UN bodies where the developing countries have a controlling voice. The replacement of the assembly's principle of "one country, one vote" by a system of weighted voting based on the size of a country's contributions to the UN? Another attempt at a power-grab by the North. The newly adopted "responsibility to protect" victims of genocide and other atrocities? Hypocritical northerners claiming the right to meddle in the domestic affairs of the South. Even proposals to expand Security Council membership to include more developing countries, which might have been expected to attract G77 support, are opposed on the ground that these would simply strengthen a body that, whatever happens, will remain dominated by four white veto-wielding northerners, plus China.

Kofi's Legacy   Will Mr. Ban, who hails from what is now the world's tenth biggest economy (in nominal terms), be able to win the co-operation of the G77 any better than his Ghanaian-born predecessor? Many doubt it. But at least he is making the right noises, announcing that his first foreign trip will be to attend the African Union summit in Addis Ababa later this month, and promising to make the Millenium Development Goals one of his top priorities.

These goals, adopted in 2000 and regarded by Mr. Annan as his proudest legacy, commit world leaders to halving poverty, slashing mortality and illiteracy rates and raising aid levels to 0.7 percent of GDP by 2015. But as Mr. Annan himself has admitted, he leaves the UN with the job "far from done." Although some encouraging progress has been made, notably on debt relief and HIV/AIDS, the world was "not on track," he said, to meet many other goals. In Africa, for example, poverty has actually risen over the past decade.

Much else, too, remained undone or unfinished on Mr. Annan's watch. The long-awaited reform of the Security Council has been pushed once again onto the back burner. The new Human Rights Council is almost as ineffectual as its discredited predecessor, and is equally stuffed with flagrant human-rights violators. Under Mr. Annan, the UN proclaimed a new high-minded "responsibility to protect"; but in Darfur the raping and killing continue unabated. The search for a definition of terrorism has been abandoned; management reform has been blocked. But Mr. Annan is not solely, or even chiefly, responsible for these failures. As Mr. Bolton himself conceded before stepping down last month, "While it is easy to blame the UN as an institution for some of the problems we confront today, we must recognise that ultimately it is member states that must take action and therefore bear the responsibility."

In some areas Mr. Annan notched up notable achievements. Thanks to an overhaul of the organisation's department of humanitarian affairs and much better coordination with NGOs in the field, the UN's once shambolic relief operations are now regarded as second to none. Around 30m people in some 50 countries currently depend on its services for survival. In March a new $500m central emergency relief fund was launched to deliver assistance within hours, rather than months, of an emergency. Another $250m fund, administered by the UN's new intergovernmental Peacebuilding Commission, has been set up to help finance reconstruction in countries emerging from conflict. Sierra Leone and Burundi have been designated as the first two beneficiaries. In return, they will have to produce evidence of good governance.

Peacekeeping, which is not even mentioned in the UN Charter, is another of the organisation's recent success stories. The explosion of civil wars and of ethnic and religious violence at the end of the cold war caught the UN by surprise. It had no standing army, no effective military staff, and very little peacekeeping experience. What troops it managed to muster, mostly from developing countries, were often poorly trained and badly equipped. Peacekeeping mandates from the Security Council tended to be far too restrictive both in scope and numbers. Some terrible mistakes were made: the UN's failure to stop the slaughter in Rwanda and the massacre in Srebrenica continues to haunt it. But over the past five years or so there has been a marked improvement.

A 2005 Rand Corporation study of American and UN peacekeeping operations concluded that the blue-helmet missions were not only cheaper, but had a higher success rate and enjoyed greater international legitimacy. Another Canadian study attributed the dramatic decline in the number of conflicts and battle deaths over the past decade to the "huge increase" in preventive diplomacy and peacekeeping over the same period, "for the most part authorised and mounted by the UN." Never has the demand for the organisation's peacekeeping services been so great. As the UN's former head of peacekeeping, Mr. Annan had a lot of experience in the field. Mr. Ban has none.

Indeed, the more people compare the UN's new secretary-general with his predecessor, the glummer they tend to become. Mr. Ban is said to be bland, given to platitudes, lacking charisma. Honest, intelligent and diligent he may be (his only hobby is said to be his work), but many fear he is unlikely to provide the strong, inspiring leadership the UN so badly needs. Some even wonder whether America deliberately chose a weak candidate in order to undermine an organisation with which it has always had problems. But the inscrutable Mr. Ban replies that, in Asia, a smiling face often hides an inner strength. He could surprise everyone.

Almost since its inception, the UN has been charged with failing to live up to its original high ideals. But big changes in world governance seem possible only after great global upheavals. At other times, the world has to be content with small incremental steps. The UN's new secretary general, eager to find consensus might be rather good at those.

Gladwyn Jebb, the British negotiator at the UN's founding conference and later its first (acting) secretary-general, reckoned that its founding fathers had simply aimed too high for "this wicked world." But as Dag Hammerskjöld, the organisation's third secretary-general, wisely noted: "The UN was not created to take humanity to heaven, but save it from hell."

Call the Blue Helmets

Can the UN Cope with Increasing Demands for its Soldiers?   Call it peacekeeping, peace-enforcement, stabilisation or anything else, but one thing is clear: the world's soldiers are busier than ever operating in the wide grey zone between war and peace.

The United Nations has seen a sixfold increase since 1998 in the number of soldiers and military observers it deploys around the world. About 74,000 military personnel (nearly 100,000 people including police and civilians, and increasing fast) are currently involved in 18 different operations—more than any country apart from the United States. And it is not just the UN that is in high demand. NATO, the European Union and the African Union (AU), as well as other coalitions of the willing, have some 74,000 soldiers trying to restore peace and stability in troubled countries. Added to their number come the more than 160,000 American, British and other troops in Iraq.

The "war on terror" is one cause of this military hyperactivity. But Jean-Marie Guéhenno, the UN's under-secretary for peacekeeping, also sees more hopeful reasons. The growing demand for blue helmets, he says, is a good sign that a number of conflicts are ending.

This is only partly true. In Congo, southern Sudan and Liberia—the UN's three biggest operations—the blue helmets are shoring up peace agreements. But in countries such as Lebanon or Côte d'Ivoire, they are at best holding the line between parties still in conflict.

One reason for the surge in UN peacekeeping is that Africa, the region most in need of peacekeepers, is least able to provide for itself. The AU is trying to improve its peacekeeping capacity, but is desperately short of resources. It has handed over its operation in Burundi to the UN. Now it wants the blue helmets to help relieve its 7,000 hard-pressed AU peacekeepers in Sudan's troubled region of Darfur.

The Sudanese government has long resisted such a deployment, accusing the UN of being an agent of the West. But under sustained international pressure to halt what Washington regards as genocide, it has grudgingly agreed to allow in a "hybrid" UN and AU force. An advance party of 24 police advisers and 43 military officers, wearing blue berets and AU armbands, has started to arrive in Darfur to test Sudan's cooperation. According to a three-phase plan, the force will be built up into a contingent of 17,000 soldiers and 3,000 police officers.

Can the UN take on another onerous peacekeeping operation? Mr. Guéhenno says the world already faces two kinds of "overstretch": the military sort, in which many armed forces of many leading countries are badly strained by foreign operations; and "political overstretch," in which the world's political energies are focused on just a few acute problems while the UN is left to deal as best it can with many chronic or less visible conflicts.

Mr. Guéhenno is cautious about what he can achieve in Darfur. He says he may get the soldiers, given the right political conditions, but is worried about getting enough "enablers"—the crucial specialised units and equipment that enhance the ability of a force to move and operate. These include army engineers and logisticians, field hospitals and nurses, heavy-lift aircraft and transport helicopters, as well as proper command-and-control and intelligence-gathering: in other words, the wherewithal of modern Western expeditionary forces. These capabilities are in short supply and are expensive; the few countries that have them are using them, and the others can't afford them.

In a region as vast as Darfur, an effective UN force would need to be highly mobile, and make use both of unmanned surveillance drones and special forces. It would need to sustain itself in a harsh environment, some 1,400km (870 miles) from the nearest harbour and with few airfields. Engineers could drill for water, but would be under pressure to share it with local populations and with refugees. And then there is the problem of time. On current plans it would take six to nine months to build up to full strength in Darfur. Having to merge with the AU adds further complications to the command structure.

Finding a Fire Engine   Apart from military capability, or lack of it, there is the question of political will. Who will risk their soldiers' lives, and their valuable military assets, in a faraway conflict? NATO, the world's foremost military alliance, has struggled for months to find a few thousand additional soldiers—and a few extra helicopters—to back up its troops fighting in southern Afghanistan.

By contrast, European countries moved with unusual speed when the UN appealed for its hapless mission in Lebanon to be reinforced last summer in order to end the war between Israel and Hizbullah. Within weeks of a ceasefire being called in August, French and Italian peacekeepers were coming ashore. It was the first time that sizeable Western forces had donned blue helmets since the unhappy days of the war in Bosnia.

But there were particular reasons for this. Lebanon, of course, is more easily accessible than Afghanistan or Darfur. But it is also less dangerous than southern Afghanistan, and European governments regard the Israeli-Arab conflict as much closer to their interests than the effort to pacify rebellious Pashtun tribesmen.

Kofi Annan, the former UN secretary-general, liked to say that the UN is the only fire brigade that must go out and buy a fire engine before it can respond to an emergency. The Security Council must first authorise an operation and pass a budget, and then the secretariat beseeches governments to contribute forces and arranges the means to transport them. This system has created a two-tier structure: powerful countries decide the missions (and pay for them) while poor countries such as India, Pakistan, Bangladesh, Nepal and Jordan supply the soldiers. They receive a payment for doing so; this becomes for some a subsidy for their own armed forces, while the deployment also provides their troops with training.

Idealists such as Sir Brian Urquhart, a former UN under secretary-general, believe it is high time the UN had its own "fire engine": a permanent force that could deploy quickly to stop conflicts before they spin out of control. The UN's founding fathers envisioned some kind of international army, but all proposals for a standing UN force have foundered—partly because of political objections to giving the UN too much power, partly because of the practical difficulties of recruiting, training and paying for such a force.

After the failure of the UN in the mid-1990s to stop blood-letting in Somalia, Rwanda and the Balkans, many argued it would be better for those who are properly equipped to deal with putting out the fires of conflict. In 1999, it was NATO that stopped the killing of ethnic Albanians in Kosovo, while a force led by Australia halted the conflict in East Timor. A year later, in Sierra Leone, the quick deployment of about 1,000 British soldiers helped save what was then the UN's largest peacekeeping mission from collapsing under attack by rebels of the Revolutionary United Front.

All this seemed to confirm that the UN could take on only soft peacekeeping and "observer" missions with cooperation from the warring sides. But in 2000 a panel headed by Lakhdar Brahimi recommended a complete rethink of UN peacekeeping. The United Nations, it acknowledged, "does not wage war"; but its operations nevertheless had to "project credible force" and be ready to distinguish between victim and aggressor.

Mr. Brahimi's central recommendation was the creation of multinational brigades around the world ready to deploy at short notice. This idea of pre-assembling bits of the fire engine has made only fitful progress. But other proposals have been acted on. They include the creation of a more powerful headquarters to oversee the UN efforts; stockpiling of equipment; compilation of lists of military officers, police and other experts who will be on call to join UN missions; and the meshing of peacekeeping with ordinary policing, government reform and economic development.

New missions are now much more likely to be given robust mandates authorising them to use "all necessary means" under Chapter VII of the UN charter: in other words, aggressive military force. In places such as Congo and Haiti, the UN has even been accused of using too much force.

Since the world is likely to need large number of peacekeepers for the foreseeable future, a further option is being explored: "leasing" the fire engine by hiring private security companies to do more of the work. Don't expect anything to happen quickly, though. The world, and especially the Americans, has moved a long way towards the privatisation of war. But for many, the privatisation of peacekeeping is still a step too far.

 # The International Monetary Fund

6.3 The IMF and Democratic Governance

Devesh Kapur and Moisés Naím

Perhaps even more controversial in today's world than the United Nations is the International Monetary Fund (IMF). On first blush, this might seem surprising. The role of the IMF would seem to be quite technical and even arcane: to stabilize international capital flows and to prevent undesirable instability in exchange rates. But the conditions imposed by the IMF as part of its loan arrangements can to a considerable degree dictate the domestic economic policies of the borrower states, with enormous human and political costs (or benefits). In the next selection, University of Pennsylvania professor Devesh Kapur and *Foreign Policy* editor Moisés Naím discuss the problematic role the IMF has come to play in promoting good governance and democracy.

The International Monetary Fund (IMF) plays many roles in the global economy, and appears to be playing a significant—and controversial—role in influencing the global prospects of political democracy as well. Created as a financial cooperative by the Bretton Woods agreement in July 1944 and made a specialized UN agency three years later, the IMF was conceived as a major element in a battery of organizations (the World Bank was another) that would help to prevent a postwar recurrence of worldwide economic depression and its associated evils by giving numerous countries a stake in the stability and sound basic management of the whole system of international payments, finance, and trade.

The Fund acts as a financial and informational go-between, a bulwark against global financial chaos, and a source of restraint on governments prone to

Kapur, Devesh and Moisés Naím, "The IMF and Democratic Governance," *Journal of Democracy* 16:1 (2005), pp. 89–102. © National Endowment for Democracy and The Johns Hopkins University Press. Reprinted with permission of The Johns Hopkins University Press.

dangerously heavy borrowing. In the eyes of some, the Fund also functions as a debt collector for lenders of international capital and a foreign policy instrument for certain nation-states that are among the largest IMF shareholders. At the same time, the Fund serves as a convenient scapegoat and punching bag for unhappy member states as well as antiglobalization activists from the left and "small-government" fundamentalists from the right. Finally, there are observers for whom the Fund, with its capital of roughly US$300 billion, represents the institutional possibilities—and unfulfilled hopes—of global governance.

In recent years, the IMF's scale and scope have expanded enormously. Its member countries have grown from 29 at its inception to 184 today. But even more importantly, world trade expanded rapidly and global capital flows grew exponentially—total foreign assets of banks rose from $775 billion in mid-1984 to $17.1 trillion in mid-2004, an increase of more than twenty-fold. This changed international economic landscape has created new demands upon the IMF as well as new problems for which answers are neither obvious nor simple. Not surprisingly, the added complexity of the issues and the institution has sparked a number of intense controversies. Politicians often accuse the Fund of mismanagement while leading economists argue vehemently both for and against the IMF stance. Debate has swirled around the potential alternatives to IMF programs, the conditions that the Fund typically attaches to its loans, and the consequences—especially in the form of painful and politically sensitive "austerity" measures—for the countries whose governments do the borrowing, and in whose macroeconomic stability the IMF has a stake. Everyone agrees that these consequences reach well beyond the economic realm and can have massive, all-too-concrete social and political effects, not least on the processes and institutions that make up the nerves and sinews of democracy. . . .

Of greatest concern, perhaps, is the inherent tension between conditions imposed by an outside lender and the cardinal democratic principle of consent. By their very nature, IMF conditions arise not from debate and discussion within a society, but come rather from unelected foreign experts. Locally made decisions lose relevance as conditionality ties the hands of domestic political actors. Does it matter what elected officials are choosing when the fate of the local economy is being decided by technical specialists and managers in an IMF office somewhere?

In recent years, the IMF's focus on "good governance" and corruption-fighting has led it into subjects with a deep and important connection to democracy and its prospects of spreading and deepening across and within whole countries and regions of the world. Does the IMF, of all the international organizations that might take on such a task, have either the mandate or the best tools for tackling it? After all, the Fund's programs tend to be of a duration much shorter than that which all prior experience suggests is needed for the slow and bumpy work of building sounder institutions for the long term. . . .

The IMF's impact on democracy is amplified during international economic and financial crises, especially the rapid and gravely consequential sort that have become more common in recent years. Money now flies across borders faster than ever, while governments struggle to keep up. Crises always tend to direct more decision-making power to the center: in borrower countries this means mostly the finance ministry and central bank, while in the IMF it means the G-7 countries (especially the United States but also some European nations and Japan) and the creditors (typically banks or large bondholding financial institutions) domiciled therein. The more representative parts of the borrower government drop into the shadows. In weak, resource-starved postconflict societies such as East Timor, Mozambique, or Afghanistan, all these concerns take on an even more intense form, since there institutions such as the Fund and World Bank face so few checks on their actions. . . .

Two interlinked sets of changes could enhance the support that the IMF lends to democracy and democratic consolidation in particular countries as well as in the international system as a whole. The first type of change would seek to reform *how* the Fund does things by bringing its decision-making methods more into keeping with such democratic principles as consent and transparency. The second sort of change would seek to improve *what* the Fund actually does (and potentially can do) so as to bolster democracy both globally and in borrowing countries.

The first issue is important for practical as well as principled reasons. Democracy is about process, not just outcomes. The none-too-democratic nature of the IMF's decision-making processes means that, even if a "good" result comes about, it may happen at a cost in legitimacy and public trust that saps the Fund's effectiveness over the long run. Participation matters, whether in domestic programs aimed at helping individuals escape poverty and improve well-being, or in international lending focused on helping whole societies reach the same broad goals. As Montek Singh Ahluwalia, head of the IMF's own Office of Independent Evaluation, pointed out in November 2003 to the Club of Madrid, the Fund's decisions seem to come from a "black box." IMF officials often neglect to explain the precise reasons for conditions placed on loans, or to spell out the assumptions (and doubts) behind programs aimed at key goals such as restoring the external financial viability of an entire national economy. The upshot is greater leeway for intervention by major shareholders, leading the Fund to a forced optimism in program design, in turn adversely affecting the quality (and effectiveness) of its programs. Forcing the adoption of ambitious goals—and mandating their rapid achievement—is often more pleasing for the small policy circles that monitor these issues in donor countries or for the international financial markets than it is for the government of a country in trouble. The latter is likely to be already embattled and may often have no option but to sign an IMF agreement which, however ambitious and even desirable in economic terms, may require policy changes with enormous short-term political costs. . . .

As we suggested above, among the most troubling issues raised by international financial crises is the degree to which elected governments must answer to external actors rather than domestic constituents. Leaders of developing democracies must steer between the Scylla of global financial markets and the Charybdis of demands from their own citizens. Campaign platforms meant to attract votes at home rarely meet with the approval of the IMF or global financial markets, and the latter may press an election winner such as South Korea's President Kim Dae Jung to change course after taking office.

On the merits, the new course might turn out to be a good idea. It may boost the economy and improve the country's standing in global financial markets and attractiveness to foreign investors. But a sharp switch spurred from outside also risks turning citizens into cynics by corroding their trust in elected leaders and perhaps even democracy as such. . . .

The Fund's strength vis-à-vis borrowing members (especially low-income countries) masks its own weakness in the global system and is symptomatic of a more general problem: the weakness of multilateral decision-making mechanisms to deal with even the most pressing global issues. At times of financial crisis, for instance, it is not the IMF but the U.S. Treasury Department whose decisions matter most. And if such crises not only continue but even get worse, as former U.S. treasury secretary Robert Rubin predicts they will, the IMF's lack of capacity (a result of shortsightedness among its major shareholders) may force the Fund to meet the next crisis by saddling borrower countries with massive adjustment burdens that are almost certain to harm democratic governance.

The lack of global means to deal with global problems seems to result in part from the uneven dynamics of globalization itself. The complex sets of changes which travel under that rubric have unfolded more rapidly and extensively in areas of greatest concern to industrialized countries (including finance and trade in consumer goods). Areas that are most urgent to countries whose economies are not so well developed, such as labor flows, have seen globalization lag. At the 2002 International Conference on Financing for Development at Monterrey, Mexico, representatives from the governments of both rich and poor countries agreed that the main responsibility for development lies within developing countries themselves. But this assumes that such countries will have due freedom of action regarding their own policies. At what point do things such as IMF conditionalities so limit a developing nation's autonomy that its responsibility for developing itself becomes moot? . . .

The IMF began just over six decades ago as a venue for international monetary cooperation. Today, it has become a tool for helping poorer countries with the immense task of achieving capitalist "development" and all the broad, deep, and disconcerting yet elusive changes which that term implies. This has meant "mission creep" and a proliferation of new aims that IMF officials say they must embrace, given their need to grapple with a plethora of complex interrelationships among numerous economic, structural, and institutional variables. While many critics decry this situation as a source of confusion, what concerns us more are the implications that such a widening agenda may hold for democracy. Students of bureaucracy have long noted that when missions begin springing up like desert flowers after a rainstorm, the clear incentives and institutional autonomy that a typical bureaucracy needs in order to function well can become prone to politicization and perhaps to other forms of distortion as well. The skewed governance structure and lack of competition that currently characterize the IMF only heighten this disturbing prospect in ways that should give grave pause to anyone who cares about the plight of democracy in borrower countries.

In many ways, the Fund's predicament reflects the sad folly of the global community's penchant for criticizing an institution, then asking it to take on more tasks, and then critiquing it all the more harshly after it fails to check off all the boxes on its new and longer "to-do" list. One cure for this might be to distribute some of the "burdens of the Fund" to other regional and international organizations (making both types stronger for the purpose). . . .

The heated nature of debates about the Fund is a sign of how great have become the tensions between the mid-twentieth-century designs of the typical multilateral institution and the realities of the early twenty-first-century world. In a sense, the Fund has become a scapegoat for stronger forces (global capital markets in general, the U.S. Treasury Department in particular) that buffet even the IMF itself. It is predictable that by taking on such ambitious agendas and trying to be all things to all members, the Fund often seems to succeed mainly in disappointing expectations and becoming an institutional stand-in for problems larger than its own failings.

Despite the Fund's technocratic persona, its actions are highly political, often driven by geopolitical calculations. Not surprisingly, its actions have significant political ramifications. The Fund is not an independent actor and decision making in the institution reflects its governance. The Fund's less-than-transparent procedures and tendency to press rapid and highly centralized decision-making styles on borrower countries are plainly in tension with democracy's emphases on deliberation and participation in the making of public policy. . . .

Democracy promotion is not a science. In truth, we know very little about it. The IMF has neither the mandate nor the skills to undertake such an enormously challenging task, and asking Fund officials to do so would be shortsighted and even dangerous. Yet the Fund can support democracy indirectly, both by promoting transparency in national economic policies and budgetary practices and by taking care to consult with key democratic institutions. At the same time, an increased awareness might lead the institution to adhere to a form of "Hippocratic oath" ("first do no harm") that would make it systematically more conscious of the harmful implications that its procedures and programs might have for democracy in a borrower nation.

 The European Union

6.4 Standard Bearer: How the European Union Exports Its Laws

Tobias Buck

Most international organizations lack the global reach of the UN, the IMF, the World Bank, and the WTO. Instead, they exist to facilitate regional coordination and help states solve regional problems. Although these regional organizations lack the global inclusiveness of a UN, in at least one case a regional organization has achieved an extraordinary degree of political integration and policy coordination, not only solving a wide range of political and economic problems but making war between its members essentially unthinkable. The European Union (originally the European Community, or EC) was established by the 1957 Rome Treaty as a free trade area. Its founding fathers, looking back on the sad history of European conflict, sought to overcome generations of Franco-German rivalry and hostility by linking their two economies and the economies of their neighbors together, thereby promoting mutual prosperity and creating inescapable bonds of interdependence that would make war self-destructive. The EC was expected to advance Europe's economic integration, while NATO provided the continent with military security. Among the consequences of the EC were a dramatic growth in trade among the original "inner six" (West Germany, France, Italy, Belgium, the Netherlands, and Luxembourg) and growing cooperation between Germany and the rest of Europe.

In December 1991, the EU took a dramatic leap forward with the signing of the Maastricht Treaty that pledged the (by then) fifteen-nation group to build a lasting union. Most internal barriers to movement between members came down in 1993. The Maastricht Treaty also committed members to form a European Monetary Union (EMU) in 1999 with a single central bank (the European Central Bank, or ECB) to set interest rates and a new currency (the euro) to replace national currencies. Eleven of the EU's members joined the EMU at its inception, including all of the major powers except Great Britain.

Thus, although its member states continue to retain their formal sovereignty, the EU plays an increasingly important role not only in coordinating government policies but also by enacting regulations that affect day-to-day lives and help solve the problems facing ordinary people and businesses. The freedom of movement and economic integration spurred by the EU have also begun to transform how many ordinary Europeans see themselves—not as Germans or Italians, for example, but as Europeans. Born in one country, many EU citizens now choose to be educated in another, to live in a third, to work for a company based in a fourth, and to marry someone from a fifth.

Even while it has worked to deepen the union by increasing the interdependence of its member states and enhancing the sense of shared identity, the EU has also engaged in widening—bringing into its membership more of Europe. In 2004 the EU added ten new states, including eight formerly communist states in central Europe (Estonia, Latvia, Lithuania, Poland, the Czech Republic, Slovakia, Hungary, and Slovenia), and two more (Romania and Bulgaria) were admitted in 2007. The expanded scope of the EU' s powers and its increased membership have raised fundamental questions about the EU's decision-making structure, which now permits single states to veto important measures. Constitutional reform of the EU thus remains very much on the agenda even as the EU struggles to define its role in areas such as security policy. The EU's size and its ability to impose regulations on its members, however, already make it an important player on the world stage. As Tobias Buck observes in the following article from the *Financial Times,* the EU's regulations affect the decisions of corporations around the world and thereby affect the behavior and options of other states.

In late March [2007], a delegation of California government officials arrived in Brussels on a most unusual mission. Governor Arnold Schwarzenegger had sent them to meet their counterparts at the European Commission and explore whether his state could join one of Europe's most ambitious and controversial projects: the emissions trading scheme.

Both sides emerged from the talks feeling optimistic that a deal was possible to link the European Union regime with a state that itself counts among the biggest emitters of carbon dioxide in the world. "We hope that California will be able in the near future to be the first non-European region that would join the emissions trading system," a Commission official said.

California's eagerness to bypass the federal government in Washington and participate in a regime developed by lawmakers and governments more than 9,000 km away may seem startling. But the U.S. state is far from alone in following Brussels' regulatory and legislative lead: on issues such as product safety, financial regulation, anti-trust, transport, telecommunications and myriad other policy areas, the EU is leaving an indelible mark on nations outside the bloc.

Sometimes voluntarily, sometimes through gritted teeth and sometimes without even knowing, countries around the world are importing the EU's rules. It is a trend that has sparked concerns among foreign business leaders and that irritates U.S. policymakers. But whether they like it or not, rice farmers in India, mobile phone users in Bahrain, makers of cigarette lighters in China, chemicals producers in the U.S., accountants in Japan and software companies in California have all found that their commercial lives are shaped by decisions taken in the EU capital.

"Brussels has become the global pacesetter for regulation," says David Vogel, a professor of business and public policy at the University of California, Berkeley. Prof. Vogel points out that even the U.S.—the world's most powerful nation and the biggest economy—is finding it increasingly hard to escape the clutches of the Brussels regulatory machine: "The relative impact of EU regulation on U.S. public policy and U.S. business has been dramatically enhanced. Even if a country does not adopt the [European] standards, the firms that export to the EU do. And since most firms do export to the EU, they have adopted the EU's more stringent standards."

The EU's emergence as a global rulemaker has been driven by a number of factors, but none more important than the sheer size and regulatory sophistication of the Union's home market. The rapid expansion of the economic bloc to 27 nations with a total of more than 480 m largely affluent consumers has turned the Union into the world's biggest and most lucrative import market. At the same time, the drive to create a borderless pan-European market for goods, services, capital and labour has triggered a hugely ambitious programme of regulatory and legislative convergence among national regimes.

This exercise has left the Union with a body of law running to almost 95,000 pages—a set of rules and regulations that covers virtually all aspects of economic

Buck, Tobias, "Standard Bearer: How the European Union Exports Its Laws," *Financial Times*, July 10, 2007, p. 9. Reprinted with permission.

life and that is constantly expanded and updated. Compared with other jurisdictions, the EU's rules tend to be stricter, especially where product safety, consumer protection and environmental and health requirements are concerned. Companies that produce their goods to the EU's standards can therefore assume that their products can be marketed everywhere else as well.

As Henrik Selin and Stacy VanDeveer, two U.S.-based academics, point out in a recent paper that examines the global impact of three recent EU laws on chemicals, electronic waste and hazardous substances: "The EU is increasingly replacing the United States as the de facto setter of global product standards and the centre of much global regulatory standard setting is shifting from Washington DC to Brussels."

Japan, for example, has copied a whole batch of EU environmental laws. Southeast Asian nations such as Malaysia and Indonesia have followed Brussels' approach on cosmetics regulation. All around the world, chemical groups are implementing the Union's so-called Reach regulation, which forces companies from BASF in Germany to Dow Chemical in the U.S. to register some 30,000 substances with a new EU agency in Helsinki.

Immediate EU neighbours such as Switzerland and Norway as well as countries in eastern Europe, the Balkans and North Africa are committed to keeping their regulatory regimes as close as possible to the EU approach to ease trade. Countries hoping to join the 27 must in any case incorporate the Union's rules and regulations down to the very last line.

This situation has not come about by accident. The Commission, the EU's executive body, states openly that it wants other countries to follow EU rules and its officials are working hard to put that vision into practice. The Union has established "regulatory dialogues" with a host of countries, most importantly China, to help them improve their domestic regulatory framework–and often to urge them to copy the EU approach.

A Commission policy paper released in February boasted that "frequently the world looks to Europe and adopts the standards that are set here." The document went on to say that the integration of Europe's economies had "spurred the development of rules and standards in areas such as product safety, the environment, securities and corporate governance which inspire global standard setting." It even advocated stronger measures to promote the global use of EU norms, for example through bilateral deals and lobbying in international organisations.

In some cases, however, the EU has to do little more than sit back and watch as other nations voluntarily copy it. This has happened, for example, with the EU's blacklist of airlines that are banned from European airspace. Saudi Arabia, Bahrain and South Korea have copied and enacted the flight bans themselves, while countries including South Africa and Kuwait use the list without putting it into national law. Commission officials also point to a recent law on mobile phone roaming rates and a proposal on solvency ratios for the insurance industry as examples that are closely followed—and may soon be copied—by non-EU countries.

For a country such as Japan the importing of foreign laws is nothing unusual, says Franz Waldenberger, an economics professor at the Japan Centre of Munich's Ludwig-Maximilians University. "Ever since Japan opened itself to the west, there has been a long tradition of turning to western laws for inspiration. There is barely a Japanese law that has not taken a western law as a model. But the key factor is having the highest standard. Global companies develop products for the global market and that means they have to follow the highest standard—which today tends to be European."

The second way in which the EU has stamped its authority on other jurisdictions is through influencing the decisions of international standard-setting organisations and global regulatory bodies such as the International Maritime Organisation or Unece, the Geneva-based branch of the United Nations that deals with economic cooperation.

Carmakers around the world—with the exception of the U.S.—follow Unece's technical standards. But these in turn are based on EU norms drafted and agreed in Brussels. This means European automotive groups such as Volkswagen or Renault can export their vehicles to Japan, India or China without having to remodel their cars or seek the approval of foreign safety authorities. Their U.S. rivals, meanwhile, are often forced to invest in additional tests and costly tweaks to their models before they can be shipped abroad.

Perhaps the most famous example of an EU standard conquering the world is in the market for mobile telephones. The GSM standard was enshrined in a 1987 EU law, then rapidly spread across the economic bloc and today forms the platform used by more than 2bn mobile phone customers around the world (though, again, the U.S. is largely an exception).

Not least thanks to Europe's first-mover advantage, companies such as Finland's Nokia, Ericsson of Sweden and Britain's Vodafone emerged as some of the biggest players in a vast and expanding market.

Officials in Brussels say the EU will in future be in even better shape to dominate global standard-setting. Though it tends to act in unison, the EU after all wields not one but up to 27 votes in bodies such as the IMO. This enabled the Union to persuade the maritime grouping to ban single-hull tanker ships from international waters earlier than many non-European countries wanted.

Indeed, the EU's emergence as a global rulemaker has not been without controversy–and the U.S. in particular has followed the Union's growing regulatory clout with concern. Washington and Brussels have clashed at the World Trade Organisation over the EU's strict limits on genetically modified crops, not least because the U.S. biotechnology industry fears that Europeans' aversion to GM foods will spread to other nations.

Even if Brazilian or Indian farmers do not share Europe's hostility to the new varieties, they must think twice before planting GM rice or maize: if they fall foul of the Union's strict GM laws, they face being shut out from the world's most lucrative market. As Berkeley's Prof. Vogel says: "In the long run it seems there will be a more permissive approach to GMOs. But in the short term there are many countries which are reluctant to use GM crops because of their fear of losing access to the EU market."

C. Boyden Gray, the U.S. ambassador to the EU, says Washington's concerns about the Union's moves reflect the fact that they often hurt businesses outside the

27 member states: "I think there is now recognition [in the U.S.] that the EU is being aggressive about exporting their approach—which tends to favour their own native companies. I think the U.S. is concerned about it because frequently it imposes higher costs across the board."

He adds: "What many in the U.S. think is happening is that EU policymakers tolerate a higher level of regulation and then worry that they are putting themselves at a competitive disadvantage. So they seek to export their regulations abroad so that every multinational is subject to the same level [of regulation]."

To EU officials, this may seem a less than charitable interpretation. But even they admit that the drive to export EU rules is motivated to a large degree by the desire to help European companies. As the February Commission paper argued, being the maker rather than the follower of global rules "works to the advantage of those already geared up to meet these standards."

Companies outside the bloc, meanwhile, are waking up to challenges posed by the EU's growing clout. Groups such as Microsoft—which has been fined close to €780m ($1.1bn, £528m) by the European Commission for breaking EU antitrust laws—now employ large teams of lawyers and lobbyists to attempt to ensure that their views are heard in the Brussels corridors of power. Others use their national governments or trade associations to seek to influence the outcome of the EU regulatory process.

They all know that Brussels is slowly but steadily emerging as the regulatory capital of the world. As much as some loathe it, it is a trend that business leaders and policy-makers from Tokyo to Washington feel they cannot afford to ignore.

Suggested Discussion Topics

1. Is it more useful to think of the UN as an organization that rules over the world or as a club at which world problems are discussed and through which its sovereign members try to coordinate their policies? Which do you think the UN should be? Why?

2. Evaluate the UN's record in maintaining international peace and security before the end of the Cold War. How have UN efforts to maintain peace and security changed since the end of the Cold War? Why have these changes occurred?

3. What reforms, if any, do you think are necessary at the UN to make it effective in today's world? Should the UN have its own army? Why or why not?

4. Discuss the following idea: "The world would be no worse off if the UN were to disappear tomorrow."

5. According to Article 2.7 of the UN Charter, the organization is not permitted to intervene in the domestic affairs of members because such intervention would violate the members' sovereignty. To what extent does this prohibition make sense today? Is it consistent with former Secretary-General Kofi Annan's concern with individual rights and his assertion of a "developing international norm in favor of intervention to protect civilians from wholesale slaughter"? What are the implications of failed states for the United Nations?

6. What does sovereignty mean when sovereign states have to depend on IMF assistance—and agree to IMF conditions, including reforming their domestic political systems—to stabilize their currencies and economies in the face of pressures from the global marketplace? Should states accept that the IMF will be able to dictate policies to them? Or should states try to insulate themselves from global forces and the need for IMF help? Explain your view. How would you feel if the IMF told the United States that it had to change its labor or welfare laws or the way businesses are regulated, or to take steps that would trigger a recession and throw Americans out of work—or even that it had to change how votes are counted in Florida?

7. How do you feel about the fact that the European Union can effectively dictate the regulatory standards that products sold around the world must meet? Should some other body—for example, one in which the United States is represented—have this ability and authority instead? Would your answer change if you acknowledged that until the growth of the European Union (and even now for many products and industries), the United States, as the world's largest economy, effectively had this power to set regulatory standards?

Chapter 7

TIES THAT BIND: THE RISE OF TRANSNATIONAL INSTITUTIONS

The widening violence of postmodern war, the growing problem of terrorism, the dark shadow of weapons of mass destruction, the expanding danger of state failure, the spread of democratic values and institutions, and the increasing power of intergovernmental organizations all testify to the turbulent transformation under way in global politics today, and to the simultaneous fragmentation and integration of politics that is taking place. Perhaps the most striking evidence of this transformation, though, is the growing importance of *transnational institutions*. Reflecting the heightened importance of issues that transcend national frontiers and the growing political activity of ordinary citizens, especially in the advanced economic areas of the world like North America and Europe, transnational institutions are changing how the global political agenda is set and empowering individuals and groups to solve a wide range of problems.

Transnational institutions link together people in different societies, enhancing cooperation and encouraging global and regional responses to the challenges posed by transnational issues. In this way, they act to integrate global politics. Transnational organizations are as varied as the Catholic Church, General Motors, the Boy Scouts, the Irish Republican Army, Greenpeace, the Cali drug cartel, the International Political Science Association, Shell Oil, Doctors Without Borders, and Amnesty International. What these organizations have in common is that their membership consists of ordinary individuals in more than one country. Transnational organizations are thus different from more traditional *intergovernmental organizations (IGOs)* like those discussed in the preceding chapter, whose members are sovereign states.

The proliferation of transnational organizations is even more explosive than that of intergovernmental organizations. This growth is creating a rapidly thickening web of institutions that bind peoples across state frontiers, fundamentally alter the nature of global politics, and reflect both the desire and ability of individuals to take their fate in their own hands. Classically, states and their governments served to mediate the wishes of citizens whose knowledge of and interest in foreign affairs was at most episodic. The growing interdependence of peoples, the erosion of state capacity, the availability of new electronic technologies that provide access to information and allow citizens to communicate easily across vast distances, growing literacy, and the seeming impotence of governments to solve problems have all accelerated transnational activity and the tendency and ability of ordinary people to take responsibility for their own future.

The variety of transnational groups is astounding. Among the most powerful are transnational corporations (TNCs), like General Electric or Coca-Cola, whose business activities span national boundaries, involving people from different societies in networks of economic activities. Other transnational organizations are motivated by goals other than economic profit. They work for environmental ends or human rights, serve educational or humanitarian purposes, and bring together people with similar professions. Together, such groups are bringing about what has been described as an "associational revolution." The spreading network of nonprofit groups is encouraged by the grassroots activities of citizens, the actions of public and private institutions, and sometimes even by official government policies. This revolution, which is taking place in the developing world and the former Soviet bloc as well as in the West, reflects growing citizen activism and participation at a time of declining state efficacy. Dramatic improvements in communication technology and the globalization of economic growth also facilitate and stimulate this associational revolution.

The expansion of transnational institutions and groups represents an exciting, if sometimes troubling, aspect of today's turbulent political transformation. Involving ordinary people, solving ordinary people's problems, and interacting with intergovernmental organizations and states, NGOs and TNCs represent powerful forces on the global political scene and promise to play an important role in addressing the new issues emerging on the world stage.

7.1 Power Shift

Jessica T. Mathews

In the first selection, Jessica T. Mathews, formerly of the prestigious New York–based Council on Foreign Relations and now head of the Carnegie Endowment for International Peace, argues that states are increasingly "sharing powers" with nongovernmental organizations as state sovereignty weakens. In her view, technological innovation, especially in computers and telecommunications, is the most important factor in the decline of states and the rise of nonstate actors because governments no longer enjoy a monopoly on information. Moreover, the new technology has made it easy for people who are physically remote to communicate and make common cause for political ends, thereby reducing government control.

Not only is the number of NGOs growing geometrically, but governments are relying upon them more and more for human and financial resources and for expertise. "Increasingly," Mathews argues, "NGOs are able to push around even the largest governments." The weakening of states has costs and dangers, Mathews observes, but she concludes that "nation-states may no longer be the natural problem-solving unit."

The Rise of Global Civil Society

The end of the Cold War has brought no mere adjustment among states but a novel redistribution of power among states, markets, and civil society. National governments are not simply losing autonomy in a globalizing economy. They are sharing powers—including political, social, and security roles at the core of sovereignty—with businesses, with international organizations, and with a multitude of citizens groups, known as nongovernmental organizations (NGOs). The steady concentration of power in the hands of states that began in 1648 with the Peace of Westphalia is over, at least for a while.

The absolutes of the Westphalian system—territorially fixed states where everything of value lies within some state's borders; a single, secular authority governing each territory and representing it outside its borders; and no authority above states—are all dissolving. Increasingly, resources and threats that matter, including money, information, pollution, and popular culture, circulate and shape lives and economies with little regard for political boundaries. International standards of conduct are gradually beginning to override claims of national or regional singularity. Even the most powerful states find the marketplace and international public opinion compelling them more often to follow a particular course.

The state's central task of assuring security is the least affected, but still not exempt. War will not disappear, but with the shrinkage of U.S. and Russian nuclear arsenals, the transformation of the Nuclear Nonproliferation Treaty into a permanent covenant in 1995, agreement on the long-sought Comprehensive Test Ban treaty in 1996, and the . . . entry into force of the Chemical Weapons Convention in 1997, the security threat to states from other states is on a downward course. Nontraditional threats, however, are rising—terrorism, organized crime, drug trafficking, ethnic conflict, and the combination of rapid population growth, environmental decline, and poverty that breeds economic stagnation, political instability, and, sometimes, state collapse. The nearly 100 armed conflicts since the end of the Cold War have virtually all been intrastate affairs. Many began with governments acting against their own citizens, through extreme corruption, violence, incompetence, or complete breakdown, as in Somalia.

These trends have fed a growing sense that individuals' security may not in fact reliably derive from their nation's security. A competing notion of "human security" is creeping around the edges of official thinking, suggesting that security be viewed as emerging from the conditions of daily life—food, shelter, employment, health, public safety—rather than flowing downward from a country's foreign relations and military strength.

Matthews, Jessica, "Power Shift," *Foreign Affairs,* January/February 1997, pp. 50–66. Reprinted by permission of Foreign Affairs. © 1997 by the Council on Foreign Relations, Inc. <www.ForeignAffairs.org>.

The most powerful engine of change in the relative decline of states and the rise of nonstate actors is the computer and telecommunications revolution, whose deep political and social consequences have been almost completely ignored. Widely accessible and affordable technology has broken governments' monopoly on the collection and management of large amounts of information and deprived governments of the deference they enjoyed because of it. In every sphere of activity, instantaneous access to information and the ability to put it to use multiplies the number of players who matter and reduces the number who command great authority. The effect on the loudest voice—which has been government's—has been the greatest.

By drastically reducing the importance of proximity, the new technologies change people's perceptions of community. Fax machines, satellite hookups, and the Internet connect people across borders with exponentially growing ease while separating them from natural and historical associations within nations. In this sense a powerful globalizing force, they can also have the opposite effect, amplifying political and social fragmentation by enabling more and more identities and interests scattered around the globe to coalesce and thrive.

These technologies have the potential to divide society along new lines, separating ordinary people from elites with the wealth and education to command technology's power. Those elites are not only the rich but also citizens groups with transnational interests and identities that frequently have more in common with counterparts in other countries, whether industrialized or developing, than with countrymen.

Above all, the information technologies disrupt hierarchies, spreading power among more people and groups. In drastically lowering the costs of communication, consultation, and coordination, they favor decentralized networks over other modes of organization. In a network, individuals or groups link for joint action without building a physical or formal institutional presence. Networks have no person at the top and no center. Instead, they have multiple nodes where collections of individuals or groups interact for different purposes. Businesses, citizens' organizations, ethnic groups, and crime cartels have all readily adopted the network model. Governments, on the other hand, are quintessential hierarchies, wedded to an organizational form incompatible with all that the new technologies make possible. . . .

. . . Both in numbers and in impact, nonstate actors have never before approached their current strength. And a still larger role likely lies ahead.

Dial Locally, Act Globally

No one knows how many NGOs there are or how fast the tally is growing. Published figures are badly misleading. . . . In fact, it is impossible to measure a swiftly growing universe that includes neighborhood, professional, service, and advocacy groups, both secular and church-based, promoting every conceivable cause and funded by donations, fees, foundations, governments, international organizations, or the sale of products and services. The true number is certainly in the millions, from the tiniest village association to influential but modestly funded international groups like Amnesty International to larger global activist organizations like Greenpeace and giant service providers like CARE, which has an annual budget of nearly $400 million.

Except in China, Japan, the Middle East, and a few other places where culture or authoritarian governments severely limit civil society, NGOs' role and influence have exploded in the last half-decade. Their financial resources and—often more important—their expertise, approximate and sometimes exceed those of smaller governments and of international organizations. "We have less money and fewer resources than Amnesty International, and we are the arm of the UN for human rights," noted Ibrahima Fall, head of the UN Centre for Human Rights, in 1993. "This is clearly ridiculous." Today NGOs deliver more official development assistance than the entire UN system (excluding the World Bank and the International Monetary Fund). In many countries they are delivering the services—in urban and rural community development, education, and health care—that faltering governments can no longer manage.

The range of these groups' work is almost as broad as their interests. They breed new ideas; advocate, protest, and mobilize public support; do legal, scientific, technical, and policy analysis; provide services; shape, implement, monitor, and enforce national and international commitments; and change institutions and norms.

Increasingly, NGOs are able to push around even the largest governments. When the United States and Mexico set out to reach a trade agreement, the two governments planned on the usual narrowly defined negotiations behind closed doors. But NGOs had a very different vision. Groups from Canada, the United States, and Mexico wanted to see provisions in the North American Free Trade Agreement on health and safety, transboundary pollution, consumer protection, immigration, labor mobility, child labor, sustainable agriculture, social charters, and debt relief. Coalitions of NGOs formed in each country and across both borders. . . .

Technology is fundamental to NGOs' new clout. The nonprofit Association for Progressive Communications provides 50,000 NGOs in 133 countries access to the tens of millions of Internet users for the price of a local call. The dramatically lower costs of international communication have altered NGOs' goals and changed international outcomes. Within hours of the first gunshots of the Chiapas rebellion in southern Mexico in January 1994, for example, the Internet swarmed with messages from human rights activists. The worldwide media attention they and their groups focused on Chiapas, along with the influx of rights activists to the area, sharply limited the Mexican government's response. What in other times would have been a bloody insurgency turned out to be a largely nonviolent conflict. "The shots lasted ten days," José Angel Gurría, Mexico's foreign minister, later remarked, "and ever since, the war has been . . . a war on the Internet."

NGOs' easy reach behind other states' borders forces governments to consider domestic public opinion in countries with which they are dealing, even on matters that governments have traditionally handled strictly between themselves. At the same time, cross-border NGO networks offer citizens groups unprecedented channels of influence. Women's and human rights groups in many developing countries have linked up with more experienced, better funded, and more powerful groups in

Europe and the United States. The latter work the global media and lobby their own governments to pressure leaders in developing countries, creating a circle of influence that is accelerating change in many parts of the world.

Out of the Hallway, Around the Table

In international organizations, as with governments at home, NGOs were once largely relegated to the hallways. Even when they were able to shape governments' agendas . . . their influence was largely determined by how receptive their own government's delegation happened to be. Their only option was to work through governments.

All that changed with the negotiation of the global climate treaty, culminating at the Earth Summit in Rio de Janeiro in 1992. With the broader independent base of public support that environmental groups command, NGOs set the original goal of negotiating an agreement to control greenhouse gases long before governments were ready to do so, proposed most of its structure and content, and lobbied and mobilized public pressure to force through a pact that virtually no one else thought possible when the talks began.

More members of NGOs served on government delegations than ever before, and they penetrated deeply into official decision-making. They were allowed to attend the small working group meetings where the real decisions in international negotiations are made. The tiny nation of Vanuatu turned its delegation over to an NGO with expertise in international law (a group based in London and funded by an American foundation), thereby making itself and the other sea-level island states major players in the fight to control global warming. ECO, an NGO-published daily newspaper, was negotiators' best source of information on the progress of the official talks and became the forum where governments tested ideas for breaking deadlocks.

Whether from developing or developed countries, NGOs were tightly organized in a global and half a dozen regional Climate Action Networks, which were able to bridge North-South differences among governments that many had expected would prevent an agreement. United in their passionate pursuit of a treaty, NGOs would fight out contentious issues among themselves, then take an agreed position to their respective delegations. When they could not agree, NGOs served as invaluable back channels, letting both sides know where the other's problems lay or where a compromise might be found.

As a result, delegates completed the framework of a global climate accord in the blink of a diplomat's eye—16 months—over the opposition of the three energy superpowers, the United States, Russia, and Saudi Arabia. The treaty entered into force in record time just two years later. . . .

The influence of NGOs at the climate talks has not yet been matched in any other arena, and indeed has provoked a backlash among some governments. A handful of authoritarian regimes, most notably China, led the charge, but many others share their unease about the role NGOs are assuming. Nevertheless, NGOs have worked their way into the heart of international negotiations and into the day-to-day operations of international organizations, bringing new priorities, demands for procedures that give a voice to groups outside government, and new standards of accountability.

One World Business

The multinational corporations of the 1960s were virtually all American, and prided themselves on their insularity. Foreigners might run subsidiaries, but they were never partners. A foreign posting was a setback for a rising executive.

Today, a global marketplace is developing for retail sales as well as manufacturing. Law, advertising, business consulting, and financial and other services are also marketed internationally. Firms of all nationalities attempt to look and act like locals wherever they operate. Foreign language skills and lengthy experience abroad are an asset, and increasingly a requirement, for top management. Sometimes corporate headquarters are not even in a company's home country.

Amid shifting alliances and joint ventures, made possible by computers and advanced communications, nationalities blur. Offshore banking encourages widespread evasion of national taxes. Whereas the fear in the 1970s was that multinationals would become an arm of government, the concern now is that they are disconnecting from their home countries' national interests, moving jobs, evading taxes, and eroding economic sovereignty in the process.

The even more rapid globalization of financial markets has left governments far behind. Where governments once set foreign exchange rates, private currency traders, accountable only to their bottom line, now trade $1.3 trillion a day, 100 times the volume of world trade. The amount exceeds the total foreign exchange reserves of all governments, and is more than even an alliance of strong states can buck.

Despite the enormous attention given to governments' conflicts over trade rules, private capital flows have been growing twice as fast as trade for years. International portfolio transactions by U.S. investors, 9 percent of U.S. GDP in 1980, had grown to 135 percent of GDP by 1993. Growth in Germany, Britain, and elsewhere has been even more rapid. Direct investment has surged as well. All in all, the global financial market will grow to a staggering $83 trillion by 2000, a 1994 McKinsey & Co. study estimated, triple the aggregate GDP of the affluent nations of the Organization for Economic Cooperation and Development.

Again, technology has been a driving force, shifting financial clout from states to the market with its offer of unprecedented speed in transactions—states cannot match market reaction times measured in seconds—and its dissemination of financial information to a broad range of players. . . .

More and more frequently today, governments have only the appearance of free choice when they set economic rules. Markets are setting de facto rules enforced by their own power. States can flout them, but the penalties are severe—loss of vital foreign capital, foreign technology, and domestic jobs. Even the most powerful economy must pay heed. . . .

The forces shaping the legitimate global economy are also nourishing globally integrated crime—which UN officials peg at a staggering $750 billion a year,

$400 billion to $500 billion of that in narcotics, according to U.S. Drug Enforcement Agency estimates. Huge increases in the volume of goods and people crossing borders and competitive pressures to speed the flow of trade by easing inspections and reducing paperwork make it easier to hide contraband. Deregulation and privatization of government-owned businesses, modern communications, rapidly shifting commercial alliances, and the emergence of global financial systems have all helped transform local drug operations into global enterprises. The largely unregulated multi-trillion-dollar pool of money in supranational cyberspace, accessible by computer 24 hours a day, eases the drug trade's toughest problem: transforming huge sums of hot cash into investments in legitimate business.

Globalized crime is a security threat that neither police nor the military—the state's traditional responses—can meet. Controlling it will require states to pool their efforts and to establish unprecedented cooperation with the private sector, thereby compromising two cherished sovereign roles. If states fail, if criminal groups can continue to take advantage of porous borders and transnational financial spaces while governments are limited to acting within their own territory, crime will have the winning edge. . . .

Leaps of Imagination

After three and a half centuries, it requires a mental leap to think of world politics in any terms other than occasionally cooperating but generally competing states, each defined by its territory and representing all the people therein. Nor is it easy to imagine political entities that could compete with the emotional attachment of a shared landscape, national history, language, flag, and currency.

Yet history proves that there are alternatives other than tribal anarchy. Empires, both tightly and loosely ruled, achieved success and won allegiance. In the Middle Ages, emperors, kings, dukes, knights, popes, archbishops, guilds, and cities exercised overlapping secular power over the same territory in a system that looks much more like a modern, three-dimensional network than the clean-lined, hierarchical state order that replaced it. The question now is whether there are new geographic or functional entities that might grow up alongside the state, taking over some of its powers and emotional resonance. . . .

For Better or Worse?

A world that is more adaptable and in which power is more diffused could mean more peace, justice, and capacity to manage the burgeoning list of humankind's interconnected problems. At a time of accelerating change, NGOs are quicker than governments to respond to new demands and opportunities. Internationally, in both the poorest and richest countries, NGOs, when adequately funded, can outperform government in the delivery of many public services. Their growth, along with that of the other elements of civil society, can strengthen the fabric of the many still-fragile democracies. And they are better than governments at dealing with problems that grow slowly and affect society through their cumulative effect on individuals—the "soft" threats of environmental degradation, denial of human rights, population growth, poverty, and lack of development that may already be causing more deaths in conflict than are traditional acts of aggression.

As the computer and telecommunications revolution continues, NGOs will become more capable of large-scale activity across national borders. Their loyalties and orientation, like those of international civil servants and citizens of non-national entities like the EU, are better matched than those of governments to problems that demand transnational solutions. International NGOs and cross-border networks of local groups have bridged North-South differences that in earlier years paralyzed cooperation among countries.

On the economic front, expanding private markets can avoid economically destructive but politically seductive policies, such as excessive borrowing or overly burdensome taxation, to which governments succumb. Unhindered by ideology, private capital flows to where it is best treated and thus can do the most good. . . .

There are . . . many reasons, however, to believe that the continuing diffusion of power away from nation-states will mean more conflict and less problem-solving both within states and among them.

For all their strengths, NGOs are special interests, albeit not motivated by personal profit. The best of them, the ablest and most passionate, often suffer most from tunnel vision, judging every public act by how it affects their particular interest. Generally, they have limited capacity for large-scale endeavors, and as they grow, the need to sustain growing budgets can compromise the independence of mind and approach that is their greatest asset.

A society in which the piling up of special interests replaces a single strong voice for the common good is unlikely to fare well. Single-issue voters, as Americans know all too well, polarize and freeze public debate. In the longer run, a stronger civil society could also be more fragmented, producing a weakened sense of common identity and purpose and less willingness to invest in public goods, whether health and education or roads and ports. More and more groups promoting worthy but narrow causes could ultimately threaten democratic government.

Internationally, excessive pluralism could have similar consequences. Two hundred nation-states is a barely manageable number. Add hundreds of influential nonstate forces—businesses, NGOs, international organizations, ethnic and religious groups—and the international system may represent more voices but be unable to advance any of them.

Moreover, there are roles that only the state—at least among today's polities—can perform. States are the only nonvoluntary political unit, the one that can impose order and is invested with the power to tax. Severely weakened states will encourage conflict, as they have in Africa, Central America, and elsewhere. Moreover, it may be that only the nation-state can meet crucial social needs that markets do not value. Providing a modicum of job security, avoiding higher unemployment, preserving a livable environment and a stable climate, and protecting consumer health and safety are but a few of the tasks that could be left dangling in a world of expanding markets and retreating states. . . .

Finally, fearsome dislocations are bound to accompany the weakening of the central institution of modern society. The prophets of an internetted world in which national identities gradually fade, proclaim its revolutionary nature and yet believe the changes will be wholly benign. They won't be. The shift from national to some other political allegiance, if it comes, will be an emotional, cultural, and political earthquake.

Dissolving and Evolving

Might the decline in state power prove transitory? Present disenchantment with national governments could dissipate as quickly as it arose. Continuing globalization may well spark a vigorous reassertion of economic or cultural nationalism. By helping solve problems governments cannot handle, business, NGOs and international organizations may actually be strengthening the nation-state system.

These are all possibilities, but the clash between the fixed geography of states and the nonterritorial nature of today's problems and solutions, which is only likely to escalate, strongly suggests that the relative power of states will continue to decline. Nation-states may simply no longer be the natural problem-solving unit. Local government addresses citizens' growing desire for a role in decision-making, while transnational, regional, and even global entities better fit the dimensions of trends in economics, resources, and security.

The evolution of information and communications technology, which has only just begun, will probably heavily favor nonstate entities, including those not yet envisaged, over states. The new technologies encourage noninstitutional, shifting networks over the fixed bureaucratic hierarchies that are the hallmark of the single-voiced sovereign state. They dissolve issues' and institutions' ties to a fixed place. And by greatly empowering individuals, they weaken the relative attachment to community, of which the preeminent one in modern society is the nation-state.

If current trends continue, the international system 50 years hence will be profoundly different. During the transition, the Westphalian system and an evolving one will exist side by side. States will set the rules by which all other actors operate, but outside forces will increasingly make decisions for them. In using business, NGOs, and international organizations to address problems they cannot or do not want to take on, states will, more often than not, inadvertently weaken themselves further. Thus governments' unwillingness to adequately fund international organizations helped NGOs move from a peripheral to a central role in shaping multi-lateral agreements, since the NGOs provided expertise the international organizations lacked. At least for a time, the transition is likely to weaken rather than bolster the world's capacity to solve its problems. If states, with the overwhelming share of power, wealth, and capacity, can do less, less will get done.

Whether the rise of nonstate actors ultimately turns out to be good news or bad will depend on whether humanity can launch itself on a course of rapid social innovation, as it did after World War II. Needed adaptations include a business sector that can shoulder a broader policy role, NGOs that are less parochial and better able to operate on a large scale, international institutions that can efficiently serve the dual masters of states and citizenry, and, above all, new institutions and political entities that match the transnational scope of today's challenges while meeting citizens' demands for accountable democratic governance.

7.2 Learning to Live with NGOs

P. J. Simmons

The increasing power and influence of NGOs raises critical questions about their nature and whether they will be a force for good or evil. In the next selection, P. J. Simmons of the Carnegie Endowment for International Peace builds on Mathews's analysis, looks at the roles NGOs play, warns about the dangers as well as benefits inherent in increasing NGO strength, and explores how to incorporate NGOs into the international system in ways that take advantage of the integration they provide without creating unnecessary dangers.

In the summer of 1994, U.S. environmental advocacy groups were getting ready to celebrate. The United States was about to join almost 90 other nations in ratifying the Convention on Biodiversity, which enjoyed broad support from U.S. environmentalists, agro-business groups, and the biotechnology sector. After hearings characterized in the press as a "love fest," members of the Senate Foreign Relations Committee were almost unanimously prepared to back the treaty. Then a group of agricultural and trade nongovernmental organizations (NGOs) previously uninvolved in the debate weighed in, warning that ratification could, in effect, destroy U.S. agriculture. As the *Chicago Tribune* reported in September 1994, evidence later surfaced that some of this opposition was based on a virulent misinformation campaign claiming, among other things, that treaty advocates were all foes of farming, logging, and fishing. But by then, the biodiversity treaty had been relegated to the back of a long line of treaties competing for congressional attention.

At a time when NGOs are celebrating their remarkable success in achieving a ban on landmines and creating an International Criminal Court (ICC), it may seem churlish to recall a four-year-old episode that many would likely regard as a defeat. But amid the breathless accounts about the growing power of NGOs, the failure of the biodiversity treaty is a useful reminder of the complexity of the role that these groups now play in international affairs. Embracing a bewildering array of beliefs, interests, and agendas, they have the potential to do as much harm as good. Hailed as the exemplars of grassroots democracy in action, many NGOs are, in fact, decidedly undemocratic and unaccountable to the people they claim to represent. Dedicated to promoting more openness and participation in decision making, they can instead lapse into old-fashioned interest group politics that produces gridlock on a global scale.

The question facing national governments, multilateral institutions, and national and multinational corporations is not whether to include NGOs in their deliberations and activities. Although many traditional centers of power are fighting a rear-guard action against these new players, there is no real way to keep them out. Instead, the real challenge is figuring out how to incorporate NGOs into the international system in a way that takes account of their diversity and scope, their various strengths and weaknesses, and their capacity to disrupt as well as to create.

Why NGOs Matter

. . . In 1948, for example, the UN listed 41 consultative groups that were formally accredited to cooperate and consult with the UN Economic and Social Council (ECOSOC); in 1998, there were more than 1,500 with varying degrees of participation and access. Until recently, NGOs clustered in developed and democratic nations; now groups sprout up from Lima to Beijing. They are changing societal norms, challenging national governments, and linking up with counterparts in powerful transnational alliances. And they are muscling their way into areas of high politics, such as arms control, banking, and trade, that were previously dominated by the state.

In general terms, NGOs affect national governments, multilateral institutions, and national and multinational corporations in four ways: setting agendas, negotiating outcomes, conferring legitimacy, and implementing solutions.

Setting Agendas NGOs have long played a key role in forcing leaders and policymakers to pay attention. In the early 1800s, U.S. and European bodies such as the British and Foreign Anti-Slavery Society were driving forces behind government action on the slave trade; by the turn of the century, groups such as the Anglo-Oriental Society for the Suppression of the Opium Trade were leading an influential antidrug movement that culminated in the 1912 Hague Opium Convention. In 1945, NGOs were largely responsible for inserting human-rights language in the UN Charter and have since put almost every major human-rights issue on the international agenda. Likewise, NGO activism since the 1960s and 1970s successfully raised the profile of global environmental and population issues.

Instead of holding marches or hanging banners off buildings, NGO members now use computers and cell phones to launch global public-relations blitzes that can force issues to the top of policymakers' "to do" lists. Consider the 1997 Nobel Prize–winning campaign by NGOs to conclude a treaty banning landmines over the objections of the United States. The self-described "full working partnership" between the Canadian government and a loose coalition of more than 350 humanitarian and arms-control NGOs from 23 countries was key to the negotiations' success. But what seized the attention of the public and policymakers was the coalition's innovative media campaign using the World Wide Web, faxes, e-mail, newsletters, and even *Superman* and *Batman* comic books. Treaty supporters won the signatures of 122 nations in 14 months. When several coalition members announced plans for a follow-on campaign against small arms, the U.S. government sprang into action, meeting with 20 other countries in July 1998 to launch official talks on a possible treaty.

Negotiating Outcomes   NGOs can be essential in designing multilateral treaties that work. Chemical manufacturing associations from around the world helped set up an effective verification regime for the 1997 Chemical Weapons Convention that could be supported by industries and militaries. Throughout the various sessions of negotiations on climate change, groups such as the Environmental Defense Fund and the World Business Council for Sustainable Development have helped craft compromise proposals that attempt to reconcile environmental and commercial interests; meanwhile, NGOs have been instrumental in helping government negotiators understand the science behind the issues that they seek to address.

NGOs can also build trust and break deadlocks when negotiations have reached an impasse. In 1990, a sole Italian NGO, the Comunità di Sant'Egidio, started the informal meetings between the warring parties in Mozambique that eventually led to a peace settlement. During talks in 1995 to extend the Treaty on the Non-Proliferation of Nuclear Weapons, NGOs from several countries working with the South African government delegation helped forge a compromise that led to the treaty's permanent extension.

Conferring Legitimacy   NGO judgments can be decisive in promoting or withholding public and political support. The World Bank learned this lesson in the early 1990s, albeit the hard way. After decades of watching the bank do business with only a handful of NGOs and brush off demands for change, more than 150 public-interest NGOs took part in a sustained campaign to spur greater openness and accountability and to encourage debt reduction and development strategies that were more equitable and less destructive to the environment. Today, partly as a result of this high-profile pressure, about half of the bank's lending projects have provisions for NGO involvement—up from an average of only 6 percent between 1973 and 1988. The bank has even included NGOs such as Oxfam International in once sacrosanct multilateral debt relief discussions—against the wishes of many World Bank and International Monetary Fund (IMF) officials. Even the IMF is beginning to change its tune. In June 1998, the IMF Board of Directors met with several NGO leaders to discuss their proposals to increase the fund's transparency.

Making Solutions Work   NGOs on the ground often make the impossible possible by doing what governments cannot or will not. Some humanitarian and development NGOs have a natural advantage because of their perceived neutrality and experience. The International Committee of the Red Cross, for example, is able to deliver health care to political prisoners in exchange for silence about any human-rights violations that its members witness. Other groups such as Oxfam International provide rapid relief during and after complex humanitarian disasters—with and without UN partners. Moreover, as governments downsize and new challenges crowd the international agenda, NGOs increasingly fill the breach. Willy-nilly, the UN and nation-states are depending more on NGOs to get things done. Total assistance by and through international NGOs to the developing world amounted to about $8 billion in 1992—accounting for 13 percent of all development assistance and more than the entire amount transferred by the UN system.

International NGOs also play critical roles in translating international agreements and norms into domestic realities. Where governments have turned a blind eye, groups such as Amnesty International and the Committee to Protect Journalists call attention to violations of the UN Declaration on Human Rights. Environmental NGOs police agreements such as the Convention on International Trade in Endangered Species, uncovering more accurate data on compliance than that provided by member nations. Perhaps one of the most vital but overlooked NGO roles is to promote the societal changes needed to make international agreements work. Signatories of the Organization for Economic Cooperation and Development's 1997 Bribery Convention, for example, are counting on the more than 80 chapters of Transparency International to help change the way their societies view bribery and corruption.

Increasingly, however, NGOs operate outside existing formal frameworks, moving independently to meet their goals and establishing new standards that governments, institutions, and corporations are themselves compelled to follow through force of public opinion. The UN moratorium on driftnet fishing in 1992 and the U.S. International Dolphin Conservation Act of 1994, for example, largely codified changes in fishing practices that NGOs had already succeeded in promoting and then winning from commercial fisheries. More recently, even as governments and multilateral institutions slowly begin to consider measures to promote the sustainable use of forests, the environmental NGO Greenpeace led a European consumer boycott that persuaded a leading Canadian logging company to announce that it would change the way that it harvests trees.

The Rise of the "Global Idiots"?

Despite the demonstrated capacity of NGOs to do good, their growing power on the ground has exposed them to heightened criticism, some of it justified. . . . In the Sudan and Somalia, NGOs have subsidized warring factions by making direct and indirect payments to gain access to areas needing assistance. In other conflict settings such as Ethiopia and Rwanda, NGO-constructed roads and camps for civilian assistance have instead been used by combatants.

Other longer-term concerns loom for these service-delivery NGOs. The UN High Commissioner for Refugees warned in 1996 that if national governments continue to favor NGOs over multilateral agencies in donor assistance, they may undermine important systems of coordination and cooperation in large-scale emergencies. Intense competition among NGOs in the relief sector has also pushed the sector toward a form of oligopoly that threatens to crowd out smaller players, especially local NGOs in developing countries. Eight major groups now control about 50 percent of the relief market. . . .

But on balance, the record for such NGOs is surely no worse than that of governments. NGOs are increasingly aware of these weaknesses and are moving to address them by adopting codes of conduct and pledging to "do no harm." Moreover, given their origins as grassroots groups, NGOs tend to be wary of organizations that become too big; this innate suspicion can serve as a mechanism for self-regulation.

Yet, the greatest challenges created by the growing influence of NGOs are not in the field but in the arena of public opinion and the corridors of power. Today, in a phenomenon that one environmental activist bemoaned as the "rise of the global idiots," any group with a fax machine and a modem has the potential to distort public debate—witness the demise of not just the biodiversity treaty but the Multilateral Agreement on Investment (MAI), which for all its apparent shortcomings still deserved more reasoned consideration than it received. . . . Even legitimate, well-established groups sometimes seize on issues that seem designed more to promote their own image and fundraising efforts than to advance the public interest: in 1995, for example, Greenpeace continued to attack the Royal Dutch/Shell Group for its plans to sink an oil rig (the Brent Spar) in the North Sea, even after independent scientific analyses showed that the environmental effects of doing so would be inconsequential. Steeped in a culture that encourages adversarial attitudes to the powers that be, many NGOs seem best suited to confrontation, a characteristic that some U.S. policymakers seized on in noting that the NGO coalition against landmines might have won U.S. support (and hence a stronger treaty) if it had been more patient and willing to compromise.

The Limits of Democracy

Governments, multilateral institutions, and corporations face inherent dilemmas in trying to work with NGOs. At their most fundamental level, these dilemmas hinge on two key questions: Who should participate, and how? On the one hand, opening up the floodgates to allow equal access to every group would frustrate decision making. More than 1,500 NGOs were accredited at the 1992 United Nations Conference on the Environment and Development in Rio de Janeiro, for example. Trying to include them all was impossible, so in the final days of the conference, government delegates increasingly retreated behind closed doors. On the other hand, narrowing the field fairly is extraordinarily difficult because no one algorithm or set of criteria can objectively rank the worth of an NGO to a participatory process. . . .

Some traditional centers for power have done a better job than others at tackling these kinds of questions about participation. Among nation-states, Canada stands out for its role in forging an alliance with NGOs on the landmine ban. As Foreign Minister Lloyd Axworthy has said, "Clearly, one can no longer relegate NGOs to simple advisory or advocacy roles. . . . They are now part of the way decisions have to be made." . . . The U.S. record in working with NGOs is mixed: generally good in areas such as the environment and relatively poor in areas such as arms control and regional issues. China represents another extreme, having chosen to banish NGO delegates at the Fourth International Women's Conference in Beijing in 1995 to a site one hour's drive away from the main negotiations.

Most multinational corporations are still struggling to figure out how to handle NGO participation. . . . Still, there are grounds for optimism: a 1998 survey of 133 NGOs found that while many rated their current relationships with corporations as "antagonistic" or "nonexistent," most predicted the development of cooperative relationships in the future. The changing attitude toward NGOs of the Royal Dutch/Shell Group may be a case in point. Stung by fierce NGO campaigns on the Brent Spar episode and its operations in Nigeria, where its ties to the dictatorship of General Sani Abacha made it a target for human-rights groups, Shell has adopted a new Statement of General Business Principles that includes commitments on human rights and the environment; in regions such as Latin America, it now consults with NGOs to ensure that its oil operations take environmental and social factors into account. . . .

Perhaps most important in the long run are systems to formalize existing means of two-way communication between decision-making institutions and "stakeholders." Although NGOs still see much room for improvement at the World Bank, it has produced better decisions and is rated accountable by more NGOs because it no longer simply provides a sounding board mechanism for selected groups to air their views. The bank now disseminates more detailed information about its decisions and activities so outside groups can weigh in. And it uses a variety of techniques to elicit feedback and track NGO expertise—including surveys, advisory groups, public meetings, and private meetings with staff. Consequently, the bank is more apt to consult and partner with the right groups when designing and implementing specific projects. Because the system is more open, groups that cannot participate directly are more likely to judge the decision-making process as accountable—even if they disagree with the results.

Letting NGOs Be NGOs

Many governments and institutions—including the WTO, IMF, and several UN bodies—will continue to resist more public participation, arguing that their issues require great secrecy. . . .

The challenge facing NGOs is more subtle but no less important. As these groups acquire the access and influence that they have long sought, they must not lose the qualities that have made them a source of innovation and progress. Some analysts already fear that formerly independent NGOs may become more beholden to national governments as they come to rely more on public-sector funding—which now accounts for around 40 percent of NGO budgets versus only 1.5 percent in 1970. And many of the schema for increasing NGO involvement may simply foster predictable and bureaucratic behavior among civil society representatives, potentially dulling the passion and richness of views that can emanate from narrowly focused groups. They may also cut off NGOs from the informal channels through which they have traditionally been most influential.

Instead, NGOs, governments, and multilateral institutions need to devise systems of public participation that draw on the expertise and resources of NGOs, their grassroots connections, sense of purpose and commitment, and freedom from bureaucratic constraints. Those NGOs that have seen the most rapid growth in their power will have to contend with inevitable limits on their influence and access. Those governments and institutions that have resisted the advance of these new players will have to permit an unprecedented level of public scrutiny and participation. Over time, this messy process of give-and-take promises to transform the way that international affairs are conducted. Yet as it plays out, both sides may realize that the new system that they have sought to create or resist is in many respects no different from the clash of competing interests that has characterized democracies since their inception.

NGOs and States

7.3 NGOs: Sins of the Secular Missionaries

The Economist

The combination of weakening or failing states and the growing capacity of NGOs has meant that in some cases NGOs have stepped in to provide basic services, such as education and health care, that states are failing to provide. Where states are failing, NGOs seem to be the big growth industry, as the following article from *The Economist* suggests. In some cases, these NGOs are closely linked to other states, and are carrying out assistance operations that these states could not conduct without clearly violating sovereignty. Thus while NGOs may find themselves at loggerheads with IGOs, and while NGOs may be infringing on the sovereign responsibilities of failing states, NGOs and nonfailing states—and NGOs and businesses—are developing complex, symbiotic relationships. Indeed, the boundaries between states, NGOs, and businesses are becoming increasingly unclear.

A young man thrusts his crudely printed calling card at the visitor. After his name are printed three letters: NGO.
"What do you do?" the visitor asks.
"I have formed an NGO."
"Yes, but what does it do?"
"Whatever they want. I am waiting for some funds and then I will make a project."
Once little more than ragged charities, non-governmental organisations (NGOs) are now big business. Somalia, where that exchange took place, is heaven for them. In large parts of the country, western governments, the United Nations and foreign aid agencies cannot work directly; it is too dangerous. So outsiders must work through local groups, which become a powerful source of patronage. "Anybody who's anybody is an NGO these days," sighs one UN official.
And not just in Somalia. NGOs now head for crisis zones as fast as journalists do: a war, a flood, refugees, a dodgy election, even a world trade conference, will draw

them like a honey pot. Last spring, Tirana, the capital of Albania, was swamped by some 200 groups intending to help the refugees from Kosovo. In Kosovo itself, the ground is now thick with foreign groups competing to foster democracy, build homes and proffer goods and services. Environmental activists in Norway board whaling ships; do-gooders gather for the Chiapas rebels in Mexico.

In recent years, such groups have mushroomed. A 1995 UN report on global governance suggested that nearly 29,000 international NGOs existed. Domestic ones have grown even faster. By one estimate, there are now 2 million in America alone, most formed in the past 30 years. In Russia, where almost none existed before the fall of communism, there are at least 65,000. Dozens are created daily; in Kenya alone, some 240 NGOs are now created every year.

Most of these are minnows; some are whales, with annual incomes of millions of dollars and a worldwide operation. Some are primarily helpers, distributing relief where it is needed; some are mainly campaigners, existing to promote issues deemed important by their members. The general public tends to see them as uniformly altruistic, idealistic and independent. But the term "NGO," like the activities of the NGOs themselves, deserves much sharper scrutiny.

Governments' Puppets?

The tag "Non-Governmental Organisation" was used first at the founding of the UN. It implies that NGOs keep their distance from officialdom; they do things that governments will not, or cannot, do. In fact, NGOs have a great deal to do with governments. Not all of it is healthy.

Take the aid NGOs. A growing share of development spending, emergency relief and aid transfers passes through them. According to Carol Lancaster, a former deputy director of USAID, America's development body, NGOs have become "the most important constituency for the activities of development aid agencies." Much of the food delivered by the World Food Programme, a UN body, in Albania last year was actually handed out by NGOs working in the refugee camps. Between 1990 and 1994, the proportion of the EU's relief aid channeled through NGOs rose from 47 percent to 67 percent. The Red Cross reckons that NGOs now disburse more money than the World Bank.

And governments are happy to provide that money. Of Oxfam's £98 million ($162 million) income in 1998, a quarter, £24.1 million, was given by the British government and the EU. World Vision U.S., which boasts of being the world's "largest privately funded Christian relief and development organisation," collected $55 million-worth of goods that year from the American government. Médecins Sans Frontières (MSF), the winner of last year's [1999's] Nobel peace prize, gets 46 percent of its income from government sources. Of 120 NGOs which sprang up in Kenya between 1993 and the end of 1996, all but nine received all their income from foreign governments and international bodies. Such official contributions will go on, especially if the public gets more stingy. Today's young, educated and rich give a smaller share of their incomes away than did—and do—their parents.

In Africa, where international help has the greatest influence, western governments have long been shifting their aid towards NGOs. America's help, some $711 million last year, increasingly goes to approved organisations, often via USAID. Europe's donors also say that bilateral aid should go to NGOs, which are generally more open and efficient than governments. For the UN, too, they are now seen as indispensable. The new head of the UN's Development Programme says the body "will put a lot more emphasis on relations with NGOs." Most such agencies now have hundreds of NGO partners.

So the principal reason for the recent boom in NGOs is that western governments finance them. This is not a matter of charity, but of privatisation: many "non-governmental" groups are becoming contractors for governments. Governments prefer to pass aid through NGOs because it is cheaper, more efficient—and more at arm's length—than direct official aid.

Governments also find NGOs useful in ways that go beyond the distribution of food and blankets. Some bring back useful information, and make it part of their brief to do so. Outfits such as the International Crisis Group and Global Witness publish detailed and opinionated reports from places beset by war or other disasters. The work of Global Witness in Angola is actually paid for by the British Foreign Office.

Diplomats and governments, as well as other NGOs, journalists and the public, can make good use of these reports. As the staff of foreign embassies shrink, and the need to keep abreast of events abroad increases, governments inevitably turn to private sources of information. In some benighted parts of the world, sometimes only NGOs can nowadays reveal what is going on.

Take, for example, human rights, the business of one of the biggest of the campaigning NGOs, Amnesty International. Amnesty has around 1 million members in over 162 countries, and its campaigns against political repression, in particular against unfair imprisonment, are known around the world. The information it gathers is often unavailable from other sources.

Where western governments' interests match those of campaigning NGOs, they can form effective alliances. In 1997, a coalition of over 350 NGOs pushed for, and obtained, a treaty against the use of landmines. The campaign was backed by the usual array of concerned governments (Canada, the Scandinavians) and won the Nobel peace prize.

NGOs are also interesting and useful to governments because they work in the midst of conflict. Many were created by wars: the Red Cross after the Battle of Solferino in 1859, the Save the Children Fund after the First World War, MSF after the Biafran war. By being "close to the action" some NGOs, perhaps unwittingly, provide good cover for spies—a more traditional means by which governments gather information.

In some cases, NGOs are taking over directly from diplomats: not attempting to help the victims of war, but to end the wars themselves. Some try to restrict arms flows, such as Saferworld, which is against small arms. Others attempt to negotiate ceasefires. The Italian Catholic lay community of Sant' Egidio helped to end 13 years of civil war in Mozambique in 1992. International Alert, a London-based peace research group, tried the same for Sierra Leone in the mid-1990s. Last year,

Unicef (a part of the UN) and the Carter Centre, founded by ex-President Jimmy Carter, brought about a peace deal of sorts between Uganda and Sudan. There are now roughly 500 groups registered by the European Platform for Conflict Prevention and Transformation. "Civil war demands civil action," say the organisers.

Larger NGOs have pledged not to act as "instruments of government foreign policy." But at times they are seen as just that. Governments are more willing to pay groups to deliver humanitarian aid to a war zone than to deliver it themselves. Last autumn, America's Congress passed a resolution to deliver food aid to rebels in southern Sudan via USAID and sympathetic Christian groups (religious NGOs earn the label RINGOs, and are found everywhere).

Perhaps the most potent sign of the closeness between NGOs and governments, aside from their financial links, is the exchange of personnel. In developing countries where the civil service is poor, some governments ask NGOs to help with the paperwork requested by the World Bank and other international institutions. Politicians, or their wives, often have their own local NGOs. In the developed world, meanwhile, increasing numbers of civil servants take time off to work for NGOs, and vice versa: Oxfam has former staff members not only in the British government, but also in the Finance Ministry of Uganda.

This symbiotic relationship with government (earning some groups the tag GRINGO) may make the governments of developing countries work better. It may also help aid groups to do their job effectively. But it hardly reflects their independence.

NGOs can also stray too close to the corporate world. Some, known to critics as "business NGOs," deliberately model themselves on, or depend greatly on, particular corporations. Bigger ones have commercial arms, media departments, aggressive head-hunting methods and a wide array of private fund-raising and investment strategies. Smaller ones can be overwhelmed by philanthropic businesses or their owners: Bill Gates, the head of Microsoft, gave $25 million last year to an NGO that is looking for a vaccine for AIDS, transforming it overnight from a small group with a good idea to a powerful one with a lot of money to spend.

The Business of Helping

In 1997, according to the OECD, NGOs raised $5.5 billion from private donors. The real figure may well be higher: as leisure, travel and other industries have grown, so too have charities. In 1995 non-profit groups (including, but not only, NGOs) provided over 12 percent of all jobs in the Netherlands, 8 percent in America and 6 percent in Britain.

Many groups have come to depend on their media presence to help with fund-raising. This is bringing NGOs their greatest problems. They are adapting from shoebox outfits, stuffing envelopes and sending off perhaps one container of medicines, to sophisticated multi-million-dollar operations. In the now-crowded relief market, campaigning groups must jostle for attention: increasingly, NGOs compete and spend a lot of time and money marketing themselves. Bigger ones typically spend 10 percent of their funds on marketing and fund-raising.

The focus of such NGOs can easily shift from finding solutions and helping needy recipients to pleasing their donors and winning television coverage. Events at Goma, in Congo, in 1994 brought this problem home. Tens of thousands of refugees from Rwanda, who had flooded into Goma, depended on food and shelter from the UN High Commissioner for Refugees and from NGOs. Their dramatic plight drew the television cameras and, with them, the chance for publicity and huge donations. A frantic scramble for funds led groups to lie about their projects. Fearful that the media and then the public might lose confidence in NGOs, the Red Cross drew up an approved list of NGOs and got them to put their names to a ten-point code of conduct.

Since then, NGOs have been working hard to improve. More than 70 groups and 142 governments backed the 1995 code of conduct, agreeing that aid should be delivered "only on a basis of need." "We hold ourselves accountable to both those we seek to assist and those from whom we accept resources," they pledged. Yet in Kosovo last year there was a similar scramble, with groups pushing to be seen by camera crews as they worked. Personnel and resources were even shifted there from worse wars and refugee crises in Africa.

As they get larger, NGOs are also looking more and more like businesses themselves. In the past, such groups sought no profits, paid low wages—or none at all—and employed idealists. Now a whole class of them, even if not directly backed by businesses, have taken on corporate trappings. Known collectively as BINGOs, these groups manage funds and employ staff which a medium-sized company would envy. Like corporations, they attend conferences endlessly. Fund-raisers and senior staff at such NGOs earn wages comparable to the private sector. Some bodies, once registered as charities, now choose to become non-profit companies or charitable trusts for tax reasons and so that they can control their spending and programmes more easily. Many big charities have trading arms, registered as companies. One manufacturing company, Tetra Pak, has even considered sponsoring emergency food delivery as a way to advertise itself.

Any neat division between the corporate and the NGO worlds is long gone. Many NGOs operate as competitors seeking contracts in the aid market, raising funds with polished media campaigns and lobbying governments as hard as any other business. Governments and UN bodies could now, in theory, ask for tenders from businesses and NGOs to carry out their programmes. It seems only a matter of time before this happens. If NGOs are cheap and good at delivering food or health care in tough areas, they should win the contracts easily.

Good Intentions Not Enough

It could be argued that it does not matter even if NGOs are losing their independence, becoming just another arm of government or another business. GRINGOs and BINGOs, after all, may be more efficient than the old sort of charity.

Many do achieve great things: they may represent the last hope for civilians caught in civil wars, for those imprisoned unfairly and for millions of desperate refugees. There are many examples of small, efficient and inspirational groups with great achievements: the best will employ local people, keep foreign expertise to a minimum, attempt precise goals (such as providing clean water) and think deeply about the long-term impact of their work. Some of these grow into large, well-run groups.

But there are also problems. NGOs may be assumed to be less bureaucratic, wasteful or corrupt than governments, but under-scrutinised groups can suffer from the same chief failing: they can get into bad ways because they are not accountable to anyone.

Critics also suspect that some aid groups are used to propagate western values, as Christian missionaries did in the 19th century. Many NGOs, lacking any base in the local population and with their money coming from outside, simply try to impose their ideas without debate. For example, they often work to promote women's or children's interests as defined by western societies, winning funds easily but causing social disruption on the ground.

Groups that carry out population or birth-control projects are particularly controversial; some are paid to carry out sterilisation programmes in the poor parts of the world, because donors in the rich world consider there are too many people there. Anti-"slavery" campaigns in Africa, in which western NGOs buy children's freedom for a few hundreds dollars each, are notorious. Unicef has condemned such groups, but American NGOs continue to buy slaves—or people they consider slaves—in southern Sudan. Clearly, buying slaves, if that is what they are, will do little to discourage the practice of trading them.

NGOs also get involved in situations where their presence may prolong or complicate wars, where they end up feeding armies, sheltering hostages or serving as cover for warring parties. These may be the unintended consequences of aid delivery, but they also complicate foreign policy.

Even under calmer conditions, in non-emergency development work, not all single-interest groups may be the best guarantors of long-term success. They are rarely obliged to think about trade-offs in policy or to consider broad, cross-sector approaches to development. NGOs are "often organised to promote particular goals . . . rather than the broader goal of development," argues Ms. Lancaster. In Kosovo last spring [1999], "many governments made bilateral funding agreements with NGOs, greatly undermining UNHCR's [United Nations High Commissioner for Refugees] ability to prioritise programmes or monitor efficiency," says Peter Morris of MSF. This spring in Kosovo, "there were instances of several NGOs competing to work in the same camps, duplication of essential services," complains an Oxfam worker.

And whatever big international NGOs do in the developing world, they bring in western living standards, personnel and purchasing power which can transform local markets and generate great local resentment. In troubled zones where foreign NGOs flourish, weekends bring a line of smart four-by-fours parked at the best beaches, restaurants or nightclubs. The local beggars do well, but discrepancies between expatriate staff and, say, impoverished local officials trying to do the same work can cause deep antipathy. Not only have NGOs diverted funds away from local governments, but they are often seen as directly challenging their sovereignty.

NGOs can also become self-perpetuating. When the problem for which they were founded is solved, they seek new campaigns and new funds. The old anti-apartheid movement, its job completed, did not disband, but instead became another lobby group for southern Africa. As NGOs become steadily more powerful on the world scene, the best antidote to hubris, and to institutionalisation, would be this: disband when the job is done. The chief aim of NGOs should be their own abolition.

7.4 What Is a Gongo?

Moisés Naím

Far from weakening state power, some NGOs actually are a means of preserving and expanding state power. As *Foreign Policy* editor Moisés Naím argues, authoritarian states have found ways to turn the "associational revolution" to their advantage, using government-sponsored NGOs to manipulate civil society at home and abroad.

The Myanmar Women's Affairs Federation is a gongo. So is Nashi, a Russian youth group, and the Sudanese Human Rights Organization. Saudi Arabia's International Islamic Relief Organization is also a gongo, as is Chongryon, the General Association of Korean Residents in Japan. Gongos are everywhere, in China, Cuba, France, Tunisia, and even the United States.

Gongos are government-sponsored nongovernmental organizations. Behind this contradictory and almost laughable tongue twister lies an important and growing global trend that deserves more scrutiny: governments funding and controlling nongovernmental organizations (NGOs), often stealthily. Some gongos are benign, others irrelevant. But many, including those mentioned above, are dangerous. Some act as the thuggish arm of repressive governments. Others use the practices of democracy to subtly undermine democracy at home. Abroad, the gongos of repressive regimes lobby the United Nations and other international institutions, often posing as representatives of citizen groups with lofty aims when, in fact, they are nothing but agents of the governments that fund them. Some governments embed their gongos deep in the societies of other countries and use them to advance their interests abroad.

That is the case, for example, of Chongryon, a vast group of pro–North Korean, "civil society" organizations active in Japan. It is the de facto representative of the North Korean regime. Japanese authorities have accused several of its member organizations of smuggling weapons technology, trafficking pharmaceutical products, and funneling hundreds of millions of dollars, as well as orchestrating a massive propaganda operation on Pyongyang's behalf. For decades, "civil society" groups based in a variety of countries have stridently defended Cuba's human rights record at U.N. conferences and regularly succeed in watering down resolutions concerning

Cuba's well-documented violations. Bolivarian Circles, citizen groups that support Venezuelan President Hugo Chávez, are sprouting throughout Latin America, the United States, and Canada. Their funding? Take a guess. Iran, Saudi Arabia, and other wealthy governments in the Middle East are also known to be generous—and often sole—benefactors of NGOs that advance their religious agenda worldwide.

But the most dangerous gongos grow at home, not abroad. They have become the tool of choice for undemocratic governments to manage their domestic politics while looking democratic. In many countries of the former Soviet Union, government-backed NGOs are crowding out and muddling the voices of the country's legitimate civil society. In Kirgizstan, for example, the Association of Non-commercial and Nongovernmental Organizations was an enthusiastic fan of former President Askar Akayev. It ran a national petition drive in 2004 asking the president, who had been in power since 1991, to run for reelection. Likewise, the Myanmar Women's Affairs Federation is a harsh critic of Aung San Suu Kyi, the Nobel Peace Prizewinner and opposition leader who has spent much of the past 18 years under house arrest. The federation is run by the wives of the military junta's top generals.

Democratic governments have their own gongos, too. The National Endowment for Democracy (NED) is a private, nonprofit organization created in 1983 to strengthen democratic institutions around the world through nongovernmental efforts. It is a gongo funded by the U.S. government. In several countries, receiving money from the NED is considered a crime. President Vladimir Putin's government has denounced foreign-funded support for political reform by groups such as NED as subversive and anti-Russian. A Chinese newspaper called U.S.-backed democracy promotion "self-serving, coercive, and immoral."

For the sake of full disclosure, it's important to note that I serve on NED's board of directors. I, therefore, disagree that its activities are criminal, immoral, or a tool of the White House. Its programs, decisions, and sources of revenues and expenditures are perfectly transparent, and its directors, who serve without pay, are completely independent. But why should you believe me?

Ideally, there should be an independent and credible source that helps you decide if the NED or other gongos backed by, say, the Canadian or Dutch governments belong in the same category as Chongryon or Nashi. The world needs an NGO rating system that does for global civil society what independent credit rating agencies do for the global financial system. The credit rating agencies play an indispensable role in facilitating the massive borrowing and lending that takes place every day by providing investors with reliable information about the financial conditions of corporations, government agencies, and individuals. These independent and professional assessments of the creditworthiness of borrowers allow major transactions to take place faster and cheaper. Ultimately, lenders make the decision. But they do so within a more transparent market where a company that has a history of always meeting its obligations is less likely to be confused with one that only pays its debtors after a court orders it to do so.

A similar set of institutions can provide accurate information about the backers, independence, goals, and track records of different NGOs. The globalization and effectiveness of nongovernmental organizations will suffer if we don't find reliable ways of distinguishing organizations that truly represent democratic civil society from those that are tools of uncivil, undemocratic governments. Such bodies will help donors and citizens decide whom and what to believe. It will also make life harder for gongos with the worst intentions.

 TNCs

7.5 Mountain of Gold Leaves a River of Waste

Jane Perlez and Raymond Bonner

The best-known private transnational groups, of course, are the increasing number of giant, often oligarchic, corporations that, while originating in the United States, Japan, Europe, South Korea, and elsewhere, no longer have a clear national home. Instead, they engage in global production and marketing, and they invest in different countries to take advantage of low labor and capital costs, fluctuating currencies, raw materials, or favorable regulatory conditions.

With financial resources at their disposal that dwarf those of many states, the largest transnational corporations wield enormous power. In their pursuit of profits, TNCs can engage in activities and strike deals that have important consequences for the stability of states and their governments. Indeed, recognition by TNCs may at times be even more important than recognition by the UN in conveying legitimacy and power to a new state or government. Agreements reached between TNCs and particular governments may provide those governments with the revenues required to defeat domestic rivals or to stand up to neighboring states. Conversely, TNCs' support of opposition groups can contribute to the overthrow of popularly elected governments; the ITT corporation, for example, was implicated in the overthrow of the Allende government in Chile, and a number of large Western agricultural and mining companies have been important players in Latin American, African, and Asian politics.

It would be a mistake, however, to see TNCs' role in global politics as limited to the "high politics" of making or breaking particular governments. TNCs also directly affect the lives of ordinary people around the globe, building the mines, factories, and agricultural plantations that provide jobs. By their policy choices, TNCs may bring employment and better lives to workers in the less-developed world; TNC policy decisions may also exploit these same workers. TNCs are often accused (frequently on good evidence) of paying wages far below those paid in the developed world, of treating workers with disrespect, of employing child or prison labor, of operating with hazardous or unsafe working conditions, and of degrading the environment. But TNCs may also play a much more positive and progressive role in today's world, exporting Western human rights and labor standards as well as capital and technology.

In some cases, TNCs have largely replaced the state as the critical institution in ordinary individuals' lives. In weak states, TNCs have assumed responsibility for building and maintaining infrastructure—roads, schools, hospitals—and, by buying off local elites and bringing in private security firms, effectively become the principal dispenser of security.

The following news story, from the *International Herald Tribune,* looks at the operations of the mining giant Freeport McMoRan in Papua, a thinly populated and economically underdeveloped province of the archipelagic Indonesian state. The corporation's relationship with key elements of the Indonesian government, including the Indonesian military, have allowed it to operate with disregard for Indonesia's environmental regulations.

As Freeport-McMoRan Copper and Gold sealed its relations with the military, the fledgling Indonesian Environment Ministry could do little but watch while the waste piled up from the company's mine in Papua, the easternmost province of Indonesia.

This year, Freeport-McMoRan told the Indonesian government that the waste rock in the highlands now covers about eight square kilometers, or three square miles, and in some places is 275 meters deep, or 900 feet.

Down below, about 230 square kilometers of wetlands, once one of the richest freshwater habitats in the world, are virtually buried in mine waste, with levels of copper and sediment so high that almost all the fish have disappeared, according to Indonesian Environment Ministry documents.

The waste, the consistency and color of wet cement, belts down the rivers and inundates and smothers all in its path, said Russell Dodt, an Australian civil engineer who managed those tailings for Freeport-McMoRan on the wetlands for 10 years until 2004. About a third of the waste has moved into the coastal estuary, an essential breeding ground for fish, and much of that "was ripped out to sea by the falling tide that acted like a big vacuum cleaner," he said.

But no government, even in the new era of democracy in Indonesia, has dared encroach on Freeport-McMoRan's prerogatives. The strongest challenge came in 2000, when Sonny Keraf, a politician who was sympathetic to the Papuans, was appointed environment minister.

As he had done once before, James Moffett, chairman of Freeport-McMoRan, which is based in New Orleans, flew out to Jakarta. Keraf initially refused to see Moffett but eventually agreed, and on the day kept him waiting on hour and a half. "He came in so arrogant," Keraf recalled of the meeting in a recent interview. Freeport-McMoRan declined to comment on the meeting. The U.S. ambassador to Indonesia at the time, Robert Gelbard, said in an interview, "It was a terrible meeting."

Keraf said Moffett had recounted that his company had never polluted. "I told him that he should spend that money he spent on paying off people not to talk about the mine to properly dispose of the waste," Keraf said. Behind the scenes, Keraf kept up the pressure, angered that the company was using the rivers, forest and wetlands for its mine waste, a process allowed during the Suharto years.

An internal ministry memorandum from 2000 said the mine tailings had killed all life in the rivers and noted that this violated the criminal section of a 1997 environmental law. In January 2001, Keraf wrote to the coordinating minister for economic affairs, arguing that Freeport-McMoRan should be forced to pay compensation for the rivers, forests and fish that its operations had destroyed.

Six months later, one of his deputies, Masnellyarti Hilman, wrote to Freeport-McMoRan, saying a special environmental commission had recommended that the company stop using the river as a waste chute and instead build a system of pipes. She also told Freeport-McMoRan to build sturdier damlike walls to replace the less solid levees that it used to contain the waste on the wetlands. The levees are still there.

Freeport-McMoRan said that local and regional governments approved its waste management plans and that the central government approved its environmental impact statement and other monitoring plans. But in a July 2001 letter, Keraf took the governor of Papua to task for having granted Freeport-McMoRan a permit in 1996 to use the rivers for its waste. The governor, Keraf said, had no authority to grant permits more lenient than the provisions of national laws. Despite all these efforts, nothing happened. Keraf was unable to secure the support of other government agencies or his superiors in the cabinet.

In August 2001, a new government came to power, and a less aggressive minister, Nabiel Makarim, replaced Keraf. At first, he, too, talked publicly of setting stricter limits on Freeport-McMoRan. Soon his efforts petered out.

The Environment Ministry has begun trying to put teeth to its rules where it can. It brought a criminal case against the world's largest gold company, Newmont Mining, that included a charge of not having a permit to dispose of mine waste into the sea. Newmont has fought the charges vigorously.

But in the case of Freeport-McMoRan, the ministry has had no traction. Freeport-McMoRan still does not hold a permit from the national government to dispose of mine waste, as required by the 1999 hazardous waste regulations, according to Rasio Ridho Sani, assistant deputy for toxic waste management at the ministry. Stanley Arkin, legal counsel for Freeport-McMoRan, said that the company cooperated well with the ministry and that Freeport-McMoRan would not otherwise comment.

"Freeport-McMoRan says their waste is not hazardous waste," Rasio said. "We cannot say it is not hazardous waste." He said his division and Freeport-McMoRan were now in negotiations on resolving the permit question.

"A Massive Die-Off"

The ministry was not the first to challenge Freeport-McMoRan over how it has disposed of its waste in Papua.

The Overseas Private Investment Corp., a U.S. government agency that insures U.S. corporations for political risk in uncertain corners of the world, revoked

Freeport-McMoRan's insurance policy in October 1995. It was a landmark decision, the first time that the agency had cut off insurance to any U.S. company for environmental or human rights concerns.

In doing so, two environmental experts, Harvey Himberg, an official at the agency, and David Nelson, a consultant, after visiting the mine for several days, issued a report critical of Freeport-McMoRan's operations, especially the vast amount of waste it had sent into rivers, something that would not be allowed in the United States. The company went to court to block publication of the report, and only a censored version was later released. A person who thought it should be made public provided an uncensored copy to *The Times*.

Freeport-McMoRan says the report reached "inaccurate conclusions." The company says it has considered a full range of alternatives for managing and disposing of its waste, instead of using the river, and settled on the best one. A storage area would not be large enough and would require a tall dam in a region of heavy rainfalls and earthquakes, it said. A waste pipeline, rather than the river, would be too costly and prone to landslides and floods.

To the U.S. auditors, such arguments were not convincing. Freeport-McMoRan "characterizes engineered alternatives as having the highest potential for catastrophic failure when the project otherwise takes credit for legendary feats," the audit noted, like the pipelines more than 100 kilometers long that carry fuel and copper and gold slurry down the mountains. At the time of the investigation, the waste was jumping the riverbanks, "resulting in a massive die-off of vegetation," the report said.

Freeport-McMoRan threatened to take the agency to court over the cancellation of its insurance. After protracted negotiations, the policy was reinstated for a few months. That was a face-saving gesture to Moffett, according to Ruth Harkin, then the head of the agency. The policy was not renewed.

Bright Green Water

Many of the same problems persist, but on a vastly larger scale. A perpetual worry is where to put all the mine's waste, which is accumulating at a rate of some 700,000 tons a day. The danger is that the waste rock atop the mountain will trickle out acids into the honeycomb of caverns beneath the mine in a wet climate that gets up to 3.5 meters of rain a year, say environmental experts who have worked at the mine.

Stuart Miller, an Australian geochemist who manages Freeport-McMoRan's waste rock, told a mining conference in 2003 that the first acid runoffs began in 1993. The company could prevent much of it, he said, by blending in the mountain's abundant limestone with the potentially acid-producing rock, which is also plentiful. Freeport-McMoRan says it collects the acid runoff and neutralizes it.

A report, obtained by *The Times*, written by Parametrix, a consulting company that did a study for Freeport-McMoRan, noted that before 2004, the mine had "an excess of acid-generating material." A geologist who worked at the mine, who declined to be named because of fear of jeopardizing future employment, said acids were already flowing into the groundwater. Bright green springs can be seen spouting several kilometers away, he said, a telltale sign that acids had leached out copper and traveled much farther from the mine than the company has acknowledged. "That meant the acid water traveled a long way," he said.

Freeport-McMoRan says the green springs are "located several miles from our operations in the Lorentz World Heritage site and are not associated with our operations." The geologist agreed that the springs were probably in the Lorentz National Park, but said this showed that acids and copper from the mine were affecting the park, considered a world treasure for its ecological diversity.

Freeport-McMoRan says that the tailings are not toxic and that the river it uses for its waste meets Indonesian and U.S. drinking water standards for dissolved metals. The coastal estuary, it says, is a "functioning ecosystem."

The Parametrix report said that copper levels in some of the surface waters were high enough to kill sensitive aquatic life in a short time, said Ann Maest, a geochemist who consults on mining issues. The report showed that nearly half of the sediment samples in parts of the coastal estuary were toxic to the sensitive aquatic organisms at the bottom of the food chain, she said.

An Uneasy Coexistence

If the accumulating waste is the despair of critics, for Freeport-McMoRan it signals ever-expanding production. To keep its mine running, the company has increasingly had to play caretaker for the world that it has created. After anti-mine sentiment erupted in riots in 1996, shutting the mine for three days, Freeport-McMoRan began dedicating 1 percent of annual revenue to a development fund for Papua to pay for schools, medical services, roads—whatever the people wanted.

The company built clinics and two hospitals. Other services include programs to control malaria and AIDS and a "recognition" fund of several million dollars for the Kamoro and Amungme tribes. By the end of 2004, Freeport-McMoRan had spent $152 million on the community development fund, the company said.

A report commissioned by the company concluded in October that the company had successfully introduced a human rights training program for its employees and had doubled the number of Papuan employees by 2001. The company is poised to double the number of Papuans in the work force again by 2006, the audit said.

Still, Thom Beanal, the leader of the Amungme, said the combined weight of the Indonesian government and Freeport-McMoRan had left his people in bad shape. Yes, the company provided electricity, schools and hospitals, but the infrastructure was built mainly for the benefit of Freeport-McMoRan, he said. Beanal, a vocal supporter of independence for Papua, has fought the company from outside and inside. In 2000, he decided that harmony was the better path, and accepted an offer to join the company's advisory board.

In November, he and other Amungme and Komoro tribal members met with Moffett at the Sheraton Hotel in the lowland city of Timika. In an interview in Jakarta not long afterward, Beanal said he told Moffett that the flood of money from the community fund was ruining people's lives. When the company arrived, he noted, there were several hundred people in Timika. Now it is home to more than 100,000 in a Wild West atmosphere of alcohol, shootouts between soldiers and the police, AIDS and prostitution, protected by the military.

Beanal said he was angry and increasingly impatient with the presence of both the soldiers and the mine. "We never feel secure there," he said. "What are they guarding? We don't know. Ask Moffett, it's his company."

NGOs and TNCs

7.6 How a Global Web of Activists Gives Coke Problems in India

Steve Stecklow

The power of both nonprofit "public-interest" NGOs and TNCs is illustrated in the following news story from the *Wall Street Journal.* One of the interesting features of this story is the leverage that modern information technology has given a small, essentially one-person NGO to battle a global giant, Coca-Cola.

A mit Srivastava doesn't own a car or a house. He runs a nonprofit, activist organization in California that has only one full-time employee—himself. But he has been helping shake up one of the world's biggest corporations, Coca-Cola Co., thousands of miles away in India.

Speaking on a tour of U.S. college campuses in April, he accused Coke of egregious offenses in India: stealing water, poisoning land and selling drinks laced with dangerous pesticides. "It is destroying lives, it is destroying livelihoods and it is destroying communities all across India," the pony-tailed, 39-year-old college dropout told dozens of students at Smith College in Northampton, Mass. "That is the story of Coca-Cola in India."

Coca-Cola, which considers India a crucial element in its plans for global growth, wasn't invited to Smith to tell its version of the story. But the Atlanta-based soft-drinks giant is well aware of Mr. Srivastava's activities. Coke acknowledges he is a central figure in a burgeoning global campaign by nonprofits—commonly known abroad as nongovernmental organizations, or NGOs—that has cost it millions of dollars in lost sales and legal fees in India, and growing damage to its reputation elsewhere.

Mr. Srivastava and the NGOs have flagged some serious issues, such as Coke's onetime practice of giving away waste material to local farmers that some studies later showed contained toxic materials. But amid the heated rhetoric, there have been some dubious claims as well. Mr. Srivastava, for example, has compared

Coke's environmental practices to the industrial accident at Bhopal, which killed thousands.

Amid the NGO's campaign, Coca-Cola has been forced to fight legal and legislative battles all across India—including challenging a court order in the northern state of Rajasthan that would require soft-drink makers to list pesticide residues on their labels. The order was prompted by laboratory tests of soft drinks by a New Delhi-based NGO. The company says the levels are safe.

In the southern state of Kerala, local officials shut down a $16 million Coke bottling plant in March 2004 over still-unproven claims by local residents and Indian activists that it drained and polluted local water supplies. The company has been trying ever since to regain the plant's license, fighting a case that has gone all the way to India's Supreme Court. But even if Coke prevails, the company hasn't yet said whether it will reopen the plant.

Now Mr. Srivastava is rallying college students in the U.S. and Europe to take up the NGOs' cause. Under pressure from student protesters, at least a half-dozen colleges have decided not to renew contracts with Coke or boycott it, and other campuses are considering similar actions. Schools that have banned Coca-Cola products include Bard College in New York, Carleton College in Minnesota, Oberlin College in Ohio and two colleges in Ireland.

Even though he lives in Northern California, Mr. Srivastava has emerged as a key figure in Coke's travails in India. Activists inside and outside the country say he plays an important role in coordinating the activities of far-flung protesters on the subcontinent, and that he has become the point-man for communicating their cause to the outside world. That a one-man NGO armed with just a laptop computer, a Web site and a telephone calling card can, with his allies, influence a huge multinational corporation illustrates the role social activists can play in a world that's going increasingly online.

"The moral high ground seems to be anyone with a Web site," complains David Cox, Coke's Hong Kong–based communications director for Asia, who has spent months in India trying to combat the NGOs' allegations with little apparent success.

Mr. Srivastava and numerous NGOs both inside and outside India accuse Coke, among other "crimes," of sucking local Indian communities dry through excessive pumping. But the water allegations remain unproven. Kerala's highest court rejected such claims in April, noting that wells there continued to dry up last summer, months after the local Coke plant stopped operating. And a scientific study previously requested by the court found that while the plant had "aggravated the water scarcity situation," the "most significant factor" was a lack of rainfall. The NGOs respond that Coke shouldn't be locating bottling plants in drought-stricken areas.

From Coke's point of view, Mr. Srivastava and other activists "are making false environmental allegations against us to further an antiglobalization agenda," says Mr. Cox.

The dispute in India does raise questions about Coke's waste-disposal practices there. Coke officials acknowledge, for example, that they violated their own global safety standards by failing to conduct any toxicity tests on a dump site used by its biggest plant in India until after a Wall Street Journal reporter visited it in March.

Meanwhile, near the holy city of Varanasi in northeastern India, a local water official blames a Coke plant—which has been the scene of many protests by NGOs and local residents—for polluting groundwater by releasing wastewater into surrounding land. A Coke official confirms there had been a drainage problem with treated wastewater several years ago but says that company built a long pipeline to correct it.

Mr. Srivastava, whose father is a management professor in India, was born in the U.S. and grew up in India. He dropped out of Southern Illinois University after becoming more interested in activism than formal education.

In 2002, while working at Corp Watch, a nonprofit corporate watchdog based in Oakland, Calif., he commissioned an article for one of the group's Web sites about a protest outside a Coke bottling plant in a poor tribal area in Kerala. Local residents accused Coke of extracting so much water that their wells dried up or yielded brackish, undrinkable water. Coke, which says it uses about four liters of water to produce a one-liter bottle of soft-drink, blames the problems on area drought conditions.

The article, which appeared on a Web site called Corp Watch India that Mr. Srivastava oversaw, proved popular. The NGO followed up with a "fax action" in which Web-site visitors were urged to send a fax to Coke via the Internet, demanding that it close the Kerala plant. More than 1,400 people responded, according to Corp Watch, although it says many faxes didn't arrive because of technical problems.

Global Resistance

In 2003, Corp Watch ran into financial problems. Mr. Srivastava lost his job but quickly launched his own NGO, called Global Resistance. He was allowed to take Corp Watch India with him, wrapping it into a new site called the India Resource Center.

The new site initially focused on various issues in India, including outsourcing and globalization. But the controversy over Coca-Cola soon began to dominate as Mr. Srivastava learned of growing protests in different parts of India and saw a need to try to bring them global attention. "It took on a life of its own," he says.

Today, the Web site, www.indiaresource.org, serves as a global platform for local activists and protesters throughout India and draws about 20,000 visitors a month, according to tracking numbers on the Web site. In contrast, a Coke Web site designed to counter NGO allegations, www.cokefacts.org, draws just 800 visitors a month, Coke officials say. Mr. Srivastava also has resumed the "fax action," relaying more than 9,000 faxes to Coke's headquarters to date, he says. In addition to frequent campus speeches, he says he's also advising potential investors who hope to launch a London-based hedge fund that would bet against the share price of Coke, among other companies, according to two other people involved in the planning. A portion of any profits would be donated to activist groups, these people said.

Activists throughout India credit Mr. Srivastava with helping to link them together. Protesters in the southern state of Kerala said that when they tried to email other activists in Varanasi, in the north, they found they couldn't communicate because they spoke different languages. Both turned to Mr. Srivastava, who became an intermediary to coordinate their efforts. Now they can help each other plan their protests for maximum impact.

"He has such enormous resources," says R. Ajayan, a Kerala activist. "We don't have a Web site or a communications system. Whenever we have a protest, we have no way to publicize it—he's doing all this."

When he isn't traveling around the U.S. or India, Mr. Srivastava operates his NGO from a house he shares with friends in El Cerrito, Calif. He says he draws no salary but covers his expenses mainly through modest fund raising.

Global Resistance, which had a budget last year of $60,000, is supported by several private foundations interested in globalization and water issues, including the Unitarian Universalist Veatch Program at Shelter Rock in Manhasset, N.Y. The Unitarian Church social-action fund has given him $45,000 to date, according to its grant administrator. Global Resistance maintains its tax-free status through Community Networking Resources Inc., an Albuquerque, N.M., nonprofit that handles its finances. Mr. Srivastava is the only full-time employee; there's a part-time Web-site editor in New Delhi. "We've been able to survive, barely," the activist says. "I have good friends who keep me going."

Controversy overseas isn't new to Coca-Cola, whose revenue last year totaled $22 billion. In 1999, quality-control problems in Europe sparked a widespread consumer scare and prompted governments to pull Coke products from shelves. The company also has been dogged in recent years by claims by U.S. activists and local union officials that it was complicit in the murder and harassment of union leaders and workers in Colombia. The company denies the claims.

In the wake of the European problems, Coke has tried to respond to critics more quickly and forcefully. Lately, it sends teams of executives to college campuses to rebut charges. But the company isn't always invited. In April, the Union Theological Seminary in New York banned the sale of Coke products on campus because of "considerable evidence" of human-rights violations and environmental damage abroad. A seminary spokeswoman says company officials weren't "invited to present their side." The decision to ban Coke was made by the seminary's president on the recommendation of the school's institutional and community affairs committee.

The president of the seminary, which has only about 300 students, later did extend an invitation to the company. Coke sent six representatives, including four from Atlanta. Mr. Srivastava says his travel schedule didn't permit him to attend. The spokeswoman says the school will re-evaluate its ban in the fall.

For years, Coke was India's leading soft drink. In 1977, the company left after a new government ordered it to dilute its stake in its Indian unit and turn over Coke's secret formula. The company returned in 1993 when the government began trying to attract foreign investment. Coke quickly gained a lead in the market by buying up popular local brands, including Thums Up soda. Its products are now produced in 76 bottling plants and officials say India is one of its fastest growing markets.

But the continuing allegations by NGOs—over excessive water use, pesticides, pollution and waste disposal—have taken their toll. During a conference call with analysts in April, Mary Minnick, who had been president of Coke's Asia division and now heads global marketing, innovation and strategy, called India a "work in progress" and noted the company still was feeling "the residual effects of the unfounded pesticide scare in 2003."

That scare occurred after the Center for Science and Environment, a New Delhi–based NGO, issued a report on lab tests of a dozen local Coca-Cola and PepsiCo Inc. soft drinks. The tests showed they contained pesticide and insecticide levels of between 11 times and 70 times the maximum set by the European Union for drinking water. Coke's product sales plummeted by as much as 40 percent.

Coke and Pepsi, which together hold about a 95 percent market share of soft-drink sales in India, disputed the lab results and say their products are safe. But an Indian parliamentary committee last year backed up CSE's findings and a government-appointed committee is now trying to develop the world's first pesticide standards for soft drinks. Coke and PepsiCo oppose the move, arguing, among other things, that lab tests aren't reliable enough to detect minute traces of pesticides in complex drinks like soda.

Coke's Mr. Cox accuses Sunita Narain, CSE's director, of "brandjacking," using Coke's brand name to draw attention to her campaign against pesticides. Ms. Narain says CSE's study of pesticide residues in soft drinks was a natural follow-up to a previous study it did on bottled water. "It's the arrogance of Coke that makes it believe that we were targeting it," she says.

"Things Grow Better"

To further publicize the pesticide issue, some NGOs last year began spreading stories online and to the news media of Indian farmers who had begun spraying Coke on their crops as a pesticide. "Things grow better with Coke," read a headline in Britain's Guardian newspaper. But Mr. Srivastava admits the whole thing was a publicity stunt by local activists and farmers, and it's unclear how many farmers participated. "We played it up as well, obviously," he says.

The controversy in India has been marked by other outlandish or misleading claims. At a recent appearance at the University of Michigan, which has been debating whether to renew its contract with Coke, Mr. Srivastava compared the possible long-term health effects of some of Coke's environmental practices in India to the devastating 1984 gas leak at a Union Carbide plant in Bhopal. "Twenty years from now we can have another Bhopal," he said. Coke officials dismiss the analogy as absurd.

A Boston-based nonprofit called Corporate Accountability International posted on its Web site a "Coca-Cola fact sheet." It suggested that as a result of Coke's extraction of water in Kerala, "Water riots and water-related murders are now an everyday occurrence as water becomes scarcer."

But there are no reports of daily water-related murders and riots in Kerala. Asked to back up the claim, Patty Linn, the group's campaign director, said after checking that she couldn't. The group later removed the statement from the "fact sheet."

Coke also has been selective with its information. On the Web site of Coke's India unit, under a section called "Facts on Kerala," there's a document that disputes allegations that plant officials there distributed dangerous waste material to local farmers to use as fertilizer.

The company acknowledges that until 2003 it had given away sludge—a byproduct of water- and sugar-treatment processes, and bottle- and equipment-cleaning operations—but maintains it was safe. "Numerous reports since the commissioning of the plant, and as recently as December 2003, have confirmed that the levels of heavy metal traces are within the [Kerala state] Pollution Control Board norms for classification as non-hazardous," Coke's Web site states.

But the document doesn't mention two other government studies of the Kerala waste material, including one by India's highest environmental regulatory authority. The study found that the material contained high enough levels of cadmium, a highly toxic metal, to deem it hazardous.

Harry J. Ott, Atlanta-based director of Coke's global water resources center, says the company didn't mention the other studies because he and other officials questioned the validity of one of them and didn't know the basis of the other. But, he added, "I guess we could show there were tests by other agencies that indicated that there were higher than acceptable levels."

The NGO-TNC-State Nexus

7.7 More Than the Sum of the Parts

Sarah Murray

While relations between nonprofit NGOs and TNCs may be oppositional and confrontational, NGOs and TNCs sometimes find ways to work together. NGO-TNC partnerships may also involve state regulators and intergovernmental organizations, like the United Nations. As Sarah Murray of the *Financial Times* reports, when these different types of actors are able to identify shared interests and goals, they can contribute their very different resources to accomplish aims beyond the reach of any of them acting alone.

There was a time when a company's interaction with non-profit organisations consisted either of fending off the ire of anti-corporate activists or of signing cheques for good causes.

While these activities continue, another, far more collaborative relationship has emerged in which companies, in pursuit of responsible business strategies, are turning to community groups, non-governmental organisations (NGOs) and UN agencies to help achieve their social and environmental aims.

Murray, Sarah, "More Than the Sum of the Parts," *Financial Times,* July 5, 2007, special section, p. 10. Reprinted by permission of the author.

Convening bodies such as the UN Global Compact are also making it easier for public and private organisations to connect with each other.

However, the process of embarking on joint projects is not without its difficulties. The business culture of fast decisions, rapid product development and swift implementation of initiatives is far removed from the slower, more bureaucratic style of many non-profit organisations. Trickier still, some partnerships involve a shift from an adversarial relationship to a co-operative one.

Coca-Cola's work with Greenpeace takes place against a background of conflict in which the environmental group had been campaigning for the elimination of hydro-fluorocarbons, refrigerant gases that are powerful greenhouse gases. "They were very much on the attack with us and other companies," says Salvatore Gabola, director of European public affairs at Coca-Cola.

Since then Coca-Cola, Unilever and others have been working with Greenpeace to develop alternative refrigeration technology and persuade suppliers to make the switch. "Instead of confronting each other, we slowly got into that mode of understanding each other and realising that we have common goals," says Mr. Gabola.

For Coca-Cola, there are several advantages of working with Greenpeace. For a start, Greenpeace's recognisable brand as an environmental campaigner gives the companies it chooses to work with credibility. "It's very powerful for a company to be associated with an NGO, especially if it's an activist one," says Mr. Gabola.

Moreover, Greenpeace has environmental and technical expertise that a company such as Coca-Cola can use to implement change to a new refrigeration technology.

Technical expertise is also at the heart of another Coca-Cola partnership, announced in June: a water conservation programme with the World Wildlife Fund to protect seven of the world's most crucial freshwater river basins. At the same time, Coca-Cola is working to continue to reduce its own water consumption with help from the WWF. "These are the kind of things we know we need to do, but we can't do on our own because we don't have the credibility or the expertise," says Mr. Gabola.

The fact that NGOs have local knowledge and experience of social and environmental issues is another form of expertise that is crucial as companies enter the development arena.

In India, for example, ICICI, the country's largest private-sector bank, has increased its microfinance loans from $15 m four years ago to more than $350 m by working through local microfinance institutions. Through this network of local organisations, the bank can reach rural borrowers it would otherwise not be able to access.

The key to the success of these partnerships lies in the different assets that companies and non-profit organisations bring. "Unless we bring the specific skills and talent that each of these types of organisations have together, we're not going to make the progress we need to make," says Pamela Passman, head of global corporate affairs at Microsoft.

"We understand the power of software and computing, but we're not experts on poverty or health. So we can make significant progress when we are partnering with NGOs, governments and international organisations such as the UN."

Microsoft has more than 1,000 such partnerships around the world through which it rolls out such programmes as its Microsoft Unlimited Potential initiative, giving skills training to disadvantaged people with the assistance of community groups and NGOs.

ICICI's microfinance model and Microsoft's global partnerships are both examples of how alliances can give large companies access to communities they might not otherwise reach. "We can learn much more about local community needs and who are the key players," says Ms. Passman. "We need people who can help make connections and get the services to those that need them."

As with access to technology and financing, access to medicine is another area where large corporations need local players to advance their social objectives. One example is the International Trachoma Initiative, founded by the Edna McConnell Clark Foundation and Pfizer, the pharmaceuticals company, to address trachoma, the world's leading cause of preventable blindness.

Pfizer had developed a treatment that was effective in eliminating the disease but needed a way of delivering it to areas where the disease was endemic.

"What we had was the medicine," says Robert Mallet, Pfizer's head of philanthropy and corporate responsibility, and president of the Pfizer Foundation. "What the initiative had was the expertise on the ground. Put those things together and you have a real solution for communities around the world."

Suggested Discussion Topics

1. How are transnational organizations different from traditional intergovernmental organizations like the ones discussed in the last chapter? How does the growth in the number and power of transnational organizations affect how global politics is conducted?
2. Describe the relationship between nonprofit transnational organizations and states. Are nonprofit transnational organizations replacing states in some roles, or are they partners of states, or are they both? Explain your conclusions. Are there some problems that transnational organizations can solve more easily than states? Why or why not?
3. How has the "telecommunications revolution" altered the relationship between states and transnational groups? Do you think the growing power of transnational groups vis-à-vis states is, on balance, a positive development or a dangerous one? Explain your reasoning and the evidence that supports your position.
4. In what ways are transnational nonprofit nongovernmental organizations similar to transnational corporations? In what ways are they different?
5. Compare the relative power of states and transnational corporations. In what ways do they have different *kinds* of power? Do you think that TNCs will get stronger or weaker during your lifetime? Explain your conclusion.
6. Should nonprofit NGOs be regulated? If so, by whom? Should organizations like Nashi (the nationalistic, pro-authoritarian Russian youth movement linked to the ruling Russian party) be regulated in some different fashion than, say, Global Resistance (the one-person NGO campaigning against Coca-Cola's operations in India)?

Chapter 8

THY BROTHER'S KEEPER: HUMAN RIGHTS AND INTERNATIONAL LAW IN THE POSTINTERNATIONAL ERA

Among the most dramatic manifestations of the turbulent change under way in contemporary global politics has been a remarkable transformation in international law. Along with the growing importance of international organizations in solving shared problems and the widening role of nongovernmental organizations in binding together communities around the world, international law has emerged as an important integrative institution in today's world, establishing new norms of collective responsibility.

Traditionally, international law applied to sovereign states, not to individuals, whose behavior was presumably regulated by the laws of the sovereign state in which they resided. Today, however, there has been a shift away from regarding sovereign states as the sole subjects of international law and toward the view that the international community can hold individuals accountable for certain actions even if the state in which they live does not.

Equally important, the view has emerged that the international community may have an obligation to intervene in order to protect human rights—inalienable rights accorded to every individual by virtue of his or her humanity—when sovereign states fail to do so, or when sovereign states are themselves directly responsible for the violations of human rights. This inclusion of human rights on the global agenda represents a significant shift. Until recent decades, it was taken for granted that states had a sovereign right to treat their subjects as they wished. No longer is this the case. Not only other states but nongovernmental organizations (NGOs) and international organizations (IGOs) are increasingly willing to disregard sovereignty in order to protect or restore human rights. Indeed, specialized NGOs and IGOs have emerged to work across borders to ensure that individuals are not abused by their governments.

This rethinking of international law was triggered by the increasingly indiscriminate violence of twentieth-century warfare. Both interstate and intrastate (that is, civil) wars were marked by the growing victimization of civilians. Although the twentieth century opened with the Hague Conferences of 1899 and 1906, where delegates celebrated a "century of peace" and optimistically concluded that war was becoming rare and that its conduct was becoming "civilized," as the century progressed wars were marked by widespread inhumanity.

The atrocities committed by states during World War II, especially the Holocaust, prompted the victors to hold the Nuremberg and Tokyo trials. These trials were noteworthy because they ignored the sovereign right of states to try their own citizens and because they established the principle that individuals could be held accountable by the international community for their actions even when those actions were ordered by superiors in the state (or military) hierarchy. Individual agents of states could be charged with a whole new category of crimes—crimes against humanity and, later, genocide—in the misuse of state power. This new concept of crimes against humanity and the argument that not only states but individual members of the government and the state's armed forces could be charged with these crimes underscored the position that decision-makers at all levels had an obligation to observe distinctions between soldiers and civilians, and between legitimate acts of warfare and criminal violence or wanton brutality. The murder of six million Jews, like later "ethnic cleansing" in Bosnia and Kosovo and genocide in Rwanda, came to be regarded by the global community as a criminal act, not an acceptable, if deplorable, wartime action by a sovereign state, and individuals who were involved in these criminal acts could be tried and punished not only by their sovereign state but by outside tribunals as well.

The Nuremberg and Tokyo trials were thus important not only because they established the notion of individual responsibility but also because their verdicts limited state sovereignty in using violence. Not only did states have an inescapable obligation to treat foreign noncombatants and prisoners of war humanely, but they also had an international obligation to ensure "universal" human rights, even in the treatment of their own subjects. For the first time, the global regulation of violence entered the shielded realm of state "domestic" jurisdiction: the use of violence by states against those within their boundaries.

Since World War II, UN conventions and international and regional human rights tribunals have reinforced and expanded the Nuremberg precedent. In 1948, the United Nations Genocide Convention was signed, as was the Universal Declaration of Human Rights: the latter provided a comprehensive listing of civil, political, social, and economic rights. In 1966, the Universal Declaration was fleshed out in more detailed international covenants.

In May 1996 the first international criminal court since Nuremberg, the International Criminal Tribunal for the former Yugoslavia, was convened in The Hague. Among those who have been indicted for war crimes or crimes against humanity, including genocide, was Yugoslav President Slobodan Milosevic. This was the first of several international criminal courts. A dramatic additional step in the direction of providing individuals with legal standing was taken in Rome in the summer of 1998 by the conclusion of a treaty to establish a permanent International Criminal Court (ICC) to try individuals charged with genocide, war crimes, and crimes against humanity. The practical fate of the court remains undecided, however, because the United States refuses to ratify the treaty.

In general, the end of the Cold War and the rapid spread of democratic norms have made it easier to disregard power considerations and to address human-rights concerns. Western countries have been increasingly prepared to extend rights and responsibilities to individuals even if doing so violates sovereignty as traditionally conceived. Indeed, even former heads of state may no longer be immune from being brought to justice by a court in another state, charged for acts they authorized in their own state: a landmark decision of the British Law Lords held that Chile's former president Augusto Pinochet, who had been visiting Britain for medical treatment, could be extradited to Spain and prosecuted there for crimes against humanity committed in Chile.

8.1 Are Human Rights Universal?

Thomas M. Franck

The first selection in this chapter addresses directly the basic questions of the universality of human rights and whether alleged human-rights violators should be tried before international tribunals or national courts outside their own states. Thomas Franck, a professor of international law at New York University, argues vigorously that human-rights standards are universal and that demands by individual countries not to be bound by these standards because of exceptional cultural or other characteristics should be disregarded. Franck contends that a human-rights consensus has emerged, not as a result of Western dominance but as a consequence of "transcultural" social, economic, and scientific modernization.

The Rise of Cultural Exceptionalism

In May 2000, the Taliban [then in control of Afghanistan], who rule most of Afghanistan, ordered a mother of seven to be stoned to death for adultery in front of an ecstatic stadium of men and children. The year before, the House of Lords—Britain's highest court—had allowed two Pakistani women accused of adultery to claim refugee status in the United Kingdom, since they risked public flogging and death by stoning at home. Women today are denied the vote and the right to drive cars in several Arab states, and harsh versions of shari'a (Islamic law) punishment are spreading to Sudan, Nigeria, and Pakistan.

Still, the Taliban's repression remains in a class by itself: denying women the right to leave home except when accompanied by a brother or husband and forbidding them all access to public education. Not only do the Taliban seek to spread their militant vision to other states, they also demand to be left alone to implement their own religious and cultural values at home without foreign interference. Leaders in Kabul insist that they not be judged by the norms of others—especially in the West.

Franck, Thomas M., "Are Human Rights Universal?," *Foreign Affairs,* January/February 2001. Reprinted by permission of *Foreign Affairs.* © 2001 by the Council on Foreign Relations, Inc. <www.ForeignAffairs.org>.

Of course the Taliban are not the only ones to reject outside scrutiny. Florida's government, after frying several prisoners in a faulty electric chair, has only reluctantly turned to other methods of execution to conform to the U.S. Constitution's prohibition of "cruel and unusual punishment." Yet when America's Western allies tell it that the U.S. system of capital punishment is barbaric, local politicians and courts reply that it is their way and no one else's business. Which is precisely what the Taliban say.

This is not to indulge in what Jeane Kirkpatrick, a former U.S. permanent representative to the UN, has called the "sin of moral equivalence." The United States is not Afghanistan. What the Islamic fundamentalist regime is doing there violates well-established global law. Article 7 of the International Covenant on Civil and Political Rights (ICCPR) echoes the U.S. Constitution in proclaiming that "no one shall be subject to cruel, inhuman, or degrading treatment or punishment," which certainly covers stoning and flogging—but not execution by lethal injection or (functioning) electric chair. And the 1980 Convention on the Elimination of All Forms of Discrimination Against Women (CEDAW) prohibits almost everything the Taliban have done to subordinate women.

The difference has been widely recognized. In October 1999, the UN Security Council duly censured the Taliban by a unanimous resolution. The General Assembly, too, has shown its disapproval by refusing to accept the credentials of the Taliban's delegation. But Taliban leaders and other radical fundamentalists in Pakistan, Sudan, and elsewhere reply to such condemnation by arguing that their codes have reintroduced social cohesion, decency, and family values into societies corrupted by colonialism and globalization. They point scornfully to the degradation of Western women through pornography, prostitution, and other forms of exploitation, and argue that their wives and daughters have been liberated from public obligations to focus instead on home and family.

Although huge differences in degree do exist between repression in Afghanistan and executions in Florida, the point is that the arguments of Islamic extremists parallel those used by U.S. courts and politicians: namely, that states have a sovereign right to be let alone and not be judged by international human rights standards. The United States insists, for example, on the right to execute persons who committed crimes as minors. Never mind that this violates U.S. obligations under the ICCPR. It is the American way, representing American values and ethics.

Such assertions are made nowadays by many varieties of cultural exceptionalists. For most of the 55 years since the collapse of Hitler's own extravagant form of cultural exceptionalism, this sort of claim tended to be suppressed, or at least muted. The Universal Declaration of Human Rights and the several ensuing legal treaties setting out civil, political, cultural, and economic rights as well as the rights of children, women, ethnic groups, and religions, were meant to create a global safety net of rights applicable to all persons, everywhere. Although these legal instruments allow some restrictions in time of national emergency, they brook no cultural exceptionalism.

But more and more, such universalist claims are being challenged. And so the argument must be joined: are human rights truly universal, or are they a product of the decadent West that has no relevance in other societies?

Common Cause

The postwar flourishing of human rights has featured two dynamic elements: globalization and individualization. Against both a backlash has emerged.

Globalization has been achieved by drafting basic codes of protection and, to the extent possible in a decentralized world, by monitoring and promoting compliance. Inevitably, this scrutiny has come into conflict with notions of state sovereignty. When the Commission of Experts overseeing compliance with the ICCPR found Jamaica to have violated the treaty through its administration of the death penalty, Jamaica responded by withdrawing from the ICCPR provision that allows individuals to make complaints to the commission. Jamaica's defense in that case was typical: respect our culture, our unique problems. When it comes to the treatment of our own people, we want sovereignty, not globalism.

Sovereignty, however, is not what it used to be. Beginning in the mid-1950s, the global system began to take humanitarian crimes more seriously. The UN barely hesitated before telling even quite seriously sovereign states—Belgium, the United Kingdom, France, the Netherlands, and the United States—to emancipate their colonies. And they did. By 1965, the Security Council was imposing mandatory sanctions on a white racist regime in Rhodesia and, in 1977, on South Africa—although they, too, had asked in vain to be let alone to pursue the cultural exceptionalism of apartheid.

By last fall [2000], the secretary-general of the UN, Kofi Annan, felt emboldened enough to tell the General Assembly that their core challenge was

> to forge unity behind the principle that massive and systematic violations of human rights—wherever they may take place—should not be allowed to stand. . . . If states bent on criminal behavior know that frontiers are not the absolute defense; if they know that the Security Council will take action to halt crimes against humanity, then they will not embark on such a course of action in expectation of sovereign immunity.

Annan called for a redefinition of national interests that will "induce states to find far greater unity in the pursuit of such basic [UN] Charter values as democracy, pluralism, human rights, and the rule of law."

This bold call drew quite a hostile reaction from member states. Governments seeking to preserve their sovereignty, however, are not the only ones offended by this most recent call for the enforcement of global values. Some cultures perceive the global human rights canon as a threat to their very identity. The Taliban may brandish national sovereignty as a shield, but they also see themselves as militant guardians of a religion and culture that should be exempted from a "Western" system of human rights that is inimical to Islam as they practice it. Other governments, notably Singapore's, have similarly advanced their claim of exceptionalism by referring to "Asian values" that are supposedly antithetical to universal or Western norms.

In taking a stand against global human rights, the Taliban have made common cause not with the tired nationalist defenders of state sovereignty, but with a powerful and growing subset of cultural exceptionalists. These include some traditional indigenous tribes, theocratic national regimes, fundamentalists of many religions, and surprisingly, a mixed bag of Western intellectuals who deplore the emphasis placed by modern human rights rhetoric on individual autonomy. Although these exceptionalists have little else in common, they share an antipathy for the whole human rights system: the treaties, intergovernmental assemblies, councils, committees, commissions, rapporteurs of the secretary-general, and the supporting coterie of nongovernmental organizations (NGOs), each seeking to advance the cause of personal self-determination and individual rights. The exceptionalists view this system as corrosive of social cohesion and a solvent of community, eroding the social customs and traditions that become unsustainable once the individual ceases to be subordinate to the group.

Rights or Responsibilities?

Although the struggle for human rights as seen through the prism of, say, Amnesty International or Human Rights Watch looks like a tug of war between governments and individual dissidents, the real action has moved elsewhere: to the battle lines between the forces of communitarian conformity and the growing network of free-thinking, autonomy-asserting individualists everywhere. And although a physical struggle is undoubtedly occurring for control of Chechnya's hills, the Khyber Pass, and the White Nile, a crucial intellectual struggle is also being waged between the forces of Lockean individual liberty and those championing communitarian values.

The communitarian argument is well paraphrased by professor Adeno Addis of Tulane University: "One cannot have a right as an abstract individual. Rather, one has a right as a member of a particular group and tradition within a given context." To this, Princeton's Michael Walzer adds that the recent emphasis on individual rights has fostered a "concept of self that is normatively undesirable" because it "generates a radical individualism and then a radical competition among self-seeking individuals." This, Addis asserts, "breeds social dislocation and social pathology among members of the group."

Harvard professor Michael Sandel, in his recent book *Democracy's Discontent*, criticizes the accommodations made by U.S. law—judge-made law, in particular—to an ethos of individual rights that, he claims, undermines the civic virtues that sustain Americans' sense of communal responsibility. Sandel complains that the emphasis placed on individualism in recent years has neutered the state and elevated personal rights above the common good. At the international level, Malaysian Prime Minister Mahathir bin Mohamad espouses a variation on the same theme. In 1997, he urged the UN to mark the fiftieth anniversary of the Declaration of Human Rights by revising or, better, repealing it, because its human rights norms focus excessively on individual rights while neglecting the rights of society and the common good. Meanwhile, Australia's former prime minister Malcolm Fraser has dismissed the declaration as reflecting only the views of the Northern and Eurocentric states that, when the declaration was adopted in 1948, dominated the General Assembly. Former German Chancellor Helmut Schmidt, too, says that the declaration reflects "the philosophical and cultural background of its Western drafters" and has called for a new "balance" between "the notions of freedom and of responsibility" because the "concept of rights can itself be abused and lead to anarchy."

Building New Bonds

The argument against this cultural relativism weaves together three strands. The first demonstrates that those advancing the exceptionalist claim do not genuinely and legitimately represent those on whose behalf that claim is made. The second shows that human rights are grounded not in a regional culture but in modern transcultural social, economic, and scientific developments. And the third maintains that individual rights are not the enemy of the common good, social responsibility, and community but rather contribute to the emergence of new, multilayered, and voluntary affiliations that can supplement those long imposed by tradition, territory, and genetics.

First, the matter of exceptionalist legitimacy—or the lack thereof. Many prominent voices in non-Western societies reject the claims of exceptionalists who supposedly speak for them. . . . Former UN Secretary-General Boutros Boutros-Ghali bluntly states that there "is no one set of European rights, and another of African rights. . . . They belong inherently to each person, each individual."

How, then, does one explain the increasing frequency and vehemence of exceptionalist claims made on behalf of culturally specific "values"? It often turns out that oppressive practices defended by leaders of a culture, far from being pedigreed, are little more than the current self-interested preferences of a power elite. If Afghan women were given a chance at equality, would they freely choose subordination as an expression of unique community values? We are unlikely to find out.

Some guidance can be drawn, however, from the parallel case of Sandra Lovelace, a Maliseet Indian from New Brunswick. Under Canadian law, which incorporates Indian customary law, she lost her right to live on tribal land when she "married out" of the tribe. When Lovelace took her complaint to the ICCPR's Human Rights Committee, she pointed out that no similar penalty applied to men. The global group of experts upheld her claim. Pushed to conform to its international human rights obligations, the Canadian government then repealed the gender-discriminatory Indian law. Although that change disturbed some traditionalist leaders, they were soon repudiated in monitoring tribal elections. As with much that passes for authentic custom, the rules turned out to have been imposed, quite recently, by those who stood to benefit. Discrimination against women by the Maliseet, far from being a traditional requisite of group survival, was shown by recent anthropological research to have been copied from male-dominated Victorian society.

In a similar fashion, many of the exceptionalist claims made in the name of cultural diversity have been challenged by others in the non-Western world. Radhika Coomaraswami, the UN special rapporteur on violence against women, says that practices such as female genital mutilation, flogging, stoning, and amputation of limbs, as well as laws restricting women's rights to marriage, divorce, maintenance, and custody, are all inauthentic perversions of various religious dogmas. Moreover, she insists that "cultural diversity should be celebrated only if those enjoying their cultural attributes are doing so voluntarily." . . . The Egyptian art historian Professor Nasr Abu-Zaid puts it simply: "It is the militants who are . . . hijacking Islam."

Just as many of the idiosyncratic customs that alienate non-Western traditionalists from the human rights system are inauthentic, so too are the attempts to portray these rights as aspects of Western cultural imperialism. The human rights canon is full of rules that, far from being deeply rooted in Western culture, are actually the products of recent developments—industrialization, urbanization, the communications and information revolutions—that are replicable anywhere, even if they have not occurred everywhere at once. . . .

What brought about the transformation to personal autonomy in religion, speech, and employment as well as equal legal rights for the races and sexes? Although these recent developments occurred first in the West, they were caused not by some inherent cultural factor but by changes occurring, at different rates, everywhere: universal education, industrialization, urbanization, the rise of a middle class, advances in transportation and communications, and the spread of new information technology. These changes were driven by scientific developments capable of affecting equally any society. It is these trends, and not some historical or social determinant, that—almost as a byproduct—generated the move to global human rights.

In the United Kingdom, it was the growth of a capitalist middle class in the eighteenth-century Industrial Revolution that fueled the demand for quality children's education and thereby compelled the admission of women to the teaching profession. In the United States, the demographic consequences of the Civil War gradually forced an opening for women in medicine and law. After World War II, veterans' benefits and the need for a large peacetime army profoundly affected the opportunities of African Americans. Improved and cheaper transportation loosened the ties that long bound people to the place where they were born and generated a demand for the right to travel and emigrate. The advent of information globalization through CNN and the Internet has profoundly affected individual participation in discourses on foreign and domestic politics, just as the invention of the printing press and Gutenberg's vulgate Bible unleashed the social forces leading to the Reformation.

These changes, wherever they have occurred, have boosted the capacity for individual autonomy and, in consequence, fueled the demand for more personal liberty. Does this trend, as the cultural exceptionalists warn, presage the unraveling of community and social responsibility? Elites in authoritarian societies have always professed to think so. When, in 1867, the Boston School Committee rejected a petition signed by, among others, Harvard President Thomas Hill and the poet Henry Wadsworth Longfellow calling for abolition of corporal punishment, the committee, employing the common Benthamite communitarian litany, defended beatings as advancing "the greatest good of the greatest number." Modern individualists, however, believe that the good of the greater number should not be achieved by sacrificing the human rights of even the smallest number. They also believe that, set free of unnecessary communal constraints, individuals will not retreat into social anomie but, on the contrary, will freely choose multilayered affinities and complex, variegated interpersonal loyalties that redefine community without the loss of social responsibility.

Modern human rights–based claims to individual autonomy arise primarily not out of opposition to community, but from the desires of modern persons to use intellectual and technological innovations to supplement their continued traditional ties with genetically and geographically based communities. Liberated from predetermined definitions of racial, religious, and national identities, people still tend to choose to belong to groups. This threatens the state and the traditional group only to the extent that traditional communities are no longer able, alone, to resolve some of the most difficult global problems facing humanity: epidemics, trade flows, environmental degradation, or global warming. Few quarrel with Aristotle's observation that "he who is unable to live in society, or who has no need because he is sufficient for himself, must be either a beast or a God." But many, freed to do so, now define themselves, at least in part, as "new communitarians," seeking additional transnational forums of association.

According to policy analyst Hazel Henderson, "Citizen movements and people's associations of all kinds cover the whole range of human concerns. . . .The rise of such organizations [is] one of the most striking phenomena of the twentieth century." For example, whereas there were 5 international NGOs in 1850 and 176 in 1909, now more than 18,000 are listed by the UN, which reports that "people's participation is becoming the central issue of our time." Most of these NGOs, from Médecins Sans Frontières to the International Confederation of Free Trade Unions, are engaged globally in socially responsible activities that promote the well-being of others.

Joining the Battle

It appears, then, that the globalization of human rights and personal freedoms is rarely an affront to any legitimate interest in cultural self-preservation. Nor do human rights represent Western cultural imperialism; instead, they are the consequence of modernizing forces that are not culturally specific. And the social consequences of expanding human rights have been far more benign than traditional communitarians have feared. To the Taliban's claim of cultural exceptionalism one might more specifically reply, first, that the Taliban's interpretation of the culture they claim to defend is considered incorrect by most Islamic historians and theologians; second, that their claim to speak on behalf of Afghan culture is undermined by their silencing of half the population; third, that the force of individual rights is becoming irresistible in a world of globalizing fiscal, commercial, cultural, and informational forces; and fourth, that many persons freed to choose their own identities will still decide to affiliate along religious, cultural, and national lines.

These arguments are unlikely to carry weight, however, with those whose claim of cultural exceptionalism is only a flimsy disguise for totalitarian tendencies. To some, the problem with freedom is not cultural or social, but political. After the recent victory of reformists in the Iranian parliamentary elections, for example, Ayatollah Mesbah-Yazdi reportedly said that the victorious reformers were more dangerous to the system than a military coup because they promote greater freedom for Iranians to write, read, and behave as they wish. Such an argument is hard to refute. It will be overcome, eventually, by the irresistible forces of modernization and the demands for personal freedom those forces unleash. Meanwhile, however, it is essential to defend the universality of human rights and expose and oppose cultural exceptionalism's self-serving fallacies.

But why bother? If the global triumph of human rights truly is predestined, encoded in the genome of scientific and technological progress, why not simply await the inevitable? One answer is that waiting is immoral. In the short run, scientific and technological progress may actually strengthen the hand of oppression. For women in Afghanistan, Kurds in Iraq, Indians in Fiji, and others, their inevitable liberation is still far away and provides scant comfort.

In harder strategic terms, too, waiting is a flawed approach. Autocratic elites have learned to fight historical inevitability by destroying the engines of social progress. The cultural Luddites of the Taliban, by disempowering women and dismantling their society's educational and health infrastructure, hope to delay their own eventual overthrow. Idi Amin had that in mind when he demolished Uganda's Indian mercantile community in the 1970s. Pol Pot almost succeeded with a similar project in Cambodia. And George Speight recently pursued the same goal in Fiji. Each sought to catapult society back to a premodern age when race or class purification justified everything.

Waiting for the inevitable globalization of personal freedoms is also made untenable by the reviving militance of cultural exceptionalism. From the Balkans to the Horn of Africa, from the southern tier of the former Soviet Union to western China, from Indonesia to Mindanao in the Philippines, extremist tribalism is on the rise. To the extent that this is a political problem—the use of terrorism and the export of guns and money—it must be countered by political and economic support for the governments and societies that firmly oppose it.

When such measures fail, international, regional, governmental, and nongovernmental means must be mobilized to carry on the fight against the more egregious forms of cultural oppression. There is no one-size-fits-all solution. In the instance of the Taliban, the UN has wielded the stick of nonrecognition and the carrot of food relief. It withdrew relief agencies when Afghan women were arrested for working with its field offices, and it sent them back when those measures were revoked. When a racist government comes to power—such as Speight's recent junta in Fiji— the international community has many sanctions that can be deployed to protect universal values. These range from diplomatic nonrecognition to the suspension of air traffic and the withholding of World Bank loans, International Monetary Fund credits, and bilateral trading privileges. They should be used.

Such steps could, for a time, harden the resolve of the cultural extremists. The principal objective of a concerted strategy against cultural extremism, however, must not be the quick reversal of any one outbreak of racism or intolerance, but the forging of a unified global stance against radical cultural exceptionalism in general.

This process will not be easy, for when it comes to global human rights norms, even some U.S. politicians, judges, and intellectuals are quite skeptical of universalism. And a superficial but subtly effective nexus joins the cause of cultural exceptionalism and other forms of resentment against globalization and its alleged parent: Western, or U.S., hegemony. For example, it is not always readily apparent to people why, if France claims the right to protect its culturally unique movie industry, Afghanistan should not protect its policy on women. Leaders of liberal societies everywhere—political, intellectual, industrial—are being challenged to defend values and clarify distinctions they may have assumed were self-evident.

If the fight against cultural exceptionalism is to be made effective, it needs military and fiscal resources. It needs a common strategy involving governments, intergovernmental organizations, NGOs, business, and labor. But let there be no mistake: the fight is essentially one between powerful ideas, the kind that shake the pillars of history. It is a deadly earnest conflict between an imagined world in which each person is free to pursue his or her individual potential and one in which persons must derive their identities and meanings exclusively in accordance with immutable factors: genetics, territoriality, and culture.

This, then, is a wake-up call. Waging this war of ideas successfully—and it cannot be evaded or postponed for long—will require intellectual rearmament for thinkers lulled by the warm, fuzzy triumph of liberalism and the supposed end of ideology.

8.2 Taming Leviathan

The Economist

The next selection, "Taming Leviathan," turns to the knotty question of the degree to which human-rights law has reduced state sovereignty and state independence of outside interference in domestic affairs.

The influence of human rights on global politics should not be overrated. States continue to cherish the prerogatives of sovereignty. Even though public support has become more vocal, western governments still tend to condemn human-rights abuses in other countries only where it suits them, and gloss over equally egregious abuses elsewhere. Strategic, military and economic interests still carry the most weight with national governments, as they always have.

Sceptics go further. The international legal system, they point out, is fragmentary and incomplete. Unlike national legal systems, it has no police force. Its single permanent court, in The Hague, deals only with disputes between states, and then only when they agree to its jurisdiction. The UN General Assembly is a talking shop, not a law-making body. Decisions by the UN Security Council, the world's "executive," are subject to the veto of any of its five permanent members. When push comes to shove, those sceptics argue, brute force, not law, remains the governing principle of international affairs.

Yet that sceptical view has become less convincing. For a start, it directly compares national and international law. Such a comparison, however tempting, is misleading. Without a world government—which would probably prove a disaster—international law could never function in the same way as national law, nor is there any support for the idea that it should. But that does not mean that international law is useless.

To understand why not, consider how national legal systems work. They do not, as is often supposed, rely solely, or even mainly, on coercion. Most people obey domestic law not because they are afraid of the police, but out of a sense of social obligation and self-respect. Even laws that carry little threat of sanction are generally observed. Coercion certainly plays a part in national legal systems, but prisons full of convicts do not stop the small minority bent on crime. This does not mean that national law does not work. It stops working only when the law-abiding majority loses respect for the law, or feels it no longer has a stake in its observance. And when that happens, no police force, however draconian its methods, can cope.

Again contrary to popular belief, international law, like national law, is generally observed, and for similar reasons. This is most obviously true in finance, trade and commerce. Without internationally observed rules, the global economy could not function. But states also abide by international law in thousands of transactions between themselves every day. Violations attract the most attention (and some times sanctions, as Saddam Hussein and Slobodan Milosevic have discovered). International law is rarely enforced by military action, and then only when it suits the political interests of the combatants, as it did in the Gulf war. But even in the absence of a global police force, that does not mean it has no effect.

Virtue for Virtue's Sake

Unless governments think survival is at stake, they rarely breach international law openly, because most government leaders and officials consider themselves law-abiding and do not want to put themselves in the wrong. Instead, governments often justify their own behaviour as legal and invoke international law against their opponents. They act as if it matters. The surprise of the past two decades has been that they are now acting as if human-rights law (which has always been at the furthest edge of international law) matters as well.

One piece of evidence for the growing importance of human rights has been the large number of risky humanitarian interventions undertaken in the 1990s. Western countries have been fiercely criticised for dithering while war raged in Bosnia and genocide in Rwanda. Their threats this year [1998] to use force to stop Serb atrocities in Kosovo have been scorned as too little, too late. And yet, judged by earlier standards, the remarkable thing is that western countries were expected to intervene in any of these conflicts at all.

It could be argued that in none of these cases, no matter how terrible the suffering, was international peace or security at stake. Humanitarian action is fraught with risks, as America discovered in Somalia, where intervention proved a political and military disaster, even though it also saved lives. America's and Europe's subsequent reluctance to intervene in Bosnia, Rwanda or Kosovo is understandable in purely political or military terms, and looks shameful only if a higher standard of responsibility is assumed.

In the same way, underlying criticism of the western response to the events in Tiananmen Square, and of the re-establishment of cordial relations with Chinese leaders some years later, is the idea that it is appropriate for other nations to judge China's treatment of its own citizens. In fact, the West's re-engagement with China was inevitable, given China's huge size and geopolitical importance. What was startling was the initial response to the Chinese government's brutal treatment of the demonstrators. The United States and the European Community quickly imposed an arms embargo, suspended high-level official contacts and froze new aid. Bilateral foreign aid dropped by 80 percent the next year. Over the following two years relations with most western countries returned to normal, although the United States delayed granting China most-favoured-nation trading status (i.e., normal trade relations) until 1994. Criticism of China's human-rights record continues, albeit in a lower tone of voice. The Chinese government now accepts that the subject can no longer be taboo. But is this enough? Human-rights campaigners rightly think not. Yet in the circumstances it is quite a lot. After all, Asia's largest and most powerful country was cracking down on its own protesters; it was posing no direct military threat to its neighbours.

Concern for human rights will always have to vie with a nation's political, strategic and commercial interests. The tools used to promote human rights—cajoling, criticism, monitoring, diplomatic protests, sanctions—will vary from case to case. Military intervention solely on human-rights grounds will remain rare, appropriate only in the most extreme cases. And yet human rights have indisputably become a factor in international relations, and not always the least important one. For example, Myanmar's political isolation is due mostly to its appalling domestic human-rights record, not its behaviour towards its neighbours.

There is growing recognition that a government's mistreatment of its own people may eventually make it unreliable or dangerous to other countries. In its final report last year, the Carnegie Commission on Preventing Deadly Conflict, a collection of former political leaders and senior diplomats, argued that human rights are becoming a key tool for promoting collective security. A top priority, the commission maintained, was to create "capable states with representative governance based on the rule of law" which, together with economic opportunity, could guarantee "protection of fundamental human rights." A crucial element in creating such governments, argued the commission, is "a network of interlocking international regimes underwritten by the rule of law."

The Price of Sovereignty

Where does this leave national sovereignty? With plenty of life left in it. For most purposes, states will continue to respect each other's sovereignty. But the doctrine is being revised. At a time when Yugoslavia's treatment of Kosovo Albanians— who live within Yugoslavia's internationally recognised borders—can elicit the threat of NATO bombing raids and visits by war-crimes investigators, sovereignty is no longer absolute, but conditional. "By joining the treaties, most governments have now signed on to the idea that human rights clearly limit their sovereignty, and create obligations to the entire community of states," maintains Theodore Meron, a professor of international law at New York University. Eventually, a government's claim to sovereignty may depend on whether it respects the basic human rights of its citizens.

That is the way in which international law is slowly moving. Other forces are pushing in the same direction. Global economic integration, the growth of international broadcasting, telecommunications and travel will all make it more difficult in future for repressive regimes to go about their business unhinderd by outside influence.

The assertion of international human rights is still in its early stages. There will be reversals. The world will not quickly become a kinder, gentler place. For some countries, establishing the rule of law may take generations, not years. Nevertheless, the treaties, conventions and other international agreements so painstakingly negotiated since the adoption of the Universal Declaration of Human Rights 50 years ago are beginning to look less like a record of pious hopes, and more like an expression of what is expected of all governments in an increasingly interdependent world.

An International Criminal Court

8.3 If Not Peace, Then Justice

Elizabeth Rubin

A critical test for international law will be Darfur, the province of Sudan where government-supported militias have waged genocidal war against indigenous agrarian tribes. The following news story from the *New York Times Magazine* examines the efforts of the International Criminal Court to bring to justice individuals responsible for this genocide.

I. A Day in Court for the Criminals of Darfur?

A thick afternoon fog enveloped the trees and streetlights of The Hague, a placid city built along canals, a city of art galleries, clothing boutiques, Vermeers and Eschers. It is not for these old European boulevards, however, that The Hague figures in the minds of men and women in places as far apart as Uganda, Sarajevo and now Sudan. Rather, it symbolizes the possibility of some justice in the world, when the state has collapsed or turned into an instrument of terror. The Hague has long been home to the International Court of Justice (or World Court), a legal arm of the United Nations, which adjudicates disputes between states. During the Balkan wars, a tribunal was set up here for Yugoslavia; it has since brought cases against 161 individuals. It was trying Slobodan Milosevic—the first genocide case brought against a former head of state—until his unexpected death last month. And now the International Criminal Court has begun its investigations into the mass murders and crimes against humanity that have been committed, and are still taking place, in the Darfur region of Sudan.

The Hague has become a symbol of both the promise of international law and its stunning shortcomings. We have reached a point in world affairs at which we learn about genocide even as it unfolds, and yet it is practically a given that the international community will not use military intervention to stop it. Militias called janjaweed, recruited from Arab tribes in Darfur and Chad and supported by the Sudanese government, continue to attack, rape and kill villagers from African tribes—more than 200,000 people have been killed in Darfur, and two million have fled their homes. For more than two years, politicians and activists have been shouting to the world that a genocide is unfolding in Darfur, calling it a slow-motion Rwanda in the hope that the shock of remembering the nearly one million people slaughtered in that African country in 1994 would prompt action. Coalitions of students, religious leaders and human rights groups have lobbied in Washington, have set up SaveDarfur.org and have made green rubber bracelets, now worn all over the United States, that quote George Bush recalling Rwanda and promising, "Not on my watch." Yet the killing rolls on, and no one intervenes to bring it to an end, as if the genocide in Darfur were already history.

Last year the United Nations Security Council referred the Darfur file to the International Criminal Court. And now the horrors of Darfur have become the preoccupation of an extraordinary international team of investigators in a plain and quiet Dutch town. They have no army, but they want to ensure that out of this history—this slow-motion genocide—they can wrest some justice.

Luis Moreno-Ocampo is the chief prosecutor of the International Criminal Court. A veteran Argentine lawyer in his 50's, he has a short, graying beard and

Groucho Marx eyebrows that are almost always in motion—excited, alarmed, disappointed. Moreno-Ocampo knows how difficult his position is. "I'm a stateless prosecutor—I have 100 states under my jurisdiction and zero policemen," he said when I visited him in The Hague in January. But he does not see his court as a token body. "No. No! Wrong!" he said, swinging his arms one Saturday afternoon as we strolled by The Hague's medieval prison. He recounted how he had explained the court to his 13-year-old son: "My son is studying the Spanish conquerors in Latin America. Yesterday he says to me, 'They killed 90 percent of the Indians, so today you'd put them in jail?' I said: 'Yes. Exactly. What happened to the native populations in the U.S. and Latin America could not happen today with the I.C.C. Absolutely. Absolutely. We are evolving. Humanity is not just sitting. There is a new concept. The history of human beings is war and violence; now we're saying this institution is here to prevent crimes against humanity.'"

The International Criminal Court was created by the Rome Statute in 1998 and began work in 2003 with two goals—to prevent crimes against humanity, genocide and war crimes; and to prosecute them. Of the two, prevention is what fires Moreno-Ocampo's ambition; it is what excites his imagination and intellect and fuels his 18-hour workdays, far away from his family, his horses and his farm in Argentina. It's not that he thinks the court can protect the villagers now being killed and maimed and raped in Darfur; his investigation into war crimes there will take years. What he is convinced of is that the prospect of prosecuting war criminals in Darfur and elsewhere will deter others from committing horrific crimes. Genocides "are planned," he told me. "They are not passion crimes. These people think in cost." The I.C.C. is intended to raise the cost. Moreno-Ocampo holds up Carlos Castaño, one of Colombia's top paramilitary commanders, as an example of the court's potential reach. After Colombia ratified the I.C.C. treaty, Castaño laid down his weapons because, according to his brother, he realized that he might become vulnerable to I.C.C. prosecution.

Colombia, however, is not Sudan, and Castaño was not carrying out a genocide. Does Moreno-Ocampo have a chance of bringing the perpetrators of the crimes in Darfur to justice?

II. The Dreams of Gustave Moynier and Luis Moreno-Ocampo

In 1989, as Soviet rule crumbled, a tiny window of historical possibility opened. For a moment, many people imagined a new world, with relations between nations rooted in human rights and international norms. It was something of a utopian vision, and the 90's—with massacres in Rwanda and Bosnia, Chechnya, Liberia, Congo and Sierra Leone—quickly swept the world back into bloodshed and genocide. Despite all the killing, an international movement was pushing the principle that government officials must be held accountable before the law. An early triumph of the movement was the successful prosecution in the mid-80's of Argentine generals responsible for the "dirty war" that led to as many as 30,000 Argentines being "disappeared." This was the first such trial—against top generals and leaders—since Nuremberg. Luis Moreno-Ocampo was the assistant prosecutor and became a household name across Argentina. The Argentine trials set a precedent for later tribunals like those for crimes committed in the former Yugoslavia, Rwanda and Sierra Leone.

The dream of an I.C.C. can be dated as far back as 1872 to a Swiss man named Gustave Moynier, who helped found the Red Cross. He saw many atrocities committed during the Franco-Prussian War of 1870–71 and realized that the 1864 Geneva Convention, on the treatment of wounded soldiers, was just paper without a court that could try violators. Nearly 130 years later, 120 countries voted to endorse the Rome Statute and began what could prove to be a small revolution in the history of nations. World leaders dared expose themselves to international law. No more immunity: they agreed to be held accountable for war crimes, crimes against humanity and genocide. Investigators and prosecutors would detail crimes and prosecute the criminals. Prisons would hold those convicted. Here was an idealistic vision designed by liberal pragmatists.

In the end, the delegations of seven states involved in the negotiations voted against the resulting treaty. Those states included Iraq, Israel, Libya, China—and the United States. But in 2000, just hours before the deadline, President Bill Clinton signed the treaty, a necessary step before sending it on to the Senate for ratification. A few weeks later, advisers to his successor, President Bush, let it be known that his administration would not respect that signature—that it regarded most international treaties as tools for the weak. In May 2002, Under Secretary of State John R. Bolton sent a letter to Kofi Annan, secretary general of the United Nations, announcing that the United States didn't consider itself bound by the Rome Statute. In one public debate, Bolton, who later became the American ambassador to the U.N., had argued: "The United States should pursue a policy of 'three nos': the United States should provide no financial support for the court, directly or indirectly; the administration should not collaborate further in efforts to make the court operational; and the United States should not negotiate further with governments to 'improve' the I.C.C. This policy will maximize the chances that the court will not come into existence." Since the court was a fait accompli, President Bush signed into law the American Service-Members' Protection Act, which requires American forces to liberate any American in I.C.C. custody. It is popularly known as The Hague Invasion Act.

Given that the reputation of the United States on human rights is today at one of its lowest points—Abu Ghraib, Bagram, Guantánamo—Moreno-Ocampo gamely regards Bush as an inadvertent boon to the court. Bush builds Moreno-Ocampo's legitimacy by being against the court. For Moreno-Ocampo's work is political as well as legal, and his approach is intensely pragmatic. As idealistic as he may be in his global post, his career is rooted in the muck of reality. He was just 32 when he prosecuted the Argentine generals. He went on to prosecute Argentina's military regime responsible for the Falklands war and other officers for murder, torture and kidnapping. He endured assassination threats while taking on corrupt officials, cabinet members and judges; preventing and fighting corruption became his unusual specialty when he went into private practice in 1992.

The challenge in Darfur is, however, greater by far than anything in Moreno-Ocampo's career. It was in March of last year that the Security Council referred the case of crimes against humanity in Darfur to the I.C.C. Soon, television footage was shown around the world of a truck delivering boxes of documents, compiled by United Nations investigators, about the crimes committed in Darfur. In New York, Kofi Annan handed Moreno-Ocampo an envelope containing the names of 51 Sudanese people recommended for indictment by the commission. News of the list's existence unnerved officials in Khartoum, Sudan's capital. Moreno-Ocampo took the envelope, flew back to The Hague and opened it among a few associates. He then locked the names away, later saying that he would compile his own list.

Moreno-Ocampo's Darfur file is a first in international justice. His investigators must work against the will of the Sudanese government. They cannot gather any forensic evidence from schools where collective rapes occurred. They cannot gather samples from wells that were poisoned. They cannot even gather shrapnel from bombs dropped on civilians by the government. The collecting of written material, however, did not stop with the U.N. commission. Sudanese dissidents and activists have been feeding the I.C.C. investigators letters and documents. A U.N. team recently returned from investigating key Sudanese officials (and singled out 17 for international sanctions). And Moreno-Ocampo is interviewing victims by every means possible, putting together the narratives of selected crimes and connecting them to command decisions in government. Slowly, too slowly for some, out of the murderous morass a case is being built.

III. What the I.C.C., and Sudan, Can Do

The government of Sudan, led by President Omar Hassan al-Bashir, contends that the I.C.C. investigation is unnecessary. After all, Sudanese courts are conducting their own investigations and prosecutions for whatever crimes may have occurred in Darfur. Immediately after Moreno-Ocampo declared in June 2005 that the people he was likely to investigate would not face justice in Sudanese courts, Bashir's ministry of justice announced the creation of the Darfur Special Criminal Court, a three-judge traveling court.

There are several ways in which a case may be brought before the I.C.C. One is by invitation of a state; this is the case in Uganda, for example, where the government asked the I.C.C. to investigate crimes committed by the Lord's Resistance Army, a murderous cult group composed of a few leaders and thousands of kidnapped children that has been terrorizing northern Uganda for nearly 20 years. A second option is for an I.C.C. prosecutor to initiate an investigation. This is the method that has made John Bolton and others apoplectic about the court and led President Bush in the 2004 presidential campaign to refer to an "unaccountable prosecutor." (In fact, the prosecutor is accountable to an international panel of judges.) The third possibility is referral by the Security Council. In every instance, a case will be inadmissible to the I.C.C. if a state is carrying out its own investigation or prosecution—unless the I.C.C. determines that the state's prosecution is seriously inadequate.

That determination is made by the I.C.C. prosecutor and the court's judges, who are nominated by the 100 states that are full parties to the Rome Statute. In short, the court is empowered to assert jurisdiction in states like Sudan that are not themselves parties to the treaty. This is the point at which the aspirations of international law meet the resistance of sovereignty and political power. For now, Sudan has set up courts with an eye toward demonstrating that the Darfur cases are inadmissible to the International Criminal Court because they're being handled perfectly well in Sudan.

The airport in Nyala, the capital of South Darfur, welcomes you with carefully tended flowers and a soft breeze that is a pleasant change from the relentless heat of Khartoum. A bustling market town on the edge of the desert, Nyala has an air of normalcy about it. Children in blue-and-white uniforms walk the dusty roads to school in the morning. Lawyers wait outside the courts to bring their cases. Women in technicolor wraps make fresh tea and coffee on little stools in the market. Arab nomads park their camels in the livestock market at the edge of a neighborhood locally known as Falluja because of the violence there.

The governor has declared it a crime to call the neighborhood Falluja, one of the many strange rules that remind you that you are in a police state. My translator during my trip to Darfur this past winter was a Fur, the Fur being one of the main African tribes of Darfur, and to protect himself he often had to lie about his tribe when we went to neighborhoods like Falluja. On the edge of town, African Union troops—they have been in Darfur since July 2004 to monitor a cease-fire and now number a mere 7,000—camp in tents provided by American companies. Just outside town, the notorious Kalma camp spreads across a stark plain alongside a dry riverbed. Some 90,000 people have come to live at the camp after fleeing their villages. The camp is nearly two years old and has sprawled almost five miles as families pack themselves in under thatch roofs and flapping walls made of canvas USAid food sacks.

In a quiet corner of Nyala, in a modest stone house, is the Amal Center, one of a handful of local institutions that offer some hope to Darfurians. The Amal Center is financed mainly by international organizations. Volunteer doctors treat victims of attacks, and a team of local Arab and African lawyers donate their time to file cases of murder, looting and rape stemming from the crisis. The center was founded in Khartoum in 2000 to help victims of torture in Sudanese prisons and later expanded to Darfur.

Among the lawyers at Amal is Muhammad Ali, a local Arab whose clients are mostly black African victims of janjaweed violence, and Thuriya Haroon Daldon, who is teasingly nicknamed Mrs. I.C.C. by local judges and, unusually for a woman here, drives herself around in a van. Thuriya Haroon's first case with Amal was in 2001, representing a group of men who said they had been tortured by national-security officers. "I submitted the names of the torturers to the attorney general, but until now there's no permission even to pursue the case, and no answer," she said, and laughed. A frank woman with a friendly but firm aspect, Thuriya Haroon uses laughter to fend off the realities of death and cruelty that now fill her workday. "Instead, we face harassment," she said. "They follow us, watch us. And until now the victims say to me: 'What do you do? We give our stories, and those who tortured us are on the streets.' Sometimes I'm ashamed. I've done nothing." She has handled hundreds of rape cases, for example, and until now: "No one has been convicted of rape in all of Darfur. We've had only two cases of immoral behavior. They were sentenced to six months."

Since President Bashir and the National Islamic Front (now known as the National Congress Party) took power in a coup in 1989, there have been dozens of rebellions all over Sudan. The deadliest predated the regime: a civil war between the north, where the Islamist regime was based, and the mostly Christian or animist south. Unlike in the south, however, in Darfur the African and Arab tribes are all Muslim. In Darfur, as elsewhere in Sudan, the rebels are fighting their people's economic and political marginalization.

The current Darfur conflict began raging after rebels ambushed the Sudanese Air Force at one of its bases in North Darfur early in 2003. It was a humiliating defeat for Bashir and his government's security apparatus. The government responded—as it had previously in the Nuba Mountains and the southern oil fields—by recruiting local militias to wage a counterinsurgency campaign, thus pitting tribes against one another. The name janjaweed means bandits or ruffians; it combines "devil" (jinn) with "horse" (jawad) and conjures a dark terror for Darfurians. The janjaweed were plucked from the mostly nomadic camel- or cattle-breeding Arab tribes of Darfur and neighboring Chad. Uneducated, destitute and landless, they are motivated mainly by promises made by Sudanese government officials of land and loot. Today the government uses them as a means of deniability: the militias are uncontrollable, the government says, and are merely carrying on an ancient tribal conflict or a cen-turies-old fight over resources between seminomadic Arabs and African farmers. Yet when the government wants to control them, it does, and many of the janjaweed have simply been incorporated into what are known as the popular defense forces.

Since August 2004, the Amal Center has compiled information on more than 72,000 cases. The documents are stored in boxes and a simple gray metal cabinet. Most are in folders sorted by the name of the targeted village. Consider the case of the town of Marla. In April of last year, after the Darfur file was referred by the Security Council to the I.C.C., the governor of South Darfur, Atta al-Mannan, announced that anyone from Marla who had a complaint could open a court case. The people of Marla took the governor at his word. "I brought all the cases of tor-ture to the governor," the omda, or community leader, of Marla, Abdul Karim, told me one hot, windy afternoon at the Kalma refugee camp. "The one tied by plastic rope who was paralyzed, the ones who were hung and have wounds on their necks, the ones who were burned with melting plastic. Sixteen cases. I told them to stand in front of the governor to tell their story and to show their wounds. One man couldn't even hold a cup of water anymore. The governor said, 'I didn't know such things happened.'" The governor said he would form a committee to investigate who committed the crimes. A prosecutor from Khartoum came and did the inves-tigation, submitted his report and returned to Khartoum. The governor proudly showed me the bound report, along with several other investigative reports that he had ordered and that sat in a glass display case behind his desk.

Abdul Karim said that when investigators found that all the Marla cases were against government or janjaweed or popular defense forces, they dropped the investigation. Several men from Marla had filed cases against specific young men who belonged to the popular defense forces. The men from Marla had a court hearing and brought witnesses. But on the way out through the courtyard that day, the plaintiffs were arrested by national security and then disappeared for months.

The men accused of the initial crimes were released. The tribal leader who the Marla men and United Nations officials say assisted in commanding the attack lives in a comfortable house in Nyala and hangs out at police headquarters and the prosecutor's office.

Justice in Nyala begins and ends with the prosecutor of South Darfur, Mauwia Abdullah Ahmed, who is from one of Darfur's Arab tribes. He decides which, if any, cases will go to the Darfur Special Criminal Court. I met him one morning in his office in a long one-story building just across a fence from Nyala's courthouse. He wore a blazer and tie and seemed bored when I asked why he hadn't transferred any of the serious cases—like those brought by the survivors from Marla—to the special court. He said it was too difficult to arrest the accused. He complained that the victims never identified their attackers, that witnesses never showed up.

I then asked him about the case of Hamada, a village attacked by janjaweed in January 2005. Muhammad Ali and others from the Amal Center filed the case on behalf of the villagers of Hamada—93 people had been slaughtered, livestock and possessions were looted and as the mayhem went on at least 19 women were raped.

The Arab tribal leader Nazir al-Tijani, who commands most of the janjaweed in that area and is said to be under control of the governor, has admitted that the attacks occurred and that he directed them. He said it was in retaliation for cattle raids. "He gave a big speech about his innocence, but he has not read the Geneva Conventions very well," one international official told me, quoting Tijani as having said, "Just because I ordered and planned the attacks doesn't mean that I was present during the attacks!"

The prosecutor told me that no individuals had been named in relation to Hamada. I asked him about Tijani. "That's a political case," he said. "People talk to the media, but no one came and gave us these details." I reminded the prosecutor that the village leader of Hamada filed the case through the Amal Center, and the prosecutor changed tactics. "We made an order of arrest, but up to now they're not arrested," he said. "The police don't know these people." But everyone knew Tijani. He came into town several times a week, or you could, as I once did, drive the two hours to his farm. "Murder cases are so common here," the prosecutor said, leaning back in his chair and scratching himself. "Hamada is no different. It's not a war crime. It's a murder case."

IV. A Visit to Sudan's Own Court

The Sudanese government's leading initiative to pre-empt the I.C.C. is its Darfur Special Criminal Court. By late last fall the special court had heard just six cases. One was a rape case that was dropped. (Thuriya Haroon, of the Amal Center, tried to obtain a closed-session hearing for the under-age girl, but the judges refused, and the girl clammed up.) Another case involved the looting of a truck and the shooting of a USAid employee; the charge was reduced to weapons possession. One of the harsher sentences went to a man convicted of stealing 80 sheep. It's not that no one has been connected by Sudanese courts to the genocide. They have convicted several men who did not want to take part in it: Darfurian Air Force pilots who refused to fly bombing missions over their homeland. They are serving 10 to 20 years in Kober prison in Khartoum.

One morning I visited the special court in El Fasher, the capital of North Darfur. I asked the president of the court, Mahmoud Abkam, why, with all the heinous crimes committed in Darfur over the past two years, so few cases of any seriousness had come before his court. He was an elderly man and had been retired when this job came up. He said, "We've found nothing of importance except those cases we heard." Why? "Because no information went to the prosecutor." What about Marla, Hamada, Deleig and all the other cases? He reiterated that no cases had come to the court's attention and suggested that this was because the victims preferred to talk to foreigners like me.

"You can serve their case better than the authorities," he said. "Here you can do nothing." He invited frustrated complainants to come to his court and tell him that the attorney general's office is ignoring their cases, but, he added, "They won't do it."

I said that many of the people who had told me their stories had no idea of his court's existence. He said, with a distinct suddenness: "To be frank, when we came here we thought there would be cases ready for trial. And we heard of mass rape, mass murder. We had the authority to see everything in the attorney general's office. But nothing on paper was shown to us." How did he explain that? "Perhaps the attorney general could not proceed due to circumstances beyond his control," he said. "Let us be optimistic and say that."

What if we were to be pessimistic?

"Higher authorities are not interested in these cases to be presented to the court," he said, "or for them to even come to the knowledge of the court." Another judge told me that, given the shortcomings of the court, the government of Sudan, far from preventing the I.C.C. from taking over justice in Darfur, is all but ensuring that the I.C.C. prosecutor will come to Sudan.

V. An I.C.C. Kind of Crime

A few days before I arrived in Nyala, the janjaweed and Arabs in military uniform attacked the Fur village of Tama. In the courtyard of a small house in Nyala, I met two women who had fled Tama and were wrapped in white shrouds, legs stretched out on the earth, eyes fixed down. One of them, Zahara Muhammad Abdullah, drew an orange cloth over the face of a young girl who was hiding in her lap. The child was petrified. A few days earlier, the two women told me, they rose before the sun for prayers in the mosque with their husband, the imam, when out of the quiet came the sounds of hoofbeats and gunfire and shouts, and janjaweed, some in uniform, burst through the mosque doors asking for the imam by name. The women watched as their husband said, "Yes, this is me," and the armed men said, "You, imam, are the one asking God to give victory to the Tora Bora"—a nickname for antigovernment rebels—"so today is the last day for you." The imam prayed and recited a sura from the Koran, Zahara said, "and then suddenly they shot him."

Then the men fired their guns randomly around the mosque. The bullets hit the imam's brother, his brother's wife, his brother's two sons and his daughter's son. They all died. Another armed man appeared and asked the other gunmen, "Did you kill Fakir Tahir"—the imam. "We did," they said. He wanted to make sure and pulled off the cloth covering the dead imam's face.

The imam's two wives and Howa, the 5-year-old girl, were kept inside the mosque and beaten periodically throughout the day while some 300 janjaweed continued to kill and loot. Meanwhile, the janjaweed women known as Hakama, a kind of Greek chorus who sing and encourage their warrior men during raids on villages, broke into song when they saw the dead in the mosque: the blood of the blacks runs like water, we take their goods and we chase them from our area and our cattle will be in their land. The power of al-Bashir belongs to the Arabs, and we will kill you until the end, you blacks, we have killed your God. It's a nonsensical ending: one thing that distinguishes the war in Darfur is that all the tribes are Muslim, and their God is the same.

The janjaweed killed 42 people that day, most of them running out of their homes or through fields of sorghum, hoping to escape. They told the imam's wives, "Go now to your father."

"We asked them, 'Who is our father?' and they said, 'The foreigners in Kalma camp.'"

VI. The Perpetrators' Point of View

A few days later, I drove to Tama with African Union officers and troops. Their mandate is a cruel one in that they are nearly powerless; they must monitor the cease-fire, and that's it, no peacekeeping. Which means that many of these men— Rwandans, Gambians, South Africans, Kenyans, Nigerians—have spent the last year picking up and burying hundreds of dead bodies, and even watching as janjaweed burn and shoot. And they can do nothing.

In Tama the fires hadn't yet gone out. Flames shot out of the freshly harvested sorghum and sesame. Ceramic storage vats of food were smoldering. Homes were ransacked. Empty toothpaste boxes, notebooks, onions and okra spilled across the floors. A dog lay dead outside the smashed basins of the midwife's house. Inside the brick mosque the floor was clean but for a bloodied turban, a bloodied djellaba, a few bullet casings and two aluminum boxes holding Korans. "This is the Islam of Sudan," said a young Fur man, a Muslim. A sheik from the village showed us the graves outside the mosque where they buried 10 men and a woman. A week had passed since the janjaweed first attacked, and still they were burning the place to ensure that the villagers wouldn't come back. The governor of South Darfur, Atta al-Mannan, explained Tama to me this way: "I warned the A.U. that this is the seasonal trip south of the nomads and there may be an accident." But according to a military-intelligence officer, who spoke on condition of anonymity because he feared he would be killed, the Sudanese military knew the janjaweed were going to attack Tama. The janjaweed, he said, are considered legal and are mostly part of Border

Intelligence Guard units. "They picked up boxes of ammunition at 2 p.m. the day before," he said. "So we knew some attack was coming. That is the usual routine."

Sudan's rulers seem to contemplate the murderous violence that sustains their power with complete serenity. One evening in Khartoum I visited the former governor of South Darfur, Lieut. Gen. Adam Hamid Musa. We sat in his garden during Ramadan, accompanied by a professor friend of his. Hamid Musa lived in a residential area cordoned off for favored military officers. He was removed as governor in 2004 and now heads the Darfur Peace and Development Forum, which is financed by Sudan's ruling party. He suggested that talk of rapes and racial cleansing in Darfur was simple propaganda. "Do you think a governor will go to kill his own people?" he asked.

Even before he was made governor in 2003, Musa was part of a group of Arab ideologues who were in Darfur recruiting Arab nomads into the militia now known as the janjaweed. In the garden that night, he noted that the allegations of rape and slaughter all came from the tribes of victims.

"And they all lied?" I asked.

"Yes," he said. "A single case of raping hasn't been proved. The women there don't even know what the word means." He chuckled happily and popped a toffee into his mouth, as did his professor friend.

VII. Moreno-Ocampo Fights on Many Fronts

For Moreno-Ocampo, working on the Darfur file is a never-ending tale of bureaucracy and doublespeak. Interviews, access and permits are given to I.C.C. investigators, then revoked, then rethought. Slow comes with the job, and in some ways this is a throwback to Moreno-Ocampo's early days against a similar regime. In prosecuting the perpetrators of the dirty war, 20 years ago, Moreno-Ocampo and his team could not rely on evidence from intelligence or police. They had no graves or remains—the desaparecidos were mostly thrown into the sea. What they had were 30,000 reported cases of desaparecidos collected by a truth commission. They decided to focus on 700 cases. They based their evidence on the testimony of survivors, many of whom were tortured alongside those who disappeared. The prosecution proved that the generals had command responsibility for the detention centers and the military pilots who had dumped the bodies into the sea. This is exactly the strategy Moreno-Ocampo plans to use in Darfur.

The Argentine trials gave Moreno-Ocampo a deeper understanding of the meaning of the law for society. Argentina's new president at the time, Raúl Alfonsín, won the 1983 elections with a promise to prosecute the guerrillas and the junta. "There was a social demand for law, but we the prosecutors were just the strawberry—the politicians were the cake," Moreno-Ocampo told me. "Trials are an expression of society. The victims finally received respect, for the first time in my country. Before the trials, if you were a victim you were under suspicion." Even his mother came around. She attended the same church as Gen. Jorge Rafael Videla, the president and leader of the junta, and was furious with her son for prosecuting him and betraying the family—after all, her father was a general. "She changed her thinking through the media, watching the trials. She said, 'I still love Videla, but he has to be in jail."'

The trials were the most potent symbols of the fundamental changes sweeping through Argentina. One disappointment with the Yugoslav tribunals, according to Moreno-Ocampo, is that people were hoping "the trials were the cake." But the trials didn't change the country. "The prosecutor cannot change job opportunities or create consensus in society," he said. "You need social movements."

But Sudan is not Argentina or even Yugoslavia. The regime is still in control, and its officials are masters at manipulating the international community. As one Sudanese foreign-ministry ambassador told me, "We just have to get one step ahead of the game so we can outmaneuver the I.C.C. when they finally request to send investigators." Referring to the Darfur Special Criminal Court, he said, "We make national trials, show no impunity"—that is, that the guilty are being punished—"and ruin the I.C.C." You have to look long and hard to find any political figure of significance in Sudan who is actively supporting the I.C.C.—while there are plenty who will draw a crowd by fulminating against the court as one more instance of foreign meddling.

Given the lack of domestic support for prosecutions in Sudan, foreign support is crucial. The European Union has been the I.C.C.'s most loyal backer but has shown some wariness in the Sudan case, not least because of justifiable worries about appearing colonialist. (There were huge anti-U.N. demonstrations in Khartoum last month, and Sudanese politicians played the colonialism card very heavily.) China and France, which are permanent members of the Security Council, have interests in Sudanese oil, and though they referred the Darfur file to the I.C.C., it is reasonable to question how deep their commitment goes. Russia, another permanent member of the Security Council, has always been uneasy about the I.C.C., given the continuing disaster in Chechnya. Neighboring countries, through the African Union, have in general supported peace efforts and in some instances have helped the I.C.C. But of course such support must be handled with care, as the Bashir regime has active disputes with several of its neighbors—notably Chad, with whom it is virtually at war.

The American position is a confused one. On one level, the Bush administration is determined to hobble the I.C.C. For a few years, the United States has pressed I.C.C. member states to sign a bilateral agreement swearing not to surrender U.S. citizens, or foreign nationals working for the U.S., to the I.C.C. But the administration's anti-I.C.C. policy has backfired. Gen. Bantz J. Craddock, head of the Pentagon's Southern Command, testified before Congress this year that the insistence on special bilateral agreements is undermining American military influence. Eleven Latin American countries have not only lost military aid; they no longer receive American training—which means no bonds are established with their American counterparts. Other countries, especially China, are taking advantage of the American withdrawal to advance their own foreign goals. On a trip to Latin America last month, Secretary of State Condoleezza Rice acknowledged that this I.C.C.-immunity policy was damaging America's interests.

The American willingness to allow, without voting for it, the Security Council's referral of Darfur to the I.C.C. may have indicated a change in attitude, though it seems to have come more from a belief that the court's investigation couldn't hurt and might help. The State Department was working hard on Darfur even before Secretary of State Colin Powell declared in 2004 that Sudan's actions in the region constituted genocide. The peace agreement between North and South Sudan last year, which ended decades of war, was a rare (and fragile) success for Bush administration diplomacy in Africa. The United States has tried to push similar negotiations on the warring parties in Darfur, so far with little result. At the United Nations, John Bolton led the administration's push in February to have the African Union force in Darfur reorganized under U.N. auspices and expanded, which will probably take place by the end of the year.

At the same time, the Bush administration has stopped calling the crimes in Darfur a genocide. The administration does not want to lose the North-South agreement and the peace it has secured, and this may make it wishy-washy on Darfur. It has also found Sudan to be a useful ally in the war on terror. At least some Sudanese leaders being investigated by the I.C.C. are, according to American officials who asked not to be named, highly valuable, if unreliable, allies in hunting down Islamic terrorists. "In 2004, when the Sudanese decided to conclude the North-South peace, they got an A− on cooperation," a senior American official said. "They rendered people and gave us information on people we didn't even know were there. Since then they've done stuff that saved American lives." The C.I.A. flew Sudan's national-security director, Salah Abdallah Ghosh, to Washington for a debriefing last year. He shared information that his office had on Islamist militants training in Sudan before 9/11. Yet he is one of a handful of top security men orchestrating Khartoum's crimes in Darfur and deploying intelligence units that have carried out targeted killings since 2003. In December, a United Nations panel recommended that Ghosh and 16 other Sudanese officials face international sanctions. "The U.S. has pressed the U.N. not to include Ghosh on the list of people who should be subject to sanctions," John Prendergast, a senior adviser at the International Crisis Group, told me. "Trying to constructively engage with mass murderers in order to gather information is the wrong policy. It reinforces the regime's willingness to perpetrate atrocities."

The Bush administration is reluctantly coming to terms with the usefulness, if not the necessity, of the I.C.C. According to Roger Winter, the State Department's special representative for the Sudan conflict, who has been involved in America's Sudan policy for 25 years, "If you want to liquidate an Islamo-fascist regime that committed genocide, the way to do it that is accepted by the international community is through the C.P.A."—the Comprehensive Peace Agreement that ended the North-South war—"and prosecutions by the I.C.C."

Despite the ambivalences, mixed messages and conflicting interests in the international community, the biggest challenges for Moreno-Ocampo and his team are in Sudan. The Khartoum government is learning how to play the game. It is pushing tribal leaders from the Fur, Zaghawa and Massalit to accept reconciliation and compensation; it has its roving Special Criminal Court. And as the new minister of justice in Khartoum told me: "We are sending 15 prosecutors to Darfur. We will try the armed forces, and convict rape offenders, just to prove to the I.C.C. prosecutor that we are willing and able to try the offenders in Darfur." He did add that under

Sudan's Constitution, the president and his cabinet members, members of the assembly and certain members of the armed forces and police may be immune from prosecution.

Leaving aside the question of sincerity, Sudan's efforts do point to deeper issues: should peace be allowed to trump justice? (The I.C.C. statute itself advises that the prosecutor suspend indictments if they are not in the interests of the victims.) Are reconciliation and compensation better justice than prosecution and punishment? In northern Uganda, many tribal groups were against the intervention of the I.C.C. at first. But some of Moreno-Ocampo's initial enemies, like the northern mayors he was meeting with when I went to visit him in The Hague, subsequently brainstormed with him on how to arrest Joseph Kony, the leader of the Lord's Resistance Army.

Sudanese intellectuals close to the government are very good at painting pictures of Armageddon to foreigners, insisting that if the international community demands justice it will only hasten war. As Ghazi Salah al-Addin, a moderate Islamist and presidential adviser, told me in Khartoum: "Those who feel threatened by the I.C.C., at a certain point, it will be a matter of life and death to them. They could block the C.P.A. The situation is so fragile. We shouldn't be complacent. Sudan is a very dangerous place. Your Somalia would be a picnic if Sudan degenerates into chaos. It would draw in the elements you fear most. It would require an influx of U.S. troops just like Afghanistan."

But that is why the I.C.C.'s work is so crucial, including to the United States: it has the potential to increase the pressure for peace as well as to deliver some justice. Darfurians and activists across Sudan see it as the only way of getting rid of one of the most murderous governments in the world. As the omda of Marla, Abdul Karim, told me, "After the intervention of the commission of inquiry and the U.N. and all of them confessed that there are crimes of war and crimes against humanity in this state, the best chance for the citizens of Darfur is that the perpetrators of these crimes should be taken to account at fair trials. Our hope is with the I.C.C."

So, quietly and doggedly, Moreno-Ocampo is stitching together his file against the top leaders of the genocide in Darfur, collecting evidence from victims, activists and international officials, and perhaps this might, in a very partial way, help keep Sudan from falling apart. In June he will present to the Security Council a report on the crimes committed, a road map of how he will proceed and probably a list of suspects to be indicted. Given that the Security Council is backing Moreno-Ocampo, if he issues arrest warrants against President Bashir and Vice President Ali Osman Taha, which is a real possibility, their political careers will effectively end.

I met Moreno-Ocampo recently at a cafe on the Upper East Side of New York to talk about his presentation at the Security Council. Sitting next to us was Hector Timerman, the Argentine consul, and his family. Timerman told me that when Moreno-Ocampo was first offered the job, Timerman was pushing him to accept. "Argentina is known in the world for the word *desaparecidos*—it is heavy for a country like us," Timerman said. "I told him, 'It's time to show the world a new Argentina committed to human rights.'" A few jokes were made between the Timermans and Moreno-Ocampo about his arrogant confidence as a lawyer and prosecutor. And then Timerman's wife said there was, after all, a reason for it: "Luis never loses."

Suggested Discussion Topics

1. Are human rights universal? Are there some rights that are, or ought to be, possessed by every human being and that no state has the right to take away, and that no culture has the right to deny? If so, what are these rights? Would all societies around the world agree about this list of universal human rights? If some universal human rights exist, what is their source—that is, who "grants" them—and who should guarantee them?

2. Should human rights be sacrificed to national interest? Or does the United States, for example, have an obligation to intervene around the world, and even to jeopardize its relations with friendly states, to uphold human rights? What are the assumptions behind your answer? Would you be willing to be drafted and sent overseas, and risk your life, in order to end human-rights abuses in Rwanda or Bosnia or Darfur?

3. What were the bases of the Nuremberg and Tokyo war crimes trials? In what ways did they violate state sovereignty? Were the trials mere examples of "victors' justice"? Why or why not?

4. What do you see as the most important developments in human rights since World War II? To what degree do states honor the growing body of human-rights international law? Is the importance of human-rights law likely to increase, or do you think we have reached the end of this process of expanding human-rights law? Explain your thinking.

5. Should the United States reverse its position and support the International Criminal Court? Why or why not? What are the costs and benefits of an international institution like the ICC?

6. The murders, rapes, and other crimes taking place in Darfur are taking place *within* a sovereign state. Why not let the sovereign state—Sudan—deal with these crimes? Many observers have complained that the activities of the Russian military in the rebellious Russian republic of Chechnya have violated human rights. Should Russian military (or civilian) leaders also be tried by the ICC? U.S. interrogation techniques at Abu Ghraib, in Iraq, violated international norms. Should the United States also be subject to the ICC's jurisdiction? Explain your reasoning.

Chapter 9

THE PROBLEM OF SOFT SECURITY: CRIME, DISEASE, AND DANGEROUS PRODUCTS IN A GLOBALIZED WORLD

The preceding chapters have focused on the changing nature of violence in today's world and on the weakening of some political institutions and the rising importance of others. These chapters have also introduced, however, another major feature of the transformation of global politics now under way: the changing meaning of "security" and the emergence of new issues on the global security agenda. Today's new global political agenda reflects the widening range of border-spanning threats to human life and happiness and the increased difficulty states face in dealing with them.

As we see in this chapter and the four that follow, what the issues on this new agenda have in common is that they reflect the increasing interdependence of people around the world and the proliferation of non-zero-sum problems—problems that threaten everyone, in spite of disagreement over who should pay the cost of their solution. Many of these issues defy solution in a politically fragmented world and encourage (but do not ensure) new forms of political integration to facilitate interstate or transnational responses. Resolving these non-zero-sum problems and dealing with heightened global interdependence will not only mean an expanding role for the intergovernmental organizations and transnational institutions but will also demand an increased, and increasingly complex, network of cooperation among states.

What we are witnessing is a transformation of the global security agenda. From the beginning of the Westphalian era until the end of the Cold War, security was defined principally in terms of safety from foreign invasion or attack. Although the threat of interstate war still exists, other issues loom larger than in the past. States may still see a danger that other states may attack them. But increasingly it is other kinds of behavior that frighten us. We fear that human-rights abuses or civil disorder in other nations may trigger massive transnational refugee flows, or that other nations may fail to control organized crime, drugs, or the spread of disease. We fear that other states may fail to control the production of biological, chemical, or nuclear weapons and that these might be used accidentally or by terrorist groups.

We fear that states may mismanage their economies and create shocks that affect markets everywhere. We fear that less-developed states may fail to develop economically and that the unmet needs of their people will result in migration, violence, and environmental damage. And we fear that they may pursue social or economic policies that disrupt or contaminate the global environment.

Issues such as human-rights abuse, crime, disease, the environment, the economy, poverty and migration are not new, of course. What has changed is that the dangers and problems they pose are now transnational, or global, in scope, rather than local or national. Changes in technology—the increasing ease with which people, ideas, products, diseases, and pollutants now move around the globe—mean that states are increasingly affected by events beyond their borders. And the increasing porosity of borders means that problems that individual states used to be able to address on their own have now become collective problems that can be solved only through collective action. They are beyond the ability of any single society, acting alone, to solve. Where the interconnectedness of states used to be primarily a matter of military security, which states could manage simply by maintaining a balance of power, what has emerged is a complex web of interdependence.

Interdependence complicates the relationship among societies. On the one hand, shared problems and opportunities create common interests. At the same time, however, they also create disputes over how to solve those problems or take advantage of those opportunities, and they create vulnerabilities that can be exploited. Although two states may see the desirability of trading with each other, for example, or the need to work together to solve environmental or health problems that cross international borders, they may disagree about the relative prices of the goods being traded or about who should pay to clean up pollution or how best to stop the spread of disease. They may also try to take advantage of the other side's vulnerability, and attempt to extract concessions on a particular issue or to link cooperation on this issue to other issues.

Increasing interdependence does not mean that the old problems of ensuring national security have disappeared, although the end of the Cold War has certainly solved some of them. But it does mean that we need to pay attention to emerging, redefined security agendas and to the ways in which states can, despite their fears and suspicions, collaborate with each other and with international and transnational institutions to deal with issues that span national borders.

Perhaps most profoundly, however, the new global security agenda reflects the idea that what ultimately matters is the security of *individuals,* not the security of states. Although the security of states remains important—not least because it presumably permits states to assure the security of the individuals living within their borders—in today's discussion of security it is seen as an instrumental goal, not an end in itself. If human security is threatened by developments outside the state's borders that do not challenge the survival of the state itself, or if states are unwilling or unable to provide for the security of their citizens, then human security becomes part of the global agenda, not just part of the national agenda.

Redefining Security

9.1 Human Security in a Globalized World

Rob McRae

Despite its growing popularity, there remains considerable confusion about what the idea of human security actually involves and how it is affected by globalization. In the first selection, Canadian Rob McRae defines and describes human security and how it is related to the many conflicts in today's global politics. He argues that human security goes well beyond the traditional concept of military security to include a wide range of threats to individual survival.

Globalization, that much overused word, is, nonetheless, the word most of us use to describe the profound changes affecting the international environment in the last few years. It means different things to different people, but for most globalization includes:

♦ the global reach of new communications technologies (the "death of distance");
♦ the emergence of global markets, and the "triumph" of capitalism (and consumerism) over its alternatives;
♦ the spread of democracy and western political values;
♦ and the nascent appearance of a global civil society.

By and large, these changes have been positive. The number of democracies in the international system has grown significantly, and most regions, with the notable exception of Africa, have experienced real economic growth and rising living standards. But what has become equally apparent is that globalization brings with it many new problems: these, if left unchecked, could reverse the gains of recent years and eventually threaten the international system itself. This is the dark side of globalization, and includes such things as international crime, mass migration, ethnically and religiously-based conflict, environmental degradation, pandemics and, last but not least, the widening gap between a rich and ageing North and an increasingly youthful and impoverished South. . . .

. . . The threats we face are more diffuse and multidimensional. In many ways, the world is less safe today, particularly for civilians. . . . Because the international system that grew up in the twentieth century was designed to protect states and state sovereignty, and to enhance security between states, the international system

McRae, Rob, "Human Security and the New Diplomacy," excerpted from *Human Security and the New Diplomacy: Protecting People, Promoting Peace* by Rob McRae and Don Hubert, McGill-Queen's University Press, 2001. Reprinted with permission.

is struggling to protect civilians within states. The tools are not there, though some are now being developed in the face of some staggering challenges. These new foreign policy instruments . . . reflect a broader change in foreign policy itself. This is the "Copernican Revolution" that makes human security, rather than state security, a new measure of success for international security, and for the international system.

The Human Security Paradigm

Of course, the concept of human security is, in principle, quite broad. It takes the individual as the nexus of its concern, the life *as lived,* as the true lens through which we should view the political, economic, and social environment. At its most basic level, human security means freedom from fear. These concerns have been traditionally the domain of nation-states, and where there was democracy those concerns were at least addressed, if not always successfully. Internationally, the security of our citizens was promoted through a set of interlocking agreements between governments, through international organizations, and through the voluntary sector. . . .

There are other antecedents of human security too. The United Nations (UN) has taken a leading role on human rights issues generally, and contributed substantially to a developing body of international human rights law. Both the UN Charter and the Declaration on Human Rights are ample testimony to this body's leading role, including the fact that the UN has woven human rights considerations into the work of virtually all of its agencies and commissions. So too has the UN been active in the investigation and condemnation of specific human rights abuses around the world, bringing to attention the plight of specific individuals and communities. . . .

International aid and development assistance have made, and still make, an enduring contribution to human security. Emergency humanitarian relief has always taken the individual—this particular woman, this child, this man—as the focus of its effort. Humanitarian action of this kind has sought to respond to basic needs in a moment of crisis, to fend off starvation, or to build temporary accommodation for the dispossessed. Development assistance has complemented humanitarian aid by building sustainable economies and by strengthening the capacity of developing societies to manage both internal and external political fault-lines. But even here, human security provides a new insight: development projects that strengthen economies at the macro level, whether through market reforms or liberalization, can produce unintended effects locally. Smaller economies, especially in the developing world, are sometimes battered by the winds of globalization in ways no economist can truly measure.

What lies behind the unhappiness of some smaller states with the World Trade Organization (WTO), the International Monetary Fund (IMF), and the World Bank is a plea to consider more carefully the micro impact of international policies and agreements on the human security of their citizens. So too environmental security proposes that we measure international economic and environmental agreements against the impact they have at the level of civil society, including the impact they have on the environmental security of individuals. Human security, viewed through an environmental lens, leads us to examine the welfare of individuals as a function of a total ecology, both physical and psychological. An environmental diplomacy that departs from this humanitarian standpoint would take quality of life and health, in addition to life-expectancy, as the real measure of successful environmental and health policies. Where environmental degradation or preventable diseases have a negative impact on health and create chronic disabilities, life-expectancy measures are rendered meaningless. It is the quality of the life lived, in addition to the abstract calculation of years, that is the focus of human security. . . .

Globalization and the New Conflicts

What has led to this reconsideration of international relations, and the diplomacy we use to pursue them? The first trend is, unquestionably, globalization. If the safety and security of civilians, and their welfare, has traditionally been the responsibility of nation-states, it has become increasingly clear that, in a globalized world, these states no longer possess all of the means to deliver. Whether developed or developing nations, all have come to recognize the need for international trade agreements to regulate commerce, arms agreements to promote international security and stability, global environmental accords to tackle truly global environmental problems, or international human rights accords to guarantee certain basic freedoms. Many more examples could be given, but the point is that we can no longer treat "domestic policy" in isolation from the international context: every domestic issue has an international dimension and vice versa.

Globalization, whether we mean markets, democratic systems of government, technology, or the spread of global values, is pushing down into the affairs of states and affecting the lives of individuals everywhere. This process is far from universal, and there are plenty of ghettos in globalization, but it is now a discernable broad-scale trend. The unanswered question is whether or not it can be managed, and by whom. . . . The future challenge here is a challenge of international governance, and the development of new instruments that both enhances the opportunities of globalization, while tackling its "dark side."

Because the dark side of globalization *does* pose a threat to human security. This is the second trend that is leading to a reconsideration of our foreign policy instruments, to our paradigm shift. The other side of the coin to globalization is localization. We see it everywhere, almost always mixed up together. The opposites converge in the image of a Coca-Cola drinking, jean-clad, AK-47 equipped paramilitary youth defending ethnic or religious purity by attacking helpless civilians from another clan, tribe, or village. Localization is both a reaction against globalization (and often the West), and yet facilitated and made more deadly by it. The retreat into tribalism (in the broadest sense of this term) is a reaction against the uncertainties wrought by globalization and the disappearance of traditional economies and ways of life, even of cultures and languages. When identities are so threatened, extremism and violence become self-affirming. The current phase of globalization is inherently dislocating, with political, economic, even psychological dimensions. If ever there was an age of anxiety, this is it.

Moreover, globalization makes localization and local conflict more deadly, for a variety of reasons. Foremost, it empowers nonstate actors as never before. Stateless international arms dealers are ready to sell to any side, even both sides, of a nascent conflict. The sides in question are as often as not nonstate paramilitaries, who support themselves through the illegal control of a local resource (diamonds, drugs, people) or black markets, who trade that resource through international markets, and then launder the criminal gains via overseas banks in order to pay for the guns. These, the conflicts of localization, of ethnic and religious homelands, spread their tentacles far and wide. They have a global impact because they promote international crime, terrorism, and extortion, often through the witting or unwitting cooperation of an ethnic diaspora, which may itself be virtually global in geographic extent. The export of deadly local conflicts to other parts of the world is exacerbated by globalization. In the future, we may find that "homeland" conflicts are directly driven by such aspects of globalization as the ongoing assault on traditional economies, and by such global phenomena as the impact of global warming, environmental degradation, and water shortages. We have a plethora of intergovernmental agreements to tackle many of these problems, but the new threats to human security in both the developing and developed world seem to be particularly resistant to such an approach. Why is this so?

In seeking to prevent conflict, the international system has long relied on the negotiation of interstate treaties and agreements as the preferred option, based on the assumption that states exercise sovereign control within their borders. There have been two problems with this approach, just now becoming apparent. While we have a web of international agreements, the way in which they interact and together have an impact on specific countries, including vulnerable communities and individuals, is still not well understood. By focusing on human security, we focus on the actual impact of these intergovernmental agreements, where the individual is the nexus of competing and sometimes conflicting international and national laws and treaties, or even policies (e.g., the IMF or World Bank strictures). We are just now coming to terms with the unintended effects on people's lives of this plethora of national and international instruments. It would seem that sometimes the policy challenge is better understood at the micro level than through macro analysis.

But the second reason that traditional intergovernmental processes are not always successful in protecting human security is that governments are sometimes not willing or able to implement their international obligations. When such states are not willing to abide by international commitments, their refusal is often couched in terms of the supremacy of national sovereignty over all other considerations. The civilians of such countries are left in a legal limbo of competing rights and responsibilities, whether they be economic, environmental, or political. Other states are simply unable to implement international obligations due to a lack of control, or governance, within their borders. This can be due to a variety of factors, ranging from a dearth of institutional capacity and resources, to the breakdown of order, or even ongoing conflict. These are weak and failing states, where disorder is often accompanied not only by conflict but by economic and social collapse, including famine and mass migration. Here, human security evaporates altogether. Indeed, we are better to speak of traumatic insecurity as the daily fare of the citizens of these noncountries. In both circumstances, where states willfully threaten the security of their citizens, or where states are unable to ensure such security, the international community must ask itself how it can best extend assistance to such civilians. The answer is not always self-evident.

The reason for this is that intergovernmental agreements and organizations do not possess all of the instruments necessary to protect the security of civilians from fear or violence. On the economic side, development assistance, both official and private, has sought to strengthen human security by establishing a basic level of *economic* security. In responding to basic human needs, and in building the capacity of developing countries so that they can profit from international assistance in a sustainable way, economic development is key to long-term political stability. But without a minimal level of security, there can be no sustainable economic development, and even international humanitarian assistance of the most basic kind can be precluded by endemic violence and insecurity. Yet, it is precisely where international assistance is most needed to protect human security that the international system is the weakest. The intergovernmental framework that has grown up since World War Two has developed mechanisms to prevent, and contain, interstate conflicts. These are wars of territorial aggression between states, fought across, and over, borders.

But current conflicts often take place within states, between rival factions, where interstate mechanisms do not penetrate, and where the claims of sovereignty can be used to block international humanitarian action. The challenge has been to develop new instruments, both governmental and nongovernmental, to protect civilians in situations of armed conflict. . . . This is the paradigm shift for international security: from a concern with protecting and enhancing the security of states, to the protection and security of civilians. The shift results both from a failure of the previous paradigm to comprehend what is going on and to provide satisfactory solutions, and from the emergence of new norms among foreign policy practitioners and in civil society more broadly. Hence, this is also a shift in value systems, representing new concerns and feeding a new international advocacy. Perhaps what we are witnessing is the emergence of a global civil society because this is precisely what seems to be energizing the new multilateralism, a multilateralism that brings together states, international organizations, nongovernmental organizations (NGOS), and individuals in radically new combinations.

Addressing the Costs of War

In the field of international security, a focus on the individual as the nexus of concern enables us to understand both the broad spectrum of threats, and their interlocking nature, in any given context. The new conflicts are unique to their local milieu, and indelibly sui generis. But there are some important similarities too: frequently rooted in ethnic rivalries, they often "benefit" from the cheap availability of small arms; paramilitaries and mercenaries almost always play an important role, including the use of child soldiers; such conflicts are often funded through local and international crime and corruption; and vital resources, such as fuel and oil, are controlled through black markets run by local warlords. In fact, it is often economic advantage, whether the control of a resource or access to the spoils of a corrupt regime, that are the hidden motives behind what first appears as a bloody ethnic conflict.

In these new conflicts, the civilians are not only pawns, they are often the targets, and vehicles, for complicated power struggles involving opposing warlords or clans. Moreover, the civilians affected by these conflicts are not just those in the immediate vicinity of the conflict. The crime and clan structures that support these conflicts are truly international: drug deals in North America might pay for small arms shipments from Europe that are intended to equip insurgents in Africa. Crime, corruption, and black markets have been not merely ancillary to the conflicts in West Africa or the Balkans, they have been key to the prosecution of the wars of ethnic-cleansing there. Civilians have even been used as instruments of war, where death and mutilation in such countries as Algeria and Sierra Leone have been used to terrorize the population and weaken public authority; or when the ethnic Albanian population of Kosovo was pushed across the border in an effort to destabilize neighbouring countries and overwhelm the North Atlantic Treaty Organization (NATO) forces stationed there. . . .

. . . In all cases, economic factors play an important role. When states fail, it is, in part, because their economies are failing. These countries live in globalization's ghettos, the places where global economic growth does not penetrate or benefit. It is precisely where globalization does not go that our development assistance programs are so crucial in building capacity. But more often than not, development assistance is ineffective or undermined if there is no human security, no security for a civilian population in pursuit of its economic well being. By developing mechanisms to protect and enhance human security, we build stability and protect the human capital upon which the prosperity of future generations depend.

   Crime

9.2 The Five Wars of Globalization

Moisés Naím

The second selection in Chapter 9, by *Foreign Policy* editor Moisés Naím, focuses on and describes five critical perils to human security that are linked to the process of globalization. These five—*drugs, arms trafficking, intellectual property, alien smuggling,* and *money laundering*—are all transnational threats to human well-being that defy solution by individual sovereign states. In all five cases, state governments find themselves fighting against criminal networks that are increasingly able to ignore or defy borders. As the author argues, fighting these sorts of transnational networks requires rethinking sovereignty, strengthening international institutions, and finding ways to work with, rather than against, market forces.

The persistence of al-Qaeda underscores how hard it is for governments to stamp out stateless, decentralized networks that move freely, quickly, and stealthily across national borders to engage in terror. The intense media coverage devoted to the war on terrorism, however, obscures five other similar global wars that pit governments against agile, well-financed networks of highly dedicated individuals. These are the fights against the illegal international trade in drugs, arms, intellectual property, people, and money. Religious zeal or political goals drive terrorists, but the promise of enormous financial gain motivates those who battle governments in these five wars. Tragically, profit is no less a motivator for murder, mayhem, and global insecurity than religious fanaticism.

In one form or another, governments have been fighting these five wars for centuries. And losing them. Indeed, thanks to the changes spurred by globalization over the last decade, their losing streak has become even more pronounced. To be sure, nation-states have benefited from the information revolution, stronger political and economic linkages, and the shrinking importance of geographic distance. Unfortunately, criminal networks have benefited even more. Never fettered by the niceties of sovereignty, they are now increasingly free of geographic constraints. Moreover, globalization has not only expanded illegal markets and boosted the size and the resources of criminal networks, it has also imposed more burdens on governments: tighter public budgets, decentralization, privatization, deregulation, and a more open environment for international trade and investment all make the task of fighting global criminals more difficult. Governments are made up of cumbersome bureaucracies that generally cooperate with difficulty, but drug traffickers, arms dealers, alien smugglers, counterfeiters, and money launderers have refined networking to a high science, entering into complex and improbable strategic alliances that span cultures and continents.

Defeating these foes may prove impossible. But the first steps to reversing their recent dramatic gains must be to recognize the fundamental similarities among the five wars and to treat these conflicts not as law enforcement problems but as a new global trend that shapes the world as much as confrontations between nation-states did in the past. . . .

The Five Wars

Pick up any newspaper anywhere in the world, any day, and you will find news about illegal migrants, drug busts, smuggled weapons, laundered money, or counterfeit goods. The global nature of these five wars was unimaginable just a decade ago. The resources—financial, human, institutional, technological—deployed by the combatants have reached unfathomable orders of magnitude. So have the numbers of victims. The tactics and tricks of both sides boggle the mind. Yet if you cut through the fog of daily headlines and orchestrated photo ops, one inescapable truth emerges: the world's governments are fighting a qualitatively new phenomenon with obsolete tools, inadequate laws, inefficient bureaucratic arrangements, and ineffective strategies. Not surprisingly, the evidence shows that governments are losing.

Drugs   The best known of the five wars is, of course, the war on drugs. In 1999, the United Nations' "Human Development Report" calculated the annual trade in illicit drugs at $400 billion, roughly the size of the Spanish economy and about 8 percent of world trade. Many countries are reporting an increase in drug use. Feeding this habit is a global supply chain that uses everything from passenger jets that can carry shipments of cocaine worth $500 million in a single trip to custom-built submarines that ply the waters between Colombia and Puerto Rico. To foil eavesdroppers, drug smugglers use "cloned" cell phones and broadband radio receivers while also relying on complex financial structures that blend legitimate and illegitimate enterprises with elaborate fronts and structures of cross-ownership.

   The United States spends between $35 billion and $40 billion each year on the war on drugs; most of this money is spent on interdiction and intelligence. But the creativity and boldness of drug cartels has routinely outstripped steady increases in government resources. Responding to tighter security at the U.S.-Mexican border, drug smugglers built a tunnel to move tons of drugs and billions of dollars in cash until authorities discovered it in March 2002. Over the last decade, the success of the Bolivian and Peruvian governments in eradicating coca plantations has shifted production to Colombia. Now, the U.S.-supported Plan Colombia is displacing coca production and processing labs back to other Andean countries. Despite the heroic efforts of these Andean countries and the massive financial and technical support of the United States, the total acreage of coca plantations in Peru, Colombia, and Bolivia has increased in the last decade from 206,200 hectares in 1991 to 210,939 in 2001. Between 1990 and 2000, according to economist Jeff DeSimone, the median price of a gram of cocaine in the United States fell from $152 to $112. . . .

Arms Trafficking   Drugs and arms often go together. In 1999, the Peruvian military parachuted 10,000 AK-47s to the Revolutionary Armed Forces of Colombia, a guerrilla group closely allied to drug growers and traffickers. The group purchased the weapons in Jordan. Most of the roughly 80 million AK-47s in circulation today are in the wrong hands. According to the United Nations, only 18 million (or about 3 percent) of the 550 million small arms and light weapons in circulation today are used by government, military, or police forces. Illicit trade accounts for almost 20 percent of the total small arms trade and generates more than $1 billion a year. Small arms helped fuel 46 of the 49 largest conflicts of the last decade and in 2001 were estimated to be responsible for 1,000 deaths a day; more than 80 percent of those victims were women and children. . . .

. . . Multilateral efforts to curb the manufacture and distribution of weapons are faltering, not least because some powers are unwilling to accept curbs on their own activities. In 2001, for example, the United States blocked a legally binding global treaty to control small arms in part because it worried about restrictions on its own citizens' rights to own guns. In the absence of effective international legislation and enforcement, the laws of economics dictate the sale of more weapons at cheaper prices: in 1986, an AK-47 in Kolowa, Kenya, cost 15 cows. Today, it costs just four.

Intellectual Property   In 2001, two days after recording the voice track of a movie in Hollywood, actor Dennis Hopper was in Shanghai where a street vendor sold him an excellent pirated copy of the movie with his voice already on it. "I don't know how they got my voice into the country before I got here," he wondered. Hopper's experience is one tiny slice of an illicit trade that cost the United States an estimated $9.4 billion in 2001. The piracy rate of business software in Japan and France is 40 percent, in Greece and South Korea it is about 60 percent, and in Germany and Britain it hovers around 30 percent. Forty percent of Procter & Gamble shampoos and 60 percent of Honda motorbikes sold in China in 2001 were pirated. Up to 50 percent of medical drugs in Nigeria and Thailand are bootleg copies. This problem is not limited to consumer products: Italian makers of industrial valves worry that their $2 billion a year export market is eroded by counterfeit Chinese valves sold in world markets at prices that are 40 percent cheaper. . . .

Governments have attempted to protect intellectual property rights through various means, most notably the World Trade Organization's Agreement on Trade-Related Aspects of Intellectual Property Rights (TRIPS). Several other organizations such as the World Intellectual Property Organization, the World Customs Union, and Interpol are also involved. Yet the large and growing volume of this trade, or a simple stroll in the streets of Manhattan or Madrid, show that governments are far from winning this fight.

Alien Smuggling   The man or woman who sells a bogus Hermes scarf or a Rolex watch in the streets of Milan is likely to be an illegal alien. Just as likely, he or she was transported across several continents by a trafficking network allied with another network that specializes in the illegal copying, manufacturing, and distributing of high-end, brand-name products.

Alien smuggling is a $7 billion a year enterprise and according to the United Nations is the fastest growing business of organized crime. Roughly 500,000 people enter the United States illegally each year—about the same number as illegally enter the European Union, and part of the approximately 150 million who live outside their countries of origin. Many of these backdoor travelers are voluntary migrants who pay smugglers up to $35,000, the top-dollar fee for passage from China to New York. Others, instead, are trafficked—that is, bought and sold internationally—as commodities. The U.S. Congressional Research Service reckons that each year between 1 million and 2 million people are trafficked across borders, the majority of whom are women and children. A woman can be "bought" in Timisoara, Romania, for between $50 and $200 and "resold" in Western Europe for 10 times that price. The United Nations Children's Fund estimates that cross-border smugglers in Central and Western Africa enslave 200,000 children a year. Traffickers initially tempt victims with job offers or, in the case of children, with offers of adoption in wealthier countries, and then keep the victims in subservience through physical violence, debt bondage, passport confiscation, and threats of arrest, deportation, or violence against their families back home. . . .

Money Laundering   The Cayman Islands has a population of 36,000. It also has more than 2,200 mutual funds, 500 insurance companies, 60,000 businesses, and 600 banks and trust companies with almost $800 billion in assets. Not surprisingly, it figures prominently in any discussion of money laundering. So does the United States, several of whose major banks have been caught up in investigations of money laundering, tax evasion, and fraud. . . . Estimates of the volume of global money laundering range between 2 and 5 percent of the world's annual gross national product, or between $800 billion and $2 trillion.

Smuggling money, gold coins, and other valuables is an ancient trade. Yet in the last two decades, new political and economic trends coincided with technological changes to make this ancient trade easier, cheaper, and less risky. Political changes led to the deregulation of financial markets that now facilitate cross-border money transfers, and technological changes made distance less of a factor and money less "physical." Suitcases full of banknotes are still a key tool for money launderers, but computers, the Internet, and complex financial schemes that combine legal and illegal practices and institutions are more common. The sophistication of technology, the complex web of financial institutions that crisscross the globe, and the ease with which "dirty" funds can be electronically morphed into legitimate assets make the regulation of international flows of money a daunting task. In Russia, for example, it is estimated that by the mid-1990s organized crime groups had set up 700 legal and financial institutions to launder their money.

. . . The imminent, large-scale introduction of e-money—cards with microchips that can store large amounts of money and thus can be easily transported outside regular channels or simply exchanged among individuals—will only magnify this challenge.

Why Governments Can't Win

The fundamental changes that have given the five wars new intensity over the last decade are likely to persist. Technology will continue to spread widely; criminal networks will be able to exploit these technologies more quickly than governments that must cope with tight budgets, bureaucracies, media scrutiny, and electorates. International trade will continue to grow, providing more cover for the expansion of illicit trade. International migration will likewise grow, with much the same effect, offering ethnically based gangs an ever growing supply of recruits and victims. The spread of democracy may also help criminal cartels, which can manipulate weak public institutions by corrupting police officers or tempting politicians with offers of cash for their increasingly expensive election campaigns. And ironically, even the spread of international law—with its growing web of embargoes, sanctions, and conventions—will offer criminals new opportunities for providing forbidden goods to those on the wrong side of the international community.

These changes may affect each of the five wars in different ways, but these conflicts will continue to share four common characteristics:

They Are Not Bound by Geography   Some forms of crime have always had an international component: the Mafia was born in Sicily and exported to the United States, and smuggling has always been by definition international. But the five wars are truly global. Where is the theater or front line of the war on drugs? Is it Colombia or Miami? Myanmar (Burma) or Milan? Where are the battles against money launderers being fought? In Nauru or in London? Is China the main theater in the war against the infringement of intellectual property, or are the trenches of that war on the Internet?

They Defy Traditional Notions of Sovereignty   Al-Qaeda's members have passports and nationalities—and often more than one—but they are truly stateless. Their allegiance is to their cause, not to any nation. The same is also true of the criminal networks engaged in the five wars. The same, however, is patently *not* true of government employees—police officers, customs agents, and judges—who fight them. This asymmetry is a crippling disadvantage for governments waging these wars. Highly paid, hypermotivated, and resource-rich combatants on one side of the wars (the criminal gangs) can seek refuge in and take advantage of national borders, but combatants of the other side (the governments) have fewer resources and are hampered by traditional notions of sovereignty. A former senior CIA official reported that international criminal gangs are able to move people, money, and weapons globally faster than he can move resources inside his own agency, let alone worldwide. Coordination and information sharing among government agencies in different countries has certainly improved, especially after September 11. Yet these tactics fall short of what is needed to combat agile organizations that can exploit every nook and cranny of an evolving but imperfect body of international law and multilateral treaties.

They Pit Governments Against Market Forces   In each of the five wars, one or more government bureaucracies fight to contain the disparate, uncoordinated actions of thousands of independent, stateless organizations. These groups are motivated by large profits obtained by exploiting international price differentials, an unsatisfied demand, or the cost advantages produced by theft. Hourly wages for a Chinese cook are far higher in Manhattan than in Fujian. A gram of cocaine in Kansas City is 17,000 percent more expensive than in Bogotá. Fake Italian valves are 40 percent cheaper because counterfeiters don't have to cover the costs of developing the product. A well-funded guerrilla group will pay anything to get the weapons it needs. In each of these five wars, the incentives to successfully overcome government-imposed limits to trade are simply enormous.

They Pit Bureaucracies Against Networks   The same network that smuggles East European women to Berlin may be involved in distributing opium there. The proceeds of the latter fund the purchase of counterfeit Bulgari watches made in China and often sold on the streets of Manhattan by illegal African immigrants. Colombian drug cartels make deals with Ukrainian arms traffickers, while Wall Street brokers controlled by the U.S.-based Mafia have been known to front for Russian money launderers. These highly decentralized groups and individuals are bound by strong ties of loyalty and common purpose and organized around semiautonomous clusters or "nodes" capable of operating swiftly and flexibly. John Arquilla and David Ronfeldt, two of the best known experts on these types of organizations, observe that networks often lack central leadership, command, or headquarters, thus "no precise heart or head that can be targeted. The network as a whole (but not necessarily each node) has little to no hierarchy; there may be multiple leaders. . . . Thus the [organization's] design may sometimes appear acephalous (headless), and at other times polycephalous (Hydra-headed)." Typically, governments respond to these challenges by forming interagency task forces or creating new bureaucracies. Consider the creation of the new Department of Homeland Security in the United States, which encompasses 22 former federal agencies and their 170,000 employees and is responsible for, among other things, fighting the war on drugs.

Rethinking the Problem

Governments may never be able to completely eradicate the kind of international trade involved in the five wars. But they can and should do better. There are at least four areas where efforts can yield better ideas on how to tackle the problems posed by these wars:

Develop More Flexible Notions of Sovereignty   Governments need to recognize that restricting the scope of multilateral action for the sake of protecting their sovereignty is often a moot point. Their sovereignty is compromised daily, not by nation-states but by stateless networks that break laws and cross borders in pursuit of trade. In May 1999, for example, the Venezuelan government denied U.S. planes authorization to fly over Venezuelan territory to monitor air routes commonly used by narcotraffickers. Venezuelan authorities placed more importance on the symbolic value of asserting sovereignty over air space than on the fact that drug traffickers' planes regularly violate Venezuelan territory. Without new forms of codifying and "managing" sovereignty, governments will continue to face a large disadvantage while fighting the five wars.

Strengthen Existing Multilateral Institutions   The global nature of these wars means no government, regardless of its economic, political, or military power, will make much progress acting alone. If this seems obvious, then why does Interpol, the multilateral agency in charge of fighting international crime, have a staff of 384, only 112 of whom are police officers, and an annual budget of $28 million, less than the price of some boats or planes used by drug traffickers? Similarly,

Europol, Europe's Interpol equivalent, has a staff of 240 and a budget of $51 million.

One reason Interpol is poorly funded and staffed is because its 181 member governments don't trust each other. Many assume, and perhaps rightly so, that the criminal networks they are fighting have penetrated the police departments of other countries and that sharing information with such compromised officials would not be prudent. Others fear today's allies will become tomorrow's enemies. Still others face legal impediments to sharing intelligence with fellow nation-states or have intelligence services and law enforcement agencies with organizational cultures that make effective collaboration almost impossible. Progress will only be made if the world's governments unite behind stronger, more effective multilateral organizations.

Devise New Mechanisms and Institutions   These five wars stretch and even render obsolete many of the existing institutions, legal frameworks, military doctrines, weapons systems, and law enforcement techniques on which governments have relied for years. Analysts need to rethink the concept of war "fronts" defined by geography and the definition of "combatants" according to the Geneva Convention. The functions of intelligence agents, soldiers, police officers, customs agents, or immigration officers need rethinking and adaptation to the new realities. Policymakers also need to reconsider the notion that ownership is essentially a physical reality and not a "virtual" one or that only sovereign nations can issue money when thinking about ways to fight the five wars.

Move from Repression to Regulation   Beating market forces is next to impossible. In some cases, this reality may force governments to move from repressing the market to regulating it. In others, creating market incentives may be better than using bureaucracies to curb the excesses of these markets. . . .

In all of the five wars, government agencies fight against networks motivated by the enormous profit opportunities created by other government agencies. In all cases, these profits can be traced to some form of government intervention that creates a major imbalance between demand and supply and makes prices and profit margins skyrocket. In some cases, these government interventions are often justified and it would be imprudent to eliminate them—governments can't simply walk away from the fight against trafficking in heroin, human beings, or weapons of mass destruction. But society can better deal with other segments of these kinds of illegal trade through regulation, not prohibition. Policymakers must focus on opportunities where market regulation can ameliorate problems that have defied approaches based on prohibition and armed interdiction of international trade.

Ultimately, governments, politicians, and voters need to realize that the way in which the world is conducting these five wars is doomed to fail—not for lack of effort, resources, or political will but because the collective thinking that guides government strategies in the five wars is rooted in wrong ideas, false assumptions, and obsolete institutions. Recognizing that governments have no chance of winning unless they change the ways they wage these wars is an indispensable first step in the search for solutions.

9.3 In Afghanistan, Heroin Trade
Soars Despite U.S. Aid

Philip Shishkin and David Crawford

The following selection, from the *Wall Street Journal,* describes how Afghanistan has become the world's largest producer and exporter of heroin despite the presence of thousands of American and NATO soldiers at war against the radical Islamic Taliban. It suggests the reasons behind this development and the deleterious consequences of Afghan heroin upon neighboring countries as well as Europe and North America. As this suggests, the new security agenda may require very different strategies, tools, and approaches than does the old security agenda of protecting states from attacks by other states.

The suspicious whirring of a motor came from somewhere in the dark skies above the river separating Northern Afghanistan from Tajikistan. Tajik border guards say they shouted warnings and then opened fire. What fell out of the sky was a motorized parachute carrying 18 kilograms of heroin.

It was a small drop in a mighty flood of Afghan heroin that is reshaping the world drug market. Once best known for opium, the active ingredient in heroin, Afghanistan has been working its way up the production ladder. Now it's the world's largest producer and exporter of heroin. Clandestine labs churn out so much product that the average heroin price in Western Europe tumbled to $75 a gram from $251 in 1990, adjusted for inflation, according to the United Nations Office on Drugs and Crime.

In Hamburg, Germany, a single hypodermic shot of Afghan heroin goes for just three euros, or about one-third the price a decade ago. "Even 13-year-old children have enough money to get into serious trouble," says Mathias Engelmann, a police detective in nearby Schacht-Audorf.

The business is also spreading disease and addiction in Central Asia and Russia, where traffickers have ramped up a smuggling route to the heart of Europe. Roughly a third of Afghanistan's drug exports go through this so-called northern route, supplementing the more-established routes through Iran and Pakistan.

In Afghanistan itself, the heroin trade jeopardizes the nation's fragile democracy, which is struggling to consolidate since U.S.-led forces ousted the extremist Taliban and their al-Qaeda allies in 2001. The drug industry dwarfs honest business activity. In 2005, Afghanistan earned $2.7 billion from opium exports, which amounts to 52 percent of the country's gross domestic product of $5.2 billion, according to UNODC estimates. "You probably can't build democracy in a country where narcotics are such a large part of the economy," says John Carnevale, a former senior counternarcotics official in the first Bush administration and in the Clinton administration.

The heroin business has blossomed despite the continued presence of thousands of U.S. and European troops. Some Afghan officials have argued that foreign soldiers should take a direct role in combatting traffickers. But Western commanders have resisted, arguing that they don't have the resources to broaden their mission. And they worry about alienating local civilians. "Our primary mission is a combat mission," says Col. Jim Yonts, a spokesman for the U.S. forces in Afghanistan. "We stay focused on our role of defeating the Taliban and al-Qaeda."

In Afghanistan, people have grown poppies since ancient times, originally for purposes ranging from medical use as a painkiller to making cooking oil and soap. In the northeast Argu district of the Northern Badakshan province, heaps of dry poppy stalks—already emptied of opium—are piled on top of nearly every mud hut, serving both as roofing material and as firewood.

Industrial-size harvesting of poppies began to develop only in the early 1990s, after war and anarchy plunged farmers into persistent poverty. Poppy cultivation became an attractive alternative to conventional crops such as wheat, as heroin merchants used the booming harvests to meet the demand for the drug abroad.

By the late 1990's, the traffickers began to make even more money by converting opium into heroin inside Afghanistan, as opposed to letting foreigners do the conversion outside and reap the profits. By locating heroin labs close to the poppy source, they were also able to save on transportation of the bulky opium, say people in the business and counternarcotics officials.

In a hurried effort to curry world favor, the Taliban in 2000 used its repressive methods to practically wipe out poppy cultivation. But since then, farming of poppies and production of heroin have quickly risen beyond their heights of the mid-1990s. The post-invasion U.S. counterterrorism operations, mostly focused in the south and east of the country, had the indirect effect of making drug business there more difficult. So some heroin merchants expanded to poppy fields in the more secluded and peaceful north, setting up hundreds of hidden labs.

"Badakshan had a really long history of opium, but not of heroin, so people from the south went to set up factories there," says a man in his late 20s from the Eastern Shinwar district on the Pakistani border. He said he spent several months working in a Badakshan heroin lab in the backyard of a house rented from a local farmer. Cooks would drop opium into a barrel and heat it over a fire, then filter it through a simple flour sack. They'd let the purified opium juice dry in the sun. Sometimes using electric mixers, they would blend the product with two kinds of acid. "And what you get in the end is a beautiful thing—pure heroin," he summed up.

Heroin's pervasive hold on the economy is on view in Argu, a town not far from the Tajikistan border. The main narrow street is lined with wooden shacks selling food, clothes and assorted necessities. Until a recent raid by Afghan special forces from Kabul, many shopkeepers acted as intermediaries in the heroin trade.

"Poppy farmers used opium as currency. They came to the Argu shops and exchanged their opium for wheat, for instance," said shopkeeper Haji Firouz, over melon slices in the office of the local police chief. "Then the heroin makers came to the shops, bought the opium, gave us cash, and we would buy more goods for the shops." Added Mohammad Nahim, the head of Argu's counternarcotics squad: "The drug trade became so normal here that everyone is involved."

The Afghan government has eradicated some poppy fields, destroyed labs and offered incentives for crop replacement. The U.S. contributed $780 million to the effort in 2005, up from $100 million to cover the three previous years combined. In Colombia, by comparison, the U.S. has spent $4.5 billion over the past six years under its "Plan Colombia" anticocaine program.

Afghan President Hamid Karzai tapped local religious leaders to expound on the evils of opium and threatened provincial governors that they would lose their jobs if they didn't reduce poppy cultivation. Those efforts had some effect. Total area under poppy cultivation fell to 104,000 hectares last year from 131,000 hectares in 2004. But excellent weather meant the actual opium yields remained virtually unchanged.

What's more, farmers who switched to other crops say the government didn't provide the help it had pledged. "The government promised cash, equipment, fertilizer, tractors, seeds, but they didn't keep their promises," fumed Abder Rahim, a poppy farmer who now has a wheat crop riddled with diseases. This year, he plans to grow poppies again.

Afghanistan's police and military are strained by confronting the heroin trade. In the provincial capital of Faizabad, the 12-person counternarcotics squad doesn't have guns, radios or steady transportation. There are supposed to be 22 of them, but not enough officers could be found. "I can tell you, I'm really tired of this job," says Major Ghulam Muheddin, the 50-year-old squad leader, who received threats on his life and has been shot at. "I make plans to arrest people, and they find out in advance." Major Muheddin recently arrested a man named Abdel who carried several kilos of heroin. He was bounced among various police offices and soon released. The major lives on roughly $90 a month. A kilo of heroin here costs $900 and up.

Afghanistan's long border with Tajikistan follows the Panj River through rugged mountain terrain that's difficult to police. It's the first step on Afghan heroin's northward journey toward Europe. One night in mid-August, Tajik border guards at the Moskovsky crossing shot down the heroin-carrying parachute.

For nearly two years, the soldiers at this riverside outpost had been hunting for an elusive airborne contraption used to transport heroin from Afghanistan to Tajikistan—but could never bring it down. This time, they had intelligence about an upcoming flight, according to border guard officials.

The next day the machine was all laid out in the courtyard of the border guards' barracks: a red, blue and white French-made parachute outfitted with a harness ring, a German-made motor, a small propeller, a plastic gas canister—and 18 one-kilo plastic bags of Afghan heroin. The harness ring was to hold a pilot, and the propeller to give him control of his direction after jumping from a mountain on the Afghan side. The soldiers' bullets had pierced the gas tank, forcing an emergency landing, but the guards never found the pilot.

A few days later, border guards at the same post intercepted a water-borne heroin vehicle—an inner tube from a heavy truck with wooden boards laid on top for the smuggler to sit on. Shudi Nurasov, a skinny 37-year-old citizen of Tajikistan, was navigating the calm waters of the Panj with 20 one-kilo bags of heroin worth $24,000, each bearing a neat oval stamp reading "AZAD PRIVATE FACTORY. The Best of all Export. Super White." But his raft was greeted by armed soldiers when it beached in Tajikistan.

Wearing a glittery green skullcap and a dirty knee-length Afghan shirt, a bedraggled Mr. Nurasov told his story. A few months earlier, he'd befriended an Afghan man in a Tajik prison where he was serving a short drug-related sentence. The Afghan eventually entrusted him with the heroin, under a typical deal: within a month, Mr. Nurasov would sell the heroin in Tajikistan and then pay his patron $16,000, keeping the rest.

Tajikistan stands as a stark example of how quickly and deeply this drug can wound a society. The northern heroin route through the country began spiking dramatically three years before the 2001 U.S. invasion next door, after the end of a brutal Tajik civil war that claimed more than 60,000 lives. The war's damage, in a country that had been the Soviet Union's poorest republic, drove the Tajiks further into poverty and dislocation. And then the Afghan heroin started flowing over the border.

"We never imagined that there would be heroin in Tajikistan," says Gen. Rustam Nazarov, who heads the country's Drug Control Agency, established in 1999 with funding mostly from the U.S. "We weren't ready." The number of Tajik drug addicts seeking treatment has increased eightfold in 10 years, according to government statistics, with half of that increase coming since 2001.

"This is worse than a nuclear bomb," says Batir Zalimov, a 36-year-old former heroin user who now works with recovering addicts. As in Europe, "the addicts are getting younger and younger," he says. These days, he says, there are users as young as 14 years old. When the first wave of heroin washed over from Afghanistan, Tajik youths had no idea how dangerous and addictive the drug was, especially when taken intravenously. "It was very prestigious, we saw drugs in movies," says one resident of the small drug clinic where Mr. Zalimov works, in the Tajik capital of Dushanbe.

The rise in shooting heroin has spun off a Tajik AIDS problem in the past five years, and 5,000 people are now estimated to have HIV. Eighty percent of all new cases are passed through dirty needles. Tajikistan has just negotiated its first-ever order of antiretroviral drugs.

Most heroin that passes through Tajikistan travels onward, through Kazakhstan to Russia. Last summer, Tajik investigators got a tip about a train-car with heroin departing from Tajikistan to a Russian town in Western Siberia. The train was eventually impounded in Russia. Hidden deep inside a shipment of onions in one car were 74 kilos of heroin packaged into round rubber containers made to resemble real onions.

In Russia, seizures of heroin reached 3.9 metric tons in 2004, the latest UNODC statistic, triple the previous all-time high in 2001, while street prices decreased in the same period. In Russia, which already has one of the world's highest growth rates in the spread of AIDS, many of the new infections are passed through dirty needles.

What's left of the contraband after the Russian journey pushes on to Western Europe through Poland and other Eastern European countries. European police and social workers say heroin fell out of favor in Europe in the 1990s, but the drug is making a comeback today.

When prices began to fall as production rose in the mid-1990s, addiction in Germany grew first among the immigrant community from Central Asia, say German police reports. Police statistics show double-digit annual percentage increases in the amounts of heroin seized in Germany as production rose in Afghanistan.

As Afghan poppy cultivation doubled, so too did the misery in Europe, with the deaths per year in the European Union rising from about 4,000 to over 9,000 during the decade. After poppy production dipped sharply in 2001, the number of heroin deaths in Europe also dipped in 2002. In Germany, drug deaths doubled to 2,030 in 2000 from 991 in 1989, then declined to 1,513 in 2002 as the effects of the Taliban's poppy ban reached Europe. Since 2003 the death rates have fluctuated, but are highest in regions such as Berlin that are dominated by heroin imported along the northern route, according to German police data.

Ivan, a 23-year-old immigrant from Kazakhstan who asked that his last name not be used, recalls a party on Christmas Eve, 1999, when he and nine friends celebrated at a friend's home in Leipzig, Germany. Among the gifts exchanged by the five couples that evening was Ivan's first shot of heroin. "I just wanted to try it once," he said. Within three years, all 10 Christmas celebrants had tried heroin, and two were dead from overdoses, Ivan said.

Heroin has more of a stigma among native Germans, says Bernd Westermann, a social worker at a center assisting drug addicts in Berlin. "It's been years since heroin was cool," he says. But German users often take heroin as a second drug to smooth the effects of ecstasy or cocaine.

Heroin from the southern and eastern routes through Iran and Pakistan also makes its way to Europe. Mr. Engelmann, the Hamburg-area police detective, says heroin is cheaper in northern Germany than in the south, in part because of cheaper smuggling costs along the route that leads to northern Germany. A German police report says better roads in the former Soviet Union compared to roads in Pakistan and Iran simplify the work of smugglers along the northern route out of Afghanistan. Russian crime organizations also take advantage of the high volume of trade between Russia and Germany to hide shipments of heroin in a handful of the thousands of trucks that ply the transit routes from Russia via Poland to northern Germany.

As the last step in the trail, some Afghan heroin is making its way to the U.S. The U.S. Drug Enforcement Administration says Afghan heroin is increasing its market share in New York because Russian and Eastern European drug cartels can buy Afghan heroin on the northern route at a price significantly below the price of South American heroin.

As in Europe, the purity of heroin on American streets has increased and the price has fallen in stride with production increases in Afghanistan, according to UN and U.S. government statistics. Most of the heroin on the U.S. market still comes from South America. But Afghan heroin increasingly is being brought in by Pakistani, West African and Eastern European traffickers, says the Justice Department report. "It is often smuggled through Central Asia and Europe," says the report, and often comes in "via air cargo and express mail services."

 Disease

9.4 Together, in Sickness and in Health

Natalie Angier

Disease is increasingly a transnational security problem. To be sure, transnational epidemics are hardly new. Many more people died during the influenza epidemic of 1919 than had been killed in World War I, and diseases like bubonic plague, cholera, malaria, smallpox, and typhoid decimated populations with little regard for national identity or borders. However as AIDS (acquired immune deficiency syndrome) demonstrates, plagues now can cross borders and spread rapidly via modern transportation systems. Other transnational problems, like drug abuse, changing sexual mores, and economic underdevelopment, exacerbate the difficulties of controlling the epidemic. In turn, AIDS exacerbates other transnational problems, like poverty. Thus, "solving" the AIDS problem, or the problem of other infectious diseases like malaria and drug-resistant tuberculosis, is likely to require both a global approach and serious progress in resolving a complicated nexus of global economic, environmental, and social problems.

According to United Nations experts, one in every one hundred sexually active adults in the world is infected with HIV, the virus that causes AIDS, and nine of every ten of them are unaware that they have contracted the virus. More than five million people are infected each year. The virus has swept across Africa, following trade routes and ignoring borders. Although Africa has been the worst afflicted continent to date, the AIDS epidemic is truly global in scope, and Asia threatens to inherit this unhappy distinction in the near future.

In the following selection, Natalie Angier describes the accelerated spread of pathogens that comes with globalization. She focuses in particular on three killer diseases—malaria, AIDS, and tuberculosis—and their rapid transnational spread. These diseases show no respect for borders and, where they are endemic, have caused serious economic and social disruption, which in turn create more ripple effects that cross borders, undercutting prospects for happy, healthy lives around the globe. Thus both directly and indirectly these diseases weaken the global fabric of human security. In today's increasingly tightly linked and interdependent world, nations will have to cooperate to solve these problems. As Angier notes, however, globalization, as well as speeding the spread of diseases and complicating national efforts, may help in the search for cures.

Not long ago, my older brother, Joe, flew in from Los Angeles for a family gathering at my home outside Washington, looking paler than a dieting vampire and muttering that he might be "coming down with something." The rest of us eyed him warily, washed our hands compulsively and broke out the echinacea and vitamin C.

By the time my brother-in-law, Dave, had flown back to Oregon, he was too sick to return to work. My daughter and I also took to bed for a day or two, but then gamely pulled ourselves together to attend a big party at my mother's apartment in Manhattan—after which we collapsed once more in fevered, achy near-delirium. Later my mother told me that party guests from two different states had called to complain that I had given them some sort of "bug."

And so from one humble plucking of the kinship bond came an Attila-scale distribution of the season's flu virus, itself a strain that most likely had its genesis in Asia. My story is hardly unusual, and that is exactly my point. Today, diseases as common as the cold and as rare as Ebola are circling the globe with near telephonic speed, making long-distance connections and intercontinental infections almost as if by satellite. You needn't even bother to reach out and touch someone. If you live, if you're homeothermic biomass, you will be reached and touched. Microbes are, after all, members of the most ancient, zealous and Darwinically gilded 24–7 delivery consortium. They travel by land, sea, air, nose, blows, glove, love, sewage, steerage, rat backs, hat racks, uncooked burritos, overlooked mosquitoes.

And, oh, how they love the global village. How readily, for microbes, that village feels like home. Whether it's the recent outbreak of cholera in Buenos Aires, after years during which Latin America was free of the disease, or the debut in the emergency rooms of Manhattan of an African-born illness like West Nile fever, the globalization of disease is an unavoidable byproduct of the high holy multicultural hustle. And though microbes have always had the traveling bug, in centuries past, it at least took a few weeks or months for sailors to deliver a ship of rats bearing fleas with bubonic-plague bacteria from the Orient to Europe. Nowadays, a mosquito infested with the malaria parasite can be buzzing in Ghana at dawn and dining on an airport employee in Boston by cocktail hour.

Every day brings fresh evidence of how intimate are the links that lash together nations, peoples, bodies, species. One land's meat, for example, seems every land's poison, as hapless Britain has struggled with a double whammy on its livestock. Since 1988, nearly 180,000 cases of bovine spongiform encephalopathy—a.k.a. mad cow disease—have been reported in British cattle, along with several thousand cases elsewhere in Europe, raising fears that we're eating tainted hamburgers capable of delivering into our brains the deadly agent of Creutzfeldt-Jakob disease, and prompting the Department of Agriculture to ban animal protein products from Europe. Vegetarianism has beckoned even more brightly in the last few weeks with the televised images of macabre mass barbecues, as Britain, the Netherlands and a number of other countries have struggled to combat the recent outbreak of foot-and-mouth disease among their livestock. Nearly five million animals in Britain and hundreds of thousands elsewhere in Europe have been killed or await execution, resulting in meat, dairy and leather shortages worldwide, not to mention the tanning of the political hide of the [former] British prime minister, Tony Blair.

"The globalization of health and disease is an incontrovertible fact," said Christopher J. Murray, a policy director with the World Health Organization in Geneva and an author of an influential report, "The Global Burden of Disease." "The travel and interaction between continents, and the exchange of people, animals, animal products, food products, disease vectors, are all vastly greater than in the past, and so is the potential for pathogens to move quickly from one place to another."

"Today I can be in a place like Mecca, where there's an outbreak of meningitis, and I would not know I was sick with it until I got home," said David L. Heymann, executive director in charge of communicable diseases at the World Health Organization in Geneva. "And think of all the people I'll expose on my trip back." Especially given the robustly recycled vaporous substances that passes for air in a modern jetliner.

The United States can give as well as it gets. In 1998, nearly 1,500 athletes from around the world competed in a triathalon in Springfield, Ill., where they were exposed during the swim portion of the event to leptospirosis bacteria, which can cause fever, chills, jaundice, meningitis and kidney failure. Of these, 72 sought medical attention, and the Centers for Disease Control and Prevention spent many weeks tracking down all the participants to warn them of possible symptoms and to seek immediate treatment should they arise, before permanent organ damage set in. Moreover, there was some risk of infected people releasing leptospirosis microbes into local water supplies through urination, further dispensing America's inadvertent gift to the spirit of international competition. "There's no epidemic in even the smallest corner of the globe that the world can afford to ignore," said Jacquelyn C. Campbell, a professor at Johns Hopkins School of Medicine's Board on Global Heath. "We're so interconnected that an isolationist's perspective is no longer an option."

A true understanding of that growing interconnectedness has to include the developing world, where most of the people on the planet live and where infectious diseases account for almost half the deaths each year. Half of those deaths can be attributed to three "pedestrian" yet persistently devastating diseases: malaria, HIV/AIDS and tuberculosis. Malaria kills more than one million people annually, the overwhelming majority of them children in sub-Saharan Africa. Many millions of other people living in more than 90 countries suffer from malaria, sometimes contracting it repeatedly year after year. Though they don't die of the disease, the debility and cost are enormous. By one estimate, Africa's gross domestic product would be $100 billion greater today than it is if malaria had been eliminated. And the warming global climate is carrying those malaria-bearing mosquitoes north. So is the 2:43 out of Kinshasa: planes landing in Charles de Gaulle Airport have recently been found to be carrying more than a few non-paying passengers, leading European airlines to step up their preflight extermination efforts.

Sub-Saharan Africa also has taken the most brutal jackhammering from the AIDS epidemic. Of the 35 million people living with HIV or AIDS in the world, 25 million are in sub-Saharan Africa. Of the 5.4 million people who are newly infected with the virus each year, 4 million live in sub-Saharan Africa. Helen Epstein, a former instructor at Makere University School of Medicine in Uganda, wrote recently in *The New York Review of Books* that "the AIDS epidemic in Africa may turn out to be the worst health crisis in the history of the human race." Thanks to the effectiveness of new drug regimens, Westerners have developed the false sense that AIDS is no longer a lethal disease. But apart from the fact that nobody knows how long patients on the new drug regimens will survive before the virus finally outmutates the current armamentarium, these drugs are expensive and difficult to take.

Moreover, the AIDS epidemic in Africa is unlikely to remain confined to Africa: the strains of HIV running rampant there, if left unchecked, are sure to gain novel malevolence that would allow them to spread elsewhere and overwhelm whatever resources we have devoted to defeating our Western-bred strains. And keep in mind that other highly populous countries like China and India are just beginning to feel the brunt of the disease. There's a perversely poetic loopiness at work: a disease that presumably had its origins in Africa made its first angry mark in America, then exploded in Africa, and is now moving onward, outward and back again, cat's-cradle style. It's not "Africa's" health crisis alone.

The only sane response to the world's AIDS crisis remains prevention—a response that hardly attracts an ounce of attention, let alone pounds, dollars or rubles. Last year, a total of $165 million from all sources was devoted to AIDS prevention in sub-Saharan Africa, compared with the $2.5 billion estimated as necessary to do even a perfunctory job. "When you see $9 billion going into the response to Creutzfeldt-Jakob disease, where you would expect a few hundred or maybe a few thousand cases at the most, while other, far greater public health problems are seriously neglected, we have to ask if we're getting the bang for our health bucks that we ought to get," said Joshua Lederberg, a Nobel-laureate infectious-disease expert at Rockefeller University. Don't look to the United States to swoop in and fix it: of the top 20 industrialized nations, the United States devotes the smallest percentage of its gross domestic product to battling these international epidemics.

But disease isn't the only thing moving around the globe with increasing speed, binding far-flung countries together in a mutual medical destiny. Medicines and methods of treatment are also part of the worldwide exchange. Pharmaceutical companies in the United States and Europe export a vast array of medications—from penicillin to protease inhibitors—to the developing world. And by seeking out alternative, local solutions from around the world, those companies, along with the best-endowed Western hospitals and research facilities, are beginning to level the balance of trade.

Where their citizens' health is concerned, some developing nations clearly have the edge over us on doing much more at fire-sale prices. In Chile, for example, the per-capita income today is about $5,000, the same as it was in the United States in the year 1900. But while the average life expectancy in our country a century ago was 47, in Chile today it is 76—pretty much the same as ours is now. And while Cuba remains an economic backwater, Castro's commitment to universal health care has paid off: the infant mortality rate there is the lowest by far in Latin America. (Meanwhile, the United States, which has the finest available health care, was ranked 54th by the World Health Organization in terms of equality of access.) Whatever our squeamishness over methodology, we have a lot to learn from these countries and from others that have demonstrated successes in treating disease with a fraction of our resources.

We also have a lot to learn about the potential medical applications of herbs and extracts native to obscure corners of the continents. Seeking them out and bringing them back to the lab for study—bioprospecting, as these hunting expeditions have come to be known—has become a big business unto itself, incorporating the quest not only for flora, fauna and fungi, but even for exotic human genes to which biotech companies now routinely purchase the rights in hopes they will yield some insight, and some profit.

Globalization has also underscored a potentially universal source of human strength: in the tribe. We are clansfolk at heart, hardly past the mutual flea-plucking stage, and evolved to traffic comfortably with a few scores of people at best. As a result, global health care workers have found that the most effective health programs are local and inclusive. For example, says Patricia L. Rosenfield of the Carnegie Corporation in New York and a former member of the Board on Global Health, "Thailand has one of the most effective AIDS programs in the world because they take the power of the community seriously." Their education efforts are concentrated locally on individual villages, schools, groups of prostitutes. The lesson of "think global, nag local" can work here too: when doctors in Minnesota took the time to contact families whose children need follow-up booster shots, the overall effectiveness of the local vaccination program rose markedly. And tuberculosis outbreaks in both Africa and New York have been tamed by keeping an eye on infected people and ensuring that they take their medications every day.

As a number of articles in this issue make clear, the world is moving beyond the old polarities of ancient and modern, global and vernacular, high-tech and no-tech. We're not just mixing our microbes; we're hybridizing our medical traditions. Elisabeth Rosenthal describes a promising treatment being used at Memorial Sloan-Kettering Cancer Center that was developed by a folk healer in rural China. Matthew Steinglass visits a tribal doctor in South Africa who dispenses Western analgesics along with his herbal potions. In an article about a family of noble Italian lineage whose members suffer from an exceedingly rare genetic disease called fatal familial insomnia, D. T. Max describes the insights that the affliction has yielded into the general nature of prions, rogue proteins believed to be responsible for a number of brain disorders, mad cow disease among them.

It's not always easy to admit that other tribes are more enlightened than we are. America refuses to adopt the metric system, by gum, and we're way behind most countries of the world when it comes to the promotion and acceptance of the finest form of disease prevention known to medicine—breast-feeding. Sara Corbett describes the outrage and disgust that a Delaware woman elicits because she nurses her 4-year-old twins, though in many traditional societies breast-feeding children of 4, 5, 6 years of age is considered a sign of superlative mothering. And despite the sustained scoffery of American doctors, a number of "folk" remedies may be every bit as worthy as their mainstream pharmaco-counterparts, as Sheryl Gay Stolberg makes clear in her discussion of herbs like black cohosh, widely used in Europe but not here, to treat the symptoms of menopause.

In the end, then, the great global agora of medicine is all about barter: buying, selling, swapping, titting, tatting, seducing and swindling. We import a malign parasite here, we export a rotten fast-food franchise there. Merck donates medicines for river blindness to Africa. Americans fly to Thailand for discount plastic surgery. Through the Internet, too, we've become an obligate if virtual superorganism, busy bees without borders, compulsively foraging through a billion sites for sensation, guidance, palliatives or cures for lupus, chronic fatigue syndrome, nailbiting, insomnia, narcissism.

There is something unnerving about the distending column of health information ricocheting through our cyberhive, much of it unexpurgated, unedited and unconfirmed. At the same time, there is something glorious—OK, I'll call it miraculous—about anybody anywhere having free, instant computer access to Medline and all the papers published in thousands of medical journals around the world. Our modems have become medical devices, and as fast as microbes can move nowadays, ideas, Google willing, will always outrun them.

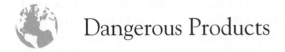 Dangerous Products

9.5 Dangers for Both Pets and People

Ariana Eunjung Cha

Although the globalized market and the outsourcing of production to other countries has reduced costs and increased the variety of products available to consumers worldwide, they made it more difficult for countries like the United States to assure the health and safety of those products. The following selection describes the use of tainted ingredients in Chinese exports of pet food to the United States, discusses the larger danger of unsafe food products made in China and exported to the rest of the world, and examines China's efforts to reduce the problem.

Something was wrong with the babies. The villagers noticed their heads were growing abnormally large while the rest of their bodies were skin and bones. By the time Chinese authorities discovered the culprit—severe malnutrition from fake milk powder—13 had died.

The scandal, which unfolded three years ago after hundreds of babies fell ill in an eastern Chinese province, became the defining symbol of a broad problem in China's economy. Quality control and product-safety regulation are so poor in this country that people cannot trust the goods on store shelves.

Until now, the problem has not received much attention outside of China. In recent weeks, however, consumers everywhere have been learning about China's safety crisis. Tainted ingredients that originated here made their way into pet food that has sickened and killed animals around the world.

Chinese authorities acknowledge the safety problem and have promised repeatedly to fix it, but the disasters keep coming. Tang Yanli, 45, grand-aunt of a baby who became sick because of the fake milk but eventually recovered, says that even though she now pays more to buy national brands, she remains suspicious.

"I don't trust the food I eat," she says. "I don't know which products are good, which are bad."

With China playing an ever-larger role in supplying food, medicine and animal feed to other countries, recognition of the hazards has not kept up.

By value, China is the world's No.1 exporter of fruits and vegetables, and a major exporter of other food and food products, which vary widely, from apple juice to sausage casings and garlic. China's agricultural exports to the United States surged to $2.26 billion last year, according to U.S. figures—more than 20 times the $133 million of 1980.

China has been especially poor at meeting international standards. The United States subjects only a small fraction of its food imports to close inspection, but each month rejects about 200 shipments from China, mostly because of concerns about pesticides and antibiotics and about misleading labeling. In February, border inspectors for the U.S. Food and Drug Administration blocked peas tainted by pesticides, dried white plums containing banned additives, pepper contaminated with salmonella and frozen crawfish that were filthy.

Since 2000, some countries have temporarily banned whole categories of Chinese imports. The European Union stopped shipments of shrimp because of banned antibiotics. Japan blocked tea and spinach, citing excessive antibiotic residue. And South Korea banned fermented cabbage after finding parasites in some shipments.

As globalization of the food supply progresses, "the food gets more anonymous and gradually you get into a situation where you don't know where exactly it came from and you get more vulnerable to poor quality," says Michiel Keyzer, director of the Centre for World Food Studies at Vrije University in Amsterdam, who researches China's exports to the European Union.

Chinese authorities, while conceding the country has many safety problems, have claimed other countries' assessments of products are sometimes "not accurate" and have implied the bans may be politically motivated, aimed at protecting domestic companies that compete with Chinese businesses. . . .

In the United States, more than 100 brands of pet food have been recalled since March 16 because of a spike in animal deaths, generally from kidney failure. The recall, one of the largest ever, included mass-market brands sold in stores such as Safeway and Wal-Mart, as well as pricey brands sold by veterinarians and specialty retailers.

Why the food is killing pets remains a focus of investigation, but the FDA and a manufacturer in South Africa have found that several bulk ingredients shipped from China, including wheat gluten and rice-protein concentrate, were contaminated with an industrial chemical called melamine. . . .

The investigations are unearthing details of the food chain that were previously a mystery to most Americans, including international dealings that determine how ingredients make their way into the food supply. U.S. companies are under pressure to cut costs, in part from consumers who demand low prices, and obtaining cheap ingredients from China has become an important strategy for many of them.

In China, meanwhile, the government has found that companies have cut corners in virtually every aspect of food production and packaging, including improper use of fertilizer, unsanitary packing and poor refrigeration of dairy products. . . .

Not surprisingly, food-related poisonings are a common occurrence. Last year, farmers raising duck eggs were found to have used a red dye so the yolks would look reddish instead of yellow, fetching a higher price. The dye turned out to be a cancer-causing substance not approved for human consumption. In Shanghai, 300 people were poisoned by a chemical additive in pork.

The Chinese government has undertaken a major overhaul of its monitoring system by dispatching state inspectors to every province, launching spot inspections at supermarkets, and firing a number of corrupt officials. . . .

In response to the pet deaths in the United States, China is carrying out a nationwide inspection of wheat gluten, but its government has refuted allegations that Chinese companies are responsible for the deaths. . . .

Investigators from the United States and China are still trying to determine how the contaminated wheat gluten got into pet food. The FDA says it had traced the ingredient to Xuzhou Anying Biologic Technology Development, near Shanghai. The company has said, however, that it is a middleman and got the wheat gluten from another source.

Suggested Discussion Topics

1. How and why is the global security agenda changing? What do you see as the major threats to your personal health and happiness? For example, are you more worried about an attack by a foreign nation or about the global spread of infectious diseases, the mass movement of refugees, or crime? Which, if any, of the major threats you see to your personal security or well-being are caused by global forces outside of the direct control of your particular nation or state?

2. What is human security? How does the idea of human security differ from the traditional idea of national security? Whom do we need to make secure—states (or nations) or individual people? Does your answer to this question affect how you think about international problems, how you rank the importance of various dangers, and what actors and institutions you see as playing an important role in providing security?

3. What role can intergovernmental and nongovernmental organizations play in coping with collective dilemmas of disease, migration, and crime? Identify IGOs and NGOs that deal with these issues and describe their contribution to solving these problems.

4. In what way is the drug problem a "transnational" one? Can the drug problem be solved by any single nation in isolation? What kind of transnational cooperation do you think would be useful in dealing with the problem of the global drug trade? What role would you envision for intergovernmental organizations? For transnational ones? Should the United States be involved in drug eradication efforts in other nations? Should it insist on "certifying" that these other states are making progress in drug eradication and making this a condition for aid?

5. Why should Americans care if AIDS spreads in Africa or Asia? In what way or ways is AIDS a security issue for the United States or for individuals in America?

6. Is it feasible to assure the safety of products imported from overseas? How might we reduce the risk posed by importing food from abroad? Should we erect trade barriers to products from countries with poor safety records? What costs would be entailed if we did so?

Chapter 10

MANAGING A GLOBAL ECONOMY

A key element in the turbulent transformation of global politics now under way is the erosion of borders between "national" economies and the declining ability of states to ensure the economic well-being of their citizens. Economic security issues that used to be national in scope now exceed the power of any individual state to handle.

Today's economic challenges illustrate both the disintegration of old political institutions and the creation of new ones. Although the globalization of economic markets has undermined the power of individual states to control what happens within their borders, it has also probably been the single most important source of political integration in contemporary global politics. As Harvard economist Jeffrey Sachs notes, "The world's economy has been dramatically transformed in recent years. Instead of separate national economies and marketplaces, producers and consumers increasingly find themselves in a single global one, posing new opportunities and new challenges as people around the world seek economic growth and stability."[1] Today, people's livelihoods depend on events far beyond the borders of their nation. Policy decisions made by other states, by intergovernmental actors such as the International Monetary Fund or World Trade Organization, and by transnational organizations, including powerful oligarchic corporations, will determine whether jobs exist and what wages they will pay.

10.1 The Challenge of Global Capitalism

Robert Gilpin

The chapter's first selection, by retired Princeton University political economist Robert Gilpin, explores the importance of today's economic globalization in understanding today's turbulence. Gilpin examines the principal features of this globalization and the forces that have driven it, as well as the political impact and reaction it has caused.

---

[1] Jeffrey Sachs, "International Economics: Unlocking the Mysteries of Globalization," *Foreign Policy,* Spring 1998.

Americans, other citizens of the industrialized world, and many peoples in other parts of the international economy have entered what the financial expert and economic commentator David D. Hale has called "the Second Great Age of Global Capitalism." The world economic and political system is experiencing its most profound transformation since emergence of the international economy in the seventeenth and eighteenth centuries. The end of the Cold War, the collapse of the Soviet Union, a stagnant yet enormously rich Japan, the reunification of Germany and its consequent return as the dominant power in Western Europe, and the rise of China and Pacific Asia are influencing almost every aspect of international affairs. Changes originating in earlier decades have also become more prominent; these developments include the technological revolution associated with the computer and the information economy and the redistribution of economic power from the industrialized West to the rapidly industrializing and crisis-riven economies of Pacific Asia. The worldwide shift to greater reliance on the market in the management of economic affairs, and what many call the "retreat of the state," are integrating national economies everywhere into a global economy of expanding trade and financial flows. . . .

These developments are having important consequences for the lives of us all. There will be many winners as a global capitalism refashions almost every aspect of domestic and international economic affairs. There will also be many losers, at least over the short term, as international competition intensifies and as businesses and workers lose the secure niches that they enjoyed in the past. Economic globalization presents both threats and challenges for the well-being of peoples everywhere. If individuals and societies are to adjust intelligently to the challenge of global capitalism, it is imperative that they understand the principal forces transforming international economic and political affairs. . . .

Economic Globalization

Since the early 1980s, economic issues and the global economy have become more central to international economic and political affairs than at any time since the late nineteenth century. Many commentators have noted a profound shift from a state-dominated to a market-dominated world. The market's increased importance, reflected in increased international flows of goods, capital, and services, has been encouraged by declining costs of transportation and communications, the collapse of command-type economies, and the increasing influence of a conservative economic ideology based on the policy prescriptions of economics. This resurgence of the market is really a return to the pre–World War I era of expanding globalization of markets, production, and finance.

At the turn of the century, issues arising from economic globalization confront national societies and the international community. Immediately after the end of the Cold War almost every economist, business executive, and political leader in both industrialized and industrializing countries expected that economic globalization would lead to a world characterized by open and prosperous economies, political democracy, and international cooperation. However, as the 1990s progressed, and especially in response to the post-1997 global economic turmoil, a powerful negative reaction to globalization arose in both developed and less developed countries. Rejections of globalization and its alleged negative consequences became especially strident within the United States, Western Europe, and some industrializing economies. Globalization has been blamed for everything from growing income inequality to chronic high levels of unemployment and even to the oppression of women, and critics have favored such nostrums as trade protectionism, closed regional arrangements, and severe restrictions on migration. Certainly the future of the international economic and political system will be strongly affected by the relative success or failure of the proponents and opponents of globalization.

According to the "globalization thesis," a quantum change in human affairs has taken place as the flow of large quantities of trade, investment, and technologies across national borders has expanded from a trickle to a flood. Political, economic, and social activities are becoming worldwide in scope, and interactions among states and societies on many fronts have increased. As integrative processes widen and deepen globally, some believe that markets have become, or are becoming, the most important mechanism determining both domestic and international affairs. In a highly integrated global economy, the nation-state, according to some, has become anachronistic and is in retreat. A global capitalist economy characterized by unrestricted trade, investment flows, and the international activities of multinational firms will benefit rich and poor alike.

Others, however, emphasize the alleged downside of economic globalization, including the increase of income inequality both among and within nations, high chronic levels of unemployment in Western Europe and elsewhere, and, most of all, the devastating consequences of unregulated financial flows. These critics charge that national societies are being integrated into a global economic system and buffeted by economic and technological forces over which they have very little control. For them, the global economic problems of the late 1990s offer proof that the costs of globalization are much greater than its benefits.

Although the term "globalization" is now used broadly, economic globalization has entailed just a few key developments in trade, finance, and foreign direct investment by multinational corporations. Since the end of World War II, *international trade* has greatly expanded and has become a much more important factor in both domestic and international economic affairs. Whereas the volume of international commerce had grown by only 0.5 percent annually between 1913 and 1948, it grew at an annual rate of 7 percent from 1948 to 1973. . . . Over the course of the postwar era, trade has grown from 7 percent to 21 percent of total world income. The value of world trade has increased from $57 billion in 1947 to $6 trillion in the 1990s. In addition to the great expansion of merchandise trade (goods), trade in services (banking, information, etc.) has significantly increased during recent decades. With this immense expansion of world trade, international competition has greatly increased. Although consumers and export sectors within individual nations benefit from increased openness, many businesses find themselves competing against foreign firms that have greatly improved their efficiency. During the 1990s, trade competition became even more intense as a growing number of industrializing economies shifted from an import-substitution to an export-led growth strategy. Nevertheless, the major competitors for most all American firms are other American firms.

Underlying the expansion of global trade have been a number of developments. Since World War II, trade barriers have declined significantly due to successive rounds of trade negotiations. For example, over the past half century, average tariff levels of the United States and other industrialized countries on imported products have dropped from about 40 percent to only 6 percent, and barriers to trade in services have also been lowered. In addition, since the late 1970s deregulation and privatization have further opened national economies to imports. Technological advances in communications and transportation have reduced costs and thus significantly encouraged trade expansion. Taking advantage of these economic and technological changes, more and more businesses have expanded their horizons to include international markets. Despite these developments, most trade takes place among the three advanced industrialized economies—the United States, Western Europe, and Japan, plus a few emerging markets in East Asia, Latin America, and elsewhere. Most of the less developed world is excluded, except as exporters of food and raw materials. It is estimated, for example, that Africa south of the Sahara accounted for only about 1 percent of total world trade in the 1990s.

Since the mid-1970s, the removal of capital controls, the creation of new financial instruments, and technological advances in communications have contributed to a much more highly integrated *international financial system*. The volume of foreign exchange trading (buying and selling national currencies) in the late 1990s has been approximately $1.5 trillion per day, an eightfold increase since 1986; by contrast, the global volume of exports (goods and services) for all of 1997 was $6.6 trillion, or $25 billion per day! In addition, the amount of investment capital seeking higher returns has grown enormously; by the mid-1990s, mutual funds, pension funds, and the like totaled $20 trillion, ten times the 1980 figure. Moreover, the significance of these huge investments is greatly magnified by the fact that foreign investments are increasingly leveraged; that is, they are investments made with borrowed funds. Finally, derivatives or repackaged securities and other financial assets play an important role in international finance. Valued at $360 trillion (larger than the value of the entire global economy), they have contributed to the complexity and to the instability of international finance. It is obvious that international finance has a profound impact on the global economy.

This financial revolution has linked national economies closely to one another, significantly increased the capital available for developing counties, and, in the case of the East Asian emerging markets, accelerated economic development. However, as a large portion of these financial flows is short-term, highly volatile, and speculative, international finance has become the most vulnerable and unstable aspect of the global capitalist economy. The immense scale, velocity, and speculative nature of financial movements across national borders have made governments more vulnerable to sudden shifts in these movements. Governments can therefore easily fall prey to currency speculators, as happened in the 1992 European financial crisis (which caused Great Britain to withdraw from the Exchange Rate Mechanism), in the 1994–1995 punishing collapse of the Mexican peso, and in the devastating East Asian financial crisis in the late 1990s. Whereas for some, financial globalization exemplifies the healthy and beneficial triumph of global capitalism, for others the international financial system seems "out of control" and in need of improved regulation.

The term "globalization" came into popular usage in the second half of the 1980s in connection with the huge surge of foreign direct investment (FDI) by multinational corporations (MNCs). . . . Throughout much of the 1990s, FDI outflows from the major industrialized countries to industrializing countries rose at approximately 15 percent annually; FDI flows among the industrialized countries themselves rose at about the same rate. In the late 1990s, the cumulative value of FDI amounts to hundreds of billions of dollars. The greatest portion of this investment has been in high-tech industries, such as those of automobiles and information technology.

These general statements, however, hide noteworthy aspects of FDI and MNC activities. Despite much talk of corporate globalization, FDI is actually highly concentrated and distributed very unevenly around the globe. Most FDI takes place in the United States, China, and Western Europe because firms are attracted to large or potentially large markets. FDI in less developed countries, with a few notable exceptions, has been modest. In addition to that in a few Latin American countries, and particularly in the Brazilian and Mexican automobile sectors, most FDI in developing countries has been placed in the emerging markets of East and Southeast Asia, particularly in China. When one speaks of corporate globalization, only a few countries are actually involved.

Despite the limited nature of corporate globalization, multinational corporations (MNCs) and FDI are very important features of the global economy. The increasing importance of MNCs has profoundly altered the structure and functioning of the global economy. These giant firms and their global strategies have become major determinants of trade flows and of the location of industries and other economic activities around the world. Most investment is in capital-intensive and technology-intensive sectors. These firms have become central in the expansion of technology flows to both industrialized and industrializing economies. As a consequence, multinational firms have become extremely important in determining the economic, political, and social welfare of many nations. Controlling much of the world's investment capital, technology, and access to global markets, such firms have become major players not only in international economic, but in political affairs as well, and this has triggered a backlash in many countries.

Economic globalization has been driven by political, economic, and technological developments. The compression of time and space by advances in communications and transportation has greatly reduced the costs of international commerce while, largely under American leadership, both the industrialized and industrializing economies have taken a number of initiatives to lower trade and investment barriers. Eight rounds of multilateral trade negotiations under the General Agreement on Tariffs and Trade (GATT), the principal forum for trade liberalization, have significantly decreased trade barriers. Since the mid-1980s, Latin American, Pacific Asian, and other developing countries have initiated important reforms to reduce their trade, financial, and other economic barriers. More and more firms have pursued global economic strategies to take advantage of these developments.

Elimination of capital controls and movement toward a global financial system along with removal of barriers to FDI have also accelerated the movement toward both global and regional integration of services and manufacturing. In both industrialized and industrializing economies, spreading pro-market thinking has strongly influenced economic policy to reduce the role of the state in the economy. The collapse of the Soviet command economy, the failure of the Third World's import-substitution strategy, and the growing belief in the United States and other industrialized economies that the welfare state has become a major obstacle to economic growth and to international competitiveness have encouraged acceptance of unrestricted markets as the solution to the economic ills of modern society. Sweeping reforms have led to deregulation, privatization, and open national economies. In the late 1990s, the debate over the costs and benefits of economic globalization became highly acrimonious.

Meanwhile, the increased openness of national economies, the enlarged number of exporters of manufactured goods, the more rapid increase in trade than in the growth of the global economic product, and the internationalization of services have greatly intensified international economic competition. Growth of the proportion of world output traded on international markets has been accompanied by a significant change in the pattern of world trade. Many less developed countries (LDCs) have shifted from exporting food and commodities to exporting manufactured goods and even services. . . . Manufactured goods have begun to provide a growing proportion of this LDC trade at the same time that the United States and other advanced industrial economies have been shifting from manufactured exports to export of services. This restructuring of the entire global economy is economically costly and politically difficult and is producing many losers as well as winners.

Intensification of global competition in manufacturing, especially in high-tech products, has resulted in increased concern in advanced economies about international competitiveness, particularly about manufacturers from the low-wage industrializing countries. The prestigious World Economic Forum reflected these concerns when it proclaimed in the mid-1990s that competition from industrializing countries was causing deindustrialization of the advanced economies. These concerns have been magnified as more and more Pacific Asian countries have sought to export their way out of economic distress; consequently, more and more groups and leaders in advanced economies worry about such competition and brand it as unfair. Some even express fear that their own living standards could be reduced to those of China. Many believe that intensified competition from the industrializing countries has, at the least, increased job insecurity, unemployment, and income inequality; growing concerns have increased pressures for trade protection and economic regionalism. . . .

Although there is general agreement on the increased importance of the market and of globalization, there is intense controversy over the role of economic factors in the determination of international economic affairs and over the likelihood of cooperation versus conflict. Oversimplifying somewhat, two schools of thought on this issue can be discerned in American and other writing. I shall call one school the "market-oriented" position because of its emphasis on free markets and its commitment to free trade and, most important, to a significant decrease in the role of the state in the economy. The other school of thought is more diverse, but, for lack of a better term, I shall call it the "revisionist" position because of its emphasis on economic conflict, trade protection, and the strong role of the state in the economy.

The market-oriented position is based on the theories and policy prescriptions of economics and asserts that, whereas in the recent past the policies of powerful states and international institutions have played the dominant role in the organization and functioning of the international economy, in the twenty-first century free markets and economic forces will increasingly determine international economic affairs. The demise of communism, the increasing integration of national markets, and the failure of inward-looking economic policies of less developed countries have resulted in a global shift toward such market-oriented policies as free trade and export-led growth and to a drastic reduction of the role of the state in the economy. As the London *Economist* has observed, since the collapse of communism, there has been universal agreement that no serious alternative to free-market capitalism exists as the way to organize economic affairs.

Many also argue that the world is moving toward a politically borderless and highly interdependent global economy that will foster prosperity, international cooperation, and world peace. In this view, with the triumphal return to the free market and the laissez-faire ideals of the nineteenth century, global corporations will lead in organizing international production and maximizing global wealth. A corollary of this position is that the American economic and political system has become the model for the world. Moreover, the United States, as the only true superpower, will lead the rest of the world. Global economic policy will focus on economic multilateralism and on strengthening international rules and institutions created within the Bretton Woods system. American leadership and the reformed Bretton Woods system will facilitate continued cooperation among the dominant economic powers and thereby ensure the global economy's smooth functioning.

Revisionist critics of globalization foresee a world characterized by intense economic conflict at both the domestic and international levels. Believing that an open world economy will inevitably produce more losers than winners, revisionists argue that unleashing market and other economic forces could result in an immense struggle among individual nations, economic classes, and powerful groups. Geo-economic adherents of this position believe (paraphrasing the German strategist Karl von Clausewitz) that international economic competition, especially in manufacturing, is the pursuit of foreign policy by other means. Many assert that this global struggle for market share and technological supremacy will be embodied in competing regional blocs dominated by one or another of the three major economic powers and that the European Union under German leadership, the North American bloc under U.S. leadership, and the Asian Pacific bloc under Japanese leadership will vie for economic and political ascendancy.

This rather pessimistic position declares that the clash between communism and capitalism has been replaced by conflict among rival forms of capitalism and social systems represented in regional economic blocs. In a provocative article in 1991, for example, Samuel P. Huntington argued that, with the end of the Cold War, Japan had become a "security threat" to the United States. Subsequently, in even more provocative writings, Huntington proclaimed that intercivilizational conflicts will dominate the agenda of world politics well into the twenty-first century. Some commentators, reflecting on the tragic events in the former Yugoslavia and in the Soviet Union in the 1990s, argue that an age of intense ethnic and nationalistic conflict has been unleashed on the world. In a world still divided by rival national ambitions in which economic factors in effect determine the fate of nations, many conclude that international economic affairs will become increasingly filled with conflict.

 # Economic Globalization

10.2 In the Shadow of Prosperity

The Economist

The most obvious feature of our global economy is trade. Whether it is shoes made in China or Vietnam, automobiles assembled in Mexico, or grapes grown in Chile, we all use products that were partly or wholly produced in another country, and many of our jobs depend on people in some other part of the world buying the products we make or the services we offer. Increasingly, the economic well-being of citizens in one country rests upon their ability to export products overseas and to import the goods and service they need from abroad. Increasingly, too, we depend on our ability to import or export "capital": the tools necessary to produce the things we want, whether this is the actual tools themselves or the money (financial capital) that can be used to purchase tools.

This economic interdependence offers mutual benefits, but the global marketplace creates losers as well as winners. The challenge is to create international rules and enforcement mechanisms to permit nations and individuals to gain as many of the benefits as possible from global markets without paying too high a price in terms of economic dislocation (as particular jobs move elsewhere), economic instability, or social or environmental damage.

The global marketplace results in disputes not only between but also within nations. Increasingly, economic issues blur the distinction between the domestic and interstate arenas. Foreign policy on trade issues, for example, is typically a matter of intense political disagreement. On one hand, governments are under pressure from domestic interest groups to limit imports, protect home markets, and subsidize exports. Labor unions, for example, frequently object to cheap foreign labor. Uncompetitive industries demand protection from foreign competition. Human-rights activists object to imports made by children or prisoners, and environmentalists oppose imports from countries with low environmental standards. On the other hand, export-oriented industries lobby to eliminate impediments to free trade, and consumers seek access to high-quality or low-cost foreign-made goods.

Those who believe in the desirability of free trade and a global market for goods and capital argue that all nations profit when countries specialize in making only those goods that, given their particular endowment of land, capital, labor, and technology, they can produce most efficiently and inexpensively and when a global market for capital allocates productive resources on an economically rational basis.

Among the losers in the global economy are workers in highly advanced societies like the United States whose jobs are lost to workers overseas who are willing to work for less pay and fewer benefits. Although new jobs are being created in the United States at the same time because of growth in those industries and services in which American workers are more skilled and efficient than those overseas, this is of little consolation to Americans who find themselves unemployed through no fault of their own. The following selection from *The Economist* illuminates some of conflicts over trade in the United States. It describes how many American workers, especially older workers, have lost their jobs to those in other countries or have seen their wages reduced or stagnate, and what measures are available to assist those who have suffered from economic globalization such as retraining.

Nestled among the wooded Blue Ridge mountains in Virginia's far southwest, Galax is a town of bluegrass music, barbecue and hardscrabble living. It is home to an annual fiddlers' convention and, less happily, a huddle of textile and furniture factories. Over the past few years, globalisation has hit hard.

Unable to compete with Mexican and then Chinese competition, the town's old industries have withered, taking thousands of jobs with them. Last year brought the biggest single blow. Three big factories closed their doors within months. More than 1,000 people, around one-sixth of the town's workforce, lost their jobs.

Galax then acquired an "Economic Crisis Strike Force" for displaced workers, sent in by Virginia's governor, Tim Kaine. Housed behind a liquor store in an old strip mall, the Strike Force helps people apply for Trade Adjustment Assistance (TAA), the government support America offers to those deemed to have lost their jobs to global competition. TAA includes up to two years of unemployment benefits while retraining, temporary subsidies to help pay medical insurance and, for those over 50, a short-term top-up to any lower-paying new job. The centre also co-ordinates more basic help, from child care to food banks run by private charities.

Thousands of people have walked through its doors in the past nine months, many several times. Around one-third of those laid off last year are being retrained. Many others have found new jobs. At 6 percent, Galax's unemployment rate is twice Virginia's average, but no higher than it was a year ago.

For some, particularly those in their 50s, the future looks bleak. At 59, Paul Rotan sees little chance of finding another job with health insurance, but he is still six years away from qualifying for Medicare, the government health plan for the old. He is terrified of what will happen in June when the temporary public subsidies for his health insurance end.

But other, mainly younger, workers are already better off. After 19 years in a textile factory, Bobby Edwards has retrained as a radiologist. Brian Deaton has set up a thriving picture-framing business and has started selling gourmet coffee. Few of these people are enthusiastic about globalisation. "No one trusts China around here," is a common refrain. But government help has cushioned the shock. "I'd be lost if they weren't here," says Mr. Rotan, nodding towards the centre's staff.

In the neat world of economics text-books the downside of globalisation looks much like Galax. Low-skilled workers in a rich country, such as America, suffer when trade expands with a poorer country with plenty of much cheaper low-skilled workers, such as China.

If labour markets are efficient in the rich country the displaced workers should find new jobs, but their wages will probably fall. Although the country overall gains handsomely, these people are often worse off. Hence the case for redistributing some of trade's gains and compensating the low-skilled losers. Traditionally, trade-displaced workers have also tended to be older and less educated than typical workers, and to have worked in only one industry. They take longer than average to find another job and, when they find one, are more likely to see their wages fall.

In America, where labour markets are flexible, the impact is felt on wages more than employment. In Europe fewer trade-displaced workers find new jobs quickly, but those who do take less of a pay cut. One study suggests that, during the 1980s–90s, 65 percent of manufacturing workers in America who lost their jobs to freer trade were employed two years later, but most took a pay cut. A quarter suffered pay losses of more than 30 percent. In Europe during the 1990s, in contrast, less than 60 percent of workers in the same situation had found a new job, but only 7 percent saw their pay fall more than 30 percent.

How Much to Spend?

Nonetheless, help for displaced workers has always been modest compared with the gains from trade. In America, where the social safety net is thinner than in other rich countries, those officially deemed hurt by trade are singled out. Their unemployment assistance lasts four times longer than ordinary workers', and they get more retraining. The United States spends around $1 billion a year on helping trade-displaced workers. But the economy overall, by one estimate, gains $1 trillion a year from freer trade.

In Europe overall public safety nets are far more generous, although in many countries they are being scaled back. European governments also spend much more money than America's on training and other "active" help for all workers. In this more comfortable environment, globalisation's losers have never been singled out.

That may be changing. Public scepticism about trade is rising in both rich countries and poor. A host of big economic shifts, such as rising income inequality, are blamed on global integration. The Doha round of trade talks has long been stalled. America's elections last November brought in a clutch of lawmakers deeply opposed to freer trade. To control this backlash, globalisation's champions are keen to appear more sensitive to the losers.

Already, some shifts are evident. One of the first bills introduced in the Democrat-controlled Senate is a big expansion of TAA, covering not merely manufacturing workers but also service workers whose jobs have been "offshored," and offering help not just to individual factories, but to whole industries.

Introduced by President Kennedy in 1962 to shore up support for tariff cuts, TAA has long been used to buy congressional support for trade deals. It was expanded as part of the North American Free Trade Agreement in 1993 and again in 2002 when George Bush asked Congress for special negotiating authority to pursue trade deals. The fate of the current bill is uncertain, but the Democrats have stressed that their support for future trade agreements depends on more help for workers who lose out.

In Europe the political pressure is similar. As Italy's shoemakers protest about Chinese competition and Germany's car-workers worry about "offshoring" to cheaper eastern Europe, the European Union has recently created a €500m ($650m) Globalisation Adjustment Fund to offer job counselling, training and other help when more than 1,000 people in a firm or industry lose their jobs because of "structural changes in world trade patterns."

But cause and effect may not be so obvious. People filter in and out of employment in huge numbers all the time. In America around 20m jobs, or about one in seven, are lost involuntarily every year. Only a small fraction of those, some 2m–3m a year or 2 percent of all jobs, are permanent "displacements," where workers have little or no prospect of returning to their old industry. The displacement rates for Europe are broadly similar. And only a small share of these permanent job losses can be directly attributed to globalisation, rather than, say, to technological change.

One study by Lori Kletzer of the University of California, Santa Cruz found that only 14 percent of displaced manufacturing workers are in industries facing intense international competition. To judge by the number of people receiving TAA, the figure is even lower: fewer than 120,000 workers were deemed eligible for it in 2005. In the much bigger services sector, the share is lower still. For all the hoopla about offshoring, the best estimates suggest that only about 1m American service-sector jobs have actually moved overseas. In short, trade's role in job losses is much smaller than the public angst suggests.

Most economists have long held that technology, rather than globalisation, is the main cause of the rising gap between the pay of the high- and low-skilled. But some argue that the distinctions between trade and technology are increasingly irrelevant. Progress in information and communication technology means that traditional trade models, and their predictions of winners and losers by skill level, are becoming outdated.

In the 21st century competition between firms and industries, such as Galax's furniture factories and their Chinese rivals, is becoming less important than competition between individual tasks within firms in different countries. Whether he is employed in a furniture company or a hospital, the American data-processor will be competing against someone from Bangalore. Rather than affecting entire industries, or whole factories, global competition will affect individual jobs—skilled as much as unskilled.

Such a shift helps explain the popular nervousness about globalisation. Many more workers are worried that their jobs will be at risk. That, in turn, increases the political appeal of assisting trade's losers. But it also makes those losers even harder to identify. And it undermines at least one reason for offering them special help. When trade-displaced workers were older, less educated and hence less easily re-employable than others, helping to retrain them improved the economy's efficiency. But as potential job losses from trade shift up the skill ladder and across industries, those displaced by trade will look much like the rest of the workforce.

10.3 How Trade Barriers Keep Africans Adrift

Juliane von Reppert-Bismarck

Although the global market has witnessed a progressive lowering of tariffs on industrial goods and services to the benefit of those countries engaged in free trade, agriculture has been largely omitted from this process. Wealthy countries and regions such as the United States and the European Union continue to protect their farmers who constitute small but significant political interests from foreign competition and routinely provide subsidies or price supports to assure that their farmers' income remains steady. The big losers in this are poor countries that still depend heavily on agriculture and whose farmers cannot compete with farmers in rich countries. Indeed, rich countries subsidize their farmers to such an extent that their products can be sold less expensively in poor countries than the produce of local farmers.

The inability of farmers in poor countries to export their products may be the single greatest impediment to ending poverty in Africa, Latin America, and Asia. The next selection describes how subsidies to farmers in rich countries perpetuate poverty in Ghana in west Africa.

On the lush savannas of northern Ghana, rice farmer Kpalagim Mome lets half his rice paddies lie fallow as he watches his community break up and leave for Europe. The 42-year-old son of a once-prosperous farmer, Mr. Mome blames his misfortunes on high U.S. and European agricultural subsidies, which have priced his own produce out of Ghana's market.

"We can't sell our rice anymore. It gets worse every year," Mr. Mome says . . . . Years of economic hardship have driven three of his brothers to walk and hitchhike 2,000 miles across the Sahara to reach the Mediterranean and Europe. His sister plans to leave next year.

Mr. Mome's plight is repeated throughout farm communities in Africa and elsewhere in the developing world. Grinding poverty, often exacerbated by Western agricultural subsidies, has compelled thousands of Africans to attempt difficult—and usually illegal—journeys to Europe, frequently by boarding rickety boats for hazardous voyages across open seas to the Spanish Canary Islands or to Italy. Thousands die every year as they cross the Mediterranean at ever-more-dangerous spots to avoid detection by European patrols.

After global trade talks at the World Trade Organization collapsed this summer, the chances that rich countries will cut agricultural subsidies—and that others will reduce their import tariffs—have become even smaller, darkening the outlook for agriculture in the developing countries of Africa, Latin America and Asia. Like Ghana, many run strict open-market regimes advocated by the World Bank and International Monetary Fund, with no payments to farmers and limited import tariffs . . . .

Yet trade ministers face strong lobbies that make it politically difficult to cut aid to their own farmers. High trade barriers in major rice-importing nations, such as Japan and Indonesia, also lower world demand and depress prices.

Defenders of farm payments say U.S. rice farmers, faced with rising exports from Thailand and Vietnam, would go out of business without subsidies. U.S. aid also helps poor consumers buy cheap staples.

Critics say U.S. and European subsidies depress world rice prices and make it harder for Africans such as Mr. Mome to compete. The U.S. paid its 9,000 rice farms $780 million of subsidies in 2006, according to the Department of Agriculture. "Acre per acre . . . rice is the most distorted market in the world," says Daniel Griswold, director of Cato Institute's Center for Trade Policy in Washington.

Ghana is the U.S.'s biggest rice market in Africa. An average ton of U.S. rough rice cost $240 to sow, tend and harvest this year. By the time that rice left a U.S. port in July, U.S. subsidies cut the price to foreign buyers to $205, the USDA says. That discount prices Mr. Mome and farmers in other developing countries out of the market. Using equipment that ensures U.S.-level rice quality, Mr. Mome's costs come in at $230 a ton, he says.

"U.S. farmers have gotten too greedy. Until there is some change in this, you'll have a huge part of the population in poor countries trying to leave and raising hell," says Stephen Gabbert, Managing Principal at international business consultancy Gabbert & Associates. Mr. Gabbert is rallying support from 25 countries—including Ghana, Mexico and India—to fight U.S. rice subsidies at the WTO. Prior legal challenges have succeeded: in 2005, Brazil won a legal battle over cotton subsidies against the U.S. at the WTO. Mr. Gabbert says the rice sector's complaints mirror those of cotton farmers.

Even so, officials in Ghana's cinderblock trade ministry in Accra point to the gulf that separates a powerful trading nation such as Brazil from African minnows. "We don't have the capacity or the legislation to sue the U.S," says Lawrence Sae-Brawusi, director at the Ghana Ministry for Trade and Industry. "We don't do so well when it comes to the arm-twisting."

In the 1970s and early 1980s, rice harvested around Tamale and further north fed Ghana and boosted exports to neighboring nations. Crop-dusters and combine harvesters worked the fields. Mr. Mome's father took bankers for rides in his Mercedes and slaughtered four bulls to celebrate the end of Islamic holy month of Ramadan.

In 1983, Ghana adopted free-market changes, followed by more in 1986. It earned accolades from the World Bank as the most promising West African economy after cutting duties and eliminating the aid that protected its rice sector. While the country's overall economy is expanding, poverty in the rural north has spiraled. Farming has been set back decades: men harvest with small, hand-held sickles; women clean and sort rice by hand. According to the Ghana Rice Interprofessional Body, the country's three-ton-per-hectare (2.47 acres) yield is half what it could be.

As farm income shrinks, communities are fragmenting. Thirteen miles east of Tamale, the 800 villagers of Tugu are saving up to send Yussif Yakubu to Europe. They hope the 32-year-old psychology graduate will find work and send money home.

Men are leaving despite the uncertainty of the journey. Though some find success—Siba Mohammed turned the soccer tricks Mr. Mome taught him into a University of Maryland scholarship—the majority struggle as illegal aliens. Patrols caught and returned Mr. Mome's younger brother, who tried to leave Ghana in the anchor cabin of a freighter. One year later, he made off again, this time hitchhiking across the Sahara. The last time Mr. Mome heard from him, he was cleaning office buildings in Libya and looking for a boat ride to Europe . . . .

"I would like to leave, but I can't," says Mr. Mome. "Who will look after my father? Who would look after all of this?"

 # Monetary and Financial Issues

10.4 The ABCs of Global Money and Finance

Peter J. Dombrowski

Although trade is the most visible element of economic interdependence, it is not the only way in which the world's national economies are tied together and not the only area in which we are seeing a turbulent transformation of institutions.

"Money matters." This terse statement by Peter Dombrowski, a political economist and the author of the next selection, summarizes why global capital flows, currency exchange rates, and the efforts by governments, either individually or in cooperation with each other, to control or stabilize these are of such concern not only to businesspeople and investors but to ordinary people around the world. Money matters because without sufficient money in circulation, trade dries up, goods sit on store shelves, factories and offices close, and unemployment rises. It matters because with too much money in circulation, prices rise and economies experience inflation. It matters because without satisfactory procedures for exchanging national currencies, international trade and investment would disappear.

In today's interdependent world, however, the ability of individual states to control the supply of money in their countries or to determine currency exchange rates—the price of their currency in terms of other currencies, for example, how many Japanese yen or German marks it takes to buy one American dollar—is ever more problematic. Transnational actors—including large corporations, investment funds, and currency speculators—and international organizations like the International Monetary Fund (IMF) make decisions that effectively negate the policy choices or preferences of even powerful states. Even before the end of the Cold War, the sovereignty of states in the realm of finance was increasingly compromised by transnational activity. More and more, investors were coming to think in global, rather than national, terms: barriers that prevented the shifting of money from one country to another were declining, and improvements in information and technology made capital flows (the movement of money from one national market to another to garner larger profits or earn higher rates of return) easier and faster. Events in recent years have accelerated these trends.

The transformation of international finance—the explosive growth of transnational investment, currency speculation, and capital markets—underpins many of the other changes taking place and is for the most part what people mean when they speak of "globalization." International financial markets have little respect for sovereign boundaries and they move vast amounts of capital around the world in the wink of an eye, undermining or reinforcing the stability of governments. Against these private transnational capital flows there is little governments can do. Nations can try to maintain their independence by opting out of global financial and capital markets, but only at great cost. With no loans or investments, economic development and modernization will grind to a halt; and, without funds to pay for imports, the range of goods available to consumers will diminish.

In the next selection, Dombrowski explains the role of money and finance in global politics. He begins by providing a brief review of the historical role of money in global political life, showing why its availability is crucial for modern market economics. He then focuses on the Bretton Woods system, established at U.S. urging after World War II to encourage economic recovery, and he explains the disappearance of that system during the 1970s and following decades. Dombrowski describes a series of critical political issues that revolve around global finance, including economic development, global debt, and competition for foreign investment, and he concludes by speculating about the future of global finance.

This article is an original contribution prepared for this text.

"Everyone can create money, the problem is to get it accepted."

—Hyman Minsky, *economist*

By reputation, international finance is the most difficult area of the global political economy for non-specialists to understand. The sums involved are huge; daily financial flows are counted in the billions of dollars and yearly balances total in the trillions. Financial jargon is complex and often inscrutable— how many of us are familiar with the terms *arbitrage*, *LIBOR*, and *forward markets*? Many important "players"—such as the Bank for International Settlements (BIS), the so-called central bank of central banks—are hardly known to the general public. Even financial scandals such as the Barings Bank collapse in 1995 remain opaque as they unfold across continents in tangled webs of insurance claims, currency violations, and bankruptcy courts. International financiers, on the rare occasions when they speak in public, often revel in the mystery of their business rather than speaking to be understood by ordinary citizens with checking accounts, mortgages, and retirement funds.

Yet global financial markets are too important to be left to experts. Global finance influences the lives of everyone from young families in Des Moines with home mortgages to villagers in China paying for food staples. Cross-border financial flows may help fuel economic growth and spread prosperity, but they can also spread inflation and unemployment. Financial crises may even bring down governments or weaken their ability to make policy choices. To be blunt, money matters. In this essay, we will explore the roles and functions of international monetary and financial systems. Before we can begin to analyze contemporary global monetary and finance systems, however, we need to review their historical development.

Brief History of International Money and Finance

For most of human history there were no international financial or monetary systems. Trade was largely local and based on barter—the direct exchange of goods or services without the use of money. There was thus little need for currencies, much less formal methods for exchanging different types of currencies. When barter was inconvenient because of the distances involved, gold, silver, and other precious metals were accepted as payment. Indeed, long distance trade in luxury goods— spices, furs, and the like—was a primary stimulant to rudimentary monetary and financial systems. By necessity merchants encouraged standardized exchange rates (the prices of one currency expressed in terms of others) and, eventually, simple forms of credit.

Rome created the first explicit monetary system; it lasted largely intact for nearly twelve centuries, from the time of Julius Caesar to the fall of Constantinople to the Crusaders in 1203. Based on gold coins, Roman and Byzantine monetary arrangements supported thriving commercial routes among the far-flung outposts of the Empire as well as with competing states throughout Europe, Northern Africa, and Asia. For centuries, Roman coins bearing busts of emperors and the gold Solidus of

Byzantium provided stable and readily acceptable means of paying for goods and services throughout much of the world. Indeed, years after the final collapse of the Roman political system its coins remained in use.

Between the fall of Constantinople in the thirteenth century and the rise of Great Britain in the eighteenth century, currencies, exchange rates, and global finance were largely private matters. Although states coined money, so did goldsmiths, great merchant houses, and, eventually, private firms resembling modern banks. For everyday use most coins were silver or even copper although gold was the metal of choice for large transactions. The quality of a coin and thus its acceptability for international transactions depended in large part upon the reputation of the issuer—the coins of leading states became de facto international currencies. Thus Florentine florins, Venetian ducats, and Dutch guilders served successively as internationally accepted methods of payment.

As the state emerged as the predominant political form in the seventeenth and eighteenth centuries, governments gradually assumed the role of providing and regulating money for both domestic and international transactions. Gradually they enacted laws denying private enterprises the right to issue or use private monies. Eventually, paper notes issued by banks and governments also entered into circulation, although once again, their usefulness for international transactions depended on the power and solvency of the issuer. In the international arena, governments imposed "mercantilist" trade and monetary policies—policies designed to accumulate a stockpile of gold and silver in their national treasuries, which could then be used to pay for armies or navies in the event of war. Mercantilism implied that states would attempt to stimulate national exports and discourage imports: by selling products abroad and receiving gold and silver in return, the nation would gradually accumulate the desired stockpile of bullion.

The first modern international monetary "system" was the classical gold standard of the eighteenth century. Under this system, money was gold and gold was money. This meant that the world's money supply—consisting of national currencies—was tied to supplies of gold available in treasuries or known mining regions. International payments were reconciled by flows of gold from deficit countries that imported more goods than they exported to surplus countries that exported more goods than they imported. By reducing the money available for making purchases, gold outflows (caused by a nation importing more goods than it exported) suppressed a nation's demand for imported goods, while gold inflows (caused by a nation importing less than it exported) stimulated demand, thus helping to balance a nation's international accounts.

By myth, the gold standard was an automatic, self-regulating, self-contained, system. In practice, however, the gold standard was not automatic, self-regulating, or self-contained. It depended on the economic strength, financial wisdom, and political will of Great Britain, operating in concert with other major powers of the day. The great powers often cooperated to ensure international liquidity—supplies of gold and national currencies sufficient to facilitate international trade—in times of crisis. Britain also exercised leadership by forcing other countries to bring their international payments (imports, exports, and financial flows) into balance and, when necessary, by adjusting its own economic growth in the interest of international economic stability. Britain was willing to bear the burdens of slowing its economy, cooperating with its political rivals, and even expending its own resources to calm international financial crises because as the world's largest national economy it benefited disproportionately from a stable monetary system. For much of the nineteenth century, British goods and investments were so competitive in overseas markets that only widespread economic disruptions could undermine Great Britain's own wealth and prosperity.

During the gold standard era, international finance was mainly the province of a few large, relatively wealthy European countries, because only they had sufficient capital to seek profits outside their own domestic economies. Most other countries were so intent on their own economic modernization that they had little capital available for foreign investment. Britain was the leading source of foreign investment. British banks and private investors funded railways, port facilities, and other infrastructure projects across the globe. France and Germany also channeled capital overseas, albeit with less global reach and a more conscious connection to foreign policy objectives. France concentrated its investments in its colonies and Russia, while Germany devoted its energies to central and eastern Europe. On the whole, investment flows were private matters and few international rules or norms governed capital movements.

The heyday of the gold standard was short-lived, lasting roughly from 1870 to 1914. As the United States and Germany began to challenge Britain for economic supremacy, Britain's ability to organize international monetary and financial relations eroded. Ultimately, the political and economic disruptions of World War I (1914–1918) severely weakened Britain and led to numerous changes in the international monetary and financial systems. During the long and debilitating war, Britain's industrial economy was surpassed by the United States and, to finance the cost of the war, it had become, for the first time in generations, an international borrower. Moreover, wartime disruptions of the global trade and investment exacerbated Great Britain's difficulties.

After World War I Britain tried to resume its role as the arbiter of international finance, but found that it was unable to fulfill its former responsibilities. It no longer had the economic strength to enforce monetary discipline at home or abroad. To make matters worse, British officials and their private banker counterparts in the City of London also made the mistake of pegging the British pound at an artificially high price relative to their own holdings of gold and demand for the pound internationally. This error helped further erode Britain's international position by weakening demand for British exports and undermining international confidence in Britain's leadership.

Ultimately, between the First and Second World Wars the classical gold standard gave way to a "gold-exchange" standard. In the "gold-exchange" standard although gold remained at the heart of the monetary system, it was no longer in general circulation. Paper money issued by national governments supplemented gold, and holdings of currencies issued by major powers augmented existing gold reserves in the vaults of national central banks.

In retrospect the center of gravity in the global economy shifted across the Atlantic from the City of London to New York City in the wake of World War I.

The Great War had been a financial windfall for American banks and a boon to U.S. industry; American financial institutions extended credits to the many combatant nations while American factories produced the materials of war. As a consequence, the United States entered peacetime as an international creditor with a booming economy. The United States, however, was not ready to assume leadership of global monetary and financial affairs. American financiers still thought in largely parochial terms. For much of the interwar period (roughly 1918–1939), American policy makers and private bankers sought to assure that debts the allied governments had incurred to finance the war were repaid, regardless of the pressures this placed on the economic health of the debtors, on the political relationships among the major powers, or on the long-term stability of the financial system. American demands that the British and French repay war debts in full encouraged both countries to force severe reparations (punitive fines imposed to offset some of the costs of the war) on the defeated Germans. This slowed both Germany's own economic recovery and the intra-European trade that was essential to the entire global economy. The unwillingness of the United States to look beyond its own short-term interest and to assume economic leadership helped doom the global economy during the Great Depression and contributed to the political instabilities that led to World War II.

Even as they struggled to defeat the Axis powers in World War II, the Allied governments began planning for the postwar years. Economic matters dominated planning meetings because many influential officials blamed the rise of fascism and the West's political weakness on the failures of international economic management after World War I. The inability to resolve the international reparations issues in a timely fashion, the protectionist measures that followed the American Smoot-Hawley Tariff of 1932, and the monetary instabilities that plagued the global economy in the 1930s had led to depression, domestic turmoil, virulent nationalism, and conflictual economic relations among the Great Powers. Territorial and military grievances had been exacerbated by competitive economic pressures. Recognizing this, Allied wartime conferences at Bretton Woods, New Hampshire, and Havana, Cuba, sought to devise a new system of economic management for the postwar years.

The Bretton Woods System

At the Bretton Woods conference in 1944, postwar planners led by Harry Dexter White of the American Department of the Treasury and John Maynard Keynes of the British Treasury Department focused on monetary and financial arrangements. Bretton Woods participants designed a fixed exchange rate regime in which all currencies were convertible with each other and with gold at a pre-established ratio. Exchange rates (known as par value) could only vary plus or minus one percentage point without the formal permission of other members of the monetary system. The par value of all currencies was set against the American dollar, which was valued at one thirty-fifth of an ounce of gold. Bretton Woods negotiators also established two new international organizations: the International Monetary Fund (IMF) and the

International Bank for Reconstruction and Development (the IBRD, better known as the World Bank). For our purposes, the IMF is of special interest because it was to serve as the keeper of the monetary rules and as a source of temporary financing for members experiencing international balance of payments deficits. When deficits occurred—meaning a country was importing more goods and capital than it was exporting—measures needed to be taken to ensure that the country met its international obligations. The IMF's role was to provide credits until the deficit country could adjust its international spending patterns.

When decisions were made regarding the "rules," Bretton Woods members were to cast weighted votes proportional to their contribution of capital to each organization; thus the United States held a dominant position in both the IMF and the World Bank because it contributed, and still contributes, the largest sums to both organizations. In contrast to its parochialism and isolationism after World War I, the United States assumed a leadership position in the post–Second World War global economy that was commensurate with the size of its economy and its political ambition to keep the world "safe for democracy."

The preferences of the Bretton Woods planners for global openness and governmental noninterference in trade did not extend to financial flows. The Bretton Woods agreements did not assume that states would let their money move freely across international borders. By letting investors move money out of one national economy and into another, unfettered financial flows would have had the effect of undercutting government control over how much money was in circulation within a nation's borders at any particular time. Governments were allowed to implement capital controls—rules, regulations, and taxes designed to limit inflows and outflows of investment. Most countries, including the United States, took advantage of this opportunity. Not until the 1970s did most of the leading economies remove most restrictions on inflows and outflows of investment capital from international financial markets.

The postwar monetary system did not function as envisioned at the Bretton Woods conference. In the immediate postwar years the only major currency that was fully convertible (that is, could be redeemed for gold) was the American dollar. Other prominent countries simply had insufficient gold reserves to maintain full convertibility (in part because, during World War II as during World War I, foreign governments had sold off their gold reserves to help pay for wartime imports). Within a few years, a de facto "dollar system" emerged with American dollars serving as the world's reserve currency—the primary financial asset held by governments (usually central banks) to support their own national currencies. That is, instead of holding gold in their vaults to pay off foreign investors and governments that wanted to redeem their holdings of the domestic currency, central banks held American dollars. The United States government accepted this role for the dollar, at least in part, because it gave the United States enormous power. In essence, it allowed the United States to avoid adjustment in response to changes in the global economy and to enjoy the privilege of seignorage—the difference between the cost of issuing a currency (for example, the cost of printing a dollar bill) and its exchange value (what the dollar bill buys), or more simply, the "profit" that accrues to the state that issues a currency.

The Bretton Woods system began to unravel in the late 1960s. Inflation in the United States had begun to weaken international confidence in the dollar. More importantly, most observers understood that the United States could not honor its pledge of convertibility—at $35 per ounce, too many dollars were now circulating outside the United States to permit everyone with dollars to exchange them for gold. It became increasingly clear that the United States would either have to disavow convertibility or revalue the dollar relative to the price of gold. In August 1971, President Richard M. Nixon acknowledged the inevitable. Without consulting American allies or members of his own government, the President announced that American dollars were no longer convertible into gold. Overnight the Bretton Woods system as embodied in the "dollar-system" was destroyed.

The Managed Float System

The 1970s and early 1980s saw efforts to construct an alternative to the Bretton Woods monetary system. For brief periods, national currencies experienced a pure "float." In a floating system exchange rates are determined by market forces—the supply and demand for a nation's currency relative to other national currencies. Governments quickly realized that this left them vulnerable to the whims of global financial markets in an era of increasing economic stress—high inflation, high unemployment, and soaring prices for natural resources including petroleum. The United States, Great Britain, Germany, Japan, France, and Italy (which, with the later inclusion of Canada, came to be known as the Group of Seven [G-7] nations) subsequently convened a series of summit meetings to rethink international monetary relations. Although these international meetings never managed a Bretton Woods style top-to-bottom restructuring of global monetary relations, a measure of stability did eventually emerge. The G-7 governments intervened periodically in foreign exchange markets to influence rates for domestic political purposes and occasionally to influence economic flows among the leading economies. This system of intervention in global markets by governments, individually or in cooperation with one another, came to be known as the "managed float" regime.

By the late 1980s the international monetary system had stabilized. Despite the challenges of the previous decades, the dollar had retained its position as the global currency of choice. While central bankers continue to be concerned because they cannot intervene effectively in international financial markets to offset the market forces increasing or decreasing the price of their currency, in recent years international monetary arrangements have remained under a managed float regime. What prevents states from exerting more control over their currencies is that the tremendous volume of private financial flows can now overwhelm the financial resources of central banks. Thus international efforts to adjust the exchange rate—for example, the dollar-yen rate—have proven notably unsuccessful for any length of time. Even if national governments are incapable of controlling specific exchange rates, though, under the managed float regime they are able to ensure some consistency within the entire system. Within this broadly stable set of arrangements regarding international money, however, a number of challenges remain unmet.

Economic Development

International financial markets remain plagued by the age old question of how to channel capital to those areas of the globe that most need investment—that is, poor underdeveloped countries and regions. Although market logic suggests that capital should flow from advanced industrial societies to the less-developed regions in a relentless search for profits—the higher risks associated with investing in the Third World earn higher rewards for hardy investors—there is little evidence that this is taking place. Indeed, in recent years financial flows among the advanced industrial societies have dwarfed flows from the economically more-developed "North" to the economically less-developed "South."

In the long run, this may not be healthy for the global economy or for international security. While much of the world's natural resources and population growth are located in precisely those areas that suffer from investment shortfalls, even local capital flees developing countries for safer investments in the developed world. Not only does this contribute to the continued impoverishment of large segments of the world's population, it means that containing demographic pressures—emigration, refugee flows, famines, and environmental degradation, for example—will be more difficult. Today, we may be witnessing not only continued economic dysfunction but the long-term breakdown of political authority in regions that have lacked sufficient investment capital for generations.

Global Debt Crisis

The long-standing shortfall of investment capital for the less developed world was exacerbated by the global debt crisis. In the 1970s, the rise of global financial markets, increased prices for imported oil, and historically high interest rates contributed to an unprecedented accumulation of commercial debt in many Third World countries. By the early 1980s, the aggregate accumulation of debt and the amounts owed by individual developing countries threatened to undermine the entire international financial regime. Many debtors found themselves unable or, in some cases, unwilling to fulfill obligations to repay the interest and principal due on external loans. For example, in August 1982, Mexico announced that it could not meet its obligations. Over the next several months, American officials, in concert with representatives of the World Bank and the IMF, officials from many creditor countries, and hundreds of commercial bankers, struggled to "rescue" Mexico by rescheduling existing loans (for example, by lowering interest rates) and extending new loans to repay past debts. Within a few years dozens of other highly indebted countries were also forced to reschedule their loans to avoid defaulting. Officials in many creditor countries such as the United States, Japan, and Germany feared that default by a major debtor might cause one or more international commercial banks (banks like Citicorp or Chase-Manhattan, which had loaned large sums to foreign governments) to fail, bringing about a collapse of the global financial system and destabilizing the global economy.

The major development of the mid-1990s, at least until the Asian financial crisis that began in 1997, was the easing of the global debt crisis. Debt rescheduling and even some debt forgiveness have helped ease pressure on the international financial system. Banks are no longer as vulnerable to foreign defaults; global financial markets are less susceptible to system failure, and the individual borrowing countries now are repaying smaller amounts spread over longer periods of time.

Although private financial flows to the developing world have turned positive after the lean post-debt crisis years, foreign direct and portfolio investment remain inadequate to jump-start economic growth. Foreign aid regimes have also faltered as donors have been unwilling to meet even modest targets such as donating one percent of their GNP each year. The IMF and the World Bank have expanded their programs in recent years but until recently they seem to have focused on their own "profitability" over the needs of impoverished nations. And, when investment has gone to the Third World, it has been the most "successful" developing countries such as China and Mexico that have benefited rather than the most needy. Cooperative efforts by the Third World, including proposals for a "New International Economic Order" in the early 1970s and the debtors' cartels proposed in the 1980s, have earned publicity but saw few significant results. In the market-oriented international climate of recent decades, there appears little sympathy or political willpower for more interventionist state policies to remedy investment shortfalls.

Private Investment

With regard to private financial flows, there has been a shift from foreign loans to foreign direct investment (building factories, opening subsidiaries, or buying up foreign companies) and portfolio investment (buying shares of stock in foreign companies). Although this trend is most pronounced among the advanced industrial societies, it has also affected capital flows to the less-developed world. Many international financial experts and some foreign officials have welcomed the move from loans to investment as the primary means for bringing capital, technology, and managerial expertise to less-developed areas. However, the long-term implications of portfolio and direct investment for the autonomy of the recipient countries and the overall health of the global economy are unclear. Some critics suggest that many states have lost the ability to control or even regulate transnational enterprises such as banks and industrial corporations. Other experts believe that global financial markets can overwhelm economic development strategies, macroeconomic policies, and, some even argue, the social welfare programs pursued by nation-states. By this logic, countries seeking foreign capital cannot afford to ignore the preferences of private foreign investors. Because investors prefer policies that maximize the rate of return on their investments and protect profits against potential instability, governments have to pursue stable macroeconomic policies (promoting low inflation and perhaps high unemployment), balanced budgets, and openness to the global economy (for example, low tariffs and easy credit for importers). Furthermore, to obtain the investment necessary for economic development, countries often give preferential treatment to transnational corporations that invest heavily. Governments thus attempt to keep foreign investors satisfied so that they do not pull out their money or move operations to other more accommodating countries.

Reduced policy autonomy is not simply a problem for the less-developed world. Increased capital mobility—the ability of financial flows to cross national borders—has reduced the political choices available even to wealthy and powerful nations like the United States. First, many governments borrow in private financial markets to finance budget deficits; credit ratings and interest rates determined in large part by private actors may adversely affect the ability of governments to attain access to capital at desirable rates. To finance deficits, then, governments may promote policies (macroeconomic, budgetary, and otherwise) that meet the approval of market players by instilling confidence and ensuring profit margins. Second, global financial markets are now open for business twenty-four hours a day and financial flows total in the many billions of dollars. Financial firms, individuals, and even some countries speculate on very small changes in interest rates (arbitrage) among national financial markets. National regulators cannot track, much less control, the volume of financial flows within the global economy both because of the sheer size of the market and because technology has advanced to the point where regulators cannot keep pace.

One of the principal motivations behind financial regulation is the prevention of "manias, panics, and shocks," in short, financial crises. Although financial regulation and international policy coordination have managed to avert major crises in some situations (witness the American Stock Market Crisis of 1987, the 1995 collapse of the Mexican peso, and the 1997 flight of capital from Southeast Asia and Korea) there are good reasons to suspect that increased financial integration may have already weakened the ability of the financial system to weather another major stock market sell-off or the collapse of a debtor country. The United States and the other G-7 nations have used the Bank for International Settlements and other international forums to facilitate greater cooperation to prevent and contain future crises. These initiatives have included greater national and international supervision of international financial institutions as well as procedures for increased cooperation during crisis management efforts by the leading financial powers. It remains to be seen—presumably after the crisis caused by the 2008 collapse of America's subprime mortgage market—whether these efforts have been successful.

A New Bretton Woods?

Since the late-1960s, there have been many calls to convene a new "Bretton Woods" conference to revise the internationally agreed upon "rules" of the international monetary system. Some participants in early G-7 meetings may have thought they were providing long-term solutions to the weaknesses of the Bretton Woods arrangements. Yet, these reform efforts did not succeed in fixing Bretton Woods or developing a superior alternative. The current system of a "managed float" has three major weaknesses. First, individual governments are unable to establish any sustained influence over exchange rates. The size and volatility of financial flows preclude effective intervention by a single government and perhaps even concerted action by the largest economies. Second, efforts to promote concerted action by the major economic powers often fail because these powers disagree on diagnoses about what is wrong with existing monetary arrangements and, even more often, on how to cure monetary ills. Finally, monetary arrangements often falter when domestic political pressures force leaders to renege on international agreements. The inescapable logic of collective action provides a powerful incentive for individual nations not to implement jointly agreed-upon monetary policies.

The political will to convene a new Bretton Woods is lacking. In the absence of a crisis comparable to the Great Depression or another major war, members of the international community will not agree to participate in the negotiations and trade-offs that would be necessary to re-engineer existing global monetary arrangements. One problem is the absence of an effective leader favoring systemic change. The United States has little motivation to lead efforts to reconstitute a fixed exchange rate system or an alternative scheme because it remains a principal beneficiary of the current system. European Union members such as Germany remain committed to completing regional monetary integration before they tackle global problems. Japan has not demonstrated the political will to initiate reform either at home or internationally.

Nor is it likely that a single global currency will emerge in the foreseeable future. Although the dollar's role as the global reserve currency has weakened, no other currency has achieved comparable status. The Japanese yen and the Swiss franc are powerful regional currencies but they do not have the dollar's global appeal. The only other potential candidate for replacing the American dollar as the world's leading currency is the European Union's "euro."

Conclusion

The relationship between global politics and global money is close. Dominant nation-states, with preponderant military, political, and ideological power, usually set the rules of the game for global issues, including monetary and financial matters. Successive international leaders—the Italian city-states, the Dutch, the British, and, finally, the Americans—have chosen to create liberal arrangements by which trade and finance are left to market allocation. The congruence between powerful nations, global monetary stability, and financial openness has led some observers to question the viability of contemporary international monetary and financial arrangements. They conclude that the declining economic preponderance of the United States weakens prospects for international cooperation and may eventually result in more chaotic and crisis-prone monetary and financial systems. Yet, given the low probability of major institutional changes or the emergence of a universal currency, what are the prospects for the existing global monetary and financial systems? For the most part, individual states will continue trying to coordinate their international macroeconomic policies. When domestic interests are threatened by international developments, however, most countries will continue to rely on their own policy instruments rather than international cooperation. As yet, few citizens

are willing to accept decisions made in Brussels, Basel, Bonn, or Tokyo that contribute to domestic inflation or unemployment. As voters, they will continue to
hold their elected officials accountable.

While nation-states struggle with financial and monetary globalization, technological innovation will continue apace, thereby reducing state capacity to regulate
financial markets and provide for a stable international monetary environment. In
only a few years electronic "virtual" money—complete with internationally acceptable debit cards linked in real time—may become available. The public policy
implications of such developments are only now being explored by policy makers.

China, India, and a New International Economic Order

10.5 The New New World Order

Daniel W. Drezner

One of the most important developments in global politics in recent decades has
been the emergence of China and India as major powers, economically as well as
politically and mililtarily. Recent years have witnessed a dramatic surge in the
economies of China and India, which prior to industrialization in Europe had been
the world's largest economies. India, until 1980, was, in the words of one observer,
"shackled" by "a mixed economy that combined the worst features of capitalism
and socialism."[1] Since 1991, however, the Indian state has gradually reduced its
role in the country's economy and encouraged greater entrepreneurship. As a
result, India's economy grew at the rate of 7.5 percent a year between 2002 and
2006, in the process reducing population growth, enlarging its middle class, raising
per capita income from $1,178 to $3,051, and becoming the world's fourth largest
economy.[2]

However, the rapid economic development of China and its transition from a
centrally controlled Marxist economy to a market-based economy is the single
most important factor in the shifting economic balance between developed and
developing countries. China alone will soon account for 10 percent of global trade,
and China and India are increasingly competing with the developed countries in a
range of high-technology as well as labor-intensive products and services. Within a
few decades, China will probably surpass the United States as the single largest

[1] Gurcharan Das, "The India Model," *Foreign Affairs*, **85:** 4 (July/August 2006), 4.
[2] Ibid., 2.

economy in the world. Its dramatic economic growth and demand for raw materials and energy have created resource scarcities and have rapidly pushed prices higher for commodities like oil. The United States and Europe import more and more from China and have ballooning trade deficits with that country. American and European corporations outsource more and more production and jobs to China and India and are investing enormous amount of capital in those countries.

While creating pockets of unemployment in the developed world as jobs are outsourced and while producing new sources of global pollution, rapid economic growth in China will also benefit the developed countries. First, the large numbers of newly enriched citizens in China and India increase the demand for products from the United States and Europe; second, the lower cost of production in China and India keeps inflation down globally. The next selection discusses these trends and their implications, the problems they pose for the United States, and the efforts of the Bush administration to adjust to the new realities of global economic and political power represented by China and India.

Rising and Falling

Throughout the twentieth century, the list of the world's great powers was predictably short: the United States, the Soviet Union, Japan, and northwestern Europe. The twenty-first century will be different. China and India are emerging as economic and political heavyweights: China holds over a trillion dollars in hard currency reserves, India's high-tech sector is growing by leaps and bounds, and both countries, already recognized nuclear powers, are developing blue-water navies. The National Intelligence Council, a U.S. government think tank, projects that by 2025, China and India will have the world's second- and fourth-largest economies, respectively. Such growth is opening the way for a multipolar era in world politics.

This tectonic shift will pose a challenge to the U.S.-dominated global institutions that have been in place since the 1940s. At the behest of Washington, these multilateral regimes have promoted trade liberalization, open capital markets, and nuclear nonproliferation, ensuring relative peace and prosperity for six decades—and untold benefits for the United States. But unless rising powers such as China and India are incorporated into this framework, the future of these international regimes will be uncomfortably uncertain.

Given its performance over the last six years, one would not expect the Bush administration to handle this challenge terribly well. After all, its unilateralist impulses, on vivid display in the Iraq war, have become a lightning rod for criticism of U.S. foreign policy. But the Iraq controversy has overshadowed a more pragmatic and multilateral component of the Bush administration's grand strategy: Washington's attempt to reconfigure U.S. foreign policy and international institutions in order to account for shifts in the global distribution of power. The Bush adminis-

Drezner, Daniel, "The New New World Order," *Foreign Affairs,* March/April 2007, pp. 34–46. Reprinted by permission of *Foreign Affairs.* © 2007 by the Council on Foreign Relations, Inc. <www.ForeignAffairs.org>.

tration has been reallocating the resources of the executive branch to focus on emerging powers. In an attempt to ensure that these countries buy into the core tenets of the U.S.-created world order, Washington has tried to bolster their profiles in forums ranging from the International Monetary Fund (IMF) to the World Health Organization, on issues as diverse as nuclear proliferation, monetary relations, and the environment. Because these efforts have focused more on so-called low politics than on the global war on terrorism, they have flown under the radar of many observers. But in fact, George W. Bush has revived George H. W. Bush's call for a "new world order"—by creating, in effect, a new new world order.

This unheralded effort is well intentioned and well advised. It is, however, running into two major roadblocks. The first is that empowering countries on the rise means disempowering countries on the wane. Accordingly, some members of the European Union have been less than enthusiastic about aspects of the United States' strategy . . . . The second problem, which is of the Bush administration's own making, stems from Washington's reputation for unilateralism. Because the U.S. government is viewed as having undercut many global governance structures in recent years, any effort by this administration to rewrite the rules of the global game is naturally seen as yet another attempt by Washington to escape the constraints of international law . . . .

Plus Ça Change

When the United Nations, the IMF, the World Bank, the General Agreement on Tariffs and Trade (GATT), and NATO were created in the late 1940s, the United States was the undisputed hegemon of the Western world. These organizations reflected its dominance and its preferences and were designed to boost the power of the United States and its European allies . . . . It was agreed that the IMF's executive director would always be a European. And Europe was de facto granted a voice equal to that of the United States in the GATT.

Today, the distribution of power in the world is very different. According to Goldman Sachs and Deutsche Bank, by 2010, the annual growth in combined national income from Brazil, Russia, India, and China—the so-called BRIC countries—will be greater than that from the United States, Japan, Germany, the United Kingdom, and Italy combined; by 2025, it will be twice that of the G-7 (the group of highly industrialized countries).

These trends were already evident in the 1990s—and the end of the Cold War presented an opportunity to adapt international institutions to rising powers. At the time, however, Washington chose to reinforce preexisting arrangements. The GATT became the World Trade Organization. NATO expanded its membership to eastern European states and its sphere of influence to the Balkans. The macroeconomic policies known as the Washington consensus became gospel in major international financial institutions. There were few institutional changes to accommodate rising powers, besides the creation of the Asia-Pacific Economic Cooperation (APEC) forum in 1989 and China's hard-won admission to the WTO in 2001. . . .

The Clinton administration had good reasons for not doing more. Remaking international institutions is a thankless task that requires holders of power to voluntarily cede some of their influence. There was no urgent need to undertake it in the 1990s. China and India were rising, but their great-power status still seemed a long ways off . . . .

Many of the rising powers believed that the existing global governance structures stacked the deck against them. The IMF's perceived highhandedness during the Asian financial crisis of the 1990s bred resentment across the Pacific Rim. New Delhi was frustrated by Washington's objections to its 1998 nuclear tests and grew tired of being viewed by Washington strictly through the prism of South Asian security. China resented the drawn-out negotiations to enter the WTO. And NATO's bombing of Kosovo was triply problematic for Beijing: the accidental hit on the Chinese embassy in Belgrade aroused nationalist passions, Washington's willingness to cross international borders to protect human rights clashed with Beijing's notion of state sovereignty, and the United States' decision to bypass the United Nations and act through NATO highlighted the limits of China's effective influence over world politics. Heading into the new millennium, the fastest-growing economies in the world were nursing grudges toward the United States . . . .

The New Deal

. . . But in part, the effort to institutionalize a new great-power concert has been a long-standing component of the Bush administration's foreign policy. And Washington-style multilateralism is above all a means to further U.S. goals. Accordingly, the Bush administration defers to institutions it sees as being effective (say, the WTO) and has consistently sought the enforcement of multilateral norms and decisions it deems important (be they IMF lending agreements or UN Security Council resolutions). But it scorns multilateral institutions that fail to live up to their own stated standards (such as other UN bodies). The 2006 National Security Strategy reiterates Washington's dual position by arguing that great-power consensus "must be supported by appropriate institutions, regional and global, to make cooperation more permanent, effective, and wide-reaching. Where existing institutions can be reformed to meet new challenges, we, along with our partners, must reform them. Where appropriate institutions do not exist, we, along with our partners, must create them."

Global institutions cease to be appropriate when the allocation of decision-making authority within them no longer corresponds to the distribution of power—and that is precisely the situation today. The UN Security Council is one obvious example; the G-7 is an even more egregious one. The G-7 states took it upon themselves to manage global macroeconomic imbalances in the 1970s. They were moderately successful at the job during the 1980s, when they accounted for half of the world's economic activity. Today, however, even when they meet with Russia (as the G-8), they cannot be effective without including in their deliberations the economic heavyweight that is China.

Incorporating emerging powers while placating status quo states is no simple feat. But the task should appear less daunting when it is understood that success will benefit ascendant states as much as it will the United States. It will bring ascendant states recognition and legitimacy to match their new power. Granted, they will have to accept a multilateral order built on U.S. principles. But they—especially China and India—have grown phenomenally by doing just that. Now that they are concerned with sustaining their current high rates of economic growth, emerging powers share some interests with the United States on issues such as the security of energy supplies and the prevention of global pandemics.

One-on-One

The Bush team has already made significant efforts to keep up with the changing world. A few years ago, it started to reallocate resources within the U.S. government. More recently, it has spearheaded multilateral efforts to integrate China and India into important international regimes.

The Defense Department was the first U.S. bureaucracy to make major changes to reflect the new new world order. It started by moving around U.S. troops stationed abroad. In 2004, more than 250,000 troops were based in 45 countries, half of them in Germany and South Korea, the battlegrounds of the Cold War. To improve troop mobility in the face of ever-changing threats, President Bush announced in August 2004 that the number of U.S. armed forces stationed overseas would be reduced and that 35 percent of U.S. bases abroad would be closed by 2014. Many of these troops will be based in the United States, but others will be redeployed in countries on the periphery of the new zone of threat: in eastern Europe, in Central Asia, and along the Pacific Rim.

The State Department is also adjusting. In a January 2006 address at Georgetown University's School of Foreign Service, Secretary of State Rice said, "In the twenty-first century, emerging nations like India and China and Brazil and Egypt and Indonesia and South Africa are increasingly shaping the course of history . . . . Our current global posture does not really reflect that fact. For instance, we have nearly the same number of State Department personnel in Germany, a country of 82 million people, that we have in India, a country of one billion people. It is clear today that America must begin to reposition our diplomatic forces around the world . . . to new critical posts for the twenty-first century." Rice announced that a hundred State Department employees would be moved from Europe to countries such as India and China by 2007.

Washington has also strengthened its bilateral relationships with China and India. After an awkward beginning—the Bush team's first foreign policy crisis came when a U.S. spy plane collided with a Chinese jet fighter—the Bush administration reoriented its approach to Beijing. "It is time to take our policy beyond opening doors to China's membership into the international system," then Deputy Secretary of State Robert Zoellick announced in September 2005. "We need to urge China to become a responsible stakeholder in that system" so that it will "work with us to sustain the international system that has enabled its success." The "responsible stakeholder" language has since become part of all official U.S. pronouncements on China, and the theory behind it has guided several initiatives. Last fall, Washington launched the U.S.-China Strategic Economic Dialogue. In December, Treasury Secretary Paulson led six cabinet-level U.S. officials and the chair of the Federal Reserve in two days of discussions with their Chinese counterparts on issues ranging from energy cooperation to financial services to exchange rates. On matters as diverse as dealing with North Korea and Darfur, reigniting the Doha Development Agenda, and consulting with the International Energy Agency, Washington has tried recently to bring China into the concert of great powers.

The United States has reached out to India as well. For most of the 1990s, the United States was primarily concerned with managing India's dispute with Pakistan over Kashmir and defusing potential nuclear crises. Even though Pakistan is a significant U.S. ally in the war on terrorism, the U.S.-Indian relationship has warmed considerably over the past five years. In November 2006, the U.S. Department of Commerce arranged its largest-ever economic development mission to India, expanding the commercial dialogue between the two countries. Last year, they also concluded a bilateral agreement to cooperate on civilian nuclear energy—a de facto recognition by the United States that India is a nuclear power. The agreement reinforces India's commitment to nonproliferation norms in its civilian nuclear program, but it keeps India's military program outside the orbit of inspections by the International Atomic Energy Agency. Critics of the deal have warned that it threatens the NPT. But the Bush administration argues that India is emerging as a great power, the nuclear genie cannot be put back in the bottle, and because India is a democracy, the genie will do no harm. According to the 2006 National Security Strategy, "India now is poised to shoulder global obligations in cooperation with the United States in a way befitting a major power."

All-Inclusive

More ambitiously, the Bush administration has tried to reshape international organizations to make them more accommodating to rising powers. In some instances, the changes have occurred almost as a matter of course. The formation of the G-20 bloc of developing countries, for example, compelled the United States to invite Brazil, India, and South Africa into the negotiating "green room" at the September 2003 WTO ministerial meeting of the Doha Round of trade talks, in Cancún. Since then, U.S. trade negotiators have been clamoring for greater participation from China in the hope that Beijing will moderate the views of more militant developing countries.

Similarly, the United States has encouraged China to participate periodically in the G-7 meetings of finance ministers and central-bank governors. Washington's aim is to recognize China's growing importance in world politics and economics and in return get Beijing to concede that its exchange-rate policies and its repression of domestic consumption contribute to global economic imbalances . . . .

Also with a view to giving greater influence to China (as well as Mexico, South Korea, and Turkey), the Bush administration has pushed hard to change the voting quotas within the IMF. China's formal quota grossly underrepresents the country's actual economic size . . . .

Meanwhile, the Bush administration has moved toward greater cooperation with emerging powers on other issues as well, especially energy, the environment, and nuclear proliferation. Washington has engaged China through APEC's Energy Working Group. It has encouraged China and India, which are anxious to secure regular access to energy, to work with the International Energy Agency in order to create strategic petroleum reserves. It has launched, along with Australia, China, India, Japan, and South Korea, the Asia-Pacific Partnership on Clean Development and Climate to facilitate energy efficiency and environmentally sustainable growth. (Because its members account for more than half of the global economy, the partnership has the potential to affect global warming more than does the Kyoto Protocol.) The United States has also relied on China and India to help halt nuclear proliferation. It is depending on Beijing to bring Pyongyang back into the six-party talks and to implement financial sanctions limiting North Korea's access to hard currency. In October 2006, following North Korea's nuclear test, for the first time China endorsed a UN Security Council resolution mandating sanctions against the regime. Similarly, Washington has relied on India's support for the United States' objections to Iran's nuclear program, as well as India's presence on the governing board of the International Atomic Energy Agency, in presenting its case against Tehran to the UN Security Council.

In the Way

It is too soon to tell whether Washington's moves to bring Beijing and New Delhi into the great-power concert will succeed. Some U.S. initiatives have failed or yielded meager results . . . .

[R]ewriting the rules of existing institutions is a thorny undertaking. Power is a zero-sum game, and so any attempt to boost the standing of China, India, and other rising states within international organizations will cost other countries some of their influence in those forums. These prospective losers can be expected to stall or sabotage attempts at reform. Although European countries are still significant, their economic and demographic growth does not match that of either the emerging powers or the United States. Having been endowed with privileged positions in many key postwar institutions, European countries stand to lose the most in a redistribution of power favoring countries on the Pacific Rim. And since they effectively hold vetoes in many organizations, they can resist U.S.-led changes. The Europeans argue that they still count thanks to the EU, which lets them command a 25-member voting bloc in many institutions. But if the EU moves toward a common policy on foreign affairs and security, it will be worth asking why Brussels deserves 25 voices when the 50 states comprising the United States get only one.

Developing countries on the periphery of the global economy can be expected to back Europe in resisting U.S.-led reform efforts: they do not want to lose what little influence they have in multilateral institutions . . . .

In or Out?

It may seem odd for the United States today to seek to disenfranchise its long-standing allies in Europe in order to reward governments that often have agendas that deviate from its own. But the alternative is even more disconcerting: if these countries are not integrated, they might go it alone and create international organizations that fundamentally clash with U.S. interests. In the past few years, fueled by anti-Americanism, dormant groups such as the Nonaligned Movement have found new life. If India and China are not made to feel like co-managers of the international system, they could make the future very uncomfortable for the United States. Nationalists in rising powers will be eager to exploit any policy fissures that may develop between their countries and the United States.

China, in particular, has already begun to create new institutional structures outside of the United States' reach. The Shanghai Cooperation Organization, for example, which consists of China, Kazakhstan, Kyrgyzstan, Russia, Tajikistan, and Uzbekistan (with India, Iran, Mongolia, and Pakistan as observers), has facilitated military and energy cooperation among its members, although still at a low level. At the SCO's June 2006 summit in Beijing, Iranian President Mahmoud Ahmadinejad proposed that the organization "ward off the threats of domineering powers to use their force against and interfere in the affairs of other states." The joint declaration issued at the end of the summit appeared to endorse this sentiment, noting that "differences in cultural traditions, political and social systems, values and models of development formed in the course of history should not be taken as pretexts to interfere in other countries' internal affairs."

China is also aggressively courting resource-rich countries. In October 2006, it hosted a summit with more than 40 leaders from Africa to ensure continued access to the energy-rich continent. And its leaders have proposed creating free-trade areas within the SCO and APEC—displaying such willingness to go ahead that President Bush was forced to remove the global war on terrorism from the top of his APEC agenda, and in November 2006, he called for an APEC free-trade zone.

China's efforts do not necessarily conflict with U.S. interests, but they could if Beijing so desired. From a U.S. perspective, it would be preferable for China and India to advance their interests within U.S.-led global governance structures rather than outside of them. The United States could get something in return for accommodating these states in institutions such as the UN and the IMF and giving them the recognition and prestige they demand: a commitment by Beijing and New Delhi that they will accept the key rules of the global game.

Suggested Discussion Topics

1. Gilpin notes that many commentators believe we are moving, or have moved, from a state-dominated world to a market-dominated world. What would such a shift imply? What would it mean for your personal economic security? Do you think this shift has taken place, or is taking place? Since the 1930s, most

Americans have assumed that if another major economic depression were to occur, the U.S. government would be able to use fiscal and monetary policy to get the economy moving again; that if extreme inflation were to occur, the U.S. government would be able to bring it under control; and that in bad times as well as good times the U.S. state would guarantee a minimum level of Social Security and welfare to all Americans. Given globalization and the growing importance of market forces, does the United States still have this ability?

2. Imagine that you are an official at the World Trade Organization or the International Monetary Fund and that you have been asked to explain why economic globalization is a good thing. Outline the strongest possible argument that economic globalization is beneficial and should be allowed to continue. Now imagine that you are a protester, marching in the street outside a WTO or IMF meeting. Explain why you think globalization is a bad thing and needs to be restrained.

3. What difference do multinational corporations (MNCs, also known as transnational corporations, or TNCs) make? How have they affected global economics and global politics? What is the relationship between MNCs and sovereign states?

4. Compare the classical gold standard with the fixed exchange rate regime of the Bretton Woods system and with the dollar system that actually developed after World War II. How did each work and how did each provide for international liquidity? What were the advantages and disadvantages of each? Why did the United States abandon convertibility in 1971 and move toward a system of floating exchange rates?

5. Why do states now have less policy autonomy and ability to control domestic and international monetary conditions? What makes today's capital flows different from those in the past? What are the costs and benefits of increased globalization of financial markets? Do you think we need better controls on international financial markets and capital flows? If so, should these be imposed by individual nation-states? Or by intergovernmental organizations like the IMF?

6. Should the United States and Europe open their markets to agricultural products from the developing world? Should the United States be willing to reduce its subsidies to farmers for commodities like sugar, cotton, and soybeans in order to help farmers in Africa? Why?

7. In what ways should the United States adjust its policies in response to the growing economic and political clout of China and India? What policy options exist for the United States? Has the Bush administration shown sufficient flexibility in its polities to these two Asian giants? Should they be treated as friends or foes?

Chapter 11

POVERTY AND DEVELOPMENT

As interdependence transforms the global security agenda, poverty emerges as one of the most pressing issues in world politics. Approximately 3.2 billion people live in low-income economies (economies with per capita gross national product [GNP] of $725 or less), in many cases at the edge of survival. Although every society has its rich and poor, the gap between the world's industrialized North (the rich First World nations of North America, Western Europe, Australia, and Japan and the ex-communist Second World nations of Eastern Europe and the former Soviet Union) and the economically less-developed nations of the world's South (Latin America, Asia, and Africa) is enormous. The developing countries, home to four-fifths of the world's population, earn only about one-fifth of the world's GNP. Although India and China still account for large numbers of the world's poor, twenty-nine of the fifty poorest countries in the world are located in sub-Saharan Africa, including the ten poorest. These regions are burdened by high population growth, widespread disease, poor education systems, and subsistence agricultural economies. In many of the poorest societies, wealth and land are concentrated in the hands of a small elite, creating huge disparities within these societies. Rural poverty and underemployment encourage immense migrations to urban centers, where people live in wretched conditions in "shanty towns" and "favelas" without sanitation or pure water.

Since 1980, the gap between rich and poor has widened rather than narrowed. During this period the income of roughly a quarter of the world's population has declined, and in forty-three countries average incomes are actually lower than they were in 1970. During the 1980s (sometimes called the "lost decade"), per capita income in Latin America fell by 7 percent. In sub-Saharan Africa, per capita GNP dropped by 10 percent, and real prices for major export commodities, notably tea, coffee, cocoa, and cotton, fell by more than 50 percent in real terms. Many African countries confronted a mountain of debt and were forced to use up all or most of their earnings from exports merely to pay interest on that debt. Overall, during the last three decades, the share of global income enjoyed by the richest 20 percent of the world's population rose from 70 to 85 percent, while the share of the poorest 20 percent declined from 2.3 to 1.4 percent.

Poverty is associated with a variety of serious problems. Approximately 17 million people die each year in the developing world from curable diseases like malaria, and 90 percent of all those infected with HIV, the virus that causes AIDS, live in these countries. Approximately 500 million people in the developing world are chronically malnourished, including more than a third of the children.

The world's poor are, in large measure, either left out of the economic globalization discussed in the previous chapter or are its victims. Globalized markets and
transnational corporations may provide opportunities, stimulating economic development and creating new or higher-paying jobs. In some parts of the world, however,
this economic development has proceeded only slowly, if at all, and gaps between
the world's rich and the world's poor continue to widen. And where economic
development has proceeded, it has come at a price, threatening social stability
and traditional values and straining the environment. Integrating the world's poor
into the global economy, and doing so in a way that does not perpetuate poverty,
thus represents a major challenge in today's world. The new integrative institutions
and actors discussed in preceding chapters—intergovernmental organizations,
nongovernmental organizations, transnational corporations, international law,
and the web of complex interdependence that is resulting in increased interstate
cooperation—all play an important role in this development process.

The way in which the world deals with poverty is likely to determine whether the
coming decades are peaceful and stable or violent and dangerous. Poverty produces frustration and anger, directed both at the governments of developing countries and at citizens of wealthy countries. It is from the densely packed slums of the
developing world's "megacities" (urban centers with a population of more than ten
million) that angry young terrorists emerge determined to take revenge on their own
rulers or on wealthy foreigners and to make the world take notice of their plight.
Civil war, lawlessness, and refugees are some of the consequences of urban overcrowding, unemployment, and poverty.

The problems of global poverty and underdevelopment thus draw together a
number of the strands we have been exploring: how the disintegration of some political institutions and the rise of others, like a global economy, are transforming life,
and how a whole new set of issues is making its way onto the global security agenda.

11.1 The Tangled Web:
The Poverty-Insecurity Nexus

Lael Brainard, Derek Chollet, and Vinca LaFleur

The first selection in this chapter emphasizes that poverty creates the conditions for
insecurity and violence and that the resulting insecurity and violence in turn intensify
poverty in the less-developed world. In this tragic cycle, poverty and insecurity reinforce each other. The complex relationship among the factors involved in poverty
and the political instability and violence in poor countries make it difficult to know
how to begin to bring an end to what the authors call the "doom spiral." The authors
show how poverty contributes to enfeebled political institutions and environmental
degradation and how these in turn foster instability and violence. These conditions
are further intensified by the relative youth of populations in the most impoverished
societies. The authors suggest, nevertheless, that there are some policies that will

help break this vicious circle, including building political and social institutions, providing timely emergency assistance, and reducing corruption. Before measures such of these can become effective, however, there is a desperate need for honest and effective leaders, as well as cooperation from nongovernmental organizations, corporations, and local civil society groups. Such cooperation in altering the conditions that perpetuate poverty and instability, the authors conclude, may transform the "doom spiral" into a "benevolent web."

The fight against global poverty is commonly—and appropriately—framed as a moral imperative. Stark images of suffering weigh on Western consciences, as images of hungry children in Niger, AIDS orphans in Tanzania, tsunami victims in Indonesia, and refugees in Darfur are beamed into our living rooms in real time. In today's increasingly interconnected world, the "haves" cannot ignore the suffering of the "have-nots." Whether or not we choose to care, we cannot pretend that we do not see.

Yet the effort to end poverty is about much more than extending a helping hand to those in need. In a world where boundaries and borders have blurred, and where seemingly distant threats can metastasize into immediate problems, the fight against global poverty has become a fight of necessity—not simply because personal morality demands it, but because global security does as well.

Extreme poverty exhausts governing institutions, depletes resources, weakens leaders, and crushes hope—fueling a volatile mix of desperation and instability. Poor, fragile states can explode into violence or implode into collapse, imperiling their citizens, regional neighbors, and the wider world as livelihoods are crushed, investors flee, and ungoverned territories become a spawning ground for global threats like terrorism, trafficking, environmental devastation, and disease.

Yet if poverty leads to insecurity, it is also true that the destabilizing effects of conflict and demographic and environmental challenges make it harder for leaders, institutions, and outsiders to promote human development. Civil wars may result in as many as 30 percent more people living in poverty[1]—and research suggests that as many as one-third of civil wars ultimately reignite.[2]

In sum, poverty is both a cause of insecurity and a consequence of it.

If the link between poverty and insecurity is apparent, the pathway toward solutions is far from clear. What, after all, is meant by "insecurity" and "conflict"—two terms that cover a wide range of phenomena, from the fear and want poor individuals suffer to the armed violence that can engulf entire regions? Is conflict driven by concrete economic factors or sociopolitical exclusion and humiliation? Should our primary concern be internal instability or the risk that destabilizing threats will be exported? Should we worry most about individual livelihoods or the health of

---

[1] "The Global Menace of Local Strife," *Economist*, May 24, 2003, 23–25; the citation here is on p. 25.

[2] See chapter 2, by Susan E. Rice, in the original volume (see source note below).

Excerpts from Lael Brainard, Derek Chollet, and Vinca LaFleur, "The Tangled Web: The Poverty-Insecurity Nexus," in Lael Brainard and Derek Chollet, eds., *Too Poor for Peace? Global Poverty, Conflict, and Security in the 21st Century* (Washington: Brookings, 2007), pp. 1–30. Reprinted by permission of Brookings Institution Press.

the state itself? Is it necessary to address insecurity before poverty can be tackled? Should U.S. policymakers characterize development assistance as an American national security priority or frame it in moral terms?

It is hard to know which strand to grasp first to untangle the poverty-insecurity web. But every day, 30,000 children die because they are too poor to survive,[3] and last year saw seventeen major armed conflicts in sixteen locations.[4] Over the next four decades, the population of developing countries will swell to nearly 8 billion—representing 86 percent of humanity.[5] Addressing poverty—and clearly under-standing its relationship to insecurity—needs to be at the forefront of the policy agenda. The world simply cannot afford to wait.

The Doom Spiral

In recent years, world leaders and policy experts have developed a strong consen-sus that the fight against poverty is important to ensuring global stability. This was the core message of the 2005 Group of Eight Summit in Gleneagles, Scotland, and it is the underlying rationale of the UN Millennium Development Goals.

American policymakers have traditionally viewed security threats as involving bullets and bombs—but now even they acknowledge the link between poverty and conflict. Former secretary of state Colin Powell notes that "the United States cannot win the war on terrorism unless we confront the social and political roots of poverty."[6] The 2006 National Security Strategy of the United States makes the case for fighting poverty because "development reinforces diplomacy and defense, reducing long-term threats to our national security by helping to build stable, pros-perous, and peaceful societies."[7] And the Pentagon's 2006 Quadrennial Defense Review focuses on fighting the "long war," declaring that the U.S. military has a humanitarian role in "alleviating suffering . . . [helping] prevent disorder from spiraling into wider conflict or crisis."[8]

Such assertions have a commonsense and compelling logic. Within states, extreme poverty literally kills; hunger, malnutrition, and disease claim the lives of millions each year. Poverty-stricken states tend to have weak institutions and are often plagued by ineffective governance, rendering them unable to meet their people's basic needs for food, sanitation, health care, and education. Weak govern-ments are often unable to adequately control their territory—leaving lawless areas

---

[3] Ibid.

[4] Stockholm International Peace Research Institute, *SIPRI Yearbook 2006: Armaments, Disarmaments, and International Security* (Oxford University Press, 2006).

[5] See chapter 4, by Colin Kahl, in the present volume.

[6] Colin Powell, "No Country Left Behind," *Foreign Policy*, January/February 2005, 28–35; the quotation here is on p.29.

[7] National Securtiy Council, "The National Security Strategy of the United States of America," March 2006, 33. <www.whitehouse.gov/nsc/nss/2006/nss2006.pdf> [September 2006].

[8] Department of Defense, "Quadrennial Defense Review Report," February 6, 2006, 12. <www.comw.org/qdr/qdr2006.pdf> [September 2006].

and natural resources to be hijacked by predatory actors. Fragile states can become breeding grounds for criminal activity, internal strife, or terrorist networks—and often all three simultaneously.

Extreme poverty is also both a source and product of environmental degradation—for example, the deforestation of the Amazon River and Congo River basins is damaging biodiversity and contributing to global warming. And in an age of global air travel, when traffic is expected to reach 4.4 trillion passenger-kilometers flown in 2008, it is easy to see how a disease—whether avian flu, Ebola, or SARS—originating in a developing country with poor early warning and response mechanisms could quickly threaten the lives of people far beyond its borders.[9]

The arguments linking poverty and insecurity are reinforced by recent scholarly research. Mainstream opinion, in the media and elsewhere, tends to characterize civil conflict as stemming from ancient ethnic hatreds or political rivalries. Yet the groundbreaking statistical analysis by the Oxford economist Paul Collier shows that ethnic diversity is in most cases actually a safeguard against violence; the most powerful predictors of civil conflict are in fact weak economic growth, low incomes, and dependence on natural resources. In Collier's words, countries with all three risk factors "are engaged in a sort of Russian Roulette,"[10] struggling to promote development before the bullets start to fly.

It is true that war itself impoverishes, but the Berkeley economist Edward Miguel and his colleagues have helped establish convincingly that increases in poverty on their own significantly increase the likelihood of conflict. Miguel examined annual country-level data for forty-one countries in sub-Saharan Africa between 1981 and 1999 whose populations depend on subsistence agriculture, and he showed that the drop in per capita income associated with drought significantly increases the likelihood of civil conflict in the following year.[11] Given that drought is a natural phenomenon, the analysis suggests that violent conflict is driven by poor economic outcomes, and not the other way round. Conversely, this research shows that as such economic factors as personal income and national growth rates rise, the risk of conflict falls. For each additional percentage point in the growth rate of per capita income, the chances for conflict are about 1 percent less; doubling the level of income cuts the risk of conflict in half. According to the U.K. Department for International Development, a country with $250 per capita income has a 15 percent likelihood of internal conflict over five years—many times greater than the 1 percent risk to an economy with $5,000 per capita income.[12]

Why is the risk of conflict higher in poor countries? Some suggest that it is because poor people have little to lose; as *The Economist* wrote, "it is easy to give

---

[9] International Civil Aviation Organization, "Strong Air Traffic Growth Projected Through to 2008," News Release PIO 08/06, Montreal, June 29, 2006.

[10] Paul Collier, "The Market for Civil War," *Foreign Policy*, May/June 2003, 38.

[11] Edward Miguel, Shanker Satyanath, and Ernest Sergenti, "Economic Shocks and Civil Conflict: An Instrumental Variables Approach," *Journal of Political Economy* 112, no. 4 (2004): 725–53.

[12] Susan Rice, "The Threat of Global Poverty," *National Interest*, Spring 2006, 76.

[13] "The Global Menace of Local Strife," *Economist*, May 24, 2003, 23.

a poor man a cause."[13] In addition, governments of poor countries often have little tax base with which to build professional security forces and are vulnerable to corruption. Moreover, poverty is often associated with political exclusion, humiliation, and alienation—a poverty of dignity and voice. Finally, while the data do not confirm a causal linkage between a country's income inequality and the risk of civil war, recent trends from Mexico to India to China suggest that rising expectations that go unmet may also fuel unrest. In the words of Oxfam USA's president, Raymond Offenheiser, "It isn't just who's poor that matters, but who *cares* about being poor."

Tragically, poverty and insecurity are mutually reinforcing, leading to what the Brookings scholar Susan Rice evocatively calls a "doom spiral." Conflict increases infant mortality, creates refugees, fuels trafficking in drugs and weapons, and wipes out infrastructure. It also makes it harder for outside players to deliver assistance and less attractive for the global private sector to invest. Thus, once a country has fallen into the vortex, it is difficult for it to climb out—as the world has witnessed with the ongoing catastrophe in the Democratic Republic of Congo, a crisis that has claimed nearly 4 million lives and sparked a massive humanitarian emergency, where most people today are killed not by weapons but by easily preventable and treatable diseases.

Violent conflict also produces considerable economic spillover for neighboring countries, as refugees flow in, investment pulls out, and supply chains and trade routes are disrupted. Moreover, mass movements of people—whether armed rebels or civilian refugees—can be regionwide conveyor belts of infectious disease.

Although the overall number of internal and interstate wars is decreasing, a group of regions and countries remains vulnerable to conflicts over protracted periods—often cycling back into conflict after stability has been established. Instability is largely concentrated in and around the poorest parts of sub-Saharan Africa, and frontline states where Islamic extremists are engaged in violent conflict, such as Chechnya, Kashmir, Lebanon, Sudan, East Timor, Iraq, and Afghanistan. Unfortunately, poor economic conditions, weak governance, and natural resource barriers in these areas mean that violent conflict and displacement are likely to continue—and worsen—without intervention.

What, then, might be useful guidelines for tackling the poverty-insecurity challenge? The first is to help policymakers better understand the issue's significance and urgency. Part of that task is educating the press and public to replace the convenient narrative that "age-old" hatreds drive violence with a more sophisticated grasp of the links between economic drivers and conflict.

The second guideline is to understand the specific conditions that heighten the risk of conflict and human insecurity. These may include deteriorating health conditions, corrupt governments, and inadequate institutions. Two areas in particular that can exacerbate instability and merit special attention are environmental insecurity and large youth demographics.

Most of all, it is clear that tackling the poverty-insecurity nexus is a challenge that demands commitment. Promoting lasting stability requires building long-term local capacity. Interventions that work at one point may lose their potency over time and need to be adjusted to new circumstances. And research suggests that assistance is most effective not in the immediate aftermath of a conflict, when donor interest is typically greatest, but in the middle of the first postconflict decade, when the recipient country's absorptive capacity has improved.

Yet such long-term attention is too often hard to secure in rich-country capitals where players, parties, and administrations change, and where the "urgent" typically trumps the "important" on the policy agenda. Until global mind-sets shift from reactive to proactive, and from responsive to preventive, breaking out of the poverty-insecurity trap will remain an elusive goal.

A State of Nature: The Environmental Challenge

Natural resource scarcity and abundance have always been intertwined with poverty and insecurity. Today, throughout West Africa, poor villagers struggle with the effects of desertification, which degrades the land on which they farm. In Haiti, forest and soil loss aggravates the country's economic woes and sparks periods of conflict. In Pakistan, women walk long distances to collect drinking water from ponds that are used by livestock, leading to tremendous health challenges and high infant mortality. Resource abundance also has its perils: in eastern Congo, innocents are terrorized by rebels whose weapons were financed with looted diamonds.

When it comes to extreme poverty, the natural resource challenge is usually seen as one of scarcity—typically of such renewable resources as water, timber, and arable land that are fundamental for daily survival. Demographic and environmental stresses can exacerbate demands on already weakened states. These grievances can foment instability from below. When demand for resources outweighs supply, when the distribution is perceived to be grossly unfair, and when tensions exist over whether they should be treated as rights or commodities, public frustration can spark civil strife.

In addition, elites may be tempted to manipulate scarce resources—controlling them for personal gain, using them to reward certain groups over others, or even fueling "top-down" violence in an effort to maintain power. Scarcity is also often the result of severe imbalances of wealth, which is almost always a key factor in the outbreak of conflict in poor areas.

The challenges of resource scarcity will only intensify over time. During the next twenty years, more than 90 percent of the world's projected growth will take place in countries where the majority of the population is dependent on local renewable resources.[14] Almost 70 percent of the world's poor live in rural areas, and most depend on agriculture for their main income—which both requires and exhausts natural resources. More than 40 percent of the planet's population—2.4 billion

---

[14] Jason J. Morrissette and Douglas A. Borer, "Where Oil and Water Do Mix: Environmental Scarcity and Future Conflict in the Middle East and North Africa," *Parameters*, Winter 2004–5, 86–101; the citation here is on p. 86.

people—still use wood, charcoal, straw, or cow dung as their main source of energy, and more than 1.2 billion people lack access to clean drinking water.[15]

Yet resource abundance poses equally dangerous challenges—generally concerning nonrenewable and more easily "lootable" mineral wealth like oil, gas, gold, or diamonds. More than fifty developing countries, home to 3.5 billion people, depend on natural resource revenues as an important source of government income, and many suffer from a poverty of plenty.[16]

This so-called resource curse leads to pathologies of authoritarian and corrupt regimes, led by elites who have few incentives to invest in social development or alleviate social inequities. Abundance can also create "rentier" states, whose resource revenues allow government officials to finance themselves without directly taxing their citizenry, enabling them to more easily restrict political and other rights in return for a measure of social welfare and stability; or leading to "honey pot effects," in which rogue groups fight to secure valuable natural resources—which, once acquired, provide additional means to buy weapons, fueling a cycle of growing instability.[17]

For example, though companies like ExxonMobil and Shell have poured money and infrastructure into the oil-rich Niger Delta, the region suffers from sustained conflict and instability. Nigeria currently earns $3 billion a month from oil exports, yet the Delta remains deeply poor. Militant groups, tapping into local frustration at the continued deep poverty in this oil-rich region awash with oil revenues, have fueled violence. Local attacks continue each day, growing more sophisticated and organized, making one of the world's most resource-rich areas also one of its most dangerous.[18]

What, then, are some of the measures states and outside actors can take to attenuate the risks that resource scarcity and dependence pose to human security?

The place to begin is with sensible government policies that promote economic diversification, capacity building, equitable distribution, enforceable property rights, demographic sustainability, and public health. . . .

Meanwhile, governments, NGOs, and private actors need to be more creative in devising tailored, targeted, emergency assistance for states facing sudden economic and environmental catastrophes. For example, foreign assistance could be quickly and routinely deployed to states that suffer a drought or commodity price collapse, *before* violence has a chance to break out. In addition, crop insurance programs and other forms of protection could be created for individuals whose livelihoods may be destroyed.[19]

---

[15] Thomas Homer-Dixon, "Scarcity and Conflict," *Forum for Applied Research and Public Policy* 15, no. 1 (Spring 2000): 28–35; the citation here is on p. 28.

[16] Publish What You Pay, "Background," 2004. <www.publishwhatyoupay.org/english/background.shtml> [September 2006].

[17] See chapter 4 in the present volume.

[18] Simon Robinson, "Nigeria's Deadly Days," *Time International*, May 22, 2006, 20–22.

[19] See chapter 3, by Edward Miguel, in the present volume.

Just as critical, especially in cases of natural resource abundance, are efforts to promote transparency—not only on the budget side of the ledger, but on the expenditure side as well. Publicizing how much money is flowing in for natural resources, and how it is being allocated, makes it harder for governments to skim from the top, and for rebels to benefit from plunder. . . .

An Age of Youth: The Demographic Challenge

As the United States braces itself for retiring baby boomers, and European welfare states struggle to support their aging populations, the developing world is getting younger. Nearly half the people on the planet are under twenty-five years old, and more than a billion people are between the ages of ten and nineteen.[20] The disproportionately large share of young people in the population—the so-called youth bulge—is in absolute and relative terms the largest cohort ever to transition into adulthood, and it will remain so over the next two decades.

This fact presents tremendous challenges, particularly for the developing world. Young people often suffer the most from poverty, lack of educational and economic opportunities, poor health, crime, and armed conflict. Nearly 17 million of the world's youth are refugees or internally displaced persons,[21] 130 million are illiterate,[22] as many as 300,000 fight as child soldiers,[23] and collectively, young people make up almost 60 percent of the world's poor.[24]

Moreover, there is strong historical evidence linking youth bulges to instability and conflict. Henrik Urdal of the International Peace Research Institute in Oslo looked into conflicts dating back to 1946 to determine whether youth bulges increase the risk of conflict significantly. Using rigorous statistical analysis, he determined that for each percentage point increase in youth population as a share of the adult population, the risk of conflict increases by more than 4 percent. Furthermore, he argues that "when youth make up more than 35 percent of the adult population, which they do in many developing countries, the risk of armed conflict is 150 percent higher than in countries with an age structure similar to most developed countries."[25]

Paul Collier adds to this assertion by noting that the mere existence of a large youth demographic lowers the cost of recruitment for rebel armies.[26] Jack Goldstone

---

[20] See chapter 7, by Marc Sommers, in the present volume.

[21] This number is from chapter 9 in the present volume.

[22] This number is found in "Youth and the State of the World," in Global Roundtable Working Group on Youth. <www.advocatesforyouth.org/PUBLICATIONS/factsheet/fsstateworld.pdf> [September 2006].

[23] This number is from chapter 9 in the present volume.

[24] This number is found in "Stress Factor One: The Youth Bugle," by Richard Cincotta, Robert Engelman, and Daniele Anastasion, in *The Security Demographic: Population and Civil Conflict after the Cold War* (Washington: Population Action International, 2003), 43.

[25] See chapter 6, by Henrik Urdal, in the present volume.

[26] Paul Collier, "Doing Well Out of War: An Economic Perspective," in *Greed & Grievance: Economic Agendas in Civil Wars*, ed. Mats Berdal and David M. Malone (Boulder, Colo.: Lynne Rienner, 2000), 91–111.

of George Mason University observes that rising youth bulges coupled with rapid urbanization have been important contributors to political violence, particularly in the context of unemployment and poverty.[27] Taken together, the research seems to suggest a clear relationship between youth bulges and an increased risk of conflict.

The problem may lie in the fact that in too many places, the next generation is caught in a troubling cycle where the opportunities to make a useful contribution to society diminish as the number of youth soars. Yet, this need not—and, in terms of economic theory, ought not—be the case. A youthful population can be a country's blessing instead of its curse, providing a "demographic dividend" of energetic workers to jump-start productivity and growth.

The problem is that a country hoping to achieve such a positive outcome must provide economic opportunities for its young people—and too often, those reaching adulthood face bleak prospects of employment. Saudi Arabia, for example, will have 4 million young people joining the labor force in this decade—a number equivalent to two-thirds of the current Saudi workforce.[28] And when these young people have had their expectations raised through education, their frustration at not being able to earn a living can render them susceptible to extremists. As Tufts University professor Mark Sommers writes, "It often seems that nations don't know what to do with their own young people, while armed groups keep discovering new ways to make use of them."[29]

Too often, assistance programs intended to make a difference for youth are driven more by donor priorities and preconceptions than by what young people themselves really need; for example, too many job programs are designed to lure urban migrants back to the land, instead of accepting that many urbanized youth do not want to leave the city.

The problem is compounded by policy inefficiencies at the national and multinational levels—including the lack of political priority attached to youth issues; the absence of an integrated approach involving not only youth ministries but also health, education, labor, and culture; the lack of empirical data on what works; and the mismatch between money spent on education and money spent on ensuring that jobs are available when young people graduate—through programs supporting entrepreneurship, job creation, and enterprise development.

In certain places and policy circles, the result has been that young people, especially males, are seen only as menaces to their communities. They are often depicted negatively, as problems to be dealt with rather than potential to be tapped; and more is made of the fact that men are disproportionately responsible for violent crime than of the fact that the vast majority of young men, even those in brutally harsh and desperate conditions, never resort to violence.

The challenge, then, in crafting an effective response to the "youth bulge" is to resist the temptation to view young people solely as a threat—and instead

---

[27] Jack a. Goldstone, "Demography, Environment, and Security," in *Environmental Conflict*, ed. Paul F. Diehl and Nils Petter Gleditsch (Boulder, Colo.: Westview Press, 2001), 84–108.

[28] See chapter 6 in the present volume.

[29] See chapter 7 in the present volume.

approach them as a valuable resource to be protected and cultivated. Indeed, as those who work with disadvantaged youth will readily argue, there is much to be learned from the incredible resilience and resourcefulness of poor young people. . . .

Such a wide array of challenges begs the question, "Where do we begin?" Regardless of whether change originates in governmental institutions, the private sector, or civil society, one constant is that leadership matters.

The Role of Leaders: Spotlight on Africa   Countries on every continent suffer from poverty and insecurity, in part because of their political leaders' decisions and actions—and no country is immune from hapless, corrupt, or even venal leadership, as citizens from the Americas to Europe to Asia would readily volunteer. And yet, some regions with weak institutions have been more deeply afflicted by poor leadership than others. Postcolonial Africa in particular has borne the burdens of a leadership deficit.

It is true that African countries have several inherent disadvantages to overcome. Their independence from outside rule is relatively recent; the United States, after all, has been engaged in its democratic experiment for more than two centuries. Africa is the world's second most populous continent, comprising fifty-three countries—fifteen of which are landlocked and many of which are tropical. At the same time, many African countries possess great human and natural resources. And yet, according to Harvard University scholar Robert Rotberg, by some measures, 90 percent of sub-Saharan African nations have experienced despotic rule in the past three decades.[30]

Poor leadership can take a devastating toll on human security. In Zimbabwe, for example, Robert Mugabe has transformed a regional economic and political success story into a repressive, chaotic mess. Fifteen years ago, a quarter of Zimbabweans were unemployed; today, the figure is 70 percent, and inflation has climbed to more than 1,000 percent a year. Meanwhile, newspapers have been closed and scores of reporters thrown in jail, while Zimbabwe's police and armed forces have forcibly eradicated slum dwellers in ways reminiscent of the horrific ethnic cleansing witnessed during the 1990s in the Balkans.[31]

Human agency is to blame for millions of civilian deaths in Africa in recent years from Congo to Sudan, Angola, Rwanda, and Darfur. Moreover, the "half-life" of damage done by bad leaders can far transcend the period of misrule. Perceptions matter, especially when countries try to attract foreign investment from half a world away, and a country that has been associated with instability or corruption in the past may find its public image hard to repair for years or even decades to come.

Polling data confirm that Africans desire honest leaders and effective governments. And the experience of countries like Botswana shows that such aspirations can indeed be achieved. Blessed with a strong tradition of open discussion, a

---

[30] Robert I. Rotberg, "Strengthening African Leadership," *Foreign Affairs*, July/August 2004, 14–18; the citation here is on p. 14.

[31] Joshua Hammer, "Big Man: Is the Mugabe Era Near Its End?" *New Yorker*, June 26, 2006, 28–34; the citation here is on p. 29.

cultural heritage that values collective wisdom and accountability, and, significantly, diamond wealth, Botswana had key resources to draw on in building a strong democracy. Yet, Botswana's success cannot be divorced from the leadership its presidents have provided. In the forty years since independence, Seretse Khama, Ketumile Masire, and Festus Mogae have used not only government tools but also their personal example to transform Botswana from a poor pastoral country into one of the continent's wealthiest and most stable—distributing the benefits of diamonds broadly, including the provision of free universal education and health care.[32] Today, President Mogae is providing a model for other African leaders to emulate in his proactive and tireless crusade against the HIV/AIDS pandemic.

Likewise, Mauritius—once a poor sugar colony—today boasts one of Africa's strongest economies, thanks to creative, honest leadership, market opening, and a political arena characterized by coalition building. During the past two decades, per capita income in Mauritius has nearly doubled, with an attendant rise in human development indicators.[33] And Mozambique, which suffered nearly two decades of civil war, has since 1997 achieved average annual growth in gross domestic product of 8.9 percent, increased enrollment in primary schools by 25 percent, and reduced extreme poverty—even as it has built one of Southern Africa's more stable new democracies.[34]

Enlightened leaders with vision and strength are especially important where the state's organizational and institutional capacity to govern is lacking. Unsurprisingly, states that successfully manage to provide their citizens with basic security, political freedom, transportation and communication infrastructure, medical necessities, and educational institutions—states like Botswana, Mauritius, and South Africa—possess the most farsighted and effective leadership. . . .

Leadership from the Private Sector and the Nongovernmental Community
Although good governance and capable public institutions are indispensable, the fight against extreme poverty can only be won with active leadership from the private sector and civil society. . . .

Jane Nelson has described three basic categories of management challenges and opportunities for corporations—and also NGOs—doing business in countries plagued by political, economic, or physical insecurity.

First and foremost is an organization's obligation to do no harm—to ensure that the enterprise itself does not spark or exacerbate insecurity or conflict. As Nelson explains, while the media spotlight in recent years has been trained on resource extraction industries, other sectors also face challenges—for example, food and beverage companies that may strain limited water resources; manufacturing companies that may lower the bar on workplace safety for poor laborers; or tourism companies that may pose risks to local environments and vulnerable cultures.

---

[32] See chapter 8, by Robert I. Rotberg, in the present volume.

[33] United Nations Development Program, "Mauritius: Country Sheet," *Human Development Report* data, 2006. <http://hdr.undp.org/statistics/data/countries.cmf?c=MUS> [September 2006].

[34] Republic of Mozambique, "Report on the Millennium Development Goals," August 2005.

New accountability mechanisms have been established in recent years to help corporations manage the "do no harm" imperative—including a wide array of global codes, compacts, and voluntary principles focused on integrating performance standards and accountability into the work of companies and NGOs, from the UN Global Compact to the banking sector's Equator Principles and the diamond industry's Kimberley Process. A growing number of global corporations are seeking to adhere to corporate social responsibility approaches that set standards for best practices and establish basic principles for operating in poor and insecure environments.

The second category of engagement is investing in local socioeconomic development and community resilience—by increasing economic opportunity and inclusion; providing access to credit and insurance; enhancing communications and technology infrastructure; and supplying basic resources to improve living conditions. Recent years have witnessed a welcome burst of new activity in these areas, driven by creative social entrepreneurs; innovative, socially conscious investors; and bold partnerships among multinational corporations, philanthropic institutions, government agencies, and others. Such innovative work has not gone unnoticed. In 2006, Muhammad Yunus won the Nobel Peace Prize for his pathbreaking efforts to provide credit to the poor in rural Bangladesh. Today, the Grameen Bank, which Yunus founded in 1976, has over 6 million borrowers, 97 percent of whom are women.

There is also a growing awareness that companies and NGOs can and should play a larger role in supporting civil society organizations, the media, and such high-risk groups as youth, women, and ethnic minorities. . . .

The third level of engagement is for organizations to participate in the broader public policy dialogue—tackling corruption, strengthening institutions, and fortifying government frameworks. Often, these are areas where collective action is especially effective; for example, business-led groups have supported efforts from strengthening the criminal justice system in South Africa to promoting the peace and reconciliation processes in Sri Lanka, the Philippines, and Guatemala. . . .

America's Role: Is Transformational Diplomacy the Route to Security?

For decades, experts have debated whether democracy or development should top the policy agenda. Today, the jury seems to have settled on a commonsense conclusion: both democracy and development are essential, and neither can endure without the other. And yet, if there is a mounting consensus on the virtues of liberal democracies for economic development and human security, disagreement persists over whether foreign intervention can transplant democracy into societies with weak institutional foundations.

Policymakers clearly need a political strategy to complement their poverty strategy. If poor governance and a lack of accountability are part of the reason that countries are poor in the first place, then simply throwing more money at the problem will not help—and could in fact make the situation worse by reinforcing corruption and the capture of the state by elites. Support for nation building and democracy promotion has been sorely tested in recent years by the United States' struggles in Afghanistan and Iraq, but support for transparent and accountable governance should remain an overarching goal of U.S. foreign assistance. Meanwhile, NGOs and others working at the grass roots can help cultivate poor citizens' familiarity with democratic practices and capacity to hold local officials accountable—even in repressive states, where government-to-government channels are not possible. . . .

There is also a risk that U.S. democracy promotion will be seen as a self-serving strategy designed to bolster America's national security, rather than to lift the lives of needy people around the globe. Critics do not deny the national security benefits of promoting democracy, but they argue for a shift of tone in the way the strategy is advanced—one that assumes more humility and appears less squarely "made-in-the-U.S.A."

Similarly, some humanitarian organizations engaged in development work feel they are on a collision course with the U.S. Agency for International Development (USAID) regarding the "branding" of U.S. foreign assistance. USAID's branding campaign was launched in late 2004, with the aim of helping American taxpayers get "the credit they deserve" for the foreign assistance programs they fund. Presumably, the hope is that global publics will regard the United States more favorably if they understand just how much assistance comes "from the American people," as the revamped USAID tagline reads. To promote the campaign, new federal regulations require all contractors and U.S. NGOs receiving USAID funding to ensure their "programs, projects, activities, public communications, and commodities" prominently bear the USAID standard graphic.

Some experienced NGOs argue, however, that the most effective way to promote sustainable development is to foster the local ownership of programs, and that if America's strategic goal is promoting security and reducing poverty, then the focus should be on empowering effective local change agents, not on getting credit for U.S. taxpayers. As these NGOs suggest, the branding campaign risks undermining the effectiveness of development and democracy programs, because local communities need to feel like they are building something themselves, not be reminded at every turn that their destiny depends on the grace of the United States.

Underlying all these concerns is the continued mismatch between the United States' stated strategic priorities and the way aid dollars are actually spent. A recent analysis by the Brookings Institution in cooperation with the Center for Strategic and International Studies counted more than fifty separate offices addressing more than fifty separate aid objectives—a laundry list that is not ranked in any consistent hierarchy.

Moreover, the bulk of U.S. assistance does not fund the things the government claims to care about. The United States would like its aid to be progovernance, but even the Middle East Partnership Initiative—the flagship democracy promotion program in that region—represented only 2 percent of overall U.S. economic assistance to the Middle East in 2005; meanwhile, strategically important Egypt received an assistance package amounting to $27 per capita, its autocratic governance notwithstanding. Ghana, in contrast, received less than \$4 per capita, even while maintaining relatively good governance.[35] . . .

A Benevolent Web

. . . In fighting against poverty and insecurity, we must confront a range of interconnected issues—from demographics to governance to resource distribution—and embrace a variety of solutions that span the governmental, NGO, and private sectors. Our fight must also include efforts too often relegated to the security field—such as enhancing the capacity for conflict resolution and peacekeeping. There are many new avenues for research that will advance how we understand the difficult problems presented by the complex relationship between poverty and insecurity—and more important, many new opportunities for innovative action to meet these challenges.

But no single person, organization, or country can meet these challenges alone. Only by working together on multiple fronts can we hope to prevail against the scourges of hunger, homelessness, disease, and suffering. Tackling poverty and insecurity is not just a matter of doing the right thing—it is a matter of doing the sensible thing to ensure global security. For the sake of our shared security, for the sake of our shared humanity, there is not a moment to waste.

11.2 The Megacity

George Packer

The next selection, from *The New Yorker,* focuses on the enormous problems of poverty in the rapidly expanding cities of the less-developed world, cities whose populations outpace services as people flock from the countryside in search of jobs. Packer describes conditions in the megacity of Lagos, Nigeria, and its vast slums, and he explains how people survive and sometimes prosper under conditions as bad as or worse than those in Europe's cities during the industrial revolution of the nineteenth century.

The Third Mainland Bridge is a looping ribbon of concrete that connects Lagos Island to the continent of Africa. It was built in the nineteen-seventies, part of a vast network of bridges, cloverleafs, and expressways

---

[35] Lael Brainard, "A Unified Framework for U.S. Foreign Assistance," in *Security by Other Means* (Brookings, 2007), 8–16.

intended to transform the districts and islands of this Nigerian city—then comprising three million people—into an efficient modern metropolis. As the bridge snakes over sunken piers just above the waters of Lagos Lagoon, it passes a floating slum: thousands of wooden houses, perched on stilts a few feet above their own bobbing refuse, with rust-colored iron roofs wreathed in the haze from thousands of cooking fires. Fishermen and market women paddle dugout canoes on water as black and viscous as an oil slick. The bridge then passes the sawmill district, where rain-forest logs—sent across from the far shore, thirty miles to the east—form a floating mass by the piers. Smoldering hills of sawdust landfill send white smoke across the bridge, which mixes with diesel exhaust from the traffic. Beyond the sawmills, the old waterfront markets, the fishermen's shanties, the blackened façades of high-rise housing projects, and the half-abandoned skyscrapers of downtown Lagos Island loom under a low, dirty sky. Around the city, garbage dumps steam with the combustion of natural gases, and auto yards glow with fires from fuel spills. All of Lagos seems to be burning.

The bridge descends into Lagos Island and a pandemonium of venders' stalls crammed with spare parts, locks, hard hats, chains, screws, charcoal, detergent, and DVDs. On a recent afternoon, car horns, shouting voices, and radio music mingled with the snarling engines of motorcycle taxis stalled in traffic and the roar of an air compressor in an oily tire-repair yard. Two months earlier, a huge cast-iron water main suspended beneath the bridge had broken free of its rusted clip, crushing a vacant scrap market below and cutting off clean water from tens of thousands of the fifteen million people who now live in Lagos.

In the absence of piped water, wealthier residents of the waterfront slum at the end of the bridge, called Isale Eko, pay private contractors to sink boreholes sixty feet deep. All day and night, residents line up at the boreholes to pay five cents and fill their plastic buckets with contaminated water, which some of them drink anyway. Isale Eko is the oldest and densest part of Lagos Island. Every square foot is claimed by someone—for selling, for washing, even for sleeping—and there is almost no privacy. Many residents sleep outdoors. A young man sitting in an alley pointed to some concrete ledges three feet above a gutter. "These are beds," he said.

In the newer slums on the mainland, such as Mushin, rectangular concrete-block houses squeeze seven or eight people into a single, mosquito-infested room—in bunks or on the floor—along a narrow corridor of opposing chambers. This arrangement is known as "face me I face you." One compound can contain eighty people. In Mushin, Muslim Hausas from the north of Nigeria coexist uneasily with mostly Christian Yorubas from the south. Armed gangs represent the interests of both groups. On the night of February 2, 2002, a witness told me, a Hausa youth saw a Yoruba youth squatting over a gutter on the street and demanded, "Why are you shitting there?" In a city where only 0.4 per cent of the inhabitants have a toilet connected to a sewer system, it was more of a provocation than a serious question. The incident that night led to a brawl. Almost immediately, the surrounding compounds emptied out, and the streets filled with Yorubas and Hausas armed with machetes and guns. The fighting lasted four days and was ended only by the military occupation of Mushin. By then, more than a hundred residents had been killed, thousands had fled the area, and hundreds of houses had burned down.

Newcomers to the city are not greeted with the words "Welcome to Lagos." They are told, "This is Lagos"—an ominous statement of fact. Olisa Izeobi, a worker in one of the sawmills along the lagoon, said, "We understand this as 'Nobody will care for you, and you have to struggle to survive.'" It is the singular truth awaiting the six hundred thousand people who pour into Lagos from West Africa every year. Their lungs will burn with smoke and exhaust; their eyes will sting; their skin will turn charcoal gray. And hardly any of them will ever leave.

Immigrants come to Lagos with the thinnest margin of support, dependent on a local relative or contact whose assistance usually lasts less than twenty-four hours. A girl from the Ibo country, in the southeast, said that she had been told by a woman in her home town that she would get restaurant work in Lagos. Upon arrival, she discovered that she owed the woman more than two hundred dollars for transport and that the restaurant job didn't exist. The girl, her hair combed straight back and her soft face fixed in a faraway stare, told me that she was eighteen, but she looked fifteen. She is now a prostitute in a small hotel called Happiness. Working seven nights a week, with each customer spending three and a half dollars and staying five minutes, she had paid off her debt after seven months. She has no friends except the other girls in the hotel. In her room, on the third floor, the words "I am covered by the blood of Jesus. Amen" are chalked on a wall three times.

A woman named Safrat Yinusa left behind her husband and two of her children in Ilorin, north of the city, and found work in one of Lagos's huge markets as a porter, carrying loads of produce on her head. She was nursing a baby boy, whom she carried as she worked. She paid twenty cents a night for sleeping space on the floor of a room with forty other women porters. In two months, she had saved less than four dollars. Considering that the price of rice in Lagos is thirty-three cents per pound, it is hard to understand how people like Yinusa stay alive. The paradox has been called the "wage puzzle."

When Michael Chinedu, an Ibo, arrived in Lagos, he knew no one. On his first day, he saw a man smoking marijuana—in Lagos, it's called India hemp—and, being a smoker as well, introduced himself. On this slim connection, Chinedu asked the man if he knew of any jobs, and he was taken to the sawmill, where he began at once, working long days amid the scream of the ripsaw and burning clouds of sawdust, sleeping outside at night on a stack of hardwood planks. After three months, he had saved enough for a room. "If you sit down, you will die of hunger," he said.

The hustle never stops in Lagos. Informal transactions make up at least sixty per cent of economic activity; at stoplights and on highways, crowds of boys as young as eight hawk everything from cell phones to fire extinguishers. Begging is rare. In many African cities, there is an oppressive atmosphere of people lying about in the middle of the day, of idleness sinking into despair. In Lagos, everyone is a striver. I once saw a woman navigating across several lanes of traffic with her small boy in tow, and the expression on her face was one I came to think of as typically Lagosian: a look hard, closed, and unsmiling, yet quick and shrewd, taking in everything, ready to ward off an obstacle or seize a chance.

In 1950, fewer than three hundred thousand people lived in Lagos. In the second half of the twentieth century, the city grew at a rate of more than six percent annually. It is currently the sixth-largest city in the world, and it is growing faster than any of the world's other megacities (the term used by the United Nations Center for Human Settlements for "urban agglomerations" with more than ten million people). By 2015, it is projected, Lagos will rank third, behind Tokyo and Bombay, with twenty-three million inhabitants. . . .

Around a billion people—almost half of the developing world's urban population—live in slums. The United Nations Human Settlements Program, in a 2003 report titled "The Challenge of the Slums," declared, "The urban poor are trapped in an informal and 'illegal' world—in slums that are not reflected on maps, where waste is not collected, where taxes are not paid, and where public services are not provided. Officially, they do not exist." According to the report, "Over the course of the next two decades, the global urban population will double, from 2.5 to 5 billion. Almost all of this increase will be in developing countries." . . .

As a picture of the urban future, Lagos is fascinating only if you're able to leave it. . . . Traffic pileups lead to "improvised conditions" because there is no other way for most people in Lagos to scratch out a living than to sell on the street. It would be preferable to have some respite from buying and selling, some separation between private and public life. It would be preferable not to have five-hour "go-slows"—traffic jams—that force many workers to get up well before dawn and spend almost no waking hours at home. And it would be preferable not to have an economy in which millions of people have to invent marginal forms of employment because there are so few jobs. . . .

Folarin Gbadebo-Smith, the chairman of a district on Lagos Island, said that globalization, in the form of mass media, attracts Nigerians to Lagos as a substitute for New York or London. A distorted picture then flows back to the village. . . . In this way, the West African countryside is being rapidly depopulated. . . .

Shina Loremikan, who runs an anti-corruption organization, lives in Ajegunle, Lagos's biggest and most dangerous slum, across a canal from the port. The drainage ditches of Ajegunle are frequently blocked, and during the rainy season they overflow into houses and across streets, which fill up with sludge, sacks, scraps of clothing, and plastic bags, so that some of Ajegunle's streets seem to be wholly composed of trash. I asked Loremikan to show me the slum areas on a map of Lagos. With his finger, he drew a line from the southeast corner all the way to the northwest. "From here to here, they are all slums," Loremikan said flatly. "Refuse is everywhere, either in Victoria Island or Ikoyi"—Lagos's two relatively upscale districts—"or in Agege or Mushin. Black water is everywhere. They are all slums."

Other megacities, such as Bombay, Dhaka, Manila, and São Paulo, have spawned entire satellite cities that house migrants and the destitute, who lead lives that often have nothing to do with the urban center to which they were originally drawn. Lagos expanded differently: there is no distinct area where a million people squat in flimsy hovels. The whole city suffers from misuse. Planned residential areas—such as Surulere, built for civil servants on the mainland—are gradually taken over by the commercial activity that springs up everywhere in Lagos like fungus after the rains. Areas reclaimed from swamps give rise to economic clusters whose nature depends on location: for example, Mushin became one of the city's central spare-parts yards when the Apapa-Oshodi Expressway was built near it, in the seventies. . . . It's hard to decide if the extravagant ugliness of the cityscape is a sign of vigor or of disease—a life force or an impending apocalypse. . . .

In the mid-eighties, under the dictatorship of General Ibrahim Babangida, Nigeria submitted to austerity measures prescribed by the World Bank and the International Monetary Fund, in order to reduce a thirty-billion-dollar debt. Over time, the country shut down or sold off inefficient state-run enterprises, including construction industries, port facilities, oil refineries, and textile and steel mills; electricity, water, and telephone services were privatized. With these structural adjustments, civil-service jobs, the mainstay of the middle class in districts like Surulere, disappeared; meanwhile, privatization often occurred at fire-sale prices, with the profits benefitting politicians or soldiers and their cronies. The remaining savings were devoured by the corrupt military regimes. (An official report released after the fall of Babangida, in 1994, could not account for twelve billion dollars.)

The effect of these policies in Nigeria has been to concentrate enormous wealth in a few hands while leaving the vast majority of people poorer every year. The rare job that still awaits young men and women who come to Lagos pays less than it did a quarter century ago; it is also less likely to be salaried, and more likely to be menial. At the same time, the cost of rent, food, and fuel has soared. If there is an element of American frontier capitalism in the unregulated informal economy of Lagos, there is much less opportunity to make hard work pay off. And if the teeming slums of Lagos recall the "darkness, dirt, pestilence, obscenity, misery and early death" that Dickens described in an essay about Victorian London, there is no industrial base to offer the poor masses at least the possibility of regular employment. . . .

What looks like anarchic activity in Lagos is actually governed by a set of informal but ironclad rules. Although the vast majority of people in the city are small-time entrepreneurs, almost no one works for himself. Everyone occupies a place in an economic hierarchy and owes fealty, as well as cash, to the person above him— known as an *oga*, or master—who, in turn, provides help or protection. Every group of workers—even at the stolen-goods market in the Ijora district—has a union that amounts to an extortion racket. The teen-ager hawking sunglasses in traffic receives the merchandise from a wholesaler, to whom he turns over ninety per cent of his earnings; if he tries to cheat or cut out, his guarantor—an authority figure such as a relative or a man from his home town, known to the vender and the wholesaler alike—has to make up the loss, then hunt down his wayward charge. The patronage system helps the megacity absorb the continual influx of newcomers for whom the formal economy has no use. Wealth accrues not to the most imaginative or industrious but to those who rise up through the chain of patronage. It amounts to a predatory system of obligation, set down in no laws, enforced by implied threat. . . .

A sign near the headquarters of Shell Oil on Victoria Island says, "Did You go to School, College, University, Polytechnic, and you still throw Refuse out of your car or from the bus? Dump garbage bags on the road medians or in drains? Build your house/shop on drains? Urinate or defecate in public places? Then why did you bother to get an education? Think about it!"

The sign is part of a government-led campaign for beautification and order in Lagos. . . . But the megacity doesn't encourage social responsibility and collective action to improve public life. The very scale of it is atomizing. The absence of government services in most neighborhoods rarely leads to protest; instead, it forces slum dwellers to become self-sufficient through illegal activity. They tap into electrical lines, causing blackouts and fires; they pay off local gangs to provide security, which means that justice in the slums is vigilante justice. In Mushin, several members of the Oodua People's Congress, a Yoruba gang, displayed for me a suspected motorcycle thief whom they had caught the night before and were holding in a dingy back room of their clubhouse: he was chained at the hands and feet, and bleeding from the head. His captors hadn't decided whether to turn him over to the police or simply kill him. Alongside the Badagry Expressway, I saw the charred remains of a corpse, recognizably human only from the buttocks and thighs, which had been burned and left to rot. No one I asked knew what it was doing there, and no one seemed particularly surprised. . . .

The most famous shantytown in Lagos, called Maroko, rose up on prime ocean-front property along the southern shore of Victoria Island. In the eighties, the Lagos business district began to move to Victoria from Lagos Island, and the land became valuable. In July, 1990, the military government sent bulldozers and soldiers into Maroko, and within a few hours a quarter of a million people had been made homeless. A few miles down the coast from the site, in a concrete public-housing apartment whose ceiling was caving in, I found Prince S. A. Aiyeyemi, a sixty-eight-year-old retired postal-authority worker and the leader of the Maroko Evictees Committee. From his desk, he brought out a letter that he wanted me to give to Bola Tinubu, the Lagos governor. The letter demanded compensation for the loss of the houses owned by committee members and for resettlement to equivalent property. In the meantime, Aiyeyemi was allowing the apartment to which he'd been removed to disintegrate around him. He was slight and frail from a stroke that had left half his face paralyzed. "We shall continue to live till we get justice," he said, slurring his words. "And, if we the elderly die, our children are ready to continue. This is our own contribution to the social engineering of Nigeria." When I asked him whether it was fair for ten people to have to live in a single room, he said, "Well, there's nothing we can do about that. We don't take that so much as a social injustice. That is their economic limitations. It's only when those ten people are tampered with by government, thrown out into the open air—*that* is social injustice."

I had never heard anyone else in Lagos speak this way. This indignant old man was going to die waiting for something called justice, while everyone else in the city struggled. . . .

Nigerians have become notorious for their Internet scams, such as e-mails with a bogus request to move funds to an offshore bank, which ask for the recipient's account number in exchange for lucrative profit. The con, which originated in Lagos, represents the perversion of talent and initiative in a society where normal paths of opportunity are closed to all but the well connected. Corruption is intrinsic to getting anything done in Lagos. . . . Even morgues demand bribes for the release of corpses. The shorthand for financial crimes is "419," from the relevant chapter in the Nigerian criminal code. The words "This House Is Not for Sale: Beware of 419" are painted across the exterior walls of dilapidated houses all over the city—a warning to potential buyers not to be taken in by someone falsely claiming to be the owner. . . .

The most widely available commodity in Lagos is garbage. It is an engine of growth in the underworld of the city's informal economy, a vast sector with an astonishing volume of supply.

Babatunde Ilufoye, an Ibo in his early forties, was brought to Lagos at the age of eighteen, by a German man whose flat tire Ilufoye had fixed one day in his village, and who decided to teach the young man the import-export business. Today, Ilufoye lives near the sawmills, in the shabby-genteel district of Ebute-Meta, where there are many three-story colonial-era buildings in various stages of neglect. He is a polite, neatly dressed, hardworking man, whose wife owns a drygoods shop next to the house; in a European city, Ilufoye would be a successful entrepreneur. In 2004, after visiting a Lagos friend who dealt in cow horns and hooves, he went to an Internet café and typed those words into Google. Nothing useful appeared, but, when he entered "plastic scraps," thousands of links came up.

Ilufoye is now a full-time exporter of recycled hard plastics, selling the ground-up fragments to Indian and South African companies for a minimum of a hundred dollars a ton. In choosing plastics, Ilufoye tapped into a growth market, but Nigeria's international reputation as a breeding ground for online scam artists makes it difficult for him to find customers, and he can't move the product fast enough to become profitable. . . .

Ilufoye's grinder is Andrew Okolie, a gloomy man who operates two crushing machines in a gloomy concrete building under an expressway. The narrow rooms are filled to the ceilings with dirty plastic kitchenware, pails, milk cartons, empty bottles of shampoo, car-wash fluid, cosmetic gels, all pouring out of open doorways in little landslides. When I visited, the power had been out for days and Okolie sat idle in the front room, chewing hard on a piece of gum. Like Ilufoye, he is frustrated by structural limitations: he could handle a capacity of one ton a day, but he can't afford a generator to keep his machines running during the frequent outages. Unless you are rich and connected, the banks charge as much as thirty-per-cent interest on loans, he said. . . .

In the recycling business, Okolie said, most of the suppliers are "dropouts, miscreants"—scavenger boys who scour the gutters and streets and municipal dumps, filling up sacks or carts, and sell what they collect to their *oga*, who has twenty or so boys working for him, in a kind of dependency that resembles that of Fagin and the pickpockets of "Oliver Twist." The *oga*, in turn, sells the refuse to Okolie, who then sells the ground bits to Ilufoye, who exports them. The scavengers, who are called pickers, can collect two or three hundred pounds of plastic a week, for which they are paid six cents per pound. They spend most of their cash, according to Okolie, on marijuana or glue.

Half a dozen miles north of Andrew Okolie's plastics-grinding shop, along the expressway, is the largest municipal dump in Lagos. The first time I visited, a line of trucks stretched from the dumping area to the highway. One badly overloaded truck had tipped over on the entrance road and taken down another, and the mound of garbage left by the spill made it difficult for other trucks to move past. . . .

Hundreds of pickers were trudging across an undulating landscape of garbage. Every minute, another dump truck backed in and released its load, with a tremendous sliding noise culminating in a crash that shook the trash underfoot. As a bulldozer pushed the fresh garbage up into a wave that crested and broke across the older landfill, the pickers rushed over it, swarming dangerously close to the vehicles. Bent under their sacks, they worked quickly and with focus, knowing what they were looking for. Some pickers wanted only copper; others specialized in printer cartridges. One man inspected a wheel axle for half a minute before tossing it aside. A girl sold water from a bucket on her head. Most of the scavengers had closed shoes and some kind of headwear, but only a few wore rubber boots and gloves. They all clawed at the trash with bent rebar, sharpened with use to a shiny point. . . .

The dump—a hole gouged out of the earth—is as broad as a small town, and surrounded on all sides by fifty-foot cliffs composed of laterite and garbage. We were standing at the edge of one such cliff, and the pickers took turns pushing their full sacks over the edge, sending them bouncing down to the bottom and then scurrying after them. Across the floor of the pit are hundreds of hovels, a sizable shantytown of dwellings made of plastic sheeting and scrap metal bound together with baling wire. A thousand pickers live down in the pit, among flocks of white cowbirds, and middlemen come to buy their stock. The pickers have built a mosque and a church, and at Christmas they celebrate by decorating their shacks.

"It is somewhere between the law of the jungle and civilization," Aremu Hakeem, a municipal worker with a master's degree, who escorted me across the dump site, said. "They have an organization, a chairman, rules and regulations. But the physically stronger prevail when the trucks come." Hakeem spoke excitedly about recent improvements to the dump, including the opening of the entrance road. He had read books about landfills and checked out garbage-related Web sites. He was extremely proud of the dump, which he called a "reference point" for all of Nigeria. Then he gazed out over the site and grew quiet. "Someday I would like to come to your country and use what I have here," he said, pointing to his head. "Here we are not using it very much." . . . .

The vision of twenty-three million people squeezed together and trying to survive, like creatures in a mad demographer's experiment gone badly wrong, fills Gbadebo-Smith with foreboding. "We have a massive growth in population with a stagnant or shrinking economy," he said. "Picture this city ten, twenty years from now. This is not the urban poor—this is the new urban *destitute*." He expressed surprise that the level of crime and ethnic violence in Lagos, let alone civil insurrection, is still relatively contained. "We're sitting on a powder keg here," he said. "If we don't address this question of economic growth, and I mean vigorously, there is no doubt as to what's going to happen here eventually. It's just going to boil over." He added, "And guess what? If all this fails, the world will feel the weight of Lagos not working out."

There is an even darker possibility: that the world won't feel the weight of it much at all. The really disturbing thing about Lagos's pickers and venders is that their lives have essentially nothing to do with ours. They scavenge an existence beyond the margins of macroeconomics. They are, in the harsh terms of globalization, superfluous.

Aid, Advice, and Governance/ Ending Poverty Forever

11.3 The Eight Commandments

The Economist

This selection addresses global efforts to end poverty for good by achieving the Millennium Goals set by the United Nations in 2000. These ambitious goals, to be met by 2015, entail

♦ Reducing by half both the proportion of people living on less than a dollar a day and who suffer from hunger

♦ Achieving universal primary education

♦ Promoting gender equality by reducing gender disparity in education

♦ Reducing mortality by two-thirds among children under five

♦ Improving maternal health

♦ Combating HIV/AIDS, malaria and other diseases

♦ Reducing by half those without access to safe drinking water and improving the lives of at least 100 million slum dwellers

♦ Developing an open and nondiscriminatory trading and financial system to provide developing states with access to markets of developed states, and reduction or cancellation of debts owed by poor states[1]

Arguing that the goals themselves were somewhat arbitrary, the article explains why it is unlikely that they will be met despite the efforts of public and private international institutions.

In 2000 the world set itself goals to cut poverty, disease and illiteracy. It will take more than aid to meet them. Rick Johnston carries his "Arsenator" with him whenever he leaves his office at the United Nations Children's Fund (UNICEF) in Dhaka to check on the handpumps, standpipes and ringwells of rural

---

[1] United Nations, "Millennium Development Goals," <www.un.org/millenniumgoals>.

Bangladesh. This device, a sort of portable chemistry set, can detect whether village groundwater is laced with dangerous concentrations of arsenic. If it finds its way into a person's organs the poison can accumulate, causing black lesions and terminal cancers.

Arsenic has contaminated over 90 percent of the shallow tubewells in Muradnagar, a subdistrict three hours from Dhaka. Drilling deeper is not an option: the low-lying aquifer is too salty. The households in this corner of the subdistrict rely instead on a gift from the United Nations Foundation: a $4,000-filtration plant, which can strip arsenic and iron from up to 2,000 litres of water a day. A small crowd gathers to watch Mr. Johnston mix water from the plant with the chemical reagent in his kit. The Arsenator will take 20 minutes to deliver its verdict.

In 1990 more than one person in four lacked access to safe water, according to the United Nations. By 2015 that scandal will be only half as large—if the world's leaders keep the grand promises they made at the UN's New York headquarters in September 2000. The pledges, which also include halving poverty and hunger, schooling the world's children, arresting disease and rescuing mothers and their infants from untimely deaths, have been translated into eight "Millennium Development Goals" (MDGs). July 7th is officially the halfway point between setting the goals and reaching the 2015 deadline.

Sadly, the UN family is better at making goals than meeting them. In 1977 in Mar del Plata, Argentina, the world urged itself to provide safe water and sanitation for all by the end of the 1980s. In 1990 the UN renewed the call, extending the deadline to the end of the century. In 1978 in what is now Almaty, Kazakhstan, governments promised "health for all" by 2000. In 1990 in Jomtien, Thailand, they called for universal primary schooling by 2000, a goal pushed back to 2015 ten years later. Kevin Watkins, the lead author of the UN's yearly Human Development Report, worries that the pledges the UN mints so readily may become a "debased currency". In the summer of 2005, at the height of a campaign to "make poverty history", only 3 percent of Britons thought the world would meet the 2015 goal of halving poverty, defined as the proportion of people who live on less than the equivalent of a dollar a day.

Such fatalism is as unwarranted as complacency. The world is making unprecedented progress against poverty. Thanks to miraculous growth in China and India, the first MDG target should be met. Almost 32 percent of people in the developing world lived on less than a dollar a day in 1990. In 2004 that figure was 19.2 percent. It should fall below 16 percent by 2015.

But if such progress inspires optimism, the goals themselves provoke scepticism. They are meant to convert worthy aspirations into quantifiable commitments, against which governments can be judged. But only 57 out of 163 developing countries have counted the poor more than once since 1990. Ninety-two have not counted them at all.

The world has promised to halt the spread of malaria by 2015. But the disease's death toll is unknown. To monitor its fourth and fifth goals, cutting infant and maternal mortality, the UN would like to cull data from death certificates. But many places lack hospitals, let alone hospital records. The UN relies instead on surveys, which net 5,000–30,000 people in a country once every five years or so.

These ask siblings whether they have lost any sisters to childbirth. But these estimates are too vague to track trends over time or to make meaningful comparisons between countries, the UN laments.

The numerical targets are also arbitrary. They are not a global totting up of what might be doable country by country. Far from it. China, for example, had more or less halved poverty from its 1990 level by the time that goal was set in 2000. Sub-Saharan Africa, by contrast, will not meet any of the goals. They remain too distant even to serve as beacons to steer by.

Although the extreme-poverty rate in Africa has fallen from an estimated 46 percent in 1999 to 41 percent in 2004, that is still way off the 2015 target of 22 percent. Hunger and malnutrition still gnaw at the region: the proportion of under-fives who are underweight has declined only marginally, from 33 percent in 1990 to 29 percent in 2005. Despite dramatic gains, Africa will not meet the goal of universal primary enrolment either; the rate is up from 57 percent in 1999 to 70 percent in 2005.

Africa lags behind partly because its population is growing so rapidly. In rural areas, mothers are giving birth to at least six children on average, doubling the population every generation. As a result, Africa's top-line numbers are improving more than its ratios. Millions more African children are going to school, but the denominator is also increasing. According to the UN, in 1990 there were 237m Africans under 14; today, that figure is 348m, and by 2015 it is expected to top 400m. What price the goal of universal schooling at that pace of population growth?

Start Where You're ATT

Yet it is still possible to get things done, even if not at the pace that the MDGs demand. Take Mali, for instance. This landlocked country, straddling the Sahel region and the Sahara desert, should be one of the least promising countries for development on earth. It is ranked third from bottom (in 175th place) in the UN's human-development index, just shutting out its neighbour Niger and poor Sierra Leone. Yet Western governments and aid agencies, to say nothing of Libya, the Islamic Development Bank and the Chinese, are all flocking to Mali with both great expectations and lots of money.

Why has Mali generated so much hope, whereas nearby Nigeria and Guinea, for example, provoke merely exasperation? Mali has a government, led by Amadou Toumani Touré ("ATT" to Malians) that devotes most of its limited resources to what it calls the "Struggle against Poverty" rather then squandering them on the baubles of office. Mr. Touré's commitment is acknowledged by Malians, who have just re-elected him for a second term. It has also been rewarded by donors. Mali is one of only five African countries to have fully qualified for America's Millennium Challenge Account (MCA), with its stringent criteria for good governance; that alone will bring in $460m over the next five years, a huge amount in a country with a government budget of only about $1.5 billion.

How will Mr. Touré spend this money? Mali's government has made agriculture and infrastructure a priority. The head of its poverty-reduction programme,

Sékouba Diarra, argues that rather than depending on aid, his government wants to raise growth to lift people out of poverty. With greater mechanisation and irrigation, the country's 3.5 m farmers will, he hopes, become self-supporting, growing much more than the traditional crop of cotton. Donors have been persuaded to give large sums to support this; the MCA, for example, is funding a 16,000-hectare (40,000-acre) irrigation project at Alatona, which represents almost a 20 percent increase in the country's drought-proof cropland.

In a desert country, irrigation is probably the most important anti-poverty tool of all, and the results can be seen in the remote villages around the desert town of Timbuktu. In recent years villagers have been shown how to build irrigation canals to capture the flood-waters of the huge Niger river, which winds its way through most of the country. This week, with the rains just about to arrive, the people of one of the villages, Adina Koira, are coming to the end of a three-month communal slog to build up their 5 km of irrigation canals. On the irrigated lands they have been able to grow traditional crops such as cotton and rice, as well as new ones such as tomatoes and onions. At the moment they can buy aid-subsidised fertiliser and seeds to do this.

So successful has some of this irrigation work been that the villagers have even reversed the usual patterns of immigration. People are coming back to the villages, from the capital Bamako, or from other nearby countries such as Côte d'Ivoire and Niger, to share in the new sense of endeavour, if not actual prosperity. One man, reflecting the experience of many villagers of the Sahel, says that without the irrigation schemes "none of us would be here today."

The hope eventually is that Mali, using the waters of the Niger, will become the bread-basket of west Africa. It would also be nice to have better access to European and American markets. But for any of that to happen, Mali needs roads and transport. The country has excellent beef, for instance. But as one UN official says, "You can't have the cattle walk 2,000 km to market—they become skeletons." During the four-month rainy season, villages just 20 km or 30 km apart can become cut off from trading with each other. Thus donors such as the European Union and China are building roads and the Americans are re-developing the international airport.

Donors now contribute about a fifth of the government's budget. Foreigners are happy to help out because they are confident that the funds they provide will not be misused. The institutional framework for reducing poverty seems entrenched and irreversible, whatever happens to ATT. Mr. Diarra is confident that even Mali will reach the goal of halving poverty in the end. Not by 2015, but perhaps by 2025.

Goal-Hanging

Such incremental progress pleases, but does not satisfy, the custodians of the MDGs, such as Jeffrey Sachs, the UN's special adviser and a tireless advocate for the goals. They are reluctant to lower their sights, arguing that the goals are akin to human rights, solemn obligations that brook no compromise. By this reckoning, the developing world's needs can be counted, the cheapest fixes can be costed, and the resulting bill can be calculated. All that remains is for the rich world to pick up the tab, so that a poor country's health and education ministries can get the job done.

This MDG-think is seductive. It is a potent mix of inspiration (saving lives and educating minds is eminently doable) and accusation (why, then, is the rich world not doing it?). But this thinking is also misleading. However laudable, the goals wrongly invite people to think of development as akin to an "engineering problem," as Lant Pritchett, now of Harvard University, and Michael Woolcock of the World Bank have argued. The task is to pour money in one end of the MDG pipeline and then count the tubewells and school enrolments emerging from the other.

Some of the duties of government can indeed be left to the technocrats. Repealing tariffs or preserving the value of the currency are tasks best handled by "ten smart people," the two authors point out. Mr. Sachs was one such person, stopping Bolivia's hyperinflation in its tracks in 1985–86, the triumph that first made his name. In Africa, such monetary mayhem is now confined to Zimbabwe. Elsewhere, inflation has fallen from an average of 17 percent in 2000 to 7 percent last year.

Other tasks, such as laying a road or delivering a measles jab, rely on the efforts of many more people. But these legionaries need not exercise much judgment or discretion, and their output (a mile of road, a shot in the arm) can be easily counted. Thus immunisation drives and road-building campaigns lend themselves to routinised programmes that can be rolled out and "scaled up," often with the help of foreign funds. International efforts against measles have helped cut the disease's death toll in Africa from 506,000 in 1999 to 126,000 in 2005.

Most of the MDGs, however, do not play to these strengths. If a country is to educate every child and spare its infants and mothers an early death, it must enlist the efforts of thousands of teachers, nurses and midwives, all of whom must exercise care, diligence and judgment. That conscientiousness is not easy to buy or import, except in showcase communities such as Mr. Sachs's Millennium Villages, of which there are several very impressive examples in Mali. For these services, the link between spending and results is notoriously weak.

Ultimate success depends not so much on field-marshals like Mr. Sachs, but on footsoldiers like Rita Dana, an auxiliary nurse and midwife in the Bardhaman district of West Bengal, who patiently examines over 60 pregnant mothers in a day. They arrive from up to 3 km away, complaining of abdominal pain, vomiting or swollen feet—a possible sign of dangerously high blood pressure. Some of these workers show up even when floodwater is "up to the knee," says Mohammed Hossain, a consultant to UNICEF. But perhaps a quarter of the centres, he adds, will not be open when they should be.

The more qualified the doctor, the more likely he is to take flight. The district hospital in Matlab, Bangladesh, boasts an operating table, lamp, oxygen cylinder and anaesthetic machine, all carrying the EU's gift tag. They gleam, partly because they are unused. Several surgeons and anaesthetists have been trained, but none so far retained. "Other than holding a gun to their head, doctors do not stay here," comments Shams Arifeen, a researcher in the International Centre for Diarrhoeal Disease Research, Bangladesh (ICDDR,B). Doubling their pay is not the answer, because they can earn five or ten times as much in private practice. Besides, specialists want to educate their children in Dhaka, not in Bangladesh's backwaters.

One response is to turn the doctor's arts into a routine programme. Outside a hut not far from the hospital, a young woman examines a child suffering from pneumonia and diarrhoea, with blood in his stool. Her diagnosis is guided by a flow-chart that leaves little room for discretion. She is one of about 4,500 villagers who have been given 11 days' training under a scheme called Integrated Management of Childhood Illness (IMCI). The IMCI protocols are a great leveller: Bangladeshi social workers can adhere to them as faithfully as qualified Brazilian physicians, and reach similar medical conclusions.

Doctors and paramedics pose one set of problems, patients and clients another. The IMCI workers cannot count on everybody taking the advice they offer, for example. Farida Yesmin advises a young mother, expecting her fourth child, of the need to rest and avoid lifting heavy pots of water. The mother's neighbour, sticking her nose in through the window, offers a second opinion: work never did me any harm, she insists.

The Customer Is Not Always Right

Villagers think a labour of three or even four days is normal for a first-born, Ms. Yesmin says; a few will also blame headaches and convulsions on evil spirits. A study published by the ICDDR,B provides an alarming catalogue of such misconceptions. Pregnant women are sometimes told to eat less than normal because an empty stomach supposedly leaves room for the baby to grow. By tradition, midwives might kick the mother's waist or break snails over her head to speed up the delivery.

Superstition is not the only source of competition. Well-stocked quacks in the private sector are adept at giving people what they want—drugs, principally—if not always what they need. One government paramedic, his desk standing in the rainwater that leaks through the roof, confesses that he sometimes prescribes vitamin pills for the sake of it, because his patients do not expect to leave his clinic empty-handed.

Efforts to tackle the plight of the poor do not always win their favour. The needy make their own judgments about outside schemes to improve their lot. In 1980, for example, the UN proclaimed that the next ten years would be the "sanitation decade." In India the government set about improving sanitation in villages where people still defecated by rivers and under trees. The need was glaring: contaminated water was responsible for countless deaths from diarrhoea. The solution seemed obvious: a toilet with a brick cubicle, squatting slab and two pits. The government set its budget and began building.

Unfortunately, the villagers themselves had not signed up to the UN's proclamations. They preferred to defecate a prudent distance from the place where they ate and slept. Besides, a walk helped to clear the bowels. So the government's construction programme failed abjectly as a sanitation programme. As the only *pukka* concrete structure in many homes, the toilets were often used for storing grain, keeping hens or even displaying deities, says Chandi Dey of the Ramakrishna Mission, a charity based in Kolkata.

In the late 1980s, his mission and UNICEF realised they could not tackle the sanitation need until they first drummed up demand. Songs, slogans and slideshows spread the message. Public meetings pressed it home. Mr. Dey describes how they would put a drop of faecal matter into a glass of water. When people refused to drink from it, the mission would point out that they imbibed such water every day from ponds and rivers where some people defecated, even as others bathed their bodies and rinsed their mouths.

Non-governmental organisations, accustomed to the role of good Samaritans, had to learn the art of marketing. They offered people a commission for persuading their neighbours to buy a toilet. One paid 13 visits to a potential client before closing the deal. Proceeds from the sales helped meet the running costs of "rural sanitary marts," which employed poor people as toilet-masons making a range of affordable models (mosaic or ceramic bowls; bamboo or brick walls; single pits or twin pits). Now, says one mission-member, "It is not a programme, it is a movement."

The government soon latched on to this campaign, adding a small subsidy in 1993–94 and a presidential prize in 2003 for villages and districts that can show they are *nirmal* or unsullied. In West Bengal, where it began, more than two-thirds of rural households now have access to a toilet. But some districts still lag. M. N. Roy, a top civil servant, puts this down to the "low equilibrium" of poor expectations and apathetic politicians.

Parish-Pump Politics

The trick is to sharpen the elbows and strengthen the hands of poor people so that they demand what they need and get what they demand. For example, a recent report on the MDGs by the World Bank's Bangladesh office lavishes praise on the efforts of Gonoshasthaya Kendra (GK), a health charity, which began life as a battlefield clinic, treating the casualties of Bangladesh's war of independence. Born in battle, the group still sees a place for "creative tension" between the poor and the people who are supposed to serve them. Whenever someone dies in a village, it holds a public post-mortem. The aim is not to blame or indict *per se*—bare-knuckled confrontation would alienate the government—but to remind public servants that someone is watching them, and that the negligent will be named and shamed.

But is this brand of feisty local politics something donors can cultivate? Aid proposals are now replete with mentions of the word "community." Sceptics argue that donors will conjure up "communities" to fit their projects and their timetables, even if no such organic political unit exists. They also worry that ceding control to the grassroots may simply put aid in the hands of the local mafia.

Perhaps all donors can do is pray for a more productive politics to evolve, then support it when it does. Mali, for example, has gone further than any other African country in decentralising its government. In 1991 it had 18 local communes, now it has 702. In many communes the people now actually pay local taxes and can see the tangible results of the money that they hand over in a school or a health centre. Alexander Newton, the head of USAID in Mali, which helps train the new layer of local administrators in 155 of the communes, argues that "local management of money tends to be much better."

Likewise, in Bangladesh, households are often asked to pay something towards the filters that strip their water of arsenic. These charges are not mean-spirited. They aim instead to turn victims into proprietors. A financial contribution is proof of a household's commitment to a scheme, which helps to ensure a filter's upkeep. Halima paid 300 takas ($4.30) for her filter. Now she wouldn't part with it for 5,000.

Across the border in West Bengal, villages are going a step further. For each well or pump, they are convening a water committee. The committees collect dues to pay for regular water-quality tests by laboratories set up in the sanitary marts. Elsewhere, such committees have not always lasted; everyone would rather someone else paid to maintain their well. But without them, villages will remain forever dependent on outside professionals from the government, UNICEF and the like.

After 20 minutes, Mr. Johnston's arsenic reading is ready. The test paper has turned an ominous shade of ochre, suggesting arsenic up to four times the allowable limit. He is phlegmatic. The filter's granules have probably reached the end of their natural life. Once informed, the company can fix it within days, and it takes years of exposure at these concentrations to suffer much harm. But as schoolchildren busily fill their *kolshi* pitchers with contaminated water, the easy promises of seven years ago feel a long way from fulfilment.

Moving People Rather than Moving Jobs?

11.4 Should We Globalize Labor Too?

Jason DeParle

The final selection in this chapter describes the idea promoted by Lant Pritchett, an economist at Harvard's Kennedy School, to alleviate poverty by sending the poor to rich countries as guest workers, working at jobs largely shunned by citizens of those countries. Such programs, he argues, will relieve poverty more efficiently than providing assistance to the poor in their own countries. His idea, however, faces strong political opposition across the political spectrum in the West for reasons from fears about security to concerns about cultural cohesion.

he Arniko Highway climbs out of Kathmandu in long wending loops that
pay twin tribute to the impassability of Himalayan terrain and the implausi-
bility of its development. Outside Africa, no country is poorer than Nepal.
Its per capita income looks like a misprint: $270 a year. Sudan's is more than twice
as high. Nearly two-thirds of Nepalis lack electricity. Half the preschoolers are malnourished. To the list of recent woes add regicide—10 royals slaughtered in 2001 by
a suicidal prince—and a Maoist insurgency.

A few hours east of the city, a gravel road juts across a talc quarry, where the work
would be disturbing enough even if the workers were not under five feet tall. Scores
of young teenagers, barefoot and stunted, lug rocks from a lunar pit. The journey
continues through a district capital flying Communist flags and ends, 12 hours after
it began, above a forlorn canyon. Halfway down the cactus-lined slope, a destitute
farmer named Gure Sarki recently bought four goats.

The story of Gure Sarki's goats involves decades of thinking about foreign aid
and the type of program often seen as modern practice at its best. Two years ago, an
organizer appeared in the canyon to say that the Nepal government (with money
from the World Bank) was making local grants for projects of poor villagers' choosing. First villagers had to catalog their problems. With Sarki as chairman, Chaurmuni village made its list:

"Not able to eat for the whole year."

"Not able to send children to school."

"Lack of proper feed and fodder for the livestock."

"Landslide and flood."

"Not able to get the trust of the moneylender."

"Insecurity and danger."

A week later, they agreed to start a microcredit fund and expand their livestock
herds. Twenty villagers would buy a total of 55 goats at $50 apiece. The plan
specified who would serve on the goat-buying committee, the per diem the goat
buyers would get and the interest rates on the loans (just over 1 percent). Those
who were literate signed their names, while others inked fingerprints, and the
papers went off to Kathmandu, where officials approved a $3,700 grant. Within
two months of the first meeting, Sarki had his goats. They doubled the value of his
livestock holdings. He prizes them so much that he sleeps beside them inside his
house to protect them from leopards. He plans to sell them next year for a profit of
about $25 each.

Lant Pritchett says he has a better idea. Pritchett, a development economist and
practiced iconoclast, has just left the World Bank to teach at Harvard and to help
Google plan its philanthropic efforts on global poverty. In a recent trip through
Chaurmuni, he praised the goats as community-driven development at its best: a
fast, flexible way of delivering tangible aid to the poor. "But Nepal isn't going to
goat its way out of poverty," he said. Nor does he think that as a small, landlocked
country Nepal can soon prosper through trade.

DeParle, Jason, "Should We Globalize Labor Too?," *New York Times Magazine,* June 10, 2007, pp. 80–85.
© 2007, Jason DeParle. Reprinted by permission.

To those standard solutions, trade and aid, Pritchett would add a third: a big upset-the-applecart idea, equally offensive to the left and the right. He wants a giant guest-worker program that would put millions of the world's poorest people to work in its richest economies. Never mind the goats; if you really want to help Gure Sarki, he says, let him cut your lawn. Pritchett's nearly religious passion is reflected in the title of his migration manifesto: "Let Their People Come." It was published last year to little acclaim—none at all, in fact—but that is Pritchett's point. In a world in which rock stars fight for debt relief and students shun sweatshop apparel, he is vexed to find no placards raised for the cause of labor migration. If goods and money can travel, why can't workers follow? What's so special about borders?

When they are being polite, Pritchett's friends say he is, ahem, ahead of his time. Less politely, critics say that an army of guest workers would erode Western sovereignty, depress domestic wages, abet terrorism, drain developing countries of talent, separate poor parents from their kids and destroy the West's cultural cohesion. Pritchett has spent his career puncturing the panaceas of others. It says something about the intransigence of much of the world's poverty that he may be in the grip of his own. . . .

The same could be said of Ireland in the 1850s, Italy in the 1880s and Oklahoma in the 1930s. In each case, large populations suffered economic shocks and responded in the same way. They left. Following the potato blight, the Irish population fell by 53 percent, at least as much because of migration as the deaths caused by famine. That benefited the migrants, of course. But Pritchett notes that it also left Ireland with fewer people to support; gross domestic product per capita never fell.

Pritchett contrasts Zambia, whose economy peaked in 1964 on the strength of copper mines. When copper markets declined, Zambians had no place to go; the population nearly tripled and per capita G.D.P. fell more than 40 percent. Pritchett likens 19th-century Ireland to a ghost town and calls places like Zambia "zombies"—lands of the living dead. While some distressed regions can adapt and prosper, by far a preferential fix, Pritchett argues that hundreds of millions of people are stuck in places with little chance for development. For them, only "out-migration can prevent an extended and permanent fall in wages."

Nepal has not suffered a sudden shock (except for the civil war, which has paused with the Maoists sharing government power). But it is a small, landlocked country with little manufacturing, daunting terrain, low literacy and scant infrastructure. What it does have—its "comparative advantage"—is cheap workers, many of whom already go abroad. While most go to low-wage countries like India, they still send home about $1 billion a year. That accounts for 12 percent of Nepal's G.D.P. and is three times its spending on "public investment," which includes efforts like education, hunger relief and electrification. Despite the country's troubles, remittances have helped cut the poverty rate by 25 percent and would cut it further, Pritchett says, if more Nepalis could work in the West. . . .

The basics are simple: the rich world has lots of well-paying jobs and an aging population that cannot fill them. The poor world has desperate workers. But while goods and capital can easily cross borders, modern labor cannot. This strikes Pritchett as bad economics and worse social justice. He likens the limits on labor mobility to "apartheid on a global scale." Think Desmond Tutu with equations.

Pritchett sees five irresistible forces for migration, stymied by eight immovable ideas. The most potent migration force is the one epitomized by Nepal: vast inequality. In the late 19th century, rich countries had incomes about 10 times greater than the poorest ones. Today's ratio is about 50 to 1, Pritchett writes in "Let Their People Come." The poor simply have too much to gain from crossing borders not to try. What arrests them are the convictions of rich societies: that migration erodes domestic wages, courts cultural conflicts and is unnecessary for—perhaps antithetical to—foreign development. When irresistible force meets immovable object, something gives—in this case legality. Migration goes underground, endangering migrants and lessening their rewards.

The key to breaking the political deadlock, Pritchett says, is to ensure that the migrants go home, which is why he emphasizes temporary workers (though personally he would let them stay). About 7 percent of the rich world's jobs are held by people from developing countries. For starters, he would like to see the poor get another 3 percent, or 16 million guest-worker jobs—3 million in the U.S. They would stay three to five years, with no path to citizenship, and work in fields with certified labor shortages. He assumes that most receiving countries would not allow them to bring families. Taxpayers would be spared from educating the migrants' kids. Domestic workers would gain some protection through the certification process. And a revolving labor pool would reach more of the world's poor.

In effect, Pritchett is proposing a Saudi Arabian plan in which an affluent society creates a labor subcaste that is permanently excluded from its ranks. His does so knowing full well that his agenda coincides with that of unscrupulous employers looking to exploit cheap workers. Many migration advocates oppose a plan, now dividing Congress, to create a guest-worker force a 15th as large as the one Pritchett wants, saying it would create a new underclass. But Pritchett calls guest work the only way to accommodate large numbers. To insist that migrants have a right to citizenship and family unification, he says, is to let men like Gure Sarki go hungry. It is cruel to be kind. The choice is theirs. Let the poor decide. "Letting guest workers in America doesn't create an underclass," he says. "It moves an underclass and makes the underclass better off."

Part of Pritchett's argument is mathematical. Drawing on World Bank models, he estimates his plan would produce annual gains of about $300 billion—three times the benefit of removing the remaining barriers to trade. But the philosophical packaging gives his plan its edge. Pritchett assails a basic premise—that development means developing places. He is more concerned about helping Nepalis than he is about helping Nepal. If remittances spur development back home, great, but that is not his central concern. "Migration *is* development," he says.

Indeed, Pritchett attacks the primacy of nationality itself, treating it as an atavistic prejudice. Modern moral theory rejects discrimination based on other conditions of birth. If we do not bar people from jobs because they were born female, why bar them because they were born in Nepal? The name John Rawls appears on only a single page of "Let Their People Come," but Pritchett is taking Rawlsian philosophy to new lengths. If a just social order, as Rawls theorized, is one we would embrace behind a "veil of ignorance"—without knowing what traits we possess—a world that uses the trait of nationality to exclude the neediest workers from the richest job markets is deeply unjust. (Rawls himself thought his theory did not apply across national borders.) Pritchett's Harvard students rallied against all kinds of evils, he writes, but "I never heard the chants, 'Hey, ho, restrictions on labor mobility have to go.'"

Even friends fear he has not come to grips with the numbers. The West is nowhere close to accepting Pritchett's 16 million—and the developing world has a labor force of nearly 3 billion; what if most of them moved? "I think Lant overdoes it in estimating migration's potential," said Nancy Birdsall, president of the Center for Global Development in Washington, which commissioned and published the book. "Do you think the U.S. would accept 300 million of the world's poorest people?" Birdsall praises Pritchett's work as a concentration starter but adds, "People think about development as being about place not person—they're more right about this than Lant believes." . . .

With more access to global labor markets, Pritchett predicts some poor countries will develop quickly while others, like Zambia, will depopulate into giant ghost towns as the world grows comfortable with higher levels of permanent migration. Eventually—over a century, say—the combination of population adjustments and policy innovation will raise the living standards of most poor countries to that of the West without pulling the West down, just as the rise of the Japanese has not meant the fall of Americans. The labor forces of the West are shrinking, which, he says, should keep wages high despite increased migration. Whether or not his forecasts are correct—the track record of his field is not reassuring—he has pondered the economics.

But the greatest risk posed by the Pritchett plan is cultural conflict, or even conflagration, which Pritchett greets with a shrug. "I don't think about it a lot because I'm an economist," he says. "If you say your culture can't survive an influx of migrants, you have a pretty dim view of your culture." Cultures change all the time, he figures, and change is not to be feared. A century hence, nations will still exist, but in a more ecumenical way. Germans will accept Turkish mosques, and Turkey will accept Christian spires, and everyone will be free to come and go as long as they obey the law. Here he sounds less like Adam Smith than Rodney King: "Can't we all just get along?"

So far, in the U.S., at least, the answer has been yes: acculturation has triumphed in every generation, despite the doubters. But Pritchett envisions cultural blending on an unprecedented scale, across societies much less skillful at it. Israel and Palestine, Hutu and Tutsi, Bosnian and Serb—the world is not exactly galloping away from the ethnic and nationalist identities that he finds anachronistic. With an Ellis Island heart in a sleeper-cell age, Pritchett is reluctant to consider the possibility that the interests of the West and its would-be migrants could diverge. "If you say you believe in open borders, you sound like a lunatic—I'm aware of that," he says. "I'm saying let's start slow and let what's already happening happen in a managed way. A hundred years is a long time. We can work it out."

Suggested Discussion Topics

1. Why should citizens in wealthy countries be concerned about the fate of the poor living elsewhere? In what ways do poverty and underdevelopment pose problems for the global community? Do you think we should regard poverty and underdevelopment as security issues? Why or why not?

2. One way to reduce global poverty would be to allow poor people to move to wherever the jobs are, regardless of national borders. How do you feel about this idea? Why? Be prepared to argue either side of this question: that the United States, for example, should allow open immigration, or that countries should strictly limit immigration.

3. If people cannot move freely to jobs, then employers are likely to move jobs to wherever labor is most readily and most cheaply available, if they are able to do so. Is this a good thing? Again, be prepared to argue either side in a debate.

4. In recent decades, economic development has rocketed ahead in East Asia and, at best, inched forward in sub-Saharan Africa. Why has development proceeded unevenly around the globe? What are the dangers of continued uneven development? Do you think economic development will become more or less uneven during your lifetime? Explain your reasoning.

5. Who should play the lead role in promoting economic development: states, nongovernmental organizations, or private corporations? What does your answer imply about the strategies for development that will be pursued? What does it imply about which institutions will be powerful in everyday life?

6. What, in your view, are the most important reasons that aid has not ended global poverty or narrowed the gap between rich and poor nations? Drawing on all of the readings in this chapter, outline your own plan for making development aid more effective.

7. Do the UN's Millennium Goals make sense? Why will they prove so difficult to achieve?

Chapter 12

Environmental Issues and the Global Commons

Perhaps no contemporary issues more clearly reflect the new security agenda, present a greater challenge to the global system, and demand greater cooperation among societies and political actors around the world than do environmental issues. Among the most perilous of environmental trends are depletion of the ozone layer, deforestation and desertification, loss of biodiversity, and global warming. Collectively, they are as much a threat to human security and survival as are weapons of mass destruction. They represent challenges that have no respect for national sovereignty or national frontiers and that are beyond the ability of any single state, however powerful, to overcome. Thus, when it comes to the global environment, human beings, regardless of nationality, have linked fates, and our continued existence as a species rests upon our ability to cooperate in confronting and overcoming environmental degradation.

To the extent that people compete for scarce resources, environmental issues promote political fragmentation and conflict. The solution to environmental problems, however, demands greater global collaboration and the creation of integrative political institutions that facilitate this collaboration.

Although humankind has faced environmental challenges before, population growth and rapid modernization have placed unprecedented stress on the world in which we live. Two problems are clear. First, more people—all of whom are demanding a higher standard of living—means greater competition for increasingly scarce natural resources such as water, energy, land, and food. Human efforts to provide sustenance, clothing, shelter, and all the comforts and luxuries that make life pleasant have had a dramatic impact on the world's ecosystems. In an attempt to turn the environment to productive use, humans have cleared land of native plant and animal species, dammed rivers for energy or water supplies, pumped water from underground aquifers, and hunted and fished certain species to the brink of extinction or beyond.

Two centuries ago, Thomas Malthus (1766–1834) predicted that population growth would outstrip food supply, causing massive famine. That the catastrophe he predicted did not occur owes much to the ability of science to increase food production. But even with improved technology, the population explosion of the last two centuries has taxed the capacity of the environment, as humans in some places have exploited renewable resources (such as fresh water, fish, and forests) past their "carrying capacity," have used other natural resources in ways that have led to their degradation (for example, farming processes that have led to soil erosion and loss of fertile topsoil), and have begun to damage highly fragile ecosystems (such as rain forests or arctic regions). In the absence of more suitable land, for example, large tracts of the Amazon jungle have been cleared for cattle ranching. This exploitation of the rain forest, however, has yielded little by way of long-term food production—the land quickly becomes compacted and nutrients leach away, leaving it unsuitable for agriculture—but has resulted in the extinction of innumerable species and created local environmental wounds that will take centuries or longer to heal. Although rates of population growth have begun to ease in recent decades, the world's population continues to explode, and many observers doubt that the world and its delicate ecology can sustain human population growth indefinitely.

Second, population growth and demands for higher standards of living in the developing world are also straining the environment's capacity to cope with the waste products human societies generate. More people, all making and using more things, translates into more air, water, and soil pollution. On the local level, this has meant cities in which the air is dangerous to breathe and land and groundwater that are contaminated with toxic chemicals. Regionally, it has meant phenomena such as acid rain (caused by sulfur emissions from the burning of carbon fuels) that has devastated flora and fauna. And globally, the byproducts of human agriculture and industry threaten to result in massive climate change, as depletion of the ozone layer allows more of the sun's ultraviolet radiation to reach the Earth and as greenhouse gases like carbon dioxide build up and produce a global warming that could melt polar icecaps, raise ocean levels, swamp island countries, and inundate coastal areas around the world.

This double-barreled environmental problem—increasing pollution and shortages of resources—is growing and is inextricably tied to the development problems discussed in the previous chapter. The United Nations projects that world population will increase from 5.7 billion in 1992 to 12.5 billion in the middle of the next century. In the last half century, the world's population has doubled and its economy has increased fivefold. In a world of global markets, shortages of food and water cease to be a matter of purely local or national concern, and the destruction of environmental capital, through overuse or by contamination with waste products, reduces the world's long-term carrying capacity for everyone.

The need for cooperative action is obvious. Concerns about the consequences of unfettered growth provided the impetus for the 1992 UN-sponsored Conference on Environment and Development (Earth Summit) in Rio de Janeiro and the 1994 UN-sponsored Conference on Population and Development in Cairo. Many of the most difficult environmental problems facing the world today transcend national borders, and solving them requires international cooperation or transnational action. Two examples illustrate this. Sulfur dioxide released by power plants in the United States precipitates out of the air as sulfuric acid, or acid rain, killing trees and increasing the acidity of lakes and streams hundreds of miles downwind: across the border in Canada. Determining whether American consumers should pay more for their electricity, or how much more they should pay, in order to save Canadian forests and fisheries is a matter for international, rather than national, negotiation. Global warming caused by the increased release of greenhouse gases from the burning of carbon fuels and the clearing of forests offers a second example. Although environments all around the world are likely to be affected, the most dramatic human suffering may well be caused by increased drought in sub-Saharan Africa, the disappearance of low-lying Pacific islands, and the inundation of highly populated coastal regions in East Asia. The principal contributors to global warming, however, have not been the nations of these areas, but the industrialized nations of Europe and North America and the nations presently clearing tropical rain forests. In general, reaching agreement on who should pay the costs, or who should forego the benefits, of exploiting natural resources will be highly contentious.

12.1 The Tragedy of the Commons

Garrett Hardin

Over thirty years ago, biologist Garrett Hardin outlined what he described as "the tragedy of the commons." Hardin noted that resources that are owned "in common," like the world's atmosphere and its oceans, tend to be overused, even to the point of environmental collapse. Although no one wants this outcome, in the absence of "ownership" that would make it rational for individuals to take responsible care of common resources, it is rational for each user to exploit them. Understanding this tragedy of the commons, and the need for some sort of international agreement or regulation—mutual coercion, Hardin would say—to prevent it, is the starting place for any discussion of today's environmental dangers.

The tragedy of the commons develops in this way. Picture a pasture open to all. It is to be expected that each herdsman will try to keep as many cattle as possible on the commons. Such an arrangement may work reasonably satisfactorily for centuries because tribal wars, poaching, and disease keep the numbers of both man and beast well below the carrying capacity of the land. Finally, however, comes the day of reckoning, that is, the day when the long-desired goal of social stability becomes a reality. At this point, the inherent logic of the commons remorselessly generates tragedy.

As a rational being, each herdsman seeks to maximize his gain. Explicitly or implicitly, more or less consciously, he asks, "What is the utility *to me* of adding one more animal to my herd?" This utility has one negative and one positive component.

1) The positive component is a function of the increment of one animal. Since the herdsman receives all the proceeds from the sale of the additional animal, the positive utility is nearly +1.

2) The negative component is a function of the additional overgrazing created by one more animal. Since, however, the effects of overgrazing are shared by all the

Hardin, Garrett, "The Tragedy of the Commons," *Science,* December 13, 1968, pp. 1243–1248. Reprinted with permission from American Association for the Advancement of Science.

herdsmen, the negative utility for any particular decision-making herdsman is only a fraction of –1.

Adding together the component partial utilities, the rational herdsman concludes that the only sensible course for him to pursue is to add another animal to his herd. And another; and another. . . . But this is the conclusion reached by each and every rational herdsman sharing a commons. Therein is the tragedy. Each man is locked into a system that compels him to increase his herd without limit—in a world that is limited. Ruin is the destination toward which all men rush, each pursing his own best interest in a society that believes in the freedom of the commons. Freedom in a commons brings ruin to all. . . .

Pollution

In a reverse way, the tragedy of the commons reappears in problems of pollution. Here it is not a question of taking something out of the commons, but of putting something in—sewage, or chemical, radioactive, and heat wastes into water; noxious and dangerous fumes into the air; and distracting and unpleasant advertising signs into the line of sight. The calculations of utility are much the same as before. The rational man finds that his share of the cost of the wastes he discharges into the commons is less than the cost of purifying his wastes before releasing them. Since this is true for everyone, we are locked into a system of "fouling our own nest," so long as we behave only as independent, rational, free-enterprisers.

The tragedy of the commons as a food basket is averted by private property, or something formally like it. But the air and waters surrounding us cannot readily be fenced, and so the tragedy of the commons as a cesspool must be prevented by different means, by coercive laws or taxing devices that make it cheaper for the polluter to treat his pollutants than to discharge them untreated. We have not progressed as far with the solution of this problem as we have with the first. Indeed, our particular concept of private property, which deters us from exhausting the positive resources of the earth, favors pollution. The owner of a factory on the bank of a stream—whose property extends to the middle of the stream—often has difficulty seeing why it is not his natural right to muddy the waters flowing past his door. The law, always behind the times, requires elaborate stitching and fitting to adapt it to this newly perceived aspect of the commons.

The pollution problem is a consequence of population. It did not much matter how a lonely American frontiersman disposed of his waste. "Flowing water purifies itself every 10 miles," my grandfather used to say, and the myth was near enough to the truth when he was a boy, for there were not too many people. But as population became denser, the natural chemical and biological recycling processes became overloaded, calling for a redefinition of property rights. . . .

Mutual Coercion Mutually Agreed Upon

The social arrangements that produce responsibility are arrangements that create coercion, of some sort. . . .

. . . Taxing is a good coercive device. To keep downtown shoppers temperate in their use of parking space we introduce parking meters for short periods, and traffic fines for longer ones. We need not actually forbid a citizen to park as long as he wants to; we need merely make it increasingly expensive for him to do so. Not prohibition, but carefully biased options are what we offer him. . . .

Coercion is a dirty word to liberals now, but it need not forever be so. As with the four-letter words, its dirtiness can be cleansed away by exposure to the light, by saying it over and over without apology or embarrassment. To many, the word *coercion* implies arbitrary decisions of distant and irresponsible bureaucrats; but this is not a necessary part of its meaning. The only kind of coercion I recommend is mutual coercion, mutually agreed upon by the majority of the people affected.

To say that we mutually agree to coercion is not to say that we are required to enjoy it, or even to pretend we enjoy it. Who enjoys taxes? We all grumble about them. But we accept compulsory taxes because we recognize that voluntary taxes would favor the conscienceless. We institute and (grumblingly) support taxes and other coercive devices to escape the horror of the commons. . . .

Recognition of Necessity

Perhaps the simplest summary of this analysis of man's population problems is this: the commons, if justifiable at all, is justifiable only under conditions of low-population density. As the human population has increased, the commons has had to be abandoned in one aspect after another.

First we abandoned the commons in food gathering, enclosing farm land and restricting pastures and hunting and fishing areas. These restrictions are still not complete throughout the world.

Somewhat later we saw that the commons as a place for waste disposal would also have to be abandoned. Restrictions on the disposal of domestic sewage are widely accepted in the Western world; we are still struggling to close the commons to pollution by automobiles, factories, insecticide sprayers, fertilizing operations, and atomic energy installations. . . .

Every new enclosure of the commons involves the infringement of somebody's personal liberty. Infringements made in the distant past are accepted because no contemporary complains of a loss. It is the newly proposed infringements that we vigorously oppose: cries of "rights" and "freedom" fill the air. But what does "freedom" mean? When men mutually agreed to pass laws against robbing, mankind became more free, not less so. Individuals locked into the logic of the commons are free only to bring on universal ruin: once they see the necessity of mutual coercion, they become free to pursue other goals. I believe it was Hegel who said, "Freedom is the recognition of necessity."

The Problem of Collective Action

12.2 Global Problems and Local Concerns

The World Bank

Our next selection uses the critical issues of the diminishing ozone layer and global warming to illustrate the problem of achieving collective action in a world divided among sovereign nation-states. The first of these provides something of a model of adaptive change and cooperation through a process of learning, building a capacity for action, and compromising between domestic and international interests. As this analysis by the World Bank observes, however, the problem of warming has been less amenable to collective action than the ozone issue. Despite some progress, the institutions needed to coerce individual states into modifying their behavior for the benefit of humanity as a whole are still being developed.

Social and environmental problems often spill over national boundaries. . . . However, there is one big difference: at the global level, there is no central authority to enforce agreements. Nations have to devise ways to keep themselves on agreed paths. . . .

Designing Institutions to Solve Global Problems

Who would have thought that leaky refrigerators, fire extinguishers, and aerosol spray cans could seriously damage the entire biosphere? The story of how stratospheric ozone depletion was diagnosed as a problem, and how the global community organized to address it, illustrates how *adaptive, learning institutions* can successfully address global issues.

Refrigerators began using chlorofluorocarbons (CFCs) around 1930. By 1970 the world used about 1 million tons of these substances each year as coolants, as propellants in aerosol cans, and for manufacturing. In that year, James Lovelock used recently invented techniques to detect trace amounts of CFC in the atmosphere over London. His request for a grant to measure CFC concentrations over the Atlantic was denied: "One reviewer commented that even if the measurement succeeded, he could not imagine a more useless bit of knowledge."

Lovelock persisted, though, and showed that CFCs were detectable far from land. Four years later, chemists F. Sherwood Rowland and Mario Molina realized that even tiny concentrations of CFCs could, theoretically, erode the stratospheric

"Global Problems and Local Concerns" from *World Development Report 2003: Sustainable Development in a Dynamic World,* pp. 157–182. Reprinted by permission of the International Bank for Reconstruction and Development/The World Bank.

ozone layer that shields life from ultraviolet radiation, an insight that won them the 1995 Nobel Prize in chemistry. It was known, too, that CFCs had a long life-time in the atmosphere and that increased exposure to ultraviolet radiation would increase the risk of skin cancer. Although a definitive cause-and-effect relationship had not yet been demonstrated, circumstantial evidence was strong enough in the early 1980s to support a precautionary approach to the threat of ozone depletion. The Vienna Convention (1985) committed the nations of the world to addressing the problem, but imposed no obligations.

Meanwhile, scientists had been monitoring stratospheric ozone since the 1920s in a widening global network that extended to Antarctica in 1957. A scientist at the British Antarctic Station, noticing declining ozone readings in the late 1970s, published definitive data by 1984. Shortly thereafter, dramatic satellite images of the Antarctic ozone "hole" captured public attention. This deepening evidence prompted the Montreal Protocol of 1987, an out-growth of the Vienna Convention, to impose obligations on developed countries to reduce the use of ozone-depleting substances. The Montreal Protocol also set up panels to assess the impacts of ozone depletion and the technology and economics of mitigating ozone-depleting substances.

By 1990 there was firmer evidence of a causal impact of chlorine and bromine compounds on ozone. In that year the London Protocol to the Vienna Convention took effect. Under this protocol, developing countries agreed to take on obliga-tions, with a grace period, and developed countries underwrote a trust fund to assist them.

The process remains dynamic. Two more amendments to the Vienna Conven-tion have been adopted. Technical panels, involving multistakeholder cooperation, have helped identify technological approaches to phasing out ozone-depleting substances. More than $1.3 billion have been committed to help developing coun-tries. The result: a foreseeable reduction in atmospheric concentrations of ozone-depleting substances and an eventual recovery of the ozone layer.

The problem of protecting the global ozone layer was, for a variety of reasons, easier to tackle than other global problems. The production and use of ozone-depleting substances is not central to any economy—unlike greenhouse gases, whose production is deeply embedded in the energy and transport sectors. It has been easy to find less harmful substitutes for most substances, at modest cost. The political economy of reaching agreement has also been favorable. At the national level, the wealthy industrial nations responsible for most production were also those at the greatest risk from skin cancer, in part because ozone depletion is far more severe at temperate than tropical latitudes. And the corporations that pro-duced most ozone-depleting substances also produced most substitutes.

The record of success in tackling this problem provides both hope and inspira-tion for other global initiatives. It also shows the key components in global problem-solving:

♦ Pick up signals of the problem and agree on its nature.

♦ Build local capacity and international networks to support adaptive learning.

♦ Reconcile domestic and international interests.

These components are explored in detail below, together with an emerging fourth:

◆ Harness decentralized mechanisms to establish incentives for socially responsible actions.

Pick up Signals of the Problem and Agree on Its Nature   Solving problems requires some consensus on the facts and on the costs and impacts of action (or inaction). The first step is to detect the problem and put it on the public agenda. . . . But detection is not enough. Especially where dispersed interests need to be mobilized, activists (sometimes including scientists) can put a problem on the public agenda. . . .

The next step is achieving some consensus on the problem's gravity, threats, and potential solutions. At the outset, activists use data to demand action, and defenders of the status quo attack the data and interpretation as inaccurate, incomplete, and biased. Progress in resolving the issue requires better information and some consensus on the diagnosis. This is not always easy. To understand such problems as acid rain and global warming, we need to understand how thousands of factories and millions of households behave—and how chemicals mix and react across the entire atmosphere. These processes can be understood only through sophisticated simulation models, and the models can be validated only against rich and accurate observations of physical, biological, and social systems. There is scope for honest disagreement on interpreting data and models. And naturally, each stakeholder group will promote interpretations favorable to its own interests. What is needed is a credible, legitimate forum for fostering consensus on diagnosis and action.

Combining credibility and legitimacy in a policy institution is a fine balancing act, especially for global issues. . . . How can this be done?

The IPCC [Intergovermental Panel on Climate Change] is one example. The IPCC was chartered by the World Meteorological Organization and the United Nations Environment Programme (UNEP) to assess the risk of human-induced climate change. It has produced three large assessments, carried out by an international team of volunteer experts, who evaluate and synthesize the vast and sometimes contradictory scientific literature through an elaborate set of working groups, subgroups, and reviews. Because the reports are thick, densely technical documents, attention focuses on distilling summaries for policymakers. Each summary is approved, line by line, by representatives of all IPCC member governments in a forum where scientists can defend their conclusions. The process results in political buy-in to scientific findings. Over the past 10 years, the IPCC's work has contributed greatly to promoting consensus on the nature and causes of climate change. . . .

Learning and Adapting   The diagnostic process is most effective when it feeds into an adaptive process of balancing interests, setting goals, taking actions, and learning from results. The Convention on Long-Range Transboundary Air Pollution (CLRTAP) illustrates adaptive learning. This Convention has forged increasingly ambitious agreements among European nations (including economies in transition) on reducing emissions that cause acid rain, eutrophication, ground-level ozone, and other environmental problems. It has done so in part by encouraging the collection, harmonization, and analysis of data on emissions and environmental conditions. This process has fostered communication among policymakers and scientists, facilitated agreement on an operational definition of goals, and promoted a rational, cost-effective approach to achieving those goals.

The CLRTAP and the Montreal Protocol illustrate the appeal of adaptive learning in forging international agreements. Countries are averse to taking on binding commitments when there is great uncertainty about the costs or impacts, about their ability to induce citizens to comply, and about the compliance of other parties. Adaptive learning allows countries—and groups whose behavior is targeted for change—to understand the problem and to acquire confidence in their own ability and others' to deal with it.

Two routes are available:

♦ One route is through "soft law": nonbinding statements of principles and sometimes targets. By gradually establishing norms, soft law lays the foundation for negotiation on binding arrangements. Nonbinding but ambitious targets can also encourage experimentation that would be too risky under a binding regime.

♦ The other route is to start with a binding agreement that is easy to achieve, but that sets up a process that allows parties to learn more about costs and benefits and to build confidence in their partners' behavior and in newly created institutions.

For both routes, the seemingly mundane requirement of reporting can be key. Reporting—for greenhouse gas emissions under the Kyoto Protocol, for consumption of ozone-depleting substances under the Montreal Protocol, or for compliance with labor standards under the International Labour Organisation—deepens domestic understanding of the problem and strengthens external confidence in the country's commitment to compliance.

Build Local Capacity for Assessment, Negotiation, and Action   How can a hundred or more governments, representing billions of people, forge sustainable agreements that touch those people's lives? These agreements need to balance the diverse interests of groups that cut across national boundaries. International labor standards affect the workers, owners, and customers of low-wage assembly plants. The Montreal Protocol touches multinational and local chemical companies, people who risk developing skin cancer, and poor families that dream of affording a small used refrigerator. Negotiations on climate change affect coal miners, oil companies, Sahelian herders, atoll dwellers, car owners, and wind turbine entrepreneurs.

To work, these agreements must reconcile interests within and between countries. This requires mobilizing concern, and demands for action, among the many who would gain some benefit from the agreement, but who are less vocal than the few who perceive their main interests to be at risk. It thus requires creative ways of framing problems and solutions to increase the perceived congruence of interests, within and across countries. And it often depends on strengthening the capabilities of people and organizations in the developing world to assess options, to negotiate provisions, and to finance and undertake actions. . . .

Reconcile Domestic and International Interests—with Commitments and Cash
International agreements are possible because of the overlap between domestic and global interests—and because participating nations agree that the benefits they gain outweigh the costs that they accept. But environmental and social agreements usually involve balancing opposing domestic interests, often supporting a broad constituency of dispersed interests against one that is more narrowly focused but influential. And national compliance is not usually achieved with the simple stroke of an executive pen, requiring instead the cooperation of a multitude of citizens, government officials, corporate leaders, and others. Think, for instance, of the issues surrounding worker rights, pollution, and protection of privately owned wetlands or forests. A nation that agrees to international commitments on these issues has to deploy domestic carrots and sticks to coax its citizens into compliance. However, international agreements themselves can help provide some of those carrots and sticks. . . .

Financial transfers are often designed to align local actions with global interests. Many international agreements recognize that developing countries may be unable to finance their commitments to improve the global environment, even when those commitments provide some domestic benefits. The GEF [Global Environment Fund] has approved about $2.7 billion in grants to reduce ozone-depleting substances, mitigate climate change, protect biodiversity, and protect international waters. Depending on how the Kyoto Protocol is implemented, developing countries and economies in transition could get billions of dollars annually in market payments that would promote clean energy technologies.

Standards, Certification, and Performance Reporting—Inducing Socially Responsible Behavior   How can society reward people, firms, organizations, and governments that behave well? Locally, a community might patronize merchants who are friendly, civic-minded, and environmentally responsible—and do so happily even if their prices are a bit higher than those of less respectable competitors. Outside the community, the scope for doing this diminishes, as information about reputation thins. . . . An emerging set of institutions and networks tries to fill this gap by generating information about performance, using that information to set up incentives for socially responsible behavior. . . .

Various initiatives are beginning to publicize information about environmental and social performance—and there is some evidence of firms responding. Indonesia's government-led PROPER program, which instituted audited self-reporting of firms' pollution levels, has now been emulated in China, India, the Philippines, and Vietnam. . . . Nongovernmental evaluation and certification systems are developing quickly. . . .

There has been rapid growth in mutual funds and other investment vehicles that screen investments on social and environmental performance. In 1984, $40 billion in professionally managed assets were socially screened; in 2001, $2 trillion, of

$19 trillion in professionally managed assets. The growing demand for socially responsible investment and the growing supply of environmental and social performance indicators can interact in a virtuous circle. Better information enables more discerning investment; greater interest in ethical investment elicits better information. Similarly, as certification starts to become the norm in an industry, non-certified products find it harder to compete.

Who sets the standards and defines the indicators—and how? This is crucial to the future of such "bottom-up" approaches to regulation. Already there are disputes about how strictly to set standards for certification. Overly lax standards could defeat the purpose of certification. But so too could overly strict standards, if they are too expensive for firms to adopt and for outsiders to monitor. . . . This tradeoff is of crucial interest in trade negotiations, especially where developing countries fear that onerous standards would freeze them out of export markets. . . .

Mitigating and Adapting to Risks of Climate Change

People are changing the planet's climate. Burning fossil fuels—and to a lesser but important extent, deforestation and other land use practices—releases CO_2 and other greenhouse gases (GHGs). Accumulating more rapidly in the atmosphere than can be removed by natural sinks, these gases trap heat, changing climate in complex ways, with widespread impacts. This is quintessentially a global problem because GHGs mix rapidly in the atmosphere and have the same impact on climate change regardless of where they are emitted. And it is a long-term problem because the great inertia in social, economic, and physical systems means that it would take decades to moderate the rate of change substantially.

Because of its characteristics, climate change has been a particularly difficult problem to solve. It has been difficult for society to pick up signals—to understand the causes, magnitude, and consequences of climate change. . . .

Dispersion of interests in mitigating climate change has been a barrier to achieving agreement on actions. Many of the people most vulnerable to climate change are poor, live in remote regions—or have not even been born. Even the vulnerable wealthy—owners of oceanfront property, for instance—may not yet rank climate change among their greatest current concerns. The voice of these numerous but diffuse interests is weaker than that of industries and consumers, especially wealthy ones, that are heavily reliant on fossil fuels and would bear the burden of control costs. Finally, climate change is an extreme example of the commitment problem. . . . Mitigation of climate change will require a concerted, decades-long effort.

With these barriers in mind this section starts by reviewing the consequences and sources of climate change. Using this information, it assesses institutional aspects of undertaking the long-run mitigation of climate change. Then, it examines issues related to adapting to the climate change that past actions have already made inevitable—and that lack of progress in mitigation will exacerbate.

Consequences and Causes of Climate Change   Climate change is already here. Over the past century, mean global surface temperature has increased by 0.4° to

0.8° Celsius (C). According to the IPCC, GHGs released by human action are likely to have been responsible for most of the warming of the past 50 years. Other observed changes are consistent with this warming. Sea levels rose 10 to 20 centimeters over the past century. Over the past 50 years, the summer extent of arctic sea-ice has shrunk by 10 percent or more, and its thickness by 40 percent. Outside the polar regions, glaciers are retreating, affecting mountain ecosystems and water flows. Droughts have become more frequent and intense in Asia and Africa. Many of the world's coral reefs have been damaged by bleaching, associated with higher sea temperatures. Animals and plants have shifted their geographic ranges and behavior. Extreme weather events may have increased.

Unchecked, these impacts are predicted to intensify, posing risks of varying kinds for different countries. Impacts will fall heavily on many developing countries, including those that have not contributed to climate change. They are physically vulnerable. Climate-sensitive agriculture bulks large in their economies. And they have less institutional capacity to adapt to change.

Low-lying islands and coastal areas everywhere will be exposed to flooding and storm damage. Bangladesh, for instance, may be severely hit. A recent study predicts that by 2030 an additional 14 percent of the country would become extremely vulnerable to floods caused by increased rainfall. A 10-centimeter increase in sea level would permanently inundate 2 percent of the country, with the additional effect of making floods more severe and longer lasting. Saltwater intrusions, and more severe dry seasons, will reduce fresh water availability in coastal areas. As coastal populations swell worldwide, a 40-centimeter rise in the sea level would increase the number of coastal dwellers at risk of annual flooding by 75 to 206 million—90 percent of them in Africa and Asia. The starkest local impacts are faced by the low islands of the Pacific, some of which could lose their freshwater and be largely inundated during storm surges if sea levels rise.

Climate change could damage developing-country agriculture. Even taking into account crop substitution possibilities, one study finds that a 2°C temperature increase decreases the value of Indian agricultural land by 36 percent. Arid and semi-arid areas in Africa and Asia will probably face higher temperatures. Feedback between vegetation loss and reduced rainfall could result in faster desertification.

Impacts on industrial countries are thought to be mixed, but may be generally negative. Agricultural productivity will likely improve, in the medium term, in some northern areas. But southern Europe will likely suffer drier summers; much of Europe could experience river flooding. The Atlantic coast of the United States will be vulnerable to rising sea levels, and Australia will likely be more subject to drought.

Current understanding also depicts the global climate as a finely balanced mechanism that goes awry when stressed, with prehistoric instances of 10°C global temperature changes occurring within the span of a decade. There is a risk of catastrophic consequences of climate change that could be irreversibly set in motion during this century. There could, for instance, be an abrupt failure of the great ocean "conveyor belt" currents that warm the North Atlantic and mix deep with surface waters. Biodiversity losses could be massive as habitat fragmentation makes it impossible for plants and animals to migrate in response to rapidly changing temperatures. The risks are difficult to evaluate, but they affect industrial as well as developing countries and are credible enough to demand attention. At the very least they put a premium, or option value, on maintaining lower levels of atmospheric GHGs while the world more carefully examines the consequences and develops options for mitigation.

What drives climate change? GHGs have built up in the atmosphere as a consequence of 250 years of emissions from burning fossil fuel, deforestation, and other sources. Currently, about 40 percent of the human-induced heating effect is from increased atmospheric concentrations of methane (from landfills, rice paddies, and cows), nitrous oxide (from industry and agriculture), and halocarbons such as CFCs. The remaining 60 percent is CO_2. Of the approximately 28.2 billion tons of annual CO_2 emissions, 23.1 billion are from energy and other industrial sources. This component is closely linked to income, across countries, though there is considerable variation in emissions per dollar of GDP and emissions per capita among the wealthier countries. The remaining 5.1 billion tons come from tropical deforestation. . . .

Mitigating Climate Change   Concerned about climatic risks, most of the world's nations agreed in 1992 to the UNFCCC [UN Framework Commission on Climate Change]. The convention's objective is defined as the "stabilization of greenhouse gas concentrations in the atmosphere at a level that would prevent dangerous anthropogenic interference with the climate system." But the Convention itself did not quantify this level or specify how to achieve it.

As a first step the Kyoto Protocol to the UNFCCC was negotiated in 1997. This agreement would require industrial nations and economies in transition—the Annex B countries—to accept specified limits on emissions of GHGs for 2008–2012. The Protocol would decrease compliance costs by allowing Annex B countries to trade their emissions allowances. It would also allow these countries to purchase emissions reductions from developing countries, the reductions being reckoned against assumed "business as usual" levels, since the developing countries' emissions were not capped. The subsequent Marrakech Accords of 2001 allowed for developing countries to generate emissions reductions from forestry projects in only a limited way. . . .

It is important to recognize that the Protocol's commitments for 2008–2012, even if observed by all major emitters, would be only a first step toward the UNFCCC goal. . . .

If the world is to stabilize atmospheric concentrations and provide good living standards to all its citizens, it must switch in the long run to energy technologies (such as wind, solar power, and hydrogen, among others) that emit near-zero net amounts of CO_2. Simple arithmetic shows why. The world's population is now expected to stabilize at about 9 billion around mid-century. Suppose that people then aspire to the current lifestyle of a prosperous country. Among the prosperous countries, Norway has one of the lowest ratios of CO_2 emissions per capita from energy, owing in part to ample use of hydropower. Yet if the global population of 2050 emitted CO_2 on average at this rate, the total would be about 2.5 times current global emissions, which would greatly exceed the planetary absorptive capacity.

Between now and the time the world switches entirely to near-zero-emissions technologies, GHGs will accumulate in the atmosphere. The amount of damage, and the risk of catastrophic changes, will be related to the cumulative amount. To reduce the damage, the world needs to accelerate the shift to lower-emissions energy technologies, increase the efficiency of energy use, and reduce the emissions of GHGs.

Although these actions provide some immediate side benefits in addition to their cumulative effect on reducing climate damages, they involve costs. Because emissions reductions represent a global public good, burden sharing is inevitably contentious. To facilitate global coordination in this effort, a strategy has to reduce the overall cost of mitigating emissions and seek to align local and global interests as far as possible. It also has to avoid free-rider problems. This requires further institutional innovation at both national and global levels. . . .

Conclusion

The distinctive feature of global problems is the lack of a central authority for coordination and enforcement. Despite this obstacle, there are encouraging examples of successful transnational institution building to tackle transborder environmental problems. Success has been greatest in cases such as stratospheric ozone and acid rain, where the problem can be made operational in precise technical terms; where international action can therefore focus on tightly defined interventions; and where the perceived benefits of collective action have been high, for key actors, relative to the cost. It will be more difficult for other environmental and social problems—where the relationship between action and impact is less well understood, and where the costs and benefits of action do not coincide.

Global Warming, Environmental Degradation, and International Conflict

12.3 Terror in the Weather Forecast

Thomas Homer-Dixon

Shortages and environmental degradation may actually bring nations and peoples into conflict with one another and pose serious security problems. In the next selection, Thomas Homer-Dixon, a Canadian political scientist, argues that severe environmental stress and resource shortages are likely to overwhelm political institutions, produce violence, and "rip apart societies from one side of the planet to the other."

Does climate change threaten international peace and security? The British government thinks it does. As this month's head of the United Nations Security Council, Britain convened a debate on the matter last Tuesday. One in four United Nations member countries joined the discussion—a record for this kind of thematic debate.

Countries rich and poor, large and small, and from all continents—Bangladesh, Ghana, Japan, Mexico, much of Europe and, most poignantly, a large number of small island states endangered by rising seas—recognized the security implications of climate change. Some other developing countries—Brazil, Cuba and India and most of the biggest producers of fossil fuels and carbon dioxide, including China, Qatar and Russia—either questioned the very idea of such a link or argued that the Security Council is not the right place to talk about it.

But these skeptics are wrong. Evidence is fast accumulating that, within our children's lifetimes, severe droughts, storms and heat waves caused by climate change could rip apart societies from one side of the planet to the other. Climate stress may well represent a challenge to international security just as dangerous—and more intractable—than the arms race between the United States and the Soviet Union during the cold war or the proliferation of nuclear weapons among rogue states today.

Congress and senior military leaders are taking heed: legislation under consideration in both the Senate and the House calls for the director of national intelligence to report on the geopolitical implications of climate change. And last week a panel of 11 retired generals and admirals warned that climate change is already a "threat multiplier" in the world's fragile regions, "exacerbating conditions that lead to failed states—the breeding grounds for extremism and terrorism."

Addressing the question of scientific uncertainty about climate change, General Gordon R. Sullivan, a former Army chief of staff who is now retired, said: "Speaking as a soldier, we never have 100 percent certainty. If you wait until you have 100 percent certainty, something bad is going to happen on the battlefield."

In the future, that battlefield is likely to be complex and hazardous. Climate change will help produce the kind of military challenges that are difficult for today's conventional forces to handle: insurgencies, genocide, guerrilla attacks, gang warfare and global terrorism.

In the 1990s, a research team I led at the University of Toronto examined links between various forms of environmental stress in poor countries—cropland degradation, deforestation and scarcity of fresh water, for example—and violent conflict. In places as diverse as Haiti, Pakistan, the Philippines and South Africa, we found that severe environmental stress multiplied the pain caused by such problems as ethnic strife and poverty.

Rural residents who depend on local natural resources for their livelihood become poorer, while powerful elites take control of—and extract exorbitant profits from—increasingly valuable land, forests and water. As these resources in the countryside dwindle, people sometimes join local rebellions against landowners and government officials. In mountainous areas of the Philippines, for instance, deforestation, soil erosion and depletion of soil nutrients have increased poverty and helped drive peasants into the arms of the Communist New People's Army insurgency.

Other times, people migrate in large numbers to regions where resources seem more plentiful, only to fight with the people already there. Or they migrate to urban slums, where unemployed young men can be primed to join criminal gangs or radical political groups.

Climate change will have similar effects, if nations fail to aggressively limit carbon dioxide emissions and develop technologies and institutions that allow people to cope with a warmer planet.

The recent report of Working Group II of the United Nations Intergovernmental Panel on Climate Change identifies several ways warming will hurt poor people in the third world and hinder economic development there more generally. Large swaths of land in subtropical latitudes—zones inhabited by billions of people—will experience more drought, more damage from storms, higher mortality from heat waves, worse outbreaks of agricultural pests and an increased burden of infectious disease.

The potential impact on food output is a particular concern: in semi-arid regions where water is already scarce and cropland overused, climate change could devastate agriculture. (There is evidence that warming's effect on crops and pastureland is a cause of the Darfur crisis.) Many cereal crops in tropical zones are already near their limits of heat tolerance, and temperatures even a couple of degrees higher could lead to much lower yields.

By weakening rural economies, increasing unemployment and disrupting livelihoods, global warming will increase the frustrations and anger of hundreds of millions of people in vulnerable countries. Especially in Africa, but also in some parts of Asia and Latin America, climate change will undermine already frail governments—and make challenges from violent groups more likely—by reducing revenues, overwhelming bureaucracies and revealing how incapable these governments are of helping their citizens.

We've learned in recent years that such failure can have consequences around the world and that great powers can't always isolate themselves from these consequences. It's time to put climate change on the world's security agenda.

12.4 Receding Aral Sea Offers Fertile Ground for Conflict

David Stern

In the following selection, British journalist David Stern describes one of the world's great man-made environmental tragedies, the virtual disappearance of the Aral Sea owing to the abuse of its water for agriculture by the former Soviet Union. The article suggests that the disappearance of the Aral Sea is already having detrimental consequences for the economies and societies of the region. The problem is likely to increase as states selfishly compete for the water that used to flow to the sea, and the potential for conflict over this water continues to increase.

The countryside in the western Uzbek region of Karakalpakstan is as white as the snow in a Christmas scene, but the reality is not so picturesque. The soil is laden with salt—a result of the steady drying-up of the nearby Aral Sea and a catastrophic loss of water in its main source, the Amu Darya river.

This is ground zero of one of the world's most extreme examples of regional water abuse, an issue which will be one of the main points on the agenda at the Group of Eight summit in the French spa town of Evian next week [June 2003]. The Aral Sea has been inexorably disappearing since the 1960s, when Soviet planners tapped the waters of the Amu Darya and Syr Darya rivers to help fulfil grandiose plans for cotton production.

Today what was once the fourth largest inland body of water is now less than one-fifth of its original size. The sea's shores have retreated more than 150 km.

The plight of the Aral is nothing new. Untold numbers of international conferences and possibly hundreds of millions of dollars—as well as thousands of lines of newsprint—have been devoted to the subject. Each year environmentalists and government officials meet and agree that more must be done and the countries of the region must co-operate. Still the sea continues to recede.

The disaster is almost entirely man-made. "The fact is that the region's basin has enough water. We have over 2,500 cubic meters per capita per year which even for irrigated agriculture should be sufficient," says Juerg Kraehenbuehl of the Swiss Agency for Development and Co-operation.

The problem, says Mr. Kraehenbuehl, is an antiquated, decaying infrastructure, with masses of unlined irrigation canals, and gross mismanagement of water resources. "It's a catch-as-catch can system with each upstream country and region taking as much as it is able," he says.

The sea's disappearance is just one more result of the fractious former Soviet states' inability to agree among themselves. Kyrgyzstan needs the water to power its hydroelectric stations, since it lacks the energy resources of its neighbours. Uzbekistan, Tajikistan and Kyrgyzstan fight over limited resources in the Ferghana Valley, the region's breadbasket. Kazakhstan is also a big agricultural producer and shares the Aral Sea with Uzbekistan.

Jacques Chirac, the French president, in a message to the World Water Forum in March, voiced concern that the 21st century could be a period of "tension and water wars." Nowhere is this threat greater than in central Asia.

For environmentalists the greatest areas of worry lie to the west and south. Turkmenistan, which already uses four to five times the amount of water that it should, plans to dig a 3,460 sq km, $6 billion . . . artificial lake in the heart of the desert.

This could prove a catastrophic drain on resources and increase the chance of conflict with neighbouring Uzbekistan, experts say. Likewise Afghanistan, which

Stern, David, "Receding Aral Sea Offers Fertile Ground for Conflict," *Financial Times,* May 28, 2003, p. 7. Reprinted with permission.

so far has not realised its agricultural potential because of its recent political turmoil, is expected to increase consumption.

And as the sea dies, economic and social tensions rise. In a bazaar in the Uzbek village of Takhtakupir a handful of tradesmen offer cheap household goods and car parts. There are few buyers though. Those that do venture a purchase can do so only on credit and the traders themselves say that they can support their families only by borrowing.

At a nearby, collective farm, most of the fields are unusable. Marat, a farm worker, says that today he works on only 40 hectares, compared with 400–500 in the past. Drinking water is heavily salinated and full of heavy metals and pesticides.

In the town hospital the number of cases of respiratory illness and anaemia have soared, doctors say. Especially acute is the level of tuberculosis, a "poor person's disease," in the words of one, which affects those who suffer from lowered immunity brought on by poor diet. According to Médecins sans Frontières, the disease sees Karakalpakstan ranked 11th in the world.

"All of the region's economy is based on the idea that people live in a river delta. And people here still live as if they were in a river delta—but the river doesn't exist anymore," says Jean Takken of MSF's Karakalpakstan office.

 # A Global Web of Pollution and Environmental Devastation

12.5 Huge Dust Plumes from China Cause Changes in Climate

Robert Lee Hotz

This selection describes how air pollution, especially in the form of microscopic particles called aerosols, originates in China, crosses the Pacific Ocean, and poisons the air in California. This pollution is actually changing the climate, intensifying storms and contributing to global warming.

One tainted export from China can't be avoided in North America—air. An outpouring of dust layered with man-made sulfates, smog, industrial fumes, carbon grit and nitrates is crossing the Pacific Ocean on prevailing winds from booming Asian economies in plumes so vast they alter the climate.

These rivers of polluted air can be wider than the Amazon and deeper than the Grand Canyon.

"There are times when it covers the entire Pacific Ocean basin like a ribbon bent back and forth," said atmospheric physicist V. Ramanathan at the Scripps Institution of Oceanography in La Jolla, Calif.

On some days, almost a third of the air over Los Angeles and San Francisco can be traced directly to Asia. With it comes up to three-quarters of the black carbon particulate pollution that reaches the West Coast, Dr. Ramanathan and his colleagues recently reported in the Journal of Geophysical Research.

This transcontinental pollution is part of a growing global traffic in dust and aerosol particles made worse by drought and deforestation, said Steven Cliff, who studies the problem at the University of California at Davis.

Aerosols—airborne microscopic particles—are produced naturally every time a breeze catches sea salt from ocean spray, or a volcano erupts, or a forest burns, or a windstorm kicks up dust, for example. They also are released in exhaust fumes, factory vapors and coal-fired power plant emissions.

Over the Pacific itself, the plumes are seeding ocean clouds and spawning fiercer thunderstorms, researchers at Texas A&M University reported in the Proceedings of the National Academy of Sciences in March.

The influence of these plumes on climate is complex because they can have both a cooling and a warming effect, the scientists said. Scientists are convinced these plumes contain so many cooling sulfate particles that they may be masking half of the effect of global warming. The plumes may block more than 10 percent of the sunlight over the Pacific.

But while the sulfates they carry lower temperatures by reflecting sunlight, the soot they contain absorbs solar heat, thus warming the planet.

Asia is the world's largest source of aerosols, man-made and natural. Every spring and summer, storms whip up silt from the Gobi desert of Mongolia and the hardpan of the Taklamakan desert of western China, where, for centuries, dust has shaped a way of life. From the dunes of Dunhuang, where vendors hawk gauze face masks alongside braided leather camel whips, to the oasis of Kashgar at the feet of the Tian Shan Mountains 1,500 miles to the west, there is no escaping it.

The Taklamakan is a natural engine of evaporation and erosion. Rare among the world's continental basins, no river that enters the Taklamakan ever reaches the sea. Fed by melting highland glaciers and gorged with silt, these freshwater torrents all vanish in the arid desert heat, like so many Silk Road caravans.

Only the dust escapes.

In an instant, billows of grit can envelope the landscape in a mist so fine that it never completely settles. Moving east, the dust sweeps up pollutants from heavily industrialized regions that turn the yellow plumes a bruised brown. In Beijing, where authorities estimate a million tons of this dust settles every year, the level of microscopic aerosols is seven times the public-health standard set by the World Health Organization.

Once aloft, the plumes can circle the world in three weeks. "In a very real and immediate sense, you can look at a dust event you are breathing in China and look at this same dust as it tracks across the Pacific and reaches the United States," said climate analyst Jeff Stith at the National Center for Atmospheric Research in Colorado. "It is a remarkable mix of natural and man-made particles."

12.6 A Corrupt Timber Trade

Peter S. Goodman and Peter Finn

The final selection in this chapter provides a complex and fascinating case study of the international timber trade, much of which entails illegal logging and produces deforestation on a massive scale. Even as China seeks to conserve its own dwindling forests, Chinese loggers scour Burma, the Russian Far East, Indonesia, Papua New Guinea, and elsewhere for timber to feed its burgeoning furniture industry, much of which is subcontracted by the Swedish home-furnishing corporation, Ikea. Ikea portrays itself as concerned with the environment, but much of the furniture it accepts from China is made from illegal timber. The article describes how the illegal trade in timber takes place, including the bribing of local officials. While enriching the Chinese involved in this industry, illegal logging is environmentally devastating in those countries where it takes place and impoverishes those who live there. The article concludes by describing the Forest Stewardship Council, a nongovernmental international body that sets standards for the sustainable use of forest. Although companies such as Ikea and Home Depot have joined the organization, it still supervises only a very small part of the global trade in lumber, and much of the furniture made with illegal timber ends up in the West, including the United States.

The Chinese logging boss set his sights on a thickly forested mountain just inside Burma, aiming to harvest one of the last natural stands of teak on Earth.

He handed a rice sack stuffed with $8,000 worth of Chinese currency to two agents with connections in the Burmese borderlands, the men said in interviews. They used that stash to bribe everyone standing between the teak and China. In came Chinese logging crews. Out went huge logs, over Chinese-built roads.

About 2,500 miles to the northeast, Chinese and Russian crews hacked into the virgin forests of the Russian Far East and Siberia, hauling away 250-year-old Korean pines in often-illegal deals, according to trading companies and environmentalists. In the highlands of Papua New Guinea, Indonesia and Africa and in the forests of the Amazon, loggers working beyond the bounds of the law have sent a ceaseless flow of timber to China.

Some of the largest swaths of natural forest left on the planet are being dismantled at an alarming pace to feed a global wood-processing industry centered in coastal China.

Goodman, Peter S. and Peter Finn, "A Corrupt Timber Trade," *Washington Post National Weekly Edition*, April 9–15, 2007, pp. 6–9. © 2007, The Washington Post. Reprinted with permission.

Mountains of logs, many of them harvested in excess of legal limits aimed at preserving forests, are streaming toward Chinese factories where workers churn out such products as furniture and floorboards. These wares are shipped from China to major retailers such as Ikea, Home Depot, Lowe's and many others. They land in homes and offices in the United States and Europe, bought by shoppers with little inkling of the wood's origins or the environmental costs of chopping it down.

"Western consumers are leaving a violent ecological footprint in Burma and other countries," says an American environmental activist who frequently travels to Burma and goes by the pen name Zao Noam to preserve access to the authoritarian country. "Predominantly, the Burmese timber winds up as patio furniture for Americans. Without their demand, there wouldn't be a timber trade."

At the current pace of cutting, natural forests in Indonesia and Burma—which send more than half their exported logs to China—will be exhausted within a decade, according to research by Forest Trends, a consortium of industry and conservation groups. Forests in Papua New Guinea will be consumed in as little as 13 years, and those in the Russian Far East within two decades.

These forests are a bulwark against global warming, capturing carbon dioxide that would otherwise contribute to heating the planet. They hold some of the richest flora and fauna anywhere, and they have supplied generations of people with livelihoods that are now threatened.

In the world's poorest countries, illegal logging on public lands annually costs governments $10 billion in lost assets and revenues, a figure more than six times the aid these nations receive to help protect forests, a World Bank study found last year.

Environmental activists have prodded some of the largest purveyors of wood products to adopt conservation policies. Industry leaders and conservationists have crafted standards meant to give forests time to regenerate. They certify operations that comply and encourage consumers to buy certified goods.

But such efforts are in their infancy and are vulnerable to abuse. Corruption bedevils the timber trade in poor countries.

"What we've done very well so far with certification is to reward the best players in the marketplace," says Ned Daly, vice president of U.S. operations for a leading certification body, the Forest Stewardship Council. "What we haven't done very well is to figure out how to exclude the worst players. We're having a hard time getting the criminals to label their products 'illegal.'"

This story is the result of a year-long *Washington Post* investigation involving reporting in China, Russia, Indonesia, Burma, Thailand, Singapore and the United States. The *Post* interviewed government officers, diplomats, logging companies, traders, retailers, environmental scientists and advocates. Given the risks of discussing illegal activity, the *Post* sometimes granted anonymity to its informants—particularly in Burma, where the agents who brokered a logging deal with military commanders displayed their bribe ledgers on the condition they not be named.

The industry that connects forests in Asia with living rooms in the United States via the sawmills of China is a quintessential product of globalization. As transportation links expand and technology erodes distance, multinational manufacturing operations can draw supplies from almost anywhere and ship goods everywhere.

No company better symbolizes this reality than Ikea, the Swedish home-furnishings giant. Ikea cultivates a green image, filling its cavernous stores—including three in the Baltimore-Washington corridor—with signs asserting that its products are made in ways that minimize environmental harm.

But in Suifenhe, a wood-processing hub in northeastern China, workers at Yixin Wood Industry Corp. fashion 100,000 pine dining sets a year for Ikea using timber from the neighboring Russian Far East, where the World Bank says half of all logging is illegal.

"Ikea will provide some guidance, such as a list of endangered species we can't use, but they never send people to supervise the purchasing," said a factory sales manager who spoke on condition she be identified by only her family name, Wu. "Basically, they just let us pick what wood we want."

China is Ikea's largest supplier of solid wood furniture, according to the company. In 2006, about 100 Chinese factories manufactured about one-fourth of the company's global stock. Russia is Ikea's largest source of wood, providing one-fifth of its worldwide supply. Ikea executives say they are confident this wood is legal, because the company dispatches auditors and professional foresters to factories and traces wood to logging sites.

But Ikea has only two foresters in China and three in Russia, the company says. It annually inspects logging sites that produce about 30 percent of the wood imported by its Chinese factories, more commonly relying on paperwork produced by logging companies and factories.

"Falsification of documents is rampant," acknowledges Sofie Beckham, Ikea's forestry coordinator. "There's always somebody who wants to break the rules."

Sending more people to inspect logging sites would make Ikea's products more expensive.

"It's about cost," says Ikea's global manager for social and environmental affairs, Thomas Bergmark. "It would take enormous resources if we trace back each and every wood supply chain. We can never guarantee that each and every log is from the right source."

Two years ago, Ikea set a goal that by 2009, at least 30 percent of the wood for its products will be certified by the Forest Stewardship Council. But now, the company says, only 4 percent of the wood used to make its wares in China meets that grade.

China's voracious appetite for foreign timber is the direct result of its campaign to protect its own forests, even as its demand for wood has exploded.

In 1998, floods along China's Yangtze River killed 3,600 people. The government, blaming deforestation, imposed logging bans—particularly in Yunnan province, bordering Burma. What logging goes on must adhere to plans for regeneration.

China also unleashed an ambitious replanting effort, expanding its forest cover by an area the size of Nebraska from 2000 to 2005. A 2005 assessment of the world's forests by the U.N. Food and Agriculture Organization pointed to China's replanting as the primary reason Asia's total forest cover grew during that period, even as deforestation continued worldwide "at an alarmingly high rate."

But in those same years, unprecedented expansion has unfolded at China's factories, requiring enormous quantities of wood. In 2005, China exported $8.8 billion worth of wood furniture, an eightfold increase from 1998, according to Chinese customs data. About 40 percent landed in the United States. China's exports of all timber products, including plywood and floorboards, exceeded $17 billion in 2005, nearly five times the 1997 level.

All that wood had to come from somewhere. In the years since China enacted its logging bans, it became the world's largest importer of tropical logs, according to the FAO. Its log imports swelled nearly ninefold in a decade, reaching $5.6 billion in 2006, according to China's State Forestry Administration.

China's imports of wood and exports of finished wood products are both expected to double again over the next decade, according to Forest Trends.

Whatever environmental benefits have resulted from China's replanting have been undone by the damage to the tropical regions now supplying so many of its logs, says Mette Wilkie, the U.N. officer in Rome who coordinated the FAO report. China is primarily adding tree plantations with little biological diversity. Much of the logging in Burma, the Russian Far East, Indonesia and Papua New Guinea is assailing natural forests that hold creatures and plants found nowhere else.

"You're losing tropical rainforest, and you're gaining areas of plantation, and that of course is a concern," Wilkie says. "A lot of the biodiversity is found in the moist forests."

The FAO report found grave environmental risks—particularly in Indonesia, home to 10 to 15 percent of all known animal, plant and bird species. Several species are imperiled, among them the Sumatran tiger, according to the World Conservation Union in Switzerland. In Burma, tigers, red pandas and leopards are threatened as logging roads open forests to a range of exploitation, a dynamic at play across Southeast Asia.

"The arrival of logging operations has an immediate and devastating effect," says Jake Brunner, a regional environmental scientist for Conservation International. "We see a fragmentation of the forest and a collapse" in wildlife.

More than 1 billion people in poor countries depend on forests for their livelihoods, according to the World Bank. As forests are degraded, and as logging proceeds on steep slopes, allowing soil to wash away, communities are suffering from flooding, forest fires and a dearth of game.

"Whole ecosystems are being wiped out," said Horst Weyerhaeuser, a forester with the World Agroforestry Centre research group who advises the Chinese government.

Meanwhile, the spoils of the timber trade are monopolized by those who control the trees, typically local authorities acting with military groups.

"For local people, it just gets more difficult," said a community leader in Kachin state, in northeastern Burma, bordering China, where Chinese logging has stripped mountains bare. He spoke on condition that he be identified only by his given name, Shaung, citing threats to his safety. "The commanders sell our natural resources and our local people get nothing."

The buzzing sawmills and clattering furniture plants in China explain why the pace of logging in Papua New Guinea is four times faster than legally permitted, according to Forest Trends. It explains why ships ferry logs to China from the African nation of Gabon, where 70 percent of logging is illegal, according to the World Bank. It explains why Chinese traders armed with cash line the Russian border, overwhelming the regulators charged with preserving trees.

"There is no strategy for forest resources," said Alexei Lankin, a researcher at the Pacific Geographical Institute in Vladivostok, Russia. "What you have is a take-and-run system."

Chinese authorities acknowledge they rarely challenge imports. As long as shipments are accompanied by harvest permits issued by authorities in the country of origin, customs officers allow the wood in, making no effort to authenticate the paperwork.

"China can only ensure that the logging companies and traders obey Chinese law," says a researcher in Beijing affiliated with the State Forestry Administration. "What they do in other countries is not something the Chinese government can control."

Each year, illegal logging costs Indonesia at least $600 million in lost royalties and export taxes, more than double what the government spent to subsidize food for the poor in 2001, according to the World Bank. Five years ago, China pledged to help Indonesia halt shipments of merbau, a threatened tree species. Shippers have evaded an Indonesian ban on exports of merbau logs by transporting them through Malaysia, forging documents saying that the trees were harvested there, Chinese traders say.

But China has done nothing to follow through.

"They said they have no authority to implement this kind of agreement," complains Tachir Fatmoni of the Indonesian Forestry Ministry. "Merbau is still getting to China."

North of Shanghai, the Zhangjiagang port has become perhaps the largest trading place on Earth for tropical logs. According to state figures, $500 million worth of wood passed through the port in 2004.

One morning a year ago, tens of thousands of logs laid stacked on the muddy banks. A four-story hotel next to the port had become a trading house where buyers from furniture and flooring factories haggled over cups of green tea. A bulletin board in the lobby was jammed with offers for logs from South America and Africa, and one trader whispered to a visitor that for the right price, he could get his hands on merbau.

In the rugged mountains of southwestern China, automobiles worth more than many villagers earn in a lifetime traverse dirt roads, a testament to the riches that Chinese timber merchants are extracting from next-door Burma. The trade amounts to a joint venture between China's frontier capitalists and corrupt Burmese generals leading one of the world's most repressive regimes.

For more than four decades, Burma's military dictatorship has plundered the country's natural resources. In the northeast, ethnic Kachin minority communities resisted the regime's rule with a long-running guerrilla war, until they signed cease-fire deals with the Burmese government in the 1990s. The Kachin had been sustained by jade mining, but as those rights went to the government, they shifted aggressively into logging, leaning on Chinese partners for capital, laborers and transport.

The cross-border log trade swelled by 60 percent between 2001 and 2004, reaching $350 million in 2005, according to a London environmental group, Global Witness. With competing Burmese generals involved and some using force to evict villagers in the way, control over land is in flux, contributing to forest destruction: Chinese logging crews work fast, cognizant that new armed forces could show up any minute and shut them down.

"You bribe one army and you get the right to cut everything," said Li Tao, a Chinese logger preparing last May to sneak across the border from the Chinese town of Ruili. "Then another army comes and threatens to arrest you, and you have to bribe them, too."

Ethnic Kachin agents working for a Chinese logging boss consented to interviews in Myitkyina, a town in northeastern Burma, on the condition of anonymity, citing fears they would be imprisoned or killed. They said they wished to publicize the details of the trade to bring international pressure on Burma's government to aid local people.

"We know what we are doing is rotten," one agent said. "There is nothing else for us to do. This is how we are surviving."

They displayed a logbook showing records of the bribes they said they paid to facilitate teak logging in the Sinpo area beginning in October 2004 through March 2006: $200 per year to the local police, $250 to the forestry department, $225 to the Burmese military special intelligence and $950 to the local brigade of the Burmese army, plus $8,000 worth of gold to battalion-level leaders. The Chinese boss independently funneled $4,000 each to five officers in the northern regional command, the Kachin men said.

In January 2005, the agents said, a crew of more than 120 Chinese workers slipped into Burma and set up camp on a mountaintop near the town of Bhamo, adding the whine of chainsaws to the screeching of jungle insects. "They cut the whole mountain," one agent said. "They cut it all."

Caravans of 10 and 20 trucks, each carrying about 20 logs, ferried the wood into China. The Kachin agents said they rode ahead on motorbikes, giving soldiers $40 per truck at eight government checkpoints. Where the government's control yields to the territory of a separatist group, the Kachin Independence Organization, they paid $125 per truck to Burmese soldiers, $83 to the forestry department and $25 to the drug police. At Laiza, the final stop before the border, the Kachin group collected a tax from the Chinese truckers, then issued documents declaring the shipments legitimate.

In the first six months of 2005, this operation hauled 150 truckloads of teak into China, with each truck carrying about 20 tons, the men said. On the other side of the border, each ton fetched nearly $1,000, making the total haul worth about $3 million.

Last May, in one hour, a reporter counted six big trucks loaded with logs as they made their way down a narrow, winding road from the border toward the Chinese town of Yingjiang.

At the opposite edge of China, along the meandering border with Russia, the logging trade has transformed backwater towns into bustling hives. Russia has become China's primary wood supplier, with shipments multiplying 20-fold in less than a decade.

In Vostok, a Russian town of 4,000 with crumbling Soviet-era apartment blocks, villagers receive about $100 a month to haul logs from the forest. Chinese workers run sawmills across the region.

South of Vostok, just outside the Russian town of Roshino, eight Chinese workers sliced oak and ash trees into planks one day last year, at a small plant where they also live, sleeping on cots in converted offices. Piles of oak and ash awaited the saw blades. At the railyard in the city of Dalnerechensk, freight cars bore loads of Korean pine and linden trees—both protected species—with the cargo bound for furniture factories in China.

Shi Diangang is typical of the entrepreneurs who control the trade. He once sold clothing to Russian tourists on the border. Now he brings laborers from China into Russia, paying them $375 per month to work 12- to 15-hour days, prying wood from the forest. He sells timber to Chinese traders who supply Chinese factories that he says make furniture for Ikea. He is shopping for a villa in Macau, the gambling mecca. He tells time with a gold watch.

"It's been hell to heaven," he said.

Shi operates inside Russia largely free of regulation, with his business partner's government pedigree rendering everything legal, he said.

"The Russian company settles all the documents," he said. "Russia has very loose controls."

Already, logging has laid bare much of the Russian forest bordering China. Crews are moving farther into the interior, penetrating officially protected terrain. In the Primorsky region—an area rich with wildlife, including 450 Amur tigers, the world's largest cat—Yappy lumber company struggles to satisfy orders from its Chinese customers for unprocessed oak and ash logs.

"The forest is exhausted," complained Alexander Sobchenko, the company's general-director.

The Russian Forest Service issues licenses for cutting in protected areas under the guise of so-called sanitation logging, to remove sick or fallen trees. In Primorsky, one-third of exported logs have been cut under such licenses, according to Josh Newell, a researcher at the University of Washington.

"Sanitation logging is a cover to get into areas that should be protected," he said.

Last year, Russia's environmental prosecutor opened a criminal investigation of Forestry Service officials after 14 firms with such licenses harvested 1.3 million cubic feet of wood in a protected zone near Vostok. The logs were exported to China with documentation, prosecutors said. How much more passed through undetected no one really knows: about the size of Florida, Primorsky has 12 forest inspectors.

"Barbaric" is one word Russian President Vladimir Putin has used to assail the "critical problem" of illegal logging. By shipping logs out of the country, Russia is exporting tens of thousands of jobs that would go to Russians if the country had more sawmills and furniture factories. "Our neighbors continue to earn billions of dollars relying on Russian timber," Putin says.

Across the border, in the Chinese city of Suifenhe, 11 freight trains were loaded with logs one morning about a year ago, some being offloaded, others bound for factory towns throughout the country. Shacks of corrugated tin and discarded tree bark encircled the rail yard—homes for migrant workers who have swelled the city's population to more than 100,000 from 20,000 a decade ago.

On seemingly every lane, sawmills filled the air with black smoke, the scent of fresh sawdust and the screech of metal blades biting wood. Some were jury-rigged operations manned by workers lacking safety goggles and gloves. At Jindi Wood company near the rail yard, four men strained to haul huge logs to the saws with slats hung over their shoulders. They earn $250 a week for seven days of work.

"This keeps my child in school," said Xiao Jifeng, 35, whose wife and son remained in his village, a six-hour bus ride away.

Construction crews were filling the horizon with brick villas for the bosses, as a modern city took shape on once-empty plains.

"Four years ago, there was nothing here," said Su Guanglin, chairman of Guofeng Wood Co., a Hong Kong firm that employs 500 workers at a floorboard plant in Suifenhe. Guofeng ships nearly all its products overseas, about one-third to the United States, mainly through Armstrong, a prominent Pennsylvania brand of floor products.

A China-Russia trading office was going up behind the factory. Empty grassland had been transformed into a public square fringed with neon-lighted restaurants and nightclubs offering Cognac and hired female companionship. Oxcarts shared dusty roads with black Audi sedans.

The Forest Stewardship Council, a body created by environmental and industry groups in 1990, sets standards for the sustainable use of forests. The movement has gained high-profile members, including Ikea and Home Depot.

Home Depot conducts top-to-bottom investigations of the products on its shelves, refusing to buy from vendors who cannot verify the wood's origin, says Ron Jarvis, the company's merchandising vice president.

Home Depot sold some $400 million in products certified by the FSC in 2005, compared with $15 million in 1999. Still, those recent sales represented less than 5 percent of the company's total wood-product sales.

"If we could get 100 percent of our wood certified, we would do it tomorrow," Jarvis said: "But we have to do it on a commercial basis."

In China, 20 companies per month are gaining certification, says Alistair Monument, the FSC's country director in Beijing. In the floorboard and furniture factories of Guangdong province in southern China, management vernacular now includes forest conservation.

"All the big Chinese companies exporting to the United States are really paying attention to this issue now," says She Xuebin, president of one of China's largest flooring companies, Yingbin (Guangdong) Wood Industry Co.

But many major Western brands have declined to join. Four-fifths of Yingbin's exports go to the United States, some to Armstrong. Much of Yingbin's wood comes from a sawmill in Indonesia, where as much as 80 percent of the logging is illegal, according to the World Bank. Yingbin's president acknowledges "there's a gap between the law and enforcement," though he says his company plays by the rules.

Armstrong does not require that Yingbin or its four other China suppliers meet the standards of a certification body such as the FSC. Armstrong buys Southeast Asian merbau for flooring that it sells as "exotic," listing only the country of final manufacture—typically the United States—but not the wood's source.

"I just don't think there's a need for it," says Frank J. Ready, chief executive of Armstrong Floor Products North America.

Ready and his counterpart at Yingbin say they do not trade in wood from one country that is synonymous with human-rights abuse—Burma. Yet as a reporter toured Yingbin's flooring factory in the Chinese city of Zhongshan last spring, a pile of teak boards sat on the floor.

"It's from Burma," a worker said.

In the southern Chinese city of Guangzhou, merchants at Yuzhu lumberyard hawked piles of Burmese teak to buyers from surrounding furniture factories. In Shanghai, marketing representatives for one of China's largest flooring companies, Anxin, boasted that they had a large and steady supply of Burmese teak.

They were exporting it to the United States, they said. Through which channels, they would not say.

Suggested Discussion Topics

1. In what ways does the environment represent a security problem? What conflicts over resources, or over the impact of pollution, do you expect to see during your lifetime? Will these be more likely to affect economically developing nations or nations in the developed world? Why?

2. Despite repeated predictions over the years that environmental catastrophe or mass starvation is just around the corner, the world has so far avoided disaster. Why do environmental pessimists think that this time we really have reason to worry? Do you think these environmental pessimists are right? Why or why not?

3. If everyone wants a clean, healthy environment, why is it so difficult to achieve this goal? What kinds of agreements, institutions, and organizations might be useful in helping to prevent the overuse of natural resources or pollution?

4. Is the environment a global problem, or is it a local or national one? Explain your reasoning. Who should have responsibility for protecting the environment and for determining and enforcing environmental standards?

5. What connection do you see between economic development and the environment? Does economic development result in increasing scarcity of resources, such as food and clean water? Will it lead to additional pollution as members of developing nations gradually attain the lifestyle, and levels of consumption, of the world's richer citizens? Why or why not?

6. How does pollution "made in China" affect Americans? What can or should the U.S. government do to protect the health of its citizens? Be prepared to form Chinese and American negotiating teams to discuss the problem and conduct a dialogue between them.

7. What role should Western corporations like Ikea or Home Depot play in dealing with the illegal trade in timber? If officials in Burma or Russia's Far East agree to let China cut timber that harms the local environment, should corporations insist on higher standards? How would corporations be able to do this? If the future development of the timber industry in Burma or Papua New Guinea is decided by China's Yingbin Wood Industry Company based on demand for furniture in the United States, then what are the obligations, if any, of the U.S. government? In a classroom discussion, be prepared to play the role of an Ikea representative, a Yingbin company official, a Burmese logger, an environmentalist, a Chinese government representative, and a U.S. State Department official.

Chapter 13

IMMIGRANTS, REFUGEES, AND DIASPORAS: POPULATION MOVEMENTS ACROSS BORDERS

One feature of globalization is the porosity of national borders and the increasing number of people moving across these borders. In 1950, the United Nations created the office of High Commissioner for Refugees (UNHCR), responsible for implementing the 1951 Convention Relating to the Status of Refugees by providing humanitarian assistance, including food, shelter, and medical assistance, and it was awarded Nobel Peace Prizes in 1954 and 1981. In recent years, its resources have been stretched to cope with refugee populations around the world.

Many refugees seek an escape from violence and human-rights abuses; and, under the 1951 convention, countries are obliged to give asylum to refugees, defined as those who are outside the country of their nationality and are unable or unwilling to return home "owing to well-founded fear of being persecuted for reasons of race, religion, nationality, membership of a particular social group or political opinion."[1] After World War II, most refugees were victims of the war or those escaping communism, but in recent decades the refugees include millions of people fleeing from persecution and violence in their homelands.

Between 1984 and 2004, the number of refugees almost doubled, peaking in 1994 following the Rwanda genocide. Although the settlement of global conflicts such as the civil wars in Liberia, Rwanda, and Sierra Leone reduced the number of refugees in 2007 to the lowest level in 25 years (9.2 million),[2] the UN High Commission for Refugees argues that refugees are becoming victims of "asylum fatigue," being denied their rights by countries that confuse them with illegal economic immigrants.[3] Currently, the largest groups of refugees are Afghans, Colombians, Iraqis, and Sudanese.

---

[1] UNHCR,"Convention and Protocol Relating to the States of Refugees," p. 16, <www.unhcr.ch/cgi-bin/texis/vtx/basics/+SwwBmeJAIS_wwww3wwwwwwwhFqA72ZR0gRfZNtFqtxw5oq5zFqtFEIfgIAFqA72ZR0gRfZNDzmxwwwwwww1FqtFEIfgI/opendoc.pdf>.

[2] UNHCR, "UNHCR says number of refugees at 25-year low but new challenges loom," July 30, 2007, <www.unhcr.org/cgi-bin/texis/vtx/news/opendoc.htm?tbl=NEWS&id=44463fed4>.

[3] "UN alarmed over 'asylum fatigue,'" *BBC News*, April 19, 2006, <http://news.bbc.co.uk/2/hi/in_depth/4919746.stm>.

Moreover, civil strife has created as many as 25 million additional refugees *within* their own countries who are termed "internally displaced persons" (IDPs), including over 7 million in Sudan and the Democratic Republic of the Congo alone. IDPs are not protected by the 1951 refugee convention as are international refugees. According to the UNHCR, the total population of concern consisting of refugees, asylum seekers, stateless persons, and internally displaced persons (IDPs) grew from 19.5 million at the beginning of 2005 to 32.9 million by the end of 2006.[4]

In fact, illegal immigration poses a larger problem than do asylum-seeking refugees. Most migrants leave poor countries for rich ones in search of a better life, and countries are under no legal obligation to grant asylum to such "economic refugees." Concern about security, especially with the threat of global terrorism, has complicated efforts to deal with illegal immigration. It is estimated that there are over 10 million undocumented aliens in the United States alone,[5] about 7 million of whom are from Mexico. Many others live in Canada and Western Europe, straining the tolerance of citizens. In Europe, much of the immigration is from South Asia and sub-Saharan Africa, creating problems of assimilation that these largely homogeneous societies previously had not faced. Today, as many as 40 percent of the world's countries have implemented policies to reduce the level of immigration.

Those who migrate from poor countries to rich countries often take low-paid jobs and remit part of their earnings to families back home that are estimated to be $75 billion a year or twice as large as the total official foreign aid from rich to poor states.[6] In 2004 alone, Mexican migrants in the United States remitted about $16.6 billion back home, accounting for more than 2 percent of Mexico's gross domestic product.[7] Remittances, then, play a major role in economic development for poor countries like Mexico or Morocco. Such migrants also benefit wealthy countries with declining birthrates that are beginning to experience labor shortages, especially in economic sectors such as seasonal farm work with demanding and low-paid jobs.

Alien smuggling, especially to Europe and the United States, has become a multibillion-dollar-a-year racket; and, as countries tighten their borders, illegal immigration has become ever more dangerous. In addition to concern about terrorism and assimilation, citizens also complain, whether fairly or unfairly, about immigrants who work for low wages and place pressure on welfare and education systems.

---

[4] UNHCR, "Basic Facts," July 30, 2007, <www.unhcr.org/basics.html>.

[5] Sylvia Moreno, "Flow of Illegal Immigrants to U.S. Unabated," *Washington Post*, March 22, 2005, p. A5.

[6] Richard H. Adams, Jr., "Migration, Remittances and Development: The Critical Nexus in the Middle East and North Africa," United Nations Expert Group Meeting on International Migration and Development in the Arab Region, April 18, 2005, <www.un.org/esa/population/meetings/EGM_Ittmig_Arab/P01_Adams.pdf>.

[7] Joan Authers, "Mexican Migrants Send $16bn in Remittances," *Financial Times*, February 1, 2005, <www.ft.com/cms/s/ccd06de6-73e7-11d9-b705-00000e2511c8.htm>.

13.1 Crossing Borders: International Migration and National Security

Fiona B. Adamson

This chapter's first selection evaluates international migration as a problem of national security. It observes that migration is part of the phenomenon of globalization, and it differentiates between voluntary and forced migration, between migration for political reasons and economic reasons, and between legal and illegal migration. The author then analyzes the degree to which migration actually limits state capacity and autonomy, arguing that this claim that states cannot control their borders is often overstated. There are, however, historical and contemporary cases where states have lost control of their borders and, as a result, migration has become an acute security problem, for example, in Eastern Europe at the end of the Cold War. Other security threats related to migration include the mobilization of refugee communities against governments and organized criminal networks facilitating illegal immigration. However, migration may be less of a direct than an indirect threat to security to the extent that it dilutes or alters a state's national identity and produces divided loyalties on the part of diasporas that may be mobilized in ways that undermine states' interests.

International migration has moved to the top of the international security agenda. Increasingly, policymakers in the United States, Europe, and around the world are making links between migration policy and national security. Much of this discussion has focused on migration flows as a conduit for international terrorism. The ability of nineteen hijackers from overseas to enter, live, and train in the United States in preparation for carrying out attacks on the World Trade Center and the Pentagon could not but raise concerns regarding the relationship between the cross-border mobility of people and international terrorism. Since the attacks of September 11, 2001, the management of migration has become a top national security priority for the United States, with concerns about migration helping to drive the largest reorganization of the U.S. government since the passage of the National Security Act of 1947.

Even before the September 11 attacks, however, interest in the relationship between globalization, migration, and security had emerged both in the policy world and in some areas of the security studies field. Migration was high on the European security agenda throughout the 1990s. The bombings in Madrid on March 11, 2004, and in London on July 7, 2005, only reinforced already-existing fears regarding the links between migration and terrorism in Europe. Earlier incidents, such as the 1995 bombings of the Paris metro system by Algeria's Armed Islamic Group and attacks in various Western European states in the 1990s by the

Excerpts from Fiona B. Adamson, "Crossing Borders: International Migration and National Security," *International Security*, 31:1 (Summer 2006), pp. 165–99. © 2006 by the President and Fellows of Harvard College and the Massachusetts Institute of Technology.

Kurdistan Workers' Party, had already raised concerns regarding the relationship between migration and security.

Some scholars have noted that the end of the Cold War and bipolarity has helped to transform both the nature and the function of national boundaries in ways that increasingly securitize migration and lead to a greater policing of national borders. In addition, concerns about the security impacts of massive refugee flows and the roles that mobilized diasporas play in fueling violent conflicts around the globe were being discussed long before September 11. Moreover, migration and migrants have a long history of being viewed as closely linked to national security concerns. States have traditionally forged their national immigration policies in response to their security and economic interests. In the United States and other countries, migrants have all too often been viewed as national security threats during times of war or crisis because of the possibility that they may possess dual political loyalties or represent a "fifth column" in a conflict.

Scholars in mainstream security studies have often dismissed such concerns as insignificant or as issues limited to matters of domestic politics and policy. Yet international security scholars and policymakers are finding it increasingly difficult to ignore the relationship between migration and security in a highly intercon-nected world defined by globalization processes. Globalization is changing the overall environment in which states operate, including how they formulate their security policies. . . .

Globalization, International Migration, and Cross-Border Mobility

Migration is not a new phenomenon. It is, however, more than ever before, a global phenomenon that is closely related to a number of other globalization processes in both its causes and its effects. The globalization of trade, finance, and production, and the general trend toward greater global economic integration—all contribute to the emergence of new and more mobile pools of labor, while creating stronger ties and networks among advanced industrial and developing economies that pro-vide new avenues and opportunities for migration. These economic processes are reinforced by cheaper and more accessible forms of transportation and communi-cation technologies, as well as an emerging global infrastructure of services, that link national economies and undergird the formation of international migration networks.

"Like other flows, whether financial or commercial, flows of ideas or informa-tion," notes a 2003 report by the International Organization for Migration (IOM), "the rising tide of people crossing frontiers is among the most reliable indicators of the intensity of globalization." . . .

An examination of some basic migration statistics offers an indication of the significance of migration as one component of the larger process of globalization. According to the IOM, approximately 180 million people live outside their coun-try of birth, up from 80 million three decades ago. The number of people who migrate across national borders in any given year is between 5 and 10 million. One out of every 35 persons in the world is a migrant, or almost 3 percent of the global population. If all migrants formed a single state, it would be the world's fifth most populous country. Migration to both Europe and the United States has continued to increase over the past two decades. In the year 2000, 40 percent of all international migrants lived in Western industrialized countries, including approximately 19 million in the European Union.

Many countries have significant portions of their populations abroad and rely on them heavily as a source of foreign exchange. Migration plays a particularly important role, for example, in the economic life of states in the Middle East. Ten percent of Moroccans live outside of Morocco, and 8 percent of Tunisians live outside Tunisia. In some of the Gulf states, up to 70 percent of the labor force is composed of migrant labor.

Among the factors contributing to these overall increases are declining transportation costs; the growing ease of travel; continuing level of economic inequality among states; the fall of the iron curtain and opening up of borders in the former Soviet bloc; the loosening of emigration restrictions in other states, such as China; refugee-generating conflict and violence, such as in the Balkans and sub-Saharan Africa; state policies of forced migration; and the growth in human smuggling networks. At the same time, as compared with other indicators of levels of globalization, levels of global migration are still relatively low. While 1 in 35 people is a migrant, 34 of 35 people in the world are not migrants. Similarly, contemporary levels of migration are not unprecedented in their volume; the late nineteenth and early twentieth centuries, for example, were also characterized by high levels of international migration. . . .

Voluntary Versus Forced Migration   Much of the general literature and political debate on migration has dealt implicitly with voluntary migration—that is, migration by individuals who have left their homes of their own accord to pursue economic opportunities, for personal enrichment, or to be reunited with their families (family reunification is a standard immigrant category in most industrialized states). A second category, forced migration, includes refugees and displaced persons. Involuntary migration can stem from a variety of causes, including human slavery, ethnic cleansing, and deportation.

Many of the major migrations throughout history have occurred as a result of forced migration or expulsion. The formation of the Jewish diaspora after the destruction of the Temple of Jerusalem in 586 B.C.; the mass migration flows that occurred during the transatlantic slave trade, in which approximately 15 million Africans were transferred to the Americas prior to 1850; the population exchanges between Greece and Turkey at the end of World War I; the forced migration of Jews during the Russian pogroms and later during the Holocaust; the expulsion of Germans from the Sudetenland following World War II; the expulsion of indigenous Arab populations with the establishment of the state of Israel in 1948; the ethnic cleansing that characterized the Balkan wars in the 1990s; and the coerced trafficking of women in many parts of the world (especially Eastern Europe and East Asia) that has been referred to by many as a contemporary form of slavery—all are examples of largely involuntary waves of migration.

The population flows of refugees and exiles produced by forced migration have, as often as not, been the product of state action rather than of nonstate or market forces. Serbian leader Slobodan Milošević, for example, employed refugee flows during the 1999 Kosovo crisis as a weapon of war in what was an asymmetric conflict with NATO. More generally, many instances of forced migration have been intimately bound up with the emergence of new states in the international system—a fact observed by Aristide Zolberg, who has characterized state making as a "refugee-generating process."

Economic Versus Political Migration   The impetus for an individual to migrate can be economic, political, or in many cases, a combination of both. Economic migrants leave their countries in search of employment or other economic opportunities. Refugees and asylum seekers leave to avoid the trauma of war or political persecution. In practice, disentangling the political and economic factors that contribute to migration flows is often difficult. . . .

In the global economy, however, the relative immobility of labor distinguishes it from other factors of production. Despite the sheer numbers and importance of labor migration, the flow of labor across national borders is generally less liberalized than other factors of production and is subject to more state intervention. In a global economy, the mobility of labor has not kept pace with the mobility of capital. As Paul Hirst and Grahame Thompson note, "A world market for labor just does not exist in the same way that it does for goods and services. Most labor markets continue to be nationally regulated and only marginally accessible to outsiders, whether legal or illegal migrants or professional recruitment. Moving goods and services is infinitely easier than moving labor."

In general, states still exercise a great degree of control over whom they admit as migrants; it is partly due to the tight restrictions on labor migration that have emerged since the 1960's economic boom in Europe that one sees a blurring of the lines between political and economic migration, on the one hand, and the corruption of the asylum process, on the other. Progress in liberalizing the global market for labor has been mostly at the high end of the skills continuum, with provisions for increased mobility in the service sector or for highly skilled professionals built into broader economic agreements such as the General Agreement on Tariffs and Trade/World Trade Organization and the North American Free Trade Agreement, although the flow of labor across borders is still much more restricted than the flow of goods and services in these agreements.

International law distinguishes between political and economic migration by assigning categories to individuals who are seeking to cross borders to escape political persecution or violent conflict, as opposed to those who cross borders in search of economic opportunities. International law defines "refugees" as those who have a well-founded fear of persecution because of race, religion, nationality, or membership in a particular social or political group. In 2001 there were approximately 12.0 million refugees in the world, as compared with 8.8 million in 1980; 47.9 percent of all refugees in 2001 were concentrated in Asia, 27.3 percent in Africa, and 18.5 percent in Europe.

Similarly, recent decades have witnessed an increase in asylum seekers. In 2001, 923,000 people filed asylum requests, up from 180,000 in 1980. Altogether, approximately 6 million asylum applications were filed in advanced industrialized countries during the 1990s. Of these, only a small percentage were by individuals eventually deemed to be legitimate asylum seekers. Asylum applications cost advanced industrial states approximately $10 billion per year; this is ten times the annual budget of the Office of the United Nations High Commissioner for Refugees. The number of false asylum seekers, combined with high levels of illegal migration, contributes to the perception that states are losing sovereign control over their borders.

Legal Versus Illegal Migration　　Many immigrants enter states through formal, legal channels; others enter through illegal channels, including those who are smuggled or trafficked, or who enter with either forged papers or none at all. So-called irregular migrants make up 30–50 percent of all migration to Western industrialized countries. The IOM surmises that approximately 4 million people are smuggled across borders every year. In the United States alone, there may be as many as 12 million illegal migrants, with approximately 4,000 illegal border crossing every day. Half of all illegal migrants have some interaction with smuggling or trafficking networks—a global industry that generates approximately $10 billion per year. . . .

Impacts of Migration on State Capacity and Autonomy

Some experts portray international migration flows as overwhelming states' capacity to maintain sovereignty across a number of areas, thus jeopardizing the very basis of their security. Ever larger flows of people across borders; increasingly multicultural populations; and the emergence of informal, migration-based, transitional networks that circulate capital, goods, and ideas—all challenge notions of the territorial state as a bounded entity with a clearly demarcated territory and population. This in turn calls into question traditional models of national security, which assume a unitary national identity from which a set of national interests can be derived. Yet this does not necessarily mean, as some more sensational accounts claim, that large migration flows are causing states to lose control. As Gary Freeman has argued, "Anyone who thinks differently should try landing at Sydney airport without an entry visa or go to France and apply for a job without a work permit."

It is still states that have the primary responsibility both for regulating borders and for conferring citizenship rights and claims to membership in a political community. States have always faced challenges to their sovereignty, and the impact of migration flows across borders is analogous to other instances in history in which states have had to respond to pressures arising from increased transnationalism. All states are not equally able to manage the challenges posed by migration, however, and those with high levels of institutional capacity are in a much better position to adapt to this new environment than are weak or failing states. Two areas in which migration influences state capacity and autonomy are border control and national identity. The ability of states to maintain control over their borders and to formulate a coherent national identity are arguably necessary preconditions for the maintenance of state security in other areas.

Regulating Borders: Migration and Interdependence Sovereignty   The ability to control who has the right to cross the borders of a states is a key dimension of what Stephen Krasner refers to as a state's "interdependence sovereignty." States have interests in controlling their territorial borders for a variety of reasons, such as maintaining control over their populations, limiting access to labor markets and public goods, and maintaining internal security. A failure to control territorial borders can precipitate serious security challenges. In weak and failing states, a lack of border control significantly jeopardizes their capacity across a number of areas. Large-scale refugee flows, for example, can overwhelm a state's capacity to provide public services and can lead to conflicts over resources.

The end of communism in Eastern Europe was symbolized by the loss of control over state borders and offers a dramatic example of the relationship between border control and state strength. The fall of the iron curtain began when thousands of East Germans escaped to the West through Czechoslovakia, Hungary, and Poland in 1989, until the border between East and West Germany was finally declared open by East Germany on November 9, 1989. Similarly, one of the characteristics of weak or failing states is the inability to control their territorial borders. The world's poorest states host most of its refugees, and the uncontrolled flow of refugees or other migrants across borders produces additional stresses on already weak state institutions, heightens competition over scarce resources, and exacerbates ethnic and sectarian tensions.

Moreover, porous borders in weak states can allow politically organized nonstate actors access to territory and population groups that can be used for political mobilization, which in turn can lead to the emergence of "refugee-warrior communities." Examples include the mobilization activities of the Palestine Liberation Organization in refugee camps in Lebanon in the 1970s, the role played by refugee camps in Pakistan as sites of mobilization for Taliban-related groups in the 1980s, and the emergence of the Rwandan Patriotic Front in Ugandan refugee camps in the 1990s. Refugee flows can act as conduits that regionalize and internationalize internal conflicts; the Great Lakes region of Africa provides just one example of the disastrous consequences that such dynamics can have on weak states.

For advanced industrial states with very high levels of internal capacity and control, the concern with maintaining secure borders is also significant. As John Torpey has pointed out, the monopolization of the legitimate means of movement of people across borders through the creation of the passport and accompanying bureaucracies has been a key feature in the development of modern nation-states. Although states are authorized to monopolize the legitimate means of movement, they do not necessarily control all movement—just as they do not always have a monopoly over the means of violence. As the earlier statistics on illegal migration demonstrate, even if states have formal control over migration processes, a number of nonstate actors—in particular, organized criminal networks and smugglers—are in competition with the state in this area.

The emergence of organized criminal networks around illegal migration can also pose a significant challenge to state authority and control. As the IOM report mentioned above notes, "Given the vast amounts of money involved, such operations erode normal governance and present real challenges and threats to national sovereignty." Globalization produces a situation that resembles a cat-and-mouse game between migration pressures and state control over borders. If migration pressures on states increase without the state adapting, then the capacity of states is indeed under threat. The record shows, however, that many states are adjusting to these pressures. As Peter Andreas argues, "Globalization may be about tearing down economic borders, as globalists emphasize, but it has also created more border policing work for the state. At the same time as globalization is about mobility and territorial access, states are attempting to selectively reinforce border controls."

Throughout the 1990s, the United States and Europe expanded the policing of their borders, increased the use of technology to monitor and regulate these borders, and generally militarized and securitized border crossings. Since 1993, for example, the budget of the U.S. Immigration and Naturalization Service (since 2003, the U.S. Citizenship and Immigration Service) has tripled, and the number of agents in Border Control has doubled. The human consequences of this strengthening, however, have been very high. The number of deaths at the U.S.-Mexican border has steadily increased, with approximately 1,700 occurring during the second half of the 1990s—a 400 percent jump from 1996 to 2000. Since the creation of the Department of Homeland Security following the September 11 attacks, the control of U.S. borders has become even more securitized. Smuggling fees from Mexico into Arizona in 2001 were 50 percent lower than what they were before the attacks, because of the higher likelihood that migrants would be interdicted. As a border crosser who was caught trying to enter the United States illegally after September 11 succinctly put it, "Because of this bearded guy, what's his name, bin Laden, it is harder now. There are more reinforcements now because America is afraid of terrorism." . . .

Thus, even though illicit migration flows provide states with clear challenges, it would appear that overall state capacity has been threatened by migration flows to a much lesser degree than many of the more sensationalist accounts in the globalization literature had predicted. Of course, for states with very weak or low capacity, monitoring borders will continue to be a challenge. Even here, however, a common interest in the regulation of migration has prompted stronger states to earmark economic, technical, and development assistance to weaker states for border control. In Europe during the 1990s, for example, approximately 50 percent of funds spent on technical assistance for the EU Phare programs to Eastern Europe were targeted at illegal immigration and border control in candidate states. . . .

Reshaping National Identity: Multicultural States and Diasporas   State migration policies generally have two main objectives: regulating who enters (e.g., controlling borders), and deciding who is entitled to membership in a polity (e.g., conferring citizenship or political membership in a community). States may be able to rely on technology to control borders, but how do they respond to challenges to their national identity? . . .

International migration processes call into question the cultural basis of a state's identity and provide incentives for states to take up more liberal and expansive national identities. The challenge that migration flows pose to unitary conceptions of national identity has deep historical roots and continues to provoke political debate. Many states have historically incorporated national, ethnic, or racial criteria into their migration policies; examples include racial restrictions on immigrants to the United States during the nineteenth and early twentieth centuries, the favoring of ethnic Germans (or *Aussiedler*) by Germany in its post–World War II immigration policy, the "White Australia" policies that defined Australian migration policies for much of the twentieth century, and the automatic right to immigrate to Israel that is granted to Jews in the 1950 Law of Return.

The spread of international norms of racial equality and universal human rights, the rise of civil rights movements and multiculturalism, and economic imperatives resulting from the changing global structure of production have increasingly delegitimized the use of ethnic and racial criteria in the formulation of immigration policy. Debates surrounding the relationship between migration and national identity, however, are still politically contentious: when established patterns of national identity formation are called into question, even highly institutionalized and liberal democratic states may experience some levels of internal instability and incoherence at the societal level—what Ole Waever has referred to as "societal insecurity." The problem is most acute for states that derive their identity and legitimacy from an ethnic version of nationalism, rather than a civic nationalism. Meanwhile, some cultural conservatives argue that even states whose identities are primarily liberal, civic, and constitutional can be threatened by migration, as they claim that liberal constitutionalism itself has its origins in a particular culture. Samuel Huntington, for example, has made the argument that recent waves of immigration to the United States threaten to undermine its core identity, which he asserts is based on an "Anglo-Protestant" heritage. . . .

The relationship between migration flows and national identity provides an example of the many ways in which market forces are challenging traditional state functions. States are increasingly using market criteria to make migration policy, with economic skills largely trumping cultural and identity criteria in evaluating potential migration requests. At the same time, a global "market" for the political loyalties of individual migrants and their descendents is emerging. Old models of incorporation or assimilation into a nation are giving way to new discourses of multiculturalism, transnationalism, and diasporic identities—all of which challenge the notion of a unitary and territorially defined national entity.

Factors such as the ease of travel, new communication technologies, and the emergence of a global media infrastructure allow migrants to maintain ties with their homelands or even take part in wholly new transnational identity communities. Migrants and their descendents can easily maintain dense social networks that stretch across national borders, are rich in social capital, and can be used for a variety of purposes—including political mobilization. . . .

The literature on diasporas points to how the emergence of transnational organization structures, such as diaspora organizations, creates identities and political loyalties that challenge conventional notions of citizenship. Gabriel Sheffer, for example, notes, "The establishment of diaspora organizations and participation in those organizations can create the potential for dual authority, and consequently also for dual or divided loyalties or ambiguous loyalty vis-à-vis host countries. Development of such fragmented loyalties often results in conflicts between diasporas and their host societies and governments." Members of diaspora groups are sometimes actively involved in the politics of their "home state." Prime examples are the political activities of Jews in the diaspora directed toward politics in Israel or of Armenians vis-à-vis Armenia. Migrants and their descendents thus form contested constituencies that can be mobilized by a variety of actors.

Some scholars have argued that the transnationalization of political participation and the existence of diaspora networks can impair a state's ability to formulate a coherent foreign policy based on a unified national interest. Huntington and Tony Smith, for example, argue that U.S. foreign policy formulation in some areas can be influenced by skilled ethnic lobbying groups whose loyalties are to a real or imagined homeland. Interestingly, Huntington makes the comparison between transnational ethnic groups and economic actors, such as multinational corporations. Both, in some sense, illustrate how increased levels of marketization and pluralization can challenge a state's ability to act coherently as a unitary rational actor in the area of foreign policy formulation. . . .

Economic Power: Human Capital in a Globalizing World Economy Some scholars argue that, in an increasingly global economy, states will inevitably see labor migration as a means of maximizing economic gains. Immigration flows are highly correlated with economic growth. The postwar economic boom in Germany and other Western European countries would not have been possible without the influx of migrant labor from Mediterranean countries in the 1960s. In the 1990s, migration flows and an increase in the foreign-born labor force were largely responsible for spurring growth in the U.S. economy. Highly industrialized countries are designing their immigration systems to harness the talent of skilled workers, attempting to outdo one another in luring talent in what the IOM has referred to as a "human capital accretion 'sweepstakes.'" This trend is especially noticeable in the area of information technology and the knowledge economy, which has become an integral component of state power. The United States, for example, has encouraged highly skilled labor migration with the H-1B visa, which brings people in to work temporarily in the information technology and communication sectors, a route that often becomes a fast-track for permanent migration. In 2000 Germany initiated a new "Green Card" program, modeled on the U.S. program, as a way of attracting highly skilled labor, especially computer specialists.

Students are another group of sought-after "migrants." The United States continues to be a world leader in issuing student visas, although other states are increasingly attempting to capture a greater share of this "market." Universities in Great Britain, for example, are turning to overseas students as a source of revenue to stem the financial crisis that has hit its education sector; in 2005, for example, Britain was host to approximately 50,000 students from China. In the wake of the September 11 attacks, U.S. leadership in attracting international talent has been called into question, as the United States has reduced the number of visas issued to foreign students and increased the time it takes for students to acquire visas: an overall drop in foreign graduate student applications to top U.S. universities has caused some to question the ability of the United States to maintain its leading edge in science and technology if such restrictions continue.

In the global competition for highly skilled workers, however, there are winners and losers. In particular, many parts of Africa continue to experience a brain drain of skilled labor. In 1987, 30 percent of Africa's skilled workforce lived in Europe, and in the 1990s more than 5 percent of all Africans were estimated to be living outside their country of origin. According to estimates, 70,000 professionals and university graduates leave countries in Africa every year with the aim of working in Europe or North America; more than 20,000 Nigerian doctors practice in North America; and in 2003 the South African economy had lost approximately $7.8 billion in human capital due to emigration since 1997. The exit of highly skilled labor from developing economies contributes to the growing gap between the wealthiest and poorest members of the international state system.

Yet the effects of emigration processes from the developing world to the developed world are multiple, and developing countries also benefit greatly from out-migration. Perhaps the most significant result of migration from developing countries is the capital flows that are generated through labor remittances. If states are able to capture the developmental benefits of remittances, this can contribute substantially to economic growth in ways that have advantages over other types of capital flows. . . .

The size of remittances has been growing steadily since the 1970s. Whereas in 1970 global remittances were estimated at slightly more than $3 billion, by 1988 the figure had increased to $30.4 billion. In the mid-1990s global remittances were estimated at $66 billion, an amount greater than the sum of all state-sponsored foreign development aid programs. Estimates for remittances in 2002 ran as high as $100 billion annually in transnational flows across national borders.

Labor remittances from migrants make up more than half of all total financial inflows in a number of countries. In Morocco, they total approximately $3.3 billion a year, accounting for 83 percent of the trade balance deficit. In both Egypt and Tunisia, they account for 51 percent of capital inflows. Labor remittances can be put to use for a variety of purposes and, if effectively utilized, can help to stimulate economic development. In the year 2000, labor remittances contributed more than 10 percent to the national economies of several developing countries, including El Salvador, Eritrea, Jamaica, Jordan, Nicaragua, and Yemen. As such, more states are trying to harness the power of labor remittances. Morocco, for example, is prioritizing migration management through the establishment of foundations that encourage the temporary return migration of skilled professionals; it is also seeking to foster a core of elite émigrés who can further the country's development and promote Moroccan culture abroad.

Military Power: Immigrant Skills, Expertise, and Recruits   Immigrants can also contribute to a state's military strength by, for example, providing technical and intelligence expertise (e.g., foreign language skills and analysis). An extreme example is the role that émigré scientists played in developing the U.S. nuclear program in the 1930s. Albert Einstein, Edward Teller, and others who fled National Socialism in Europe put their scientific expertise to work in developing the first atomic bomb. This is but one of many examples of the ability of states to harness the skills and expertise of immigrants for military ends.

The state can also draw on immigrant populations when fighting a war. The use of noncitizens mirrors, in some respects, the recent increased use of private contractors in U.S. military operations. In 2004 it was estimated that 40,000 noncitizens were enrolled in the U.S. military, or 4 percent of all enlistees. In fact, joining the military is one way to expedite the naturalization process for noncitizens. U.S. military recruiters regularly seek new recruits in immigrant communities. In some areas of California, up to half of all enlistees do not have U.S. citizenship, and five of the first ten Californians who perished in the war in Iraq were noncitizens. The U.S. military also attempted to mobilize recent immigrants or their descendents when it sought to create a separate division of approximately 3,000 Iraqi expatriates and exiles known as the Free Iraq Forces.

Diplomatic Power: Migrants and Ambassadors   Migration can enhance a state's ability to engage in diplomacy. In some respects, this is the flip side of the earlier discussion regarding a state's ability to maintain a coherent national identity. Small states in the international system can involve their diasporas in diplomacy by drawing on emigrants and their descendents within a target country, and by sponsoring lobbying and public relations activities. In the United States, for example, NATO enlargement was helped along by the domestic lobbying activities of Americans of Eastern European descent. Armenia has a diaspora desk in the ministry of foreign affairs. The Republic of Cyprus draws on its diaspora in the United Kingdom and elsewhere to represent its interests abroad in the Cyprus conflict. . . .

Cross-Border Mobility and the Changing Nature of Violent Conflict

. . . Migration flows can interact with other factors in three ways to exacerbate conditions that foment violent conflict in the international system: by providing resources that help to fuel internal conflicts; by providing opportunities for networks of organized crime; and by providing conduits for international terrorism. The degree to which each of these factors affects a state depends on the level of its capacity. Organized crime, for example, presents itself as a law enforcement problem to highly institutionalized states; but for weakly institutionalized states, organized crime can lead to much more serious consequences, corrupting, challenging, or even hijacking state institutions. . . .

Internal Conflict: Mobilized Diasporas and Refugees   International migration processes, combined with the availability of new technologies and media markets, allow for migrants and their descendents to remain connected to their home country and co-ethnics through diaspora networks. These transnational diaspora networks, in turn, can be used as a political resource, including in violent conflicts.

Studies have shown that diaspora funding played a key role in providing resources for violent conflicts during the 1990s. According to a World Bank study, countries experiencing violent conflict that had significant diaspora populations abroad were six times likelier to experience a recurrence of conflict than states without such populations. The author of this report, Paul Collier, argued that "diasporas appear to make life for those left behind much more dangerous in post-conflict situations." . . .

A similar dynamic exists with regard to refugee populations and violent conflict. Just as political entrepreneurs can mobilize resources and political support for a conflict within diasporas in Western industrial states, refugee populations can also provide a base for political mobilization activities in conflicts. Not all refugee populations are likely to become the targets of political mobilization activities, but when they are targeted, dilemmas are created on multiple levels. Humanitarian assistance operations that target refugee populations, for example, can fuel violent conflicts by providing material assistance, support, and legitimacy to militants who are embedded in or linked to refugee camps and populations. This is what occurred in refugee camps in the Democratic Republic of Congo (at that time, Zaire) following the 1994 Rwandan genocide and in camps in Pakistan following the 1979 Soviet invasion of Afghanistan.

Organized Crime: Human Smuggling and Gray Economy Networks   Perhaps the most obvious link between migration and organized crime is the global industry in human smuggling and trafficking that has emerged to meet the demands of individuals seeking to cross national borders. This is an instance in which market-based mechanisms take over when the demand for opportunities to immigrate outstrips the supply provided by official channels in state migration policies. Smugglers command high prices for their services, ranging from $500 for passage from Morocco to Spain to as much as $50,000 from some countries in Asia to the United States. Like other nonstate actors, smuggling networks have been able to take advantage of new technologies to achieve their goals. Albanian smuggling groups operating in the Czech Republic during the 1990s, for example, were equipped with night-vision equipment, cell phones with network cards, and other high-technology gear that were used to help smuggle some 40,000 "clients" across the Czech-German border. . . .

Global organized criminal networks are often defined by a particular ethnicity and are able to operate transnationally by forging networks of solidarity that take advantage of migration-based networks and migration circuits. Again, organized criminal networks are not new. Chinese criminal networks, or "Triads," for example, smuggled Chinese into California during the Gold Rush in the 1840s. What is new, however, is the globalization of ethnically based criminal networks and their ability to forge alliances with one another—organizing themselves internationally, just as any legitimate business might do in a global economy. Peter Lupsha details how contemporary "Chinese illegals in Naples produced counterfeit French perfume in bottles made in Spain, with faux Chanel perfume made in Mexico, and covered in gold wrappings and labels printed in Belgium." Just as globalization provides opportunities for legal operations to transnationalize production structures, so too does it provide opportunities for criminal operations that rely on networks of individuals that stretch across national borders. . . .

Conclusion

The management of international migration flows is a key challenge facing states in a globalized international security environment. . . .

Ultimately, however, it is how states respond to global migration flows through policy formation and implementation that will determine the extent to which national security is enhanced or diminished by international migration. . . . The challenge facing states is to adopt an expansive, long-term view of migration, taking into account the many benefits of international migration and devising comprehensive migration policies that enhance overall levels of international security. States that are best able to "harness the power of migration" through well-designed policies in cooperation with other states will also be the best equipped to face the new global security environment.

 # Political Causes and Effects of Migration: Poverty, Misgovernment, and Violence

13.2 Europe's Huddled Masses

The Economist

This brief selection describes the movement of people from the former communist states of Eastern Europe like Poland westward to richer countries like Britain. The author explodes a number of myths about this movement. For example, Western Europe is not the main destination for migrants in Europe; America and Russia are. Also, expectations about the future are more important in motivating migrants than income differentials. The author also observes that opinions are divided on whether migration benefits the migrants' countries of origin, with some observers arguing that the money that migrants remit home is highly beneficial, while others bemoan the loss of skills as talented young people leave their home countries. In all events, the tide of migration westward is unlikely to continue as populations in their home countries decline and conditions improve.

Robert, the Polish-born head of a group of British removal men, can read and write English easily, unlike his British colleagues who after packing their cardboard boxes label them as "clovs" and "shuse." Two years ago, when he moved to Britain, Robert lugged heavy loads like them. He still lives worse than they do, in a shabby rented house crammed with compatriots. But the remittances he sends home are paying for his family, a car, a house and—eventually—his own business there.

That dream, of hard work abroad leading to success at home, has inspired millions of people to move across Europe since the collapse of communism—a peacetime migration exceeded only by the upheavals that followed the end of the second world war. But remarkably little is known about the nature of this movement of people one way, and money the other, not least because so much is undocumented or illegal. Now a new report from the World Bank attempts to fill some gaps and explode some misconceptions.

The first is that the main migration is from the ex-communist world to what used to be called the West, when in fact Russia is the main destination for immigrants, surpassed only by America. That is due partly to ethnic Russians returning to the motherland after the break-up of the Soviet Union, but also to Tajiks, Georgians, Moldovans and other non-Slav citizens of ex-Soviet republics moving to Russia in search of work. In the process, Georgia, for example, lost a fifth of its population in the 14 years from 1989.

The money-flows from migration—around $19 billion annually, the authors estimate—are surprising too. In some countries they matter more than foreign investment. For example, remittances make up more than a quarter of Moldova's GDP—a figure exceeded worldwide only in Haiti and Tonga. For nine ex-communist countries, remittances provide 5 percent or more of national income. In the region as a whole, three-quarters of the money come from migrants working in the European Union; about a tenth from those in the former Soviet Union.

The big question is the impact on the home country's development. Optimists think that remittances prop up current accounts and help development. "Whereas aid to governments is often wasted or siphoned off into Swiss bank accounts, migrants' remittances end up directly in poor people's pockets," says Philippe Legrain (formerly of *The Economist*) in a book arguing the case for migration.

But pessimists reckon that having the best and brightest working abroad, often in menial jobs, is a dreadful loss. Remittances may also keep currencies artificially high, harming growth. The World Bank's authors think only a third of remittances go on education, savings and business investment. The overall result, they surmise, has been a mild stimulus to growth in the recipient countries, but without a measurable effect on poverty: it is better-off, urban families that tend to send someone abroad, and then reap the benefits.

The final misconception is about what motivates migration. "Everyone thinks it is all about income differentials, but actually it is all about expectations. Even in poor countries we can expect low levels of migration if people think that conditions there will improve," argues Brice Quillin, one of the report's authors.

From one viewpoint, the huge migration of recent years to western Europe seems unlikely to continue. Populations are declining in all countries (except Albania) in the western half of the post-communist region. That tightens their labour markets and may stimulate migration from farther east. By contrast, populations in the southern states of the former Soviet Union—countries such as Tajikistan—will keep growing until the middle of this century. "If the typical migrant of the 1990s was a Pole moving to Britain, his successor in the next decade may be a Tajik moving to Poland," says Mr. Quillin. Even Turkey, previously a big exporter of workers, now imports migrants.

What really helps putative migrants stay at home is not just higher wages but the prospect of fast, effective reform, bringing better public services and a dependable legal system. Employers in post-communist countries, particularly those outside big cities with a local monopoly in the job market, still treat their employees with remarkable casualness. A sawmill in a small town, for example, may fail to pay wages, and then declare bankruptcy, only to restart under a new name with the same owners, managers and workforce.

The catch is that reform throughout the region is flagging. No country between the Baltic, Black and Adriatic seas can boast a strong reformist government, and with a few exceptions the farther east you go, the worst it gets.

13.3 A Massive Migration

Sudarsan Raghavan

The war in Iraq and the civil violence among Shia, Sunni, and Kurds that followed have produced a massive migration from the country. Iraq's neighbors—Jordan, Syria, and Lebanon—have been overwhelmed by Iraqi migrants, many of whom are Iraq's most skilled and wealthy professionals and who constitute an additional burden on host countries already burdened by large Palestinian refugee populations. The number of internal refugees—the victims of sectarian threats and violence—constitutes an additional humanitarian disaster.

Inside his cold, crumbling apartment, Saad Ali teeters on the fringes of life. Once a popular singer in his native Baghdad, he is now unemployed. To pay his $45 monthly rent, he borrows from friends. To bathe, he boils water on a tiny heater. He sleeps on a frayed mattress, under a tattered blanket.

Outside, Ali, 35, avoids police officers and disguises his Arabic with a Jordanian dialect. He returns home before 10 p.m. to stay clear of government checkpoints. Like hundreds of thousands of Iraqi refugees here, he fears being deported. Six

Raghavan, Sudarsan, "A Massive Migration," *Washington Post National Weekly Edition*, February 12–18, 2007, pp. 6–7. © 2007, The Washington Post, reprinted with permission.

months ago, near his home in Baghdad, two men threatened to kill him. Singing romantic songs, they said, was un-Islamic.

So when his pride hits a new low, he remembers that day.

"Despite all the hardships I face here, it is better than going back to Baghdad," said Ali, long-faced with a sharp chin, who wore a thick red sweat shirt and rubbed his hands to keep warm. "They will behead me. What else can I do? I have no choice."

As the fourth year of war nears its end, the Middle East's largest refugee crisis since the Palestinian exodus from Israel in 1948 in unfolding in a climate of fear, persecution and tragedy.

Nearly 2 million Iraqis—about 8 percent of the prewar population—have embarked on a desperate migration, mostly to Jordan, Syria and Lebanon, according to the U.N. High Commissioner for Refugees. The refugees include large numbers of doctors, academics and other professionals vital for Iraq's recovery. Another 1.7 million have been forced to move to safer towns and villages inside Iraq, and as many as 50,000 Iraqis a month flee their homes, the U.N. agency said in January.

The rich began trickling out of Iraq as conditions deteriorated under U.N. sanctions in the 1990s, their flight growing in the aftermath of the 2003 U.S.-led invasion. Now, as the violence worsens, increasing numbers of poor Iraqis are on the move, aid officials say. To flee, Iraqis sell their possessions, raid their savings and borrow money from relatives. They ride buses or walk across terrain riddled with criminals and Sunni insurgents, preferring to risk death over remaining in Iraq.

The United Nations is struggling to find funding to assist Iraqi refugees. Fewer than 500 have been resettled in the United State since the invasion. Aid officials and human rights activists say the United States and other Western nations are focused on reconstructing Iraq while ignoring the war's human fallout.

"It's probably political," says Janvier de Riedmatten, U.N. refugee agency representative for Iraq, referring to the reason why the world hasn't helped Iraq's refugees.

"The Iraq story has to be a success story," he says.

For decades, Jordan welcomed refugees. Roughly a third of its 5.9 million residents are Palestinian refugees. According to the United Nations, 500,000 to 700,000 Iraqi refugees live in Jordan, but aid officials say the actual number is nearer to 1 million because many Iraqis live under the radar. Jordan's tolerance has waned, however, since a group of Iraqis bombed three hotels in November 2005, killing 60 people, according to Iraqis, aid officials and human rights groups. The government fears that Iraq's mostly Sunni Arab refugees could remain in the country permanently or become recruits for Iraq's insurgency.

Now, the exodus is generating friction and anger across the region, while straining basic services in already poor countries. Iraqis are blamed for driving up prices and taking away scarce jobs. Iraq's neighbors worry the new refugees will carry in Iraq's sectarian strife.

"The Jordan government does not want to encourage Iraqis to stay for a long time," says Gaby Daw, project officer for the Catholic charity Caritas Internationalis, one of the few aid agencies assisting Iraqi refugees.

Into their new havens, Iraqis are bringing their culture and way of life, gradually reshaping the face of the Arab world. But the cost of escape is high. Feeding the bitterness of exile is a sense that outside forces created their plight. Many Iraqis here view the U.S.-led invasion that ousted President Saddam Hussein as the root of their woes.

"We were promised a kind of heaven on earth," says Rabab Haider, who fled Baghdad last year. "But we've been given a real hell."

The road out of Iraq begins on Salhiye Street in Baghdad.

On Jan. 13, knots of Iraqis waited to board 14 buses to Syria. Inside a travel agency, Raghed Moyed, 23, sat solemnly with her 12-year-old brother, Amar. It had become too dangerous for her to attend college, so she was heading to Damascus to continue her education. As she sat, her head bowed, she recalled the previous night, when she bade farewell to her friends.

"It's really sad," said Moyed, her voice cracking as tears slid down her face. "I cried the whole way from the house to here. I don't want to leave Iraq, but it is hard to stay."

Sameer Humfash, the travel agent, watched her cry. By his estimate, 50 to 60 families were fleeing each day on the buses lined up outside. Nowadays, Iraqis were heading mostly to Syria, he said.

"They are not letting Iraqis in at the Jordanian border," interrupted Ahmed Khudair, one of Humfash's employees.

Humfash makes all his passengers sign waiver forms that read: "I am traveling on my own responsibility and God is the only one that protects us." On the roads to both Jordan and Syria, Sunni insurgents have dragged Shiites from buses and executed them. Humfash stays in radio contact every hour with the bus driver, usually a Syrian. He always asks three questions, he said:

"How is the road?"

"Did they take any passengers?"

"Did they hurt any passengers?"

Along the Iraq-Jordan border Jan. 16, a brisk wind howled across the barren landscape. It was 1:45 p.m. Until recently, hundreds of cars and buses filled with Iraqis would have been lined up to enter Jordan. On this day, there were four vehicles. A Jordanian border security official said many Iraqis were afraid to travel through Anbar province, one of Iraq's most violent regions.

Abu Hussam al-Khaisy, an Iraqi taxi driver, offered another explanation. The day before he had brought a family of seven Iraqis to the border, but Jordanian officials, he said, denied them admission with no explanation.

"They are not giving permission to enter because they are scared about security," said Khaisy at a restaurant in Ruwayshid, a Jordanian rest stop about 55 miles from the border. In other instances, he said, officials have turned away young Iraqi men who could take jobs away from Jordanians.

Today, the government is making it increasingly difficult for Iraqis to reside legally in Jordan. It views Iraqis as temporary visitors, not refugees, and has not sought international assistance. Human rights activists and U.N. officials have accused Jordan of shutting its border to many Iraqis fleeing persecution and deporting others.

Nasir Judah, a government spokesman, says Jordan has kept its door open to Iraqis even as they have become a burden on Jordan's economy and natural resources. In recent years, the influx was largely unregulated, but now tighter security measures are needed, he says. Iraqis, he adds, have tried to enter Jordan using fake passports and identity cards.

"There are no mass deportations of Iraqis," Judah says. "Otherwise the numbers would be dwindling, and they are not."

On this day, Khaisy was driving Abu Wisam al-Azzawi, 35, back to Baqubah, a city about 35 miles northeast of Baghdad. Two months ago, members of Azzawi's immediate family were refused entry into Jordan, even though he owned a car dealership in Amman. Azzawi still remembers his son, on the Iraq side of the border, pleading through the cellphone: "Daddy, don't leave us."

Now, he was planning to fetch them from Baqubah and take them to Syria.

"I haven't told my family I am coming back," said Azzawi, before getting into Khaisy's maroon Caprice Classic in Ruwayshid. "Maybe I am not going to see them."

"Maybe I will get killed on the road."

Outside the restaurant, two sport-utility vehicles passed by, heading to Amman. One carried Abu Saif al-Ajrami's family. The other vehicle carried their possessions.

The Jordanians let them in after the family waited more than 24 hours at the border. It helped that Ajrami's father was Jordanian. At night, they arrived in Amman near a place refugees call Iraq Square, where taxis drop off recent arrivals. Two relatives, whom the family had not seen in five years, met them. There were hugs and kisses, and praises to God.

"I feel psychologically relieved. You can see it is very safe," said Ajrami, waving his hands at the cars flowing by. "But I have left my family, friends, my neighbors, my memories back in Baghdad. The first day there is security, I will go back."

Then he declared he would find a job the next day. "From the border to here, we felt like we had entered paradise," he said.

Widad Shakur, 53, said that when she arrived in Amman in October, she felt the same way. A Shiite Muslim, she fled after Sunni extremists threatened to behead her daughter, a teacher. But Iraqi's chaos is never far away. Now Shakur has learned that a Sunni family has occupied her house. She cannot sleep at night.

And she cannot afford to return to Iraq. Her daughter, a saleswoman, earns barely $300 a month, half of which goes to their rent. "I wish I was a bird and I could fly back to my house," said Shakur, as tears welled in her eyes.

"Who expected it would turn out like this—Sunni against Shia?" she continued. "We were like brothers. Why is this happening?"

She has a more pressing problem. Her legs hurt, she said. But she cannot afford a doctor. She worries that seeking help at a Jordanian hospital might lead to deportation, even though she has a three-month residency permit.

"I don't know whether we have the right to go to it or not," said Shakur, who wore a black, sequined head scarf. "I am afraid to go there."

At the Royal Association for Iraq Immigrants, Salah al-Samarai had 28 pink and yellow folders stacked on his desk. They belonged to Iraqis in need of surgeries.

"I don't know what to do," said Samarai, the head of the nonprofit that helps Iraqis, as visitors waited outside.

In front of him sat Waad Abdul Rahim, a solemn Iraqi professor dressed in a tweed jacket. His 14-year-old daughter, Mina, needed an intestinal operation. It cost $5,000. For the past month and a half, he has visited Samarai's office.

"I come every day, and then I go back to suffer," Rahim said. "Her life is in danger. The longer it takes, the more dangerous it is going to be."

Samarai nodded in sympathy and said, "We have four or five more-serious cases."

Most of the organization's funds come from donations, he said. He doesn't blame the Jordanian government. "It's enough they opened their doors for us to stay here," Samarai said. But he wished the international community would do more to help.

"Lots of Americans tell us we don't need money. 'You are wealthy.' I even went to the European Union. They also said, 'You don't need money.'"

Rabab Haider and her husband, Ibrahim Al-Shawy, live in an elegant, sunlit apartment in Amman. Along with other middle-class Iraqis, they live in a parallel Iraq. Many of their relatives and friends are here. Iraqi's sectarian divisions rarely enter their lives.

The richest Iraqis can get residency permits by depositing $70,000 in a Jordanian bank, buying property or investing. Others simply pay a $2 daily fine for expired permits.

"I see more Iraqis here than I do in Baghdad," said Shawy, who travels every few months to Iraq, where he own land.

Qaduri, a popular restaurant nearby, was once an institution in Baghdad. Then it was bombed. Seven months ago, its owners decided to resurrect it in Amman. Now it serves tashreeb, a traditional Iraqi stew, from midnight to noon, just as it did in Baghdad.

Next door, a sign reads that another restaurant plans to open soon. Its specialty: pacha, the dish of boiled lamb's head that Iraqis consider a delicacy.

At a recent Iraqi wedding in the upscale Bristol Hotel, an Iraqi singer sang songs and guests moved to the drumbeats of the jobee, an Iraqi folk dance. In Baghdad, with the car bombs, checkpoints and kidnappings, large weddings are all but extinct.

"You turned the clock back four years," Um Ammar, a guest who had recently arrived from Baghdad, told the groom's mother.

The singer began to hum a patriotic Iraqi hymn. In the audience, eyes filled with tears. Others sobbed.

Moments later, the singer crooned: "Baghdad."

The audience responded: "In my eyes is Heaven."

"Baghdad," the singer sang again.

"Is our one and only love," the audience sang. "Baghdad is our sole mother, may God safeguard you from the evil surrounding you."

On a January afternoon, over cake and coffee in their Amman apartment, Haider and Shawy spoke of nostalgia, guilt and uncertainty.

"What about the torment?" said Haider, a pleasant, short-haired woman with a faint British accent. "You being safe and your people in Baghdad are not."

They have six months of savings left, Shawy said. He's sending résumés around the world.

"How long can we keep this?" asked Haider, looking at their plush sofas, the purple vase, the glass dining table.

On January 18, a curly-haired artist named Qais Mohammed Ateih sat inside singer Saad Ali's two-room apartment, which is nestled near a warren of shops and narrow alleys. A third Iraqi refugee, Razzaq al-Okaeli, 35, joined them. The trio spoke about being like beggars, depending on friends for meals. Ateih said he knew at least 70 Iraqis who have been deported since 2003.

In the wake of Hussein's execution in December, many Iraqi Shiites say they have been targeted because of their sect. Jordan, a mostly Sunni nation, is home to many supporters of Hussein, who was a Sunni and a benefactor of Palestinians.

"Is the government targeting us for being Shiites? No. But from individual policemen, we feel this," said Ateih, 36. "They say, 'You betrayed Saddam.'"

If they are lucky, Ateih said, they find jobs as day laborers, earning $7 for a 14-hour workday. But Jordanian employers, they say, often exploit Iraqis. Okaeli said he recently worked for two months as an air-conditioning repairman; his employer paid him for only 10 days of work.

"They know we cannot complain to the authorities," said Okaeli, a short man with brushed-back hair and long, trim sideburns. "If we complain, we will get deported."

Ali sat on a worn brown sofa, rubbing his hands, taking in the conversations. He had hoped to earn enough money to help his parents in Baghdad. Now, when he speaks to them, he never reveals the truth.

"They are inside Iraq. They should have to worry only about themselves," said Ali, his eyes lowered at the dusty red carpet. "So I tell them I am fine."

He paused, then glanced at the tiny heater, and said, "I never expected it would be like this."

Diasporas and International Politics

13.4 A World of Exiles

The Economist

Inevitably, people retain an interest in their countries of origin long after they emigrate elsewhere. The final selection is this chapter, taken from the British journal *The Economist,* turns to the question of whether or not communities of people from one country who are living in another—"diasporas"—divide their loyalties between the country from which they have come and that in which they reside. The article focuses on how these overseas communities relate to their new countries and how they try to participate or affect events back home.

W hy does Macedonia have no embassy in Australia? Why might a mountain in northern Greece soon be disfigured by an image of Alexander the Great 73 metres (nearly 240 feet) high? Who paid for the bloody war between Ethiopia and Eritrea? How did Croatia succeed in winning early international recognition as an independent country? And why do Mexican candidates for political office campaign in the United States?

The short answer to each of these questions is a diaspora—a community of people living outside their country of origin. Macedonia has no embassy in Australia because Greeks think the former Yugoslav republic that calls itself Macedonia has purloined the name from them, and the Greek vote counts for a lot in Australia. So as a sop to local Greeks outraged by its decision to recognise the upstart Macedonia, the Australian government has not yet allowed it to open an embassy in Canberra.

The case of the missing embassy is an extreme, but typical, example of how diasporas have long exerted their influence: they have lobbied in their adopted countries for policies favourable to the homeland. But now something new is taking place: diasporas are increasingly exerting influence on the politics of the countries they have physically, but not emotionally, abandoned. An example of this trend is the case of the monumental Alexander. The Greek diaspora is so proud of Alexander the Great, whose Macedonian kingdom encompassed what are now parts of northern Greece, and so keen to establish him as Greek, that it wants to carve his effigy on a cliff face on Mount Kerdyllion. The Greek authorities in Athens are horrified, but the Alexander the Great Foundation, based in Chicago, is eager to get chipping, and says its members will cover the $45 million cost. Grotesque as it may consider the scheme—the monument would be four times the size of the American presidents carved on Mount Rushmore—the Greek government may yield. It is to rich Greek-Americans that it turns when it wants to promote its interests in America.

Similarly, it was to its citizens abroad that Eritrea looked when it decided to wage a pointless border war between 1998 and 2000. Small, poor and just six years old, the country was in no position to fight its much bigger neighbour, Ethiopia. But of Eritrea's 3.8 million people, about 333,000 were émigrés and, astonishingly, the government was able to tax their personal income at 2 percent a year. This helped to finance, and thus to perpetuate, a terrible war.

Croats abroad also did their bit for their country, both before and after independence in 1991. In the early 1990s, not long after European communism had collapsed but before the Yugoslav federation had begun to disintegrate, the cry went up in Croatia for Croats of the diaspora to come home. Some did, returning to fight in the war that broke out in 1991. Other Croats abroad raised money: as much as $30 million had been mustered by 1991. Meanwhile, Croat exiles were lobbying hard in Germany, which in turn bounced the European Union into early recognition of the new state. Fiercely nationalist exiles forked out at least $4 million for the 1990 election campaign of Franjo Tudjman, Croatia's arch nationalist president, and in return were awarded representation in parliament in 1992, by which time the country had won its independence. Twelve out of the 120 seats were allotted to diaspora Croats, who cast their votes in consulates abroad, or in community centres, clubs and churches designated by the authorities in Zagreb. By contrast, only seven seats were set aside for Croatia's ethnic minorities.

Since 1996, Mexicans abroad have also had the right to vote in national elections although the legislation to allow them to do so without coming home has yet to be passed. Still, with 10.8 million citizens of voting age out of the country, many political candidates reckon it is worth their while to campaign in the United States, where 99 percent of the absentees live. Even if just a small proportion comes back on polling day that may be enough to tip an election.

The diaspora's new right to vote, however theoretical it remains, was a right reluctantly given. The Institutional Revolutionary Party (PRI), which ruled Mexico uninterruptedly for over 60 years, thought expatriate Mexicans were unlikely to support it. It was probably right. Although the diaspora was not composed of political exiles implacably hostile to the government of the country they had left, the émigrés were probably sophisticated enough to dislike the PRI's self-serving policies. Moreover, nationalism, which so often makes exiles sympathetic to the government back home, was hardly an issue in Mexican elections.

As a rule of thumb, though, émigrés are nationalists, even though they may at the same time be loyal citizens of their adopted country (96 percent of Australia's Croats are naturalised, and not known as lukewarm in their Ozziness). Perhaps the strength of nationalist feeling has something to do with feelings of guilt among those fortunate enough to live abroad, especially when the home country is under some kind of threat. Perhaps it has something to do with not having to live with the consequences of nationalism *pur et dur*. Perhaps it is because exile sharpens the sense of the country left behind. Issues may simply seem clearer from afar. In any event, absence certainly seems to make the heart grow fonder—and fiercer.

If you doubt that, just imagine what would happen in Ireland, north and south of the border, if Irish-Americans were allowed to vote in Ireland's or Ulster's elections. Irish-Americans tend to be strong supporters of republicanism, and in the 1970s and 1980s they raised huge amounts of money for republican terrorist groups such as the IRA. Or imagine what would happen to Cuba's politics if the exiles of southern Florida could vote as well as rant.

Wired and Wonderful

In the past, absence also made the power of the diaspora grow weaker. Scatter a few million émigrés across the globe, and, being everywhere in a minority, they are weak. They are influential only where they are concentrated, as, say, Swedes are in southern Finland; or where they are especially well-organised, as Jews are in the

United States and Armenians are in France. That is certainly the way it used to be. But nowadays jet planes, rapid communication and in particular the Internet have enabled dispersed exiles to come together cheaply and effectively for the first time in history.

This change is most evident not among the best known, older-established diasporas but among the younger ones. Thus the influence on China of the huge community of overseas Chinese is, so far at least, chiefly felt through commerce and investment; it is not yet directly political. Similarly, émigré Indians have yet to exert much out-of-body-politic influence on the homeland. Expatriate Scots count for little in Scotland. And, though passionately interested in Israel and ready to support it financially, the Jewish diaspora—the first to be given the name, after the Babylonian captivity—is probably more influential outside than within the Jewish state.

Look instead at the Tamils, and in particular at the long war fought by the Tamil Tigers against the government of Sri Lanka. Superficially, this looks like a classic struggle between an oppressed group trying to win the right to secede and an intransigent government unwilling to let it. The Tamils have indeed been hard done by in the past, and Sri Lanka's government forces have committed their share of atrocities. The guerrillas have a skilful leader, some useful exiles abroad and foreign friends who lend support. Such has been the pattern often enough in struggles elsewhere—as, for instance, when the United States wanted to break away from Britain.

But the Sri Lankan civil war has not been a standard affair. For a start, it has been unusually brutal: 65,000 lives have been lost. The Tigers have ruthlessly exploited not just child soldiers but also suicide bombers. And they have done so for most of the past 19 years with the support of a generous community of exiles. Some 60 million Tamils live in India, and Sri Lanka's politics have on at least one occasion fatefully affected India's: Rajiv Gandhi, a former prime minister of India, was assassinated by a Tamil suicide bomber in 1991 in retribution for India's involvement in Sri Lanka's civil war. But the truly Sri Lankan Tamil diaspora lies not in India but in Europe and North America. In 2001 the United Nations put the number of Tamil refugees abroad at 817,000. Taking into account those with citizenship of other countries, the total may be even bigger.

Many are poor, but a glance at the *Tamil Guardian*—"a weekly update for the global Tamil community"—suggests that the diaspora includes many others who are educated, prosperous and committed to the homeland. A broadsheet, it reprints serious articles from such papers as the *New York Times,* as well as covering the politics of Sri Lanka and the sporting and cultural activities of the diaspora; the Tigers receive uncritically fulsome coverage. Nor does it appear to want for advertisements.

Expatriate Tamils do not rely on their newspaper alone. Anything judged to be of interest to the community—a critical article in *The Economist,* for instance— may be circulated on the Internet among Tamil émigrés, particularly academics, and a flood of rather similar protests may ensue. A demonstration can be similarly conjured up if necessary, as when, in 2001, Sri Lanka appointed as high commissioner to Australia a general accused of brutality.

Both through voluntary contributions and through extortion, the diaspora has been used to help pay for the Tiger's long military campaign, which involves boats and naval forces as well as rockets, missiles and the usual paraphernalia required by soldiers—plus the cyanide pills that all Tigers are sworn to swallow if captured. At the same time, the diaspora has given succour to the exiled leadership, whose main base was for decades in London.

Second Thoughts from Abroad

If for many years the diaspora helped to sustain its side of Sri Lanka's vicious war, all the while condoning rather than condemning Tamil atrocities, so it has recently started to exercise a more benign influence. A few years ago, America, Britain and India all decided that the Tigers were not an entirely wholesome liberation group, and took steps to declare them terrorists instead; Britain proscribed them in February 2001. The disconcerted diaspora began to close its wallet.

Then came September 11th 2001, followed by a string of hideous suicide bombings in Israel, and the diaspora realised that the Tigers' record of 150 or more such bombings did not put them in good company. It was time to call a halt. A ceasefire was signed in December 2001 and talks have since been held in Thailand and Norway. Unexpectedly, the Tigers' leaders have even dropped their insistence on a completely independent homeland, saying they will settle for "substantial autonomy" instead. The outlook is now hopeful. For this, the diaspora can take some credit.

Arrivederci, Buenos Aires

With luck, the Tamil diaspora will soon be called upon to perform a more traditional role, that of helping to pay for the development of their homeland. Some diasporas are poorer than the people they left behind: so impoverished are the 537,000 Argentines of Italian origin that regions of Italy like the Veneto have organised "emigrant re-entry projects" to try to find jobs for those who want to come home. Most exile groups, however, are relatively well off. Even refugees who have fled their country with little or nothing tend either to go home eventually or to make good in a new country. It is largely the prosperity of emigrants, combined with their levels of education, that gives them their influence back home. All in all émigrés of one kind or another send about $100 billion home each year through official channels, 60 percent of it to poor countries, which may receive another $15 billion unofficially.

Much of this money is sent by underpaid Filipinas in Asia or exploited Bangladeshis in the Gulf. Yet exiles' earnings may well be higher than those at home, sometimes much higher, thanks not only to wage differentials but also to their qualifications: perhaps a third of highly educated Ghanaians live abroad, and three-quarters of Jamaica's population with higher education can be found in the United States alone. El Salvador values its emigrants' remittances ($1.75 billion in 2000) so much that it has made provision for legal aid in the United States to those of its citizens who want to claim or prolong political asylum.

Most poor countries are now resigned to losing their exiles physically, but that does not mean they cannot get hold of some of their money, or their expertise. Increasingly, this is an organised endeavour. So, for example, if you had been flying into Accra on July 22nd 2001, you might well have been going to a Ghana Homecoming Summit, organised by the country's Investment Promotion Centre to harness the skills of the Ghanaian diaspora and get it to cough up even more than the $300 million–400 million that it already sends home each year.

Why should it? Leaving aside sentimental considerations, one inducement is increasingly frequently offered: in return for money, voting rights. Apart from Mexico, Croatia and Eritrea, Armenia and India have also promised them. Filipinos would like them. Turkey, like Eritrea and Mexico, has amended its constitution to give them, but Germany, where the Turkish diaspora is heavily concentrated, is not keen to have foreign elections held on its soil.

Other countries have found other ways of exploiting their expatriates' political energies. Eritrea is one of the most advanced, perhaps because about 90 percent of eligible Eritreans abroad voted in the 1993 referendum on independence. Diaspora Eritreans then helped to draft the constitution, which guarantees them voting rights in future elections.

An alternative is to bring the exiles home in person. Turkey's Islamist party, now in government, has parachuted diaspora leaders into safe electoral seats in Turkey to reward them for fund-raising abroad. Afghanistan has pondered putting its ex-king back on the throne. Bulgaria has turned its ex-monarch into a prime minister. The Balts have been émigré importers on an almost industrial scale. Since becoming independent in 1991, Estonia has recruited from the diaspora two foreign ministers and a defence minister, plus lots of civil servants, especially in the foreign ministry. Latvia's popular president was brought back from Canada. It has also had the services of an American-Latvian defence minister, a bunch of members of parliament and a handful of diplomats, all mustered from the ranks of its émigrés. Lithuania's huge diaspora has supplied it with a president, the current chief of general staff (both Lithuanian-Americans) and several historians, novelists and poets. Unlike most expatriate Balts, Lithuania's are not all fierce nationalists.

The diaspora's influence is not always welcomed. Some exiles are simply mistrusted, especially if they were abroad when the going was hard. Thus Thabo Mbeki and those of his colleagues who struggled against apartheid from outside South Africa do not always command the respect of those who stayed and fought it from within. These exiles, though, were more like political exiles of the conventional kind—the enemies of English monarchs who plotted from France, the Cubans who launched the Bay of Pigs invasion from the United States, Russian revolutionaries who wandered Europe to escape the tsar, and so on. Diaspora exiles are different: their motives for leaving are often economic as much as political, and many have no intention of going home.

Home and Away, All at Once

Still, they can be a pain in the domestic neck. Kosovo's ethnic-Albanian émigrés helped to pay for and arm the guerrillas who proved crucial in NATO's war to rid Kosovo of its Serb oppressors. But those same émigrés, many of them left-wing in ideology and criminal in their connections, were less welcome when the time came to build the peace. Similarly, Albania's diaspora, smaller and on the whole right-wing, disastrously backed Sali Berisha, until the pyramid schemes that briefly beguiled his countrymen came crashing down. The Turks of northern Cyprus are not always convinced that the Turkish-Cypriot community in London, almost as numerous, is lobbying for the objectives they really seek.

Since September 11th, diasporas have come under new scrutiny to see whether they harbour or breed terrorists. They were already the object of growing interest among academics; and think-tanks such as the Rand Corporation in California had issued warnings that some diasporas might become fifth columns for hostile governments. Yet the influence of émigrés can be exaggerated. Eva Ostergaard-Nielsen, of the London School of Economics, points out that diasporas seldom make a government adopt a policy unless that policy is also in the country's national interest. But they do undoubtedly, and increasingly, mingle homeland interests with those of their adopted country, and carry their own concerns back home. As Tip O'Neill, an American politician of the old school, once said, "All politics is local." Now more than ever.

Suggested Discussion Topics

1. Do you think that migrants constitute a threat to America's national security? Why or why not? Do illegal migrants enrich the United States culturally and economically, or do they constitute an undue burden on American citizens? What policies are available to politicians to deal with the wave of illegal migrants, especially from Mexico and Central America? Are these realistic? What policy would you advocate, and how would it achieve its objectives?

2. What are the major causes and consequences of migration? Are massive movements of people an inevitable by-product of globalization and the growing porosity of states' borders, or can wealthy states manage the flows of refugees and migrants from the developing world?

3. Do you believe that individuals or groups being persecuted in their own country have a right to asylum in other countries? Should the United States accept groups threatened by genocide, such as European Jews in the 1940s, Tutsis from Rwanda and Muslims from Bosnia in the 1990s, or Iraqis today? What about individuals threatened with bodily harm, such as African women in traditional societies faced with female genital mutilation? If we refuse to accept these people into our country, do we have a responsibility to make sure that they are safe in their own country? Explain your thinking.

4. What about the migration of people seeking to improve their economic status? Should the flow of such people be impeded or encouraged? Why? How might the flow be limited, and what would be the economic consequences for their home countries and for the countries to which they seek to migrate?

5. Do diasporas pose a security threat to host countries? Should their divided loyalties make them suspect? Do you think that Mexicans in the United States or Muslims in Europe assimilate sufficiently in their host countries? Should more be done to make diasporas assimilate? Why or why not?

Chapter 14

THE CLASH OF CULTURES AND IDENTITIES

Previous chapters have suggested that, in part, the turbulence in today's global politics reflects the emergence of a new set of security problems, such as the increasingly transnational problems of crime and disease, the threat to ordinary lives generated by global economic forces, the tragedy of global poverty and underdevelopment, and the looming risks of environmental disaster. Part of the ongoing transformation of global politics, however, can be understood as the resurgence of an old problem, that of conflicting identities. As the boundaries of states weaken, as globalization facilitates the movement of large numbers of people farther and farther and faster and faster, as individuals are better able to communicate with people far away and discover common interests or shared beliefs, and as states are less and less able to control this communication and to shape how people think about or define themselves, how individuals and communities identify themselves and direct their loyalties becomes increasingly problematic and increasingly important. Identity politics has critical implications for how individuals interact and how they organize politically, and for the kinds of institutions, alliances, and conflicts that will emerge in coming years. Will new conflicts be based on cultural differences and be global in scope rather than be waged between sovereign states as in recent centuries? Will existing societies be torn apart along civilizational lines as peoples from very different cultures within these societies find it impossible to mix together?

In this chapter we examine the recent debates over whether a "clash of civilizations" will bring one or more of the world's great civilizations—for example, the West, the Islamic world, Orthodox Christian societies, China, and the Hindus of India—into conflict with another. The destruction of New York's World Trade Center at the hands of Islamic militants and America's subsequent invasion of the Islamic nations of Afghanistan and Iraq and announcement of a global "War Against Terror" have led some observers to speculate that a bloody clash of civilizations is already underway.

In this chapter we also examine the impact of colliding identities *within* societies. Migration and the mixing of cultural traditions raise questions about the future of "national" identities and about the survival of the nation-state. Continuing with our examination of identity politics in the next chapter, we will turn to the increasing importance of gender in world affairs and to questions about how gender identities and gendered ways of looking at the world affect world politics.

Cultural collisions are hardly new. Indeed, before the emergence of the modern territorial state global politics can be told largely as the story of encounters among different civilizations—for example, between the Mongols and Chinese around 1200 C.E., or between the Romans and Greeks around 200 B.C.E., or between the Spaniards and Aztecs in the fifteenth century. Some of these meetings ended in violence; some ended in the absorption of one culture by another; and still others ended in new "multicultural" societies. Conflict pitting different religious communities against each other was a central feature of European political life until the seventeenth century and has continued elsewhere to the present day. In some ways, the upsurge in importance of identities today, whether this is defined in national, ethnic, or religious terms, represents a return to this historic past.

The rise of a system of sovereign states complicated these cultural encounters and the ways in which identity politics is played out. Europe's colonial conquests in Asia and Africa, especially its later imperialism, represented the forcible subjugations of a tribal-based civilization by European conquerors, who imposed not only elements of their own culture but the idea of state-centric political authority. Both in their colonial dominions and within their own boundaries, states sought to repress or transform the identity of their subjects to strengthen the legitimacy, authority, and power of the state and to increase the state's ability to prevent, control, or manipulate violence. Tension between the state and individuals who feel emotional ties to groups whose membership does not conform to the boundaries of the state has always been a problem for political authority, however.

From the mid-nineteenth century through the mid-twentieth century, *nationalism*—the idea that one was part of an extended familylike group called a nation, that one should be willing to make sacrifices for the good of this nation, and that nations inevitably competed with each other for resources and power—was a major factor and source of conflict in world affairs. Nationalism can be constructed from a variety of attributes (such as a common history, language, or culture), and it overlaps with other attributes like common ethnicity or religion. Thanks to changes in communication technology and in economics that linked individuals in the countryside and in small villages with people in cities, "national" identity became increasingly important in the mid-1800s. Ordinary people, not simply the educated elite, identified themselves as part of a larger nation, not merely as members of a local or regional community, and were willing to work for what they saw as the common good of the nation. Increasingly, too, they were willing to fight for their nation: to throw off foreign rulers, to unite with other members of their nation in a single political unit, to expel outsiders from lands claimed by the nation, and to defeat neighboring states ruled or controlled by other nations either to gain control of valued resources or to demonstrate national superiority. The wars of Italian and German unification in the second half of the nineteenth century reflected this growing importance of national identity. Across most of Europe, there was pressure to adjust state boundaries to match the distribution of national groups. Where this was not easily accomplished—for example, in the case of the Austro-Hungarian Empire, whose territory included Germans, Hungarians, Czechs, Slovaks, Poles, Italians, Slovenes, Croats, and Romanians, among others—tensions were high. The two great global upheavals of the twentieth century, the First and Second World Wars, featured explosions of nationalist fervor.

In the wake of World War II, however, many of these historic national animosities (for example, between the Germans and the French) were put aside. In Europe, where conflict between nations had been fiercest, national identity was tempered: not only did most national groups have their own state (the multinational Yugoslav state and the Soviet Union being important exceptions) but international institutions such as the European Economic Community and the Warsaw Pact, and the overarching East-West conflict, encouraged rival nation-states to work together for common economic, political, or ideological purposes. Although there were a number of bloody identity-based conflicts during the Cold War—for instance, between Greeks and Turks on Cyprus—communal tensions usually took a back seat to the East-West contest.

The resurgence of identity-based violence since the end of the Cold War appears to be tied to a number of factors. The reduced autonomy of states in the face of globalized economic, technological, and social trends has encouraged people to seek psychological security in their roots. In doing so, they redefine "we" and "they" to emphasize identities other than those of citizen of a state. In addition, in many cases identity-based conflicts have been manipulated by cynical politicians to achieve their own ends. Thus the bloody struggle that raged in Bosnia among Muslims, Serbs, and Croats between 1992 and 1995 and the war and ethnic cleansing in Kosovo that began in 1999 were kindled by politicians like Serbia's leader Slobodan Milošević who sought to increase their personal power.

Although Europe has not been immune to this outbreak of identity-based violence, as the Bosnian and Kosovo examples illustrate, the less-developed world has been particularly vulnerable, for several reasons. First, in much of this area, particularly in Africa, state boundaries do not conform to identity groups. Drawn along the lines of old colonial partitions that were imposed with scant concern for whether or not they comported with identity-based divisions, state boundaries divide members of the same tribal or national groups and combine members of different ones. In many cases, the coercive apparatus of the state—the armed forces, police, secret police, and tax authorities—has simply been used by one identity group to enrich itself at the expense of the others.

Second, many less-developed states are relatively recent creations and, for a variety of reasons, failed to develop effective domestic institutions. During the Cold War, many of these states could count on support or aid from one of the superpowers, which enlisted them as allies or client-states in the East-West rivalry. With the end of the Cold War, however, superpower interest and backing largely dried up, and with it the resources these states could use to suppress warring identity-groups or to buy their common loyalty.

Third, as noted in the preceding chapters, environmental stress, rapidly increasing populations, and grinding poverty create a volatile mixture in states that were weak to begin with. Relative deprivation makes nationalism and tribalism particularly explosive, as feelings of grievance boil over.

One of the striking features of the present period of global turbulence, then, is the identity-based conflict we see around the world. Africa is the scene of a variety of tribal-based contests, for example, between Hutu and Tutsi in Burundi and Rwanda, Krahn and Mano in Liberia, and Mende and Temne in Sierra Leone. In

Asia, too, countries are riven by ethnicity and religion: Afghanistan is divided among Pashtuns, Tajiks, and Uzbeks; in Myanmar (or Burma), various national groups such as the Karens have attempted to assert their independence from the dominant Burmese; India has witnessed violence among Hindus, Muslims, and Sikhs; and even in China there is conflict between the Han Chinese and smaller identity groups such as the Tibetans and Muslim Uigurs. Many countries in Latin America, including Mexico, are plagued by divisions between descendants of the Spanish conquerors and indigenous Indians. The Middle East remains divided between Muslims and Jews, and Palestinian nationalism must be assuaged before permanent peace can come to the region. Even the developed world suffers from conflict between identity groups. Europe, for example, has identity-based cleavages between Catholics and Protestants in Northern Ireland, Walloons and Flemings in Belgium, and Basques and Spaniards in Spain, to name a few. North American states have divisions based on nation and race as well: in the United States, tensions exist among African Americans, whites, Hispanics, and Native Americans, while in Canada the divide between French- and English-speakers periodically threatens to result in the dissolution of the Canadian state. The ability of human beings to develop institutions that limit the pernicious, fragmenting effects of identity politics and permit "us" and "them" to live together to solve the shared problems we face is a key issue in today's turbulent transition.

While identity-based conflict is often local or regional in scope, as one group attempts to throw off the authority of another or seeks to protect resources or power that it regards as rightfully its own, in today's increasingly interconnected world we are also experiencing concerns about a *global* clash of civilizations. Some of these concerns have been triggered by violence of militant Muslims against the West and against governments in the Islamic world that they perceive as untrue to Islamic culture or as subservient to the West. There are other ways, too, in which the globalization we are now experiencing appears to be transforming the problem of managing identity-based conflicts. As we will also discuss in this chapter, the ease with which individuals can move in today's world while still retaining close ties to their cultural roots and to others who share these roots create new political issues and new questions about the future of the nation-state.

14.1 The Clash of Civilizations?

Samuel P. Huntington

Identity is not simply a matter of nationality, ethnicity, or race. It also may be rooted in deeper, broader cultural ties. It may reflect a widely shared understanding of what gives life meaning, of how to behave, and of how to arrange societies in order to achieve happiness. Different civilizations offer individuals different answers about how they should live their lives. Different civilizations provide different social norms and rules that guide individuals' relationships with each other and permit individuals to have what they regard as fulfilling existences. The world is fragmented between these different civilizations. How important the cleavages between them are—how much a barrier to global integration they will represent and how big an obstacle to collaboration between people and nations around the world they will be—is very much in dispute today. Thus following the destruction of the World Trade Center in September 2001, terrorist leader Osama bin Laden announced the beginning of what he regards as a war between civilizations, and many in the West shared the view that the secular Western world and the world of fundamentalist Islam were now on a collision course. If identities based on civilization are now critical, and if conflict rather than cooperation between civilizations emerges as the norm, this will mark an important departure from the recent past.

For over three centuries, global politics has revolved around the relations of Europe's states with one another, and most of our theories of global politics grew out of Europe's experience. Conflict and cooperation *within* the West and *within* the state system established in Europe have been the principal features of world politics.

Beginning in the fifteenth century, Europe's influence spread outward, first through explorers like Vasco da Gama and Christopher Columbus, then through conquistadors like Hernando Cortez and Francisco Pizarro, and still later through adventurers, missionaries, and settlers. After the last wave of European imperialism in the late nineteenth century, most of the non-European world was governed by European colonial authorities or by descendants of European settlers. Europe's world dominance was reinforced by the industrial and scientific revolutions, which began in Great Britain in the late eighteenth century, and by the adoption of European culture and customs among non-European elites, many of whom were sent to Europe for education. Until recently, non-European countries like Japan and India with ambitions to become major players in global politics sought to emulate Europe's social, political, and economic practices.

Europe's outward expansion and colonization of the rest of the world did not take place in a cultural vacuum and was not uncontested. The European empires were constructed on top of older civilizations, and the spread of Western power involved the destruction or subjugation of existing cultures. Many non-European civilizations have a rich history even older than Western civilization. Europe was still in the Dark Ages when Islam was in flower in Arabia, the Near East, North Africa, and Spain. The Ch'in unification of China (221–206 B.C.) was contemporary with the Roman republic and took place almost one thousand years after China's first imperial dynasty. The Aztecs, Mayas, and Incas, who were conquered by the Spaniards, lived in complex societies of considerable cultural achievement. The spread of European influence thus involved repeated collisions with sophisticated cultures, including the Indians of the New World, the Ashanti of Ghana, and the Ottomans of Turkey.

The end of colonialism and the growing military and economic might of regions like East and Southeast Asia are challenging the West today. At the same time, however, the telecommunications revolution and the global economy are exposing people all over the world to customs and tastes that first arose in the West. This "Coca-Cola" or global culture is a challenge to local customs and cultures and is profoundly disturbing to the advocates of traditional ways. In some cases, a backlash has taken place against foreign influences. The combination of growing assertiveness among non-European peoples and resistance to Western values has produced conflict in a variety of countries. In Iran, for example, the Westernizing and secular policies of Shah Reza Pahlavi were abruptly ended with his overthrow in 1979 by the Islamic fundamentalist followers of the Ayatollah Khomeini.

With these events in mind, in 1993 Harvard political scientist Samuel Huntington argued that, with the end of the European epoch of global politics, the most important source of conflict will be cultural and that this will pit peoples from different civilizations against one another. Huntington defines a civilization as "a cultural entity" in which people may share a common language, a common history, religion customs, and institutions. He identifies eight major civilizations in the world today, most of which include people from a number of different nation-states. Huntington offers six reasons he believes a clash of civilizations is likely, and he cites a variety of cases, such as the Bosnian civil war, to illustrate the proliferation of conflicts at the "fault lines" between civilizations, such as the one between the Islamic world and the West. He writes of the "kin-country" syndrome where people in a civilization seek to help others in their civilization who are involved in a war with those from another civilization. Thus, Iranian Muslims have fought alongside of their co-religionists in Bosnia, Afghanistan, and Chechnya in conflicts with Slavic-Orthodox Serbians and Slavic-Orthodox Russians. For Huntington, then, the decentralized and fragmented world of sovereign states is being replaced by a world that is still decentralized and fragmented, but on the basis of culture rather than sovereignty. Where other, more optimistic observers see the rise of powerful global institutions, Huntington sees continued division.

Huntington believes that the end of the Cold War has left the West at the peak of its power and that people in other regions are coming to resent the West's use of "international institutions, military power and economic resources" to maintain its hegemony. This resentment, Huntington believes, is likely to result in conflict between the West and the other civilizations.

The Next Pattern of Conflict

Worldpolitics is entering a new phase, and intellectuals have not hesitated to proliferate visions of what it will be—the end of history, the return of traditional rivalries between nation states, and the decline of the nation state from the conflicting pulls of tribalism and globalism, among others. Each of these visions catches aspects of the emerging reality. Yet they all miss a crucial, indeed a central, aspect of what global politics is likely to be in the coming years.

It is my hypothesis that the fundamental source of conflict in this new world will not be primarily ideological or primarily economic. The great divisions among humankind and the dominating source of conflict will be cultural. Nation states

Huntington, Samuel P., "The Clash of Civilizations?," *Foreign Affairs,* May/June 1994, pp. 100–112. Reprinted by permission of *Foreign Affairs.* © 1994 by the Council on Foreign Relations, Inc. <www.ForeignAffairs.org>.

will remain the most powerful actors in world affairs, but the principal conflicts of global politics will occur between nations and groups of different civilizations. The clash of civilizations will dominate global politics. The fault lines between civilizations will be the battle lines of the future.

Conflict between civilizations will be the latest phase in the evolution of conflict in the modern world. For a century and a half after the emergence of the modern international system with the Peace of Westphalia, the conflicts of the Western world were largely among princes—emperors, absolute monarchs and constitutional monarchs attempting to expand their bureaucracies, their armies, their mercantilist economic strength and, most important, the territory they ruled. In the process they created nation states, and beginning with the French Revolution the principal lines of conflict were between nations rather than princes. . . . This nineteenth-century pattern lasted until the end of World War I. Then, as a result of the Russian Revolution and the reaction against it, the conflict of nations yielded to the conflict of ideologies, first among communism, fascism-Nazism and liberal democracy, and then between communism and liberal democracy. During the Cold War, this latter conflict became embodied in the struggle between the two superpowers. . . .

These conflicts between princes, nation states and ideologies were primarily conflicts within Western civilization. . . . This was as true of the Cold War as it was of the world wars and the earlier wars of the seventeenth, eighteenth and nineteenth centuries. With the end of the Cold War, international politics moves out of its Western phase, and its centerpiece becomes the interaction between the West and non-Western civilizations and among non-Western civilizations. In the politics of civilizations, the peoples and governments of non-Western civilizations no longer remain the objects of history as targets of Western colonialism but join the West as movers and shapers of history.

The Nature of Civilizations

During the Cold War the world was divided into the First, Second and Third Worlds. Those divisions are no longer relevant. It is far more meaningful now to group countries not in terms of their political or economic systems or in terms of their level of economic development but rather in terms of their culture and civilization.

What do we mean when we talk of a civilization? A civilization is a cultural entity. Villages, regions, ethnic groups, nationalities, religious groups, all have distinct cultures at different levels of cultural heterogeneity. . . . European communities . . . will share cultural features that distinguish them from Arab or Chinese communities. Arabs, Chinese and Westerners, however, are not part of any broader cultural entity. They constitute civilizations. A civilization is thus the highest cultural grouping of people and the broadest level of cultural identity people have short of that which distinguishes humans from other species. It is defined both by common objective elements, such as language, history, religion, customs, institutions, and by the subjective self-identification of people. People have levels of identity: a resident of Rome may define himself with varying degrees of intensity as a Roman, an Italian, a Catholic, a Christian, a European, a Westerner. The civilization to which he belongs is the broadest level of identification with which he intensely identifies. People can and do redefine their identities and, as a result, the composition and boundaries of civilizations change.

Civilizations may involve a large number of people, as with China . . . , or a very small number of people, such as the Anglophone Caribbean. A civilization may include several nation states, as is the case with Western, Latin American and Arab civilizations, or only one, as is the case with Japanese civilization. Civilizations obviously blend and overlap, and many include subcivilizations. Western civilization has two major variants, European and North American, and Islam has its Arab, Turkic and Malay subdivisions. Civilizations are nonetheless meaningful entities, and while the lines between them are seldom sharp, they are real. Civilizations are dynamic; they rise and fall; they divide and merge. And, as any student of history knows, civilizations disappear and are buried in the sands of time.

Westerners tend to think of nation states as the principal actors in global affairs. They have been that, however, for only a few centuries. The broader reaches of human history have been the history of civilizations. . . .

Why Civilizations Will Clash

Civilization identity will be increasingly important in the future, and the world will be shaped in large measure by the interactions among seven or eight major civilizations. These include Western, Confucian, Japanese, Islamic, Hindu, Slavic-Orthodox, Latin American and possibly African civilization. The most important conflicts of the future will occur along the cultural fault lines separating these civilizations from one another.

Why will this be the case?

First, differences among civilizations are not only real; they are basic. Civilizations are differentiated from each other by history, language, culture, tradition and, most important, religion. The people of different civilizations have different views on the relations between God and man, the individual and the group, the citizen and the state, parents and children, husband and wife, as well as differing views of the relative importance of rights and responsibilities, liberty and authority, equality and hierarchy. These differences are the product of centuries. They will not soon disappear. They are far more fundamental than differences among political ideologies and political regimes. . . . Over the centuries . . . differences among civilizations have generated the most prolonged and the most violent conflicts.

Second, the world is becoming a smaller place. The interactions between peoples of different civilizations are increasing; these increasing interactions intensify civilization consciousness and awareness of differences between civilizations and commonalities within civilizations. North African immigration to France generates hostility among Frenchmen and at the same time increased receptivity to immigration by "good" European Catholic Poles. Americans react far more negatively to Japanese investment than to larger investments from Canada and European countries. . . . The interactions among peoples of different civilizations enhance the civilization-consciousness of people that, in turn, invigorates differences and animosities stretching or thought to stretch back deep into history.

Third, the processes of economic modernization and social change throughout the world are separating people from longstanding local identities. They also weaken the nation state as a source of identity. In much of the world religion has moved in to fill this gap, often in the form of movements that are labeled "fundamentalist." Such movements are found in Western Christianity, Judaism, Buddhism and Hinduism, as well as in Islam. In most countries and most religions the people active in fundamentalist movements are young, college-educated, middle-class technicians, professionals and business persons. . . . The revival of religion . . . provides a basis for identity and commitment that transcends national boundaries and unites civilizations.

Fourth, the growth of civilization-consciousness is enhanced by the dual role of the West. On the one hand, the West is at a peak of power. At the same time, however, and perhaps as a result, a return to the roots phenomenon is occurring among non-Western civilizations. Increasingly one hears references to trends toward a turning inward and "Asianization" in Japan, the end of the Nehru legacy and the "Hinduization" of India, the failure of Western ideas of socialism and nationalism and hence "re-Islamization" of the Middle East, and now a debate over Westernization versus Russianization in Boris Yeltsin's country. A West at the peak of its power confronts non-Wests that increasingly have the desire, the will and the resources to shape the world in non-Western ways.

In the past, the elites of non-Western societies were usually the people who were most involved with the West, had been educated at Oxford, the Sorbonne or Sandhurst, and had absorbed Western attitudes and values. At the same time, the populace in non-Western countries often remained deeply imbued with the indigenous culture. Now, however, these relationships are being reversed. A de-Westernization and indigenization of elites is occurring in many non-Western countries at the same time that Western, usually American, cultures, styles and habits become more popular among the mass of the people.

Fifth, cultural characteristics and differences are less mutable and hence less easily compromised and resolved than political and economic ones. In the former Soviet Union, communists can become democrats, the rich can become poor and the poor rich, but Russians cannot become Estonians and Azeris cannot become Armenians. In class and ideological conflicts, the key question was "Which side are you on?" and people could and did choose sides and change sides. In conflicts between civilizations, the question is "What are you?" That is a given that cannot be changed. And as we know, from Bosnia to the Caucasus to the Sudan, the wrong answer to that question can mean a bullet in the head. Even more than ethnicity, religion discriminates sharply and exclusively among people. A person can be half-French and half-Arab and simultaneously even a citizen of two countries. It is more difficult to be half-Catholic and half-Muslim.

Finally, economic regionalism is increasing. The proportions of total trade that were intraregional rose between 1980 and 1989 from 51 percent to 59 percent in

Europe, 33 percent to 37 percent in East Asia, and 32 percent to 36 percent in North America. The importance of regional economic blocs is likely to continue to increase in the future. On the one hand, successful economic regionalism will reinforce civilization-consciousness. On the other hand, economic regionalism may succeed only when it is rooted in a common civilization. The European Community rests on the shared foundation of European culture and Western Christianity. The success of the North American Free Trade Area depends on the convergence now underway of Mexican, Canadian and American cultures. Japan, in contrast, faces difficulties in creating a comparable economic entity in East Asia because Japan is a society and civilization unique to itself. . . .

Common culture, in contrast, is clearly facilitating the rapid expansion of the economic relations between the People's Republic of China and Hong Kong, Taiwan, Singapore and the overseas Chinese communities in other Asian countries. With the Cold War over, cultural commonalities increasingly overcome ideological differences, and mainland China and Taiwan move closer together. . . .

As people define their identity in ethnic and religious terms, they are likely to see an "us" versus "them" relation existing between themselves and people of different ethnicity or religion. The end of ideologically defined states in Eastern Europe and the former Soviet Union permits traditional ethnic identities and animosities to come to the fore. Differences in culture and religion create differences over policy issues, ranging from human rights to immigration to trade and commerce to the environment. Geographical propinquity gives rise to conflicting territorial claims from Bosnia to Mindanao. Most important, the efforts of the West to promote its values of democracy and liberalism as universal values, to maintain its military predominance and to advance its economic interests engender countering responses from other civilizations. Decreasingly able to mobilize support and form coalitions on the basis of ideology, governments and groups will increasingly attempt to mobilize support by appealing to common religion and civilization identity.

The clash of civilizations thus occurs at two levels. At the micro-level, adjacent groups along the fault lines between civilizations struggle, often violently, over the control of territory and each other. At the macro-level, states from different civilizations compete for relative military and economic power, struggle over the control of international institutions and third parties, and competitively promote their particular political and religious values.

The Fault Lines Between Civilizations

The fault lines between civilizations are replacing the political and ideological boundaries of the Cold War as the flash points for crisis and bloodshed. The Cold War began when the Iron Curtain divided Europe politically and ideologically. The Cold War ended with the end of the Iron Curtain. As the ideological division of Europe has disappeared, the cultural division of Europe between Western Christianity, on the one hand, and Orthodox Christianity and Islam, on the other, has reemerged. The most significant dividing line in Europe . . . may well be the east-ern boundary of Western Christianity in the year 1500. This line runs along what are now the boundaries between Finland and Russia and between the Baltic states and Russia, cuts through Belarus and Ukraine separating the more Catholic west-ern Ukraine from Orthodox eastern Ukraine, swings westward separating Transyl-vania from the rest of Romania, and then goes through Yugoslavia almost exactly along the line now separating Croatia and Slovenia from the rest of Yugoslavia. In the Balkans this line, of course, coincides with the historic boundary between the Hapsburg and Ottoman empires. The peoples to the north and west of this line are Protestant or Catholic; they shared the common experiences of European his-tory—feudalism, the Renaissance, the Reformation, the Enlightenment, the French Revolution, the Industrial Revolution; they are generally economically better off than the peoples to the east; and they may now look forward to increas-ing involvement in a common European economy and to the consolidation of democratic political systems. The peoples to the east and south of this line are Orthodox or Muslim; they historically belonged to the Ottoman or Tsarist empires and were only lightly touched by the shaping events in the rest of Europe; they are generally less advanced economically; they seem much less likely to develop stable democratic political systems. The Velvet Curtain of culture has replaced the Iron Curtain of ideology as the most significant dividing line in Europe. As the events in Yugoslavia show, it is not only a line of difference; it is also at times a line of bloody conflict.

Conflict along the fault line between Western and Islamic civilizations has been going on for 1,300 years. After the founding of Islam, the Arab and Moorish surge west and north only ended at Tours in 732. From the eleventh to the thirteenth century the Crusaders attempted with temporary success to bring Christianity and Christian rule to the Holy Land. From the fourteenth to the seventeenth century, the Ottoman Turks reversed the balance, extended their sway over the Middle East and the Balkans, captured Constantinople, and twice laid siege to Vienna. In the nineteenth and early twentieth centuries as Ottoman power declined Britain, France, and Italy established Western control over most of North Africa and the Middle East. . . .

This centuries-old military interaction between the West and Islam is unlikely to decline. It could become more virulent. The Gulf War left some Arabs feeling proud that Saddam Hussein had attacked Israel and stood up to the West. It also left many feeling humiliated and resentful of the West's military presence in the Persian Gulf, the West's overwhelming military dominance, and their apparent inability to shape their own destiny. Many Arab countries, in addition to the oil exporters, are reaching levels of economic and social development where auto-cratic forms of government become inappropriate and efforts to introduce democ-racy become stronger. Some openings in Arab political systems have already occurred. The principal beneficiaries of these openings have been Islamist move-ments. In the Arab world, in short, Western democracy strengthens anti-Western political forces. This may be a passing phenomenon, but it surely complicates rela-tions between Islamic countries and the West.

Those relations are also complicated by demography. The spectacular population growth in Arab countries, particularly in North Africa, has led to increased migration to Western Europe. The movement within Western Europe toward minimizing internal boundaries has sharpened political sensitivities with respect to this development. In Italy, France and Germany, racism is increasingly open, and political reactions and violence against Arab and Turkish migrants have become more intense and more widespread since 1990. . . .

Historically, the other great antagonistic interaction of Arab Islamic civilization has been with the pagan, animist, and now increasingly Christian black peoples to the south. In the past, this antagonism was epitomized in the image of Arab slave dealers and black slaves. It has been reflected in the on-going civil war in the Sudan between Arabs and blacks, the fighting in Chad between Libyan-supported insurgents and the government, the tensions between Orthodox Christians and Muslims in the Horn of Africa, and the political conflicts, recurring riots and communal violence between Muslims and Christians in Nigeria. The modernization of Africa and the spread of Christianity are likely to enhance the probability of violence along this fault line. . . .

On the northern border of Islam, conflict has increasingly erupted between Orthodox and Muslim peoples, including the carnage of Bosnia and Sarajevo, the simmering violence between Serb and Albanian, the tenuous relations between Bulgarians and their Turkish minority, the violence between Ossetians and Ingush, the unremitting slaughter of each other by Armenians and Azeris, the tense relations between Russians and Muslims in Central Asia, and the deployment of Russian troops to protect Russian interests in the Caucasus and Central Asia. Religion reinforces the revival of ethnic identities and restimulates Russian fears about the security of their southern borders. . . .

The conflict of civilizations is deeply rooted elsewhere in Asia. The historic clash between Muslim and Hindu in the subcontinent manifests itself now not only in the rivalry between Pakistan and India but also in intensifying religious strife within India between increasingly militant Hindu groups and India's substantial Muslim minority. . . . In East Asia, China has outstanding territorial disputes with most of its neighbors. It has pursued a ruthless policy toward the Buddhist people of Tibet, and it is pursuing an increasingly ruthless policy toward its Turkic-Muslim minority. With the Cold War over, the underlying differences between China and the United States have reasserted themselves in areas such as human rights, trade and weapons proliferation. These differences are unlikely to moderate. . . .

The same . . . applie[s] to the increasingly difficult relations between Japan and the United States. Here cultural difference exacerbates economic conflict. People on each side allege racism on the other, but at least on the American side the antipathies are not racial but cultural. The basic values, attitudes, behavioral patterns of the two societies could hardly be more different. The economic issues between the United States and Europe are no less serious than those between the United States and Japan, but they do not have the same political salience and emotional intensity because the differences between American culture and European culture are so much less than those between American civilization and Japanese civilization. . . .

Civilization Rallying: The Kin-Country Syndrome

Groups or states belonging to one civilization that become involved in war with people from a different civilization naturally try to rally support from other members of their own civilization. As the post–Cold War world evolves, civilization commonality, what H. D. S. Greenway has termed the "kin-country" syndrome, is replacing political ideology and traditional balance of power considerations as the principal basis for cooperation and coalitions. It can be seen gradually emerging in the post–Cold War conflicts in the Persian Gulf, the Caucasus and Bosnia. None of these was a full-scale war between civilizations, but each involved some elements of civilizational rallying, which seemed to become more important as the conflict continued and which may provide a foretaste of the future.

First, in the Gulf War one Arab state invaded another and then fought a coalition of Arab, Western and other states. While only a few Muslim governments overtly supported Saddam Hussein, many Arab elites privately cheered him on, and he was highly popular among large sections of the Arab publics. Islamic fundamentalist movements universally supported Iraq rather than the Western-backed governments of Kuwait and Saudi Arabia. Forswearing Arab nationalism, Saddam Hussein explicitly invoked an Islamic appeal. He and his supporters attempted to define the war as a war between civilizations. . . .

Muslims contrasted Western actions against Iraq with the West's failure to protect Bosnians against Serbs and to impose sanctions on Israel for violating UN resolutions. The West, they alleged, was using a double standard. A world of clashing civilizations, however, is inevitably a world of double standards: people apply one standard to their kin-countries and a different standard to others.

Second, the kin-country syndrome also appeared in conflicts in the former Soviet Union. . . .

Third, with respect to the fighting in the former Yugoslavia, Western publics manifested sympathy and support for the Bosnian Muslims and the horrors they suffered at the hands of the Serbs. Relatively little concern was expressed, however, over Croatian attacks on Muslims and participation in the dismemberment of Bosnia-Herzegovina. In the early stages of the Yugoslav breakup, Germany, in an unusual display of diplomatic initiative and muscle, induced the other 11 members of the European Community to follow its lead in recognizing Slovenia and Croatia. As a result of the pope's determination to provide strong backing to the two Catholic countries, the Vatican extended recognition even before the Community did. The United States followed the European lead. Thus the leading actors in Western civilization rallied behind their coreligionists. Subsequently Croatia was reported to be receiving substantial quantities of arms from Central European and other Western countries. Boris Yeltsin's government, on the other hand, attempted to pursue a middle course that would be sympathetic to the Orthodox Serbs but not alienate Russia from the West. Russian conservative and nationalist groups, however, including many legislators, attacked the government for not being more forthcoming in its support for the Serbs. By early 1993 several hundred Russians apparently were serving with the Serbian forces, and reports circulated of Russian arms being supplied to Serbia.

Islamic governments and groups, on the other hand, castigated the West for not coming to the defense of the Bosnians. Iranian leaders urged Muslims from all countries to provide help to Bosnia; in violation of the UN arms embargo, Iran supplied weapons and men for the Bosnians; Iranian-supported Lebanese groups sent guerrillas to train and organize the Bosnian forces. In 1993 up to 4,000 Muslims from over two dozen Islamic countries were reported to be fighting in Bosnia. The governments of Saudi Arabia and other countries felt under increasing pressure from fundamentalist groups in their own societies to provide more vigorous support for the Bosnians. By the end of 1992, Saudi Arabia had reportedly supplied substantial funding for weapons and supplies for the Bosnians, which significantly increased their military capabilities vis-à-vis the Serbs. . . .

Civilization rallying to date has been limited, but it has been growing, and it clearly has the potential to spread much further. As the conflicts in the Persian Gulf, the Caucasus and Bosnia continued, the positions of nations and the cleavages between them increasingly were along civilizational lines. Populist politicians, religious leaders and the media have found it a potent means of arousing mass support and of pressuring hesitant governments. In the coming years, the local conflicts most likely to escalate into major wars will be those, as in Bosnia and the Caucasus, along the fault lines between civilizations. The next world war, if there is one, will be a war between civilizations.

The West Versus the Rest

The West is now at an extraordinary peak of power in relation to other civilizations. Its superpower opponent has disappeared from the map. Military conflict among Western states is unthinkable, and Western military power is unrivaled. Apart from Japan, the West faces no economic challenge. It dominates international political and security institutions and with Japan international economic institutions. Global political and security issues are effectively settled by a directorate of the United States, Britain and France, world economic issues by a directorate of the United States, Germany and Japan, all of which maintain extraordinarily close relations with each other to the exclusion of lesser and largely non-Western countries. Decisions made at the UN Security Council or in the International Monetary Fund that reflect the interests of the West are presented to the world as reflecting the desires of the world community. The very phrase "the world community" has become the euphemistic collective noun (replacing "the Free World") to give global legitimacy to actions reflecting the interests of the United States and other Western powers. Through the IMF and other international economic institutions, the West promotes its economic interests and imposes on other nations the economic policies it thinks appropriate. . . .

Western domination of the UN Security Council and its decisions, tempered only by occasional abstention by China, produced UN legitimation of the West's use of force to drive Iraq out of Kuwait and its elimination of Iraq's sophisticated weapons and capacity to produce such weapons. . . . After defeating the largest Arab army, the West did not hesitate to throw its weight around in the Arab world.

The West in effect is using international institutions, military power and economic resources to run the world in ways that will maintain Western predominance, protect Western interests and promote Western political and economic values.

That at least is the way in which non-Westerners see the new world, and there is a significant element of truth in their view. Differences in power and struggles for military, economic and institutional power are thus one source of conflict between the West and other civilizations. Differences in culture, that is basic values and beliefs, are a second source of conflict. . . . At a superficial level much of Western culture has indeed permeated the rest of the world. At a more basic level, however, Western concepts differ fundamentally from those prevalent in other civilizations. Western ideas of individualism, liberalism, constitutionalism, human rights, equality, liberty, the rule of law, democracy, free markets, the separation of church and state, often have little resonance in Islamic, Confucian, Japanese, Hindu, Buddhist or Orthodox cultures. Western efforts to propagate such ideas produce instead a reaction against "human rights imperialism" and a reaffirmation of indigenous values, as can be seen in the support for religious fundamentalism by the younger generation in non-Western cultures. The very notion that there could be a "universal civilization" is a Western idea, directly at odds with the particularism of most Asian societies and their emphasis on what distinguishes one people from another. . . . In the political realm, of course, these differences are most manifest in the efforts of the United States and other Western powers to induce other peoples to adopt Western ideas concerning democracy and human rights. Modern democratic government originated in the West. When it has developed in non-Western societies it has usually been the product of Western colonialism or imposition.

The central axis of world politics in the future is likely to be . . . the conflict between "the West and the Rest" and the responses of non-Western civilizations to Western power and values. Those responses generally take one or a combination of three forms. At one extreme, non-Western states can, like Burma and North Korea, attempt to pursue a course of isolation, to insulate their societies from penetration or "corruption" by the West, and, in effect, to opt out of participation in the Western-dominated global community. The costs of this course, however, are high, and few states have pursued it exclusively. A second alternative, the equivalent of "bandwagoning" in international relations theory, is to attempt to join the West and accept its values and institutions. The third alternative is to attempt to "balance" the West by developing economic and military power and cooperating with other non-Western societies against the West, while preserving indigenous values and institutions; in short, to modernize but not to Westernize.

The Torn Countries

In the future, as people differentiate themselves by civilization, countries with large numbers of peoples of different civilizations, such as the Soviet Union and Yugoslavia, are candidates for dismemberment. Some other countries have a fair degree of cultural homogeneity but are divided over whether their society belongs to one civilization or another. These are torn countries. Their leaders typically wish to pursue a bandwagoning strategy and to make their countries members of the West, but the history, culture and traditions of their countries are non-Western. The most obvious and prototypical torn country is Turkey. The late twentieth-century leaders of Turkey have followed in the Atatürk tradition and defined Turkey as a modern, secular, Western nation state. They allied Turkey with the West in NATO and in the Gulf War; they applied for membership in the European Community. At the same time, however, elements in Turkish society have supported an Islamic revival and have argued that Turkey is basically a Middle Eastern Muslim society. . . .

Historically Turkey has been the most profoundly torn country. . . . Globally the most important torn country is Russia. The question of whether Russia is part of the West or the leader of a distinct Slavic-Orthodox civilization has been a recurring one in Russian history. That issue was obscured by the communist victory in Russia, which imported a Western ideology, adapted it to Russian conditions and then challenged the West in the name of that ideology. The dominance of communism shut off the historic debate over Westernization versus Russification. With communism discredited Russians once again face that question. . . .

Implications for the West

This article does not argue that civilization identities will replace all other identities, that nation states will disappear, that each civilization will become a single coherent political entity, that groups within a civilization will not conflict with and even fight each other. This paper does set forth the hypotheses that differences between civilizations are real and important; civilization-consciousness is increasing; conflict between civilizations will supplant ideological and other forms of conflict as the dominant global form of conflict; international relations, historically a game played out within Western civilization, will increasingly be de-Westernized and become a game in which non-Western civilizations are actors and not simply objects; successful political, security and economic international institutions are more likely to develop within civilizations than across civilizations; conflicts between groups in different civilizations will be more frequent, more sustained and more violent than conflicts between groups in the same civilization; violent conflicts between groups in different civilizations are the most likely and most dangerous source of escalation that could lead to global wars; the paramount axis of world politics will be the relations between "the West and the Rest"; the elites in some torn non-Western countries will try to make their countries part of the West, but in most cases face major obstacles to accomplishing this; a central focus of conflict for the immediate future will be between the West and several Islamic-Confucian states.

. . . If these are plausible hypotheses . . . it is necessary to consider their implications for Western policy. These implications should be divided between short-term advantage and long-term accommodation. In the short term it is clearly in the interest of the West to promote greater cooperation and unity within its own civilization, particularly between its European and North American components; to incorporate into the West societies in Eastern Europe and Latin America whose cultures are close to those of the West; to promote and maintain cooperative relations with Russia and Japan; to prevent escalation of local inter-civilization conflicts into major inter-civilization wars; to limit the expansion of the military strength of Confucian and Islamic states; to moderate the reduction of Western military capabilities and maintain military superiority in East and Southwest Asia; to exploit differences and conflicts among Confucian and Islamic states; to support in other civilizations groups sympathetic to Western values and interests; to strengthen international institutions that reflect and legitimate Western interests and values and to promote the involvement of non-Western states in those institutions.

In the longer term other measures would be called for. Western civilization is both Western and modern. Non-Western civilizations have attempted to become modern without becoming Western. To date only Japan has fully succeeded in this quest. Non-Western civilizations will continue to attempt to acquire the wealth, technology, skills, machines and weapons that are part of being modern. They will also attempt to reconcile this modernity with their traditional culture and values. Their economic and military strength relative to the West will increase. Hence the West will increasingly have to accommodate these non-Western modern civilizations whose power approaches that of the West but whose values and interests differ significantly from those of the West. This will require the West to maintain the economic and military power necessary to protect its interests in relation to these civilizations. It will also, however, require the West to develop a more profound understanding of the basic religious and philosophical assumptions underlying other civilizations and the ways in which people in those civilizations see their interests. It will require an effort to identify elements of commonality between Western and other civilizations. For the relevant future, there will be no universal civilization, but instead a world of different civilizations, each of which will have to learn to coexist with the others.

14.2 What Clash of Civilizations?

Amartya Sen

In this selection, Amartya Sen, an Indian economist, Harvard professor, and Nobel Prize winner, argues vigorously against Huntington's thesis of clashing civilizations because of what he sees as its reliance on religion to define and differentiate civilizations. Sen contends that religion is only one of numerous identities that characterize every individual and is rarely the most important of these identities. People, he suggests, can be classified in many ways—nationality, location, class, occupation, social status, language, and politics, among others. Indeed, Sen suggests that those who seek to dampen violence actually promote it when they identify Muslims solely by their religion, and he claims that doing so distorts the Western effort to combat global terrorism. Such a one-dimensional identification also fails to recognize the differences among Muslims who reflect many different cultural traditions and have vastly different political and social beliefs. Sen also argues that Huntington's claims reflect "a foggy perception of world history" that overlooks diversity within civilizations as well as the many interactions that occur among people from the different civilizations that Huntington identifies. Most important, Sen contends that identity does not determine the beliefs and actions of individuals, who are capable of reason and choice.

That some barbed cartoons of the Prophet Mohammed could generate turmoil in so many countries tells us some rather important things about the contemporary world. Among other issues, it points up the intense sensitivity of many Muslims about representation and derision of the prophet in the Western press (and the ridiculing of Muslim religious beliefs that is taken to go with it) and the evident power of determined agitators to generate the kind of anger that leads immediately to violence. But stereotyped representations of this kind do another sort of damage as well, by making huge groups of people in the world to look peculiarly narrow and unreal.

The portrayal of the prophet with a bomb in the form of a hat is obviously a figment of imagination and cannot be judged literally, and the relevance of that representation cannot be dissociated from the way the followers of the prophet may be seen. What we ought to take very seriously is the way Islamic identity, in this sort of depiction, is assumed to drown, if only implicitly, all other affiliations, priorities, and pursuits that a Muslim person may have. A person belongs to many different groups, of which a religious affiliation is only one. To see, for example, a mathematician who happens to be a Muslim by religion mainly in terms of Islamic identity would be to hide more than it reveals. Even today, when a modern mathematician at, say, MIT or Princeton invokes an "algorithm" to solve a difficult computational problem, he or she helps to commemorate the contributions of the ninth-century Muslim mathematician Al-Khwarizmi, from whose name the term algorithm is derived (the term "algebra" comes from the title of his Arabic mathematical treatise "Al Jabr wa-al-Muqabilah"). To concentrate only on Al-Khwarizmi's Islamic identity over his identity as a mathematician would be extremely misleading, and yet he clearly was also a Muslim. Similarly, to give an automatic priority to the Islamic identity of a Muslim person in order to understand his or her role in the civil society, or in the literary world, or in creative work in arts and science, can result in profound misunderstanding.

The increasing tendency to overlook the many identities that any human being has and to try to classify individuals according to a single allegedly pre-eminent religious identity is an intellectual confusion that can animate dangerous divisiveness. An Islamist instigator of violence against infidels may want Muslims to forget that they have any identity other than being Islamic. What is surprising is that those who would like to quell that violence promote, in effect, the same intellectual disorientation by seeing Muslims primarily as members of an Islamic world. The world is made much more incendiary by the advocacy and popularity of single-dimensional categorization of human beings, which combines haziness of vision with increased scope for the exploitation of that haze by the champions of violence.

A remarkable use of imagined singularity can be found in Samuel Huntington's influential 1998 book *The Clash of Civilizations and the Remaking of the World Order.* The difficulty with Huntington's approach begins with his system of unique categorization, well before the issue of a clash—or not—is even raised. Indeed, the thesis of a civilizational clash is conceptually parasitic on the commanding power of a unique categorization along so-called civilizational lines, which closely follow religious divisions to which singular attention is paid. Huntington contrasts Western civilization with "Islamic civilization," "Hindu civilization," "Buddhist civilization," and so on. The alleged confrontations of religious differences are incorporated into a sharply carpentered vision of hardened divisiveness.

In fact, of course, the people of the world can be classified according to many other partitions, each of which has some—often far-reaching—relevance in our lives: nationalities, locations, classes, occupations, social status, languages, politics, and many others. While religious categories have received much airing in recent years, they cannot be presumed to obliterate other distinctions, and even less can they be seen as the only relevant system of classifying people across the globe. In partitioning the population of the world into those belonging to "the Islamic world," "the Western world," "the Hindu world," "the Buddhist world," the divisive power of classificatory priority is implicitly used to place people firmly inside a unique set of rigid boxes. Other divisions (say, between the rich and the poor, between members of different classes and occupations, between people of different politics, between distinct nationalities and residential locations, between language groups, etc.) are all submerged by this allegedly primal way of seeing the differences between people.

The difficulty with the clash of civilizations thesis begins with the presumption of the unique relevance of a singular classification. Indeed, the question "Do civilizations clash?" is founded on the presumption that humanity can be preeminently classified into distinct and discrete civilizations, and that the relations between different human beings can somehow be seen, without serious loss of understanding, in terms of relations between different civilizations.

This reductionist view is typically combined, I am afraid, with a rather foggy perception of world history that overlooks, first, the extent of internal diversities within these civilizational categories, and second, the reach and influence of interactions—intellectual as well as material—that go right across the regional borders of so-called civilizations. And its power to befuddle can trap not only those who would like to support the thesis of a clash (varying from Western chauvinists to Islamic fundamentalists), but also those who would like to dispute it and yet try to respond within the straitjacket of its prespecified terms of reference.

The limitations of such civilization-based thinking can prove just as treacherous for programs of "dialogue among civilizations" (much in vogue these days) as they are for theories of a clash of civilizations. The noble and elevating search for amity among people seen as amity between civilizations speedily reduces many-sided human beings to one dimension each and muzzles the variety of involvements that have provided rich and diverse grounds for cross-border interactions over many centuries, including the arts, literature, science, mathematics, games, trade, politics, and other arenas of shared human interest. Well-meaning attempts at pursuing global peace can have very counterproductive consequences when these attempts are founded on a fundamentally illusory understanding of the world of human beings.

Increasing reliance on religion-based classification of the people of the world also tends to make the Western response to global terrorism and conflict peculiarly ham-handed. Respect for "other people" is shown by praising their religious books, rather than by taking note of the many-sided involvements and achievements, in nonreligious as well as religious fields, of different people in a globally interactive world. In confronting what is called "Islamic terrorism" in the muddled vocabulary of contemporary global politics, the intellectual force of Western policy is aimed quite substantially at trying to define—or redefine—Islam.

To focus just on the grand religious classification is not only to miss other significant concerns and ideas that move people. It also has the effect of generally magnifying the voice of religious authority. The Muslim clerics, for example, are then treated as the ex officio spokesmen for the so-called Islamic world, even though a great many people who happen to be Muslim by religion have profound differences with what is proposed by one mullah or another. Despite our diverse diversities, the world is suddenly seen not as a collection of people, but as a federation of religions and civilizations. In Britain, a confounded view of what a multiethnic society must do has led to encouraging the development of state-financed Muslim schools, Hindu schools, Sikh schools, etc., to supplement pre-existing state-supported Christian schools. Under this system, young children are placed in the domain of singular affiliations well before they have the ability to reason about different systems of identification that may compete for their attention. Earlier on, state-run denominational schools in Northern Ireland had fed the political distancing of Catholics and Protestants along one line of divisive categorization assigned at infancy. Now the same predetermination of "discovered" identities is now being allowed and, in effect encouraged, to sow even more alienation among a different part of the British population.

Religious or civilizational classification can be a source of belligerent distortion as well. It can, for example, take the form of crude beliefs well exemplified by U.S. Lt. Gen. William Boykin's blaring—and by now well-known—remark describing his battle against Muslims with disarming coarseness: "I knew that my God was bigger than his," and that the Christian God "was a real God, and [the Muslim's] was an idol." The idiocy of such bigotry is easy to diagnose, so there is comparatively limited danger in the uncouth hurling of such unguided missiles. There is, in contrast, a much more serious problem in the use in Western public policy of intellectual "guided missiles" that present a superficially nobler vision to woo Muslim activists away from opposition through the apparently benign strategy of defining Islam appropriately. They try to wrench Islamic terrorists from violence by insisting that Islam is a religion of peace, and that a "true Muslim" must be a tolerant individual ("so come off it and be peaceful"). The rejection of a confrontational view of Islam is certainly appropriate and extremely important at this time, but we must ask whether it is necessary or useful, or even possible, to try to define in largely political terms what a "true Muslim" must be like.

A person's religion need not be his or her all-encompassing and exclusive identity. Islam, as a religion, does not obliterate responsible choice for Muslims in many spheres of life. Indeed, it is possible for one Muslim to take a confrontational view and another to be thoroughly tolerant of heterodoxy without either of them ceasing to be a Muslim for that reason alone.

The response to Islamic fundamentalism and to the terrorism linked with it also becomes particularly confused when there is a general failure to distinguish between Islamic history and the history of Muslim people. Muslims, like all other people in the world, have many different pursuits, and not all their priorities and values need be placed within their singular identity of being Islamic. It is, of course, not surprising at all that the champions of Islamic fundamentalism would like to suppress all other identities of Muslims in favor of being only Islamic. But it is extremely odd that those who want to overcome the tensions and conflicts linked with Islamic fundamentalism also seem unable to see Muslim people in any form other than their being just Islamic.

People see themselves—and have reason to see themselves—in many different ways. For example, a Bangladeshi Muslim is not only a Muslim but also a Bengali and a Bangladeshi, typically quite proud of the Bengali language, literature, and music, not to mention the other identities he or she may have connected with class, gender, occupation, politics, aesthetic taste, and so on. Bangladesh's separation from Pakistan was not based on religion at all, since a Muslim identity was shared by the bulk of the population in the two wings of undivided Pakistan. The separatist issues related to language, literature, and politics.

Similarly, there is no empirical reason at all why champions of the Muslim past, or for that matter of the Arab heritage, have to concentrate specifically on religious beliefs only and not also on science and mathematics, to which Arab and Muslim societies have contributed so much, and which can also be part of a Muslim or an Arab identity. Despite the importance of this heritage, crude classifications have tended to put science and mathematics in the basket of "Western science," leaving other people to mine their pride in religious depths. If the disaffected Arab activist today can take pride only in the purity of Islam, rather than in the many-sided richness of Arab history, the unique prioritization of religion, shared by warriors on both sides, plays a major part in incarcerating people within the enclosure of a singular identity.

Even the frantic Western search for "the moderate Muslim" confounds moderation in political beliefs with moderateness of religious faith. A person can have strong religious faith—Islamic or any other—along with tolerant politics. Emperor Saladin, who fought valiantly for Islam in the Crusades in the 12th century, could offer, without any contradiction, an honored place in his Egyptian royal court to Maimonides as that distinguished Jewish philosopher fled an intolerant Europe. When, at the turn of the 16th century, the heretic Giordano Bruno was burned at the stake in Campo dei Fiori in Rome, the Great Mughal emperor Akbar (who was born a Muslim and died a Muslim) had just finished, in Agra, his large project of legally codifying minority rights, including religious freedom for all.

The point that needs particular attention is that while Akbar was free to pursue his liberal politics without ceasing to be a Muslim, that liberality was in no way ordained—nor of course prohibited—by Islam. Another Mughal emperor, Aurangzeb, could deny minority rights and persecute non-Muslims without, for that reason, failing to be a Muslim, in exactly the same way that Akbar did not terminate being a Muslim because of his tolerantly pluralist politics.

The insistence, if only implicitly, on a choiceless singularity of human identity not only diminishes us all, it also makes the world much more flammable. The alternative to the divisiveness of one pre-eminent categorization is not any unreal claim that we are all much the same. Rather, the main hope of harmony in our troubled world lies in the plurality of our identities, which cut across each other and work against sharp divisions around one single hardened line of vehement division that allegedly cannot be resisted. Our shared humanity gets savagely challenged when our differences are narrowed into one devised system of uniquely powerful categorization.

Perhaps the worst impairment comes from the neglect—and denial—of the roles of reasoning and choice, which follow from the recognition of our plural identities. The illusion of unique identity is much more divisive than the universe of plural and diverse classifications that characterize the world in which we actually live. The descriptive weakness of choiceless singularity has the effect of momentously impoverishing the power and reach of our social and political reasoning. The illusion of destiny exacts a remarkably heavy price.

 Identity Clashes in Europe

14.3 Cartoon Uproar Exposes Muslim Divide

Andrew Higgins

This selection deals with a little-known aspect of the tension that accompanied the publication in a Danish newspaper of cartoons satirizing the Prophet Muhammad, that is, the divide between militant and moderate Muslims. Although the event highlighted the cleavage between Muslims who denounced the "blasphemy" involved in depicting the Prophet and many Europeans who viewed the issue as one of freedom of speech, as this reading points out the event also deepened the rift between Muslims in Europe who wish to assimilate and who accept Western values and those who wish to maintain their Islamic identity even if it contradicts European values.

Under fire for helping to stir a global wave of Islamic rage against Denmark, Copenhagen cleric Ahmed Abu-Laban used his sermon Friday to praise his adopted homeland as "a lovely country, a good and tolerant country."

But his tone shifted sharply when he spoke of what he and many like-minded Muslims across Europe consider the real menace: self-declared moderate Muslims, who put European values ahead of Islam.

"These people are rats in a hole," thundered the Palestinian preacher in a hall packed with mostly Arabic-speaking faithful. They are, he said, "cowards" who are "making our real crisis in Europe." Worshippers in the converted automobile workshop cried "God is great, God is great!"

Mr. Abu-Laban's sermon shows how the uproar over cartoons depicting the Prophet Muhammad published by a Danish newspaper isn't just hardening differences between Islam and the West. It reveals deep divisions among Europe's Muslims over how to engage with broader European societies. The rivalry highlights the current tension within Islam, a faith born in Saudi Arabia in the seventh century and now in flux as it puts down deep roots in modern Europe. Muslims make up about 5 percent of the European Union's population and are the fastest growing demographic group.

"Islam has been petrified . . . but now we are in the middle of a complete change." says Abdul Wahid Pedersen, a Danish former schoolteacher who converted to Islam more than 20 years ago. "Islam [in Europe] is finding new ways to express itself, and this is going to change . . . Islam in the world. This is the biggest challenge for Islam in over 1,000 years."

In London on Saturday, Muslim groups organized a rally against the cartoons. Yet invitations to the protest set out a second goal: to dissociate mainstream British Muslims from radical protesters, who a week earlier had carried placards such as "Butcher those who mock Islam" as well as from mobs at Middle East rallies who had burned Danish flags and embassies.

"Most Muslims are left between a rock and a hard place. There is an extreme element that is stabbing them in the back. Every time we move a step forward, they bring us one step back," said Anas Altikriti of the Muslim Association of Britain, which helped set up the rally. Meanwhile, Turkish protesters pelted the French consulate in Istanbul with eggs, and on Saturday Denmark pulled its diplomats out of Indonesia because of security concerns.

In Denmark, the principal target of Mr. Abu-Laban's fury is a fellow immigrant of Syrian-Palestinian origin, Naser Khader. An elected member of the Danish parliament, he last week announced the formation of a "moderate Muslim network," a group of mostly professional and established immigrants. "This is not a clash of civilizations. It is a clash of democracy and antidemocracy," says Mr. Khader, who accuses the preacher of hijacking the cartoon crisis to advance a fundamentalist agenda.

Mr. Khader, 42 years old, who has the word "democracy" tattooed on his arm in Arabic, and Mr. Abu-Laban, 60, who stresses the sanctity of Shariah, or Islamic law, stand at opposite ends of the debate. Each claims to speak for a majority of European Muslims. One represents those who are well integrated in European society and are often very flexible in their faith, the other those who are far more comfortable speaking in Arabic and are sternly pious.

At the start of the cartoon imbroglio this past fall, Danish Prime Minister Anders Fogh Rasmussen invited both men to a meeting to discuss what to do. When Mr. Khader learned Mr. Abu-Laban would attend, he boycotted the session. He has his own meeting with Mr. Fogh scheduled for this week. Mr. Khader says Mr. Abu-Laban "thinks he is Mr. Islam in Denmark, but he represents only a tiny minority." Mr. Abu-Laban, meanwhile, derides the Muslim lawmaker as a turncoat who "is no longer a real Muslim." Each appears regularly on television to insult the other.

Mr. Khader has received death threats and travels about Copenhagen with two bodyguards. Mr. Abu-Laban is pilloried in the Danish media as a terrorist supporter, welfare scrounger and more. "They think he grows hair on his teeth," says Mr. Pedersen, the convert, who disagrees with both.

Mr. Abu-Laban helped globalize the cartoon conflict by sending delegations to the Middle East. He has demanded a clear apology from the Danish government and the newspaper. Mr. Khader says the cartoons, though offensive, didn't break the law and so don't require an apology.

The feud between the men, which mirrors similar conflicts across Europe, began in the 1990s when Mr. Khader wrote a book entitled *Honor and Shame*. It attacked Muslim immigrants who cling to the mindset and customs of their home countries instead of embracing those of Europe. Mr. Khader's father, who at the time worshipped at Mr. Abu-Laban's mosque, brought his son and the cleric together for a peace meeting. It only fueled their hostility.

Since then, Mr. Abu-Laban has had to deal with his own son, who has become even more doctrinaire than his father. He supports Hizb ut-Tahrir, a radical group banned in parts of Europe and that advocates a restoration of the Muslim caliphate, a super-state governed by a supreme Islamic leader. The son was expelled from school last year for spreading the group's intolerant message. Hizb ut-Tahrir has held protests against the cartoons featuring banners reading: "An apology is not enough!"

In his sermon Friday, Mr. Abu-Laban warned of a "third global war" if Europe doesn't accommodate Islam. The following day, Mr. Khader gathered with his supporters to draft a charter for their new organization. The group, they decided, would welcome "all Muslims who are committed to the constitution, to law-based state, to democracy and human rights." Mr. Abu-Laban, said Mr. Khader, wouldn't qualify.

14.4 New Russia: From Class to Ethnic Struggle

Steven Lee Myers

The principal identity encouraged in the Soviet Union was based on class; that is, Soviet citizens saw themselves as members of the international proletariat, and their conflict with the West pitted socialism against capitalism. With the end of the Cold War and the collapse of the Soviet Union, identity in Russia based on class gave way to identities based on nationalism and ethnicity. This selection describes the national and ethnic cleavage between Russia's largely Slavic population and migrants from the mountainous Caucasus region, especially Chechens as well as Azerbaijanis and Georgians. The attacks on Chechens described in the article also reflect the anger of Russians at the violence waged by many Chechens against Russian rule of their "country."

Ethnic animosity runs so close to the surface of Russian society that almost anything can cause it to boil over. Here in this quiet mill town on the shore of Lake Onego, 960 kilometers, or 600 miles, north of Moscow it was a bar fight outside a club called Seagull.

Two ethnic Russians had died by the time the brawl ended, but the violence had only just begun. Their deaths, allegedly at the hands of men from Azerbaijan and Chechnya, provoked angry protests and on the night of Sept. 2, a rampage through the town, followed by sporadic acts of vandalism that have continued since.

Mobs of young men—fueled by anger and, officials said, alcohol—burned the Seagull club, owned by a businessman originally from Azerbaijan. Then they attacked a series of precisely chosen targets: the homes and businesses of migrants from the Caucasus, mostly from Chechnya. The mobs destroyed makeshift stalls in the town's open-air market, threw rocks through apartment windows, overturned and burned cars and kiosks, sacked two shops and burned a third store still under construction.

Dozens of the town's residents, Chechens mostly, but also ethnic Azerbaijanis and Georgians, fled that night. A group of 49 are now staying in a tourist camp outside the regional capital, Petrozavodsk, having escaped what is being widely called a pogrom, one that many here welcomed. "They need to leave," said Denis Doronin, 19, who said he took part in the protests that led to the violence. "They arrive from another country and they act like kings."

Russia has experienced a surge in racist violence in recent years, from isolated acts of assault and murder to the bombing last month of a Moscow market, which killed 12 people, most of them from Central Asia. Three university students have been charged in the bombings.

But the events in Kondopoga have exposed a strain of ethnic strife that extends beyond the acts of neo-Nazis and skinheads, infecting society as a whole 15 years after the collapse of the Soviet Union discredited the enforced harmony of the many nationalities in Russia. "What happened was a shift from class struggle to ethnic struggle," said Viktor A. Shnirelman, an anthropologist with the Russian Academy of Sciences who is writing a book on racism in Russia. "And it is very dangerous."

Ethnic tensions across Russia have been fueled by the latent racism common among many Russians, who freely use the pejorative "blacks" when describing people from the Caucasus, even in casual conversation. It also reflects a growing political opposition to migrant workers not unlike those movements in Europe and the United States and the indifferent, or at times hostile, responses from elected officials when violence erupts.

The police in Kondopoga have arrested more than 100 people, including the three accused of murder in the bar fight. But Sergei Katanandov, governor of Karelia, the region near Finland that includes Kondopoga, did not blame the mobs for the violence, but rather the people who were singled out. "The behavior of certain young men who moved here from the Caucasus and other territories in recent years—not that many of them, but they were visible—has been beyond the pale," he said in an recent interview with Izvestia newspaper.

It is not clear exactly how many people fled Kondopoga as the violence flared, but in addition to the 49 Chechens now staying at the camp near Petrozavodsk, many are believed to be staying with friends or relatives. They described Sept. 2 as a day and night of terror. Many hired taxis and left after speakers at the first large protest on the central street of Kondopoga called for all migrants to leave within 24 hours. "The police could not protect us," one of them, Adlan Taikhinneki, said in an interview at the camp.

The Chechens in Kondopoga arrived in search of work and security. Hamzat Magamadov said he joined his sister, Tayissa, who had married a Russian and lived in Kondopoga, after the first war in Chechnya erupted in 1994. He had lived here since, mostly peacefully, he said, though strains existed beneath the surface. "They held all these tensions inside," he said. "After two wars, maybe they did not tell us everything, but it all came out."

Like migrants from across southern Russia and the former Soviet republics, they found work as traders, setting up shop in the new market economy of Russia. Several of the traders had pooled their resources to build a new store, which is now a charred hulk.

The economic success of migrants is at the source of many xenophobic statements, even ones by prominent officials. The country's leading nationalist politician, Vladimir V. Zhirinovsky, said that migrants should be barred from owning markets, shops, hotels, restaurants and bars.

"Restaurants and retail outlets should be in the hands of local residents first and foremost," he said in a radio interview after the violence in Kondopoga. "Otherwise clashes with local residents are inevitable."

Such views resonate in Kondopoga, a town of 37,000 people with a large pulp-and-paper factory. The town and its surrounding district are overwhelmingly Russian, with a smattering of Karelians and Finns. According to the last census, in

2002, migrants from the Caucasus account for less than 1 percent of the population, but they have become the focus of residents' complaints about crime and, especially, economic inequity.

Outside the apartment of a Chechen family—its windows shattered by rocks—an elderly woman who would give only her first name and patronymic, Valentina Ivanova, said that the brawl was a catalyst that unleashed widely held anger at the newcomers. "They completely control the prices at the market," she said of the Chechens. "They buy all the potatoes in Karelia. Potatoes are like our second bread. They buy them for 7 rubles and sell them for 15. They do not even work. They just speculate."

Kondopoga remains tense. Little of the damage has been repaired. The open-air market's stalls are half empty. The families who fled remain afraid to return. "We were refugees from the war and are refugees again," Taikhinneki said. "We are guilty just because we are Chechen."

The New Divide in World Politics?
The West Versus the Islamic World

14.5 Mutual Incomprehension, Mutual Outrage

The Economist

The final selection in this chapter describes the global uproar that accompanied the publication in a Danish newspaper of cartoons caricaturing the Prophet Muhammad (see reading 14.3). Islam forbids pictures of human images because of fear that they might become objects of worship, and Muslims in many countries regarded the publication of the cartoons as an intentionally provocative insult to Islam. Most Europeans, the product of a relatively secular and individualistic culture, view the issue differently, as a question of press freedom and freedom of speech. All in all, the controversy seemed to highlight the "clash of civilizations."

When, last September [2005], the Danish newspaper *Jyllands-Posten* published a dozen cartoons of the prophet Muhammad, it knew it was testing the limits of free speech and good taste. But it could never have imagined how much. For Denmark itself, this has been the biggest crisis since the Nazi occupation during the second world war. But the implications for the already vexed relations between the West and Islam go far wider. Denmark's prime minister, Anders Fogh Rasmussen, summed it up: "We are today facing a global crisis that has the potential to escalate beyond the control of governments."

At least ten people have died so far in protests against the cartoons. Several were killed in Afghanistan as police shot into a crowd besieging a Norwegian peacekeepers' base. More were shot dead as they tried to storm an American military base in the south of the country, setting cars alight and hurling rocks.

Western embassies in Syria, Lebanon, Indonesia and Iran have been attacked. Mosque sermons from Senegal to Sumatra have blasted the insult to the faith. Demonstrators in Karachi burned an effigy of the Danish prime minister. In Khartoum, some enraged marchers among a crowd of 50,000 chanted "Strike, strike, bin Laden." Saudi Arabia, Syria, Libya and Iran have all withdrawn their ambassadors from Denmark. Iran has formally banned imports from Denmark, while consumer boycotts across the Middle East have emptied supermarket shelves of all Danish products.

Western governments have reacted with shock and muddle. There is a growing feeling in continental Europe that Britain and America should have taken a principled stand on grounds of free speech, but have failed. In France, home to Europe's biggest Muslim minority—roughly 10 percent of the population—there has been surprise at the relatively conciliatory response of Jack Straw, Britain's foreign secretary, who called the publication of the cartoons "insensitive" and "unnecessary." Many in France are baffled at the reluctance of the British and American press to publish the cartoons themselves. (On February 8, three editors and a reporter quit the *New York Press* over a decision not to reprint the cartoons, and President George Bush called on world governments to stop the violence and be "respectful".)

To be sure, the official French reaction has been measured. President Jacques Chirac declared that freedom of expression was "one of the foundations of the republic" but added a plea for "respect and moderation" in its application. And one editor at *France-Soir,* a small newspaper that was the first to claim the "right to caricature God," was sacked after publishing all 12 caricatures. Yet it seemed that the paper's owner, a Franco-Egyptian, had been seeking an excuse to get rid of him anyway. The rest of the press, along with those who see the matter as a test case of the ability of French democracy to withstand the demands of political Islam, have taken an increasingly muscular position.

Several big national papers, including *Le Monde* and *Libération*, have republished some of the cartoons to make a point about their right to do so. This week they were joined by *Charlie Hebdo,* a satirical weekly—despite a last-minute attempt to secure an injunction against it by several French Muslim organisations. *Charlie Hebdo* reprinted a text from the Manifesto of Liberties Association, a French secular Muslim body, arguing that the orchestrated violence was a warning to Europe's Muslims from abroad that "You don't have the right to think 'like Europeans,'" and urging the West to reaffirm Europe's tradition of free thought.

That some offence should be taken is understandable. The Muslim injunction against picturing recognised prophets is well known. Yet the point of proscribing images is to ensure that they do not become objects of worship in themselves. Muslims generally shrug indifferently at Christian representations of Jesus or Moses, both of whom Islam also venerates.

In this case, however, the caricaturing of Muhammad was clearly meant as a challenge. Several of the images were frankly insulting, particularly those that pictured the Muslim prophet as a terrorist. It adds to the sense, which has grown among Muslims since America launched its war on terror after September 11, 2001, that their faith itself is being branded as violent and criminal. In addition, pious Muslims believe that Muhammad, while mortal, is the embodiment of manly perfection; at the same time a prophet, a moral example and a political leader. "He is not a believer," runs one of the prophet's sayings, "if he does not love me more than his father or son or all people."

Muslims worldwide have also grown keenly sensitive to what they see as western double standards. Freedom of speech is an admirable thing, says a Syrian member of parliament, but why do European countries forbid questioning of the Holocaust? Why are Muslim preachers jailed for incitement while anti-Muslim slurs go unpunished? And why, as a natural extension of this thought, does the West ignore Israel's atomic arsenal while questioning Iran's nuclear ambitions?

At the same time there is little understanding, in many Muslim countries, either of how Western democracies function, or how they have evolved historically towards enshrining maximum personal freedom. Danish protests that there are no laws empowering the government to intervene are met with disbelief. In both Yemen and Jordan, editors who republished the cartoons (which have now appeared in 22 different countries) were promptly arrested and their newspapers shut down.

Leaders and Manipulators

Some protests seem to have been spontaneous; others have been deliberately manipulated by Islamist elements. While demonstrations have been widespread, the number of participants has generally not been large. Moderate leaders, from Iraq's foremost Shia authority, Grand Ayatollah Ali al-Sistani, to Ekmeleddin Ihsanoglu, who heads the Organisation of Islamic Conferences, have called for Muslims to express their feelings peacefully. A *fatwa* issued by Egypt's highly respected grand mufti, Ali Gomaa, states that Muslims should understand that others will attack their faith; and although they should reject this "perverted behavior," he said, they should protest peacefully, with "wisdom and fair exhortation."

This stand presents a clear contrast to the rabble-rousing tactics used by others. A Danish imam, Abu Laban, may have started the whole thing by touring the Middle East to drum up outrage, including distributing far more offensive cartoons of the Prophet (as a pig, as a paedophile) which he said had been "received" by Muslims in Denmark. Iran's supreme guide described the furore as a plot "concocted by Zionists angered by the victory of Hamas in the Palestinian elections"— though the Palestinian vote took place four months after the publication of the cartoons. In Syria, a police state allied to Iran where rioters have torched the Danish and Norwegian embassies, witnesses noted men with walkie-talkies directing the crowds. Security was so ineffectual that camera crews accompanied arsonists into the buildings. In neighbouring Lebanon, authorities say that one-third of the 400 people arrested for setting fire to the Danish embassy and vandalising the surrounding Christian district were Syrians. On February 8th Condoleezza Rice,

America's secretary of state, remarked that Iran and Syria had so stirred up the violence for their own ends that "the world ought to call them on it."

Some analysts have speculated that the Muslim Brotherhood, a global fraternity of Islamist groups with branches in some 70 countries, may have a hand in the uproar. This is unlikely. The most vigorous Palestinian protests, for example, were led by militants from ostensibly secular Fatah, not Hamas, a Brotherhood offshoot. Protests in other Brotherhood strongholds, such as Egypt, Jordan and Morocco, have been relatively muted. A Brotherhood spokesman in Egypt accused some politicians of playing a "dirty game . . . to distort the image of the Islamic movement—to get the people to say they are not peaceful, not democratic, against free speech."

It is more likely that Islamist forces of varying stripes have seized the opportunity both to assert their presence and to reinforce the sense of Muslim embattlement that suits their goals. Recent electoral advances by Islamists, in Turkey, Iraq and Egypt as well as Palestine, had already emboldened these forces. Other competing voices, too, have found the cartoon issue an ideal platform for promoting their version of the faith. On Egyptian television, one dapper preacher aimed a sermon at the West, urging westerners to love Muhammad; another, his rival for ratings, advised Muslims to dedicate a two-day fast to the victory of their prophet.

Some Muslims find all the hullabaloo distressing. "What it shows is that we lack confidence," says the headmaster of a Cairo school. "If we were confident about our faith we wouldn't have to react so hysterically." Many others, however, feel it marks an important precedent. In a Friday sermon at the Grand Mosque in the holy city of Mecca, Saleh bin Humaid, a Saudi preacher, extolled the spirit of defiance that was unifying Muslims. "A great new spirit is flowing through the body of the Islamic nation," he said. "The world can no longer ignore the nation and its feelings."

By midweek, moderate Muslims in Denmark, Britain and elsewhere were appealing for calm. Cool-headed leaders, including clerics in Indonesia, the most populous Muslim country, urged restraint. International efforts were also under way to ease tension. A joint statement issued on Tuesday by the United Nations, the Organisation of the Islamic Conferences and the EU condemned violent protests while calling for respect for religion. The EU's foreign-policy supremo, Javier Solana, said he would travel to Arab and Muslim countries to try to calm their anger. He may be gone for some time.

Suggested Discussion Topics

1. Was the U.S. war against Iraq an "identity conflict"? How do you think an Iraqi would answer this question? Was the al-Qaeda attack on the World Trade Center and the Pentagon an "identity conflict"? How do you think Osama bin Laden would answer this question? Do you think Huntington's argument regarding a "clash of civilizations" is a useful tool in understanding these events? Why or why not?

2. Does the West pose a threat to Islamic civilization? Be prepared to argue whichever side of this question your instructor assigns you to present.

3. Can people or nations from different "civilizations" get along? Why or why not? If peaceful coexistence is possible, are there particular institutions or arrangements that are necessary?

4. How should Europe deal with its Muslim population? Should it force Muslims to assimilate? Or should it expel Muslim residents? Or should it continue to tolerate and encourage cultural diversity? What are the consequences of each policy? Should provocative behavior like the publication of cartoons satirizing the Prophet Muhammad be permitted? Should provocative sermons in mosques and provocative statements on Islamic websites be allowed? Given your answers to these questions, now think about how the United States should deal with cultural, religious, and ethnic diversity in America. Does this affect your answer to these questions?

5. What does it mean to have a "hyphenated identity"? For example, what would it mean to be a "Chechen-Russian" or a "Tamil-Canadian" or an "Estonian-American"? What do multiple identities mean for the functioning of nation-states? Can someone be a member of two nations simultaneously? Can someone be a member of one nation and a loyal citizen of a different state? Should an individual be allowed to be a citizen of two nation-states at the same time—for example, to vote both in Mexico and in the United States, or to carry both an Irish passport and an American one?

6. Does a nation like Chechnya need to have its own state in order to protect itself and advance its common interest? Can you think of nations that do not have their own state? What has their experience been? Would you feel safe if the state that ruled over you was dominated by a different national group? Why or why not? What kinds of assurances would you want if you were to live as part of a state dominated by a different national group? Would international guarantees, or commitments by your own state to protect the autonomy or special status of your nation, reassure you? Why or why not?

7. Why are multiethnic states—states whose citizens see themselves as belonging to different national, ethnic, or tribal groups—difficult to maintain? Should they be preserved? What kinds of measures can make this possible? The United States is often described as a melting pot of different national, ethnic, and racial groups. What do you think this means? How have different groups managed to live together in the United States? What kinds of political arrangements have facilitated a melting pot?

8. Why are national groups in much of the world increasingly at odds with the existing states? How can this tension between identity-based loyalties and territorially-defined states be resolved?

9. Why do individuals sometimes conclude that particular characteristics, such as language, religion, or skin color, matter? Why might states adopt policies that deliberately emphasize race or national identity, even when these policies divide their own citizens?

10. How do you define or identify yourself? What does this mean in terms of how you interact with others?

Chapter 15

GENDER AND GLOBAL POLITICS

Historically, the study of global politics has focused on the activities of states: that is, on the interaction among groups of individuals who are divided and organized according to their citizenship. Individuals define their own identity and the identity of "others" in a number of ways, however. "Us" and "them" distinctions are constructed on a variety of different superficial but observable markers, for example, language, religion, clothing, and skin color or other physical features. As we saw in the previous chapter, these other socially constructed identities can be important in global politics, dividing or uniting people in ways that can make it easy or difficult to solve shared problems and develop institutions that create security for oneself and one's own group without threatening the security of others.

In recent years, gender has become an increasingly important identity and source of division in global politics. Dividing the world along gender lines—dividing people into male or female categories and allotting different roles and opportunities to them simply because of the category they fall into—has a number of consequences for global politics.

First, because nearly all societies are dominated by men, women as a group find themselves discriminated against. Most states are ruled by men, and many states do not offer women equal legal or economic status. Even in countries in which the state attempts to treat men and women equally, social institutions, typically dominated by men, discriminate against women and limit their choices, denying them career and lifestyle options available to men.

Historically, gender-based discrimination has had an impact not only on women's quality of life but also on their chances of survival. In traditional agricultural societies, parents preferred male children who would carry on the family name and support their parents in old age. By contrast, female children were regarded as economic burdens. In such societies, it was not uncommon for female babies to be "exposed," that is, left outside the home to die. Their only crime was that they would grow up to be women rather than men. And even today, in some countries, including India and China, modern medical techniques such as ultrasound and amniocentesis are used to identify female fetuses, which are then aborted. More widely around the world, families discriminate against their daughters in providing education, health care, and even nourishment, saving family resources for the males in the household. Estimates of the number of "missing" women in today's world—individuals who were killed or allowed to die simply because they were female—fall in the range of 60 to 100 million. As a result populations in some parts of the world are increasingly skewed. The overabundance of young men and scarcity of women promises to cause social and political problems.

Gender-based discrimination extends into the most personal aspects of life, with consequences that affect not only individual happiness but the well-being of society as a whole. In many societies, women are forced to bear children, regardless of their preferences, and are denied access to birth control. In such societies, maternal mortality rates remain relatively high. Perhaps even more shocking, some African societies still encourage (and others tolerate) the genital mutilation of young women to prevent them from ever enjoying sex.

Discrimination also extends into the economic realm. Around the world, societies undervalue "women's work," jobs that are assigned to women. In most countries women are paid less than men for the same work. Even today, in some Islamic countries women cannot leave home without an escort, cannot hold jobs outside the home, and cannot drive a car. Not surprisingly, women and children make up the bulk of the poorest of the world's poor.

To focus solely on the victimization of women, however, would be to miss much of why gender is so important in global politics. A second consequence of dividing the world along gender lines and of men's control over political and social power is that women's insights are ignored, and problems are defined and addressed exclusively in ways that men see them. Feminist scholars argue that the tendency of men to see relationships as competitive and to define situations in zero-sum terms—that is, to assume that one side can gain only at the expense of the other—has resulted in a global political system that is unnecessarily conflictual. Alternative views of politics—views that are more natural for women, that give less emphasis to boundaries, separateness, and autonomy in relationships—are ignored or ridiculed. If only men could be more like women; that is, if only males were trained to value the things that women value, instead of being taught to despise them, politics would be transformed. Men, like women, are trapped in the gender roles and identities that society has constructed for them, and this limits their ability to solve the problems they face. Equally important, some feminists argue, men's efforts to retain dominance over women traps them in certain mindsets and behavior patterns that prevent the discovery of creative, cooperative solutions to shared problems. Because men are taught that being a man means dominating (dominating women, dominating weaker men, dominating nature), they ignore or reject options that would undercut rigid power hierarchies, even in their own minds.

A third consequence of gender-based divisions is that women have often been excluded from the political process of developing and implementing solutions to the world's problems. Women have been seen as the target or object of (man-made) state policies rather than as equal and active participants in problem solving. Addressing today's global security problems, such as economic underdevelopment, overpopulation, pollution, and resource depletion, requires the full involvement of both women and men. Indeed, an abundance of research has shown that the surest way to accelerate economic development is to provide women with education, contraceptive information, and access to credit, and to allow them the same freedom to make choices that men have.

To whatever degree the new issues on today's security agenda are global issues—problems that threaten us collectively and require a transnational or global effort to solve—the way individual societies around the world define women's roles becomes a matter of global concern. If women are denied capital (the tools needed to be productive), the education needed to make more productive use of their labor, and the freedom to make decisions for themselves simply because they are women, then many of today's security problems are likely to be insoluble, with tragic consequences for all. And if successful resolution of many of today's problems requires women's thinking—that is, finding the kinds of solutions that women are taught to look for—then exclusion of women from power, and the socialization of men to think as men, may prove disastrous. Many feminists therefore reason that the inclusion of women in positions of power and authority, where they can join fully in solving today's problems, is a critical step.

One of the important developments in today's global transformation has been the rise of a global network of problem-solving nongovernmental organizations, working side by side with the existing structure of sovereign states. These NGOs tend to be relatively nonhierarchic and to focus on finding cooperative solutions. Perhaps not surprisingly, these NGOs have in many cases been relatively open to women's participation and women's solutions: even while states have generally remained dominated by men, some NGOs have offered a parallel avenue for women's inclusion in problem solving and for women's insights to be heard.

At the heart of most feminist analyses of global politics is a critique of patriarchy. Patriarchy—a construction of gender roles that concentrates social and political power in the hands of men—perpetuates gender-based stereotypes and increasingly is a source of conflict in global politics. Patriarchy is not simply an infringement on human rights, victimizing individuals because they are women, but has also resulted in a distorted, conflictual view of politics and, by disempowering women, has served as an obstacle to solving some of the world's most pressing problems.

Gender-based identities are hardly new; what is new, and what may be contributing to today's turbulent global transformation, is an increased awareness of the problems posed by patriarchy, its human costs, and the barriers it creates to human fulfillment and security. Growing recognition of gender inequality was apparent at the UN-sponsored Fourth World Conference on Women that convened in Beijing in September 1995. At the conference, Hillary Clinton voiced the view of most of the 50,000 people who had gathered from over 180 countries when she declared that women's rights were also human rights. The preamble of the final conference declaration denied claims that national or religious customs could justify unequal treatment of women: "It is the duty of states, regardless of their political, economic and cultural systems, to promote and protect all human rights and fundamental freedoms." The final declaration of the conference declared the "full realization of all human rights and fundamental freedoms of all women" to be "essential for the empowerment of women." The declaration included demands that women be permitted to control their own sexuality; that violence against women, including rape in wartime, domestic abuse, genital mutilation, and sexual harassment in the workplace, be ended; that an end be brought to discrimination against female infants and girls; and that women be provided access to credit.

Gender identities thus promise to play an important role in global politics. Our ability to build integrative political institutions will depend in large measure on our ability to overcome "we/they" distinctions based on gender and to recognize how gender-based identities have shaped (and limited) how we approach collective dilemmas.

15.1 Women, the State, and War: Feminist Incursions into World Politics

Franke Wilmer

Increasingly, feminist scholars are offering students of world politics insights into the importance of gender identity and gender construction in understanding conflict and violence around the globe and an alternative framework for conceptualizing world affairs. In the first selection in this chapter, Professor Franke Wilmer of Montana State University provides an overview of feminist perspectives on global politics. She points out that gender is an important factor in many cultures and helps determine what individuals can or cannot do. In most societies, men are dominant, and they view the world in terms of stereotypic opposites. As a result, positive qualities are associated with masculinity and negative ones with femininity. When thinking about global politics, men tend to focus on abstractions like states and classes. Women, she says, unlike men, view people as individuals and focus on real people and what happens to them when thinking about global politics.

Wilmer observes that women rarely appear in accounts of global politics. "Where are they?" she asks, and answers that although their activities are frequently ignored in men's accounts, women are everywhere: providing men for wars, caring for children, working without pay, fostering peace movements, fighting as soldiers, and being coerced to provide sexual services. She then asks how women's perspectives differ from men's and argues that one important difference is that, whereas men see interstate war to be the greatest threat in global politics, women see violence in general—whether interstate, within families, or in other settings—to be the key problem. Much of the violence in the world, including organized warfare, feminists argue, grows out of men's dominance of women; that is, violence is "part of a more pervasive social process in which male dominance is reproduced in social organizations ranging from the family to the state." Males, feminists argue, find it necessary to assert their masculinity and their independence from women over and over again. Their assertion of independence is complicated by the fact that most male children are cared for by women. In adulthood the assertion of independence may take the form of preoccupation with sovereignty and boundaries, including those of the nation-state. It reflects, Wilmer argues, men's fear of being "reengulfed" by women.

More than any other issue, the reconceptualization of war as a "problem" during the twentieth century, rather than an acceptable option for implementing the foreign policy goals of states, provided the impetus for international relations to develop as a distinct field of academic inquiry. For the most part, until the first half of the twentieth century international relations as such was subsumed by the discourse of diplomatic history. Until women as feminists recently entered the academy, however, we all seemed oblivious to the fact that all of these discourses, as well as the institutions they produced and legitimated, were conducted from a *masculine* perspective.

Those engaged in academic projects which speak to the masculinization of "public" life[1] are now commonly referred to as "feminists." One aspect of feminism is that it signals an analysis undertaken from the cognitive perspective of women. But more importantly, the presentation of a distinctly feminist perspective as a special case or approach to international relations or world politics implicitly reveals that both the discourses about and the conduct of politics in the West (and by its hegemony, much of "the" world today) have proceeded from a masculine perspective. The study of international relations has been conducted largely by and from (until very recently) the cognitive perspective of men. Therefore, a course on international relations that does not take into account feminist research, theory, and perspectives is really a course on "masculinist international relations."

We Are All Gendered

While I do not want to perpetuate a masculinist perspective that the world and our knowledge about it can be conveniently divided into a dichotomous representation of masculine and feminine, one of the most important insights of feminist scholars has been to reveal the process of *gendering*. To the extent that individuals have been socialized as male and female and identify themselves as male and female, their behavior and the ways they think about the world will reflect those differences. Men have built states distinguished from other kinds of polities by their "monopoly of force," and men have defined politics as a struggle over and management of coercive power. Men, in other words, have created both states and war, without which there would be no "international relations," as we know it, to study.

Revealing the gendered nature of how we think and act is but one of the many contributions of feminist scholarship. The issue of *gendering* is a good place to begin because it helps us think about how and why patterns of gendered social relations

---

[1] I use quotes because the distinction between public and private is one of the dichotomies called into question by feminist theorizing.

This article is an original contribution prepared for this text.

have marginalized (or rendered invisible in some cases) women. What are the consequences of marginalization; how and why do women's perspectives differ from men's; and why are women's perspectives significant? These issues will be taken up as a way of organizing the rest of this essay. But first, there are at least four consequences that thinking about the process of gendering reveals that are particularly important for framing a discussion of feminism and world politics.

The first is the notion that identity categories such as "masculine" and "feminine" are *socially constructed*. Of course, there are biological differences, but what is important is the *meaning* associated with difference, indeed, the way difference itself is constructed, not the "differences" themselves. Women have the potential to bear children; men do not. Women have the potential to lactate; men do not. Men and women are biologically characterized in general by different hormone mixes. This much is cross-cultural. But cross-cultural analysis also reveals that the significance assigned to biological difference varies. Furthermore, how these categories are constructed through social processes and interactions becomes the basis for legitimating and even institutionalizing certain configurations of gender relations. Patriarchy (a community in which the father is the supreme authority in the family, clan, or tribe), for example, posits the dominance of women by men and the privileging of masculine over feminine as the basis for social order. A social order constructed in terms of the complementarity of gender roles and relationships, on the other hand, sees the interdependence of women and men and feminine/masculine as the bases for social order.

A second contribution of feminist scholarship is to highlight differences commonly ascribed to masculine and feminine. Typically, masculine and feminine are spoken of in terms of positive and negative attributes. What masculine "is," feminine "is not," and vice versa. Men are aggressive, women are submissive. A submissive man is less manly, more feminine. An aggressive women is unfeminine. Masculine is: rational, resolute, competitive, assertive, calculating, disciplined, restrained, physical, detached. Feminine is: emotional, flexible, cooperative, compliant, intuitive, undisciplined, expressive, verbal, passive, caring. And so on. To be "masculine" is to be "not feminine."

Thus a third contribution is to eliminate dichotomous thinking about gender (as well as other identity issues). Such thinking, called "essentialism," ascribes to individuals immutable qualities owing to their membership in mutually exclusive categories: male/female, nature/culture, rational/irrational. The problem with such thinking is that it stereotypes people and so hides their individuality. What is worse is that usually that which is male/masculine is viewed as superior to female/feminine.

Feminist thinking demands that we attend to the particular, and formulate alternatives to dichotomous thinking. I have recently begun to incorporate feminist research and perspectives into my courses wherever it seems relevant. After a recent lecture on international relations theory when I concluded with a feminist critique of militarization, a student approached me at the end of class. "One thing I do not understand," she said, "is what the feminist position on the military is. Some feminists critique the military, while others want to gain admission to it on the same basis and in the same capacities as men." I explained that one of the most important revelations of feminist thinking is to reject homogenized categories and male-female stereotypes altogether and to focus instead on the diversity of stand-points taken by *real people*. For feminists the actors in international relations are not states, regimes, classes, or movements. Instead, the real actors are people. Feminists resist categories wherever possible because categories deny the subject-status of people, relegating them instead as a category of objects. How does this produce a different reading of world politics and a different methodology for making sense of world politics?

Cynthia Enloe begins her book *The Morning After: Sexual Politics at the End of the Cold War* with the sentence: "Now that the war is over, Esmerelda has had her IUD removed." "Esmerelda," she goes on,

> is a Salvadoran woman who spent many of her young adult years as a guerrilla in the Farbundo Marti National Liberation Front, the FMLN. She pounded out tortillas and washed her boyfriend's clothes as well as wielding a gun. Now it was the "morning after." . . . Her country's strife had been brought to an end by a peace accord signed by government men and opposition men up in New York, under the watchful eye of the men from Washington. So Esmerelda was going to hand her gun over to the United Nations peacekeepers and try to remake her life. One of her first postwar acts was to have her IUD taken out. During the war her guerrilla tasks had made it seem politically irresponsible to get pregnant. But now she was being urged by men in the political leadership to imagine her postwar life as one devoted to being a good mother.
>
> Some Salvadoran women, however, had quite a different vision of postwar relationships between their country's women and men. They were imagining an end to police rape and domestic violence. Men's violence against women had escalated under the pressures of a civil war fueled by Cold War anxieties.[2]

From her analysis of the significance of both Esmerelda's "personal" choice to use an IUD during the war and to remove it afterward, and of women's political activism both during the war and following the peace accords, Enloe concludes that "the civil wars in Central America and the global Cold War, which intensified so many local conflicts during the last forty years, have not come to a neat end. They must have ending processes, ones not as elegant or as conclusive as, say, an operatic grand finale. These messier processes may go on for years, even generations."[3]

Enloe's point is that when we only look at men's experiences and the institutions and events designated as significant by men, we will miss something critical about international relations in general, and in this case, war and violence in particular. We will not see the continuing processes of postwar conflict as they affect the lives of *people*, and we will therefore not perceive, for instance, the necessity of postconflict reconciliation among *people*, in *communities*, and in *relationships*. We will not see how the "event" of signing a peace accord or treaty among categories of people (mostly men) called "governments" and "rebels" takes place within a historical and social context of continuous relationships, man to woman, family to community, one generation to the next. It is not simply a matter of "seeing" women's perspec-

---

[2] Cynthia Enloe, *The Morning After: Sexual Politics at the End of the Cold War* (Berkeley: University of California Press, 1993), p. 1. Copyright © 1993 The Regents of the University of California. Reprinted by permission.

[3] Ibid., p. 2.

tives. Missing the "personal" is missing the human, historical, and social context in which the conflict emerged, became violent, and became part of the interpretive framework in which configurations of power and human relationships continued after "the war." When we ignore the personal we fail to understand the social, psychological, and historical processes in which conflict, civil strife, social injustice, dominance, and power relations repeatedly erupt. It is not enough, Enloe argues, to demilitarize our institutions. We must demilitarize ourselves, our self-consciousness, the ways in which masculinity and femininity are constructed in relation to the maintenance of the garrison state if we are to find a stable world order the morning after the Cold War.

Finally, feminist explorations into the construction of feminine and masculine identity have done the most interesting and important work on the question of how identity is politicized and the consequences of politicization. Ultimately, global politics features groups whose adherents distinguish between "themselves" and "others." Ending conflict necessarily entails overcoming the opposition between people posed by "self/other" distinctions.

To summarize thus far, then, feminist scholarship has made at least five important contributions to the study of world politics. First, it reveals the gendered nature of how we think and act. Second, it focuses on the socially constructed aspect of gendered identity. Third, it highlights the mutually constitutive nature of feminine/masculine constructions. Fourth, it shows how dichotomous categorization generates stereotypes. And finally, feminist scholarship has opened new avenues for interdisciplinary work on the problem of identity.

The remainder of the essay will provide an overview of the questions that have guided feminist scholarship in recent decades. In the mid-1980s feminist perspectives were just beginning to find their way into political science, and somewhat later entered into examinations of international relations. Since then there has been a literal explosion of research.

The "Invisibility" Question: Where Are the Women?

Women have never been *absent* in world politics. They have, however, for the most part, been *invisible* within the discourse conducted by men from a masculine perspective about politics and the world. Women, along with slaves and children, were the noncitizens who "achieved the production and reproduction that was a precondition of the public"[4]—in other words, generated the resources required for the development of ancient Greek city-states, modern European states, and the settler states in North America, Australia, and New Zealand. Women's unpaid labor within the family, like the unpaid labor of slaves, contributed to the accumulation of wealth in industrial societies (concentrated in the hands of men). Without

---

[4] V. Spike Peterson, "Security and Sovereign States: What's at Stake in Taking Feminism Seriously?" in Peterson, ed., *Gendered States: Feminist (Re)Visions of International Relations Theory* (Boulder: Lynne Reinner, 1992), p. 36.

mothers socialized as "good citizens" to value the sacrifice of their sons in war, there could be no reliable military defense of the state. Enloe draws attention to the Russian women who undertook hunger strikes and formed civic organizations to resist the conscription of young Russian men as a critical factor in undermining the military support on which the Soviet regime relied for legitimacy and essential support.

Another way of rendering women visible historically is to study the contributions of specific women. Joan D'Arc, Catherine de Medici, Catherine the Great, Queens Victoria and Elizabeth I, Indira Gandhi, Clara Barton, and Golda Meir are not "invisible," although they have been scarcely considered in their roles as political actors and as women, as particular women.

In the twentieth century women have played an enormous role in fostering and sustaining peace movements, disarmament initiatives, and the processes that led to the creation of the League of Nations and the United Nations. Elise Boulding reports that the first "women's peace groups with international contacts date back to 1852 (Anglo-American Olive Leaf Circles)," that between 1880 and 1900 five international women's organizations were founded, and that the "first great congress of women" occurred at the Chicago Exposition in 1893.[5] The Women's International League for Peace and Freedom was founded in 1915 "to seek disarmament, social and economic justice, and an end to all war."[6] Women organized successful petition drives leading to the 1930 European Conference on Disarmament and the Limited Test Ban Treaty of 1963.

In 1981 "thirty-six women and a 'few' men and 'children'" initiated a protest against basing American nuclear weapons in England by camping out at Greenham Common in England. The camp lasted more than two years—through two winters. It generated a series of court cases in which women protesters were charged with "behavior likely to cause a breach of the peace" under an obscure 1361 act as well as a court case in the United States (rejected by a U.S. appeals court) against then President Ronald Reagan, undermined public support for the basing program, and opened the "mainstream" disarmament movement to "feminist argument and practice."[7] An International Women's Peace Camp in 1985 in Geneva highlighted the continued deep commitment of women to and their exclusion from international disarmament processes, and in 1986 the U.S. National Women's Conference to Prevent Nuclear War convened in Washington, D.C.

Women are economically and physically coerced into sexual tourism and slavery, and the provision of sexual services to men stationed at foreign military bases. They are rape victims in men's wars of emasculation, diplomatic wives, maids, nannies, and campesinas. Women are soldiers, revolutionaries, and the nucleus around which the social structure of the family revolves. Women's invisibility, like the invisibility of other marginalized "groups" (with women as a "class" cutting across

---

[5] Elise Boulding, *Women in the Twentieth Century World* (New York: John Wiley and Sons, 1977), p. 188.

[6] Catherine Foster, *Women for All Seasons: The Story of the Women's International League for Peace and Freedom* (Athens: University of Georgia Press, 1989), p. 7.

[7] Christine Sylvester, *Feminist Theory and International Relations in a Postmodern Era* (Cambridge: Cambridge University Press, 1994), p. 193.

all groups), renders our efforts to understand the causes, consequences, and possible futures of international relations incomplete and in all likelihood, inaccurate.

The "Voice" Question:
What Are Women's Perspectives on Global Politics?

There is no monolithic "women's perspective," but rather a variety of shared and particular perspectives about women and world politics. Women are directly concerned with the rights of children, and many of the issues highlighted by women's activism fall into the realm conventional international relations calls "low politics" (and which is marginalized in relation to men's concern with the "high" politics of militarization). Women, of course, have many of the same concerns men have. Women wish to live in secure and peaceful social environments, with equal opportunities to participate in and benefit from an economic life that provides basic needs, and where one's contribution to social processes is limited only by one's choices and aptitude. Women's conception of security, however, may be different than men's. Women, as men, do not wish for war. But they also wish to be physically secure within spheres (men have) designated as "private," like the home.

National security, for example, includes not only freedom from attack by other states but freedom from attack within the domestic sphere of marriage, family, and intimate relationships. During the height of the Vietnam War, an average of 5,750 Americans were killed annually. Around 1,500 women are murdered every year by husbands or boyfriends in a "war against women" that has been going on much longer and continues with no end in sight. If 1,500 Americans were killed each year in an "international" war, the public would be outraged.

National security means living in a social world in which one feels secure against the threat of rape. In the United States, 1.3 women are raped every minute—78 per hour, 1,872 per day, 56,160 per month, and 683,280 per year.[8]

According to the FBI, attacks on women by intimates result in more injuries requiring hospital treatment than robbery, mugging, rape, and automobile accidents combined.[9] The U.S. Department of Justice reports that on yearly average, women are victims of 572,032 violent acts committed by intimates, compared to 48,983 attacks against men in intimate relationships.

Children's security is inseparable from women's security. Where violence is directed toward women, children are observers, or victims themselves. When women lack basic resources, children are malnourished or hungry, homeless, and lacking in basic health care. Fifty percent of all homeless women and children in the United States have taken to the streets because of domestic violence; women who leave violent partners are at a 75 percent higher risk of being murdered by them than those who remain in the relationship.

---

[8] Chris Bartley, *Sexual Assault Information Page* (1997), <www.cs.utk.edu>.

[9] *Myths and Facts About Domestic Violence* (1997), <www.iquest.net/~gtemp/dv_facts.htm>.

Feminist scholarship argues that these data suggest the central problem of international relations is not "war," but *violence*. Defining the problem as "war" focuses our attention on certain institutions—the state and military—and how these institutions "behave." Thus research programs like The Correlates of War project at the University of Michigan ask question such as: are states more likely to go to war when they are in alliances? Are states less likely to go to war when power is "balanced" among them? Are democratic states more war-prone than nondemocratic states? And so on. Other studies focus on human behavior as a cause of war, but the fact that the "humans" studied and theorized about are (socially gendered) masculine and that they act as they do within socially constructed and *gendered* institutions is not regarded as significant in these accounts, if it is considered at all. War—groups of men (or states built and governed by men) carrying out institutionalized violence against other groups of men—is made to seem normal by this historical account (written largely by men) of interstate relations.

From a feminist perspective, the problem is *gendered* human violence, and the state and war are consequences of the way in which men are gendered, the way in which men are masculinized in relation to violence. Feminist perspectives problematize the distinction between "good" and "bad" violence implicit in concepts of the state and war. "Good" violence—the use of force in defense of family and community—supports order and social stability, whereas "bad" violence—that is, antisocial uses of force, violence that is disruptive of existing relationships—threatens national and international social order.

But what if the social order itself is violent, or is constructed in such a way as to legitimate and even require violence (or "coercion")? In its relations with indigenous peoples, British imperial authorities evaluated how "developed" an indigenous people's political system was by whether or not the social order relied on coercion: that is, by the extent to which it was organized to carry out violence.[10] Such a construction of violence and the identification of "good violence" as a political "necessity" carried on by "good men" not only obscures questions of interpersonal violence and structural violence, but sanctions violence itself as a necessary social behavior. Order in social groups, from the family to the state, is perceived as depending on a willingness to use violence to exert control. The "problem" then becomes regulating it (the good violence/bad violence problem). Violence is viewed as a normal component of maintaining social order. The question is not asked whether the basis of the social order itself—patriarchy—is constructed to require violence. Yet as some feminists point out, patriarchy can be interpreted as institutionalized violence: by its nature patriarchy is "a means to maintain privilege and hierarchy, so physical violence is used to demonstrate power or superiority."[11]

---

[10] It was on this basis that Australian Aboriginal peoples, for example, were determined not to have constituted political entities capable of occupying the land, leaving the land, conveniently, as "unoccupied." The High Court of Australia in 1993 overturned this doctrine and has begun a process of reconciling Aboriginal land claims.

[11] Betty Reardon, ed., *Women and Peace* (Albany: State University of New York Press, 1993), p. 41.

The roots of violence, institutional, structural and direct, private and public, from the perspective of some feminist scholars lie in the construction of social dominance in the form of patriarchy, which is then reproduced in gendered states, gendered state violence, and gendered international relations. Patriarchy is the institutionalization of unequal gender relations where *men* and *masculine* dominate *women* and *feminine*.

War—which, viewed as a problem, has provided the main impetus for the development of international relations as a distinct field of study—is, from a feminist perspective, part of a more pervasive social process in which male dominance is reproduced in social organizations ranging from the family to the state to interstate relations and regimes. More importantly, male dominance both constructs and limits the way we think about the actors and problems within the sphere called "international relations" or "world politics." At least until very recently. Instead of viewing war as either an enduring feature or a bounded problem in world politics, feminists tend to view war as one of many forms of violence. From the perspective of some feminists (particularly peace researchers and advocates of nonviolence), violence represents a failure of humanity. "Solving the problem of war" may be less a matter of "scientifically" studying war than changing the way we, living in gendered states, think about ourselves in relation to violence. By constructing nonviolent mechanisms for dispute resolution, by adopting nonviolent strategies to maintain social order, and by restructuring our thinking so that privilege, hierarchy, and violence are unacceptable in interpersonal, familial, communal, and social relations, we can collapse many points along the continuum of violence.

The "Significance" Question: What Is Signified by Man/Woman?

After acknowledging gender inequality and demanding equality in public spheres, feminists began to wrestle with the question: what difference does difference make? Are "men" and "women" merely receptacles for sets of ascribed characteristics, the former privileged and the latter the residue of "qualities society does not wish to promote as public virtues"?[12] Does acknowledging difference lend legitimacy to the continued domination of men/masculine over women/feminine?

The building and legitimating of the nation-state itself was a masculine project. The state is constructed as *boundaried* and (militarily) *defended* territory. Or, as Enloe says, "States had militaries; that's how you could tell they *were* states."[13] Feminists have explored the psychoanalytic implications of masculine identity's reliance on, even obsession with, boundaries and autonomy as a consequence of the need for the masculine self to emerge in opposition to the feminine caretaker

---

[12] Sylvester, *Feminist Theory and International Relations in a Postmodern Era*, p. 23.
[13] Enloe, *The Morning After*, p. 246.

as the original "other" against which infantile autonomy must struggle. Sovereignty, the bounded state, and autonomous political actors as the basic components of the state system are directly linked to the way in which masculine identity is formulated. Masculine identity, formulated under conditions of female-monopolized early childhood, is chronically at risk of feminization. The identification of the infant as a bounded self, according to this view, is always initially formulated in relation to the mother or "woman" as long as women are primary caretakers of infants. By some accounts, for girls this produces less anxiety, because for them the development of identity as "self" and "feminine" occurs in the same turn. The self is "mirrored" in a feminine other. For boys, however, gendered identity requires a further differentiation from the "other." Self is mirrored first in a feminine other, and subsequently a distinctly masculine identity must also be constructed. Behind the construction of a man as masculine lies his original identification with the female (m)other, so that sustaining masculine identity relies on his reminding himself and others that he is "not-feminine." This explains the prevalence of patriarchy as well as misogyny, and by some accounts, is reproduced in virtually all of men's activities, including the construction of the state as a *militarized* and thus *masculinized* institution. Thus to demilitarize the state necessitates no less than a reconstruction of masculine identity.

In this vein, Christine Di Stefano argues that, owing to the male's childhood struggle for autonomy against primarily feminine caretakers, adult masculinity, at least in the Western tradition, has been concerned with the maintenance and defense of boundaries as a mechanism for securing autonomy. The notion of sovereignty, as well as the state it sustains, reflects this preoccupation with securing autonomy. "Within this symbolic frame of meaning," Di Stefano writes, "maternal and natural reengulfment become the constitutive threats to autonomy, masculinity, and 'civilization' itself."[14] Is this fear of "reengulfment" at work in the idea of the state as a bounded territory (never quite) secured by a ready military? Is fear of "reengulfment" at work in the perception of international relations as anarchic, as an environment in which one must always imagine and expect attacks by powerful adversaries who wish to violate the boundaries of one's state, where one must be prepared to fight and win imagined potential wars? Is this fear at work in domestic politics, revealed as resistance to regional and international organization? Does the idea of a fear of "reengulfment" help explain the growing support, in the aftermath of the Cold War, for fringe groups in the United States which believe that the United Nations is really an instrument for the development of a world government that will invade and conquer the country?

Male efforts to protect masculinity appear in support for the military. "Man" or "masculine" and "warrior" are inseparable. That is, the qualities that make a "good" warrior are indistinguishable from those that "make a man masculine." Male mili-

---

[14] Christine Di Stefano, *Configurations of Masculinity: A Feminist Perspective on Modern Political Theory* (Ithaca: Cornell University Press, 1991), p. 51.

tary recruits must be bound to male state officials and military officers. "The glue," Enloe says, "is camaraderie; the base of the glue is masculinity."[15] And nothing reflects this masculinization gone amok in the U.S. military better than Marine "pin-hazing."[16]

Taking a step further, some feminist theorists argue that "woman" and "feminine" have been used to signify chaos, and "man" and "masculine" to signify order in Western political philosophy. In this reading, state building aims to bring order out of chaos, indeed, to control chaos; it represents the triumph of (masculine) rational culture over (feminine) irrational anarchy. Women/feminine as anarchy/chaos/unpredictable/irrational is the problem for *masculinist* constructions of world politics. And man as statesman and soldier fights his foe with order, predictability, and rationality. Attempts to solve the problems of world politics which are emotional, flexible, cooperative, relationship-oriented, intuitive, verbal, and caring (as feminized qualities) are dismissed as "unrealistic" in favor of those which are rational, resolute, competitive, dominance-oriented, calculating, physical, and tough. The portrayal of world politics as hostile legitimates a male "protection racket." Men in control of states portray—even create—an international environment that is hostile in order to legitimize the state and the state's (and therefore predominantly men's) monopoly of force as a defense against anarchy.

Conclusion

The necessity of rethinking sovereignty, the state, and war is apparent. A growing number of global problems—the stalling out of "development" in the less-developed countries, terrorism, environmental degradation, nuclear proliferation—have less to do with preserving "territorial integrity" (the objective of a militarized state) than with deeply embedded and complex relationships and perceptions of dominance, struggles for dominance, perpetual fear of domination, and struggles against domination. Territorially organized states that, by the doctrine of sovereignty, may use any means necessary in "defense" of their interests/autonomy may not be suited to our contemporary needs for problem solving. Feminists are providing important critiques of the state and state system that call into question the cognitive and philosophic underpinnings of international relations. Is war the problem and the state the solution? Or is the way the state is currently constructed—reproducing a certain conception of masculinity—the problem, and violence and domination consequences of that construction of the state?

---

[15] Enloe, *The Morning After*, p. 52.

[16] Reuters reported February 1, 1997, on a broadcast newsfilm which showed Marine paratroopers at Camp Lejeune, North Carolina, "writhing and crying out in pain as others pounded the spiked medals into their chests through tee-shirts."

Gender, Human Security, and National Security

15.2 Infanticide, Abortion Responsible for 60 Million Girls Missing in Asia

Sherry Karabin

The devaluation of women is nowhere more clearly revealed than in the age-old practice, especially in some Asian countries, of killing daughters or letting them die, supplemented by the newer practice of selectively aborting female practices. The following selection describes this practice and some of its effects.

There is a little-known battle for survival going in some parts of the world. Those at risk are baby girls, and the casualties are in the millions each year. The weapons being used against them are prenatal sex selection, abortion and female infanticide—the systematic killing of girls soon after they are born.

According to a recent United Nations Population Fund (UNFPA) State of the World Population Report, these practices, combined with neglect, have resulted in at least 60 million "missing" girls in Asia, creating gender imbalances and other serious problems that experts say will have far reaching consequences for years to come.

"Twenty-five million men in China currently can't find brides because there is a shortage of women," said Steven Mosher, president of the Population Research Institute in Washington, D.C. "The young men emigrate overseas to find brides."

The imbalances are also giving rise to a commercial sex trade; the 2005 report states that up to 800,000 people are being trafficked across borders each year, and as many as 80 percent are women and girls, most of whom are exploited. "Women are trafficked from North Korea, Burma and Vietnam and sold into sexual slavery or to the highest bidder," Mosher said.

State-Sanctioned Infanticide?

Mosher, the first American social scientist allowed into China, puts much of the blame on Beijing's one-child policy, which took effect in 1979. The policy encourages late marrying and late childbearing, and it limits the majority of urban couples to having one child and most of those living in rural areas to two. Female infanticide was the result, he said.

"Historically infanticide was something that was practiced in poor places in China," Mosher said. "But when the one-child policy came into effect we began to see in the wealthy areas of China, what had never been done before in history—the killing of little girls."

In recent years, female infanticide has taken a back seat to sex-selective abortion or female feticide, due to the advent of amniocentesis and ultrasound technology as well as other prenatal sex selection techniques, many of which are now readily available in clinics and doctors' offices.

"We feel it's a serious problem that everybody should be concerned about and aware of," said Wanda Franz, president of the National Right to Life Committee. "This is a form of abortion that, from our point of view is especially egregious. Abortion is claimed to help women; obviously in these cases, females are the direct victims, because women in these cultures are not valued. In our family we adopted a Chinese baby," she continued. "There have been thousands and thousands of them adopted since China's one-child policy created this overabundance of baby girls in orphanages."

How bad are the imbalances between males and females in Asia? Generally, the normal sex ratio at birth (SRB) is between 103 and 105 males per 100 females, and in rare cases 106 or a bit more than that. Countries that are known to have or have had higher sex ratio at birth numbers include South Korea, which peaked at 115 in 1994, Singapore where the SRB registered 109 in 1984 and China, which has seen the numbers increase over the past two decades.

Published reports in China show the gender ratio for newborns in 2005 was 118 boys for every 100 girls, and in some southern regions like Guangdong and Hainan, the number has reached 130 boys for every 100 girls. The 2000 Chinese census put the average sex ratio at 117, with Tibet having the lowest number at 103 and Hainan registering the highest at 136.

Nicholas Eberstadt, a researcher at the American Enterprise Institute for Public Policy Research in Washington, D.C., attributes the large sex-ratio imbalances in places like China to a combination of factors: an enormous and enduring preference for boys reinforced by the low socioeconomic status accorded to women; the use of rapidly spreading prenatal sex determination technology for gender-based abortion; and the rapid drop in fertility in different populations, making the outcome of each birth even more important.

"The one-child policy intensifies this problem, but if that policy stops and fertility levels stay at one or two, the problem won't entirely go away," Eberstadt said. "When the average number is down to one or two, there is an incentive for parents to meddle with the outcome. In places where fertility levels are high, there are few signs of sex selection." In his presentation before the World Youth Alliance in New York City last April, [he] warned that "The Global War Against Baby Girls" is expanding.

"There are gender imbalances in almost every East Asian country, but Japan," said Eberstadt, who has also noted alarming irregularities in Western Asia in places like Cyprus, Qatar and Pakistan, as well as in some countries on the African continent, including Egypt, Libya and Tunisia.

Indian Girls Bear Dowry Burden

In India, where the child sex ratio is calculated as the number of girls per 1,000 boys in the 0–6 years age group, the problem is severe. The 2001 Census shows there are only 927 girls per 1,000 boys, representing a sharp decline from 1961 when that number was 976. In certain parts of the country there are now fewer than 800 girls for every 1,000 boys.

"India is a very mixed bag," Eberstadt said. "In some parts there are no signs of any unnatural imbalances; in other parts the numbers are grotesque." For instance, 2001 census reports show that Punjab and Haryana reported fewer than 900 girls per 1,000 boys. "The problem is more prevalent in the northern and western states, where prosperity, rapid fertility decline and patriarchal (male heads the family) mindsets combine to put girls at risk," said Ena Singh, the assistant representative at UNFPA.

Like China, there is a strong son preference for various socio-economic reasons, such as the son being responsible for carrying on the family name and support in old age. Furthermore, in some sections of India it is believed that only sons can perform the last rites for parents. In addition to sharing a strong son preference, both India and China lack a national social-security system. As it is assumed that a daughter will become a part of her husband's family, parents must rely on their sons to take care of them.

Since the 1970s, India's government has promoted a two-child family as "ideal." While no formal laws exist, the general fertility decline in the country has led to smaller families, with couples still preferring to have at least one son. But the government has done more than just suggest this number. "In India it has been done state by state, village by village," Mosher said. "There have been sterilization campaigns and there is enormous pressure. Villages that won't comply have been denied fertilizer, access to irrigation water, etc."

Complicating matters even further in India is the dowry system, where families pay large sums in order to marry off their daughters. Although prohibited in 1961, newspaper reports illustrate the continuing phenomenon. This can be very expensive for families, adding to the perception that girls can be a financial burden.

Abortion is legal in India under certain conditions, but sex-selective abortions or female feticide is a crime. In 1994, the government enacted the Preconception and Prenatal Diagnostic Techniques Act (PC & PNDT), which prohibited those conducting such tests from telling or otherwise communicating to the woman or her family the sex of the fetus. The law was amended in 2003 to prohibit sex selection before or after conception.

"In recent years, prenatal sex selection and female feticide in India has increased," Singh said. "Though it is against the law for ultrasound technologies to be used to detect the sex of the child, it is still done illegally."

In 2006 a doctor and his assistant in the northern state of Haryana were sentenced to two years in jail and fined for revealing the sex of a female fetus and agreeing to abort it. It was the first time medical professionals were sentenced to jail time under the (PC & PNDT) Act. Three years earlier, a doctor in Punjab received a fine. Singh estimates that hundreds more cases are being investigated across the country and taken to court.

Experts who have analyzed the National Family Health Survey 2 (NFHS2) estimate that about 300,000 girls go "missing" in India each year. Other studies have put the number between 150,000 and 500,000. While many people see this as a problem of the poor, analysts say it is more prevalent among those in the wealthier and educated segments of society. Men in parts of India are also beginning to have difficulties finding brides, causing some to leave the country to do so.

"Hindu girls are being smuggled and purchased from poor countries like Nepal and Bhutan to be brides for Indian men," said Bernard Dickens, professor emeritus of health law and policy at the University of Toronto Law School.

Combating the Problem

In recent years various Indian state governments and media houses have launched initiatives to address the gender imbalances, including "Save the Girl Child" campaigns. Last February, the Indian government announced its "cradle scheme," whereby orphanages would be set up to raise unwanted baby girls. Other incentives include tax rebates on ownership of properties and reserving seats for female candidates in villages, districts and at municipal levels.

Community groups, corporations and individuals have also started various efforts to enhance the status of the girl child. In March 2007, politician Sonia Gandhi, chairwoman of the United Progressive Alliance, spoke out against female feticide and the need for gender equality at the International Women's Day celebrations in New Delhi. Lara Dutta, UNFPA's goodwill ambassador, a popular actress and Miss Universe 2000, has also been working extensively with young people to raise awareness about the issue.

China too has enacted laws in an effort to meet its goal of lowering the sex ratio at birth to normal levels by 2010. In 1994, the Mother and Child Health Law of the Peoples Republic of China outlawed the practice of sex identification of the fetus and sex-selective abortions without medical requirements. This was reaffirmed in the 2002 Population and Family Planning Law. Officials also started the "Care for Girls" campaign to promote equality for men and women and economic support is being offered to girl-only families in the countryside.

"Raising awareness is important," said William Ryan, an Asia and Pacific regional information advisor for the United Nations Population Fund. "I think the effort to emphasize equality of the sexes and the value of women in society will help reduce the problem in the long run."

China Holds On to One Child

However, China has pledged to keep its one-child policy in place until the year 2050, a policy which it admits is "related" to the large sex imbalances in the country.

"The implications are potentially disastrous," Mosher said. "The answer is economic development, not restricting the number of people."

This year, the United States sponsored a resolution at the U.N.'s Commission on the Status of Women that called for eliminating infanticide and gender selection. The resolution was withdrawn due to opposition from several countries, including China and India; however, the issue of prenatal sex selection was included in the final conference document. Interestingly South Korea was one of the countries to support the resolution. Like China and India, it too has had its own problems with sex imbalances; however, progress is being made.

If the imbalances continue, Adam Jones, executive director of Gendercide Watch, sees another possible outcome. "Because of the disparity, surviving women have greater market value," he said. "As a result, it may become more economically viable for families to have girl children, thus reducing rates of female infanticide and sex selection."

As China and India work toward solving their problems, Eberstadt points out that three large European countries are also showing disturbing signs. "Greece, Macedonia and Yugoslavia betray some hints of prejudicial death rates for little girls in the post-war period," he said. While the numbers are very small, he notes they are "nonetheless curious and unusual. In the western hemisphere, Venezuela and El Salvador both have unnatural death rates for little girls and now also display unnatural sex ratios at birth," he continued.

Published reports point to problems among some immigrant groups in Canada as well. And even in the United States, Eberstadt said, some Asian-American populations have begun to "exhibit sex ratios at birth that could be considered biologically impossible."

"Since the mid-1990s, the issue of female infanticide and sex selection has been highlighted in several conferences and in several U.N. documents," said Samantha Singson, chief U.N. liaison for the Catholic Family and Human Rights Institute. "Unfortunately the issue isn't getting as much attention as we feel it deserves."

15.3 A Surplus of Men, a Deficit of Peace

Valerie M. Hudson and Andrea Den Boer

This selection by two insightful political scientists picks up on the previous essay, exploring the consequences of the gender inequality that occurs when "one child is allowed to live while another is actively or passively killed." The authors of this selection make a persuasive connection between the resulting surplus of males in a population and the problems of domestic and international peace and security. Looking particularly at emerging conditions in Asia, the authors argue that "young surplus males" are a source of belligerence and strife both at home and abroad and that action should be taken immediately to bring an end to preferential sex selection of fetuses and newborn babies.

International security and stability rest in large measure on the internal security of nations. Analysts have long examined factors such as arms transfers and ethnic violence in this regard, but the list now includes variables that were not traditionally viewed as related to national security. Unemployment rates, water tables and river flows, infant mortality, migration patterns, infectious disease epidemiology, and a whole host of other variables that tap into the general stability of a society are now understood to affect security. . . .

. . . One overlooked wellspring of insecurity, we argue, is exaggerated gender inequality. Security scholarship is theoretically and empirically impoverished to the extent that it fails to inquire into the relationship between violence against women and violence within and between societies. . . .

Admittedly, there is probably no society in which women do not experience some gender inequality, meaning subordinate status or inferior treatment in political, legal, social, or economic matters. Indeed, what would constitute a perfect society between men and women is a controversial topic with which we are not concerned here. However, *exaggerated* gender inequality is hard to miss: we define it to be present when, because of gender, one child is allowed to live while another is actively or passively killed.[1] Offspring sex selection, almost universally used to favor male offspring, indicates that the life of a female in the society is not only not valued but actually despised. There can be no greater evidence of the extremely unequal and subordinate status of women in a society than the presence of prevalent offspring sex selection therein.

If violence against women within a society bears any relationship to violence within and between societies, then it should be possible to see that relationship at work in societies where violence against women is exaggerated—that is, where offspring sex selection is prevalent. Specifically, internal instability is heightened in nations displaying exaggerated gender inequality, leading to an altered security calculus for the state. Possibilities of meaningful democracy and peaceful foreign policy are diminished as a result. . . .

Selection against female offspring produces an excess proportion of males in society: surplus males. Given the long history of son preference in China, it is not surprising that the Chinese have a special term for such surplus males: *guang gun-er* (also transliterated as *guanggun, guangguer,* or *guanguen*), alternatively translated as "bare sticks" or "bare branches," indicating those male branches of a family tree that would never bear fruit because no marriage partner might be found for them. . . .

---

[1] "Passive killing" refers to such phenomena as withholding food from a newborn or abandoning a newborn in the wild. Though not an active killing, such as smothering a child, the intent to kill is clear, and so is termed passive killing.

Hudson, Valerie M., and Andrea Den Boer, "A Surplus of Men, a Deficit of Peace: Security and Sex Ratios in Asia's Largest States," *International Security*, 26:4 (Spring 2002), pp. 5–38. © 2002 by the President and Fellows of Harvard College and the Massachusetts Institute of Technology.

Who are these young surplus males? First, they are not equivalent to the bachelors of the West. Single men in the West are not surplus males: indeed they can and often do form semipermanent attachments to women and produce children in that context. Surplus males, on the other hand, do not have such possibilities. In a marriage market where women are scarce and thus able to "marry up," certain characteristics of young surplus males are easily and accurately predicted. They are liable to come from the lowest socioeconomic class, be un- or underemployed, live a fairly nomadic or transient lifestyle with few ties to the communities in which they are working, and generally live and socialize with other bachelors. In sum, these young surplus males may be considered, relatively speaking, losers in societal competition.

The behavior of young surplus males also follows a broadly predictable pattern. Theory suggests that compared with other males in society, bare branches will be prone to seek satisfaction through vice and violence, and will seek to capture resources that will allow them to compete on a more equal footing with others. These theoretical predictions are substantiated by empirical evidence so vast and so compelling as to approach the status of social science verity. Cross-culturally, an overwhelming percentage of violent crime is perpetrated by young, unmarried, low-status males. . . .

Some may question whether marital status plays an important role in such behavioral dispositions, but this is another widely confirmed research finding. David Courtwright notes, "It is when young men cannot or do not marry that socially disruptive behavior is intensified."[2] . . .

In conclusion, there is both strong theory and persuasive historical evidence that the bare branches of high sex-ratio societies can contribute significantly to intrasocietal violence. In some cases, this domestic threat has led governments to create foreign policy initiatives designed to disperse bare branches. The strategies that bare branches choose to better their position in society erode the stability of the societies in which they live. . . .

The Security Logic of High Sex-Ratio Societies

The repercussions of artificially high sex ratios pose grave problems of insecurity for a society which, in turn, create vexing policy dilemmas for governments. . . .

High sex-ratio societies will tend to develop authoritarian political systems over time, for these are better equipped to deal with possible large-scale intrasocietal violence created by society's selection for bare branches. As Christian Mesquida and Neil Weiner note, "Choice of political system made by the members of a population is somewhat restricted by the age composition of its male population."[3] Robert Wright is even more blunt: "Few things are more anxiety-producing

---

[2] David T. Courtwright, *Violent Land* (Cambridge, MA: Harvard University Press, 1996), p. 202.

[3] Christian G. Mesquida and Neil I. Weiner, "Human Collective Aggression," *Ethology and Sociobiology*, Vol. 17, No. 4 (1996), p. 257.

for an elite governing class than gobs of [unmarried] and childless men with at least a modicum of political power. . . . Leaving lots of men without wives is not just inegalitarian: it's dangerous. . . . A nation, in which large numbers of low-income men remain mateless, is not the kind of country many of us would want to live in."[4] . . .

. . . Speaking more generally about Asia, however, we are on the cusp of the time period wherein these larger proportions of bare branches will become socially active. As they do, we believe that governments in such societies will begin their predicted shift toward greater authoritarianism. In countries with high sex-ratio societies that are not ethnically homogeneous, such as India, this shift may start as rule by the majority ethnic group which group will, in turn, actually promote interethnic violence.

Indeed, governments of high sex-ratio societies must often cultivate a political style crafted to retain the allegiance and respect of its bare branches. This tends to be a swaggering, belligerent, provocative, martial style—to match that of the bare branches themselves. In the rhetoric accompanying such a posture, there is inevitably an "other," who is weak and contemptible and whose attempt to find a place in society or in the international order must be opposed. The society is then enjoined to muster its strength so that these "insults" can be answered with appro-priate action. Though all governments at one time or another may engage in these types of tactics, they take on a particular urgency for governments of high sex-ratio societies. These governments understand that its bare branches are a formidable club—if it is in your hand it can be very useful, but if it is poised over your head, it may constitute a greater threat than external enemies. . . .

There is only one short-term strategy for dealing with a serious bare-branch problem: reduce their numbers. There are several traditional ways to do so: fight them, encourage their self-destruction, or export them. Longer-range strategies to address the problem, such as decreasing offspring sex selection, are also viable (and laudable), but are not likely to improve the government's situation for a generation or more. Furthermore, though economic prosperity is useful in placating disgrun-tled members of society, including bare branches, no amount of wealth will turn surplus males into nonsurplus males. . . . Prosperity is thus no panacea in this situ-ation, though economic downturns are likely to trigger violent resource capture by bare branches.

Governments will always seek to suppress societal violence that threatens their authority. Indeed the government may actually recruit bare branches into military or police units that are used to fight bare-branch criminals. . . .

Another approach is to simply let bare branches destroy each other, either turn-ing a blind eye when rivals dispatch one another or encouraging ethnic divisions that will lead to intergroup violence. Once again, however, the level of societal dis-location may in the end threaten the government, as it will appear that the gov-ernment has lost control over the level of violence in society. A second variant of

---

[4] Robert Wright, *The Moral Animal* (New York: Pantheon, 1994), pp. 98–101.

this strategy is to provide large, dangerous public works that pay well. Building intercontinental railways or huge new dams, reclaiming vast tracts of swampland or desert—if done the old-fashioned way using primarily manual labor—can both occupy and sustain bare branches, while also ensuring significantly increased mortality among that population subgroup. Nevertheless, there may be a limit to how many such works can be undertaken by a given society.

Finally, governments seek to send bare branches elsewhere. "Elsewhere," in the government's perspective, may include distant frontier regions of the country or may in fact be other countries. This may be a peaceful export of colonists to a frontier or an exodus of migrant workers to other nations. There is, however, a martial variant of this strategy as well: a strategy that has been consciously used in history to reduce bare-branch numbers. If the bare branches threaten national security if they live at home, the government may prefer to let them die in some glorious national cause far from home instead. . . .

Conclusions

. . . In a way, the very type of government to which a nation can aspire may be tied to the status of women in society. When that status is very low, the possibilities for a full and meaningful democracy and for a peaceful foreign policy are distinctly less. High sex-ratio societies, denoting a very low status for women, cannot be expected to emulate normal sex-ratio societies either in terms of their form of government or in terms of their tendency toward peacefulness. Any attempts at that emulation may prove, historically speaking, to be short-lived. And any attempts by scholars from normal sex-ratio societies to project their own security logic onto a high sex-ratio society will lead to miscalculation. High sex-ratio societies simply have a different security calculus. . . .

. . . The relationship we see is not straightforward cause and effect: strife and war obviously take place within and between normal sex-ratio cultures as well. Nevertheless, exaggerated gender inequality, as we have seen, may provide an aggravating catalyst to the mix of insecurity factors leading to conflict. All we have found suggests that high sex-ratio societies in contexts of unequal resource distribution and generalized resource scarcity breed chronic violence and persistent social disorder and corruption. . . .

. . . The scale on which sex ratios are being artificially altered in Asia today is, generally speaking, unprecedented in human history. What are the consequences of this vast demographic shift? What happens to societies that explicitly *select* for increasing and disproportionate numbers of bare branches? We suggest that societies with young adult sex ratios of approximately 120 and above are inherently unstable, and both China and India are, at this writing, nearing that level and will probably surpass that level in the next two decades.[5] We stand at the threshold of

---

[5] In the historical time periods we examined, sex ratios of greater than 120 have been noted. With regard to China and India, such very high sex ratios were usually regionally or temporally bounded (a particular region

a time in which these young surplus males will increasingly figure into the deliberations of Asian governments. Not only the nations of Asia, but the nations of the world will want to pay close attention to the ramifications of Asia's spiraling sex ratios and the policy choices they force upon Asian governments. How ironic it would be if women's issues, so long ignored in security studies as simply irrelevant, became a central focus of security scholars in the twenty-first century.

 # Women's Rights as Human Rights—or as Western Cultural Imperialism?

15.4 Yet Another Problem in the Middle East

The Economist.com

Do Arab societies discriminate against women, as widely believed in the West, or do these societies protect women, as they claim? The next selection confronts this question in its discussion of the ways in which Arab women are perceived as repressed and discriminated against and the efforts of the Western-influenced United Nations Development Program (UNDP) to empower them in the way in which Western women have been empowered during the past century. In the West, gender equality is widely regarded as a universal human right. By contrast, many Arabs regard Western efforts to change the status of Arab women as disrespect for Arab culture and as an effort to impose Western mores on the Arab world.

Arab Women Are Suffering, Says a UN Report

It is not an easy time to be an Arab criticising the Arab world on the international stage. The authors of the hard-hitting series of Arab Human Development Reports sponsored by the UNDP—a frank, self-critical analysis by Arabs, for Arabs, of the well-being and the ills of the Arab world—have taken on a brave

---

would embrace female infanticide for a time). Never before in history, however, have entire nations engaged in such high rates of offspring sex selection. It is the new, cheap technology that allows for this heightened and nationwide prevalence. Thus the scale (in terms of what percentage of the country's population is practicing offspring sex selection) is unprecedented in human history. Also, never before have China and India had such huge populations. For example, China's population at the turn of the twentieth century was about 460 million persons. Today it is more than 1.2 billion persons. The combination of these two factors means that the sheer number of bare branches being created in Asia is also unprecedented in human history. Yet, given the pockets of high sex ratios in history, we can also say with some confidence that societies that reach and exceed 120 males per 100 females in the young-adult age group are inherently unstable.

task. This is especially so since they have broadened the notion of human development from traditional areas of health, education and per-capita income to include political freedom, good governance and what they have called the Arab world's knowledge deficit.

Previous reports have been selectively invoked by outside commentators as evidence of the defects of Arab culture, in turn leading Arab critics to accuse the reports' authors of pursuing a "Western" agenda. And in 2004, the authors said, the U.S. administration, displeased by sections that strongly criticised its presence in Iraq, threatened to cut its funding of the UNDP unless the language was toned down (a charge that U.S. officials have denied). The fourth report in the series deals with perhaps its most controversial subject yet—the empowerment of women in the Arab world. Its broad scope includes some of the most marginalised groups in the region, from foreign prostitutes in the Gulf to unemployed female squatters and rural Arab women rendered into "neoslavery" as household servants.

Women Lag Behind in Health and Education

Tangled as it is with the sensitive areas of religion and culture, at a time when many Arabs and Muslims feel under attack, the issue of the status of women is a political minefield. The idea of women's empowerment is all part of a Western agenda, the conservative argument goes: Western-style feminism turns women into bikini-clad anorexics, idealising models rather than motherhood; and its misguided individualism undermines the family, the fundamental building block of society.

Rather ingeniously, the report's authors have chosen to begin their assessment of women's inequality with the issue of health—an area where it is particularly difficult to argue for cultural relativism. According to the report, women in the Arab world lose more years of their life to disease than their male counterparts, even in countries with higher standards of living, which, it says, "is attributable to general lifestyles that discriminate against women." Women between the ages of 15 and 24 are twice as likely as their male counterparts to contract AIDS.

The report notes that half the women in the Arab world are illiterate, compared to one-third of men. Across the region as a whole, girls make up less than 50 percent of students at school and university, though they account for more than 50 percent of the top-scoring secondary-school-leavers in all countries for which data is available. Only one in three Arab women over the age of 15 works, compared to more than two out of three in East Asia, reflecting both conservative social attitudes and the slow growth of employment opportunities for either sex in much of the Arab world.

These conservative social attitudes also mean no one has bothered or been able to collect much information on gender disparities in the workplace in the Arab world. But, intriguingly, the report says that, in the few areas for which details are available, there is no great divergence in pay for salaried workers of either sex.

However, the report unfortunately does not publish the actual figures that its claim is based on. Meanwhile, many women work as part-time or informal employees rather than receiving salaries.

Perhaps most daringly of all, the report argues than in much of the region, the family "has been transformed from a place of safety and security into a place where any type of violence against women may be practiced." It cites World Health Organisaiton statistics from 2000 saying that in Egypt, 97 percent of women have been circumcised, even though the practice was banned in 1997. (A major Egyptian feature film, *Dunia,* recently tackled this issue but few Arab cinemas have been willing to show it.)

Islamic Inspiration

So what to do? A detailed set of recommendations includes prescriptions for improving women's access to healthcare and education, wiping out Arab female illiteracy by 2015, and introducing quotas for women's representation in parliament.

But none of this will be achieved without a major shift in attitudes. The battle needs to be fought in the realm of ideas. Much of the report is dedicated to arguing for an Arab model of women's empowerment, drawing in particular on Islam—on the basis that it is not Islam itself, but conservative interpretation of Islam, combined with local cultures, that has retarded women's progress.

In particular, the report calls for a revival of *ijtihad,* the independent interpretation of the sources of Islamic law (the Quran and the Sunna) as opposed to reliance on the existing interpretations produced by the established schools of Islamic jurisprudence. This advice is explicitly aimed at the region's Islamist opposition movements, suggesting a sense that in the long term, these may become the real powers in the region.

Window Dressing

Indeed, a central theme of the report is that women's empowerment is only sustainable if it has a popular base, involves the broad mass of Arab women, and comes as part of an overall drive for freedom and representation. It warns that "pro-women" policies imposed by undemocratic governments may risk a popular backlash (as was seen, for instance, in Bahrain last year when thousands of women demonstrated against government plans for a codified family law).

In particular, the authors are highly sceptical about the utility of moves by authoritarian governments to elevate a few elite women to high office. Female cabinet ministers rarely hold key portfolios, with the notable exception of the UAE's Sheikha Lubna al-Qasimi, the region's only female economy minister. Having women in parliament does not mean much if parliament itself is toothless. Compared with the threatening business of democratisation or freer expression, the report argues, making women more equal is one of the easier ways to address Western pressure for reform.

But is there any hope for popular moves to empower women? The report cites a survey conducted in four Arab states, Egypt, Jordan, Morocco and Lebanon, which found that strong majorities in each country answered "yes" to questions from, "Does gender equality relate to the total concept of freedom?" to, "Should women have an equal right to work?" This is arguably a less than representative selection of countries, especially with no Gulf state included, but the results are more encouraging than many would have predicted.

The report is also sharply critical of "foreign powers" that seek to "liberate" Arab women, saying that this leads some Arabs to associate all women's movements with external intervention. In a cutting critique, author Haifa Zangana argues that most Iraqi women have no interest in the women's organisations that the U.S. has set up on their behalf, because these groups avoid dealing with broader issues of national sovereignty and independence.

Moreover, the report says, continued infringements on national sovereignty have contributed to "a renewed emphasis on male-centred notions of honour and glory arising from an overwhelming feeling of humiliation."

15.5 Female Genital Mutilation on Rise in Britain

MSNBC.com

Patriarchy is deeply rooted in many cultures. On a number of specific issues, however, there is a growing divide between world opinion and the cultural practices of particular societies. Behavior that the modern world regards as a violation of human rights is still widespread in traditional societies, and these societies consider international pressure to end such practices as a form of cultural imperialism.

Genital mutilation is perhaps the clearest example. In much of Africa, women who come of age are forced to go through a painful procedure misnamed "genital circumcision." The purpose is to reduce a woman's capacity for sexual pleasure and, it is believed, the possibility that she will have sexual relations with anyone other than her husband. The practice is most widespread in parts of East Africa, where over 80 percent of women are subjected to it, and across a broad swath of the Sahelian region to West Africa, but, as the final selection in this chapter describes, the practice has been brought by African migrants to Europe, where it is regarded as a crime.

L ondon's Metropolitan Police, Britain's largest police force, hopes a campaign beginning on Wednesday [July 11, 2007] will highlight that the practice is a crime here.

To make their point, police are offering a $40,000 reward for information leading to Britain's first prosecution for female genital mutilation, Detective Chief Superintendent Alastair Jeffrey said.

In Britain, the problem mostly involves first-generation immigrants from Africa and the Middle East. Police say they don't have comprehensive statistics about the number of victims. But midwife Comfort Momoh, who specializes in treating them at London hospitals and clinics and who works with police, told the news conference she treats 400 to 500 victims every year.

Criminal Offense

Arranging or carrying out the procedure—in Britain or abroad—is a criminal offense punishable by up to 14 years in prison, but no one has been prosecuted since it was banned under British law in 2003, Jeffrey said. Police estimate up to 66,000 girls in Britain face the risk of genital mutilation. "The timing of this campaign is for one good reason: so we can get in before the summer holidays, a time when young girls are taken abroad and subjected to genital mutilation," he told a news conference Tuesday.

Mutilated infants, girls and women face irreversible lifelong health risks—both physically and mentally, according to UNICEF and other charity groups. Authorities believe the number of genital mutilation cases peaks in the summer, because the extended school vacation gives girls more time to recover—thereby making it easier for those responsible to cover up their actions.

Female genital mutilation usually involves the removal of the clitoris and other parts of female genitalia. Those who practice it say it tames a girl's sexual desire and maintains her honor. It is practiced by Muslims and Christians alike, deeply rooted in the Nile Valley region and parts of sub-Saharan African, and is also done in Yemen and Oman. Through migration, the practice has spread to Western countries like Britain.

U.S. federal law specifically bans the practice.

Millions of Victims

Between 100 million and 140 million women are believed to have been subjected to the practice in Africa and an additional 3 million girls face the threat of female genital mutilation every year, according to UNICEF.

Detective Inspector Carol Hamilton, who has been investigating the practice since 2004, said some immigrants in Britain may bring practitioners from their home country to mutilate several children because it is cheaper. She said children not only suffer terrible physical injuries, but can also be left emotionally scarred.

Salimata Badji-Knight was mutilated when she was 4 years old in her native Senegal. Now married and living in London, she fears she may not be able to have children because of the procedure. She hopes that by sharing her experiences she can prevent parents from subjecting their daughters to similar abuse. "Why do they need to go and mutilate a young innocent person without her knowing what is going to happen, just for culture?" Badji-Knight said. "It does not add up for me."

Somali-born supermodel Waris Dirie survived a traditional form of the practice that kills hundreds of girls each year. French President Nicolas Sarkozy is set to present the "Chevalier de la Legion d'honneur" to her on Thursday for her work as a leading critic of female genital mutilation, which has seen her tour parts of Africa to speak out against the practice.

Suggested Discussion Topics

1. Are gender identities important? If you believe they are, give examples from your life. If you believe they are not, explain your view. Feminist scholars have pointed out that the importance and meaning of being a man or a woman are constructed by societies. Explain what this means. Are the categories male and female constructed by societies? Explain why or why not.

2. How does a feminist account of global politics differ from a masculinist one? Make the strongest argument you can that our political institutions, such as war, and our understanding of global politics are influenced by gender. Now make the strongest argument you can that they are not influenced by gender.

3. What is patriarchy and how does it affect relationships such as those between individuals and states or between states themselves? Does patriarchy legitimate oppression and violence? Why or why not?

4. Are underdevelopment and poverty gender issues? Why or why not? Do you think giving women more control over their lives and equal access to social and political power would help resolve problems such as economic development, the environment, and overpopulation? If you think so, explain how and why. If not, explain why not.

5. Is violence against women a global problem? Why have women organized transnational networks to put violence against women on the global political agenda? What difference do NGOs and transnational networks make?

6. Is female genital mutilation a cultural practice that countries should be able to allow their citizens to practice, or is it a violation of basic human rights? Should the United States grant political asylum to women fleeing from societies that engage in this practice? The United States sometimes imposes economic sanctions or breaks diplomatic ties with states that violate the human rights of their people. Should the United States do so in the case of states that allow or encourage female genital mutilation?

7. Why do some families, particularly in the developing world, prefer sons to daughters? What measures, if any, should they be allowed to take to act on this preference? Should they be allowed to abort a fetus just because it is female? Should they be allowed to feed sons more than daughters? Should they be allowed to favor sons over daughters in schooling? Should states or international groups have the right to intervene in family life to prevent these practices?

8. Are gender rights and gender discrimination global issues? Or should they be dealt with by each society as it sees fit? Are transnational women's groups a healthy development or a sign of Western cultural imperialism and an infringement of sovereignty and a threat to cultural integrity? Should intergovernmental organizations become involved in legislating gender rights? What if a majority of states in the UN concluded that the United States discriminated against women by failing to provide adequate public funding for abortion? Should the United States have to change its laws?

9. Should the United States support international agencies and NGOs that provide medical assistance to women around the world, even if these agencies and NGOs provide information on abortion? U.S. courts have determined that American women have a right to abortion. In other countries where abortion is legal, should the United States support organizations that provide this medical service? Or should the United States seek to deny to non-American women a right that is guaranteed to American women?

Chapter 16

GLOBALIZATION, LOCALIZATION, AND POLITICS

In today's world, transnational processes, transnational institutions (including economic markets) and practices, and transnational norms and tastes are creating a global identity, threatening the survival of distinct local or national identities, and, most importantly, eroding the autonomy of sovereign states and their ability to protect the uniqueness of their national cultures. Globalization has many fans, especially in the economic realm, but a growing number of opponents want decisions affecting their lives to be made locally by their own elected representatives and fear that increasingly the welfare of people is ignored by global institutions.

The Antiglobalizers

The antiglobalization movement is characterized by a belief in the sovereign state as the pinnacle of political organization. Its advocates point to the successes of the state: how states established clear and secure boundaries, formed legal systems, and reduced crime. Order within a domestic realm was created and defended against enemies in the external world. To be sure, many of the early kings were pretty rough characters—one had to be in the context of the times—but over the years in the transition from king's domain to sovereign state, the harsh, arbitrary, or abusive character of many of the early states moderated substantially. Monarchs became constitutional rather than absolute rulers, themselves subject to the law and more respectful of traditional liberties and "the rights of man." Representative assemblies became more powerful, and democracies began to evolve. Although the notion of a people harked back in some cases to earlier eras, a healthy sense of nation and nationalism came to fruition in the nineteenth century, and the notion of the state as an embodiment of the public will and an instrument for advancing the national interest became firmly established. The concept of Citizen took on a new element of dignity, like that associated with ancient Athens. Conscription and regular drill created proud and patriotic citizen armies that gave young men a sense of true participation in the defense of their country. States began to regulate commerce with greater care and gradually began to assume more responsibility for the health and welfare of their citizens. Between the late nineteenth century and the 1960s, full-blown welfare states gradually developed. Many late-twentieth-century states provided meaningful physical and economic security to their citizens and gave them a sense of belonging to something greater than themselves—a patriotic identity that was not dependent upon religious belief, but also that was not inherently incompatible with most other identities.

Thus antiglobalizers believe that states have represented and protected their interests, and have been responsive, in however limited a way, to their preferences. To them, globalization reduces the rights and responsibilities of citizenship, the state's capacity to ensure public welfare, and the possibilities for meaningful democratic participation. For two decades, the social guarantees associated with the welfare state have been under attack. Is there a possibility that increasing globalization might reduce political rights as well?

From the perspective of the antiglobalizers, the territorial state is under siege, and national governments are less and less able to control their own destinies and provide psychological security and material benefits to their own citizens. In the name of interdependence and neoliberal economic doctrines of competitiveness, national sovereignty is being sacrificed. National economic and social policies are undermined by the machinations of giant multinational firms and financial institutions in the global marketplace. Reductions in living, working, and environmental standards achieved over years of struggle in the more advanced countries are threatened by the movement of investment capital to countries with low environmental and labor standards. In this new era, oligarchic TNCs scour the world for cheap labor, shifting job opportunities from country to country, often placing employees in sweatshop conditions, condoning child labor, and destroying the environment as they expand operations. And, transnational violence, exotic diseases, and dangerous pathogens travel globally with trade. Such problems are expensive to fix, but the IMF, World Bank, and giant banks place harsh conditions on loans.

Public authority is moving to the private sector. Huge corporate alliances, banks, and hedge funds, motivated strictly by greed, increasingly dictate public policies and outcomes. International organizations like the UN, the EU, or the IMF may include national government members, but national interests get submerged in voting blocs in such institutions and their bureaucracies also operate with no real constituency or accountability. Transnational NGOs may do some good, but whom do they actually represent?

Antiglobalizers have other concerns as well. National cultures are being overwhelmed by the homogenized culture of globalization, which is predominantly the "Coca-Cola/McDonald's" culture of the American hegemony. Television programs, movies, radio, pop music, and the Internet all carry glossy messages of individual self-gratification, declining moral standards, and violence that are antithetical to any sincere community spirit or religious practice. The global market is also menacing the planet with unsustainable development. Not only are humane working standards under threat but also the very future of humanity, with the pollution of the air we breathe, the loss of rain forests and species, energy exploration in the Earth's last wild places, overfishing, and the contamination of oceans and streams.

In the traditional area of security, the declining authority of states has encouraged a proliferation of fractured nationalism, tribal conflicts, breakaway polities, and private security firms and mercenaries subject to no law but their own. Violence is less and less governed by rules and military traditions, trained soldiers in uniform fighting for their country on fields of honor and sacrifice, but it is, as often as not, perpetrated against innocent civilians by religious fanatics and ethnic terrorists. Increased migrations of people are disrupting communities, creating cultural ghettos, providing opportunities for a host of new mafias, and generating a profitable illegal industry in the trafficking in humans, from desperate laborers seeking a better life to women tricked or trapped into domestic or sexual slavery. Nor is the new global technology completely innocent and constructive. The computer and Internet that enable us to get our bank balances and buy sports tickets online also facilitate money laundering, hate groups, terrorists, and reckless financial speculators. Finally, on an individual level, the computer permits users to withdraw from society and social responsibility into cyberspace.

A new global elite plays the game of globalization for their own benefit, increasing the psychological as well as material-welfare distance between themselves and the great mass of citizens at home and abroad. We are dividing into a world of the few who benefit, often outrageously, from globalization and the many who do not, or whose lives have become even worse. The cohesion traditionally provided by the state and national identity is giving way to a numbing sense of alienation created by large anonymous institutions and a homogenized high-tech global marketplace.

The Proglobalizers

The proglobalization account begins with a different view of states. In this version, the state was created by thugs, whose principal virtues were aggressiveness and guile. Rulers and nobles were exploiters, who extracted heavy taxes from an impoverished peasantry and borrowed from prosperous merchants to finance expansionist wars. To be sure, monarchs and aristocrats were forced to become more constitutional and less arbitrary over time, but even the best of the representative democracies were, until well into the twentieth century, narrowly elitist.

The nineteenth-century shift in Europe to citizen armies, coupled with new myths of the nation and its destiny, signaled a change from the limited wars fought by mercenaries to major wars waged for patriotism. The birth of nationalism divided rather than united people, as evidenced by the senseless slaughter of a generation of young men in the trenches of World War I, the bombing of Coventry, Dresden, and Tokyo in World War II, and the nuclear attacks on Hiroshima and Nagasaki. To be sure, some wars have been worth fighting, not least perhaps World War II, but that too was against the state in its most militaristic, totalitarian, and racist incarnation. When loyalty to state fused with the essentially ethnic idea of nation, and patriotism was touted as the highest fulfillment of self, the world was bound to be in for a bad time.

Now, in the globalizers' view, after a century that pushed interstate conflict to the edge of nuclear annihilation, humanity is getting the state under control. There is a marked decline in interstate wars. Although identification with country is slow to erode around the world, public opinion polls indicate that most governments and politicians who *are* the state are held in low esteem. Attentive publics seem to be increasingly aware that states simply cannot deliver on many of their promises and that, like it or not, citizen welfare is affected by wider global processes.

Fortunately, the globalizers argue, the needed expansion of global governance is already under way, exercised by more diverse groups of actors. Recent years have witnessed an explosion of international law, IGOs and NGOs, transnational firms, and financial institutions—and regimes and networks combining many of these actors—that are beginning to address collective dilemmas that no state has the capacity to deal with alone. At long last international law and institution building are advancing to wrestle with such urgent problems as violations of human rights, peacekeeping, environmental protection, organized crime, terrorism, refugees, telecommunications, shipping, aviation, disease, monetary instability, barriers to trade, and corporate bribery.

To say the least, the activities of transnational firms and banks too often do not meet the highest moral standards. However, the tremendous growth of the world economy that they have engendered—notwithstanding some inevitable instability that mainly reflects growing pains—has been very good for human welfare. Although it has enlarged the wealth gap between rich and poor, globalization has brought countless workers around the world new jobs and higher living standards. Consumers have benefited from an ever wider range of cheaper products. NGOs and attentive publics are having considerable success in persuading governments, as well as TNCs, to accept and to enforce improved working conditions and environmental standards. From the globalizers' perspective, demonstrators at WTO, World Bank, IMF, and Davos meetings consist of an odd alliance of old socialists, anarchists, and xenophobic nationalists. Demonstrators should leave the picket lines and lobby their governments for the causes they support. If they feel their jobs are threatened, they should give up employment in uncompetitive industries and reeducate themselves for more promising careers. In any event, the processes of globalization are inexorable and can only be guided and tamed in modest ways.

The threat of Western-style cultural homogenization is vastly overstated, globalizers contend, so resilient are local cultures. What is called American cultural hegemony is actually "modernization." Moreover, concern for cultural threats often involves either romantic sentimentality and condescension, or a blind eye turned to local practices and conditions that *should* be eliminated, such as the treatment of women in conservative Muslim societies.

The Internet and other improvements in telecommunications can be misused, but their impact has generally been positive. These improvements have provided the technological foundation for much of the tremendous expansion in the world economy and in the ranks of politically active individuals. Citizens around the world are getting more and more information, making it harder for governments to dupe or control them. Far from encouraging users to play computer games in lonely rooms, computers and the Internet have opened up not only vast amounts of information but also a new means of communication and organization that is the driving force behind global civil society. Globalization critics are quick to point out that those wired into the new technology are often those closest to the business sector, but technology is becoming cheaper and moving further into less affluent communities. Although in China seven out of ten people currently live in rural areas with no access to the new technology, would anyone dare to guess what the access figure will be ten or twenty years from now?

Finally, like worries about cultural homogenization, the claim that democracy is declining because of globalization is grossly exaggerated. Historically, few states have been democracies, and by far the majority of states today are either authoritarian or very imperfect democracies at best. In much of the developing world, particular ethnic, racial, religious, or regional groups control governments at the expense of other groups. There was an expansion of aspiring democracies at the end of the Cold War, but every previous expansion of democracy has been followed by a partial retreat from it.

16.1 The Globalization Index

A. T. Kearney, Inc., and the Carnegie Endowment for International Peace

Both antiglobalizers and proglobalizers see globalization as an expanding phenomenon. But is it? In fact, what exactly is globalization, and how can we measure it? We all agree that globalization refers to the degree to which people around the world are interconnected and have linked fates, but there have been few efforts to measure this interconnectedness. The A. T. Kearney/*Foreign Policy* Globalization Index was developed to measure which countries are comparatively highly globalized and which are comparatively nonglobalized, and to measure trends in globalization over time. The index uses a variety of indicators including trade, finance, political involvement, information technology, and personal contact among citizens from different societies. Using these indicators, it concludes that globalization has survived recent challenges and is prospering. The degree to which countries are integrated into a global community and the rate at which globalization is proceeding in different countries vary enormously. A few countries, like Singapore, rank high on all measures of globalization; others, like France, rank at or near the top on only one or two measures of globalization. For its part, the United States ranks highest in technology and is seventh overall, ranking only 71st in economic globalization. Some large countries, such as Brazil, Russia, India, and China, that previously were only poorly integrated into the global community are now in the process of becoming globalized.

Never before have the forces of globalization been so evident in our daily lives. An estimated 2 billion people witness Live Earth, a series of concerts held in 11 locations around the world to raise environmental awareness. Chinese manufacturers decorate toys with paint containing lead, and children around the world have to give up their Batmans and Barbie dolls. Mortgage lenders in the United States face a liquidity crunch, and global stock markets go berserk. Good, bad, and ugly—the effects of our supposedly "flattened" world are undeniable. But just how strong are these ties that bind? As former U.N. Secretary-General Kofi Annan once remarked, "Globalization is a fact of life. But I believe we have underestimated its fragility."

That fragility is particularly apparent in this edition of the Globalization Index. . . . This year's index draws on data from 2005, a year that, on the surface, exemplified the limitations of globalization's reach. It began with the fall-out from the devastating Indian Ocean tsunami, which left at least 300,000 dead, in part because there was no transnational network for emergency alerts in the region. Eight months later, similar scenes unfolded when Hurricane Katrina hit New Orleans, where the benefits of globalization failed to reach the poorest citizens of the world's wealthiest country. Not long afterward, an earthquake devastated Pakistan-administered Kashmir, where officials put the death toll at 75,000, with more than 2.5 million left homeless.

The limits of globalization weren't evident only against the backdrop of natural disasters; there were political fault lines, too. Sectarian violence continued to escalate in Iraq. Iran traded the conciliatory Mohammed Khatami for a more isolationist president, Mahmoud Ahmadinejad, who called for Israel to be "wiped off the map." North Korea announced it had nukes. Voters in France and the Netherlands rejected a new European Constitution. And four suicide bombers terrorized London on July 7 with coordinated attacks on public transportation.

Despite the turmoil in many parts of the world, nations did prove they could play nice with each other. The Middle East was home to some unexpected moments of cooperation, with Israel's withdrawal from settlements in Gaza and the West Bank, and Syria's pulling its forces from Lebanon after a 29-year occupation. On the economic front, cooperation in regional trading blocs grew, even as the Doha round of global trade talks continued to stumble. The United States approved a free trade agreement with the Dominican Republic and Central American nations, and Southeast Asian economies implemented several bilateral agreements of their own.

The inevitable push and pull of globalization plays out in the index's rankings, which incorporate indicators such as trade, foreign direct investment, participation in international organizations, travel, and Internet usage to determine rankings of countries around the world. . . . Together, the 72 countries account for 97 percent of the world's gross domestic product and 88 percent of the world's population. The index measures 12 variables, which are grouped into four "baskets": economic integration, personal contact, technological connectivity, and political engagement.

The results provide an assessment of how much, or how little, countries are opening themselves up and connecting with others. For example, the International Convention for the Suppression of the Financing of Terrorism welcomed new participants including Argentina, Brazil, Egypt, and Ireland, which boosted their political engagement scores. On the other hand, many countries made fewer contributions to U.N. peacekeeping, both in terms of financial aid and personnel—showing that even the most globalized countries face challenges in maintaining openness.

Cultural factors can curb the benefits of globalization, too. For instance, France's collective nationalism tilts the scale in favor of home-grown agriculture, and the United States' fears of terrorism make foreign management of ports an unpalatable prospect—cultural clues that may partially explain why both countries have a relatively low economic ranking on the index. Perhaps the area of the world that bears the brunt of globalization's economic failures is sub-Saharan Africa. Despite attempts to increase regional trade—Kenya, Tanzania, and Uganda launched an East African Community Customs Union that established common external tariffs—a large informal economy, accounting for more than half the workforce, makes it nearly impossible for governments to raise the revenue they need.

In 2005, the world's richest nations took some steps to acknowledge that not everyone has reaped globalization's rewards. As part of its summit in Gleneagles, Scotland, leaders of the Group of Eight industrialized nations pledged $40 billion worth of debt forgiveness and an additional $50 billion in foreign aid to Africa. They also promised more peacekeeping troops and assistance in eradicating disease. . . .

The Winner's Circle

For the fourth time in seven years, Singapore tops the list as the most globalized country in the world. But there was plenty of movement in the rest of the top 20. Many of the countries that previously ranked high fell off because of stiff competition from newcomers to the index. The top new addition was Hong Kong, which debuted in second place and distinguished itself with the highest scores in both the economic and the personal contact dimensions. The Netherlands made its way back into the top three for the first time since 2001, mostly due to the merger of the Royal Dutch Petroleum Company and Britain's Shell Transport and Trading Company. Worth about $100 billion, the deal helped to increase foreign direct investment outflows for the Netherlands by more than 590 percent over the previous year. Meanwhile, the United States slipped four places in the overall rankings to end up at seventh. Although U.S. trade grew by 12 percent, foreign investment shrank by more than 60 percent, mostly due to the effects of the 2004 American Jobs Creation Act, which granted tax incentives for hiring domestically. Clearly, the forces of globalization can turn on a dime.

Small But Powerful

If there is one big factor that many of the most globalized countries have in common, it's their size: they're tiny. Eight of the index's top 10 countries have land areas smaller than the U.S. state of Indiana; and seven have fewer than 8 million citizens. Canada and the United States are the only large countries that consistently rank in the top 10.

So, why do small countries rank so high? Because, when you're a flyweight, globalizing is a matter of necessity. Countries such as Singapore and the Netherlands lack natural resources. Countries like Denmark and Ireland can't rely on their limited domestic markets the way the United States can. To be globally competitive, these countries have no choice but to open up and attract trade and foreign investment—even if they're famously aloof Switzerland.

Indeed, economic integration is where these top-performing, tiny countries flex their muscle. All 8 rank in the top 11 on the economic dimension of globalization, which incorporates trade and foreign direct investment. Hong Kong and Singapore, the top two performers in this category, leave other economies in the dust. Additionally, the World Bank placed all the high-ranking, small countries except Jordan in the top 25 out of 175 economies in ease of doing business. Jordan, though, ranks first on the index's measure of political engagement, due to its participation in treaties and U.N. peacekeeping missions.

And if you're living in a small country, reaching out beyond your country's borders may be the only way to find new opportunities. Not surprisingly, six of this year's tiny globalizers also ranked in the top 10 on the personal dimension of globalization, which measures international phone calls, travel, and remittances. People in small countries boosted their countries' rankings by chatting it up on the phone, or in the case of Jordan, by sending large sums of money home. It all goes to show that mini can be mighty.

Olympic Ambitions

There is perhaps no greater—or more expensive—stage in the world than the Olympics. Just ask China, which is pouring $40 billion into its preparations for next year's games. Beijing has already completed construction on all but one of 37 new sporting venues. The government has disseminated etiquette booklets, and Olympic organizers are teaching conversational English to millions of residents in order to welcome an expected 300,000 foreign tourists. Beijing has even set up an Office of Weather Manipulation, which has employed scientists to investigate how to prevent rain during outdoor events. Other Olympic-sized projects could push the total to $67 billion by the time the games roll around next summer, more than four times the record-breaking amount that Athens spent in 2004.

But does all the copious cash and international publicity really pay off? Maybe not. If you look at recent host countries, the Olympic effect was negligible at best. . . .

All this, of course, may not mean much for China. Recent hosts already ranked fairly high on the index, and so may have had less to gain. China, on the other hand, is still a bastion of authoritarianism and ranks only 66th overall, lagging behind in international telephone contact and political engagement. There's still hope that the games will goose communications with the outside world, encourage Beijing to loosen its grip, and perhaps even make businesses more accountable to international standards. But as with any Olympic event, we won't know the outcome until it's over.

Trafficking in Information

An advanced highway system is often credited for the rise of the Roman Empire; goods, soldiers, and tax revenues could move across great distances at remarkable speed for the age. But if all roads once led to Rome, today's Internet superhighway leads to the world's most open countries. More-globalized countries tend to have more international Internet bandwidth, a measure of the size of the "pipe" through which e-mail and Web pages cross borders. The United States leads the way in the amount of international cybertraffic it can handle; indeed, its capacity is so large, most e-mails zooming between Latin America and Europe pass through the United States. Likewise, London is a leading transit point for trans-Atlantic traffic destined for Europe. The sun may have set on the British Empire, but it is still a Heathrow of cyberspace.

Urban Outfitted

Cities can be a blessing or a curse. Millions leave their villages each year and head to bustling cities to find a better life. But urban centers can also be home to massive slums or sprawl—and the crime, disease, and poverty that come with it. It is generally true that the more urban a country, the more globalized it tends to be. Top-ranking Singapore is the best example; it is 100 percent urban, and its citizens are well educated and relatively affluent. Meanwhile, a less globalized society like Bangladesh is a quarter urban. In fact, less globalized countries often have faster-growing cities. And that is hardly good news. For example, in low-ranking Nigeria, the urban jungle grows by more than 2.5 million people each year. Dhaka, the capital of Bangladesh, was originally designed for a population of 1 million people; today that number stands at 12 million, and demographers predict that the city will be home to more than 23 million people by 2015. Pressures that great can push any city beyond its breaking point.

Baltic Tiger

Milton Friedman would be at home in Estonia. That's because the small former Soviet republic has put many of the late Nobel Prize-winning economist's ideas to the test. The result? Estonia, having shaken itself free from its communist-era shackles, may now qualify as the first Baltic Tiger; it debuts this year at number 10 in the index.

In keeping with Friedman's free-market philosophy, the country's government has moved aggressively to open itself up to the outside world. For all practical purposes, Estonia has no corporate income tax, and shareholder dividends are subject to a simple flat tax. Bureaucracy isn't a problem, either; the government just steps aside to let investors do their thing. The World Bank ranks Estonia 17th among 175 economies in ease of doing business, and sixth in ease of trading across borders. Additionally, the government places no restrictions on foreign ownership of real estate, which has fueled a property investment boom among overseas buyers.

Although the index ranks Estonia 21st in technological connectivity, the country seems poised to pounce higher. The country, dubbed by some as "E-Stonia," has launched a large online government initiative and even declared Internet access a fundamental human right. In March, it held the world's first general election that allowed e-voting over the Web.

Standing Still

In 2005, member states of the Association of Southeast Asian Nations (ASEAN) implemented bilateral free trade agreements with Australia, India, Jordan, and New Zealand, were negotiating for eight more trade pacts, and started early talks for regional agreements with four other countries. Exports in the region jumped nearly 15 percent, and inflows of foreign direct investment rose 45 percent. Overall trade was up more than 70 percent from four years earlier.

It would seem that ASEAN has fully recovered from the Asian financial crisis of 10 years ago. Multinational corporations continue to invest in the region, increasingly adopting business strategies in which they build a second manufacturing plant in an ASEAN nation as a backup in case things go downhill in China. Yet, with the exception of perennial champion Singapore, the region's countries place relatively low on the index. And if the addition of new countries is taken into consideration, Southeast Asian nations' relative rankings remain virtually unchanged from last year. Why the stagnation? Simply put, there's been little trickle-down effect. As former U.S. President Jimmy Carter once said, "If you're totally illiterate and living on $1 a day, the benefits of globalization never come to you." Take Thailand, for example. The country ranks an impressive seventh in trade, with exports growing 14 percent and imports jumping 25 percent between 2004 and 2005. But the fruits of economic growth, such as improved technological infrastructure, are still not available to most people in Thailand; the country ranks 49th in Internet access. Although the number of Internet users in Thailand is growing between 20 and 30 percent each year, nearly 85 percent of them are concentrated in urban areas. Unsurprisingly, Thailand's cities are home to better education systems, higher investment in infrastructure, and more employment. The benefits of globalization rarely reach the 68 percent of the population that lives in rural areas.

Southeast Asian countries also continue to rank poorly in international political participation. Malaysia may rank third in trade, but it places an abysmal 63rd in the political dimension. You don't exactly see a lot of Malaysian troops deployed around the globe on U.N. peacekeeping missions. Nor do you see Southeast Asian nations donating much foreign aid. The region certainly has been a beneficiary of international political cooperation—most notably with relief efforts in the aftermath of the devastating tsunami in December 2004. Perhaps the political rankings of ASEAN states will go up as they find ways to give back. Indonesia, which ranks 67th in participation in U.N. peacekeeping missions, recently offered to contribute troops to a joint U.N.- African Union effort in Darfur. Such initiatives may help it lead the ASEAN pack in the years ahead.

16.2 English as the Language of Global Education

Doreen Carvajal

English has become the language of globalization just as French dominated diplomacy in the eighteenth century and Latin was the language of elites during Europe's Middle Ages. This selection describes how English has become the language of instruction at major universities around the world. Business schools have led the way, but disciplines in science and technology are not far behind, and English is becoming the language of choice in other fields as well.

W hen economics students returned this winter to the elite École Normale Supérieure here, copies of a simple one-page petition were posted in the corridors demanding an unlikely privilege: French as a teaching language. "We understand that economics is a discipline, like most scientific fields, where the research is published in English," the petition read, in apologetic tones. But it declared that it was unacceptable for a native French professor to teach standard courses to French-speaking students in the adopted tongue of English.

In the shifting universe of global academia, English is becoming as commonplace as creeping ivy and mortarboards. In the last five years, the world's top business schools and universities have been pushing to make English the teaching tongue in a calculated strategy to raise revenues by attracting more international students and as a way to respond to globalization.

Business universities are driving the trend, partly because changes in international accreditation standards in the late 1990s required them to include English-language components. But English is also spreading to the undergraduate level, with some South Korean universities offering up to 30 percent of their courses in the language. The former president of Korea University in Seoul sought to raise that share to 60 percent, but ultimately was not re-elected to his post in December.

In Madrid, business students can take their admissions test in English for the elite Instituto de Empresa and enroll in core courses for a master's degree in business administration in the same language. The Lille School of Management in

France stopped considering English a foreign language in 1999, and now half the postgraduate programs are taught in English to accommodate a rising number of international students.

Over the last three years, the number of master's programs offered in English at universities with another host language has more than doubled, to 3,300 programs at 1,700 universities, according to David A. Wilson, chief executive of the Graduate Management Admission Council, an international organization of leading business schools that is based in McLean, Va.

"We are shifting to English. Why?" said Laurent Bibard, the dean of M.B.A. programs at Essec, a top French business school in a suburb of Paris that is a fertile breeding ground for chief executives.

"It's the language for international teaching," he said. "English allows students to be able to come from anyplace in the world and for our students—the French ones—to go everywhere."

This year the university is fluidly celebrating its 100th anniversary in its adopted tongue. Its new publicity film debuted in English and French. Along one of the main roads leading into Paris loomed a giant blue billboard boasting of the anniversary in French and, in smaller letters, in English.

Essec has also taken advantage of the increased revenue that foreign students—English-speaking ones—can bring in. Its population of foreign students has leapt by 38 percent in four years, to 909 today out of a student body of 3,700.

The tuition for a two-year master's degree in business administration is 19,800 euros for European Union citizens, and 34,000 euros for non-EU citizens.

"The French market for local students is not unlimited," said Christophe N. Bredillet, the associate dean for the Lille School of Management's M.B.A. and postgraduate programs. "Revenue is very important, and in order to provide good services, we need to cover our expenses for the library and research journals. We need to cover all these things with a bigger number of students so it's quite important to attract international students."

With the jump in foreign students, Essec now offers 25 percent of its 200 courses in English. Its ambition is to accelerate the English offerings to 50 percent in the next three years.

Santiago Iñiguez de Ozoño, dean of the Instituto de Empresa, argues that the trend is a natural consequence of globalization, with English functioning as Latin did in the 13th century as the lingua franca most used by universities.

"English is being adapted as a working language, but it's not Oxford English," he said. "It's a language that most stakeholders speak." He carries out conversation on a blog, deanstalk.net, in English.

But getting students to feel comfortable speaking English in the classroom is easier said than done. When younger French students at Essec start a required course in organizational analysis, the atmosphere is marked by long, uncomfortable silences, said Alan Jenkins, a management professor and academic director of the executive M.B.A. program.

"They are very good on written tasks, but there's a lot of reticence on oral communication and talking with the teacher," Dr. Jenkins said, adding that he used role-playing to encourage students to speak. He also refuses to speak in French. "I have to force myself to say, 'Can you give me that in English?'"

Officials at Ewha Womans University in Seoul are also aware that they face a difficult task at the first stage of their Global 2010 project, which will require new students to take four classes in English, two under the tutelage of native English-speaking professors. The 120-year-old university has embarked on a hiring spree to attract 50 foreign professors.

At the beginning, "teaching courses in English may have less efficiency or effectiveness in terms of knowledge transfer than those courses taught in Korean," said Anna Suh, program manager for the university's office of global affairs, who said that students eventually see the benefits. "Our aim for this kind of program is to prepare and equip our students to be global leaders in this new era of internationalization."

The Lille management school is planning to open a satellite business school program next fall in Abu Dhabi, United Arab Emirates, where the working language will also be in English.

"Internationally, the competition is everywhere," Dr. Bredillet said. "For a master's in management, I'm competing with George Washington University. I'm competing with some programs in Germany, Norway and the U.K. That's why we're delivering the curriculum in English."

16.3 Soccer vs. McWorld

Franklin Foer

The next selection uses the sport of soccer to illustrate some of the limits to globalization. It reveals that, although professional soccer has become a globalized economic enterprise with players traded among teams regardless of nationality, the sport remains "a tangle of intensely local loyalties." Even in a world of globally recruited and financed teams, human beings desire to be part of some identified, local "us" and to oppose some identified "them" and develop rituals and traditions that institutionalize these attachments—though the author concludes hopefully that perhaps the desire to win may prove stronger than attachments to local prejudices.

Two omens of apocalypse, or perhaps global salvation: during the 2002 World Cup, the English midfielder David Beckham, famed bender of the ball, styled his hair in a mohawk. Almost instantly, Japanese adolescents appeared with tread marks on their shorn heads; professional women, according to the Japanese newsmagazine *Shukan Jitsuwa*, even trimmed their pubic hair in homage. A bit further west, in Bangkok, Thailand, the monks of the Pariwas

Buddhist temple placed a Beckham statuette in a spot reserved for figures of minor deities.

It should surprise no one that this London cockney has replaced basketball icon Michael Jordan as the world's most transcendent celebrity athlete. After all, more than basketball or even the World Bank and the International Monetary Fund, soccer is the most globalized institution on the planet.

Soccer began to outgrow its national borders early in the post-World-War-II era. While statesman Robert Schuman was daydreaming about a common European market and government, European soccer clubs actually moved toward union. The most successful clubs started competing against one another in regular transnational tournaments, such as the events now known as Champions League and the Union of European Football Associations (UEFA) Cup. These tournaments were a fan's dream: the chance to see Juventus of Turin play Bayern Munich one week and FC Barcelona the next. But more important, they were an owner's dream: blockbuster fixtures that brought unprecedented gate receipts and an enormous infusion of television revenue. This transnational idea was such a good one that Latin America, Africa, and Asia quickly created their own knockoffs.

Once competition globalized, the hunt for labor resources quickly followed. Club owners scoured the planet for superstars that they could buy on the cheap. Spanish teams shopped for talent in former colonies such as Argentina and Uruguay. Argentina plundered the leagues of poorer neighbors such as Paraguay. At first, this move toward an international market inspired a backlash. Politicians and sportswriters fretted that the influx from abroad would quash the development of young local talent. In Spain, for example, dictator Francisco Franco prohibited the importation of foreign players. Brazil's government declared Pelé a national treasure in 1961 and legally forbade his sale to a foreign team. But these stabs at nationalist economics could not ultimately stave off the seductive benefits of cheap, skilled labor from abroad. And, after a while, the foreign stars were needed to compete at the highest levels of European soccer. The game evolved to the point where an English club might field a team without any Englishmen.

By the 1990s, capital frictionlessly flowed across borders in the global soccer economy. European clubs not only posted scouts throughout the developing world, they also bought teams there. Ajax of Amsterdam acquired substantial shares of outfits in Cape Town and Ghana. Newcastle United began using China's Dalian Shide Football Club as a feeder. The biggest clubs started to think of themselves as multinational conglomerates. Organizations such as Manchester United and Real Madrid acquired a full portfolio of cable stations, restaurants, and megastores, catering to audiences as far away as Kuala Lumpur and Shanghai. Even with last year's dull markets, Manchester United's pretax profits for the 12 months ending on July 31, 2003, exceeded $65 million.

It is ironic, then, that soccer, for all its one-worldist features, doesn't evince the power of the new order as much as expose its limits. Manchester United and Real Madrid may embrace the ethos of globalization by accumulating wealth and diminishing national sovereignty. But a tangle of intensely local loyalties, identities, tensions, economies, and corruption endures—in some cases, not despite globalization, but because of it. . . .

Winning the Peace

Local hostilities, even outright racism, ought to be the easiest sort of legacy for global soccer to erase. When people have a self-interested reason for getting along, they are supposed to put aside their ancient grudges and do business. But there's a massive hole in this argument: Glasgow, Scotland.

Glasgow has two teams, or rather, existential enemies. Celtic represents Irish Catholics. Its songs blame the British for the potato famine, and its games have historically provided fertile territory for Irish Republican Army (IRA) recruiters. Across town, there is Rangers, the club of Tory unionism. Banners in the stadium trumpet the Ulster Defense Forces and other Northern Irish protestant paramilitaries. Before games, fans—including respectable lawyers and businessmen—shout a song with the charming line, "We're up to our knees in Fenian blood." They sing about William of Orange, "King Billy," and his masterminding of the Protestant triumph in 1690 at the Battle of the Boyne. Until 1989, Rangers consciously forbade the hiring of Catholic players. Crosstown rivalries are, of course, a staple of sports, but the Celtic-Rangers rivalry represents something more than the enmity of proximity. It is the unfinished fight over the Protestant Reformation.

The Celtic and Rangers organizations desperately want to embrace the ethos of globalism, to convert themselves into mass entertainment conglomerates. They've done everything possible to move beyond the relatively small Scottish market— sending clothing catalogs to the Scottish and Irish diasporas in North America, and campaigning to join the bigger, better, wealthier English league.

But the Celtic and Rangers clubs don't try too hard to eliminate bigotry. Rangers, for example, continues to sell Orange jerseys. It plays songs on the stadium loudspeaker that it knows will provoke anti-Catholic lyrics. The club blares Tina Turner's "Simply the Best," which culminates in 40,000 fans screaming "F—— the Pope!" Celtic, for its part, flies the Irish tricolor above its stadium. At Glasgow's Ibrox Park, I've watched Protestants celebrate a goal, egged on by former team captain Lorenzo Amoruso, a long-haired Italian with the look of a 1980s model. He applauds the fans. Flailing his arms, he urges them to sing their anti-Catholic songs louder. The irony is obvious: Amoruso is Catholic. Since the late 1990s, Rangers has routinely fielded more Catholics than Celtic. Its players have come from Georgia, Argentina, Germany, Norway, Portugal, and Holland, because money can buy no better ones. But ethnic hatred, it seems, makes good business sense. In fact, from the start of their rivalry, Celtic and Rangers have been nicknamed the "Old Firm," because they're seen as colluding to profit from their mutual hatreds. Even in the global market, they attract more fans because their supporters crave ethnic identification—to join a fight on behalf of their tribe.

There are plenty of economic causes for illiberal hatreds—unemployment, competition for scarce jobs, inadequate social safety nets—but none of those material conditions is especially widespread in Glasgow. Discrimination has faded. The city's unemployment problem is no better or worse than the rest of Britain. Glasgow has kept alive its tribalism, despite the logic of history, because it provides a kind of pornographic pleasure. Thousands of fans arrive each week from across the whole of Britain, in ferries from Belfast and buses from London, all aching to partake in a few hours of hate-filled tribalism. Once they release this bile from their system, they can return to their comfortable houses and good jobs.

If there were any place one would expect this sort of hostility to get messy, it would be Chelsea. During the 1980s, the club was the outfit most associated with English hooliganism. Its fans joined the xenophobic British National Party and merged with violent racist gangs like the notorious Combat 18. There are famous stories of Chelsea fans visiting Auschwitz, where they would walk around delivering *Sieg Heil* salutes to the tourists and try to climb inside the ovens. When the Holocaust denier David Irving went on trial for libel in 2001, the hooligan group Chelsea Headhunters provided security for his rallies.

Like a college alumni association, older, retired Chelsea hooligans make a point of sticking together. They stay in touch through an online message board, where they exchange war stories and debate the fortunes of their beloved club. The board makes a point of declaring, "WELCOME TO THE CHELSEA HOOLIGANS FORUM, FOR CHELSEA AND LOYAL FANS. PLEASE DONT LEAVE RACIST MESSAGES AND DONT USE THIS BOARD TO ARRANGE VIOLENCE." The warning is intended to inoculate the site against any exceptionally offensive posts, but it doesn't exactly deter the anti-Semitism. Almost immediately after oil baron Roman Abramovich, the second richest man in Russia, and a Jew, bought Chelsea, a guy calling himself West Ken Ken referred to Abramovich as a "yid," and moaned, "I like the money but the star of David will be flying down the [Stamford] bridge soon."

However, as the Abramovich era began and the new owner spent more than $150 million stocking his new team, the complaints became less apparent. And then, when Chelsea jumped to the top of the English Premier League table, the anti-Semitism vanished altogether.

Chelsea, it seems, has discovered the only effective palliative for the vestiges of localism—not global cash or global talent, but victory.

Managing the Problems of a Globalized World

16.4 How Globalization Went Bad

Steven Weber, Naazneen Barma, Matthew Kroenig, and Ely Ratner

This selection describes the "dark side" of globalization and argues that the combination of globalization and unipolarity in which the United States is the world's sole superpower is exceedingly dangerous. The authors contend that the presence of several major states—a multipolar world—would improve global capacity for coping with this dark side. They present three axioms that they believe illustrate the dangers arising from America's unique power in a globalizing world. The first is that global problems will ultimately prove too great for American power; the second is that a single superpower cannot by itself deal with the problems that arise in areas that lie largely beyond globalization—failed and failing states, for example—and the third is that without the possibility of entering an alliance to balance American power, opponents of U.S. policies will go "bad," most dangerously by acquiring weapons of mass destruction. The authors conclude that what is needed to cope with globalization's perils, ranging from nuclear proliferation to the spread of infectious diseases, are additional great powers that could share the burdens of managing a globalized world.

The world today is more dangerous and less orderly than it was supposed to be. Ten or 15 years ago, the naive expectations were that the "end of history" was near. The reality has been the opposite. The world has more international terrorism and more nuclear proliferation today than it did in 1990. International institutions are weaker. The threats of pandemic disease and climate change are stronger. Cleavages of religious and cultural ideology are more intense. The global financial system is more unbalanced and precarious.

It wasn't supposed to be like this. The end of the Cold War was supposed to make global politics and economics easier to manage, not harder. What went wrong? The bad news of the 21st century is that globalization has a significant dark side. The container ships that carry manufactured Chinese goods to and from the United States also carry drugs. The airplanes that fly passengers nonstop from New York to Singapore also transport infectious diseases. And the Internet has proved just as adept at spreading deadly, extremist ideologies as it has e-commerce.

Weber, Steven, Naazneen Barma, Matthew Kroenig, and Ely Ratner, "How Globalization Went Bad," *Foreign Policy (Washington)*, January/February 2007, pp. 32–40. © 2007 by Foreign Policy. <www.foreignpolicy.com>. Reproduced with permission of Foreign Policy in the format Textbook via Copyright Clearance Center.

The conventional belief is that the single greatest challenge of geopolitics today is managing this dark side of globalization, chipping away at the illegitimate co-travelers that exploit openness, mobility, and freedom, without putting too much sand in the gears. The current U.S. strategy is to push for more trade, more connectivity, more markets, and more openness. America does so for a good reason—it benefits from globalization more than any other country in the world. The United States acknowledges globalization's dark side but attributes it merely to exploitative behavior by criminals, religious extremists, and other anachronistic elements that can be eliminated. The dark side of globalization, America says, with very little subtlety, can be mitigated by the expansion of American power, sometimes unilaterally and sometimes through multilateral institutions, depending on how the United States likes it. In other words, America is aiming for a "flat," globalized world coordinated by a single superpower.

That's nice work if you can get it. But the United States almost certainly cannot. Not only because other countries won't let it, but, more profoundly, because that line of thinking is faulty. The predominance of American power has many benefits, but the management of globalization is not one of them. The mobility of ideas, capital, technology, and people is hardly new. But the rapid advance of globalization's evils is. Most of that advance has taken place since 1990. Why? Because what changed profoundly in the 1990s was the polarity of the international system. For the first time in modern history, globalization was superimposed onto a world with a single superpower. What we have discovered in the past 15 years is that it is a dangerous mixture. The negative effects of globalization since 1990 are not the result of globalization itself. They are the dark side of American predominance.

The Dangers of Unipolarity

A straightforward piece of logic from market economics helps explain why unipolarity and globalization don't mix. Monopolies, regardless of who holds them, are almost always bad for both the market and the monopolist. We propose three simple axioms of "globalization under unipolarity" that reveal these dangers.

Axiom 1: Above a certain threshold of power, the rate at which new global problems are generated will exceed the rate at which old problems are fixed. Power does two things in international politics: it enhances the capability of a state to do things, but it also increases the number of things that a state must worry about. At a certain point, the latter starts to overtake the former. It's the familiar law of diminishing returns. Because powerful states have large spheres of influence and their security and economic interests touch every region of the world, they are threatened by the risk of things going wrong—anywhere. That is particularly true for the United States, which leverages its ability to go anywhere and do anything through massive debt. No one knows exactly when the law of diminishing returns will kick in. But, historically, it starts to happen long before a single great power dominates the entire globe, which is why large empires from Byzantium to Rome have always reached a point of unsustainability.

That may already be happening to the United States today, on issues ranging from oil dependency and nuclear proliferation to pandemics and global warming. What Axiom 1 tells you is that more U.S. power is not the answer; it's actually part of the problem. A multipolar world would almost certainly manage the globe's pressing problems more effectively. The larger the number of great powers in the global system, the greater the chance that at least one of them would exercise some control over a given combination of space, other actors, and problems. Such reasoning doesn't rest on hopeful notions that the great powers will work together. They might do so. But even if they don't, the result is distributed governance, where some great power is interested in most every part of the world through productive competition.

Axiom 2: In an increasingly networked world, places that fall between the networks are very dangerous places—and there will be more ungoverned zones when there is only one network to join.   The second axiom acknowledges that highly connected networks can be efficient, robust, and resilient to shocks. But in a highly connected world, the pieces that fall between the networks are increasingly shut off from the benefits of connectivity. These problems fester in the form of failed states, mutate like pathogenic bacteria, and, in some cases, reconnect in subterranean networks such as al-Qaeda. The truly dangerous places are the points where the subterranean networks touch the mainstream of global politics and economics. What made Afghanistan so dangerous under the Taliban was not that it was a failed state. It wasn't. It was a partially failed and partially connected state that worked the interstices of globalization through the drug trade, counterfeiting, and terrorism.

Can any single superpower monitor all the seams and back alleys of globalization? Hardly. In fact, a lone hegemon is unlikely to look closely at these problems, because more pressing issues are happening elsewhere, in places where trade and technology are growing. By contrast, a world of several great powers is a more interest-rich environment in which nations must look in less obvious places to find new sources of advantage. In such a system, it's harder for troublemakers to spring up, because the cracks and seams of globalization are held together by stronger ties.

Axiom 3: Without a real chance to find useful allies to counter a superpower, opponents will try to neutralize power, by going underground, going nuclear, or going "bad."   Axiom 3 is a story about the preferred strategies of the weak. It's a basic insight of international relations that states try to balance power. They protect themselves by joining groups that can hold a hegemonic threat at bay. But what if there is no viable group to join? In today's unipolar world, every nation from Venezuela to North Korea is looking for a way to constrain American power. But in the unipolar world, it's harder for states to join together to do that. So they turn to other means. They play a different game. Hamas, Iran, Somalia, North Korea, and Venezuela are not going to become allies anytime soon. Each is better off finding other ways to make life more difficult for Washington. Going nuclear is one way. Counterfeiting U.S. currency is another. Raising uncertainty about oil supplies is perhaps the most obvious method of all.

Here's the important downside of unipolar globalization. In a world with multiple great powers, many of these threats would be less troublesome. The relatively weak states would have a choice among potential partners with which to ally, enhancing their influence. Without that more attractive choice, facilitating the dark side of globalization becomes the most effective means of constraining American power.

Sharing Globalization's Burden

The world is paying a heavy price for the instability created by the combination of globalization and unipolarity, and the United States is bearing most of the burden. Consider the case of nuclear proliferation. There's effectively a market out there for proliferation, with its own supply (states willing to share nuclear technology) and demand (states that badly want a nuclear weapon). The overlap of unipolarity with globalization ratchets up both the supply and demand, to the detriment of U.S. national security.

It has become fashionable, in the wake of the Iraq war, to comment on the limits of conventional military force. But much of this analysis is overblown. The United States may not be able to stabilize and rebuild Iraq. But that doesn't matter much from the perspective of a government that thinks the Pentagon has it in its sights. In Tehran, Pyongyang, and many other capitals, including Beijing, the bottom line is simple: the U.S. military could, with conventional force, end those regimes tomorrow if it chose to do so. No country in the world can dream of challenging U.S. conventional military power. But they can certainly hope to deter America from using it. And the best deterrent yet invented is the threat of nuclear retaliation. Before 1989, states that felt threatened by the United States could turn to the Soviet Union's nuclear umbrella for protection. Now, they turn to people like A.Q. Khan. Having your own nuclear weapon used to be a luxury. Today, it is fast becoming a necessity.

North Korea is the clearest example. Few countries had it worse during the Cold War. North Korea was surrounded by feuding, nuclear-armed communist neighbors, it was officially at war with its southern neighbor, and it stared continuously at tens of thousands of U.S. troops on its border. But, for 40 years, North Korea didn't seek nuclear weapons. It didn't need to, because it had the Soviet nuclear umbrella. Within five years of Soviet collapse, however, Pyongyang was pushing ahead full steam on plutonium reprocessing facilities. North Korea's founder, Kim Il Sung, barely flinched when former U.S. President Bill Clinton's administration readied war plans to strike his nuclear installations preemptively. That brinkmanship paid off. Today North Korea is likely a nuclear power, and Kim's son rules the country with an iron fist. America's conventional military strength means a lot less to a nuclear North Korea. Saddam Hussein's great strategic blunder was that he took too long to get to the same place.

How would things be different in a multipolar world? For starters, great powers could split the job of policing proliferation, and even collaborate on some particularly hard cases. It's often forgotten now that, during the Cold War, the only state with a tougher nonproliferation policy than the United States was the Soviet Union. Not a single country that had a formal alliance with Moscow ever became a nuclear power. The Eastern bloc was full of countries with advanced technological capabilities in every area except one—nuclear weapons. Moscow simply wouldn't permit it. But today we see the uneven and inadequate level of effort that non-superpowers devote to stopping proliferation. The Europeans dangle carrots at Iran, but they are unwilling to consider serious sticks. The Chinese refuse to admit that there is a problem. And the Russians are aiding Iran's nuclear ambitions. When push comes to shove, nonproliferation today is almost entirely America's burden.

The same is true for global public health. Globalization is turning the world into an enormous petri dish for the incubation of infectious disease. Humans cannot outsmart disease, because it just evolves too quickly. Bacteria can reproduce a new generation in less than 30 minutes, while it takes us decades to come up with a new generation of antibiotics. Solutions are only possible when and where we get the upper hand. Poor countries where humans live in close proximity to farm animals are the best place to breed extremely dangerous zoonotic disease. These are often the same countries, perhaps not entirely coincidentally, that feel threatened by American power. Establishing an early warning system for these diseases—exactly what we lacked in the case of SARS a few years ago and exactly what we lack for avian flu today—will require a significant level of intervention into the very places that don't want it. That will be true as long as international intervention means American interference.

The most likely sources of the next ebola or HIV-like pandemic are the countries that simply won't let U.S. or other Western agencies in, including the World Health Organization. Yet the threat is too arcane and not immediate enough for the West to force the issue. What's needed is another great power to take over a piece of the work, a power that has more immediate interests in the countries where diseases incubate and one that is seen as less of a threat. As long as the United States remains the world's lone superpower, we're not likely to get any help. Even after HIV, SARS, and several years of mounting hysteria about avian flu, the world is still not ready for a viral pandemic in Southeast Asia or sub-Saharan Africa. America can't change that alone.

If there were rival great powers with different cultural and ideological leanings, globalization's darkest problem of all—terrorism—would also likely look quite different. The pundits are partly right: today's international terrorism owes something to globalization. Al-Qaeda uses the Internet to transmit messages, it uses credit cards and modern banking to move money, and it uses cell phones and laptops to plot attacks. But it's not globalization that turned Osama bin Laden from a small-time Saudi dissident into the symbolic head of a radical global movement. What created Osama bin Laden was the predominance of American power.

A terrorist organization needs a story to attract resources and recruits. Oftentimes, mere frustration over political, economic, or religious conditions is not enough. Al-Qaeda understands that, and, for that reason, it weaves a narrative of global jihad against a "modernization," "Westernization," and a "Judeo-Christian" threat. There is really just one country that both spearheads and represents that threat: the United States. And so the most efficient way for a terrorist to gain a reputation is to attack the United States. The logic is the same for all monopolies. A few years ago, every computer hacker in the world wanted to bring down Microsoft, just as every aspiring terrorist wants to create a spectacle of destruction akin to the September 11 attacks inside the United States.

Al-Qaeda cells have gone after alternate targets such as Britain, Egypt, and Spain. But these are not the acts that increase recruitment and fundraising, or mobilize the energy of otherwise disparate groups around the world. Nothing enhances the profile of a terrorist like killing an American, something Abu Musab al-Zarqawi understood well in Iraq. Even if al-Qaeda's deepest aspirations lie with the demise of the Saudi regime, the predominance of U.S. power and its role supporting the house of Saud makes America the only enemy really worth fighting. A multipolar world would surely confuse this kind of clear framing that pits Islamism against the West. What would be al-Qaeda's message if the Chinese were equally involved in propping up authoritarian regimes in the Islamic, oil-rich Gulf states? Does the al-Qaeda story work if half its enemy is neither Western nor Christian?

Restoring the Balance

The consensus today in the U.S. foreign-policy community is that more American power is always better. Across the board. For both the United States and the rest of the globe. The National Security Strategy documents of 2002 and 2006 enshrine this consensus in phrases such as "a balance of power that favors freedom." The strategy explicitly defines the "balance" as a continued imbalance, as the United States continues "dissuading potential competitors . . . from challenging the United States, its allies, and its partners."

In no way is U.S. power inherently a bad thing. Nor is it true that no good comes from unipolarity. But there are significant downsides to the imbalance of power. That view is hardly revolutionary. It has a long pedigree in U.S. foreign-policy thought. It was the perspective, for instance, that George Kennan brought to the table in the late 1940s when he talked about the desirability of a European superpower to restrain the United States. Although the issues today are different than they were in Kennan's time, it's still the case that too much power may, as Kennan believed, lead to overreach. It may lead to arrogance. It may lead to insensitivity to the concerns of others. Though Kennan may have been prescient to voice these concerns, he couldn't have predicted the degree to which American unipolarity would lead to such an unstable overlap with modern-day globalization.

America has experienced this dangerous burden for 15 years, but it still refuses to see it for what it really is. Antiglobalization sentiment is coming today from both the right and the left. But by blaming globalization for what ails the world, the U.S. foreign-policy community is missing a very big part of what is undermining one of the most hopeful trends in modern history—the reconnection is societies, economies, and minds that political borders have kept apart for far too long.

America cannot indefinitely stave off the rise of another superpower. But, in today's networked and interdependent world, such an event is not entirely a cause for mourning. A shift in the global balance of power would, in fact, help the United States manage some of the most costly and dangerous consequences of globalization. As the international playing field levels, the scope of these problems and the threat they pose to America will only decrease. When that happens, the United States will find globalization is a far easier burden to bear.

Paradoxes of Globalization

16.5 Loves Microsoft, Hates America

Adam Davidson

The final selection in this chapter illustrates a paradox of globalization in which people willingly accept a culture, much of which originates in the United States, while hating the United States itself. The article tells the story of a young Muslim in the country of Jordan whose life's dream is to work as a computer programmer for Microsoft even as he is prepared to be a suicide bomber in a jihad against the United States.

Fadi is a 23-year-old unemployed computer programmer who lives in his parents' apartment in a nice, middle-class neighborhood in Amman, Jordan. Down one street is the big Amman McDonald's, down another is Fadi's mosque, where he prays several times a day. Stocky, with a big, messy beard, Fadi speaks softly, hunched over, looking at the ground. When he makes an important point, he asks you to repeat it, and when you show you understand, he lifts his head, leans back with a great smile and says, "*Sah*," "correct." One day, he explained to me in careful detail why he wants to be a *shaheed*, a suicide bomber against the United States, quoting at length from the Koran. But when he's not talking about blowing himself up and killing American troops, Fadi talks about his other great dream. "I want to be a programmer at Microsoft," he says. "Not just a programmer. I want to be well known, famous."

Fadi gives me a tour of his parents' apartment: it is long and narrow, with a private living room for the family and another, more ornate one, for guests. Fadi's bedroom is in the back, and it is small and bare. Everything Fadi has on display sits on a small desk: a copy of the Koran, in blue leather with ornate gold Arabic script on the cover, and a few boxes of audiotapes that he listens to every day.

"This is NLP," he explains. "It's very good. Neuro-Linguistic Programming." NLP, which originated at the University of California, Santa Cruz, is a sort of modern "The Power of Positive Thinking," and Fadi says it has helped him overcome the barriers to his dreams. "Six months ago, I was much more negative," he says. "I would get frustrated." For example, Fadi says he finds it frustrating that it is so difficult to get a visa to the United States, so he can't train for a job at Microsoft. But the tapes teach him to remain positive about reaching his dreams.

Fadi doesn't see anything strange about using American self-help tapes to get a job at an American company, while at the same time harboring hatred of the American government to the point of self-annihilation. Self-help, computer programming, the Koran and jihad are all aspects of the same thing, he says: a search for a way for a good Muslim to live in the modern world.

On the level of governments, Jordan is America's best friend in the Arab world: the most moderate, most pro-Western Arab state. But Fadi's Jordan is a different place, where just about every citizen has developed a deep loathing for the United States. I haven't seen any polls that determine how many Jordanians hate the United States; it seems very unlikely that the king's government would allow them to be taken. But the estimates never change.

"You can start thinking of a number above 95 percent," says Laith Shubeilat, a leading Jordanian Islamist.

"I think it's close to 100 percent," says Sari Nasir, a prominent secular sociologist at the University of Jordan. There have always been pockets of anger against the United States—you could have found it in any of Jordan's poor Palestinian refugee camps any time in the last few decades—but that anger has spread to everyone: the poor, the middle class, the upper class, Islamists, the secular, Christians, liberals.

Still, just like Fadi, almost everyone in Jordan sees his own future, his own happiness, tied up with America. American movies and TV shows and fast food have never been more popular. American computers are everywhere. It's difficult to find a professional who didn't study in the United States, and harder still to find an ambitious young person who isn't eager to do the same.

Fadi prays at his local mosque five times a day. But he is never satisfied with the imam's speeches. Occasionally, there are tame jabs at the United States, but Fadi says—and Jordan's minister of state for political affairs and information, Mohammad Adwan, confirms—that the government keeps a close watch on imams and won't allow them to say anything that could incite the population to violence.

Oddly, the place Fadi feels the most free to express his anti-American views is a pizza restaurant near his house that is modeled after one in Bay Ridge, Brooklyn. It's small: only room for two round tables, the pizza oven and a counter. It has red and white tiles like any American pizza place. It is run by two brothers, friends of Fadi's who both lived in the United States for a long time.

Y., the younger brother, is chubby and short. He was the first Arab barber in Brooklyn, he says, pulling out a contact sheet of photos of his customers, all with variants of a stylized buzz cut. "Bay Ridge is beautiful," he says.

The older brother, O., says his pizzas are as good as any in New York.

"It's very good," Fadi says and orders the special: a large pie with mushrooms, olives, sausage and tomatoes. Fadi comes here about once a week and sits with Y. and O. to discuss jihad and America.

O., who is tall and lean, was an electrician in the United States and wasn't impressed by the Americans he worked with. He worked hard, he says, but his co-workers loafed around, knowing they would be paid more if the job took longer. He wants to commit jihad against America, but he says it's too difficult. "The Mukhabarat are everywhere," he says, referring to the Jordanian secret police. He can't find a group to join. But, he says, the biggest barrier to jihad is himself. "I am too much in love with this life," he says apologetically. "I'm in love with my family and my business. I'm too weak. But I'm getting stronger."

Y., the chubby brother, doesn't want to be a jihadi, he says. He won't sit at our table; he stands a few feet away, listening attentively and every now and then laughing, a bit derisively.

O. and Fadi say they talk a lot about which jihad would be best.

"We have a few jihads we can do: Palestine, Chechnya, Kashmir or Iraq," O. says. "Palestine is too difficult. You can't get across the border. Chechnya, they already have enough people. Kashmir is easiest."

"Yes," Fadi says. "You fly to Pakistan, and someone will help you to Kashmir." But the best jihad, they both agree, is Iraq, which means a jihad against the American troops they expect will soon invade Iraq.

"If I see an American soldier in Jordan on his way to Iraq, I'll kill him," O. says.

This begins a long argument between Fadi and O. Fadi says the Koran is strict on this: you can't kill anyone who came to your country expecting peace. So, an American soldier here now cannot be harmed. O. says this isn't true. "If an American soldier comes in to my place, I will poison his pizza," O. says. "I will kill him."

"You can't do it," Fadi argues.

"I'd just give him his pizza," Y. says, laughing. "Business is business."

"If you feed an American soldier, I will fire you," O. tells him.

"You mustn't feed a soldier," Fadi says. "You can't help them. But you also can't kill them."

The biggest blow to Fadi's Microsoft dream came a few weeks ago. He was let go from his job as in-house programmer for a customer-service call center. Fadi's job search is not going well. Occasionally he lands an interview, but then he is told that the company isn't hiring.

Fadi's father, Rasem, is furious. "His beard is the main problem," Rasem says, flicking his hands wildly in the air. "That's why he can't find a good job. They're afraid he's a religious Muslim. They don't want problems. Fadi doesn't know anything about business. Fadi is very good, but he has to shave. He has to help his brothers."

Rasem is sitting in his furniture store, a small, dirty, overpacked place, and he's crumpled into one of the couches he's hoping to sell. For the past year and a half, Fadi provided the family's main income. Now that his son is unemployed, Rasem is desperate, he says, living off a 3,000-dinar loan (roughly $4,000) from a bank. He points at a framed photocopy of Fadi's college diploma hanging on the wall. "He has to work," he says to me. "Tell him to shave his beard."

Fadi has heard about a job at the University of Jordan, and he takes me along to check it out. It is a massive campus—about 27,000 students, huge utilitarian concrete buildings. He says it will be a good place to work, because many people here wear beards and are religious.

After he drops off his résumé at the administration building, Fadi and I sit on a bench at the center of campus and watch a constant parade of young men and women walking by or sitting on other benches. Fadi says this is where he sees some of the worst influences of American culture on young Jordanians. "They want to look like Americans," he says. "They want to go on dates," he says.

It's hard to see what Fadi is talking about. About 90 percent of the female students wear the hijab head scarf. About 1 in 10 of those also wear the *khimar*, a scarf that covers their faces as well. The hijab and khimar are not part of Jordanian traditions. Twenty-five years ago, few Jordanian women wore them, but recently more and more Jordanians—and more young women than old—have put on the scarf. In the last two years, as a form of protest against Western culture, student groups have called upon all Muslim women to cover their hair. But Fadi isn't impressed; the campus is still too American for him, especially the female students. "You can tell which ones mean it," he says, "and which ones are just doing it."

He points to one woman in a hijab wearing blue jeans and those overly thick-soled shoes popular among American teenagers. "She wouldn't dress like that if she was serious," he says.

America, Fadi says, is just too powerfully present in the lives of his generation of Arabs. America decides what young people will wear and what music they'll listen to. America decides whether there will be war or peace. It's so hard for a young man to feel proud of being an Arab, he says, when it is America that determines his chances for happiness and success.

Every now and then as we talk, a woman or a group of women walk by looking completely Western: no hijab, heavy makeup, a T-shirt, sometimes with several earrings or sexy boots.

"Do you look at the pretty girls here, or just ignore them?" I ask.

"Of course I look," he says. "I'm a human being."

"Do you prefer the girls with hijabs or the Western-looking girls?"

"I prefer the hijab, of course."

"You think the girls with hijabs are prettier?"

"Let's be realistic," he says, laughing. "Maybe they're not prettier. Maybe I prefer the Western-looking girls. But I wish they would wear the hijab."

Suggested Discussion Topics

1. What does globalization mean to you? In what ways do you experience globalization in your daily life?
2. To what extent do you think the antiglobalizers are right or wrong? Make a strong argument for both cases.
3. Do you favor unfettered global economic markets? Why or why not? Do global markets impinge upon you personally? How?
4. Do you think it is possible to protect local cultures from cultural homogenization? If so, how would you go about doing this?

5. Fadi, the Jordanian computer programmer, wants to work for Microsoft, enjoys American-style pizza, and uses American-made self-help tapes. Yet he hates America enough to consider being a suicide bomber. Explain this. Is it possible for someone simultaneously to enjoy the fruits of globalization and to oppose the loss of autonomy and the erosion of cultural values that goes with it? Which of these conflicting identities—Fadi the consumer of Western, global products and ideas, or Fadi the opponent of Western imperialism—is more important? Explain your thinking.

6 Do you think that the United States should take the lead in dealing with globalization's dark side? Why or why not? Do you agree that unipolarity, with America as the world's sole superpower, is dangerous? Why or why not?